The
WELL-DESIGNED
MIXED GARDEN

The
WELL-DESIGNED
MIXED GARDEN

Building Beds

and Borders

with Trees,

Shrubs,

Perennials,

Annuals,

and Bulbs

Tracy DiSabato-Aust

Timber Press
Portland ~ Cambridge

All photographs are by the author unless otherwise noted.

Design renderings are by Megan H. King, as indicated.

Color model, value scale, and color scheme watercolors by Stacey Renee Peters, as indicated; color scheme icons by Martin Knapp.

The color wheel that appears on page 39 is copyright 2001 The Taunton Press, Inc. Reprinted with permission from issue no. 78 of *Fine Gardening*, Box 5506, Newtown, CT 06470-5506. To order a copy of *Fine Gardening*, call 1.800.888.8286 or visit their website at www.taunton.com

Published in 2003 by

Timber Press, Inc.
The Haseltine Building
133 S.W. Second Avenue, Suite 450
Portland, Oregon 97204, U.S.A.

Timber Press
2 Station Road
Swavesy
Cambridge CB4 5QJ, U.K.

Reprinted 2003

Printed through Colorcraft Ltd., Hong Kong

Library of Congress Cataloging-in-Publication Data
DiSabato-Aust, Tracy.
    The well-designed mixed garden : building beds and borders with trees, shrubs, perennials, annuals, and bulbs / Tracy DiSabato-Aust.
        p. cm.
    Includes bibliographical references (p.).
    ISBN 0-88192-559-4
    1. Landscape gardening. 2. Landscape plants. I. Title.

SB473.D57 2003
712--dc21   2002023191

In memory of my mother and my greatest
cheerleader, Therese DiSabato, who taught me strength
and persistence, and my father-in-law,
Jim Aust, who taught me gentleness and patience.

CONTENTS

FOREWORD

Designing a garden, like riding a bicycle, is both an art and a science. On a bike, science keeps you upright and propels you forward. The art lies in the finesse with which you ride. To avoid scrapes and bruises, many people start off with training wheels, which help build confidence and proficiency. *The Well-Designed Mixed Garden* is like a set of training wheels for fledglings, as well as experienced and professional designers. Every page propels you forward with excellent, easy-to-understand information that you can put to use each step of the way.

Readers familiar with Tracy's best-selling book *The Well-Tended Perennial Garden* know she is an excellent teacher and skilled gardener. Garden design is another of her talents. She has spent years honing her skills at home and in the gardens of her clients. It is only natural that Tracy would turn her pen to design. In this new book she shares her enthusiasm and knowledge to help you create a garden that utilizes the wealth of plants available today, from perennials and annuals, to bulbs, shrubs, and flowering trees.

If you think design happens mysteriously after a soaking rain, or by the light of the full moon, then this book is for you. Do you long to get into the dirt but do not know how to build a stunning border? Have you gone wild at the nursery and arrived home with no idea how to use the plants you just bought? Even old hands occasionally come up short on inspiration. Read on, this lavishly illustrated book will guide you! No matter what your experience or expertise, this book will help you become an artful designer. Tracy takes the mystery, and the missteps, out of designing a mixed bed or border.

In every chapter, *The Well-Designed Mixed Garden* encourages you to have fun with design and use the process to personalize your garden. Tracy demonstrates that art is a compelling yet personal design element that can make the difference between a mundane garden and an extraordinary one. The book starts off with an overview of the design process, giving a nod to the history of gardening in America and abroad. Tracy presents historical precedent not as an end point but as a jumping-off point for exploring the garden as a rich canvas for artistic expression.

The first step is to put down your trowel and open your eyes. The most important lesson you can learn is to match your garden to your needs, taste, and budget. Once you know where you are heading, it's onto your bike and off you go, with Tracy skillfully instructing you along each leg of the journey.

If you want a garden that will give the maximum impact with the least input (and who doesn't?), you must understand your site. Site evaluation is a woefully neglected step in the design process, though it is the foundation on which a successful garden is built. You must learn the dictates and limitations inherent in your property's boundaries and context so you can work with, rather than against, your site. Tracy tells you how.

If color confounds you, then you will devour the chapter devoted to this compelling characteristic of plants and gardens. Tracy covers color theory thoroughly yet in an easily understood fashion. She teaches you ways to blend color and how to use it to elicit varied emotional responses. The chapter also includes dynamic illustrations depicting the often misunderstood factors affecting color, such as light, intensity, and color association. Once you master color, its time to move on to heavy-duty design theory. Always enthusiastic and never dogmatic, Tracy presents simple rules without demanding that we slavishly adhere to them. Terms such as order, unity, and rhythm are often bandied about by designers. Far from abstract notions, these useful tenets are clearly presented and interpreted to help you artfully combine plants and build gorgeous borders.

Now that you are versed in the theories of color and composition, and armed with your knowledge of plants and your site, Tracy guides you through the design process from start to finish, using actual gardens with real challenges and opportunities. From site selection and setting realistic design goals to the fun part, plant selection, you see firsthand how the design process really works.

An encyclopedia features 27 well-designed, expertly photographed combinations, accompanied by notes covering design and maintenance considerations. What makes the combination work? Is it a contrasting color scheme? Tracy critiques the color theory and composition of each one. Appendixes of design and maintenance characteristics make this book even more useful; the culture and design charts, and handy lists arranged by flower color, texture, winter interest, and fragrance, are just a few of the pages that are sure to be well thumbed and dog-eared. Looking

for a plant for dry shade or wet, sunny sites? Consult the maintenance lists. Want a hard-to-find plant? Check the list of sources for some great nurseries.

What about maintenance, you ask? The undisputed "Queen of Deadheading" provides information on nurturing your mixed garden, including all the fundamentals from pruning of cut-back shrubs to overwintering tropicals. In short, *The Well-Designed Mixed Garden* gives you all the tools you need to design a stunning border, island bed, or mixed garden. Even if garden design is too daunting for you to undertake on your own, this book gives you the language and the tools to work effectively with a design professional to create the garden of your dreams. So start pedaling your way down the path for the garden adventure of a lifetime.

C. Colston Burrell
Free Union, Virginia

PREFACE

The idea for this book has been brewing for years. While writing my first book, more than seven years ago, I struggled continually not to include information relating to design, which wouldn't have been relevant in a book on plant maintenance. But as I toured and lectured, I sensed a need for more education, not just about perennials but about a wide palette of plants and, most importantly, not just about the plants (we have all sat through lecture after lecture with slide after slide of plants!) but about how to properly bring a variety of plants together in artfully designed mixed gardens.

Although there are many wonderful references on design, I wanted to provide practical, fairly in-depth information about design in a way that would dispel the mystery that often surrounds it. I didn't want simply to show beautiful pictures of gardens and vaguely discuss design, leaving the reader inspired but without the tools to carry through with the process. I hope that by first discussing the basic steps of the design process and then showing how to actually lay out a simple design—applying what was discussed, using real garden designs and combinations—the reader will be equipped either to design mixed gardens or to understand the process well enough to be effectively involved with the person who is designing the garden. Above all, I hope that you, the reader, will gain a greater appreciation for the elements (particularly color) and principles of design—and take the time to really "see" these elements and principles, not only in gardens but wherever they are present in our daily lives. Joy comes with awareness!

This book, a combination of the academic and practical designer in me, is based on my 15-plus-years' experience in designing mixed gardens. I have a great love for herbaceous perennials, but I am so pleased to be discussing exciting woody plants, annuals, and bulbs as well. My academic base is actually in woody plants: my first job at The Ohio State University was as a teaching assistant in a woody plant identification course, when I was still an undergraduate. (Being a plant nerd had its benefits!) At that time, herbaceous perennials were just starting to be taught at the university, and woody plants ruled.

I hope you will be able to take your time to digest the information, the detail in the designs large and small, and the often simple beauty that makes the work effective. All the plants in the designs are referenced in the three appendixes and may be illustrated and further discussed in the encyclopedia (Part Three); if there are photographs of a plant, it is indicated in the Design Chart in Appendix B and the Culture Chart in Appendix C.

May the entire book inspire the artist in every one of you.

ACKNOWLEDGMENTS

I feel truly blessed to have had the kind of overwhelming support, from so many people, that enables a book of this kind to come to fruition. My husband, Jim, and my son, Zachary, are always at the top of my list to thank: their love and ability to keep me focused on what is really important, even during the frustrating times, are treasures. A special thanks goes to my talented and able assistant Kristen Cady, who spent months working on details of plant names, data entry, and many other annoying book tasks at the expense of her own design business—her help was invaluable. A huge thanks also to Bess Heiberger (a.k.a. Tsarina of Data), who unselfishly volunteered her time to assist with hours of computer support and programming; when she volunteered, I'm sure she had no idea how computer-illiterate I was. Kris and Bess' cama- raderie helped me avoid the isolation that one normally feels when doing a work of this kind. I want to thank the very talented Megan H. King and Stacey Renee Peters, whose beautiful artwork adds so greatly to the message of the book. Thanks to Stacey, also, for spending hours discussing color theory with me. A big thanks to Ian Adams, for making such beautiful slides of my gardens and my clients' gardens and generously allowing me to use them in this book; to my clients, for allowing me to share their designs and photographs of their gardens—and also for their patience with me during the writing of another book; and to the talented designers and gardeners who allowed me to share pho- tographs of their gardens. I especially want to thank everyone at Timber Press for believing in me again and for taking such good care of me, particularly my acquisitions editor, Neal Maillet; my editor, Franni Bertolino Farrell; and my publicity manager, Debby Garman.

The following people have helped in various ways—thanks to them all for their time: Dave Dannaher (for growing great conifers for my design work and providing information on nomenclature), Kevin Reiner (great tropical plants and informa- tion), Brent Heath (hardy and tender bulb information), Chris Baker (unusual annuals and perennials and help with nomencla- ture), Denise Adams (historical perspective and the ongoing support and encouragement of a close friend), Cole Burrell (inspiration, insight, and support), my father, Louis DiSabato, and my mother-in-law, Jeanne Aust.

I would also like to thank everyone who supported my first book: the warmth, encouragement, and kindness you showed— during book signings, conversations at speaking engagements, in your cards—inspired me to write this one. Thank you for making every ounce of hard work worth it.

PART ONE

Mixed Garden Design Basics

Chapter 1

WHY A MIXED GARDEN?

When gardens that you've visited linger pleasantly in your memory, what do they look like? Do they have trees above to protect you? Are the trees underplanted with rhododendrons, hellebores, and daffodils? Perhaps there are old-fashioned roses, whose fragrance you can almost still smell. Around the roses are alliums, foxgloves, and dianthus, the wall behind may be covered with honeysuckle and clematis. A group of nigella in soft blue, seeded from the previous season, adds a soft grace to the romantic scene. Maybe you remember a garden with the bold tropical foliage of cannas, the bright yellow flowers of heliopsis, the swaying panicles of miscanthus. The enlivening scene was grounded by the solidity of a boxwood hedge. These picturesque images are of mixed gardens, the gardens I find to be the most spectacular and emotionally rewarding.

A mixed garden is one that is planted with a combination of herbaceous (soft-stemmed) and woody plant material. Trees and shrubs, roses, and perhaps large-growing ornamental grasses may give the garden its outlining structure. Herbaceous perennials and annuals, along with spring- and summer-flowering bulbs, vines, and sometimes vegetables, fill the remaining space. The planting is diverse, derived from a wide palette of plant material, making for a garden that has interest and function year-round. Varied textures, forms, and colors abound in a mixed garden. The rhythm of undulating plant heights and habits makes for a dynamic scene. Planting in layers, utilizing all available space, frees the designer and gardener to choose from a wider variety of plant material; space is used more creatively and efficiently. Sections of light and shadow provide the ability to grow sun- and shade-loving plants in close proximity. Mixed gardens are particularly important for small spaces, where the

Plate 1. A mixed garden in spring speaks to our emotions like no other type of planting can. Featuring *Humulus lupulus* 'Bianca', *Abies lasiocarpa* 'Arizonica Compacta', *Hesperis matronalis*, *Iris* 'Flavescens' viewed through *Fagus sylvatica* 'Tricolor'. Author's garden, Sunbury, Ohio.

luxury of separate spaces for a shrubbery (shrub border), an annual bed, and a perennial garden are not possible.

What I call mixed gardens or borders are often an extension of the traditional perennial border, yet they offer several advantages over a strictly herbaceous garden. The framework of deciduous and evergreen shrubs or trees can add tremendously to the winter garden. Annuals, tropicals, and early spring, summer,

Plate 3. This wild and eclectic mixed garden, which combines trees, perennials, herbs, tropicals, annuals, and vines, harmonizes with its natural surroundings. Besides providing plant support, the arbor breaks the horizontal plane and makes it possible to utilize some of the vertical space in the border. Featuring *Canna* 'Striata' (Pretoria), *Ocimum* 'African Blue', *Ipomoea tricolor* 'Heavenly Blue', *Rudbeckia triloba*. Author's garden.

Plate 2. A closer look at a summer vignette from the garden shown in Plate 1 illustrates the multi-seasonal dynamics of a mixed border. Featuring *Eupatorium purpureum* ssp. *maculatum* 'Gateway', *Miscanthus sinensis* var. *condensatus* 'Cosmopolitan', *Humulus lupulus* 'Bianca', *Abies lasiocarpa* 'Arizonica Compacta'. Author's garden; photograph by Ian Adams.

Plate 4. I'm a plant collector *and* a designer, and I hope my own gardens reflect that. In this photograph (shot with morning sidelighting) and in Plate 5 (shot with evening backlighting), various plants are wed together with consideration to color, including the effects of light, texture, and form, and the principles of design. The photographs were taken within 5 ft. of each other, from different angles; the magenta *Phlox paniculata* 'Look Again' in the center of each is a good reference point. Also featuring *Eryngium yuccifolium*, *Pinus parviflora* 'Yatsubusa', *Hemerocallis* 'Alluring Peach', *Phlox paniculata* 'Fesselballon', *Molinia caerulea* ssp. *arundinacea* 'Skyracer'. Author's garden.

Plate 5. Who says you can't have it all—tons of plants and good design? Featuring *Miscanthus* 'Purpurascens', *Euphorbia cotinifolia*, *Acer griseum*, *Agastache* 'Blue Fortune', *Phlox paniculata* 'Look Again', *Lespedeza cuneata*, *Rudbeckia fulgida* var. *speciosa* (*newmannii*), *Panicum virgatum* 'Rehbraun'. Author's garden.

and autumn bulbs further extend the season of interest in a mixed garden. We need not rely on flowers for the predominant interest but can look to fruit, bark, and autumn color from the woodies to provide further drama. Vines incorporated to utilize the vertical space in the garden can add scale if used on a free-standing structure such as an obelisk, or they might soften a wall or hide a fence. Aligned as it is with plantings in nature, a mixed garden often has a more natural feel to it than a purely perennial or annual planting. Hearken back to fourth-grade science (yikes!) and its lessons about the layers of the forest: canopy, understory, shrubs, and herbaceous groundcovers. For planta-holics—those of us who love all kinds of plants, no matter if they are herbaceous or woody—planting a mixed border better satisfies our fanatical plant-lust. It turns a collection of plants into an artistic garden.

The origins of the American model of the mixed border can be traced back more than two centuries, to Britain, most likely to the late 18th-century British concept of a shrubbery, according to my friend and gardening historian Denise Adams. At that time, thoughtful combinations of trees, shrubs, and herbaceous plants adorned the landscape. The plants in these grouping were typically arranged according to height; the emphasis was on the shrubs themselves, and the herbaceous plants filled in. Bernard M'Mahon (1806), who "borrowed" most of his design precepts from 18th-century English garden writers, was among the first Americans to discuss ornamental gardening; he describes what we now call the mixed border thus:

> First an open lawn of grass-ground is extended on one of the principal fronts of the mansion or main house, widening gradually from the house outward, having each side bounded by various plantations of trees, shrubs, and flowers, in clumps, thickets, etc., exhibited in a variety of rural forms, in moderate concave and convex curves, and projections, to prevent all appearance of stiff uniformity. . . . Each boundary must be planted with a choice variety of ornamental trees and shrubs, deciduous and ever-greens, arranged principally in several clumps; some consisting of trees, shrubs, and herbaceous plants together; in all of which, arrange the taller growing kinds backward, and the lower forward, according to their graduation of height; embellishing the front with the more curious low flowering shrubs, and ever-greens, interspersed with various herbaceous flowering perennials, all open to the lawn and walks.

William Robinson and Gertrude Jekyll are normally credited with the resurgence of interest in herbaceous and mixed borders in England in the late 19th century (see Diagram 1 for an early indication of this renewed interest). Robinson began the crusade to work with more natural-looking combinations, eliminating gaudy bedding schemes from the landscape. Jekyll carried out the idea to perfection, incorporating color theory into border design.

In early 20th-century America, many garden writers, primarily female, followed the precepts of Gertrude Jekyll but adapted them for American gardens. Among these were Helena Rutherford Ely, Mrs. Francis King (Louisa Yeomans King), and Louise Beebe Wilder. In *Color in My Garden* (1918), Wilder mentioned some of her favorite combinations: "*Magnolia stellata* with a ground cover of the common grape hyacinth, *Muscari botryoides*, [and] purple barberry . . . behind Irises of the pinky-mauve tones, Fraxinella, hybrid Pyrethrums." In 1906, Liberty Hyde Bailey referred to this era as the "renaissance of the flower border."

We now have many talented "border-builders." One of particular note is Ann Lovejoy, author of *The American Mixed Border* (1993), the only previous American book that directly addresses the subject of mixed garden design. Ann's varied works (she has written more than 18 gardening books and countless magazine articles) often discuss a wide palette of plant material and reference their use in her mixed gardens.

Although the traditional border was backed by a hedge, fence, or wall (and was often on the border or edge of the lawn), we will use the term "mixed border" to describe any mixed garden, whether it be a freestanding bed or a bordered bed. Mixed gardens offer many different types and levels of sophistication. They can be relaxed in appearance, with no definable plan, or they can appear very organized, with distinct color themes or prominent styles. Planning a mixed border is complex but extremely gratifying, no matter what level of gardening experience one has. Success requires an understanding of order, unity, and rhythm—design principles that will be discussed in detail in Chapter 4. With the recent profusion of new plant introductions, an overwhelming number of creative options are now available for every site or gardening objective. And although, I guess, it is a mixed garden in the most pitiful sense of the term, I hope we can move on from the typical American foundation planting: yews and burning bush in predominance, a crabapple tree, and a token group of black-eyed susan, flanked by a row of annual salvias, marching like bright red soldiers along the front of the entire boring lot.

What are the maintenance considerations of a mixed border compared to other types of plantings? Just as we can create perennial gardens requiring less maintenance, we can select low-maintenance plants for mixed borders. Or we may select some higher-maintenance plants, if they fit our objectives. It is misleading and inaccurate to say that a mixed border always requires less maintenance than a perennial garden. Yes, they never require

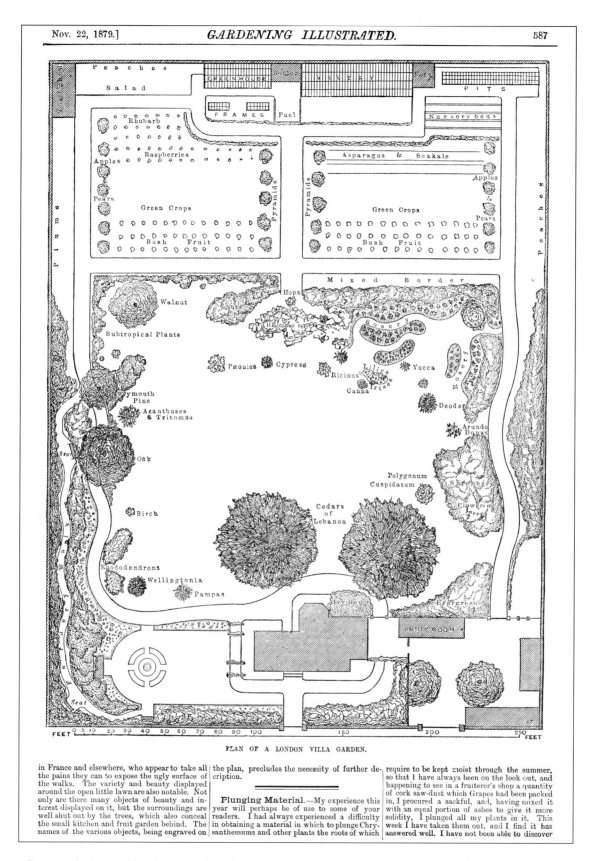

PLAN OF A LONDON VILLA GARDEN.

in France and elsewhere, who appear to take all the pains they can to expose the ugly surface of the walks. The variety and beauty displayed around the open little lawn are also notable. Not only are there many objects of beauty and interest displayed on it, but the surroundings are well shut out by the trees, which also conceal the small kitchen and fruit garden behind. The names of the various objects, being engraved on the plan, precludes the necessity of further description.

Plunging Material.—My experience this year will perhaps be of use to some of your readers. I had always experienced a difficulty in obtaining a material in which to plunge Chrysanthemums and other plants the roots of which require to be kept moist through the summer, so that I have always been on the look out, and happening to see in a fruiterer's shop a quantity of cork saw-dust which Grapes had been packed in, I procured a sackful, and, having mixed it with an equal portion of ashes to give it more solidity, I plunged all my plants in it. This week I have taken them out, and I find it has answered well. I have not been able to discover

Diagram 1. A mixed border on a plan of a London villa garden, *Gardening Illustrated* (22 November 1879).

as much work as the labor-intensive traditional borders in England around the time of World War I. But a mixed garden can be comparable in maintenance to our current perennial gardens, depending on which plants are selected. A good deal depends on the ratio of woody to herbaceous plants: a garden that is predominantly woody, or even close to being a shrubbery, with just a few herbaceous plants, will generally require less care than a mixed border that is predominantly herbaceous, with woody plants used mainly as outlining structural elements. Woody plants, of course, don't need as much care as herbaceous plants (which require daily deadheading, cutting back, pinching, or division), but they do require periodic care in the way of feeding and pruning at certain times to keep growth in check. Select lower-maintenance woody plants just as you would lower-maintenance herbaceous plants (see Chapter 7 and Appendix C). Mixed borders require seasonal adjustment to give maturing plants required space and to maintain the proper proportions of the planting. As always, putting the right plant in the right spot helps keep the degree of maintenance in check.

So, if we want to create dynamic, year-round gardens that give us endless choices and options, if we yearn for gardens that appeal to our hearts and souls—mixed gardens are the answer.

Plate 6. Not your typical foundation planting, this mixed garden incorporates strong structure, outstanding and ususual plants, and good design. Featuring *Pinus parviflora* 'Glauca', *Musa basjoo*, *Clematis terniflora* (hanging down wall), *Phormium* 'Yellow Wave' (in container), *Hosta* 'Sum and Substance', *Quercus robur* 'Pectinata' (foreground). Author's design, Marous garden, Ohio.

Chapter 2

FIRST STEPS IN THE DESIGN PROCESS

The art of garden design brings intense energy and passion to the creator, in the same way that working on a watercolor inspires a painter. And just as painters must be familiar with proper technique and the characteristics of paper, paint, and brushes, so garden designers must ultimately know the site on which they want to make a garden, the elements that impose on the site, the characteristics of the plants to be included, and the design elements and principles that make it all happen. But, whereas the visual artist eventually finishes his painting, the garden artist's work is never done. The creation of a good garden can take years, even a lifetime, so it is the journey that must be enjoyed. You will need time, desire, patience, and sometimes a touch of insanity along the way.

To decide what type of "picture" you want to create, you must come to grips with your, or your client's, objectives for the garden; these goals serve as an essential foundation, upon which you can build. Site evaluation and objectives are really the one-two nitty-gritty punch of the first three steps of the design process (the third is plant selection), and when, unfortunately, it's time to keep in touch with reality.

SITE EVALUATION

Light, soil, moisture, minimum and maximum temperatures, wind, contour of the land, microclimates, existing vegetation—all these aspects must be evaluated to properly design a new border or to make appropriate additions or subtractions to an existing border. Keep in mind that many of these variables are in constant flux. Changes such as the maturing or loss of plant material (which, for example, will increase or decrease light, while perhaps

decreasing moisture and increasing wind) are inevitable. Mother Nature, who keeps us humbled and guessing from year to year with unpredictable weather conditions, adds to the complexity of the equation—hence the importance of getting as complete an understanding of the site as possible, at the start, to have the greatest success with our design.

I travel a lot around the country, speaking, and I find that, wherever I go, almost everyone thinks they have difficult conditions for gardening, so don't feel you are alone. We all have some cross we must bear: poorly draining, heavy clay soil; overly fast-draining sandy soil; a short growing season; too long a growing season; too much humidity; too little rain, and on and on. But this is part of the challenge of gardening, and I feel it's important for us to bloom where we are planted, so to speak, and learn to find the positive aspects of our site and expand on these. A mixed border full of exciting plants can be a reality even in the most difficult gardening situation if you understand the limitations of the site and select plants that will prosper in such conditions. But do feel you have license to experiment and have fun. We all kill plants (some kill more than others), yet we learn what doesn't work from our mistakes and we move on. Sometimes small miracles happen, and something works that really shouldn't—and we can bask in those moments of glory and remember them during our failures.

LIGHT
We are bombarded with terms to describe light requirements for plants: full sun, partial sun, partial shade, light shade, full shade, dappled shade, deep shade. What conditions does our site have? The site may have many or all of these conditions. An area with

existing mature trees may have full-sun locations right next to full-shade locations. Track the sun for an entire day during the growing season to determine true patterns of the sun, then select appropriate plants for the available light.

Full sun normally means at least six hours of strong sun each day; the south side of a house generally receives at least six hours of sun. Partial sun, partial shade, or light shade means three to five hours of direct sun per day, with protection during the hottest part of the day; partial shade is often found on the east side of a house, which will receive morning sun and perhaps part of the early afternoon sun but no hot, burning late sun from the west. Partial shade may also occur in areas that receive morning sun but are protected by the shade of trees during hot afternoon sun. Areas on the west side of the house have shade in the morning but then are blasted by very intense afternoon sun for a few hours late in the day. This is the worst kind of sun and not an area that will be suited to many plants. Choices of plant material for such areas must be made carefully; do not select plants that will scorch in such a setting. I find plants that will tolerate some shade but prefer full sun work best in these spots.

Full shade or dappled shade translates to less than two hour of direct sun, and full-shade sites will have some filtered sun during part of the day. The north side of the house, directly against the house, is normally full shade. It may receive a touch of early morning sun and a touch of late afternoon sun. Full shade or dappled shade most often is provided by trees. The extent and depth of the tree roots will determine what you can grow, but this is normally a great location for many shade-loving plants (see Appendix C). Deep shade, where direct sunlight seldom reaches, can be a difficult site for growing plants. Plants may not be the best option for such a site; pine needle mulching or a structural element, such as a sculpture, may be a better choice.

Keep in mind that the farther out from the house or building the bed extends, the longer that area will be exposed to sunlight if it is not blocked by trees. For example, the area of the border right up against the north-facing wall of your home may be in shade for most of the day, but the area of the border that reaches, say, 10 or 12 ft. out from the house will get great morning sun and then some late afternoon sun. It may even receive some mid-day sun, depending on the angle of the house and time of year. Plants requiring different light conditions can be grown in different areas of such a border.

The intensity, or strength, of the sun is also an important consideration. The sun's strength varies during different times of the day, and the south and west sun is more intense than the east sun. Spring and winter sun is normally less intense than summer sun. The sun is more intense at higher elevations and in southern regions, so a plant that can take full sun in northern regions may need some protection from afternoon sun in the South. Factors such as reflective heat from hardscaping surfaces or snow can increase the intensity of the sun's power; reflected light can burn leaves, crack bark, and increase the transpiration rate of broadleaf evergreens, leading to excessive moisture loss.

Watching your site and determining the intensity and duration of the sun in different locations during the growing season will help you choose the best location for your selected border or borders. If you admire shade-loving plants but only have sunny areas, perhaps it's time to start planting some trees to develop shade areas for the future. Remember, in a mixed border small trees and shrubs will create pockets of shade. More often than not, though, people want to grow sun-loving plants and have too much shade. Can certain less-than-desirable trees be removed from the site to create more light? Perhaps just proper pruning of the tree will open up the area, increasing brightness.

Whatever your light conditions, learn them and then choose plant material that best fits them. Only then can you create a successful garden. Read more about light and its effect on the colors of selected plants in Chapter 3.

SOIL

While researching my first book, *The Well-Tended Perennial Garden* (1998), I was startled to learn that approximately 80% of all plant problems, not just those of herbaceous perennials, are related to poor soil (Patterson et al. 1980). Obviously, good soil is a must if the plants in our mixed borders are to give their best performance.

Testing the soil is an important first step. Determine the soil type (sand, clay, loam, or a combination of these?), pH (level of acidity or alkalinity), organic matter content, and available phosphate, potash, and nitrogen. Remember: to reduce maintenance and frustration down the road, match plants to conditions as much as possible. If your soil is alkaline, it is pointless to try to grow acid-loving plants in it. If you have an extremely wet area, steer away from the drought-lovers and select trees, shrubs, and herbaceous plants that will thrive in such conditions (see Appendix C).

Preparing the soil in a mixed border is the same as preparing the soil in a herbaceous perennial border (I urge you to refer to Chapter 2 of *The Well-Tended Perennial Garden* if you are not familiar these techniques, as they are covered in great detail there). Above all, be sure that the area is free of weeds and that the soil is well draining and contains sufficient organic matter. Organic matter is key: it increases plant growth, improves drainage in clay soils, increases moisture and nutrient retention in sandy soils, increases microbial and earthworm populations, reduces compaction and erosion, and in most cases reduces the incidence of many soil-borne diseases. For best results, work 4 in. of different types of organic matter into the soil to a depth of 9–12 in. For the mixed borders presented in this book, my company, Horticultural Classics & Consultations, used 2 in. of Canadian sphagnum peat moss and 2 in. of a compost blend (1 part leaf humus, 1 part composted biosolids, 1 part topsoil). All the gardens started with an organic matter content of 2–5%; after bed preparation, they were 16–18% organic matter and growing strong! Take time for the soil, and it will reward you for years.

OTHER CONSIDERATIONS

Most of us know which USDA hardiness zone we garden in (see map on page 437). The hardiness zones are determined by the average annual frost-free days and minimum winter temperatures. When selecting a plant, one of your first considerations should be its cold hardiness—and whether or not your area will support it. Following the work of Marc Cathey and the American Horticultural Society (1997), many more of us are just as aware of our heat zones, which are based on average number of days per year above 86°F (30°C). As important as these two ratings are, it's also important to understand the effect of humidity on plants where you garden. We are seeing more plants lost to increased heat and humidity all the time.

Hardiness ratings give the designer a good basis on which to work but remember: many times a plant hasn't had complete testing for hardiness, and the ranges given for it are conservative. "Zone denial" is a common affliction of gardeners of all calibers. You know the symptoms—sweaty palms and unrealistic optimism when reading a nursery catalog whose plants you would die to grow but that are only suited for areas one or two zones warmer than your garden. Many times we order a plant, give it a try. We're given a break by warmer-than-normal winters for a while, but then the inevitable happens: a real winter, and we realize that the zone listing was correct. The plant is not suited to our climate in the least. A property can be on the borderline of a zone and, depending on its location and proximity to a lake, may be warmer or cooler than the zone. We will have areas on our site that are microclimates, spots sheltered from the wind and warmed by the morning sun, where we can push the limits of the hardiness zone. Read your site and identify these areas, as well as any spots that may remain colder than other areas (frost traps). Sometimes plants are not killed by cold but moisture, particularly over the winter, or by high heat and humidity over the summer. How many of us in the Midwest or South have lusted for plants from the Pacific Northwest that only succumb, ungracefully at that, to our oppressive summers?

Record the existing vegetation when evaluating the site. Is there competition from tree roots? Approximately how far out does the root system go? Are there surface roots, or is it a tap root system? The answers will tell you how deep to prepare the soil in that area. They are also important for determining what to design into that space—which plants will take the competition? Is there shade cast in the afternoon onto the site from a neighbor's overgrown shrubs? Will all the existing plant material stay and the bed be designed around it? Will anything need to go? Be ruthless. This is the time for a change for the better. If you're a professional, do what you have to do to convince clients to remove undesirable plants. They'll love you for it in the end.

How do the buildings or other structures on the site, such as gazebos or pool houses, affect proposed planting spaces? Do they cast shadows? If so, how long does the area stay in the shade? Are there any overhangs on these buildings that will prevent rain from hitting the bed space below? Which windows on the house shouldn't be blocked by plant material?

How about eyesores on the site? Electrical boxes, heat pumps, fuel tanks, concrete foundation blocks, compost areas—all need to be recorded so they can be concealed with plant material during the design process. Sometimes these ugly spots go unnoticed during the excitement of thinking about the design possibilities, so I like to take multiple, unforgiving pictures of the site, from various angles.

OBJECTIVES

Just as it's important to evaluate the site, you must evaluate the needs, goals, and tastes of the garden owner. Factors such as maintenance, budget, type and size of border, its style, location, and function, and preferences as to color, texture, form, and peak season(s) of interest need to be determined. Although it may sound easy, it can sometimes be difficult to drag this information out. Nonetheless, it is always worth the effort.

MAINTENANCE AND BUDGET

As most of you are aware, I'm just a bit of a stickler when it comes to garden maintenance. I always preach that the first thing to consider in any garden design is the amount of time the owner has for maintenance. This is reality. Perhaps maintenance contractors will help with some of the gardening needs. Are there skilled professionals available for this in the area? What level of detail can the design take to be maintained properly? Available time for maintenance helps dictate the size and style of the border, as well as the number of higher-maintenance plants to be included. Lower-maintenance plants would have at least four of the following six traits: long-lived, insect and disease resistant or tolerant, noninvasive, minimal pruning requirements, minimal division and staking requirements, and minimal fertilizer requirements. I like to see gardens comprised of at least 70% lower-maintenance plants. If your goal is even less maintenance, strive for a design with an even higher percentage of the "toughies" (see Chapter 7 and Appendix C).

Plate 7. The bold colors and forms of *Yucca flaccida* 'Golden Sword' and *Berberis thunbergii* var. *atropurpurea* 'Rose Glow' are located in a garden viewed from my conservatory. The border was designed for the prime times that we spend in the glass structure: autumn, winter, and very early spring. It was also designed to be backlit by morning sun. The plants in the border reflect the conservatory's style of bold colors and forms (see Plates 8–9). Author's garden.

This brings us to the budget. Consider what budget is available for the cost of the design, the plants, the soil preparation, and the labor (if you are not the extent of the labor force). Then give thought to a long-term budget to maintain the garden. I see this as a potential problem in all gardens—residential, commercial, and public. People are always eager to donate things like plants, benches, and artwork to public gardens, but money for the long-term upkeep of the gardens is also vital.

Plate 8. The colorful boldness of *Canna indica* 'Red Stripe', growing in the conservatory in early spring, harmonizes dramatically with the plants in the border beyond (shown in Plate 7). Author's home.

STYLE

What better form of creative expression than the making of a garden? The style of your borders should reflect *your* style and the mood you want to create. Will they be formal, informal, naturalized, or none of the above? Some basic style guidelines may help you, but remember that these are presented as suggestions, not as strict rules. Be patient and open to "listening" to your site. In many ways, it will speak to you. Is there a certain energy associated with the space? If possible, don't rush into garden-making before you've lived in the area for a while. If you are a professional designer, try to visit the site at different times of the day or even in a couple different seasons. Watch the play of light through the space. Note existing trees on the property and adjacent properties. What feelings do you get for the site from the style of the home, the style of the owners, the style of the town? Keep in mind: as a designer, what you feel may not be exactly what the owners feel, so be open to their vision as well. I love talented garden designer Lauren Springer's philosophy: let your garden celebrate who you are and where you are. I think the "where you are" can refer to regional location as well as emotional state.

Definitely avoid the trap of trying whatever is in at the moment, at the expense of individuality. Don't worry about whether or not cottage style is cool, or think you must go with only native plants, or that it is better to use large masses of fewer perennials—when you love it busy, with lots of different plants! What makes a garden truly special is its uniqueness. Visiting other gardens, reading about gardens, or attending gardening lectures are all great ways to get creative energy and ideas that should be used to help you formulate your own style. You may want your garden style to reflect the interior style of your home. Or you may prefer to have a slightly different style for the gardens, as a change from the mood you experience inside the house. As a professional designer you may find, with time, that you have a certain style that comes through in many of your designs, even though each is individual.

Almost a century ago, Gertrude Jekyll asked important, time-less questions of style in her gardens: "Is it right?" and "Does it fit?" We must always remember to ask these questions. In my own gardens, which frame our log home and are surrounded by 35 acres of natural woodland, I have created mixed borders appro-priate to the location as well as to my style objectives. The borders at Hiddenhaven (what we call our gardens as a whole) are relaxed, literally wild-looking at times, yet full of both classic treasures and new and unusual plants from around the world. Some borders have specific color themes, in others, anything goes. Asters, gold-enrods, and ironweed occupy sections of the borders, much as they do the fields and woods that share this sacred space of ours, yet they mingle with tropicals, dwarf conifers, and countless other nonnative species that satisfy my horticultural desires. Maybe this mix wouldn't please you, but that's what makes me happy, and so to me, that's what's right and that's what fits. The native plants that are on our land have seeded into our gardens, creating a con-nection and a sense of place. Formal clipped evergreens or strong lines would not fit as well in my garden as they do in some of my clients' gardens, just as my style of garden wouldn't fit in their more urban sites.

Just because you want to stay harmonious with the location, however, doesn't mean you can't create a garden that is fun, eclectic, and filled with surprise. For more than a decade, the garden furniture and accessories at Hiddenhaven were natural-looking, made of branches and vines that were very harmonious with the surroundings. Within the last few years, I have had a desire to bring more vibrant colors into the gardens through the furniture and some of the art. Perhaps I sought out these high-energy colors as a change from all the earth tones that surrounded me. I wasn't sure if it would work, but the cobalt-blue Lutyens bench, the orange Waldo chair, and the bright yellow and blue dock chairs are dynamic accents that add major attitude to the gardens (see Plates 56–57). This story also demonstrates that the style of a garden can evolve with the owner. Change is good! You may find, as I have, that one goes through different phases with style, of art as well as of plants.

Different plants evoke different styles. Classical genera often impart a romantic Victorian image, while some of the modern tropicals say the garden is hip. I've been through a dianthus phase, a geranium phase, a lily phase, where I had to have as many of these plants as possible; and it continues, with tropical, dwarf conifer, and even poppy phases. Experimenting with

Plate 9. The yellow and red walls and chair coverings in the conservatory are in union with the plant colors inside the room and out. Author's home.

garden accessories and different plants is an easy and less expen-sive way to play with style, without making any major changes to the garden.

Large masses of fewer types of plants and smaller groups of a variety of plants are two different but equally valid styles. Massed plantings are often more appropriate in large commercial sites, large gardens of large houses, or borders located some distance from the house. In these sites the larger masses are needed to carry the garden. The effect can be dynamic, with huge sweeps of plants creating movement and form. This style, however, does not fit as well in small gardens, where the huge masses are often out of scale with the site. I find large masses of fewer plants in small spaces can often be boring, even if they are long-flowering peren-nials or annuals; the scene just doesn't have the changing dynamic offered by smaller groups in a more varied plant palette.

Is a formal or informal style appropriate to the border? It is often recommended that the gardens be more formal close to the house and progressively less formal as you move out and away from the house. Sometimes people opt for formal borders at the front entryway to the home, which may be more formal in nature, and informal borders on the sides and back of the home. The back of the home is often the location for a patio or terrace used for relaxed entertaining, and the gardens that sur-round them should support this cutting-loose theme. In other homes, this back area may still be somewhat formal in appear-ance, and so then should the gardens be; perhaps as you move further out into the property, which is often wooded and more natural, the gardens can become more informal. Of course, if the home is very informal in all locations, the style of the borders would also be informal. A very effective combination of

Plate 10. The strong vertical line and formal style of *Pinus sylvestris* 'Fastigiata' add weight and permanence to the large ephemeral mass of light-textured wildflowers planted at its base. This vignette demonstrates how effective formality and informality can be when combined. Author's garden.

Plate 11. The wildflowers, particularly the poppies, contribute to-die-for color and flowers for cutting—added benefits to the mixed combination shown in Plate 10. Author's home.

styles is to have the strictest formality in the outlining structure of the garden, with the most lax informality of planting within. Strong rectangular lines suggest formality; curvilinear lines suggest informality.

The style you choose is only one aspect in determining the mood of the garden. A garden's mood is also affected by color, texture, and form; plant selection; light and shadow; movement and line; structural and art elements. Gardens can evoke endless emotions, from refinement, grace, and tranquility to the free-spirited border that says it's time to let your inner child out! Find a style that is your own and have fun with it.

LOCATION

Can you choose the location of your border or borders? Sometimes, yes. But other times the site, existing structural elements, or other conditions dictate where the gardening space will be. A blank canvas is great to work with but can be overwhelming, particularly if it is a large blank site. Live with your location. Are there areas of the site that would not support a mixed border because of poor soil or other cultural conditions? Where will you best see the border, from inside the house or on the patio? If possible, plan your garden to take advantage of these views. If you're a professional designer, you need to go into your client's home, where you and your client will work together to determine these locations. If at all possible, I always select a border location that will marry the garden with the house. I designed our back gardens to be viewed from our screened porch, where we eat our meals and entertain during most of the growing season.

If you are interested in Asian gardening principles, you or your client may want to explore basing your garden layout on feng shui. Feng shui is the ancient Chinese art of design and placement that balances the chi, or energies, within your surroundings. Many wonderful references address this topic (Rawlings 1998, Wydra 1997, to name two).

One way to visualize the garden is to use a garden hose or outdoor extension cord (bright orange really stands out) to outline your intended border. You can experiment with different sizes, shapes, and placements at this stage. Spray paint the outline once you have a good idea of the right location. Walk around or through the area; play with incorporating paths or seating areas, if they will be included in the design. Bring a sample of the material being considered for the path, and place it to get a feel for how it works. Place bamboo stakes where focal areas may be. Are you thinking of incorporating walls? Then erect a small section of wall to see what the material looks like on the site, and to see if you like the feeling of enclosure you have planned. Check out your location from various angles and at different times of the day. Visualize what it will look like with some of the plants you are considering.

Does a garden in this location relate well to its surroundings? A border smack-dab in the middle of a large expanse of lawn is going to be out of place, even if it may be the best view from inside the home. Will trees or shrubs need to be added to the site as backdrops for the border, to create enclosure, or to act as a transition between existing larger mature trees and the border, bringing it into scale with the area? Trees or shrubs may be needed to screen unsightly views or provide privacy. At this time, consider what other things would enhance the border, perhaps some sort of water element or other artistic feature?

It is better to experiment with your options on site at this early stage. A garden hose is a lot easier to move than an entire border that is badly placed.

TYPES AND SIZES

You can create mixed gardens in borders or island beds, or a combination of the two. A border is a garden that is bordered on at least one side by a wall, fence, or hedge—a foundation planting, for example, which is backed by the wall of the house. A dark background provided by a dark-colored fence or deep green hedge can really set off the colors in a mixed border. A wall or fence also provides a vertical plane on which to grow vines, which will help soften the bordering structure as well as extend the interest of the garden into the vertical space. This wall or fence may be useful for creating boundaries for the garden as well.

What size and shape should the border be? Many variables come into play when determining this. Most important is that the border or garden be large enough to balance the scale or mass of the area, existing plant material, or structure with which it is associated. Many people have a good sense of proper scale and proportion; by just looking at an area, they can determine the garden size and preferred shape naturally, by eye. New border-builders, however, may require some guidelines to get started, so here's some food for thought.

Scale and proportion relate all parts of the design to each other and to the whole composition. Scale refers to the relative size of an element or area; proportion refers to the relationship of the elements' sizes to each other. To take a hypothetical example, the individual trees in a redwood grove on a parking strip might be in

Plate 12. The gardens are just a natural extension of our home. Author's home and garden.

proportion to each other but out of scale with their surroundings. Keep scale and proportion in mind through all the steps of the design, from the size and shape of the border to the proper mature size and shape of the plants we are selecting and even the groupings of plants. Proper scale and proportion create a balance between the positive (masses) and negative (areas between masses) spaces in the garden.

In a garden, many different things set scale. It may be the house, an arbor or other structural element, or existing trees. We have all seen improper scale in landscapes. The 2-ft.-wide bed, planted with 12-in.-tall impatiens, that borders a 20-ft.-tall house is one example, as are the massive junipers devouring the front of a ranch-style home. It pains me every time I see these all-too-frequent travesties. On several occasions we have removed existing sidewalks from a client's property, staked out the proper bed size, and poured new walks. If you are a professional designer, try to be involved with the site as early as possible and determine the bed layout as the house is being built. Colors, textures, artwork, and patterns in paths are just a few things that can be used to manipulate scale in a garden.

Proportion is the ratio of one dimension to another, as in the length of our border compared to the width. The Golden Mean, a rule of proportion common throughout nature and taught in art schools for centuries, is simply a ratio: 1 to 1.618 (multiply by 1.618 to get a larger dimension or multiply by 0.618 to get a smaller dimension). The ancient Greeks believed it to be a proportion of divine beauty—when we see something that just seems right proportionally, it is most likely close to this ratio. For example, according to the Golden Mean, a border that is 13 ft.

long should be approximately 8 ft. wide. The Fibonacci Series is an incremental series of numbers based on the Golden Mean, as follows: 0, 1, 1, 2, 3, 5, 8, 13, and so on. Each number added to the previous number yields the next number; each number divided by the previous number yields an answer of approximately 1.6—very close to the Golden Mean! Even more fascinating is that everything in nature, from a sunflower to a snowflake, has its parts arranged according to the Golden Mean. Many elements in our everyday lives, such as credit cards, cassette tapes, and even the handle on your cup, have these proportions.

We can use this rule as a tool in the garden for many things, including the placement of an important structural element, such as a specimen tree in the border or an art element. Is there an easy way to apply this classical approach to proportion? Yes! Use the dimension of one-third in your calculating: look at the total length of the border and place the tree one-third of the way in from one end of the bed. The curves of free-form beds or paths can also be based on golden geometry.

Different styles of architecture are based on different sets of proportions. By taking a few measurements on the site, you can get an idea of what they are and add them to the list of things to think about in your design.

A more modern recommendation proposes that the width of a border should be about one-third the height of the background. This may be a helpful gauge in some cases, but it doesn't hold true in all. What if you were planting in front of a 4-ft.-high fence,

Plate 13. Plants prosper in this raised island bed, located in what would normally be a tough growing area—the turnaround in a driveway. Raising the bed provides good soil and drainage for the plants as well as protection from vehicles and large rowdy dogs. The lines of the bed follow the lines of the turnaround. See Combination 8 in Part Three for plant descriptions. Author's garden.

would you make the border only 1½ ft. wide? Again, it's something to think about.

From my experience in many different landscape sites, I feel that a mixed border should be a minimum of 8 ft. wide to create anything decent horticulturally. If you carve from this a 2-ft.-wide catwalk at the back, for maintenance and to allow air circulation (this is also usually the area under the roof overhang, which doesn't get any rain), you've reduced your space even more. Realize that the remaining 6 ft. of bed space doesn't give much room for planting. This may be the more typical size for a small garden, but larger gardens will require borders that are 10 ft. wide at least. If you have a choice, always go for more room over less. Remember to plan access paths into larger borders to avoid compaction of the soil during maintenance. Use your outdoor extension cord or garden hose to lay out the bed and visualize how the size and shape fits with the site. Professional designers do this all the time when making new gardens. Live with the proposed bed for a while to see how you like it from different angles, different locations both inside and outside the house, and during different times of the day.

One of my front borders averages about 12 ft. in width and runs 45 ft., along our garage to the front entrance of our home. A 3- to 4-ft.-wide stone path runs along this garden, and another bed, 8 ft. wide by 43 ft. long, is on the opposite side of the path. Our home is approximately 25 ft. tall at the peak. A willow trellis supports a huge honeysuckle and clematis vine on the front wall, further softening the difference in scale. These gardens, which create a welcoming entrance to our home, work well in terms of scale and proportion; they were placed by eye and not any rules (see Diagram 18 in Chapter 8).

An island bed is freestanding in a lawn or perhaps paved area; it is not bordered by a structure. It can take on a variety of shapes and forms. Rectangular or square shapes appear more formal, while free-form or oval shapes are more casual. Keep in mind the design element of line when deciding on bed or border shapes. Line is related to eye movement or overall flow. In a landscape, line is inferred by bed layout and the way the different beds work or meld together. To keep a garden unified, stick with the same or similar bed lines, whether straight or curved, throughout. Pick a theme and go with it.

Again, the size of the island bed should be in proper scale and proportion to the surrounding areas. Don't forget the Golden Mean. Avoid the common traps of making the island bed too small, or of sticking it out in the middle of the lawn, by itself, without any other beds, plants, or structural elements to connect it to the rest of the landscape. I have found that a functional island bed should be at least 6–8 ft. wide; you can work in a bed this size from both sides. Another simple guideline is that the island bed be three times as long as it is wide; and it is often recommended that the tallest plant in the center of the bed be one-half the width of the bed. For example, an island bed that was 10 ft. wide would be 30 ft. long, and its tallest plant would be approximately 5 ft. tall. I hope this gives beginners a starting spot, but feel free to think outside the box, as I always try to do, and create your own dimensions, suitable to your style and garden.

I like to create mixed gardens that comprise perhaps the entire front yard or very large area of the site (see Plates 30, 115–116). These gardens don't really fit our description of borders as such or island beds. I see them as a combination of the two and have seen them referred to as open borders. Whatever we want to call them, I think of them as gardener's gardens. This style is particularly effective on small lots, where a small amount of grass is nothing but a bother anyway—it's much more desirable to give the whole area over to gardens. Paths in these gardens are essential for access and maintenance, although they may at certain times of the year be barely visible, overgrown with plant material. I like to have paths in most of my designs: the act of actually bringing people into the garden (rather than just having them look at it from the outside) heightens the experience and is one aspect of my style.

FUNCTION

It is critical before designing the mixed border to have an understanding of all the functions the garden is expected to serve, not just the obvious one of being a source of aesthetic beauty. Will it be used for cut flowers, or to attract birds, butterflies, or other wildlife into the gardens? Is it to provide fragrance? Will it be the focus during entertaining? If so, predominantly in the daytime or evening? Should the garden provide privacy from neighbors? Will children be playing in or around the garden? Is it to be educational, a public garden? Will it perhaps serve as a place for meditation or prayer? Knowledge of these factors will help you create a visually spectacular garden that serves many purposes.

COLOR, TEXTURE, AND FORM

I discuss color in great detail in Chapter 3, but it is important to think about preferences regarding it, texture, and form in the early stages of the design process, while formulating the overall objectives for the border. Color is everywhere in gardens, not just in the flowers. We need to take into account color in foliage, fruit, bark, soil, mulch, surrounding grass, vegetation, hardscaping. Will we create a garden that has a limited color palette, or will a variety of colors be used? Will the colors be soft pastels or bold hot colors? Perhaps the color theme will change with the seasons. The colors of the accompanying home and hardscaping need to be taken into consideration. As the designer, are you involved in selecting these colors? Try to be. Are there certain interior colors that are to be repeated in the garden? Color has a dramatic effect on the mood of the garden. It is extremely subjective and, of course, wonderfully artistic: it is how we as gardeners paint. Many people get carried away with color in the border, forgetting structure, form, texture, and other important design elements. Remember, even though it is great fun, color is just a part of the mixed border puzzle.

PEAK SEASON OF INTEREST

A truly well-designed mixed border should provide year-round interest. Still the garden will go through waves. At times it really shines; at other times, it rests. This is normal and occurs in all living things. I know this may sound funny, but occasionally we must remind ourselves, and others, that gardens are just that—living things. It will not be breathtaking at every moment of the year, with everything flowering in all seasons. A great part of the beauty of a garden and nature is this dynamic of change.

With this in mind, I like to have clients tell me a season that they would really like to have the border in full orchestration, so to speak. Often we will select borders at different locations throughout the site to peak at different times, based on their function. The border in the front of our house peaks in late spring and early summer; the border across from it has a predominant autumn theme (see Plates 87–89). The gardens in the back, adjacent to the screened porch, are in full glory for a long period in the summer and early autumn. The gardens always have something beautiful happening in them, but these are times when everything gels.

I hope you will find in the designs and combinations in this book some great examples for putting plants together with season-long interest in mind. For instance, if you want to have some outstanding spring-flowering shrubs and trees in the garden (which may also exhibit autumn color and perhaps ornamental fruit), then some of the perennials and bulbs should coincide with this interest. Summer-flowering annuals and tropicals and other plants should provide interest in the summer. Vines with either spring, summer, or autumn interest can further add to the display. Evergreens, either woody or herbaceous, can carry the winter garden, along with attractive seedheads and the outlining structure of perennials, ornamental grasses, and deciduous plant material. Long-flowering plants, outstanding textures and forms, and artwork are all ways to ensure continual interest in gardens and are particularly vital in very small gardens, where it may be difficult to have many plants.

Sometimes a garden needs to perform for a very limited time. The owner may only use the property as a summer or winter home. The gardens would be designed accordingly, making the most of the season when it will be appreciated.

Obviously, in order to create plant combinations with a certain season or seasons of interest, one must know, roughly, when a plant is supposed to flower (see the Design Chart in Appendix B).

Seasonal weather conditions always have the last say and ultimately determine when a particular plant will actually flower in a given year; regional conditions too will influence bloom times. Even small differences in locations can affect time of flowering; our growing season here at Hiddenhaven, for instance, can be one to almost two weeks shorter than it is in a city 30 miles to the southwest. It's great if you can note actual dates when plants flower in your area. In the very early spring, when there isn't much flowering, I always do so well—and then, of course, as my busy season gets in full swing, it becomes more difficult. Precise dates are particularly helpful when you need to design for a specific date, as sometimes happens, such as an open garden tour that occurs the first Saturday in May, or a graduation on the second Sunday in June.

Planning with consideration to seasonal interest is among the most detail-oriented, dynamic, and challenging parts of the mixed border design process. Take the time to think of each plant in all moments of its life. How does it emerge? Will there be contribution from color or form at that time? What does it look like throughout the growing season? Will the foliage or bark be a constant contributor to the garden or does the plant require pruning, leaving minimal interest? Are the deadheads or fruiting capsules exciting or distracting? Do the flowers die gracefully? Will the autumn color clash with other colors on the site? Give this step in the design process your thorough consideration, and your border will reward you with constant beauty.

PLANT SELECTION

The moment we have all been waiting for: it's time to think about the plants! As a gardener, isn't buying plants one of your favorite things to do in the whole world? The adrenaline starts pumping, your heart is light, and often you can't help buying more than you really need. Actually, I use the term "need" loosely. A firm plan does help to set limits.

Everything we have discussed in this chapter so far—including light, soil, maintenance and budget, size and type of bed, function, color, and peak season of interest—must be kept in mind when choosing plants. We also need to consider things we will discuss in more detail in the rest of the book, such as texture, form, balance, repetition, rhythm, and focal points. And we must determine if there are any plants that will help us or our clients make connections to past memorable experiences of gardens, nature, or loved ones. Every time I smell basil, I think of my grandfather, who gardened until he was close to 90 years old. Even though I often select the purple-leaved cultivar 'African Blue', which he never saw in his life, it still has that connection for me. As designers we want to include, whenever possible, plants that will stir pleasant memories in our clients.

When designing a mixed border, it is important to select plants that will work together, not only from an aesthetic standpoint but from a cultural, or maintenance, standpoint. How do we combine perennials, trees, shrubs, vines, and various other plant material with success? Unless your objective is to cover some major ground, your main priority when choosing permanent plants is to stick with species that are not extremely quick growing, invasive, or stolonizing. Trying to fight an aggressive root system—be it from a tree, a stolonizing shrub, grass, or bamboo—is a major high-maintenance pain. Having to constantly prune shrubs or trees to keep them in their allocated space is also undesirable. Of course, many nonpermanent plants, such as certain annuals (particularly tropicals), will be expected to put on major growth in the season to earn their place in the border. Most plants should have similar cultural requirements. Is the plant an environmentally sound choice? If it doesn't fit well with the site, if it requires huge amounts of supplemental water or chemical fertilizers or pesticides to maintain it, then it's not. No matter how much we or our clients might want such a plant in the garden, it should be admired only in books or other people's gardens, where it can grow without contributing to our declining resources. Also, consider if there is a danger of the plant's invading native habitats and destroying the natural ecosystem—and act accordingly (I confine *Pistia stratiotes*, water lettuce, to a whiskey barrel in my garden; see Plate 71).

Throughout the book, I offer many suggestions for outstanding plant material to use. Here we will look at some general considerations when selecting plants.

TREES

Normally there isn't room for many trees in a mixed garden; depending, of course, on the size of the garden, we may be able to incorporate up to about five. This doesn't include trees that may be used for hedging or screening around the perimeter or outer edge of the garden. Select smaller trees for design of a mixed border, preferably those that grow to about 20 ft. (small trees are in the 15–30 ft. range). Understanding the rate of growth will be a key consideration as well. Certain trees may ultimately reach 30 ft. but are so slow growing that under normal landscape conditions they would never reach that height (slow-growing plants grow about 12 in. or less in a year; medium-growing plants, 13–24 in. per year; fast growers can gain 25 in. or more annually). Usually, plant heights listed in references are the ultimate height of trees growing under ideal or native conditions; many times, smaller-growing selections of a particular species are available.

Size should really be the first consideration when selecting the right trees: one of the most frequently encountered problems in landscapes is trees that are too large for the site. There are trees for almost any size garden. Keep in mind that periodic pruning may be in order—trees may need to be limbed-up or opened for

Plate 14. Large-growing trees may be selected for large hedges in large gardens. Here, white pines (*Pinus strobus*) back a 6,000-sq.-ft. border in three acres of gardens. The dwarf conifer within the border, *Chamaecyparis obtusa* 'Fernspray Gold', is an ideal plant for mixed borders: its pyramidal habit is treelike, but it is slow growing, reaching only 6–8 ft. Author's design, Hendley garden, Ohio.

Plate 15. Large-growing shrubs, such as this *Aralia elata* 'Aureovariegata', add dramatic color, texture, and form to mixed gardens. Trellis artist, Mark Bokenkamp; author's garden.

the plant material growing around them, or pruned to keep their branches off the house or bordering structure. But regular pruning to control a tree's size detracts from the natural beauty of the plant and is a bother to the gardener.

Trees are normally the first plants placed in a design. They are almost always a very dominant feature (helping to form, as they do, the structural outline, the "bones" of the garden), so their proper selection should be given some thought. Small trees link the border or garden to the surroundings, much in the way that understory trees tie the canopy to the lower-growing vegetation in a woodland. They can be used to bring the border into proper proportion with the rest of the site.

Because the number of trees we can include in a mixed border is so limited, we want to select trees that will provide as many good qualities as possible year-round. My favorite is paperbark maple (*Acer griseum*) because it offers peeling cinnamon-colored bark through the entire year. It is a small slow-growing tree, with a good habit, narrow and upright; it also has outstanding autumn color, handsome pest- and disease-resistant trifoliate leaves, and interesting fruit. What more could you ask for?

A winter garden must have a good balance of deciduous and evergreen species. Too many of one or the other (better yet, think of too much relative mass) can be disturbing to the eye. Likewise, a tree needs to be balanced properly with the number of small shrubs or perennials and annuals in the summer garden.

Often large trees already exist on the site. It is critical to understand each species (the type and extent of its root system, the amount of shade it casts), and its contribution or hindrance to views. Live with the area and consider the value of the trees before making any decisions regarding pruning or removal. Often smaller trees are needed in such gardens to smooth the transition to the ground level, creating a more comfortable space for humans.

SHRUBS AND VINES

I most often select shrubs that are 3–5 ft. in height for mixed gardens, but larger shrubs, 6–10 ft. or more in height, can be limbed-up and used as you would a small tree, particularly where space is limited. These larger-growing shrubs are also useful as a background or hedge. Some larger-growing shrubs or small trees, such as smokebush (*Cotinus coggygria* 'Velvet Cloak') or Sutherland Gold European red elder (*Sambucus racemosa* 'Sutherland Gold'), are selected for their outstanding foliage color and are stooled (pruned heavily; see Chapter 7) at the beginning of the season for use as a foliar plant in the mixed border. Shrubs link the trees to the perennials, annuals, and lower-growing herbaceous material. On a design, shrubs are normally placed after the trees, as part of the garden's structural bones. Of course, the form and texture of the shrub determines the impact it will carry. Some are more noticeable and better used as accents; others are better blenders. Properly selected shrubs can be of relatively low maintenance.

Keep the width of shrubs in mind when selecting them, as this can often be more of a concern in a mixed border than the height. Some of what I call the "Big Bertha" shrubs are so broad and

Plate 16. Unusual perennials, such as this *Paeonia obovata*, contribute both flowers and attractive fruit to the mixed garden. Author's garden.

heavy that they can be hard to balance in the border. Look again for a multi-season offering from shrubs; many of the dwarf or slow-growing conifers, for instance, offer evergreen or colorful foliage. Shrubs with ornamental fruit, outstanding autumn color, and interesting branching—along with great flowers—should be sought out. Disease-resistant shrub roses are an integral part of this group, as are many sub-shrubs, such as lavender.

Vines are often overlooked in American mixed borders, but they offer qualities and uses that other plants lack. I love vines and use them whenever possible—on trellises, arbors, fences, and other support structures, such as obelisks or pillars—to take full advantage of the vertical space. Often this space is the side of a house or fence and needs the uniquely beautifying softening vines offer. When space is too limited for the width of a tree or large shrub, vines used on freestanding structures provide a necessary vertical element. Planting vines on something as simple as a post can break up the horizontal plane of a garden, offering variety and interest. Besides, there are so many cool vines available for foliage color, flowers, and fruit that we would be missing out if we didn't include them. Some delicate vines can even be grown on strong shrubs or on a tree in the border. In a more naturalized area, a sturdy dead tree can act as an interesting and unusual support. Allowing vines to grow along the ground is also a fun and unusual alternative to the same old groundcovers; I have done this for years with porcelain berry (*Ampelopsis glandulosa* var. *brevipedunculata* 'Elegans').

HERBACEOUS PLANTS

Herbaceous perennials (trees and shrubs are *woody* perennials), annuals, bulbs, ornamental grasses, and grasslike plants form our next layer in a mixed border. In most gardens I design, there are more herbaceous perennials than any other group of plants. They are the very dynamic element of constant change in the border. They knit the entire garden together, marrying the trees to the shrubs and the shrubs to the annuals and other perennials. Depending on their size, texture, form, and color, they will have a variety of different effects. Tall-growing perennials, such as *Eupatorium purpureum* ssp. *maculatum* 'Gateway' (joe-pye weed), and many of the ornamental grasses, such as *Miscanthus sinensis* 'Malepartus', can be used as structural elements. Architectural plants, such as spiny bear's breeches (*Acanthus spinosus*), make a wonderful accent or focal point. Soft mounding plants, particularly many of the hardy geraniums, are excellent blenders and can be used easily as a repeating element. Groundcovers crawl around the base of more prominent plants, and some, such as golden creeping speedwell (*Veronica repens* 'Sunshine'), reflect brightness onto them. Color offered by foliage and flowers can be used to draw attention or to unify. Herbaceous perennials are the workhorses of the mixed border, attracting butterflies and hummingbirds, providing cut flowers and fragrance. They offer interest in spring, summer, autumn, and, in many cases, winter. When it comes to herbaceous perennials and their exciting varieties, the choices are already innumerable—and still growing.

Complementing the herbaceous perennials are the annuals or tender perennials. Many hot new annuals are now readily available in nurseries—gone are the days when petunias and marigolds were the primary selections. Thank goodness! When I first started designing gardens, I used very few annuals, not because I didn't see their merit, but because the selection was so pitiful. Now I love the variety, particularly in the tropicals. In fact, I've gotten so into these plants that I built a 400-sq.-ft. conservatory so that I could overwinter many of them (see Chapter 7 for information on overwintering tropicals). The wild foliage and flower colors and bold leaf shapes of tropicals are just the spark we needed—back—in our gardens (they were popular during the Victorian era). Large tropicals, such as the bloodleaf banana (*Musa zebrina*), elephant's ear (*Colocasia esculenta* 'Fontanesii'), and many of the cannas, make striking structural plants in the border. What could be more exotic, to extend the season, than a ginger lily flowering in late summer?

In the annual line I'm also particularly fond of the colored-foliage plants, such as *Plectranthus argentatus* and the endless array of coleus and sweet potato vines. Also of great use in the mixed border are the annuals that reseed and act perennial, returning after most winters. Plants such as tall verbena (*Verbena bonariensis*), love-in-a-mist (*Nigella damascena*), larkspur (*Consolida ajacis*), and corn poppies (*Papaver rhoeas*) are fabulous minglers, filling gaps among perennials, shrubs, and trees that are difficult for the border-builder to squeeze a plant into. But these helpful seeders do the work on their

Plate 18. Although not uncommon, morning glories (here, *Ipomoea tricolor* 'Heavenly Blue') are still wonderful interplanted among more unusual plants to add color. Author's garden.

Plate 17. An exciting, long-flowering annual vine that is normally sold as a tropical houseplant, *Thunbergia battiscombei* is an unusual addition to a small obelisk in the garden. Author's garden.

own: I will often take seeds from these plants and sprinkle them into areas where I want filler for the next season. In the final stages of design, we put the last touches on the picture with these fillers.

Many of the tropicals we have been discussing are really tender bulbous plants arising from corms, bulbs, rhizomes, or tubers. Other tender summer-flowering bulbs of great interest are such classic plants as dahlias and gladioli. These bulbs really deserve further study. *Gladiolus* 'Atom' and *G.* 'Violetta' have won my heart by working so cooperatively into thin gaps in borders.

Hardy bulbs are usually one of the final layers in our planting. As far as hardy summer-flowering bulbs go, the alliums are nothing less than versatile and gorgeous. *Allium schubertii*, with its huge 12-ft.-wide flower, is crazy, a real conversation piece, while many of the others are a bit more subdued but still dramatic. The foliage on the large-flowered alliums comes up early and starts to die back about the time they start to flower, so it is best to underplant them with low- or medium-growing plants.

For spring-flowering bulbs, I'm partial to many of the small minor bulbs, such as *Chionodoxa forbesii* (luciliae) (glory of the snow) and *Iris reticulata* (netted iris). The iris blooms so early here in Ohio, often in late February, when you really need to see life in the garden. The foliage is fine on the minor bulbs and hides easily among perennials, and they are nice grouped en masse under trees and shrubs. But it is difficult to create many good combinations with these early bulbs, since, for the most part, the rest of the border is still asleep. Most often, I just appreciate them on their own. The netted iris are spectacular in combination with other early bloomers, such as witchhazels or hellebores. Daffodils are good among groundcovers, tucked under shrubs, and in naturalized areas, where the large leaves of hostas can help conceal their declining foliage. I have grown very fond of the gaudy parrot tulips; I use them and some of the other "artist" tulips as cut flowers and as subjects in watercolors, but otherwise we include very few in our borders. We generally treat tulips as annuals and replace them yearly for best performance; this way, they can be removed without worrying about them detracting from the rest of the garden while their foliage dies down. Besides, they require

Plate 19. We often think of the bold foliar effect of tropical plants, but gingers add a touch of rare tropical flowers to our gardens. Compare the effect of this ginger lily, *Hedychium coccineum*, with the one in Plate 20. Hendley garden, Ohio.

Plate 20. *Hedychium* 'Daniel Weeks' is both gorgeous and delightfully fragrant. Author's garden.

paths. For late-season interest, autumn-flowering bulbs, such as *Colchicum speciosum*, are fun and often novel.

Keep in mind that several perennials, such as lilies and crocosmias, are bulbous plants and may be available from both perennial nurseries and bulb growers. I remember in college trying to recall what type of root structure was associated with different bulbous plants, as it sometimes affected planting, propagation, and storage. Since I always forget, maybe you do too, so f.y.i.: tulips and daffodils are examples of true bulbs. Dahlias are tubers; crocus, crocosmia, and gladioli are corms; and cannas are rhizomes (see the Glossary for descriptions).

If you are a designer, it is important to establish your client's specific plant preferences, if any, early in the design process. (If you are not a professional designer, just imagine how fun it would be to be a personal plant shopper for others!) Of course, these will need to be incorporated into the design if at all possible. If the preferred plants simply don't work with the site, or with the overall objectives of the garden, then it is important that we educate the client about other, more suitable choices. On smaller projects, it's normally possible to determine some plants that might work on the first visit, and I share these ideas with the client by showing them pictures in books or catalogs. This brainstorming session helps me get a better feel for their tastes and preferences as well, which will be a guide as I design.

I compile lists of selected plants while designing. Sometime these lists will be by color, sometimes they are divided into plant groups. For example, I may have a list of trees that would be possible choices as a specimen; a list of shrubs that would serve as a backdrop and attract butterflies; a list of tropicals for accent and

sunny, dry, baking conditions over the summer, which is not normally the case in our borders. For more permanence, select the early blooming Kaufmanniana (waterlily-flowered) and Fosteriana (emperor) types, or the midseason-blooming Darwin hybrids; these are usually the longest-lived tulips. Some of the species tulips, such as *Tulipa batalinii* and *T. clusiana* var. *chrysantha*, which are also more perennial in nature, are effective among rock garden plants or stuck into the cracks of flagstone

Plate 22. *Tulipa* 'Carmine Parrot' is not long-lived in the border, but I use limited numbers in my designs for their pure decadence and usefulness in arrangements—and as inspirations for artistic watercolor interpretations. Author's garden.

Plate 21. *Gladiolus* 'Violetta' is a choice, must-have tender bulb for mixed borders. Author's garden.

fragrance. If you are just beginning and still getting familiar with the plants, you may find it helpful to make lists by flower time, habit, form, texture, and so on. I read catalogs constantly and take notes on plants from lectures I've attended, articles or books I've read, and gardens I've visited, which leaves me with a file bulging with new plant ideas. This helps me stay fresh and excited while designing. Sometimes a "new" plant, which hadn't been right for any of my designs for years, finally fits perfectly into the one I'm

working on. Sometimes I select a more common, tried-and-true plant but use it in the design in an uncommon way. This is when we really dream. As designers, we visualize what the plants will look like in the setting and what combinations we can create. Often we select some of the plants for the design very easily, while at other times or in certain areas of the design, we may take a while to find the right plants. We are always adding and layering plants into the design, which we will discuss further in Chapter 5.

So, we've looked at the first steps in the design process, from site evaluation, through determining the objectives for the garden, to plant selection. Now we have a solid basis on which to create an exceptional design. Keep reading to get a more in-depth understanding of mixed border design and to see firsthand some examples to help you create a well-designed mixed border.

Chapter 3

COLOR, TEXTURE, AND FORM

COLOR

To plant and maintain a flower border, with a good scheme for colour, is by no means the easy thing that is commonly supposed.

GERTRUDE JEKYLL
Colour Schemes for the Flower Garden (1908)

It is an understatement to say that we gardeners are enamored of color. We are often obsessed with color, particularly flower color. Many times color is the feature that sells us on a plant, whether we are first seeing it in a nursery or as a picture in a book or catalog. Many gardeners and nongardeners alike share a common color preference in their gardens or landscapes: more is better. Although a colorful garden can be eye-catching, it should be created with consideration to all design elements. Color is dynamic, exciting, and fun to work with, but the many variables involved in designing color in a garden can be overwhelming at times. By understanding some basic color theory and some of the principles of using color, the beginner and advanced designer alike can creatively use color to make outstanding mixed gardens that are harmonious and unified.

It can seem like the more you learn about color, the less you know. This is due to the subjective nature of the topic and the often contradictory schools of thought when it comes to color systems and theory. Hang with me during our discussion here, as I have tried to gather an applicable and digestible approach to color that I feel can be used by gardeners for mixed border design. This chapter will lay the foundation for color, and then I will continue to point out examples of these principles throughout the book—repetition through examples should help

solidify the information. Also, try to take time to observe in your garden, or in nature, the different points that we discuss. This will really pull it all together. Remember, everyone sees color differently, so appreciate your unique approach.

We must consider several different aspects of color when we are designing. Let's start with the three dimensions of color: hue, value, and intensity. The original choice of hue is relevant, of course, but a sensitivity to value and intensity will greatly affect the outcome of the plant combination.

HUE

Hue, the first dimension of color, is by definition pure color, containing no white, black, or gray. The primary hues are red, yellow, and blue. The secondary hues, each a combination of two primaries, are orange, green, and violet (the classic term for purple—both words will be used interchangeably in this text). Mixing a primary hue and a secondary hue creates what are called tertiary, or intermediate, hues: red-violet, red-orange, yellow-orange, yellow-green, blue-green, and blue-violet. The six tertiary hues, together with the three primary and three secondary hues, make up the 12-part color wheel. For simplification, we will use these colors as the basis of our discussion here, but keep in mind: other color systems have slightly different classifications for the components of color. One fairly standard American variant used by artists and scientists alike is the Munsell Color-Order System (Turner Luke 1996), which discriminates ten (not six) primary and secondary colors; Sandra Austin, in her exceptional book *Color in Garden Design* (1998), does a great job of explaining and using this system as well as clarifying color theory in general. Many of you may be aware of the RHS (Royal Horticultural

Diagram 2. A color wheel of shades (inner ring), pure hues (middle), and tints (outer). Photographs of red, orange, yellow-orange, and violet flowers by Ian Adams.

Plate 23. This combination features mostly analogous colors of yellows, oranges, and yellow-oranges. The spot of blue-violet from the agapanthus creates needed contrast. Also featuring *Kniphofia triangularis*, *Verbascum bombyciferum*, *Rudbeckia hirta* 'Irish Eyes'. University of British Columbia Botanical Garden, British Columbia.

Plate 24. The contrast between the complementary colors of red and green is very evident in this backlit combination of opium poppy (*Papaver somniferum*) and miscanthus foliage. Author's garden.

Plate 25. Hues that are close to being pure, such as this blue and red, can create unappealing contrast when juxtaposed. Featuring *Crocosmia* 'Lucifer', *Picea pungens* 'Thomsen'. Author's garden.

Society) Colour Chart (2001), a British classifying system that we use regularly (or should!) in horticulture when assigning colors for various plant parts, particularly those of new introductions.

Analogous colors are adjacent to each other, or nearly so, on the color wheel—orange and yellow, for example. Colors that are opposite each other, such as green and red, are called complementary or contrasting colors. We do not normally encounter pure spectral hues in nature because they do not occur on the flat, uniform surfaces we need to see them as such. Furthermore, most colors share an element of pigment from an adjacent hue and are further influenced by value, intensity, light, size, shape of the color area, and other elements, which we will soon discuss. Combinations that include only flower colors that are close to pure hues are often glaringly contrastful and don't work. For example, the pairing of a Lucifer crocosmia, with its close-to-red flowers, and a blue spruce, such as *Picea pungens* 'Thomsen', makes me shudder, even though the combination happened by chance in my own garden. It is more effective to lighten or darken one or both of the hues: a flower that is pink (a lighter value of red, which we will delve into shortly), such as *Phlox paniculata* 'Tracy's Treasure', works much better with the spruce.

Accepted Western tradition has it that blue appears cool, while the opposite group, yellow-orange-red, looks warm. But this is a bit of an oversimplification. The great colorist Josef Albers, in his book *Interaction of Color* (1963), offers a more realistic picture of color: "As any temperature can be read higher or lower in comparison with other temperatures, these qualifications are only relative. Therefore, there are also warm blues and cool reds possible within their own hues." In other words, there are warm and cool ranges of all colors. It is important that we, as designers, remember this rather than simply thinking red will *always* impart a warm feeling in our plant combination. Also according to Albers, green and violet are neither hot nor cool but neutral. Violet, however, is very close to the cool range occupied by blue

Plate 27. In the larger context of the garden, the blue of *Picea pungens* 'Thomsen' works well with the greens, pinks, and whites. Author's garden.

mally the most advancing. Because of this, blue flowers usually seem distant, while warmer orange or red flowers seem closer. By applying this knowledge, we can make a combination, border, or even art element, appear closer (and hence more prominent) or more distant (and less prominent) by our color selection. Remember though: a color's appearance is affected by many other factors, some controllable, others not, as we will soon discuss.

VALUE

Value, the second dimension of color, refers to the degree of a color's luminosity (the amount of light reflected back from it). Lighter colors, or tints, of a color contain more white and have a higher value. Darker colors, or shades, contain more black and have a lower value. For example, pink is a high-value tint of red, and maroon is a low-value shade of red. The hues have differing values as well. Yellow, the lightest color in the spectral wheel, has the highest value of any pure hue, while the darkest color, violet, has the lowest value.

Many different values, or areas of lightness and darkness, can be apparent in a single leaf, a single plant, a combination of plants, throughout a garden, depending not only on the actual value of the color but on how the light reflects off flowers, leaves, branches, or stems located on various parts of the plant. As the source of light changes, so can the value, the amount of reflected light. Light on a subject increases the apparent value of colors; shade decreases the apparent value. Contrast between light and shadow within foliage creates depth and interest.

Garden designers should think not only of value contrast with colors but also of the value changes that can occur as people travel

Plate 26. This color combination is more pleasing than the one in Plate 25 because the pink is a lighter value of red, and the contrast between it and the blue is not as great. Featuring *Phlox paniculata* 'Tracy's Treasure', *Picea pungens* 'Thomsen'. Author's garden.

and often shares the qualities of a cooler color. When we think of violet containing red (warm) and blue (cool), and green containing yellow (warm) and blue (cool), we see how these colors can be thought of in the mid-range. Again, green appears warmer if it leans more toward yellow, cooler if it is more blue.

With its shorter wavelength (as compared with the longer wavelength of warmer colors), blue is perceived as receding, being far away. Warmer colors are usually read as being near; red is nor-

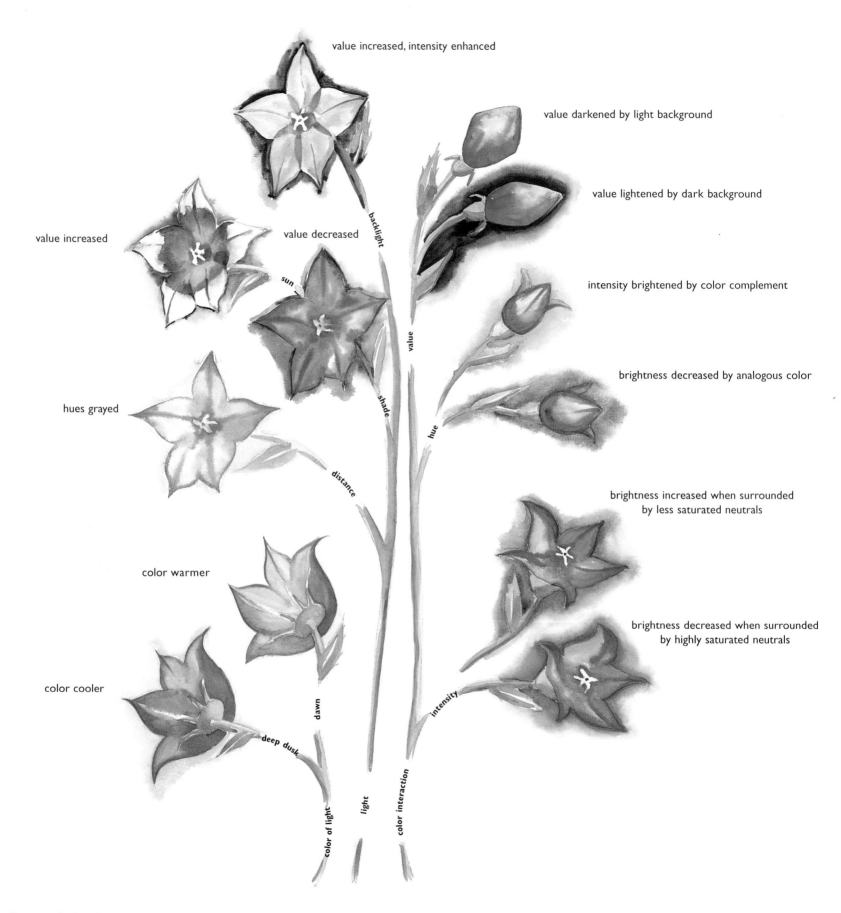

value increased, intensity enhanced

value darkened by light background

value lightened by dark background

value increased

value decreased

backlight

sun

shade

value

intensity brightened by color complement

brightness decreased by analogous color

hues grayed

distance

hue

brightness increased when surrounded
by less saturated neutrals

color warmer

dawn

color cooler

deep dusk

color of light

light

color interaction

intensity

brightness decreased when surrounded
by highly saturated neutrals

Diagram 3. A color model, in which a single flower of *Platycodon grandiflorus* shows how color of light, type of light, and interaction between surrounding colors affect a color's hue, value, and intensity. Artist, Stacey Renee Peters.

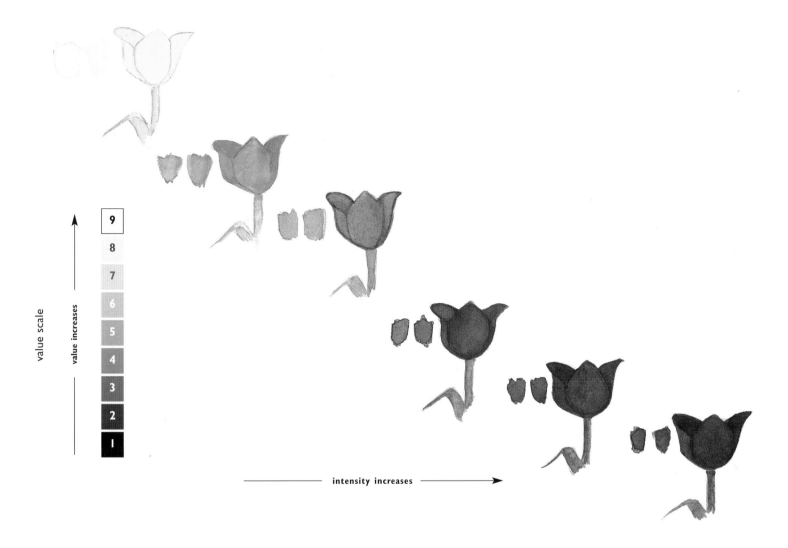

Diagram 4. Value scale and saturation of hues, showing how intensity increases from left (grayer) to right (more saturated). Artist, Stacey Renee Peters.

from one area of the garden to another. For example, as they move from the sunny to the shady section of the border, a value shift occurs, and their eyes must take some time to adjust. Too much of such contrast can create an unsettling space.

Some lighter colors—those with higher values—may even appear more prominent than certain pure hues because of their high reflectance. They can seem closer to the viewer, particularly if contrasted against a darker background. So a cooler color of a higher value may actually be more obvious to the viewer than a warmer color that is darker or lower in value, particularly if the cooler color is contrasted against a darker subject.

All elements in the garden are affected by value, and this goes for hardscaping material as well. Keep the value of the maintenance path in your border similar to the planting around it, to make it inconspicuous. Too much value contrast can be overwhelming; too little is boring.

Tints of colors imply lightness or fragility, while shades of colors imply weight or solidity. Looking back to our example of tints and shades of red: pink flowers appear almost weightless at times, whereas maroon foliage adds depth and heaviness to a garden.

Tints of colors—peach, pink, and lavender, for example—are often referred to as pastels. Some pastels are bright; others are not so bright but rather slightly faded, or grayed, to appear pale or soft. Be aware of this, as such a subtle difference will affect how they appear and act in the garden. Bright pastels are prominent; pale pastels are good blenders.

As distance increases, pastel colors will fade, or gray. We can use this quality to manipulate the sense of space or perspective in our

Plate 28. This combination of a dark orange with a light blue doesn't work because the natural order of the colors is wrong. Featuring *Amsonia tabernaemontana*, *Euphorbia griffithii* 'Fireglow'. Author's garden.

gardens. For example, siting tints (and cooler colors and finer textures) in the background of our border, or at the far end of the garden or path, has the effect of creating more depth or length. These colors can make a small garden seem larger. Conversely, planting shades (and warmer colors, stronger contrasts, and bold forms) in the background has the effect of reducing the apparent length or depth of the garden by making more-distant areas seem closer. These colors can make a large garden seem smaller and more intimate. Darker colors or shades also have a tendency to reduce dimensions (that's why black is a favorite color for clothing!). A dark fence or hedge around a garden will reduce the sense of space.

A simple rule of color harmony: keep lights light, and darks dark. It is more pleasing to combine tints of lighter colors with shades of darker colors than shades of lighter colors with tints of darker colors. Yellow is the lightest color and has the highest value; colors darken, becoming increasingly lower in value, through orange, green, red, and blue (in that order), finishing with violet, the darkest color and the lowest value. Penelope Hobhouse (1985) is a fan of sticking to this "natural order": "The deepest yellow will look 'wrong' with a pink, lavender, or pale blue (all tints of darker spectral hues) if it becomes higher in value— and competes with the normally more luminous yellow." The color police have been telling us forever that pink and orange mustn't be used together—now we know why they don't usually work. Effective combinations can also be made by either darkening (lowering the value) or lightening (increasing the value) of all the colors that are used. The mutual link would then be either all tints (pastels) or all shades. To balance colors, you generally

Plate 29. This blue and orange combination is more effective because the blue is dark and the orange is light, almost peach, which is more in line with the natural value order of the colors. Featuring *Lilium* 'Apricot Brandy', *Geranium* 'Johnson's Blue'. Carolyn Stroombeek garden, Ohio.

need more of a darker color than a lighter color, if both are at full intensity. For proper proportion (remember the Golden Mean), we should use about two-thirds blue flowers (darker hue) and one-third orange flowers (lighter hue), if both are fairly pure.

INTENSITY
Intensity, the third dimension of color, refers to the tone (relative brightness or grayness) of a color, distinguishing the colorful from the dull. It is also known as saturation, purity, or chroma. I like to

think of color saturation, or intensity, in this easy way: think of a sponge or rag taking up as much paint as it can—it will be fully saturated (see Diagram 4). A pure hue, without the addition of another color, has the highest saturation. Yellow and red are more highly saturated colors than purple, blue, or green. This, in part, is why they get our attention. As a color becomes grayer or duller, it is desaturated. These grayer colors are referred to as tones, so, to recap: the addition of white makes a pure hue a tint, the addition of black makes a pure hue a shade, and the addition of gray makes a pure hue a tone. Saturated hues appear closer than grayed hues, so a saturated purple will attract more attention than a gray-purple. Lower-toned versions of colors are less dazzling, since they share a degree of grayness.

Similar to our earlier pastel example, if we plant grayed, or less saturated, hues in the background, with saturated hues nearby, the gray-hued plants will recede into the distance, creating a feeling of depth. Conversely, placing saturated colors in the background reduces the feeling of depth.

Low-saturated colors are apparent in bricks (unsaturated orange or red with a medium value), mulch (unsaturated orange with a low value), and gray-foliaged plants (low saturation and high value). Muted colors in stones or plants are grayed and thus of low saturation; they form the background for our plantings and may seem more natural than some of the more highly saturated hues that are common in many flowers. We often speak of rich flower or leaf colors in autumn; these colors are dark (low in value) but high in saturation—they are full of color. Vivid colors are also highly saturated but not as dark as rich colors. High contrast occurs when saturated and unsaturated hues are combined, while lower contrast is created by keeping the saturation (either pure or grayed) constant.

Distance, as well as light that is too strong or too weak, can gray hues, making them appear less saturated (see Diagram 3). For good proportion and color balance, combine a larger group of lower-toned colors with a smaller amount of more intense color; in this case, following the Golden Mean, we would use two-thirds lower-toned colors and one-third intense colors.

FACTORS AFFECTING COLOR

Color is never viewed in isolation. Many elements—light, associations among colors, textures, and forms; time of day; the distance from which it is viewed—affect the way colors appear in the garden. If we understand the effects of these variables, we will be able to design the garden in an appropriate way, one that emphasizes the true color of the plants.

LIGHT
Only sometimes can we see the actual color of a subject; we will perceive it differently in various lights—skylight, sunlight,

Plate 30. An approaching storm affected the apparent color of all elements in the garden, as it turned the color of the light this strange yellow-orange. Author's garden.

reflected light. We have already briefly discussed how much light alters the apparent value and intensity of colors. The cast of daylight at different times of the day, with changing weather, at different seasons, also impacts the color of plants. Leonardo da Vinci, as quoted in Goethe's *Theory of Colours* (1840), was clearly aware of the effect: "All illumined objects partake of the colour of the light they receive." This color will change in the course of a day. Predawn light, for instance, usually has a bluer cast; with the sun, it can warm to reddish or pinkish, then orange, then yellow, and finally to white, normally with still a tinge of yellow. Skylight is a bluish light. Early evening light can appear golden, perhaps with some reddish tones as well. At dusk, colors move to blue or violet and eventual blackness (see Diagram 3).

Because of this variation in the color of light, colors may be more or less visible at different times during the day. In average daylight, red, yellow, and orange will be most apparent, followed by green, then blue and purple. In the blue-violet light of dusk, red darkens, while the color of blue flowers or bluish foliage may appear heightened. This phenomenon explains why blue balloon flowers seem to glow in the evening as the light dims into deep dusk (see Diagram 3).

In sunny situations or climates, vividly colored flowers and foliage shine, while pastel colors appear washed out. Pastels come into their own on overcast days or in cloudier regions. It is worth noting that many pastel-colored flowers are naturally more adapted to shady sites (which suits their true color), while most richer-colored flowers require sunny sites for best growth. Whites, pastels,

Plate 31. With backlighting, the leaves of *Crocosmia* 'Lucifer' appear fascinatingly transparent. Author's garden.

Plate 32. Do you want to add sheer magic to your mixed garden? Designing for backlighting transforms the ordinary into the extraordinary. Featuring *Eupatorium pupureum* ssp. *maculatum*, *Panicum virgatum* 'Dallas Blues'—and Charlotte's web. Author's garden.

and yellows, because of their higher value, are more brilliant in the shade than are deeper colors. Colors of flowers and foliage in direct sunlight are tinged yellow; in indirect or diffused sunlight they are their truest colors; in shade, the reflected light of the sky turns them toward blue. Light can also be reflected from leaves, flowers, buildings, water, and hardscaping—all alter the apparent colors of plants. Some of these elements themselves, such as leaves, change colors with the seasons, further changing our view.

The direction and angle of light changes through the day and the seasons create mystery, shadow, and intrigue and alter value and apparent depth. In early morning or late afternoon, or during the winter months, when the sun is low in the sky and weaker, contrast is reduced. This light, often known as sidelighting, emphasizes depth and the three-dimensional nature of gardens. Backlighting causes translucent objects almost to glow, while frontlighting makes objects appear more flat and imparts a more two-dimensional feel (see Diagram 3). As designers we can capitalize on different lighting by strategically placing certain plants to take advantage of these conditions.

DISTANCE

Distance also affects how colors are viewed. Distant colors in the garden normally appear cooler, more neutral, or faded. A phenomenon known as visual mixing can also occur when we view colors from a distance. Nineteenth-century French Impressionists, particularly the Pointillist painters, understood and used this principle. Thousands of individual dots or points of pure pigment were put on the canvas so that, when viewed from a distance, they would mix to create different tones. In the garden, if numerous

small or fine-textured red and blue flowers were planted together, they would mix and appear violet when viewed from a distance. Red and green flowers would blend to create a neutral brown, orange and blue would create gray, from afar. Keep in mind the distance of the border from the main vantage point when combining colors, as it will greatly affect the overall picture. Even humidity plays a part, by making light soft and muting colors.

COLOR INTERACTIONS

Interactions among colors can be used to enhance an intended effect. One phenomenon, simultaneous contrast, is responsible for heightened contrast in hue, value, and intensity. Simultaneous contrast occurs immediately when two colors are placed side by side and each color is tinged or hazed with the neighboring color's complement. We can brighten the intensity of a color by surrounding it with its complement, the opposite color on the color wheel. For example, if we place orange flowers next to blue flowers, the orange will be intensified by an orange haze (blue's complement), thus making it even more opposite the blue, which itself is intensified by a blue haze (orange's complement). We can use this principle in designing limited-palette borders or combinations: in a yellow border, including some small areas of violet flowers (opposite yellow on the color wheel) can create dramatic relief and brighter focal areas that are more stunning than a sea of yellow alone. In the same way, the effect of green foliage in a red garden is a ready-made brightening contrast (see Plates 23–24; Diagram 3).

Simultaneous contrast can also have the effect of driving colors further apart. For example, if orange is placed directly next to yellow, the orange will appear more reddish (due to the violet haze) and the yellow more greenish (due to the blue haze). Simultaneous contrast can be tricky and makes creating certain color schemes, particularly monochromatic ones, more challenging. For example, a flower that may appear red when isolated from other red flowers suddenly may look too pink, plain wrong, among truer reds. This is the time when a spade becomes the weapon of choice for the colorist, and the offending plant is moved to a new location.

Successive contrast is similar to simultaneous contrast but involves the element of time: have you ever noticed that, having stared at a color for 15 to 30 seconds, you have the tendency to see a ghost or afterimage of that color's complement when you then look at a third color, particularly white? In creating color transitions through the border, or from one color garden to another, the designer can make effective use of this phenomenon. Gertrude Jekyll (1908), a master at orchestrating colors, writes (while describing a chain of five variously colored gardens) that the gray garden, which also contained blue flowers, "is seen at its best by reaching it through the orange borders [because] the strong, rich colouring has the natural effect of making the eye eagerly desirous for the complementary colour. . . . One never knew before how vividly bright *Ageratum* could be, or lavender or *Nepeta*."

Other color associations have different types of impact. Surrounding a color with neutrals, such as grays or browns, or with less saturated colors, is another way to dramatize a color. For example, a purple garden is enlivened with splashes of gray foliage. A color's brightness can be decreased by surrounding it with analogous colors (those adjacent on the color wheel); it can be decreased by surrounding it with more highly saturated colors. The value of a flower color can be lightened by placing the flowers against a darker background or with darker foliage; conversely, we can darken a color's value by placing it next to a lighter background. See Diagram 3 for illustrations of these various effects.

On this note, consider too how the colors of nearby hardscaping, such as a wall or pavement, and elements like pots or benches affect the appearance of colors in a planting. For example, the yellow spires of *Ligularia* 'The Rocket' will look dramatic against a wall painted black or dark blue, whereas these flowers will look more subdued next to a beige house.

TEXTURE AND FORM

Texture and form also affect color, and orchestrating them for balance and contrast must be considered when we are choosing color combinations (we'll look more at texture and form later in this chapter). Vivid colors in soft, airy textures have less impact than the same colors in bolder, heavier textures. Bold flower or

Plate 33. There is no better way to really "see" plants and colors than to try to draw and paint them—even if you're not a Picasso. Also, it will probably be one of the few times you actually sit down in your garden. Author's garden.

leaf forms have more surface area, thus carrying more color impact than delicate shapes of the same value. For example, the blue in the spiky-textured spherical flowers of globe thistle (*Echinops ritro*) has one effect, the similar shade of blue in the petite flowers of perennial flax (*Linum perenne*) quite another.

Smooth-surfaced leaves, flowers, stems, or fruit, which reflect more light, will look higher in value and seem purer in color (more saturated or intense) than matte or rough-surfaced ones. And changes in color and intensity of light create greater contrasts on smooth surfaces.

Fine-textured flowers and leaves will mix colors at a distance more than coarse-textured ones. Only at extreme distances will colors mix optically on bold leaves. So bolder leaves will show more distinct colors at a distance, which can be important in certain mixed border situations.

COLOR SCHEMES

Working with living plants can, at times, be more complicated than combining colors of stagnant objects for the home or wardrobe. Not only are colors affected, among other things, by the constantly changing light and weather, but the colors on a plant can change from the time the plant emerges, to when it is in bud, to when it is flowering and on through its decline. And everywhere there is an inescapable context of green. Thought must also be given to form, texture, repetition, balance, and contrast, besides the endless choices of colors.

Where does one begin? How do you choose color themes? I get ideas by visiting gardens and noting which colors move me. I often review slides I've taken at other gardens, and use colored pencils to sketch on paper the colors that were used in an appealing combination or vignette. This really gets the creative juices flowing. Art books, tapestries, fabrics, and, of course, nature—all are excellent sources of inspiration. Taking watercolor classes has really heightened my awareness and appreciation for color. In fact, while painting in my garden, my teacher Stacey Renee showed me how sometimes a single plant, with its varying tints and shades of a color, can work as a model for color in a bed, a border, an entire garden: it was she who pointed out how the purples, blues, and yellows in *Cerinthe major* 'Purpurascens' were the colors I had chosen for the bed in which it was planted (see Diagram 18 in Chapter 8). Remember, the style, size, and situation of the garden may dictate color choices or when certain colors will predominate. The color itself may dictate where and how it is used. And our own attitudes toward color may change with the seasons. Some people feel that soft pinks are a suitable spring color but find them offensive in the autumn, when they yearn for the rich saturated shades naturally associated with that season.

You can vary the color scheme of a garden or a section of the garden in different seasons. You may want to focus on soothing blues in spring, exploding yellows in summer, and muted oranges in autumn. Or spring may include a variety of colors, while the summer theme is limited to fewer colors. Plants with foliage in blues and purples, such as *Helictotrichon sempervirens* 'Saphirsprudel' or *Heuchera* 'Velvet Night' could be used as the unifying link in all seasons. Since color is subjective, go with colors that you like, and be brave. Plants can always be moved, so have fun playing with them.

Plate 34. The appealing colors in the foliage and flowers of *Cerinthe major* 'Purpurascens' (foreground) are the model for the color scheme in one of my borders. Its diverse tints and shades harmonize well with a wide variety of other plants, including this *Stachys macrantha*. Author's garden.

You can always test color choices by starting with your chosen theme in container plantings or in a small area of the garden, using only annuals. It's a great way to ease into a color decision and to clarify your personal preferences. Another very simple approach to checking colors is to cut a collection of plants, place them together in a bunch or in a trug basket (one that is fairly flat and wide), and observe their association together. Arranging flowers is not only therapeutic and beautifying to the home but a great way to see combinations that you would never have thought of before. If you don't want to create a whole new garden,

Diagram 5. Monochromatic color scheme. Artist, Stacey Renee Peters.

consider rearranging plants in an existing border to concentrate a color theme.

Colors can be combined in the garden in innumerable ways. Color schemes can be monochromatic, analogous (harmonious), complementary (contrasting), or polychromatic, to name just a few.

MONOCHROMATIC

Monochromatic schemes incorporate shades, tints, and tones of a single pure hue, such as violet (purple). Using a limited color palette, particularly a monochromatic one, helps to simplify the design process by reducing the number of variables and is an effective and rewarding way to design combinations.

I'd like to start with an explanation of this scheme first, as this style or approach to color has quickly become a favorite of mine. A key advantage of this approach to color is that it focuses attention on the details and subtleties of a design. Structure and rhythm of a planting are emphasized. Plant form and the textures of leaf, stem, flower, and fruit are more easily appreciated. A design that is simple and cohesive in terms of color can also convey an air of sophistication. With a monochromatic scheme, the scene is less distracting, since the eye doesn't need to constantly refocus on ever-changing color. Shifts in light deepen the mystery of a monochromatic scheme's elegance.

My preference for this approach to color was strengthened when a client asked me to create a garden that was a departure from what one usually sees in the United States. The proposed border was within a larger garden in central Ohio full of unusual plants and mixed colors. To develop something that would fit, I

Plate 35. A monochromatic combination allows the simple beauty of forms and textures to shine. Featuring *Kniphofia* 'Primrose Beauty', *Picea orientalis* 'Skylands'. Author's garden.

decided to design a garden similar in style and spirit to Hadspen Garden in Somerset, England, now managed by outstanding colorists Nori and Sandra Pope, authors of *Color by Design* (1998).

The garden I designed takes the visitor through the different areas of the color wheel, with individual monochromatic sections gracefully melding into one another. The 6,000-sq.-ft. mixed border starts with the color red and moves through orange, peach, yellow, blue, and on to purple. There's a seating area in the tranquil purple section, and then the colors continue through the border in reverse order. Colored foliage (including green) is used

Plate 36. Sophistication is the message of this monochromatic vignette. Notice how green will always be a part of any garden color scheme. Featuring *Galium odoratum*, *Betula utilis* var. *jacquemontii*. Longwood Gardens, Pennsylvania.

Plate 37. The cohesive monochromatic unity among the flowering plants and their gray foliage is beautifully and thoughtfully orchestrated into the whole scene, with the gray trellis, fencing, and pavers. Featuring *Perovskia atriplicifolia*, *Clematis* 'Elsa Späth', *Nepeta sp.* Morton Arboretum, Illinois.

for accent and repetition; for example, using contrasting yellow foliage in the purple section really makes the purples pop, an effect enhanced by simultaneous contrast. Each section is designed to evoke a different mood. There are no high-value tints of red (pinks) or whites—if we can help it—in the garden; see Diagrams 21–28 and Plates 134–200 in Chapter 9.

Your monochromatic scheme can be accomplished in different ways. Perhaps you want to focus predominantly on tints of the color and use shades of the color for accent. You may want to start with tints of the color and build to shades of the color as you move down the border and then progress back to tints. You may decide that what will work best in your setting is mostly shades, with tints in moderation. Many design techniques must be incorporated to bring all the tints, shades, and tones together in a unified fashion. You may want to consider tying two or more monochromatic color schemes together with the use of analogous colors, as I did in this colorist garden. Varying shades of green also make excellent transitional colors, since green is present in almost all plants. Of course, the monochromatic scheme could itself be green, but most monochromatic schemes or limited color schemes are not truly, totally, the chosen color alone—they always include green (see Plate 36).

Once you settle on a color—say, blue—you may find that every time you see a new blue flower in someone else's garden, at a lecture, or in a picture, you're eager to find it for your blue garden. I have seen stunning displays in gardens using black, gray, and blue—all different values and intensities of blue. Developing monochromatic color schemes can take you to a new level of design and pleasure in your garden. As I've explored the subtle beauty of varying tints, tones, and shades of a single color, I've found both solace and excitement in discovering that less is more.

ANALOGOUS
Analogous, or harmonious, schemes use predominantly two or three colors that are adjacent to each other on the color wheel, such as red, orange, and yellow. You can start anywhere on the wheel and go forward or backward. The eye does not need to

Diagram 6. Analogous color scheme. Artist, Stacey Renee Peters.

refocus when related colors are used. Harmonious schemes, in the strictest sense of the word, are created when colors are related by a shared hue. For example, orange, yellow, and yellowish green are truly harmonious as they all share yellow as a parent color; blue-green, blue-violet, and violet have blue as a common parent color. Remember what we talked about in color theory: the best combinations will be with lighter light colors and darker dark colors; for example, with violet and red, tint the red to pink, which blends nicely with any shade of violet, rather than lightening the violet into pale lavender, which doesn't work as well with purer reds. Rarely are we simply combining the pure hues of colors.

Remember, we can decrease a color's brightness by surrounding it with analogous colors. This seems to have the effect of making gentle transitions between contrasts. Some of my favorite garden designers have used harmonious schemes in their gardens. Color combinations such as pinks, maroons, and purples, or grays, blues, and purples are stunning. Warmer notes of gold, yellow, and green also work beautifully.

With color, extreme unity leads to under-stimulation, extreme complexity leads to overstimulation. Harmony is a dynamic equilibrium between the two.

COMPLEMENTARY

Complementary, or contrasting, schemes focus on two colors opposite one another on the color wheel, such as blue and orange. Again, this approach requires skill. Too much contrast through a border creates confusion, forcing the eyes to refocus constantly. To avoid too many intense contrasts, which would be jarring and unsettling, just the right shades, tints, and tones of the colors must be chosen. Keep in mind, some of the best combinations are

Plate 38. Related analogous colors of blue-green, blue, and violet create harmony in this combination. Featuring *Veronica austriaca* ssp. *teucrium* 'Crater Lake Blue', *Geranium ×magnificum*, *Picea pungens* 'Iseli Foxtail'. Author's design, Hendley garden, Ohio.

between plants that have one element in common and one in contrast, be it related to color, texture, or form. Playing with subtle differences in foliage color is an effective approach for this scheme.

Using contrasting colors in an analogous color scheme is an extremely effective way to cause the eye to stop, thus creating a focal point. Try this in a border, to direct the eye and create a pause in an area that may include less-brilliant plants that you nevertheless want to highlight. Remember, you can have two-thirds of one color juxtaposed with one-third of its contrasting

Diagram 7. Complementary color scheme. Artist, Stacey Renee Peters.

Plate 40. Not exactly opposite each other on the color wheel according to many color theories, blue or blue-violet and yellow or yellow-green still make a striking contrast and are often successfully designed together for such effect. Featuring *Aquilegia alpina*, *Caryopteris* ×*clandonensis* 'Worcester Gold'. Author's garden.

Plate 39. Contrasting colors of violet (which appears a bit red-violet in this photograph) and yellow create a focal point in the garden. Featuring *Iris* 'Flavescens', *Hesperis matronalis*. Author's garden.

Plate 41. Yellow and purple foliage are strikingly contrastful, but you wouldn't want an entire garden of this combination. Notice how the textures and forms of plants are appreciated without the presence of flowers. Featuring *Cimicifuga ramosa* 'Hillside Black Beauty', *Dicentra spectabilis* 'Gold Heart', *Euphorbia cyparissias* 'Fen's Ruby'. Homewood Farm garden, Ohio.

Diagram 8. Split complementary.

color, as in monochromatic schemes. Yellow and purple foliage are a wonderful contrast but shouldn't be overdone; black, purple, and gold is really cool—figuratively—but again, in moderation.

A split complementary scheme combines analogous and complementary colors. In the approach I prefer (and the one that is illustrated above), any three adjacent colors (primary, secondary, or tertiary) can be used, plus the complement of the middle hue—for example, blue-violet, violet, red-violet, and violet's complement, yellow. Another approach is to use only three colors: a color plus the two colors on either side of its complement; for example, green (whose complement is red), red-violet, and red-orange.

Diagram 9. Polychromatic color scheme. Artist, Stacey Renee Peters.

POLYCHROMATIC

A polychromatic scheme includes a little of every color. Often this is what people want, particularly if space is a consideration and they are reluctant to limit their color choices. Polychromatic schemes appeal to people who don't care for a more disciplined approach to color; they want less discipline in their lives, particularly in their gardens. Color riot, parti-colored, motley—whatever you want to call it, it can be crazy or controlled. All the issues we have been discussing—combining different values, use of repetition and contrast,

Plate 42. This gorgeous garden incorporates a polychromatic color theme with style. The strong formal structure and horizontal line of the background hedge adds needed control. Marion Jarvie garden, Ontario.

focal points, and so on—need to be considered for optimal effect. Gertrude Jekyll often effectively combined many colors in the border, placing them so that they moved fluidly, without abrupt transitions, from restful blues, greens, and grays to cool creams and whites, into paler colors of yellows and pinks then into the stronger colors of yellows, oranges, and reds, and then back through the softer colors, ending in purples and lilacs. The approaches are endless. You can throw fluidity to the wind, and go crazy with a bit of everything, here and there. Remember: your style should be reflected in your garden. Do whatever makes you happy.

OTHER COLOR SCHEMES

Another approach to color is triadic harmony. As the icon shows, triadic harmony exists among three colors that are equidistant from each other on the color wheel, such as red, yellow, and blue (be careful to avoid a preschool look with these three!) or green, violet, and orange. This approach gives you more color than some of the other schemes, yet the colors are still harmonious. Using a personalized limited color palette of two or three colors that you like—say pinks and whites, or apricots and plums—is another approach. I knew an artist-gardener who loved chartreuse and red and used this theme very effectively in his garden. In my front border at Hiddenhaven, I use fairly saturated purple and blue flowers (soft blue foliage) for the predominant colors, with unsaturated yellows in the spring, and saturated oranges and reds in the

Diagram 10. Triadic color scheme. Artist, Stacey Renee Peters.

summer as accents; see Diagram 18 and Plates 86–112 in Chapter 8. Remember my earlier example of getting a color theme from a single plant? Use your imagination with this and be creative.

USING COLOR

Even though great garden combinations can happen by chance, taking the time to plan a color scheme is usually essential to creating awe-inspiring results and to making strong, purposeful associations. I suggest making a list of all the plants that fit into your chosen scheme, including those with colored foliage that will work (see lists of plants by color of flowers, fruit, and foliage in Appendix B). Keep in mind that colors may differ slightly from how they are pictured in books or catalogs. Consider too what colors you might want to use for accents, and list potential plants in that category. For each plant, consider the color of all its aspects—flowers, foliage, fruit, bark, and autumn color. Many times, attributes other than flower color contribute far more to the overall aesthetics of the garden.

Throughout this chapter we have discussed balance and proper proportion of hues, values, and intensities; we have talked about harmonious color schemes, the use of contrasting colors to create focal points and heightened interest in an area, and the effect of contrasting or constant values and saturations. Remember these design elements when painting your garden! In the next chapter, you can read more about the principles of design, which we also want to apply when using color. Repetition—of colors, values, and saturations—is a basic consideration. Repetition unifies your plan and directs the flow of movement—and the eye—through the garden.

Color is believed to influence our thoughts, health, and actions, thus profoundly affecting the mood of the garden and gardener. Warmer colors of yellow, orange, and red can evoke feelings of liveliness, vitality, and cheer. Cooler colors of blue-violet, blue, and blue-green are soothing. Green is a balanced hue, neither hot nor cool, and is said to promote feelings of harmony in the viewer. According to color theorists, each color has subtle meanings that are worth considering. Note that as the colors become lighter or purer, the connotation is positive; as they darken or become grayer, the meaning is negative. Colors can have different healing powers; a color selected for its healing properties should comprise two-thirds of the garden, while the remaining one-third would be composed of its complement. Now let us consider the six primary and secondary colors in turn, around the color wheel, beginning with red, and then two key neutrals, white and gray.

RED

Red is energizing and is said to help people cope with the demands of life. It encourages activity in the area in which it is used. Too much can be overstimulating, particularly in a small garden, or to those under stress. Lighter or purer colors of red symbolize affection and sensuality; darker reds, desire and anger. Large masses of red create impact, small touches create tension. Purer hues and shades are best positioned in bright sun. Reds are the first colors to fade in the evening. Tints will shine in shade, evening light, or overcast conditions. "Red hot" tells us something. Vivid reds advance, creating a horticultural exclamation point in the border. Red is most effective as a surprise in the garden.

Green, its complement, brightens red. It is often best to position red so that it is seen after the viewer has experienced soft, restful greens. Gray foliage will also enrich dull red flowers, although the combination doesn't work for me: the gray becomes hazed with green. For more appealing results, mix grays with tints of red—pink and gray are great together. Colors analogous to red—orange and violet, for example—will decrease a red's brightness. If you want to make a red border, you will find that the range of plants in truer reds is somewhat limited. I urge you to press on, though, because this can be a very satisfying color for monochromatic schemes.

Tones and shades such as burgundy, maroon, and plum (which are reds or purples shaded with an element of blue, brown, or black) are cooler in nature than the hotter scarlet-reds, which contain warming yellow. These cooler tones, most often found in foliage, are more somber. Too many of them can create a heavy feeling of doom. Just the right balance makes a dramatic accent, adding depth and mystery to many color schemes. A dark-foliaged plant will anchor a planting, adding weight. But again, if not balanced properly with other green foliage and flowers, the anchor will pull the ship down. When used among brighter reds, burgundy, bronze, or coppery foliage will decrease the dominance of the otherwise overbearing red, creating beautiful harmony. Purple leaves have a stabilizing effect among hotter colors without dulling their vibrant nature. When plum-colored plants are used with very pale tints of blues, violets, and pink, the effect is sheer coolness. If reddish leaves are used, the effect is warmer. Purple foliage absorbs light, while silver, whites, and grays reflect light, creating suspense. Purple or red foliage is extremely versatile and works well with most colors, including peaches and oranges.

Tones and shades of red are difficult to read at a distance, as they become increasingly black. Keep them up-close-and-personal in the border, where they can be seen and appreciated. Purple and red foliage looks its best and really shines when backlit by the rising or setting sun. They are lost in heavy shade. Purple foliage is a great attraction for many of us and can easily be overdone.

Black flowers, which are usually dark reds or purples, have long been prized for their seductive qualities. To me, they are to-die-for. Elusive and sophisticated treasures found only in limited numbers, black flowers have the same qualities and design considerations as purple foliage.

Pink, a tint of red, is often cool but—as you know by now—can appear warm (think hot pink!), depending on many variables. It is believed that pink restores youthfulness and brings people in touch with their feelings. It has a value similar to other pastels. It can brighten a shady garden. It is light, airy, and often comes with the connotation of being cute or sweet—the less courageous side of red. Don't lose sight of the mood you are trying to convey. No matter what kind of a pink it is, it still maintains its characteristic redness. When blushed with yellow, pink warms to peach.

Peach, a combination of various shades or tints of red with yellow or white, combines with a great many colors. High-value, highly saturated peaches will be light and bright and prominent if contrasted with darker colors.

ORANGE

Orange promotes a feeling of well-being, optimism, and joy. It is warm, welcoming, and stimulating—but slightly less so than red. It represents wisdom and justice. Due to its power (remember orange punch!), a little orange can go a long way. A secondary color, orange is normally dominated by one of the colors that combine to make it (in this case, red and yellow). Orange seems to be a misunderstood color, and I find many people are opposed to having it in their gardens. I know that for years I didn't want orange in any of my clients' gardens—or in any garden of mine. Little did I realize that all the terra-cotta pots, rusted ornaments, and clay bricks in the gardens were contributing different earthy tones and shades of orange. Actually, when I think about it, I'm

not sure why I didn't want orange around—probably some preconceived notion that it was "bad" in some way, and it might mistakenly get next to a pink and we would have to call 911. I now have developed an appreciation for orange (one of the few advantages to age—wisdom?) and enjoy using it whenever possible. I find I need the stimulating energy it offers (again, an age thing, I'm sure). Full sun does orange the greatest justice; it becomes muddy in the shade. The range of plants for the orange garden is fairly limited.

Blue, its complement, can intensify orange and vice versa. Small sections of bright orange in a blue garden can have a dramatic effect, but a bright orange garden with patches of blue can be out of balance and a leap for even the most adventurous colorist! Combining too many warmer colors, such as reds, oranges, and yellows, at full intensity can also be a bit much. Alter the strength of the different colors for more pleasing results.

YELLOW

Yellow has the warmth and power of the sun. As a lighter, purer color, it is inspirational and is said to give intellectual stimulation. As it darkens or becomes lower-toned, its presence suggests cunning or selfishness. Yellow, the highest-valued hue, is a dominant color, acting like a magnet for the eyes—think about the draw of a candle flame. It can increase the feeling of space: yellow areas may be hard to define and detail can be lost in them. Yellow can be hot or cool, depending on the colors it is tinged with; yellow tinged with red, for example, is a warmer yellow, whereas bluish yellow appears cool. The association of other colors can also affect yellow's relative warmth or coolness: greenish yellow looks cooler next to red, while yellow-orange looks warmer next to blue. Yellow has the ability to harmonize with almost all colors. Your choices among yellow flowers and plants are innumerable—perhaps because yellow is an easy color for bees to see.

Yellow foliage can add warmth in all layers of our plantings, from trees and shrubs and down, to the tiniest groundcovers. Lime-yellow and gold-greens create great relief among darker greens. Yellow-foliaged plants are luminous at dusk and on overcast days, and bring a touch of "sun" to shady nooks; they will be brightened against a dark background. Keep in mind that gold-leaved plants may burn or turn coppery if exposed to too much sun (full sun in the North may be tolerable, full sun in the South may be excessive). If planted in too much shade, some will turn chartreuse or green. As always, siting plants correctly is paramount.

Yellow's complement is violet, although blue is also a natural match. With blue flowers or foliage, yellow has a bright, clean appearance. When combined with violet, or purple, the effect is more dramatic and stunning. For some people, using a pure yellow with a strong purple is too high a contrast. If this is the case, tinge the yellow with green for a lower-keyed approach, or create better balance by using two times the amount of purple to yellow. Pastel yellows work both with other pastels and with the rich tones of purples and blues, while warmer yellows work with fellow hot colors, adding a touch of lightness to the grouping. When thinking hot colors, yellow and orange (being closer together on the color wheel) work together more harmoniously than yellow and red. Green and yellow too can create rich harmonies.

Yellow-variegated foliage is another way of bringing yellow into the garden, but discipline is required. Don't get carried away, or the effect is like plaids and stripes combined. Variegated plants should be used purposefully, not steal the show at the expense of good design. Keep the pattern of variegation in mind when you are selecting plants, choosing either a bolder, more extroverted pattern or a refined, more introverted look, based on your overall design objectives. Variegation varies, from yellow-green leaves with yellow variegation, to blue-green leaves with creamy yellow variegation, to—I could go on and on, as breeders seemed to have supplied us with all the colors of the rainbow, but I think you get the point. All these different color combinations will affect the pairing of such plants. Yellow-variegated foliage works nicely with reds and oranges; more contrast will occur when it's combined with cooler colors. Variegated plants are best placed where they can be examined closely.

GREEN

Yes, green is a color and a remarkable one at that! Lighter tints and purer colors stand for charity and a love of nature, the darker shades imply malevolence. Green is a secondary color, this time a combination of yellow and blue, and offers a huge variation in color: true-green is neutral, easing transitions; gray-green cools hot colors yet blends with pastels; yellow-green signals spring and warmth; blue-green, being cooler, creates a sense of greater space in the garden; brownish greens signify summer and autumn. Each of these greens creates a slightly different atmosphere in the garden.

The first thing that comes to mind when we think of green is foliage, but green flowers, because they are so unusual, add an air of sophistication to a planting and look good with every color (see list in Appendix B). Since they don't read well from a distance, they are best placed where they can be observed at close range. Many flowers are beautiful in their green, immature stage. If the green flowers are more yellowish, emphasize the green in them by giving them a companion or background that is pure yellow or a warm, orange-tinged yellow. I love to use the chartreuse flowers of *Alchemilla mollis* as a unifier in jarring color combinations. It's a great peacemaker.

Greens and grays, another neutral, harmonize well together. Red, green's complement, sharpens green, but too much in the pure hues of red and green is overwhelming and can create a Santa Claus atmosphere. Green will mellow out orange.

BLUE

Blue, a healing color, encourages relaxation and tranquility. Believed to inspire patience and calm thought, it is great for a meditative spot in the garden. As a stress reliever, it may be too calming for a lively entertaining area. On the negative side, blue can suggest distance and depression (we have all felt blue). Remember, blue is cooler than other hues and recedes from view, thus increasing the apparent size of a space or leading the eye toward a distant focal point. If blue is tinged with red, however, it will be warmer. Blue can be used to create shadows in a planting—picture a pool of blue-leaved hostas. True-blue flowers are prized and hard to find, as they often move toward lavender or violet. Blue leaves often border gray and green.

Blue blends well in any color scheme, but because it does not define dimensions or set limits, a spattering of blue here or there may create a sense of instability. Lack of contrast may cause blue to disappear in the shadows and green leaves of the garden; it is heightened against a light background or combined with high-value yellows. Orange is its complement—together the two dazzle. Blue is striking with neutral gray. Blue can be deep or luminous, and it glows at dusk.

VIOLET

Violet, or purple, is believed to inspire creativity and foster self-worth and inner calm. Throughout history it has been used as a sign of royalty, wealth, and knowledge—a color fit for a king. And what a great, fun color to use. Too much, though, can be depressing or lead to a feeling of isolation. It can be lifeless if not charged with the vitality of the sun, which will increase its apparent value. Violet,

Plate 43. The combination of variegations in this duo works for me but may not for everyone. Caution is advised—don't go overboard. Featuring *Aralia elata* 'Aureovariegata', *Canna* 'Phasion'. Author's garden.

like blue, decreases in contrast in the shade and is often lost in it; violet benefits greatly from contrast of texture, form, and tone. Silver (and yellow, violet's complement) enliven violet. Softer tints, lilac and mauves, are peaceful but may appear weak when used in large groups; include stronger shades and forms to break the monotony. Violet, with its short wavelength, usually recedes from the viewer. Its different tints, tones, and shades have quickly made purple one of my favorite colors to design with, and happily a wide range of plants is available in this color.

WHITE

White is associated with purity, cleanliness, and good. In most societies, white represents higher ideals and loftier values. A white garden usually has a sense of crispness, class, sophistication, and formality. White gardens are an easy way for beginners to try a monochromatic scheme, and most species seem to have a white-flowering form, opening up a wide range of choices. White doesn't clash with anything, although most whites in the garden won't be true—they are off-white, creamy yellow, or slightly tinted with other colors, such as pink, green, or lavender. Colorful stamens or venations in white flowers further influence the color of white we see, and texture and form also greatly affect white's appearance. Soft, airy white flowers are going to carry less impact than solid, coarser-textured ones. White flowers are also easily tinged by the blue of shadows or by the complementary color of a neighboring color—for example, adjacent red flowers give white a greenish cast.

White brightens shade and comes alive at dusk. In full sun, white can often be too harsh. White creates a feeling of space. Most whites are usually of a high value (pure white is the lightest color), meaning they are normally light, bright, and prominent. Some white flowers may even appear larger than other colored flowers or have a halo effect under certain lighting conditions. Purer whites are not normally useful as blenders, uniting inharmonious colors; rather, they act as a negative space or separation in the combination. If, however, white occurs at the base or in the venation of the flowers that need to be united, a truer white flower can serve as the common link, tying the plants together.

Other colors deepen and increase in contrast and saturation against white because white reflects any color that surrounds it, enhancing it. As I write this, the point is driven home by a male cardinal, which appears redder than red against the snow outside my window. Dark colors, such as deep glossy green, create a large degree of contrast with white; such a juxtaposition can be used to create a focal point in the garden. Mid-textured grays and greens blend whites, softening the effect. A white garden is usually crying for a touch of another color, but take care when incorporating whatever you settle on, as this other color will be strongly emphasized against the white. Avoid pure or saturated colors; tones of any color are more effective with white.

Purple foliage works well with white flowers, as does white- or cream-variegated foliage. White variegation, which creates a cool effect, harmonizes with cooler colors but creates too strong a contrast with reds and oranges.

GRAY

Gray is a versatile neutral, making dark, intense colors more intense and soft-tinted colors more delicate. A gray is often tinted by the complement of the color it is combined with. Most grays are not true but have underlying colors in them, such as pale green, yellow-green, blue-green, or even red in the case of the bark on certain trees and shrubs. Gray foliage is usually pubescent (hairy) and soft-textured, although glaucous grays and blue-grays are available; the hairs or wax reflect light, which causes the graying effect. Gray-foliaged plants require well-draining soil and are therefore difficult to grow in many parts of the country. Gray foliage is enriched by blue-green or gray-green variegated plants.

A gray's value affects how it works in the garden. Some grays, such as certain bright silvers, are higher in value; others are darker and less saturated. Higher-valued grays appear more bright and prominent, while muted grays work better as blenders. White normally works well with light grays because they share a common brightness. Gray recedes and appears more chromatic (colorful) on overcast days and at dusk, when blue light is cast upon it.

Plate 44. The gray of this *Artemisia* 'Huntington', a light and bright silver, attracts attention, especially when contrasted with the dark red-violet of *Perilla frutescens* var. *crispa*. Author's design, Hendley garden, Ohio.

Before we move on, let's summarize the steps for using color in the mixed garden:

1. Consider color in its three dimensions: hue, value, and intensity.
2. Remember the factors that affect color: light, distance, interactions among colors, texture, and form.
3. Purposefully select your desired color scheme: monochromatic, analogous, complementary, split complementary, polychromatic, triadic, or personalized limited palette.
4. Make a list of plants suitable for your color theme, keeping in mind repetition, contrast, harmony, balance, and focal points.
5. Think about the mood of the garden and the use and effect of each color.
6. Have fun!

TEXTURE AND FORM

Texture refers to the surface quality of an object; we can both see and feel texture. Form refers to the overall size and shape of an object. The plants we select have texture and form; so do paths, mulches, structures, and art in the garden. Form and shape exist in individual plants as well as in the mass that is created by a group of plants. Line is related to form. When we see the outline of a plant, flower, or flowerhead, or the branching of a tree, we are in essence seeing lines. These lines create different structures. Plants with strong lines are often described as architectural and make excellent structural elements. Different sizes and shapes of plants and hardscaping create different planes in the garden, from the horizontal to the vertical to the overhead. When properly united, they create a three-dimensional space.

Texture and form often take a backseat to color when a garden is being planned, but not giving significant thought to these two very important elements of design is usually what leads to failure. Texture and form need to be considered at all levels, from leaf to branch, flower, fruit, and bark, to the overall form and texture of the plant. A plant may have fine-textured leaves and coarse bark. Up close, the more prominent element sets the overall textural

Plate 46. The soft foliage of *Salvia argentea* screams to be touched; here, it creates a contrastful textural statement with *Ipomoea batatas* 'Ace of Spades'. Author's garden.

Plate 45. On close inspection, the interesting and contrasting textures and forms of these plants can be appreciated. Featuring *Ampelopsis glandulosa* var. *brevipedunculata* 'Elegans', *Pinus pumila* 'Nana'. Author's garden.

Plate 47. Contrasts of texture and form, as in this combination, add subtle and beautiful diversity to mixed gardens. Featuring *Acer palmatum* var. *dissectum* Dissectum Atropurpureum Group, *Pachysandra procumbens*. Holden Arboretum, Ohio.

look and feel of a plant. From a distance, the play of light creates different value patterns of dark and light, implying texture.

The terms we use when we talk about texture—soft, fine, airy, delicate, lacy, coarse, rough, bold—have either a masculine or a feminine connotation, and a balance between this yin and yang, if you will, is needed. Often we use too many—or even all—fine-textured plants, making the garden appear weak, unfocused, and lacking in structure. Often we hesitate to use a strong texture or form—perhaps it would not be polite? But working with these bolder textures and forms is fun and exciting, and creates a dynamic contrast with the delicate. Although to keep a balance, a greater number of fine-textured flowers or plants are needed to equal the weight of fewer bolder ones, we don't need to overdo it with the softer textures. It's best to use fine-textured plants against a backdrop of bolder textures and forms.

Earlier in this chapter, we looked a bit at texture and form and their impact on color. Remember, smooth-textured leaves and flowers, since they reflect more light, often appear more chromatic than rough ones. Rain has a similar effect on plants and hardscaping elements, creating a shiny surface that is more reflective. Remember too how textures and forms are emphasized in limited color palette schemes. Texture is most prominent in soft light, such as early morning or late evening light. Many shade-loving plants have wonderful textures to their leaves; when designing shade gardens, it's easy to emphasize texture and form and let flower color take a secondary role.

Texture and form also affect perception. Finer-textured plants increase the feeling of space or depth in a border, while bolder plants have the opposite effect. Bolder shapes, forms, and textures cause the eye to stop. Bold plants create relief among a sea of frill. Both succulent and soft pubescent leaves invite people to touch, adding another level to our enjoyment of them; too many very coarse plants may give us the heebie-jeebies, recalling visions of a haunted forest.

A variety of leaf, flower, and plant forms adds to a garden's diversity. Again, balance, contrast, and repetition of these features creates harmony in our gardens. Rounded or heart-shaped leaves set a different mood from linear leaves offset by spines along the margins. Flowers arranged in spires add a strong vertical dimension, while daisylike flowers balance the scene with a horizontal element.

Plant forms can be mounding, vertical, conical, weeping, creeping, or irregular. Mounding forms bring the eye down; vertical forms force the eye to rise. The form of a plant can change during the season or through its life, as it matures. A tree may be upright when young but wide-spreading with age. Open forms create interesting patterns of light, changing the apparent value of colors within the plant and creating suspense as the viewer deals with a more complicated pattern. Gradual changes in form create smooth transitions in a border; throwing in a prominent contrast of form creates a focal point.

Balancing color, texture, and form in a garden takes time and practice. Have fun with the process.

Chapter 4

DESIGN PRINCIPLES

To create aesthetically pleasing compositions, the designer of mixed gardens relies on three basic design principles: order, unity, and rhythm. Different references use slightly different terminology, different experts organize these principles in various ways—yet the message is similar. Our discussion follows the well-organized, easy-to-follow approach set out by Norm Booth and Jim Hiss in *Residential Landscape Architecture* (1991).

In earlier chapters we looked at elements of design—color, texture, form, scale, proportion, line. These forces are never independent of each other; they are the tools that we use, in shifting combinations, to meet various design principles: the fundamental concepts of composition that have developed over time and through experience in a variety of design fields, including interior design and photography. Although they are very useful for beginning designers, these principles are not formulas—many factors contribute to a good overall design. And as in any field of creative expression, the reward for departing from the rules is, in many cases, a masterpiece. Let's look at the design principles of order, unity, and rhythm.

ORDER

Order should be considered early in the design process: it is the underlying visual structure of a design. When we think of how the border or garden will function, and we put together a seating area, a path, and so on, in a organized fashion, order is established. If the elements are not organized, chaos reigns.

Order is accomplished through symmetry, asymmetry, and mass collection. Here is where balance comes into the picture. Balance is the feeling that different elements of the design are in equilibrium. Symmetry establishes balance by arranging elements of a design in an equal fashion around an axis. Symmetry is easily attained and can create a formal feeling to the design—but not always. We are all familiar with the two identical trees or shrubs on either side of a front door. But on several occasions when designing large borders, I have created balance by repeating similar colors and plant materials, in mirror image, on either side of a nonapparent central point in the bed. For example, a garden I designed that was 116 ft. long by approximately 16 ft. wide had *Rosa* 'Hansa', *Miscanthus sinensis* 'Morning Light', and *Achillea* 'Moonshine' on the north and south ends of the border, and various other plants repeated north and south of the central axis, giving balance to the entire garden. This type of symmetry is not obvious as two equal halves without closer study of the design or border, yet the viewer has a feeling of balance in the garden, even if they don't know this is part of what makes the composition work. You know you've accomplished your goal when the design feels right for the viewer but your use of the various principles is not readily apparent.

We create asymmetrical balance (balance of unequal parts) by proper placement. We laid the groundwork for an understanding of this sort of balance in the previous chapter, when we talked about balancing colors, textures, and forms. To combine intense colors with lower-toned colors, we need two-thirds lower-toned to balance one-third intense. Since a bold texture carries more weight in a design, we need a predominance of fine-textured plants to balance that weight. A large tree in the garden can be balanced by a large garden space. Remember our guidelines for proper balance or proportion, the Golden Mean and the Fibonacci Series.

Mass collection is established in a mixed border by grouping like plants together in masses or drifts. In general, avoid separating similar plants within the masses. Certainly a few plants can be used individually or as accents, particularly some of the bold plants, to create drama. It is also nice, periodically, to have a smaller grouping of a plant that is represented in a larger mass; this smaller mass appears then to have self-sown. Avoid the plop-plop, fizz-fizz approach to design commonly seen in collections of plants, with one of this here and one of that there. Drifts or masses of plants create greater impact and order in the design.

UNITY

Unity is the design element that brings everything together, the elusive quality that binds the design into an aesthetically pleasing and functional whole. Unity has been achieved when there is harmony, a feeling of oneness, or when it appears that all the elements of the composition are working together. We can create unity in a design by selecting a certain theme—of color, of type and size of bed shape, of materials. A limited color palette is an easy way to provide a strong sense of unity in a mixed border. We already looked at the importance of having some consistency in the lines that are used throughout the garden, if unity is to be achieved. Simplicity—the elimination of unnecessary detail or elements—adds to unification. Unity is further bolstered by the use of dominance, repetition, interconnection, and unity of three.

Dominance is set when one element or group of elements is more dominant than other elements—think of creating an accent or focal point or focal element. All the other elements in the composition are not as important as the dominant feature—and this less-important status unites them. Still, the dominant feature should have something in common with the other elements. As we have seen, the opportunities for establishing dominance in mixed borders, through contrast of form, size, hue, value, intensity, and texture, are many. The resulting focal point gives the eye a place to stop in an otherwise busy atmosphere. But again, we want to keep a balance, as too many accents can be too complex.

Repetition of similar elements also unites a garden, and this includes repeating a botanical grouping, such as ornamental grasses or dwarf conifers. Many designers, especially certain landscape architects, are big proponents of limiting the number of different types of plants that are used and repeating the same plants over and over again in the design; many collectors, by contrast, create gardens that are more like botanical museums. But keep in mind: by following basic design principles, you can use a wide variety—and, may I say, a more interesting variety—of plant material and still create a united design. Again, as in all aspects of our lives, finding the right balance is key.

Plate 48. The eye moves unobstructed through this lush planting, a great example of unity through dominance, repetition, and interconnection. A limited color theme (purples, blues, and greens) imparts a feeling of harmony. The maple, with its mass of purple and size, is well balanced by the sea of green and blue-green that surrounds it. Psychologically, the interesting and dominant form of the bamboo helps to balance the composition, and the hostas and *Salvia verticillata* 'Purple Rain' repeat subtly along the edges. Gary Koller design, Massachusetts.

Interconnection is established when various elements of the design physically link together. With good interconnection the eye moves, uninterrupted, from one element to another. I love to design and plant gardens that are lush and full, with very little, if any, mulch showing. The plants are touching or in some cases hanging over one another. This ties the garden together. Certain perennials, shrubs, and groundcovers are good melders, pulling the whole composition together. Paving material that links various planting areas together is another way to establish interconnection.

Unity of three is when three elements of the same kind are grouped together to create a sense of unity. In fact, planting groups of plants in odd numbers is generally recommended; if the grouping is an even number, the eye has a tendency to split the group in half. When the group of plants is totally interconnected to create a large mass, it is harder, of course, to divide it into its individual parts, and do keep in mind that even numbers may be desirable if you are trying to achieve symmetry.

RHYTHM

Rhythm is related to time and movement in the garden. This is a fun principle to incorporate in design. Very seldom do we see a garden or design all at once. Spacing and timing of elements

Plate 49. Notice how the different rhythms through repetition are set in this photograph and in Plates 50–51. Here, bright containers of agaves set fairly close together, within large masses of green plants, send a clear message to visitors to move along this formal path. Alan Haskell garden, Massachusetts.

Plate 50. The rhythm is slower in this garden because the repeating shapes are more widely spaced and squat in form. It is still somewhat formal, so we get the feeling we should keep marching along and not dally too long. Holden Arboretum, Ohio.

create different patterns of movement, for the eye as well as the body. Rhythm can be established through repetition, alternation, and gradation.

In contrast to repetition for unity, repetition for rhythm creates an obvious pattern. Repeating the same plant or vertical form (fence posts, for example) at close intervals speeds movement through a space; repeating at larger intervals slows the rhythm.

Alternation, when we repeat elements that are different from each other, is often more stimulating than repeating the same thing over and over. We can alternate size, shapes, or colors. For example, I like to give a border rhythm by designing an undulation of heights along its length. The plants may all be rather tall at one end of the border, followed by a dip of shorter plants, followed by a return to taller plants, and so on, in a repeating sequence. This establishes a graceful flow to the garden.

We can also establish rhythm through gradation, or transition—a gradual change in one or more elements in a sequence. We can gradually move from cooler colors to warmer colors, from tints to shades, from fine textures to coarse textures, from low forms to tall forms. Gradation also affects a scene's perspective.

We mustn't forget the movement and rhythm that plants and wind create in our gardens. Ornamental grasses and many perennials are exceptional at bringing the garden to life with movement and, consequently, sound. Even though this is not a design principle as such, it is a key consideration.

Plate 51. The rhythm set in this garden—by the soft, undulating line of the bed and the informal repetition of hostas, astilbes, and daylilies—gives an impression that strolling and relaxing while passing through this space is the designer's objective. Blanchette Gardens, Massachusetts.

I think you can see how the principles of order, unity, and rhythm all interrelate and overlap to affect our compositions. Keep them in mind but remember: the end product is often just as dependent on the designer's intuition of what works.

Chapter 5

PUTTING IT ON PAPER:

Drawing the Design

Now that we have a solid grounding in the fundamentals and theory of mixed garden design, it's time to put our objectives, thoughts, and dreams onto paper. Drawing the design to scale can seem a bit intimidating. The approach that I will share with you is fairly basic—you don't need to be an artist to execute a workable design. As I used to tell my design students at Ohio State, the most important purpose of a design is to render a functional, enjoyable, and—one hopes—beautiful garden. If we are drawing a plan for the homeowner or subcontractors to follow for installation, it's critical that it be simple and easy to follow and understand. Glitzy, showy graphics doesn't mean that the design will create even an adequate garden; I have seen some drawings that were beautiful works of art even though the plant material and design principles they depicted were pitiful. I also know some extremely creative and talented designers who may only pencil-sketch some rough ideas on paper, if that, and never really work from a formal design. Their gardens are spectacular nonetheless. For most, however, it is better to follow thoughtful steps for drawing a border design.

SUPPLIES

Some basic drawing supplies are helpful for starting out. Although there is a temptation to buy many of the fun and stimulating items sold in art supply stores, the supplies I list here will really be all you need. I use 8½ × 11 in. graph paper, with four squares to 1 in., for almost all my border designs. This way, we can work with a scale of ¼ in. = 1 ft. (one square on the paper is equal to 1 sq. ft. of bed space). This is the scale I prefer to use because it makes it easy to design everything from drifts to single specimens. I also use an engineer scale, choosing the side that reads 40 and represents 1 in. = 4

ft. We will draw the shape of the border, and any paths, hardscaping, walls, and so forth, on this graph paper, to scale, to be used as our base map (see Diagram 12). Just a note: to measure the border on the site, whether an existing garden or a new installation, I use one or two 30-ft. metal tape measures, two 100-ft. cloth measuring tapes (for larger borders), or a measuring wheel. You can accurately measure almost any size or shape garden with these devices.

A pencil (HB lead or No. 2) can be used for all the drafting. Professionals usually render the final drawing in pens with different size tips. A drawing table or drawing board and T-square are helpful for professionals but not essential for most border building. A straight edge provided by a plastic 30-60-90 triangle is useful, as is a circle template, with a variety of sizes, to mark grasses, shrubs, trees, and other individual plants. Also essential, of course, is a good eraser! I use a battery-operated one on large projects. And my electric pencil sharpener is also always close at hand. You will need a calculator for figuring the number of plants per drift. I use colored pencils as I design to keep a check on the color progression through the border. Tracing paper, or design vellum, overlaid on the graph paper, is where we will do our drawing. Drafting tape is used to hold the graph paper steady and keep the tracing paper in place over the graph paper. With inexpensive tracing paper, you can play with design ideas, trash it, if necessary, and start over—it is easy to pull it up. You will still have your original base drawing of the border on the graph paper.

PLANT SIZE

What sizes of plants should you order or purchase when first installing the garden? This issue, along with spacing, is best weighed while designing and must be considered before we look at how to lay out a design. I often shift back and forth from the design I'm drawing to plant catalogs, checking for availability and sizes. I can then keep records on which nursery might have what plants and which one has the best size. Checking catalogs after the design has been completed can be a problem, as certain plants may not be available anywhere in a given season. Because our jobs are so large, we computerize our orders by plant, nursery, and client, inputting information regarding size and cost as well. We can then print our orders by nursery or client and use them for ordering and pulling plants for our jobs. Ordering large numbers of plants, particularly uncommon herbaceous plants, can be a nightmare, entailing hours, days, and even weeks of searching and calling for availability through nurseries across the country (see Sources). Although the fun in this quickly wears thin, I urge you to persevere, as utilizing more than the same-old will set your or your client's garden apart. Substitutions are part of the program. A designer may not even be aware that the plants are not available until delivery occurs. Just another of the uncertainties we deal with in the gardening world!

The plant size you select can depend a great deal on the budget that you are working with and the sizes available. Smaller sizes are sometimes all you can find of unusual species. Plants will grow, of course, but keep in mind the nature of the planting. A puny tree or shrub is going to get lost in the first year among a group of vigorously growing herbaceous plants. As I have seen in more than one instance, woodies can be "consumed" by herbaceous plants—never to recover—if pruning is not diligent. I really prefer, as do most of my clients, to start with decent sizes for the outlining structural plants, the trees and shrubs in particular, so the garden looks proportionally correct fairly early in its life. I normally prefer small-growing trees, depending on the species and ultimate function, to be 5–6 ft. tall at planting. Keep in mind, though, that trees over about a 2-in. caliper can sometimes be more difficult to establish.

In wholesale catalogs, balled-and-burlapped (B&B) trees are often sold by the caliper size (trunk diameter). When ordering plants, I've often needed to know what height a certain caliper measurement translates to. I had always hoped there was a quick, simple way to understand the relationship between caliper and height, but unfortunately there isn't—too many variables. The ratio of caliper to height differs from region to region, from species to species, and from one type of tree to another (shade versus small trees, for example). National guidelines, useful for professionals, are published by the American Nursery & Landscape Association (*American Standard for Nursery Stock* 1996), which lists caliper-to-height relationships for different types of trees as well as other helpful information, such as expected ball size. For example, a small upright tree, 5–6 ft. tall, will usually have six or more branches and a caliper of $1\frac{1}{16}$ in. Regional guidelines may also be available. Keep these references handy when writing landscape specifications.

With shrubs, my preference is always to plant the best size available. Keep in mind the growth rate of a particular shrub; if it

is fast to mature, you may be able to get away with a smaller size. Shrubs are often listed by height if they are balled-and-burlapped. Dwarf conifers or slow-growing conifers are just that; start with a good size if at all possible, bearing in mind the expense.

Trees and shrubs can be purchased in 2-, 3-, or 5-gallon containers (listed as No. 2, 3, or 5 Cont.). If you are writing specifications for a job, and someone else, such as a subcontractor, is purchasing the plants, then indicate the size of the plant, not the size of the container. I have to admit—I'm a cherry-picker. I like to handpick specimen trees and shrubs for my clients and my own gardens whenever possible, to ensure the best quality plant. This extra time and effort is definitely worth it, particularly if you have ever experienced the disappointment of receiving an inferior plant. Fortunately, I've become friends with many nursery operators; they have patience with me and understand the high business standards I'm trying to achieve. If ornamental grasses are going to be prominent features, I prefer to plant them in the 1- or 2-gallon size, at least. I like to start with 2-gallon roses as well, unless they are only available in bareroot.

Our perennials and annuals double or triple in size the first season, so I don't usually use larger sizes of these in the spring. We normally use healthy, quart-sized ($4\frac{1}{4}$- in.) perennials at that time. Later in the season, we often use gallon sizes, or 5-pint, as these tend to be available then; the larger sizes seem to establish better than smaller sizes for the winter. Many perennial nurseries seem to be shifting to these larger containers as a standard size year-round. We may purchase certain annuals or annual vines as larger-growing plants if we are looking to create a fairly instant impact, particularly in containers.

SPACING

Many gardeners have questions about the proper spacing of plants. We all want full gardens, but we don't want to have to be moving or dividing plants constantly. It is particularly important to space woody plants properly at the start. It is fairly simple to move a few herbaceous perennials, but moving a 10-ft. tree is a bit more involved. Proper spacing of plants will normally be determined by the ultimate mature width of the plant, as well as its function for that particular garden; the size at planting is sometimes a factor, too. Nor should soil and regional conditions be ignored: a plant may become a giant in the South but never have a chance to reach such heights in northern gardens, or vice versa. Some trees and shrubs are very slow growing, and their ultimate width may never be seen in our lifetime. I usually space such plants closer together. As with most aspects of design, spacing is a personal issue. I will share with you some of the approaches and guidelines that I utilize.

TREES AND SHRUBS
I very seldom have to worry about the spacing between trees or dwarf conifers in mixed borders, as these are normally planted as individ-

uals. If screening is needed, however, I often select evergreen trees and space them closer than their normal width. For instance, when using Canadian hemlocks (*Tsuga canadensis*) as a screen around an open border, I planted 6- to 7-ft.-tall plants, on a mound (to keep the majority of roots out of our heavy clay soils), approximately 5 ft. (on center) apart, so that the outer tips of the branches were just touching (see Diagram 20 in Chapter 9). This created an effective screen starting the second season and was simply gorgeous in the sixth season. They are kept informally pruned to control their spread. I space 4-ft. specimens of eastern arborvitae (*Thuja occidentalis* 'Techny') 3 ft. apart, even though they can eventually have a 4–5 ft. spread. Swiss stone pine (*Pinus cembra* 'Silver Sheen'), with a spread of 12–15 ft., works nicely spaced 8 ft. apart, while Lawson falsecypress (*Chamaecyparis lawsoniana* 'Sullivan'), a great hemlock substitute, with a spread of 12–14 ft., also prospers at 7–8 ft. spacing.

Various boxwoods are sometimes useful as hedging or to create a defined edge. I space *Buxus* 'Green Velvet', planted when 18–24 in. tall, at 1½–2 ft. on center. The plants can ultimately reach 3–4 ft. in width but are kept sheared.

Many shrubs that I enjoy using—Nordic® inkberry (*Ilex glabra* 'Chamzin'), *Rhododendron* 'Mist Maiden', Virginia sweetspire (*Itea virginica* 'Henry's Garnet'), dwarf fothergilla (*Fothergilla gardenii*), Hummingbird clethra (*Clethra alnifolia* 'Hummingbird'), *Rosa* 'The Fairy' and *R.* 'Nearly Wild', to name a few—have similar spacing. I usually space them 3–4 ft. apart with great results. I once created a breathtaking Meserve holly hedge by planting 4-ft. specimen plants of *Ilex ×meserveae* 'Mesog' (China girl) 3½ ft. apart.

Some large-growing shrubs I love to use, such as bottlebrush buckeye (*Aesculus parviflora*), are very slow to mature. Large plants are almost impossible to find in nurseries. So I give a 2-gallon container plant (which may be 2 ft. tall and 1 ft. wide) 4–5 ft. of space on the design. I may then interplant with a nonaggressive perennial that will grow peacefully with the shrub, filling the space but allowing the shrub to get light, moisture, and nutrients.

HERBACEOUS PLANTS

Most herbaceous plants, perennials and annuals, are best planted in odd numbered drifts or groups, preferably with at least three of each kind. Larger-growing plants may require "drifts of one," as I have heard avid plant collectors refer to them. One *Colocasia esculenta* 'Fontanesii' (elephant's ear), growing to 6 ft. tall and wide, is all most of us need in a border. Not that en masse it would be anything less than spectacular—but to plant any more would be out of scale and balance with most sites and plantings. Large gardens with large borders can get away with larger groupings of big plants, if that is the desired style, and often that is what is most appropriate for the scale and viewing points.

As a general guideline, small plants (under 1 ft. in height) or plants at the front of the border are spaced 8–12 in. apart. Many low-growing annuals require this type of spacing. Medium-sized plants (1–2½ ft. tall) are best spaced 15–24 in. apart; spacing of 15–18 in. seems to work great for the majority of perennials. Larger-growing plants—ornamental grasses, for instance, and cannas and other tropical annuals—are spaced 2–3 ft. apart.

I hate to see mulch in a garden, but as a planting matures and is fine-tuned, holes happen. Fine-textured annuals can be seeded among perennials while the perennials are maturing, giving the garden a more finished look early in its life. Interplanting with love-in-a-mist (*Nigella damascena*), California poppies (*Eschscholzia californica*), or larkspur (*Consolida ajacis*) is an easy and effective way to give the illusion of a more mature garden.

BULBS

General guidelines are often given for the spacing of bulbs. Recommendations such as "space bulbs three times the width of the bulb" are helpful—if you know the width of the bulb, which is not usually the case when you're sitting at the drawing table, designing! Small bulbous plants (sometimes called minor bulbs), such as crocus, snowdrops, and winter aconites, are generally planted 3–4 in. apart. Tiny-growing snow crocus may go as close as 2 in. apart. Most daffodils, tulips, and hyacinths, as well as larger-sized alliums, are planted about 6 in apart; smaller-growing types or species tulips may be planted as close as 4 in. apart, while giant alliums may need 12-in. spacing. With bulbs, I think it's best to err on the side of planting extra, for a full effect, rather than to skimp and not have enough of a show. Bulb catalogs usually list the number of bulbs they recommend per square foot of each kind of bulb, which is a vital guideline in most cases. For recommended spacing of the bulbs discussed in this book, see the Design Chart in Appendix B.

When you design a drift of bulbs, or any other plant, you first need to know the square footage of the area it encompasses; you can find this out easily by counting the number of squares in the drift on your graph paper. Multiply this square footage by the number of bulbs, or plants, per square foot for the desired spacing:

Spacing	Plants per sq. ft.
4 in.	9
6 in.	4
8 in.	2.25
12 in.	1.0
15 in.	0.64
18 in.	0.45
24 in.	0.25
36 in.	0.11

This will tell you how many plants you need. So the equation is this: square footage of drift × number of plants per sq. ft. = number of plants needed for drift.

MIXED BORDER DESIGN EXAMPLE

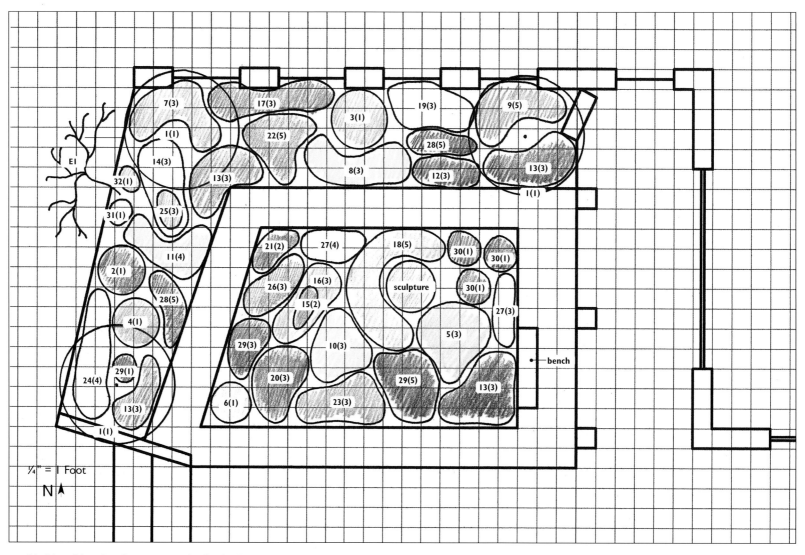

Diagram 11. Mixed border design example: finished product. Artist, Megan H. King; author's design, Harbrecht garden, Ohio.

DIAGRAM 11

Trees

I	(3)	*Malus* 'Lanzam' (Lancelot®)	flowering crabapple

Existing trees

E I	(I)	*Pyrus* sp. (espaliered)	pear

Shrubs

2	(I)	*Buddleia davidii* 'Mongo' (Nanho blue)	butterfly bush
3	(I)	*Rosa* 'Meidomonac' (Bonica®)	rose
4	(I)	*Rosa* 'Nearly Wild'	rose

Perennials

5	(3)	*Achillea* 'Anblo' (Anthea)	yarrow
6	(I)	*Artemisia* 'Powis Castle'	artemisia
7	(3)	*Chrysanthemum* 'Pumpkin Harvest'	mum
8	(3)	*Coreopsis verticillata* 'Moonbeam'	threadleaf coreopsis
9	(5)	*Crocosmia* 'Blacro' (Jenny Bloom)	crocosmia
10	(3)	*Digitalis grandiflora*	yellow foxglove
11	(4)	*Hemerocallis* 'Happy Returns'	daylily
12	(3)	*Heuchera* 'Chocolate Ruffles'	coralbells
13	(12)	*Lavandula angustifolia* 'Munstead'	lavender

(continued on next page)

Plate 52. The "before" shot of our mixed garden design example. Harbrecht garden, Ohio.

Plate 53. Four months after the design was implemented (the sculpture is not yet in place). Author's design, Harbrecht garden, Ohio.

(plant list cont.)

14	(3)	*Lilium* 'Casa Blanca'	lily
15	(2)	*Limonium platyphyllum* 'Violetta'	sea lavender
16	(3)	*Papaver orientale* 'Lighthouse'	oriental poppy
17	(3)	*Penstemon digitalis* 'Husker Red'	foxglove penstemon
18	(5)	*Perovskia atriplicifolia* 'Longin'	Russian sage
19	(3)	*Phlox paniculata* 'Pax' (peace)	border phlox
20	(3)	*Salvia* ×*sylvestris* 'Blauhügel' (blue hill)	perennial salvia
21	(2)	*Salvia verticillata* 'Purple Rain'	perennial salvia
22	(5)	*Scabiosa* Butterfly Blue®	pincushion flower
23	(3)	*Scabiosa* 'Pink Mist'	pincushion flower
24	(4)	*Veronica spicata* 'Icicle'	spike speedwell

Annuals

25	(3)	*Ageratum houstonianum* 'Blue Horizon'	ageratum
26	(3)	*Gomphrena haageana* 'Lavender Lady'	gomphrena
27	(7)	*Nierembergia scoparia* 'Mont Blanc'	nierembergia
28	(10)	*Nigella damascena* Miss Jekyll Series	love-in-a-mist
29	(9)	*Ocimum basilicum* 'Red Rubin'	basil
30	(3)	*Pennisetum setaceum* 'Rubrum'	purple fountain grass

Vines

31	(1)	*Clematis* 'Lanuginosa Candida'	clematis
32	(1)	*Lathyrus latifolius*	perennial sweet pea

Let's turn to a real-world design to see how all the steps involved in drawing a mixed border come together. It will be easy to draw lessons from this simple yet functional and attractive design, which I created for a client some years ago. Although it is an older design, it still contains exceptional plants, even if they are not the very latest (be sure to check out the designs in Part Two for examples of the latter!). I chose this design to address the fundamentals of all design—not to select the best plant choices for your region or personal tastes. If you live in California, for example, the design steps and all the fundamentals we have discussed will apply, but your plant material may be quite different: depending on the site, you may use Australian tree ferns (*Cyathea cooperi*) instead of crabapple trees—rather than lavender, you might select agaves!

We will go through the practical steps and the points we have discussed so far to show how they are used in the process. When designing we may not always proceed in this exact order, but this is generally the path to follow.

Site: Located in Worthington, Ohio, zone 5, this garden is in an entry courtyard with a southern exposure; most sections of the garden receive full sun (six hours a day for the most part). The courtyard is enclosed and protected from wind on the north, east, and west sides by the brick walls of the house. This enclosure also decreases air circulation on the site. The house is brick, and the hardscaping that surrounds the beds is cobblestone and brick. This project was a renovation of an existing garden: some previous bed preparation had been performed, but a soil test revealed that the organic matter content was still only 6%—better than most established gardens we work with but not to our preferred

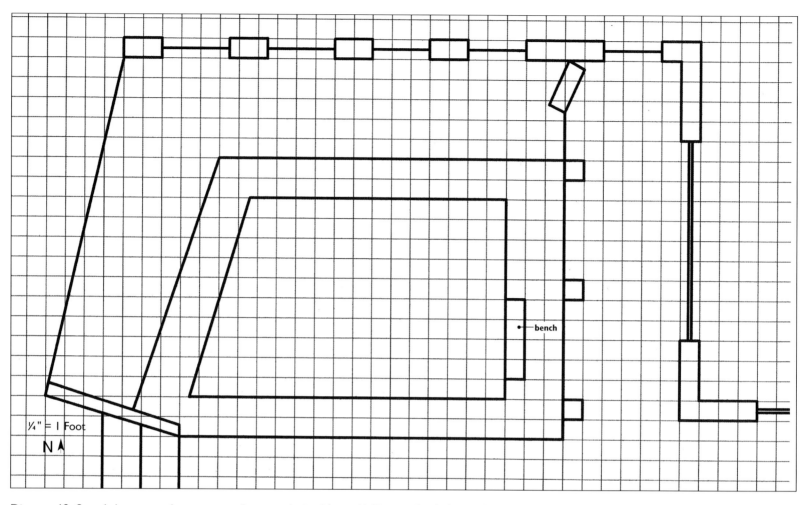

¼" = 1 Foot

N

Diagram 12. Step 1: base map drawn on graph paper. Artist, Megan H. King; author's design, Harbrecht garden, Ohio.

standard of approximately 18% organic matter. So the soil was amended with 4 in. of organic matter (2 in. of Canadian sphagnum peat moss and 2 in. of a compost blend). The pH was alkaline, 7.4. There is approximately 560 sq. ft. of bed space.

Objectives: The clients had very specific, typed-out objectives for the garden. This is uncommon. They specified a "finished" look for the courtyard, complete with containers of flowers, as the previous design never jelled. They requested an informal but "orderly" English style using traditional perennials and annuals with soft colors, accented by strong colors. The existing plants were to be upgraded, where appropriate, and a small sundial in the center bed was to be replaced with a sculpture, 5 ft. tall and 2 ft. wide, that was more appropriate in scale and impact. Lighting would provide soft highlights and safety on the front walkway and steps. They also made provisions for ongoing maintenance (how brilliant!).

Because this was a renovation, I had to decide which plants would stay and which would go. We removed a large, pest-plagued crabapple tree, some junipers and spirea, a contorted filbert, and a group of unsightly boxwood. The existing perennials and bulbs were not choice, nor were they appropriate for the conditions, so these were also removed. The already small bed spaces had been further divided into small sections with cobblestone, which created too many lines and resulted in a very busy patchwork effect; these too were removed to allow for greater bed space and to simplify the lines in the garden. An espaliered pear was kept in its existing location on the west wall.

Plant Selection: This is the step when it's a good idea to brainstorm and make a list of the plants that would work or that you would like to have in the border. Think about all the attributes of the plant—its season(s) of interest, color of foliage, flowers, fruit, bark, texture, and form. You can even organize your lists accordingly. Do the plants work well together from a cultural standpoint? We will discuss some of the plants selected for this design—and why—as we progress, but be sure to check out the

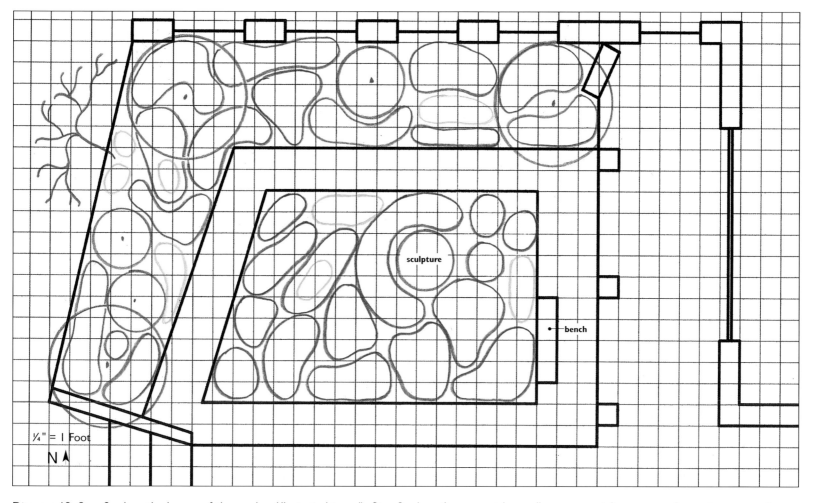

Diagram 13. Step 2: place the bones of the garden (illustrated in red). Step 3: place the perennials, smaller ornamental grasses, and prominent annuals (illustrated in blue). Step 4: place the filler or seeding plants (illustrated in yellow). Artist, Megan H. King; author's design, Harbrecht garden, Ohio.

appendixes on design and maintenance characteristics for detailed info on all the plants.

Because this is a small garden, every plant needs to perform for a long period to earn its spot in the design. The peak season of interest for this garden is summer, but there is interest through the year. The predominant colors are blues, greens, purples, soft pinks, yellows, and whites, with splashes of silver and purple-red foliage. These colors mimic colors found in the home's hallway. Ultimate plant height and width was considered: we incorporated small trees and roses that would require only periodic pruning to keep them in scale.

FIVE STEPS TO SUCCESS

Get your thinking caps on! To put together a mixed border design requires that we think about many different elements at the same time. All the issues we have discussed to this point in the book— site, objectives, plant selection, the design elements of color, form, and texture, the principles of order, unity, and rhythm— must be considered with every plant that is drawn on the paper. It means thinking about several things at one time, and it can be challenging but very dynamic. Let's get going!

Step 1. Draw the border or garden to scale on graph paper with pencil. Be sure to indicate existing plant material that is going to stay in the garden, as well as windows, doors, unsightly electric meters, air conditioners, or anything else that needs to be considered during the design process. Draw in the paths, walls, and other hardscaping elements that will be retained and those that are to be added.

Things to think about: remember colors and textures, house style, and region. Write them down, if necessary. Think about the surrounding landscape. Are there views to be hidden or framed?

Are there focal areas to be accentuated in the border? They need to be indicated on the plan. Place tracing paper over graph paper. Trace the bed or garden outline on tracing paper.

Step 2. Place the outlining structural plants (trees, shrubs, roses, large grasses, and large tropicals) and prominent artwork—the bones of the garden (hardscaping elements are also sometimes referred to as bones, the bones of the design). The three Lancelot flowering crabapples (*Malus* 'Lanzam') are dominant features, reaching a maximum height of only 10 ft.; their oval upright habit, white flowers, persistent orange fruit, and disease-resistant foliage make them ideal for the courtyard. I have drawn them with a 6-ft. spread; with pruning, they can easily be kept at roughly that width. A butterfly bush (*Buddleia davidii* 'Mongo' (Nanho blue)) and disease-resistant *Rosa* 'Nearly Wild' and Bonica® rose (R. 'Meidomonac') effectively work as an intermediate layer. The existing espaliered pear (*Pyrus* sp.) softens the vertical plane of the west wall; it combines well with the crabapples and gives a feeling of an English potager.

Things to think about: Is the mature size of the trees or shrubs going to be in proper scale with the site? Do the shrubs work as effective transitions between the trees and the herbaceous material? Do these plants provide multi-season effect? Are they the very best selections for the site?

Step 3. Place the perennials, smaller ornamental grasses, and prominent annuals. I like to think of this as the icing on the cake. Once you have made the cake structurally sound, then it's time for the fun of decorating. Eighteen different perennial and seven different annual genera are used in the garden. Most of the plants have a very long bloom period with proper deadheading.

If a perennial or annual has been selected to repeat at various locations along the front or back of the border, it is sometimes placed first in the design. For example, drifts of Munstead lavender appear three times along the back section of the garden and once in the middle section. I may draw such groupings in first, or I may simply look at the overall design and make a notation in the spot that I want a plant repeated—I work through each border differently. Sometimes I design from the front to the middle and then to back as I move along the border. If a prominent woody, tropical, or piece of art has already been placed, I will often work out from that feature. If a large-growing or bold-textured perennial or annual is being used, it is often placed first and then less dominant plant groupings are drawn in. I like to fill in an entire section of the garden before proceeding down the border. In this way, interesting combinations of colors, textures, and forms are considered together for neighboring plants. I like to color the design as I draw it to keep in touch with how it is developing.

Let's look at the thought process of the designer for this third step, starting in the northeast corner of the garden. The Lancelot crab, whose year-round qualities we have noted, has already been placed. I chose Munstead lavender (*Lavandula angustifolia* 'Munstead') because it is one of the hardiest cultivars for central Ohio, providing fragrance, long bloom, and a mounded habit with vertical flowers. Although the individual leaves are fine in texture, this woody subshrub, to me, appears coarse in its overall texture. And, of course, it is so English! Three lavenders create a nice amount of weight at the base of the crab. Their 18-in. height works well, as the crab's lower branches start at about 2½ ft. off the ground. I then chose to use five *Crocosmia* 'Blacro' (a.k.a. Jenny Bloom, after the youngest daughter of British perennial aficionado Alan Bloom). It is a narrow plant, only about 12 in. in width, so we need to use more of it, and at closer spacing, to balance the size of the other plants. The saturated yellow-orange flower color of the delicate six-parted flowers contrasts with both the color (lavender-purple) and shape of the lavender's flowers, and the two combined create a nice focal point. A similar color combination is repeated between the lavender and the daylily (*Hemerocallis* 'Happy Returns') and the yarrow (*Achillea* 'Anblo' (Anthea)). The crocosmia, with its lance-shaped leaves, lighter, more open habit, and finer texture, is also a nice contrast to the solidity of the lavender and the trunk of the crab. Crocosmias create nice vertical lines, and their airy flowers catch the slightest breeze, adding rhythm to the combination. Growing to about 2 ft., they flirt with the lower branches and leaves of the small tree, and their flower color harmonizes well with the brick wall beyond.

Coralbells (*Heuchera* 'Chocolate Ruffles') now come into the scene. Their scalloped leaves, in tones and shades of purple and red, absorb light while the gray leaves of the lavender reflect it. The result is intriguing. Contrast in leaf shapes adds to the excitement. Both foliage colors will be present for most of the year, extending the interest of this vignette. Blue love-in-a-mist (*Nigella damascena* Miss Jekyll Series), unintentionally making another British connection, is added to harmonize with the underlying blue present in the coralbells and lavender; its very fine airy texture is a nice relief from the heaviness of the coralbells and lavender, and the interesting form of its seedheads will further enhance the grouping. This kind of thought process continues throughout the designing of the garden.

As you make your drifts, you need to think about the area you are covering. With perennials, for example, I often create 5- to 7-sq.-ft. drifts, allowing for three to five plants per drift at 15- or 18-in. spacing. Look through the tracing paper to the number of squares or sections of squares in your drift. Add these up to find the square footage of irregularly shaped drifts. For example, the drifts of Munstead lavender and crocosmia in the northeast

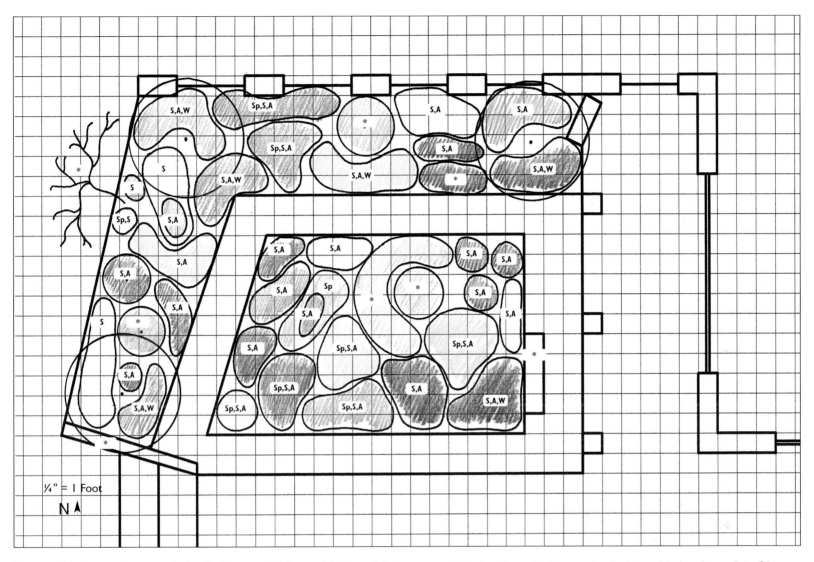

Diagram 14. Seasonal interest: Sp[ring], S[ummer], A[utumn], W[inter], * [year-round]. Artist, Megan H. King; author's design, Harbrecht garden, Ohio.

corner of the garden are each approximately 7 sq. ft., so I planned three lavender plants to be spaced 18 in. apart (0.45 plants per sq. ft. × 7 sq. ft. = 3 plants), and five crocosmia to be spaced 15 in. apart (0.64 plants per sq. ft. × 7 sq. ft. = 4.48 plants—close enough to five). The coralbells are in a space of about 5 sq. ft. and spaced 15 in. apart (0.64 plants per sq. ft. × 5 sq. ft. = 3 plants). We talked earlier about the unity of three, and the majority of the time, I use odd numbers in my drifts. Occasionally, if the space isn't appropriate, I choose an even number of perennials or annuals—I find that once they fill in, it is impossible to determine the numbers that are planted. Notice too that a small amount of space is allotted between various drifts of plants.

Keep in mind that we are normally creating irregular drifts that wind and weave among and around each other. Drifts should not come to a point, although students new to the art are often tempted to design them this way. Groups of plants very seldom form a point, especially those whose overall habit is horizontal.

Step 4. Place the filler or seeding annuals and perennials and mingling vines, as well as any bulbs. This is the time to check the layers of the garden and think about interplanting. Are there any groundcovers that could mingle at the base of certain plants? Keep a plant's season of interest in mind: can other plants or bulbs be grown around them that come up at the same time, so they can perform together? Or, if certain plants have a fairly short season, could we plan for successive interest and choose additional plants to fill the lull?

Because love-in-a-mist is an excellent reseeding annual, I use it a great deal in designs as filler. Although, for example, the design indicates five nigellas between the border phlox (*Phlox paniculata* 'Pax') and the coralbells, the five plants are actually spread out into a wider area; seed is also gathered each season and sprinkled about that area for a spontaneous result. The three ageratums (*Ageratum houstonianum* 'Blue Horizon') were added at the base of the lilies (*Lilium* 'Casa Blanca') to prolong the seasonal interest in that area. Two sea lavender (*Limonium platyphyllum* 'Violetta') were placed to fill the void created when the oriental poppies (*Papaver orientale* 'Lighthouse') go dormant in the summer. Perennial sweat pea (*Lathyrus latifolius*) and vining clematis (*Clematis* 'Lanuginosa Candida') were interplanted, with the espaliered pear as the support, to prolong interest through the season.

The clients had spring bulbs in the previous design and weren't crazy about the effect. They particularly didn't like to see the dying foliage sprawled about in their front entry garden. I can't remember if they requested they not be included in this design, but for some reason they weren't. I would like to have seen them in the garden, so let's look at some possible options. *Tulipa* 'Angelique' could be used in the nonseeding annual holes and dug and replaced yearly, just as you would annuals, after flowering but before foliar decline; this could be labor-intensive and costly, depending on the size of the job, but in this case, it isn't too bad. And keep in mind: this tulip normally returns reliably, and if declining foliage is tolerable, they could remain in the garden. The available annual space for bulbs in this garden is small, only about 35 sq. ft., and we would plant five bulbs per sq. ft. of this tulip, so we'd need about 175 bulbs.

Crocus, colchicum, netted iris (*Iris reticulata*), striped squill (*Puschkinia scilloides*), glory of the snow (*Chionodoxa* spp.), and other minor bulbs would be nice interplanted and repeated in large groups through and around the perennial plant material. Their foliage is so fine, it is easily hidden by emerging perennial foliage. More filling in, if needed, could be done by using *Allium sphaerocephalon* or other alliums. *Gladiolus* 'Violetta' would fit the style and color preference of the garden; it and other tender bulbs would work as slender additions in and among the other plants.

Step 5. Review the entire design to be sure the objectives were met. Have all the design principles been considered? Does the garden serve its intended function? How is the flow of color, texture, and form from the front to the back of the border as well as through the seasons? Are there any holes to be filled? changes or substitutions that should be made? Of greatest importance is that you are happy with the design. Better still—if you are a professional—is your client happy?

Let's do a brief review of this design. The objective of creating an English-style design, informal yet orderly, was met. I had worked with many of the genera I selected in gardens in England, but I chose species or new and improved disease- and insect-

resistant cultivars that were more adaptable to Ohio conditions. Year-round interest was created. In the spring, we have interest from the crabs, poppies, roses, foxglove, and lavender. Summer is a riot of perennials and annuals. Autumn is brilliant, with the annuals continuing and certain perennials, such as the Pumpkin Harvest mums, coming into their own. Long- and repeat-blooming perennials and ornamental grasses also carry on in this season. In the winter, the outlining structure of the crabs and pear, along with the ornamental grasses, various interesting seedheads, ornamental fruit, and the ever-gray foliage of the lavender, is appreciated.

Strong structure is provided by the walls of the house, the paving, the sculpture, and even a bench. The verging of the horizontal, vertical, and overhead planes creates a good three-dimensional relationship. Scale and proportion have been addressed nicely, and, although it was done unintentionally, many of the dimensions are actually Fibonacci numbers. The paths are 2–3 ft. wide around the center bed. The border along the walls is approximately 5 ft. in width; the length along the north edge of the middle bed is 13 ft. Is it coincidence that these dimensions work well and feel right? The planting is lush and full, with plants billowing over the walks. Containers were added and filled with drought-tolerant plants, such as sedum and blue fescue, to suit the hectic schedule of the clients. Lighting was improved.

The color objectives of the client were addressed by staying with softer colors of pink, restful greens, blues, and purples. The whites are bright, as are the yellows, which are fairly true and of a high value. Both hues make nice accents and contrast, as does the higher-valued silver foliage. The purple foliage adds stabilizing depth to the garden; its lower value creates needed contrast.

Colors are harmonious for the most part, sharing either their pastel or pale qualities. The brighter pastels, such as the rose (*Rosa* 'Nearly Wild'), yarrows (*Achillea* 'Anblo' (Anthea)), and mums (*Chrysanthemum* 'Pumpkin Harvest'), are more eye-catching, along with the bright whites of the border phlox (*Phlox paniculata* 'Pax') and spike speedwell (*Veronica spicata* 'Icicle'). Color blending is aided by the paler, more grayed or slightly less saturated flower colors of the pincushion flowers (*Scabiosa* Butterfly Blue® and S. 'Pink Mist') and the love-in-a-mist (*Nigella damascena* Miss Jekyll Series), as well as by the more muted foliage of the perennial salvia (*Salvia verticillata* 'Purple Rain') and artemisia (*Artemisia* 'Powis Castle'). Note that the finer texture of the pincushion flowers and the love-in-a-mist decreases the impact of their flower colors.

As in an English-style cottage garden, many soft, airy textures predominate, balanced by fewer, coarser textures. A nice variety—of overall plant shapes and their lines, of rounded and vertical flower forms—provides interest, contrast, repetition, and harmony. Note individual combinations within the planting and see how texture and form interplay. The garden bed lines are strong, as are the vertical lines of the trees, sculpture, and walls.

Let's consider the design principle of order: we find that the garden is more orderly because it has fewer lines (remember, we removed all the cobblestone that divided the small bed spaces into even smaller sections). Order is also established by the feeling of balance, of equilibrium, among the different elements. The many groupings of perennials and annuals nicely balance the weight of the woody plants and the sculpture. Colors and textures are balanced: we have used approximately two-thirds lower-toned or cooler colors and finer textures to one-third more intense or accent colors and bolder textures. Our drifts or groupings of perennials and annuals establish order through mass collection.

Harmony prevails in the design, which gives us a sense of unity. The dominance of the crabapples and the sculpture (a year-round focal point) unifies the less dominant features. Repetition occurs throughout—the crabs and various other plants repeat, as do textures, colors, forms, and lines. Unity is further strengthened by interconnection: most plants in the lushly styled design touch or hang over one another. Unity of three is present in the many groupings of three or five perennials; the three flowering crabapples also create more unity than if three different types of trees were selected for the design.

The rhythm of alternation is obvious. We have a tall crab on the corner, and then a layer of shrubs, perennials and annuals, whose height is lower; this sequence repeats at the next crab, and the third. Rhythm is also created by the many undulating heights of our perennials and annuals, and it is sensed in the movement of the purple fountain grass and vertical spires of the perennial salvia and spike speedwell.

Keep in mind that even the most well-designed mixed border is going to require on-site adjustments. A vision on paper and reality don't always coincide exactly! I place all the plants in my designs myself—which can take hours, even days—to be certain that I'm making those little shifts that are necessary (in plant material or whatever) for the drawn design to work.

I hope this information has taken the mystery and intimidation factor out of designing a mixed border. Now all that is left is for you to "just do it"!

Chapter 6

ART IN THE MIXED GARDEN

It is exhilarating to incorporate artistic works into the garden. In fact, I sometimes find choosing artwork (ornaments, benches, arbors, gates, containers—even creative paving material) more rewarding than selecting outstanding specimen plants. And let's face it, art provides great pleasure and serves many functions, without the degree of care—or, worse yet, the chance of death—that every plant carries with it. It is certain that art will enhance a garden if used properly, and a garden in turn enhances the art that becomes a part of it.

Art, garden ornaments, and other peripherals function as design elements in the garden in any number of ways. They can provide spatial control, focal points or dominance, structure, and permanence. They can create movement, direction, and sound, or define a sense of time or place. Artwork can create a mood, stir emotions, or evoke memories. Even ornaments can be functional and provide support for plants, food for birds, or water for butterflies. Art is invaluable for expressing individuality and a personal interest or style in a garden.

When using art in the garden, it is advisable to consider aspects of design we have already touched on, such as appropriateness, scale, and the design principles of order, unity, and rhythm. Restraint could also be added. Remember, with art as with color, less is often more.

Let's first consider appropriateness. It is easy to see how, for example, a stone Buddha would be out of place in a lively cottage garden. And, in turn, a bee skep in the middle of a formal Japanese garden would be ludicrous. But when we are out shopping, it is easy to select items on impulse that may not be exactly appropriate, in character or scale, for the intended space—if we even have a space in mind beforehand! Bear in mind the style of the garden and its location. Choose art that is in keeping with the natural materials or styles of the region and home to intensify a sense of place. Select pots, for example, that carry the same hues as the hardscaping material or house. Yet don't feel limited by these—you can take an eclectic approach, with class and style, if you take care that things aren't too extreme, as in the Buddha example; pieces of art from other regions or even countries, such as colorful glazed pots, can carry the viewer to a faraway land in the Mediterranean, for example, providing a much-needed escape from the "same old same old." I know several gardeners, by contrast, whose goal it is to get as outlandish and tacky as possible with art in their gardens. To each his own.

Consider the mood you want to create when purchasing ornaments. The ornament's colors, the material it is made from, and its character, if applicable—all transfer their energy to the space and the viewer. Brightly colored or lighthearted pieces bring that same vitality to the garden, while natural tones and more serious pieces set their own tone. The mood in the garden changes constantly, with the weather and the time of day or year; garden ornaments can create a needed permanence among this flux, even as they too subtly change with the season or time of day (see Plate 63). Art can carry a garden through its low times, when plantings are not at their peak. Lighting brings charm and a romantic atmosphere to the garden, be it from strings of small white lights, a simple lantern, or highly ornamental fixtures (see Plates 59, 127, and 129). There is also the "art" created by shadows and reflections from the light itself.

Ornaments are very effective as anchors for a planting, but they need to be of appropriate size for such a function. Be sure the ornament is in scale with the space. Many times people err by

Plate 55. The ambience committee would approve of this romantic effect. Featuring *Clematis recta*. Author's garden.

Plate 54. Bright and shiny cobalt-blue pots add good energy and an other-worldly sense of adventure. Visualize the drab results of a typical terra-cotta pot in place of this one. Featuring *Phyllostachys nigra*. Author's garden.

Plate 56. This gorgeous eye-stopping bench, which combines the classic and the modern, was created cooperatively by two artists. It was custom-designed to illustrate poppies, but when its neighbor *Paeonia* 'Burma Ruby' began to flower, the resemblance and connection between the two was uncanny—proving once again that the best design often occurs by chance! Note the live green frog on the bench's arm. Bench construction, Jacob E. Miller; tile inlay, Connie Huston; author's garden.

selecting art or pots that are too small—they wind up lost among the planting. Does the size and the placement feel right? In general, it is better to select one large item over several small items, which will only add clutter to the garden and have no impact on the overall design.

Ornaments within the garden can be unified by selecting similar materials or colors. For example, I wanted to liven up our country garden and add an artistic mood, so I got away from an entirely rustic palette and brought in some brightly colored pieces. Cobalt-blue is the unifying color in several of these

elements, including the bench, containers, and birdbath. The use of bright colors in general (the blues just mentioned, the orange Waldo chair, the yellow trellises) is unifying. But there are still many rustic pieces made of wood, which is in harmony with our log home and surrounding woodland. One, the arbor in our back garden, is the logo for my company and has thus become an identifying feature; it also creates a sense of entry into a new space.

Plate 57. Go wild and have fun with art in your garden. Remember paint colors can always be changed. Author's garden.

Plate 58. The yellow trellises betray my new penchant for bright colors. They add light to the dark logs on the west side of our home, and their style ties in with other lively art and colors throughout the gardens. Trellis artist, Mark Bokenkamp; author's garden.

Plate 59. This arbor, one of the first ornaments in my garden, is a unifying link between our rustic home and its location. Besides providing plant (and lighting!) support, it marks the entry into a magical space and serves as the logo for my company. Author's garden; photograph by Ian Adams.

The two styles—bright and artistic, rustic and natural—add contrast and harmony, create excitement and mystery, and express this gardener's varied personality. Another way to tie ornaments to the garden is to select ornaments in hues similar to those of the garden's color scheme. Or, if you really like a certain piece, design your garden palette and plants around it.

Selecting a theme or repeating an art element—gazing balls, sundials, lanterns, finials on fence posts—is another way to unify a garden. For instance, watering cans are set about our gardens, our conservatory, and our home. Some are both attractive and functional, evoking a feeling of industriousness; the old ones take us back in time.

Above all, garden ornaments should express individuality. Some of the most prized pieces of art have personal associations. Working with a variety of artists to create custom pieces of work is especially inspiring. The bronze sculpture of our son, Zachary—captured at around the age of three, holding his favorite flower, *Lychnis coronaria*, and wearing his wellies—stirs emotions in all who see it. It is a priceless treasure that to me makes the garden complete.

Plate 60. In this harmonious vignette, the art and plants all share yellow as a parent color (the brown in the pot is a shade of orange). I'm not sure what came first, the plants or the ornaments, but it works. Mary Jane Baker garden, North Carolina.

Plate 61. A collection of watering cans repeated throughout various garden spaces connects different areas—one is always handy to rescue a dry plant. This particular one, however, is tied up with *Lathyrus odoratus* 'Henry Eckford'. Author's garden.

Art directs the eye's movement through a garden. An ornament often serves as a place for the eye to rest, creating a focal point and dominance in an otherwise endless mass of plants. For this reason, it is best not to have two or more different, yet equally dominant, features in the same field of view: the result is confusion and distraction rather than harmony and order. Art in the garden usually slows a visitor's movement through the garden. Placed in the center of the bed, it anchors the garden. Sited in the intersection of converging paths, it acts as a dominant structural element of the design and draws the eye forward, pulling the visitor into the garden. A visitor is compelled to walk in the direction of the sound coming from a fountain, in an attempt to locate it. The presence and weight of art or containers placed at the entrance to a path or home signifies that this is the correct way to go, that a new space waits to be discovered. Art can be repeated at regular intervals along a path or through a bed to create rhythm

Plate 62. This depiction of our son, Zachary, as a young child exemplifies the theory that art should express individuality. Sculptor, Renate Burgyan; author's garden.

Plate 63. Although this sculpture provides permanence, it is not stagnant. Its appearance alters with the changing rhythms around it—the birth and death of plants, the subtle differences in light and weather. Author's garden.

in the garden; it sets the pace to be followed (see Plate 49). If two different items, such as a large pot and a smaller pot, are repeated alternately, we create a different type of rhythm. Art, perhaps a bench or statue, placed at the end of a long path draws visitors toward it. Ornaments can be used to separate or divide a space, thus altering the perceived sense of space. They can block an area or cause movement into it.

Order within the most informal garden can be perceived through symmetry: simply place matching planted containers or identical pieces of art on either side of a door, path, or gate. This is also an effective way to frame a view. Asymmetrical balance can

be achieved by balancing the weight of one large pot with three smaller pots.

We talked about utilizing all possible space in a garden, including the vertical space of walls; this applies to art as well, from trellises to fountains to containers. The trellis may be simply functional or extremely ornamental in itself, as mine are (see Plate 58). Obelisks add verticality to gardens; they provide support for a variety of interesting vines and are invaluable as repeating elements.

Fences, gates, and walls are more venues for an artistic touch. Think outside the box with materials and paint colors for walls and fences. Gates don't have to be boring—they can add tremendously

Plate 64. The sound of water moves people through space. The mood of the character they encounter here will affect their journey. Artist, Daniel Mathewson; author's garden.

Plate 65. Containers and ornaments on walls can help to soften structures as well as connect the house to the garden. Featuring *Ipomoea batatas* 'Margarita', *Tropaeolum majus* 'Blush Double', *Verbena* 'Homestead Purple'. Author's garden.

to the garden's spirit, depending on their style and composition. They don't even have to be part of a fence but can stand alone to signify a change of space.

Hardscaping, besides being a critical structural element in the garden, can also add to a garden's artistry: do remember to approach it that way, whether you are using traditional or nontraditional materials. For instance, you can create intriguing patterned surfaces with stones or colorful whole or broken tiles.

Containers are major design elements, extending the mixed garden to a porch, deck, or steps and bringing it to life. They can be placed in a border to fill the void left by a plant that has gone

dormant, or sited where soil is so poor that nothing will grow. Many are so attractive, you don't even need to enhance them with plants. Bamboo evokes the exotic, and you can use it and other invasive plants, such as water lettuce, in containers without fearing they'll snatch you from your bed at night (see Plates 54 and 71). Containers can be filled with plants that are similar to those repeated throughout the garden, unifying the container area with the garden as a whole. Long gone are the simple pots full of impatiens or petunias. Dynamic perennials, annuals, tropicals, vines, herbs, vegetables, and woody plants can be combined to create mixed containers that echo the style of the garden, with outstanding plants featured as specimens. Stressing foliage plants in containers and playing with texture, form, and some wild leaf colors is another fun route.

Small and slow-growing trees and shrubs are particularly suited to container culture and may be nice additions where space or the design style limits their use in the garden. But many larger-growing trees and shrubs can also be incorporated into pots and kept in bounds with pruning, if desired. Plants are usually container-hardy to two zones warmer than their "in-ground" USDA hardiness zone rating. If, for example, you wanted to overwinter your container plants outside, and you garden in zone 7, you would need to select plants that are cold hardy to at least zone 5. Plants with colorful stems, such as redosier dogwood (*Cornus sericea*; zone 2), or with ornamental winter fruit, such as winterberry holly (*Ilex verticillata*; zone 3), can be grown in containers to enhance the winter garden (Keim 2001).

Plate 66. This obelisk carries *Ipomoea lobata* (*Mina lobata*) above the heads of tall perennials, so it can be appreciated. Author's garden.

Plate 67. An exceptional gate welcomes the visitor into this artist's garden and studio. It is a brief introduction to the wonderful ornaments that lie ahead. It also diminishes the scale of the large overhead trees, providing an intimate transition into the garden. Artist, Walt Rickli; The Garden Studio, Ontario.

Depending on their size, woody plants can also create a feeling of an understory layer around a living space to comfortably reduce the scale of the surrounding property. Delicate, unusual plants that would otherwise get gobbled up in the mixed border can be coddled along under close supervision in a container. Troughs full of alpines that would never survive our heavy garden soils will prosper. And containers, with or without aquatic plants, can bring water into the smallest garden. The water brings light from the sky down to the horizontal plane. It reflects the clouds, ripples with the wind, and sparkles in the sun. It implies coolness on the hottest day.

Don't skimp on the pots or soil when potting containers. All pots must have drainage, unless they are being used as a water feature or for moisture-loving plants. Select a well-draining yet sufficiently water-retentive soilless mix that is heavy enough to hold the pots stable. Avoid heavy black soils.

Although it may seem to be stating the obvious, containers must be watered—watering is really the most critical aspect of

Plate 69. In this raised container built into our deck, a mixed planting mimics the mixed plantings of the borders. Perennials such as *Kniphofia caulescens* mingle with *Beta vulgaris* 'Bull's Blood', *Helichrysum petiolare* 'Limelight', *Tropaeolum majus* 'Moonlight', and other annuals. Author's garden.

Plate 68. Its ornamental features attract us to this gate. The stylized leaf cutouts give us just a glimpse of the adjoining space, urging us to take a peek. Carolyn Stroombeek garden, Ohio.

Plate 70. The unusual horizontal branching habit of *Ginkgo biloba* 'Autumn Gold' makes it ideal for container culture. The tight confines of the container slow its growth, and the plant offers fantastic texture and form through the season as well as shocking autumn color. Regular watering, periodic pruning, and winters in our barn are its only requirements. Cat sold separately. Author's garden.

Plate 71. This whiskey barrel, transformed into a small, low-maintenance water garden, includes fish, snails, and tadpoles. Featuring *Iris pseudacorus* 'Variegata', *Pistia stratiotes*, *Nymphaea* 'Marliacea Chromatella', *Cyperus alternifolius* 'Stricta'. Author's garden.

Plate 72. This creative water bowl, even though it's not very large, brings coolness and the light of the sky down to the ground plane of the garden. Featuring *Ligularia* 'The Rocket'. Artist, Walt Rickli; The Garden Studio, Ontario.

the art of container culture. Losses can occur from just one hot day in excessively dry soil. Water plants thoroughly and then allow them to approach dryness before watering again. This may sound like a long period of time, but in most cases containerized plants require watering every other day. Once you watch your plants, you will get on a routine based on their individual needs. Remember, there is nothing artistic about a group of otherwise outstanding plants drooping about in dire need of a watering— even if they are in an expensive pot. I have gone round and round with clients on this issue. Water-absorbing polymers (hydrogels) are available to help reduce watering needs; be sure to follow label directions.

The only fertilizing of container plants we do is with fish emulsion every two weeks through the growing season. Avoid high-nitrogen fertilizers. Some gardeners like to use a pelletized, slow-release fertilizer at planting to give container plants an extra boost. Reduce fertilizing as the days begin to shorten.

Pruning of container plants is similar to pruning in the garden. Using foliage plants obviously reduces deadheading, however disbudding may be needed. For example, it is best to prevent silver-foliaged plants and coleus (*Solenostemon* spp.) from flowering; disbudding reduces the overall decline of such plants. Most trees and shrubs will benefit from root pruning every two to five years to help maintain their size, unless they are extremely dwarf or slow growing. This should be done in late winter during dormancy, before buds break in the spring. Simply remove all circling roots and cut away about one-fourth (2–3 in.) of the bottom of

the root ball using a pruning saw or sharp knife. Then, using a knife or pruners, make several vertical cuts into the root ball. Replant in fresh soil. Top pruning may be needed to maintain size or improve habit.

Overwintering containerized perennials, woody plants, tropicals, and aquatic plants is economical and a great way to save your favorites. Plus, in many cases you will have a more mature specimen to start out the following season; sometimes, however, depending on your time and inclination, it may be best to just start with new plants the next season. Most of these plants require a cold or dormant period. Pots for woody and perennial plants that are to be overwintered outside must be able to tolerate freezing. Plants may be considered container-hardy, but there is no guarantee that they will make it through every winter. Soil is a good insulator, so plants growing in large pots will normally have more insulation over the winter. For better insulation, protect pots from wind, or group pots together, if possible. Pots can be heavily mulched with straw, and, for further protection, the sides of the pots can be wrapped in a few layers of bubble wrap. Pots could be sunk into the ground and mulched, but this is pretty labor-intensive. Most of the time I bring my potted woody and herbaceous plants into our pole barn for the winter. I sometimes put straw around the top and sides of the pot, for extra insulation, but I have had good success without in most cases. A slightly heated garage or unheated greenhouse can be used the same way. Of key importance: be sure the potting soil is moist when plants are going into storage. Move plants into more light as the days warm but protect from frost, which will kill the new buds and often the entire plant if hit hard enough.

Many tropicals, such as elephant's ear and canna, can simply be stored dry in pots in cool, dark or low light areas, for the winter. As warm temperatures return in the spring, increase light and water sparingly until new growth is evident. See Chapter 7 for other overwintering techniques for tropical plants.

The grower that I purchased my aquatic plants from overwinters the plants for me for a fee. It is worth it! Plants can also be stored in a plastic tub and mulched with straw and stored in the basement. Keep moist.

Art in the garden is both a very usable design tool and a critical element to a complete garden (see Sources for artist listings). It is the spice we add—the finishing touches to the painting, if you will, of the garden picture. We have looked at why we use art, what function it plays, and how to use it. But remember: with art in the mixed garden, no rules are the rule, so enjoy!

Chapter 7

MAINTAINING THE MIXED GARDEN

Even the best garden design is only as successful as the care the garden later receives. So, although this book is primarily concerned with design, I feel it is important to include some information on how to maintain the mixed garden. Complicated mixed borders require especially careful management to preserve design integrity. In addition to normal pruning and fertilizing, one must evaluate and record successes and failures, not to mention total losses, and make replacements or substitutions. Bare spots need to be recorded so additional plants can be ordered and added. Such evaluations should be made at least four times each season, and sometimes more often, depending on the complexity of the design. A special spring check-up is needed to note winter losses. Summer reports should be done to record plant performance and record additions necessary for autumn planting. The autumn evaluation should note performance but also any areas that may need to be redesigned over the winter as well as any plants that will need to be ordered for the following spring. Observation of the garden in winter keeps a check on structural integrity and reveals any room for changes. As a professional designer, I have found it is best if I can be involved in the actual maintenance of the gardens I've designed, or at least consult on a regular basis.

Let's look at some basic maintenance considerations with a variety of plant types that we may select for our or our client's garden. Although I would love to provide more detailed information on this topic, it is impossible to truly do it justice without writing an entire book on the subject. Fortunately this has already been done in most cases, so don't forget to check out the Bibliography in the back of the book. Remember, by selecting the proper pest- and disease-resistant plants for the site and following sound horticultural practices, such as proper soil preparation,

plants will be stress-free and thus maintenance will be minimized. See Chapter 2 for information regarding proper soil preparation.

Topdressing provides nutrients to all the plants and keeps the need for additional fertilizing to a minimum; in an already amended mixed border, topdress in the early spring, before the plants break, with about 2 in. of a high-quality aged compost every three years or so, depending on the organic matter content of the soil. Most plants resent excess fertilization. In soils of average fertility, trees may have greater stress tolerance, and insect and disease resistance if not fertilized. This is because trees that are moderately nutrient-stressed make better use of water, develop larger root systems, and contain more defensive chemicals and carbohydrates (Hartman et al. 2000). Plants that prefer a more acidic soil can be fertilized annually, with a mixture of one-third cottonseed meal (which provides nitrogen and is acidifying), one-third alfalfa meal, and one-third pelletized sulfur. This has proven successful in our neutral to alkaline soils. Other fertilizing exceptions are noted below within each plant category.

Although clay soils will be lighter and better drained once amended with organic matter, poor drainage may continue to affect the woody plants. Unless I am planting into a raised bed, I normally plant woody plants slightly higher than our surrounding clay soils. This gets the root systems up out of the heavy soil; it also allows for settling after planting. Our success with certain plants that are prone to root rot, such as rhododendrons and azaleas, is greatly enhanced if we plant them so that at least one-half of the ball is above the natural soil level.

Do not allow plants to dry out for any extended period while they are still becoming established, or losses will be inevitable. Woody plants need to be watered every seven to ten days during dry spells during the first full year after planting and to be watched closely during dry times into the second year. If the autumn is dry, plants should be watered until a hard frost so that they don't go into the winter dry, making them more susceptible to winter damage. Annual plants need to be watered thoroughly and regularly once or twice a week until fully established. Keep a rain gauge in the garden, and watch for at least 1 in. of water per week, either from rain or with supplemental irrigation. Dig into the soil and feel if it is wet; it is particularly important to check at the base of dense, low-branched trees or shrubs to see if enough water has penetrated into the root ball. Once plantings are established, many plants, particularly woody plants, spring-flowering bulbs, and perennials, can tolerate some drought but this all depends on the species. Moisture-loving plants wilt and possibly scorch in dry conditions; decreased growth is the result and, if dry conditions continue, plants eventually die. In wet (particularly wet winter) conditions, many plants—especially herbaceous perennials, which favor dry soils—will be lost. Understanding the natural tendencies of the site will help direct plant selection and aftercare. Striking the middle ground of a moist yet well-draining soil with minimal use of supplemental water is always the rather elusive goal.

Mulching the mixed border conserves moisture, reduces fluctuating soil temperatures, and prevents weeds. To me, moisture retention is the most important of these consideration. In dry climates, mulching is critical to help reduce the need for supplemental water; in such climates—on the West Coast, for instance—annual mulching will normally be necessary. If soils are moisture-retentive and poorly drained, however, mulch (especially excessive mulch—more than 2–3 in.) can aggravate the problem. Mulch should not be applied annually just to make everything look neat and tidy. Excess mulch around the base of shallow-rooted woody plants, such as some of the acid-loving ericaceous woodies, can lead to lack of necessary oxygen at the root zone and possible increase in root diseases. Excess mulch around the crowns of herbaceous perennials can lead to rot. Mulch should be kept 2–3 in. away from the trunks of trees.

A general recommendation: prune to remove diseased, weak, or dead branches of woody plants. Crossing or rubbing branches should also be removed. Any other detailed pruning advice is included in the plant groups that follow.

DECIDUOUS TREES

Beyond mulching with 2 in. of composted organic matter about every three years, no additional fertilizing is normally needed for healthy trees growing in a mixed garden with compost-amended soil. Even this may not be necessary after trees are mature. Results concerning the proof of the benefit of fertilizer to trees have been mixed. If trees are fertilized using something such as a soil injector feeder, it may be that the increase in aeration is doing

just as much good as the fertilizer. High-nitrogen fertilizers are definitely to be avoided. Acid-loving trees, such as sweetbay magnolia (*Magnolia virginiana*) and Kousa dogwood (*Cornus kousa*), that are grown in alkaline conditions normally benefit from application of the cottonseed-alfalfa-sulfur fertilizer described earlier.

Selecting small-growing trees, as discussed in Chapter 2, is your best bet to help minimize pruning of deciduous tress in a mixed garden.

CONIFERS

Dwarf or slow-growing conifers are normally the best conifers for the mixed garden, except in the case of plants for hedges. I have found the American Conifer Society to be a great source of information and follow many of their guidelines (see the Bibliography). It is best to plant or transplant conifers in the spring or early autumn, when temperatures are cooler and there is some rain. Conifers in amended soil don't normally require additional fertilizing; topdressing is usually sufficient. Some conifers, however, such as hemlocks, prefer a slightly acidic soil and would benefit from the cottonseed-alfalfa-sulfur fertilizer described earlier. If conifers look like they are failing, they can be given a boost with iron sometime during January, February, or March. Mulching is essential for conifers; it helps to maintain a cool, moist root zone, but no more than 2–3 in. is necessary, and it shouldn't come in contact with the trunk of the plant.

Pruning of most conifers will be minimal if the proper plants were selected in the first place. But even slower-growing conifers may outgrow their space in a mixed border before one is ready to part with them. One recommendation: when the conifer gets to within one foot or so of the desirable size, it is best to cut back the new growth so that about 1 in. of it is left. This will cause side branches to form and create a dense plant. Once this growth has established, continue to maintain the size of the plant by cutting off any undesirable new growth. Conifers may also require some thinning to allow air and light into the plant. Fairly commonly, cultivars of dwarf and variegated conifers revert to the typical form; remove the wayward branch, pruning well into the area where the mutation originated. Pruning for size control of conifers varies from genus to genus, and care must be taken not to damage their natural shape. It is best not to remove more than one-third of the total growth of a conifer with pruning. Most pruning for size or shape control should be done when the conifer is dormant.

Pines can be pruned by a technique called candling. The soft new growth that develops on the tip of the branches in the spring is called a candle. It can be pinched or cut off by one-half or two-thirds before the needles fully elongate. Buds will then develop below the cut. Pines do not develop buds along the stem, so shearing or heavy pruning into old wood will not rejuvenate the plant.

Plate 73. *Clethra alnifolia*, one of my favorite shrubs, is very adaptable. Shown here mingling with *Phlox paniculata* 'Laura', *Miscanthus* 'Purpurascens', and *Clematis terniflora* in a section of a condominium garden. Author's design, Aust garden, Ohio.

Douglas fir (*Pseudotsuga menziesii*), spruces (*Picea* spp.), and firs (*Abies* spp.) have visible buds along the current season's growth and often along the stems of the previous season's growth. Prune the tips of stems back to a side or lateral bud, or branch, for size control; this heading back, as it is sometimes called, produces denser foliage and a smaller plant. If a formal effect is desired, these conifers can be pruned or sheared when the current season's growth is soft.

Arborvitaes (*Thuja* spp.), falsecypress (*Chamaecyparis* spp.), and junipers (*Juniperus* spp.) can be pruned or sheared lightly,

just after new growth emerges but with care because they lack viable buds on the leafless inner portions of the branches. Cutting back into this woody zone normally will not produce new foliage, nor will heavy pruning of these plants rejuvenate an overgrown plant. It is best to perform periodic pruning, so that a major rejuvenation of the plant is not necessary. Avoid heavy pruning of specimen plants, as their natural habit will be lost.

Hemlocks (*Tsuga* spp.) and yews (*Taxus* spp.) have buds on old and new wood, making them the easiest conifers to prune or shear for use as hedges. Pruning in the spring before new growth develops produces a soft, more natural-looking effect. These plants do respond well to rejuvenative pruning; still, it is advisable to shear them annually to keep hedges in shape. Remember to prune hedges so that the upper portion is narrower than the base, allowing light to reach lower foliage.

Horticultural oils, applied during the dormant season, may be needed as a preventive measure against outbreaks of mites, scale, or aphids on susceptible evergreens.

SHRUBS

Besides the topdressing and fertilizer for acid-loving plants described in this chapter's opening section, additional fertilizing of shrubs is not routine in the mixed border. Some gardeners like to use a balanced organic fertilizer on flowering shrubs. Many great shrubs for the mixed garden fall into the acid-loving category. Virginia sweetspire (*Itea virginica*), summersweet clethra (*Clethra alnifolia*), dwarf fothergilla (*Fothergilla gardenii*) are among my very favorite shrubs to use in mixed gardens, and they all prefer acidic soil. These shrubs are fairly adaptable, though, and may only become chlorotic after several years of growing in alkaline conditions without fertilizer. Often a simple application of cottonseed meal clears the problem up. Rhododendrons and hollies are a bit more particular and benefit from regular application of a complete acidic fertilizer. Roses can be fertilized with Epsom salts after pruning, which supplies magnesium to promote strong growth of new canes from the base. Some rose gardeners use equal parts of a homemade organic mixture, such as alfalfa meal, fishmeal, greensand, bone meal, and gypsum.

When pruning shrubs, it is important to know if they flower on current year's wood or last year's wood. If pruning occurs too early or too late, flower buds may be removed. Shrubs that flower on old wood should be pruned after the shrub flowers; this way, the plant has time to put on growth for flowering the next year. Shrubs that flower on new wood can be pruned both before (when dormant in early spring) and after flowering. Michael Dirr (1997, 2002) has excellent lists of pruning times for shrubs in his illustrated encyclopedias. Most shrubs flower on old wood, particularly spring-flowering shrubs, including *Hydrangea macrophylla*, *H. quercifolia*,

Plate 74. Rugosa roses have so much to offer in a mixed garden: fragrant flowers, disease resistance, and ornamental fruit. Prune by about one-third in early spring, before buds break, for more flowers and fruit. Also featuring *Clematis terniflora*. Author's garden.

and certain species of *Clethra, Fothergilla, Genista, Hamamelis* (witchhazel), *Itea, Rhododendron, Spiraea, Syringa* (lilac), *Viburnum,* and *Weigela.* Shrubs that flower on new wood include *Hamamelis virginiana, Hydrangea arborescens* and *H. paniculata, Potentilla fruticosa,* many roses, and summer-flowering *Spiraea.* Certain shrubs that actually die back to the base or have tip dieback in midwestern and northern gardens—such as *Buddleia davidii, Caryopteris ×clandonensis, Vitex agnus-castus* var. *latifolia,* and certain species of *Callicarpa* and *Lespedeza*—also flower on new wood, fortunately.

These plants, which are sometimes referred to as dieback or cut-back shrubs, should be cut back just as new growth is about to begin, to viable buds at the base of the stems if present, or, if top growth was completely killed, to within a few inches of the ground, for new growth to emerge from the roots. Be patient. Some of these plants (*Vitex agnus-castus* var. *latifolia,* for one) can take their time and won't emerge from the base until the ground gets really warm. It may be into May or later before signs of life are evident. Sometimes just the tips or portions of the upper sections of the shrub may be killed, particularly with *Caryopteris ×clandonensis.* If this is the case, and plants are not killed completely back, it is often preferable to leave a woody framework at the base of the plant for a bit of height in the border, especially in cooler climates. In such circumstances, simply cut off the dead portion of the stems. Some of the larger flowering branches from last season can be cut back to the base to make room for new flowering stems if needed.

A heavier pruning known as coppicing or stooling can also be beneficial to cut-back shrubs, shrubs that flower on new wood, or

Plate 75. *Caryopteris ×clandonensis* (foreground) has a tendency to get tip dieback most winters in Midwest gardens. Also featuring *Heliopsis helianthoides* var. *scabra* 'Sommersonne' (summer sun), *Platycodon grandiflorus* 'Komachi', *Canna indica* 'Red Stripe', *Ricinus communis.* Author's garden.

shrubs grown for their ornamental foliage or stems. This technique can help create a better habit, more flowering, brighter-colored stems, better fruit production, and bolder, more intensely colored foliage. To coppice a shrub or small tree, cut back the entire plant to 4–6 in. above ground about a month before growth begins. With the more tender cut-back shrubs, it is best to wait a bit longer, or until the buds are just starting to swell and severe cold weather is no longer a threat. Leave some buds to be safe, although many of the plants will return from below ground. Know the plant before you do this intense pruning—it should be at least one year old, and it's best if it is vigorously growing. With weaker shrubs, it may be best to cut only one-third to one-half of the stems severely. This technique may not be desirable every season, depending on the climate or the gardener's own objectives. After pruning, an application of composted organic matter or a balanced organic fertilizer can be beneficial.

Many shrubs grown for their outstanding foliage or stem color are often large-growing and need to be kept heavily pruned, not only for aesthetics but to maintain a more appropriate scale for the mixed border. Variegated or colorful foliage plants such as *Catalpa bignonioides* 'Aurea', *Sambucus racemosa* 'Sutherland

Plate 76. Wonderful foliage form and texture make *Vitex agnus-castus* var. *latifolia* a useful addition to many mixed gardens, even though it acts like a herbaceous perennial and dies to the ground in most Ohio winters. Also featuring *Helianthus salicifolius*. Author's design, Hendley garden, Ohio.

Gold', or selections of *Cotinus coggygria* are outstanding with coppicing. Dogwoods grown for their colorful winter stems benefit from this technique as well.

VINES

Most vines growing in organically rich soil don't require additional fertilizing beyond topdressing or mulching with compost, as we have discussed for trees and shrubs. Annual vines, however, will have an increase in growth if fed periodically; we do it about once a month during the summer, with an organic fertilizer.

Vines that flower on current season's growth should be pruned in late winter or early spring before new buds develop. Vines in this category include species of *Campsis* and *Passiflora*, large-flowering clematis, and most honeysuckles (*Lonicera* spp.). Vines that flower on last year's growth, such as hydrangeas and wisterias, should be pruned immediately after flowering to allow hardening before winter.

Vigorous summer shoots of wisterias need to be pruned to conserve the plants' energies for flower production. Cut long shoots in the summer to about 6 in., leaving approximately four to six leaves. Leave only what stems may be needed to create the framework. In late winter, cut back stems to 3–4 in., leaving only two or three buds. As with all the plants we have been talking about, avoid high-nitrogen fertilizer (which will promote vegetative growth) and provide full sun and sufficient moisture. Root pruning, preferably in early spring, may also increase flower production.

I am constantly asked about the pruning of clematis. First, one needs to know to which of three pruning groups a given clematis belongs. I'll briefly list these different groups and their pruning requirements, but it is really best to check a thorough reference and see where your specific cultivar falls.

Group 1 clematis are early flowerers, including *Clematis alpina*, *C. macropetala*, and *C. montana*; these require little if any regular pruning. Pruning to restrict size or improve the appearance of the vine should be done after flowering. Group 2 are the early to midsummer large-flowered clematis, including many popular cultivars such as *C.* 'Elsa Späth', *C.* 'Nelly Moser', and *C.* 'The President'. This group of clematis flowers on stems arising from last year's growth. Prune in late winter or early spring, as the buds begin to swell, to a pair of healthy buds. This pruning usually removes anywhere from the top third to half of the old stem. The further back the plants are cut, or if killed back by cold temperatures, the later the plants will flower. Flowering may also occur on new wood in late summer and autumn.

Group 3 are the late-blooming large-flowered cultivars, late-blooming species, and the viticellas. This group includes the most notable large-bloomer, *Clematis* 'Jackmanii', and such popular cultivars as *C.* 'Ernest Markham', *C.* 'Hagley Hybrid', and *C.* 'Ville de

Lyon'; wonderful small-flowering species, such as *C. tangutica* and sweetautumn clematis (*C. terniflora*); and viticellas, such as *C.* 'Betty Corning', *C.* 'Polish Spirit', and *C.* 'Royal Velvet'. Group 3 clematis flower on current season's growth. Most stems die back in the winter and should be pruned off before new growth begins in the spring. If plants are not killed back, prune to a pair of healthy buds close to the base of the plant. Hard pruning is best for new shoot development in this group. An organic mulch will help provide the cool root zone that clematis prefer.

PERENNIALS

For maintenance of perennials, I refer you to my first book, *The Well-Tended Perennial Garden* (1998), if you are not already familiar with it—it contains all the general maintenance information plus very detailed pruning advice. Let's touch on just a few key points here. Proper soil preparation, with 4 in. of organic matter, cannot be overemphasized. Organic matter improves the structure of the soil, thus improving drainage in heavy clay soil and increasing the moisture- and nutrient-holding capacity of sandy soil. More perennials are killed by the wet overwintering conditions caused by poorly draining soil than they are by cold temperatures.

Perennials will double or triple in size the first season if the soil is properly prepared. The organic matter content of soil for perennials should be a minimum of 6–8%. (Yes, this means you will have to perform a soil test for organic matter content!) To repeat, all the gardens featured in this book were 16–18% organic matter after bed preparation.

Organic matter supplies all the nutrients most perennials will require for many years, as they are not heavy feeders and resent overfertilizing. If the soil is at least 6–8% organic matter, topdressing with 1–2 in. of compost every three years is normally all that is needed to supply necessary nutrients. Gardens that are in the 16% organic matter range may not need topdressing for four or five years after preparation. If the garden is lower than 6% organic matter, topdress with 1–2 in. of organic matter for three consecutive years to build up the organic matter content; test again in the fourth year to see where things are.

Pruning perennials is a very exciting and dynamic area. We don't just prune to extend the bloom period: we prune to encourage lush new growth, regenerate or extend the life of plants, stagger plant heights or bloom times, reduce plant height, keep plants in their own space, increase flower size or numbers, prevent or control pests, enhance the overall appearance (habit) of the plant, remove unsightly or insignificant flowers, and clean up the garden. What, when, and how we prune varies from region to region, from year to year, and with the age of the plants. Factors such as soil fertility, annual weather conditions, and the gardener's personal objectives all have a part in determining pruning needs.

Deadheading and cutting back perennials after they flower are extremely beneficial practices. Most spring-flowering perennials benefit from being cut back by one-half; this prevents the unsightly hole so commonly seen from developing in the center of the plant. But pruning a plant before it flowers—in a effort to reduce its height, eliminate the need for staking, improve its habit, or delay the bloom time, so that it coincides with the bloom times of other plants—is beyond the normal maintenance routine. In a mixed border, this cutting-edge "tweaking" type of pruning can really enhance our designs. Most autumn-flowering plants benefit from this type of pruning, as do many summer-flowering perennials. The timing and technique of pruning perennials is very species-specific. Be sure to learn more about this area of gardening, if you haven't already.

HARDY BULBS

I think by now we all know to avoid the dreaded "hair statement" of tying bulb foliage into neat ponytails, which reduces carbohydrate storage for the next year. Most spring-flowering bulbs benefit from good summer drainage; many—alliums and tulips, for example—will rot under the constant spray of irrigation in an overly moist mixed border. Timing of fertilization is also important. Many people think they should fertilize in the spring, but the best time to feed bulbs is in the autumn after a hard frost, with a slow-release fertilizer that can percolate into the soil while the roots grow in autumn and winter. Brent and Becky's Bulb Supplement from Brent and Becky's Bulbs (see Sources) is complete and high in potassium, which many others are not, with an analysis of 5-10-12. If you missed fertilizing in autumn, use a water-soluble fertilizer in the spring.

ANNUALS, TROPICALS, AND TENDER BULBS

Annuals, tropicals, and tender bulbs are normally heavy feeders, heavier than the other plant groups we have discussed. They prosper in nutrient-rich compost-amended soil. To really promote strong growth, it is helpful to fertilize every two weeks with fish emulsion and once a month with a balanced granular organic fertilizer. Tropicals in particular seem to do better with a boost of fertilizer to help them reach the colossal sizes we expect from many of them. Coleus, elephant's ear (*Colocasia esculenta* and cultivars), and other annuals grown for foliage are among the few plants in the mixed border that actually prefer high-nitrogen feedings. If they are shy to get moving, this may be the help they need. *Hot Plants for Cool Climates* by Susan Roth and Dennis Schrader (2000) offers outstanding species-specific information on the culture of tropicals, including great tips for overwintering them; anyone infected by canna-banana fever will want to refer to this book.

Deadheading keeps most annuals flowering and in good shape. Remember, though: annuals that will reseed and act perennial—some of my favorites are love-in-a-mist (*Nigella damascena*), *Verbena bonariensis*, and larkspur (*Consolida ajacis*)—should be allowed to go to seed. It may be desirable to collect seed and distribute some of the seed into areas that are bare for filler the next season.

I have seen and tried numerous methods for overwintering tropicals and tender bulbs over the years. I'm sure the plethora of information out there on the subject has made your head swim as well. A lifelong dream come true was to have a conservatory attached to our home (see Plate 9). This exciting addition houses many tropicals for the winter, my own plants and plants from my clients' gardens as well. But even at 13 × 32 ft., it can't hold all the plants, and some of the large-growing guys who have found permanent homes there—such as bloodleaf banana (*Musa zebrina*)—have hit their head on the 13-ft. ceiling after just one season! Phormiums usually make the cut to overwinter in the conservatory, although I have good luck with them under lights as well. I brought in various salvias one year, only to fight whitefly on them all winter; I now purchase new salvias for the gardens each spring rather than working to save them over. Some gingers, such as hidden gingers (*Curcuma* spp.), eventually go dormant but return when given higher temperatures and more light. Butterfly gingers (*Hedychium* spp.) are also brought in. These could be given just enough water in pots to maintain leaves (some of their old leaves die off and can be cut back once new foliage has emerged), or they could be stored in the method I am about to describe.

Plate 77. Tropicals being grown-on following winter dormancy, so large plants will be ready for summer borders after the danger of frost has passed. Author's home.

We have had good luck overwintering most tropicals or tender bulbs (remember, they can also be corms, tubers, or rhizomes)—cannas, elephant's ear, dahlias, gladioli, hymenocallis, bananas—with a simple technique that most people could follow. We don't have time to try a variety of storage media—vermiculite for some, moist peat or sawdust for others, and so on (one year I just threw canna tubers in old apple baskets and left them in the dark). For best results with these bulbs, we simply wait until after several frosts (the plants are not always completely blackened), cut the stems to 4–6 in. above the ground, dig the plants, be sure everything is tagged, let them dry on our screened porch with a ceiling fan for about one week, and then shake excess soil off the roots. Waiting for several frosts may be too late in our climate, especially for glads, which we dig as early as late September if they appear to be going dormant. Some people like to use an anti-desiccant before storing the bulbs to reduce moisture loss and fungus. When completely dry, the roots are wrapped in newspaper. We put these little packages into unsealed black plastic garbage bags, to block the light; they are stored on shelves in a lighted room in our basement that remains at 60–65°F.

You often see the elusive storage temperature recommendation of 35–50°F—and frost-free, of course. I tried for years to find such a location at our home. Garages are often recommended, but this can spell death for most bulbs as temperatures can drop into the 20s in garages, as I recorded with a minimum-maximum thermometer one winter (losses were monumental that year). And most modern or even fairly modern homes don't have root cellars.

In mid-late March we pot the bulbs and grow them on in the conservatory as well as on heat mats under lights. Most benefit from bottom heat to get started. Acclimating them before putting them back into the garden is essential, or all the lush upper leaves will be scorched (bottom leaves are sometimes spared, and plants will usually rebreak from lower on the stems). Put plants out in dense shade for a few days and then move them into slightly brighter light; finally, give them several hours daily of early or very late sun. Move them back into the garden on a cloudy day.

In the garden, we have had success overwintering tender plants such as cardoon (*Cynara cardunculus*) by folding the leaves around the crown and tucking the plant under a bell-shaped glass cloche. Evergreen boughs keep it from heating up on sunny days.

With the variety and diversity of plant material involved, maintaining a mixed border is never dull! The degree of care a garden requires depends on many different factors. As you can see from our discussion here, the types of plants selected will greatly affect the type and amount of care required. But the efforts put forth to maintain a well-designed, diverse mixed border are definitely repaid, in numerous ways, to the gardener and all who experience it.

PART TWO

Mixed Garden Design Examples

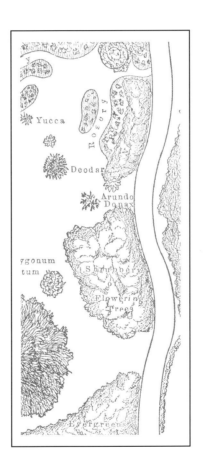

Chapter 8

SMALL AND MEDIUM GARDENS

As houselots shrink in urban and suburban areas, small- or medium-sized gardens are more often the norm. There are some wonderful advantages to designing gardens in limited spaces: because there is less space to fill, fewer plants and design elements are needed to achieve dramatic effects. Quantity should never be confused with quality!

No matter the size of the garden, all the elements and principles of design we have discussed so far (color, texture, form, order, unity, rhythm) come into play; however, we often need to address these areas in particular ways for smaller gardens. We must also consider specific approaches or techniques that are designed to enhance a small area. Everything in small gardens should have an aesthetic or practical purpose. And every space, including the vertical and overhead space, should be utilized to its fullest. With limited resources, there just isn't enough room for fluff or waste.

We will look at small and medium gardens of two types, enclosed and open. Enclosed gardens, in particular, must have an especially strong relationship with the interior design and architecture of the house directly adjacent. The garden becomes another room of the house and should reflect its style. The space should be organized clearly and creatively. The main axis and views from windows and doors need to be taken into account. Enclosed gardens should have a strong structural outline, starting with the walls of the house and extending out into either living or nonliving boundaries; these walls, fences, hedges, or mixed shrub borders create a feeling of privacy and intimacy, and it is often best that they be so high, they can't be seen over. The walls and fences should be utilized for support, to grow vines or to espalier trees or shrubs (as they are in Diagram 11 in Chapter 5 and Diagram 15 in this chapter). Trelliswork can be attached to aid the climbing of the vines. Adding a cutout to solid fences or walls can hint at distant spaces.

Screens of plant material can also be used to frame a distant view; such highlighting of a borrowed landscape enlarges the garden's feel tremendously. Always take advantage of the longest view available. Screens can also hide a less-than-desirable sight. Dividing a smaller garden into different sections, with different themes, functions, or moods creates an element of surprise and heightens the experience of delighting in small spaces. Plants, walls, fences, gates, arches, and pergolas can be used effectively for this task (see Diagram 15). Arches and pergolas provide strong vertical structure, focal points, and plant support, as well as entrance and exit corridors; they create a frame through which one passes into a new experience. Pergolas can form interesting shade patterns that are often difficult to discern at first glance, thus developing the illusion of greater space. Raised planters too can be used for division of space; they can be filled with soil that is often better suited to healthy plant growth than the existing disturbed soil of an urban garden.

A change in levels in a smaller garden greatly enhances the feeling of spaciousness. This can be accomplished by a small change in elevation, of perhaps just two steps. Making the steps or stairs wide also increases the sense of space. A deck or other seating area may be slightly elevated in relation to the rest of the garden, bringing the visitor to a new height and experience. If there is a natural slope to your property, take advantage of this to create a garden with different sections at slightly different levels. If possible, take advantage of different sun or shade areas.

Paths give a garden focus and structure; they direct the eye and the journey through the garden. Take time to carefully plan this

Plate 78. From the deck of this small condominium garden, larger-growing shrubs frame and accentuate the beautiful borrowed landscape. Larger-growing plants are used in the garden to provide the proper scale as a transition from the surrounding plant material to the ground plane. Exclusive use of small or diminutive plants would dwarf this garden in its surroundings. Featuring *Buddleia davidii* 'Mongo' (Nanho blue), *Rosa* 'F. J. Grootendorst', *Pennisetum setaceum* 'Rubrum'. Author's design, Aust garden, Ohio.

experience. Paving material can be used to define different areas of the garden, but to keep the garden unified, be sure to limit yourself to two (certainly no more than three) different types of paving, or a busy, restless effect will result. Stick to simple patterns in the paving, and, of course, be certain that the colors are appropriate to the house. An old trick that I like to use to give a greater illusion of depth to paths in small gardens is to place bricks on their narrow side (see Plate 81). Narrowing a path at its far end is another great way to make a garden appear more spacious. Keep the lines of the beds simple and perhaps geometrical, unifying with the lines on the house. Don't use a lot of unnecessary curves, and keep textural contrast low.

An area not conducive to growing plants may be a great candidate for a paved area, perhaps for a table and chairs. Consider a circular form for this space to create intimacy and make a nice contrast of line from the more symmetrical paths and beds that may be present. A rough guideline that I often refer to: a 64-sq.-ft. paved area seats six to eight people comfortably. Under an existing red maple in a section of our back gardens, I developed a low (4-in.) raised bed on one side of the tree for shade-loving plants. On the other side of the tree, I created a small seating area mulched in pine needles for the Lutyens bench (see Plate 56). This area is full of tree roots, so the tree is happy—and I'm not struggling to make plants survive here. Seating is such an integral part of the garden. Depending on your objectives, a seating area can be placed to take advantage of the best views or perhaps tucked into a secluded spot, where it can be visited for meditation and peace.

Your bench may serve as a focal point in the garden. Ornaments, containers, water features, or a specimen plant can also serve as focal points. In a very small garden, one nice piece of art may be all that is needed. The prominent focal point in a small or medium garden is usually best placed as far as possible from the main viewing point to attract attention and make the visitor want to approach it to see it in detail. Containers add greatly to a small space by extending the growing area as well as the aesthetic pleasure. Be sure their style is in harmony with the house and rest of the garden colors and materials.

A lawn is often inappropriate for smaller gardens—and besides, the high level of maintenance a lawn requires is a great waste of natural resources, whatever its size. Still, the green space it provides can sometimes be a source of relief and simplicity, a balance to the activity provided by the high variety of plants in the borders. A grassed area can also add a sense of form if given a distinct shape. Weigh a lawn's virtues and vices carefully when planning the garden.

Ponds are nice—the benefits of the wonderful reflective quality of water cannot be overstated—but they also require a great deal of maintenance. Consider instead a large bowl-type container for a few aquatic plants or even a whiskey barrel lined with a plastic liner (see Plate 71). These provide the imagery of water and a few fish, and snails can be added without the enormous commitment of a pond. The trickle of water from a fountain can be appreciated throughout the confined space of a smaller garden and adds a nice touch.

Plants in small or medium gardens should have at least two seasons of interest and preferably four. They must be performers to earn a spot where space is limited. Of course, ultimate size is of great importance, and aggressive, rampant species should be avoided. But the tendency to plant only small diminutive plants in such gardens only makes the garden appear smaller. Create the feeling of depth with layers of plants in contrasting colors and foliage sizes. Small trees, or large shrubs trained as trees, and dwarf or slow-growing conifers should all be a part of smaller garden whenever possible. Large-growing perennials,

ornamental grasses, and some of the large tropicals can add interesting height, architectural effect, and scale to a small garden—particularly if the garden is too small for trees. These larger plants may need to serve as the outlining structural layer, or canopy, in a tiny space.

Maintenance must not be neglected in a smaller garden, where every little thing is magnified. It is easier to hide neglected areas or doggy plants in the ornamental masses of a large garden, but in a small space the flaws are usually very obvious (not to say, in-your-face). On the plus side, because it is a smaller space, the amount of overall care is reduced. Nonetheless, such care as is required must be addressed on a regular basis.

Remember, when it comes to color in a small garden, less is more. Keep it simple and limit the palette to reduce the fuss. Cooler colors will make an area appear larger. Bright or warmer colors and bold textures can be effective as focal areas or planted in the foreground, with cooler or paled colors and finer textures in the background to give the illusion of greater space. Textural contrast with plants should be high. Variegated foliage creates contrast and fools the eye, blurring true boundaries. Place cut-leaved plants on the edge of paths to create interesting views through the foliage.

Other techniques used to create a false perspective include planting trees and shrubs closer together as they recede from the main view, or planting progressively smaller or smaller-leaved varieties in the background, which makes them seem farther off. We talked about narrowing the path as it recedes; borders, steps, and lawns can also gradually narrow as they move away, giving the illusion of increased depth. Tall plants in small clumps surrounded by much lower ones also gives an effect of space. Positioning an outdoor-grade mirror on a shady wall and surrounding it with vines is a great space enhancing technique that still impresses me every time I see one, whether in a smaller garden or a small section of a larger garden.

SMALL-SPACE DESIGNS

In this section, we will look at a small, enclosed garden plan and a couple of examples of designs for trouble spots. It will be most useful if you take some time to review the three designs and their acccompanying plant lists before reading my discussion about each one. I don't expect anyone to make a carbon copy of the design; what I do hope is that sections or combinations within a design may be inspirational in planning your or your client's mixed garden. And don't forget to refer to the designs for medium gardens later in this chapter as well as the large gardens illustrated in Chapter 9: many ideas can be garnered from these plans and used in smaller locations.

Diagram 15. Small garden: Design I. Artist, Megan H. King; author's design, Verzella garden.

⊢————————⊣ = 6 feet

N→

DIAGRAM 15

Trees

1	(1)	*Cornus kousa*	Kousa dogwood
2	(1)	*Syringa meyeri* (standard)	Meyer lilac

Shrubs

3	(12)	*Buxus* 'Green Velvet'	boxwood
4	(3)	*Fothergilla gardenii*	dwarf fothergilla
5	(1)	*Hydrangea quercifolia*	oakleaf hydrangea
6	(3)	*Itea virginica* 'Henry's Garnet'	Virginia sweetspire
7	(1)	*Pinus strobus* 'Nana'	dwarf eastern white pine
8	(3)	*Rhododendron* 'Chionoides'	Catawba rhododendron
9	(1)	*Rosa* 'Hansa'	rose
10	(2)	*Yucca flaccida* 'Golden Sword'	yucca

Perennials

11	(3)	*Aster novae-angliae* 'Purple Dome'	New England aster
12	(3)	*Chrysanthemum* 'Viette's Apricot Glow'	mum
13	(12)	*Coreopsis verticillata* 'Moonbeam'	threadleaf coreopsis
14	(8)	*Dicentra* 'Luxuriant'	fringed bleeding heart
15	(5)	*Geranium sanguineum* 'New Hampshire'	blood-red geranium
16	(7)	*Hemerocallis* 'Happy Returns'	daylily
17	(3)	*Hemerocallis* 'Welcome Mat'	daylily
18	(4)	*Hosta plantaginea* 'Aphrodite'	plantain-lily
19	(5)	*Iris* 'Perfume Counter'	bearded iris
20	(3)	*Iris sibirica* 'Caesar's Brother'	Siberian iris
21	(5)	*Liatris spicata* 'Kobold'	spike gayfeather
22	(1)	*Miscanthus sinensis* 'Gracillimus'	miscanthus
23	(5)	*Phlox paniculata* 'David'	border phlox
24	(3)	*Platycodon grandiflorus* 'Komachi'	balloon flower
25	(14)	*Scabiosa* Butterfly Blue®	pincushion flower
26	(5)	*Scabiosa* 'Pink Mist'	pincushion flower
27	(5)	*Sedum* 'Herbstfreude' (autumn joy)	sedum
28	(5)	*Stokesia laevis* 'Klaus Jelitto'	Stokes' aster
29	(5)	*Tradescantia* (Andersoniana Group) 'Zwanenburg Blue'	spiderwort
30	(5)	*Veronica* 'Goodness Grows'	veronica
31	(11)	*Viola labradorica*	Labrador violet

Vines

32	(2)	*Clematis terniflora*	sweetautumn clematis
33	(1)	*Hydrangea anomala* ssp. *petiolaris*	climbing hydrangea

Plate 79. The "garden" photographed on the first design consultation visit. Verzella garden, Ohio.

Plate 80. The garden nine years later. Author's design, Verzella garden, Ohio; photograph by Kristen Cady.

This example of a small, enclosed, Victorian-style garden design illustrates many of the techniques discussed in this chapter. The garden style connects with the home it complements, which was completed in 1899. The main view from the stained-glass front window is emphasized. Vines cover the side fence and wall of the house, utilizing the vertical space. The front fence was left uncovered, for a cleaner and more formal appearance as the house is viewed from the street.

A gate was used to divide the side garden into separate areas and create a sense of greater space and more privacy for the back section of the garden. Elevation change occurs with the porch,

Plate 81. Placing the bricks on their narrow end increases the feeling of space through this small garden. The wooden gate increases the sense of space, provides privacy for the back garden, and stirs anticipation as to what lies beyond. Author's design, Verzella garden, Ohio; photograph by Kristen Cady.

Plate 82. Located directly along a public sidewalk, this garden is shared by and enhances the community. Author's design, Verzella garden, Ohio; photograph by Kristen Cady.

which houses containers of plants. The straight, geometrical lines of the beds are unified with the lines of the house. Brick was selected for the paving, again to keep the material consistent with the house. The bricks were placed on their narrow end to increase one's perception of the length of the path.

The clients preferred pastel colors and specified no orange, although they did like peach and blue together. They wanted lots of color, but they didn't want it to look wild. The style of the garden, like the house, was to be refined yet not stuffy. Notice that, even though the beds are generally only 2–5 ft. in width, plant selection was not confined to small-growing plants alone. The larger trees and shrubs are needed for the scale of the house. The planting is layered, and no aggressive species are included.

References were consulted to determine which plants were most commonly grown in gardens between 1850 and 1900. These species, or at least the genera, were selected, often along with a newer cultivar if it was more desirable. Plants not only needed to be of the period of the house, but they also needed to be able to tolerate this site: urban, zone 5, neutral pH, eastern exposure.

This is a multi-season mixed garden. Spring kicks off with the lilac (2), dwarf fothergilla (4), Catawba rhododendron (8), fringed bleeding heart (14), spiderwort (29), and two iris: *Iris* 'Perfume Counter' (19) and *I. sibirica* 'Caesar's Brother' (20). The lilac (pruned as a standard) serves as a dominant focal

point in this garden. *Iris* 'Perfume Counter' is one of the few bearded iris I use; it is spectacular for its large purple fragrant flowers, self-supportive stems, and its reblooming nature in the autumn—at which time it makes a great combination with sweet-autumn clematis (*Clematis terniflora*) (32). I've never had a borer problem with this iris.

Summer is alive with numerous performers, including Virginia sweetspire (*Itea virginica* 'Henry's Garnet') (6), *Rosa* 'Hansa' (9), *Coreopsis verticillata* 'Moonbeam' (13), daylilies (16–17), hosta (18), and *Phlox paniculata* 'David' (23). This phlox cultivar was selected not only because of its disease resistance (it was named

Perennial Plant of the Year 2002 by the Perennial Plant Association) but also because it is the namesake of this client. I favor *R.* 'Hansa' for its intense "real" rose fragrance, the romantic shape of its flowers, and its glossy foliage, which turns golden in the autumn.

Autumn is also alive with *Clematis terniflora* (32), *Miscanthus sinensis* 'Gracillimus' (22), *Chrysanthemum* 'Viette's Apricot Glow' (12), and *Sedum* 'Herbstfreude' (autumn joy) (27); continuous bloom comes from the pincushion flowers *Scabiosa* Butterfly Blue® and *S.* 'Pink Mist' (25–26) as well as many other perennials. Autumn color is stunning on the *Hydrangea quercifolia* (5), *Fothergilla gardenii* (4), *Itea virginica* 'Henry's Garnet' (6), *Cornus kousa* (1), *Geranium sanguineum* 'New Hampshire' (15), and *Iris sibirica* 'Caesar's Brother' (20). Winter interest is provided by the outlining structure of the trees, shrubs, perennials, and grasses. *Pinus strobus* 'Nana' (7) and boxwood (3) bring a touch of green to the scene.

When this garden was designed in 1994, I wasn't yet into tropicals, or I'm sure cannas, castor beans, and elephant's ear would have made the lineup! As for the annuals, the clients asked that I leave a small amount of space and let them select their own in different seasons for these areas, and as filler.

Textures and forms prevail, particularly in the boldness of the yuccas (10) and oakleaf hydrangea (5) contrasted with the airy nature of the pincushion flowers (25–26) and various other perennials that surround them. The distinct rounded lines of the head of the lilac and the strong vertical line of its trunk contrast with the horizontal lines of the boxwood.

My company performed maintenance for the first two years, and then another company took over while I wrote and promoted my first book. The schedule involved about five visits: one in spring, three or four over the summer, and one in the autumn. The clients do the maintenance between visits and requested that the garden not require any more than three or four hours of work per week.

Periodic pruning of the trees and shrubs is necessary to keep habit and size in check. The herbaceous plants receive routine deadheading and cutting back. No spraying for pests and disease is required, as resistant plants were selected. Cottonseed meal provides the nitrogen and acidity required by the Virginia sweetspire (*Itea virginica* 'Henry's Garnet'), dwarf fothergilla (*Fothergilla gardenii*), Catawba rhododendron (*Rhododendron* 'Chionoides'), and Kousa dogwood (*Cornus kousa*). This garden is very visible from the sidewalk that runs along the front of it—keeping it performing well is critical.

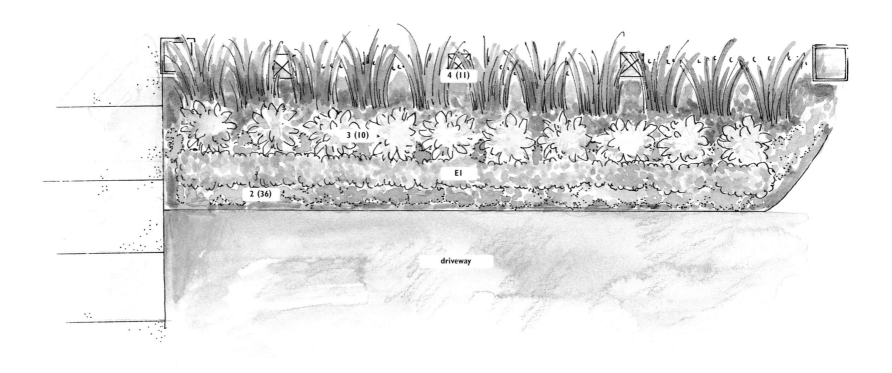

Diagram 16. Small garden: Design II. Artist, Megan H. King; author's design, DiSabato garden.

⌐_____⌐ = 4 feet
N◄—

DIAGRAM 16

Existing shrubs

| 1 | | *Buxus* 'Green Gem' | boxwood |

Annuals

2	(36)	*Brachyscome* 'Ultra'	Swan River daisy
3	(10)	*Cynara cardunculus*	cardoon
4	(11)	*Pennisetum setaceum* 'Rubrum'	purple fountain grass

Many properties come with a ridiculously narrow strip of bed somewhere, perhaps along the driveway or along the front of the house. It is apparent that the builder or architect didn't have any real gardening in mind for the new owners—if gardening ever crossed their minds at all. One is tempted to plant a row of begonias or marigolds and call it a day. But we can do better than that by thinking outside of the box.

In this simple yet dynamic design, the bed is actually not extremely narrow, but about 5½ ft. wide and 29 ft. long. An existing hedge of boxwood (*Buxus* 'Green Gem') (1) runs along the front side of the bed, along the driveway, and a white fence runs along the back. The bed is part of a nicely sized property with a massive home. Something bold was needed to stay in scale with these elements. Many neighbors walk by on the sidewalk along the north side of it. Could we provide them with something more than what they had seen at every other house they passed? Mind you, this was a jump for these clients ("Why did we plant thistle?" and so on). At times like these, I have to remind myself that educating people about different plants and styles is all part of the process.

Plate 83. Can we do something different with small, otherwise useless spaces? I think so. Author's design, DiSabato garden, Ohio.

I selected bold annuals for this mixed border because I wanted it to have as much impact during the summer months as possible. Across from this bed was another of several mixed borders I designed on this property, this one with a silver, purple, and blue color theme. This strip was to repeat that color theme. I didn't want to get too busy with a high variety of plants in this fairly limited space, so, to create drive-by impact, I selected only three types of plants, to be used in masses, in addition to the existing boxwood. The high-value gray or silver foliage of the cardoon (*Cynara cardunculus*) (3) is full of light and attracts the eye; it shares a common unifying brightness with the white fence and enlivens the purple foliage of the purple fountain grass (*Pennisetum setaceum* 'Rubrum') (4). The fountain grass in turn serves as a good balance among the two bright colors while also adding weight, depth, and intrigue to the composition.

The very bold dominant characteristics of the overall form and texture of the cardoon are further balanced and contrasted by the finer texture of the grass, the boxwood, and the Swan River daisy (*Brachyscome* 'Ultra') (2). Movement provided by the panicles of the grass is a needed contrast to the static nature of the rest of the composition. Maintenance is minimal in this planting except for a periodic shearing of the daisies (to keep them blooming) and the boxwood (if a small uniform hedge is desired). It is critical that cardoon be provided with excellent drainage through proper soil preparation and even perhaps some added grit at planting. A wet season could spell doom for the cardoon and the design.

Even in this small space, the design principles of order through balance, unity through dominance, repetition, and interconnection, and rhythm through movement are achieved.

Plate 84. High contrast catches the eye of passing cyclists, power walkers, and drivers in this planting located perpendicular to the street. Notice how the lines of the grass's panicles complement the curves of the fence. Their movement adds needed rhythm. Featuring *Cynara cardunculus*, *Pennisetum setaceum* 'Rubrum'. Author's design, DiSabato garden, Ohio.

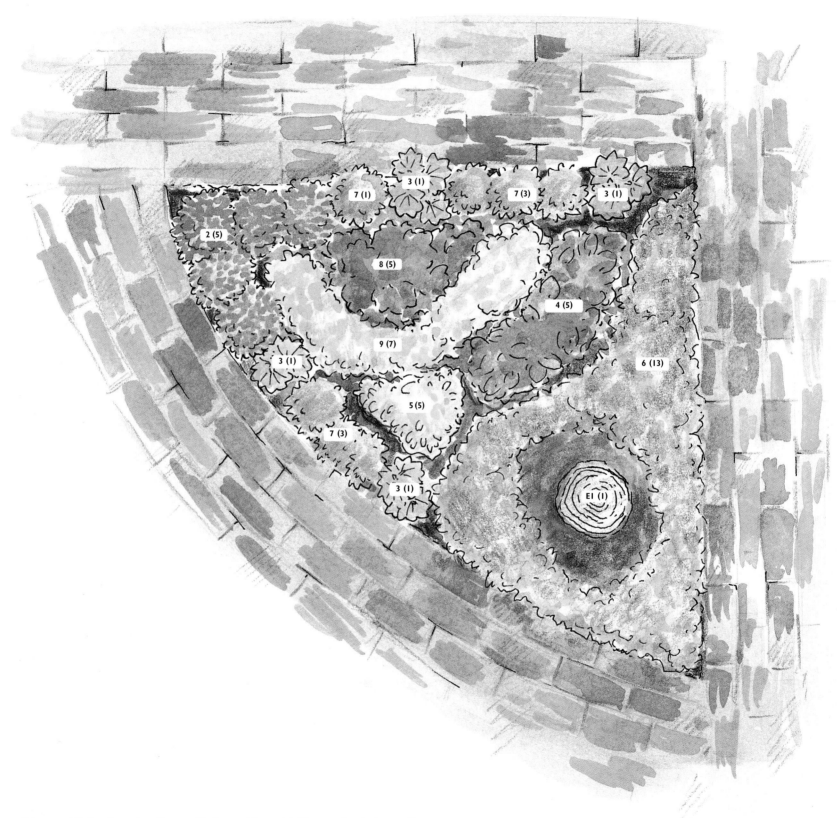

Diagram 17. Small garden: Design III. Artist, Megan H. King; author's design, Edgar garden.

⊢————————⊣ = 3 feet

N→

DIAGRAM 17

Existing trees

1	(1)	*Quercus palustris*	pin oak

Shrubs

2	(5)	*Buxus microphylla* 'Winter Gem'	boxwood

Perennials

3	(4)	*Alchemilla mollis*	lady's mantle
4	(5)	*Brunnera macrophylla*	Siberian bugloss
5	(5)	*Digitalis grandiflora*	yellow foxglove
6	(13)	*Epimedium ×rubrum*	red barrenwort
7	(7)	*Geranium macrorrhizum* 'Ingwersen's Variety'	bigroot geranium
8	(5)	*Heuchera micrantha* var. *diversifolia* 'Palace Purple'	coralbells
9	(7)	*Lamium maculatum* 'White Nancy'	dead nettle

I'm frequently asked about plantings for dry shade. This small bed is located under a pin oak and surrounded on all sides by brick. Irrigation was added, but many of these plants were selected because they tolerate dry shade. The border is one of four located in the shady front yard of a small colonial-style home. Boxwood (*Buxus microphylla* 'Winter Gem') (2) is repeated on the corners of the beds, which helps emphasize movement to the front door and harmonizes with the style of the home. The client's requested colors were pink, white, purple or blue, yellow, and some red. The peak flower color season is spring, yet there is foliage texture and form for interest in all seasons. Red barrenwort (*Epimedium ×rubrum*) (6), a premier plant for dry shade once established, was used as a large drift over a good portion of the driest area. The size of this group is balanced by several smaller groups of different species. The barrenwort's red spring flowers, heart-shaped leaves, and bronzed winter foliage make this plant not only functional but also beautiful in all seasons. Melding plants of bigroot geranium (*Geranium macrorrhizum* 'Ingwersen's Variety') (7) and lady's mantle (*Alchemilla mollis*) (3) soften the edges of the bed and create interconnection and repetition of pink and yellow-green. These plants are also repeated along the edge of other beds in the yard, serving as unifying elements. The bright foliage and flowers of *Lamium maculatum* 'White Nancy' (9) add light to this composition and balance the weight of the coralbells (8). The vertical form of the yellow foxglove (5) is a much-needed contrast to the general mounded and rounded nature of the rest of the planting. Its soft yellow flowers combine pleasantly with the blue flowers of *Brunnera macrophylla* (4) and the various pink, yellow-green, and white flowers that surround it.

Plate 85. Beautiful things can happen in dry shade. Author's design, Edgar garden, Ohio.

Diagram 18. Medium garden: Design I. Artist, Megan H. King; author's garden.

⌐——————⌐ = 4 feet

N➞

MEDIUM-SPACE DESIGNS

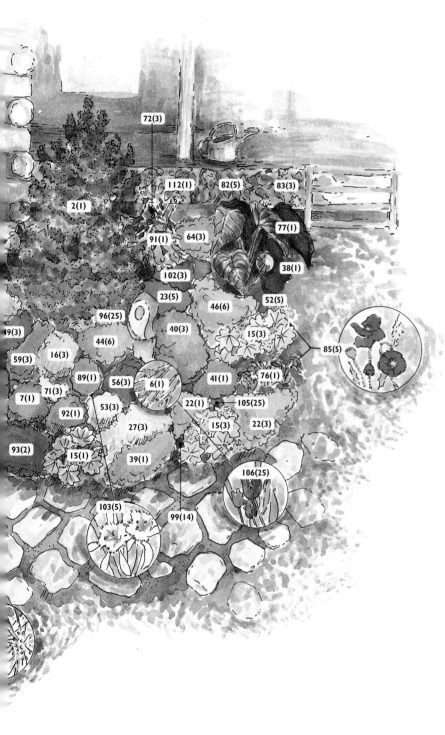

DIAGRAM 18

Trees

1	(1)	*Acer griseum*	paperbark maple
2	(1)	*Pseudotsuga menziesii* 'Astro Blue'	Douglas fir

Shrubs

3	(3)	*Berberis thunbergii* 'Monler' (Gold Nugget™)	Japanese barberry
4	(1)	*Callicarpa dichotoma* 'Issai'	purple beautyberry
5	(1)	*Chamaecyparis obtusa* 'Mariesii'	Hinoki falsecypress
6	(1)	*Chamaecyparis pisifera* 'Golden Mop'	Japanese falsecypress
7	(1)	*Hypericum androsaemum* 'Albury Purple'	st. johnswort
8	(1)	*Pinus densiflora* 'Oculus Draconis'	dragon's eye pine
9	(1)	*Pinus sylvestris* 'Albyn'	Scots pine
10	(1)	*Vitex agnus-castus* var. *latifolia*	chastetree

Perennials

11	(3)	*Acanthus spinosus*	spiny bear's breeches
12	(1)	*Aconitum carmichaelii* (Wilsonii Group) 'Spätlese'	monkshood
13	(3)	*Acorus gramineus* 'Oborozuki'	sweet flag
14	(3)	*Agastache* 'Blue Fortune'	anise hyssop
15	(11)	*Alchemilla mollis*	lady's mantle
16	(3)	*Alstroemeria* 'Sweet Laura'	Peruvian lily
17	(3)	*Anthriscus sylvestris* 'Ravenswing'	anthriscus
18	(5)	*Aquilegia alpina*	alpine columbine
19	(1)	*Aster laevis* 'Bluebird'	smooth aster
20	(3)	*Campanula* 'Kent Belle'	bellflower
21	(3)	*Carex dolichostachya* 'Kaga Nishiki' (gold fountains)	sedge
22	(7)	*Ceratostigma plumbaginoides*	plumbago
23	(11)	*Crocosmia* 'Lucifer'	crocosmia
24	(3)	*Delphinium cashmerianum*	delphinium
25	(3)	*Delphinium exaltatum*	delphinium
26	(1)	*Dianthus barbatus* 'Sooty'	sweet william
27	(9)	*Digitalis grandiflora*	yellow foxglove
28	(3)	*Digitalis lutea*	straw foxglove
29	(1)	*Dracocephalum ruyschiana*	dracocephalum
30	(1)	*Eryngium variifolium*	sea holly
31	(1)	*Euphorbia amygdaloides* 'Purpurea'	purple wood spurge
32	(1)	*Euphorbia dulcis* 'Chameleon'	spurge
33	(1)	*Euphorbia* 'Golden Towers'	spurge
34	(1)	*Euphorbia* ×*martinii*	spurge
35	(3)	*Geranium phaeum* 'Lily Lovell'	hardy geranium
36	(3)	*Geranium* 'Phillippe Vapelle'	hardy geranium
37	(3)	*Geranium pratense* 'Victor Reiter Jr.'	meadow cranesbill
38	(1)	*Geranium* 'Salome'	hardy geranium
39	(3)	*Geranium sanguineum* 'New Hampshire'	blood-red geranium

(*continued on next page*)

(plant list cont.)

40	(6)	*Helictotrichon sempervirens* 'Saphirsprudel' (sapphire fountain)	blue oat grass
41	(1)	*Heuchera* 'Plum Pudding'	coralbells
42	(3)	*Heuchera* 'Velvet Night'	coralbells
43	(1)	*Kniphofia* 'Prince Igor'	red-hot poker
44	(6)	*Lilium henryi*	Henry's lily
45	(6)	*Lilium lancifolium* var. *splendens*	lily
46	(6)	*Lilium pumilum*	lily
47	(3)	*Linaria* 'Natalie'	toadflax
48	(S)	*Linaria purpurea*	purple toadflax
49	(3)	*Lobelia* 'Dark Crusader'	lobelia
50	(3)	*Lobelia* 'Grape Knee High'	lobelia
51	(3)	*Lobelia* 'Purple Towers'	lobelia
52	(S)	*Lychnis coronaria*	rose campion
53	(3)	*Lysimachia nummularia* 'Aurea'	golden creeping jenny
54	(1)	*Miscanthus* 'Purpurascens'	miscanthus
55	(1)	*Oenothera fremontii* 'Lemon Silver'	sundrops
56	(3)	*Papaver nudicaule* 'Red Sails'	Iceland poppy
57	(3)	*Papaver orientale* 'Curlilocks'	oriental poppy
58	(3)	*Papaver orientale* 'Harvest Moon'	oriental poppy
59	(3)	*Papaver orientale* 'Patty's Plum'	oriental poppy
60	(1)	*Papaver orientale* 'Saffron'	oriental poppy
61	(3)	*Penstemon* ×*mexicale* 'Pike's Peak Purple'	penstemon
62	(3)	*Persicaria microcephala* 'Red Dragon'	persicaria
63	(3)	*Phlox divaricata* 'Eco Texas Purple'	woodland phlox
64	(3)	*Phlox divaricata* 'Sweet Lilac'	woodland phlox
65	(3)	*Rumex sanguineus*	bloody dock
66	(1)	*Sedum telephium* ssp. *maximum* 'Atropurpureum'	sedum
67	(S)	*Tradescantia* Andersoniana Group	spiderwort
68	(3)	*Verbena hastata*	American blue vervain
69	(3)	*Veronica austriaca* ssp. *teucrium* 'Crater Lake Blue'	Hungarian speedwell
70	(3)	*Veronica austriaca* ssp. *teucrium* 'Royal Blue'	Hungarian speedwell
71	(3)	*Veronica repens* 'Sunshine'	golden creeping speedwell
72	(3)	*Veronicastrum virginicum* 'Fascination'	culver's root

Annuals

73	(1)	*Agave havardiana*	agave
74	(3)	*Angelonia angustifolia* 'Purple Pinnacles'	angelonia
75	(3)	*Canna* 'Roi Humbert' (red King Humbert)	canna
76	(4)	*Cerinthe major* 'Purpurascens'	cerinthe
77	(1)	*Colocasia esculenta* 'Fontanesii'	elephant's ear
78	(S)	*Consolida ajacis* 'Blue Spire'	larkspur
79	(1)	*Duranta erecta* 'Golden Edge'	pigeon berry
80	(3)	*Helichrysum petiolare* 'Limelight'	licorice plant
81	(1)	*Hibiscus acetosella* 'Red Shield'	hibiscus
82	(5)	*Lathyrus odoratus* 'Henry Eckford'	sweet pea
83	(3)	*Lathyrus odoratus* 'King Size Navy Blue'	sweet pea
84	(1)	*Musa zebrina*	bloodleaf banana
85	(S)	*Papaver rhoeas*	corn poppy
86	(S)	*Papaver somniferum*	opium poppy
87	(S)	*Papaver somniferum* 'Black Peony'	peony-flowered poppy
88	(S)	*Papaver somniferum* 'Pepperbox'	opium poppy
89	(1)	*Phormium cookianum* 'Chocolate'	New Zealand flax
90	(1)	*Phormium* 'Platt's Black'	New Zealand flax
91	(1)	*Salvia guaranitica* 'Black and Blue'	salvia
92	(1)	*Solenostemon* 'Purple Emperor'	coleus
93	(3)	*Tropaeolum majus* 'Tip Top Mahogany'	nasturtium
94	(S)	*Verbena bonariensis*	tall verbena

Bulbs

95	(25)	*Allium cristophii*	downy onion
96	(25)	*Allium hollandicum* (*aflatunense*) 'Purple Sensation'	ornamental onion
97	(10)	*Allium schubertii*	ornamental onion
98	(25)	*Allium sphaerocephalon*	drumstick allium
99	(14)	*Camassia leichtlinii* ssp. *suksdorfii* 'Blauwe Donau' (blue Danube)	camass
100	(25)	*Chionodoxa forbesii* (*luciliae*) Siehei Group	glory of the snow
101	(25)	*Crocus chrysanthus* 'Blue Bird'	crocus
102	(8)	*Gladiolus* 'Violetta'	gladiolus
103	(5)	*Hymenocallis* 'Sulphur Queen'	Peruvian daffodil
104	(25)	*Iris* 'Blue Magic'	Dutch iris
105	(75)	*Iris reticulata* 'Harmony'	netted iris
106	(25)	*Tulipa* 'Black Parrot'	tulip
107	(25)	*Tulipa* 'Blue Heron'	tulip
108	(25)	*Tulipa* 'Blue Parrot'	tulip
109	(35)	*Tulipa* 'Carmine Parrot'	tulip

Vines

110	(1)	*Aconitum episcopale*	climbing monkshood
111	(1)	*Clematis* 'Polish Spirit'	clematis
112	(1)	*Hydrangea anomala* ssp. *petiolaris*	climbing hydrangea
113	(1)	*Lonicera periclymenum* 'Graham Thomas'	honeysuckle

This design is a renovation of my front herbaceous border at Hiddenhaven. A section of this border was the cover photograph for my first book. Although beautiful at one time, the border needed a makeover for many reasons. It was about ten years old, and with time the design had gotten further and further away from the initial plan. Certain perennial thugs were getting their way and dominating the garden. Most importantly, my objectives as a gardener had also changed—I wanted something different in this section of our gardens, in terms of style, type of plants, colors, textures, and so forth. The border as originally conceived was predominantly perennials. That was my strong focus when it was planted. With the renovation, I wanted more woody material, in particular dwarf conifers, as well as room for tropicals and just plain different, newer perennials and grasses. Foliage color, form, and texture would take precedence over flower color, which is the strong emphasis in many of our other borders. I definitely wanted to create a more varied mixed border. Some of the old plants were still favorites and in good condition, so they would stay. Although for sentimental reasons I was reluctant to make changes to this garden for a couple of years, it became apparent that it was time to take charge and accept that change is good!

Site: Located in the country, just north of the town of Sunbury, Ohio, this is a zone 5 garden. It is an almost ideal location with an eastern exposure, warmed by the morning sun until about one o'clock in the afternoon. Most of the border is blocked from the harsh west sun and winds by the house, making it one of the most protected locations in our gardens. The border is 45 ft. long and varies in width, from 16 ft. at its widest to about 9 ft. at its most narrow. The scale is in keeping with the size of the house. It is flanked on one side by a flagstone path, which leads to our front door, and on the other side by the front wall of our log home.

The soil was a clay loam, improved slightly from the original clay texture by years of topdressing with organic matter. Still, a thorough soil amending was performed to help further improve the soil structure, increase the organic matter content, and get the organics more deeply into the soil. Since some of the plants along the front of the border were not removed during the renovation it involved working around them. The pH is neutral. No automated irrigation system is in place; any necessary watering is done with sprinklers.

Objectives: The new design was not implemented to change the amount of maintenance required in the garden. About the same amount of time is involved in the upkeep with the new plan as was with the old—perhaps more because of all the fussing I do over it! This type of complex mixed border definitely requires a watchful eye to keep everything managed and performing optimally. Pruning, of course, of the herbaceous material—to keep them in their planned space, to deadhead, to improve their habits and so on—is the primary maintenance. A bit of staking is required on a few of the tender plants. Pests and diseases are experienced minimally, if at all, so no spraying is required. Tropicals and annuals are fertilized with fish emulsion and other organic fertilizers.

The woody plants that replaced some of the original perennials require a bit less care than their herbaceous counterparts, but the additional tropicals and annuals add time in the labor and energy required to overwinter them in our conservatory, to start them from seed, or to order and replace them annually. This is probably the most time-consuming aspect of this border, but we really enjoy this facet of the mixed garden.

With this new design, I wanted a style that was a bit more sophisticated. The original garden very much reflected a relaxed cottage-garden style. While this new design is still informal and appropriate to our country setting, there is more of an emphasis on strong structure, courtesy of the woody plant material. The tropicals and ornamental grasses add bold touches and create a more eclectic feel than the perennials did on their own. The new limited color palette also creates a more savvy sense, while the incorporation of bold colors creates a stimulating appeal. This new style better reflects my current style. The gardens are lush, bulging with plants. I despise seeing a hole or mulch. Holes are usually quickly filled with an appropriate plant or pot of plants. You will notice a great deal of interplanting occurs—the well-known concept of layers in the garden is paramount. And a touch of art was added: a simple yet attractive stone sculpture and orb.

The function my gardens serve is a bit different from the function of most people's gardens. As a professional designer,

Plate 86. Hiddenhaven front gardens. The appeal of well-designed mixed gardens is apparent. Author's garden; photograph by Ian Adams.

Plate 87. Hiddenhaven gardens in the spring. Author's garden.

Plate 88. Hiddenhaven gardens in the summer. Author's garden.

Plate 89. Hiddenhaven gardens in the autumn. The asters in the adjoining bed contribute extra color to this autumn scene. Author's garden.

consultant, speaker, and author, I see my gardens as living labs, if you will, where I can test plants for both cultural and aesthetic performance. I need to be able to experiment with combinations that can be inspirational for other designs I may create, or that will provide the opportunity for photographs for lectures or books (such as this one!). One objective for this renovation was to accomplish these goals.

This design features a disciplined use of color, in a fairly limited color palette, with a refined emphasis on the use of texture and form. I enjoyed selecting my favorite colors for the border. The predominant colors in the spring are the cooler analogous

blues and violets and, of course, the more neutral greens. This creates an overall calming effect, and these colors are wonderful viewed up close while walking along the path. Warmer, contrasting hues of yellow, in the spring, and red and orange, predominantly in the summer, create striking and stimulating focal points in the composition. These colors attract the eye; while driving up the lane to our home, the viewer wants to see more. The warmer tones of red and orange also heat up the mood of the garden a bit during the summer and autumn.

Many variations of tertiary hues are also present in the garden, such as blue-violet, red-violet, red-orange, and yellow-green. If we

Plate 90. Contrasting colors of the blue from *Agastache* 'Blue Fortune' and the orange from *Lilium lancifolium* var. *splendens* complement each other. Author's garden.

Plate 91. Red and green create an arresting contrast and focal point. Featuring *Papaver rhoeas*, *Cerinthe major* 'Purpurascens'. Author's garden.

can help it, there are no pinks, whites, or yellow-orange. Sometimes plants will seed into the garden in these colors, and a quick yank keeps the intended color scheme intact. Foliage color plays as important a role as flower color in this garden. Plants grown for foliage color that flower, for example in white, are preferably disbudded before the blooms open.

Simultaneous contrast abounds (a quick review of Chapter 3 may be in order!). When colors such as red and green, orange and blue, or purple and yellow are adjacent to one another, it has the effect of brightening the intensity of each color. In the spring and summer, poppies such as *Papaver orientale* 'Harvest Moon' (58)

and *P. rhoeas* (85), with their red to red-orange flowers, are electric against the various greens that surround them at those times. Also in the summer, *Tropaeolum majus* 'Tip Top Mahogany' (93) creates its own contrast of yellow-green leaves and deep red flowers, making both colors more alive than if viewed alone.

Successive contrast also comes into play. For example, in the spring the purples of *Allium cristophii* (95) and coralbells (*Heuchera* 'Velvet Night') (42) are intensified because, before seeing the purple, the eye is saturated by the yellow of *Digitalis grandiflora* (27) and the yellow-green of the repeating lady's mantle (*Alchemilla mollis*) (15). The colors are further enhanced by placing these plants together.

Plate 92. Simultaneous contrast is at work again with this plant's foliage and flowers. Featuring *Tropaeolum majus* 'Tip Top Mahogany'. Author's garden.

Plate 93. Thanks to successive contrast, the purple in this border appears intensified: the eye has been saturated with purple's complement, yellow. Author's garden.

Plate 94. A touch of yellow among the purple brightens both. Featuring *Allium cristophii*, *Heuchera* 'Velvet Night', *Alchemilla mollis*. Author's garden.

Plate 95. Contrast of textures and forms is the foundation of the garden's beauty. No flowers needed. Featuring *Acanthus spinosus*, *Lilium lancifolium* var. *splendens*, *Helictotrichon sempervirens* 'Saphirsprudel' (sapphire fountain). Author's garden.

Plate 96. Fine textures work as good visual relief among bolder textures in the garden. Featuring *Consolida ajacis* 'Blue Spire'. Author's garden.

Plate 97. The strong vertical lines of *Gladiolus* 'Violetta' create provocative tension among other forms. Also featuring *Colocasia esculenta* 'Fontanesii', *Crocosmia* 'Lucifer'. Author's garden.

Plate 98. A vignette in the border in the spring. Featuring *Pseudotsuga menziesii* 'Astro Blue', *Allium hollandicum* 'Purple Sensation', *Tulipa* 'Black Parrot', *Chamaecyparis pisifera* 'Golden Mop', *Heuchera* 'Plum Pudding', *Cerinthe major* 'Purpurascens'. Sculptor, Phil Kimball; author's garden.

Plate 99. The same view in summer. Replacing the spring-flowering bulbs are *Lilium henryi* and *Crocosmia* 'Lucifer'; splashes of red come from *Papaver rhoeas*. Author's garden.

Plate 100. The view in late autumn. The groundcover mass is *Ceratostigma plumbaginoides*, and the prominent grass near the sculpture is *Helictotrichon sempervirens* 'Saphirsprudel' (sapphire fountain). Author's garden.

Plate 101. The scene in winter. Author's garden.

Plate 102. With its small stature and multi-season effect, *Acer griseum* works well in mixed gardens. The cinnamon color of its exfoliating bark harmonizes with other warm colors, such as those of *Kniphofia* 'Prince Igor' (foreground). Author's garden.

Plate 103. *Acer griseum* works equally well with cooler colors, as here with *Aquilegia alpina*. Author's garden.

The neutral color of the dark brown logs of our home makes a great backdrop for the plants; it intensifies the colors while also lightening their values (see Plate 91). Colors selected for this sunny garden are generally rich or vivid, and they shine. In other words, most of the colors are fairly dark (shades low in value or of mid-value) and high in saturation (full of color). Very few tints of colors are incorporated, except for the lighter- or higher-valued yellows and yellow-greens. It's a pleasing proportion of one-third tints to two-thirds shades.

With the limited color palette, textures and forms play a key role in this design, and balance, contrast, and repetition of texture and form were chief considerations. You will see within plant combinations that not only the overall form (vertical or mounding) and overall texture were considered but also individual leaf surface (dull versus smooth), leaf shape, and leaf size. As you look through the overall border you will see these various textures and forms repeated to create harmony in the garden. These elements occur in a nice proportion; the bolder overall forms in the trees, shrubs, conifers, and tropicals, which add weight and stability to the design, are balanced with the softer

Plate 104. High values of yellow (blonde hair, banding on needles) ignite against the low values (black dress, brown logs) in this photograph of me with one of my favorite woodies, the luminescent *Pinus densiflora* 'Oculus Draconis'. Sidelighting is responsible for this effect. Author's garden; photograph by Jim Aust.

Plate 105. The same pine frontlit creates a dramatic analogous combination with the dazzling *Lilium lancifolium* var. *splendens*. Author's garden.

forms and finer textures of the masses of herbaceous annuals, perennials, and grasses. These bolder forms also create a place for the eye to rest among this busy design. A proportion of approximately one-third bold to two-thirds fine balances the composition. This higher proportion of finely textured plants gives the border a feeling of greater size. Fine texture is provided

Plate 106. Two exceptional vines, *Lonicera periclymenum* 'Graham Thomas' and *Clematis* 'Polish Spirit', carry the color scheme of the garden into the vertical space. Author's garden.

by the larkspur (*Consolida ajacis* 'Blue Spire') (78), which reseeds in the border (a perennial in effect); the toadflaxes *Linaria* 'Natalie' and *L. purpurea* (47–48); and the different ornamental grasses, such as *Helictotrichon sempervirens* 'Saphirsprudel' (40). Like the different colors, different forms and textures create different visual effects. For example, the bold forms attract the eye from a distance, while the softer forms and finer textures are better appreciated while walking down the path. The diverse and tantalizing textures are most prominent when the early morning sun hits this border.

The different sizes and shapes of the plants in the border occur in varied planes in the garden, from vertical to horizontal to overhead, creating a dynamic three-dimensional space. Contrasting forms of mounded versus vertical also create a place to pause in the border. Strong verticals are provided by several genera but of particular note is *Gladiolus* 'Violetta' (102), whose vertical flower spikes lead the eye up from the lower plantings to feast on their spectacular flower color, texture, and form.

Another objective was to create a multi-season garden, and this garden truly is one. It has the most flower color in late spring to early summer, but with its strong bones and interesting foliage colors, it is appealing year-round. The diverse mixed palette of plants creates never-ending interest.

Plant Selection: Selecting plants for this border was really too much fun! I was excited to be adding some outstanding specimen plants to the gardens as well as many unusual plants that I had been longing to try.

Plate 107. *Berberis thunbergii* 'Monler' (Gold Nugget™) continues to amaze me—this Japanese barberry looks good no matter the season or what it is paired with. Note the red-tinged new growth. Also featuring *Allium schubertii*, *Hymenocallis* 'Sulphur Queen', *Phormium cookianum* 'Chocolate', *Pseudotsuga menziesii* 'Astro Blue'. Author's garden.

Plate 108. Yellows, yellow-green, and blue-green combine with great appeal. Featuring *Berberis thunbergii* 'Monler' (Gold Nugget™), *Tropaeolum majus* 'Tip Top Mahogany', *Cerinthe major* 'Purpurascens', *Acorus gramineus* 'Oborozuki'. Author's garden.

Plate 109. Even into early winter, *Berberis thunbergii* 'Monler' (Gold Nugget™) excites. Author's garden.

Let's look through the design at some of the woodies first, starting at the south end of the border with the paperbark maple (*Acer griseum*) (1). This tree, a stunning specimen of my all-time favorite woody plant, existed in the garden before the renovation. Of course it made the cut to remain: it's a great vertical element and offers structure, autumn color, and year-round interest in leaf texture and bark color and texture.

Other woody plants include the dragon's eye pine (*Pinus densiflora* 'Oculus Draconis') (8), whose needles, banded with yellow, create a fine texture and look great against the brown logs. Next to it, on a willow trellis against the house, is *Lonicera periclymenum* 'Graham Thomas' (113) and *Clematis* 'Polish Spirit' (111), both of which were existing. They soften the scale of the wall, utilizing the vertical space, and their contrasting flower colors of yellow and purple are harmonious with the new color scheme. The honeysuckle adds the charm of fragrance that has become part of our emotional connection to this part of the garden; it greets us as we enter the house and wafts into open windows.

Below them is *Callicarpa dichotoma* 'Issai' (4), which was selected for its profuse purple berries. The primary focal point in the garden is *Pseudotsuga menziesii* 'Astro Blue' (2); once this conifer was procured (and it was love at first sight!), a great deal of the design—around it and through the garden—was driven by its qualities (see Plates 98–101). It is truly an aristocrat in the garden and an excellent addition to many combinations, with its deep blue color and interesting fruit and bark. Its placement too is satisfying: it is approximately one-third of the way down the bed, in keeping with our Fibonacci thinking. It is a stable force among the ever-changing garden around its feet.

Plate 110. Another awesome shrub is *Hypericum androsaemum* 'Albury Purple', combined here with the foliage of *Hymenocallis* 'Sulphur Queen', the cool seedhead of *Allium schubertii*, and a stray stem of *Consolida ajacis* 'Blue Spire'. Author's garden.

Shrubs, such as the dwarf conifers *Pinus sylvestris* 'Albyn' (9) with its interesting wide-spreading habit, *Chamaecyparis obtusa* 'Mariesii' (5), and *C. pisifera* 'Golden Mop' (6), add color and weight among the "lighter" herbaceous plants. Stunning deciduous additions include *Berberis thunbergii* 'Monler' (Gold Nugget™) (3), with its breathtaking yellow summer foliage and red and orange autumn color, and *Hypericum androsaemum* 'Albury Purple' (7), with its purple spring growth.

Plate 111. *Duranta erecta* 'Golden Edge', a primo foliage plant, is a tropical that I willingly go to the trouble of digging and overwintering in my conservatory annually. Also featuring *Canna* 'Roi Humbert' (red King Humbert). Author's garden.

Plate 112. New Zealand flax (*Phormium cookianum* 'Chocolate') adds structure, color, and exotic flair to gardens—while tolerating dry conditions and neglect. Also featuring *Hypericum androsaemum* 'Albury Purple', *Lysimachia nummularia* 'Aurea', *Alstroemeria* 'Sweet Laura'. Author's garden.

Perennials that remained from the original garden include *Alchemilla mollis* (15), which is one of my signature perennials, Hungarian speedwell (69–70), and *Geranium sanguineum* 'New Hampshire' (39). Their mounded habits make great melders at the front of the garden, unifying the length of the border, and their colors of yellow-green, blue, blue-violet, and red-violet are again in keeping with the new color palette. Several other outstanding blue and blue-violet geraniums (35–38) were also added to the repertoire.

I have a passion for poppies and so selected many perennial and annual forms for the garden, from the oriental, including the to-die-for violet-flowering *Papaver orientale* 'Patty's Plum' (59), to the seductive *P. somniferum* and other opium forms (86–88). My interest in art and watercolors spurred me to include not only poppies in the garden but also painterly parrot tulips (106–109), even though these need to be replaced annually, lilies, and even some old-fashioned favorites, such as orange and blue sweet peas (82–83) and *Tropaeolum majus* 'Tip Top Mahogany' (93). My favorite annual, *Cerinthe major* 'Purpurascens' (76), with its varying tints and shades of green, blue, yellow, and violet, is a painter's delight. I can't have enough of this plant; besides its color, its succulent texture greatly appeals to me.

The garden often has an impressionist, free-spirited feel to it, with the seeding (S) that occurs with *Aquilegia alpina* (18), *Verbena bonariensis* (94), and blue *Tradescantia Andersoniana* Group (67).

The tropicals are instant topics of conversation; among them are *Musa zebrina* (84), with its massive red-striped leaves and large habit, and *Colocasia esculenta* 'Fontanesii' (77), with its equally massive elephant's ear–shaped leaves, which are a deep green complemented by striking dark red-violet, almost black veins and stems (see Plate 97). Again, foliage color is of key importance in this design, and these two plants, along with *Duranta erecta* 'Golden Edge' (79), *Hibiscus acetosella* 'Red Shield' (81), and other tropicals, really look stunning. Other favorites for foliage color include blue from *Helictotrichon sempervirens* 'Saphirsprudel' (40), yellow and green from *Acorus gramineus* 'Oborozuki' (13) (see Plate 108), yellow groundcovers in *Lysimachia nummularia* 'Aurea' (53) and *Veronica repens* 'Sunshine' (71), and shades of red-violet from *Anthriscus sylvestris* 'Ravenswing' (17), whose white flowers are disbudded, *Heuchera* 'Velvet Night' (42), *H.* 'Plum Pudding' (41), *Phormium cookianum* 'Chocolate' (89), *P.* 'Platt's Black' (90), and *Solenostemon* 'Purple Emperor' (92).

Design Principles: (See Plates 86–112 for examples of each principle—order, unity, and rhythm.) Order has been established in the design in several ways. Balance has been accomplished by having the different elements of the design in equilibrium. We have already looked at how different elements such as colors, textures, and weight in the design are balanced in an asymmetrical one-third to two-thirds fashion throughout the border. Mass collection is evident through the many drifts and masses of herbaceous plant material.

Unity or the feeling of oneness starts with the garden as a whole. The stone path that accompanies this border is repeated in our back borders as well. Another border on the other side of this path is surrounded by two layers of stone. This stone edging is repeated throughout six other gardens on the property. The combination of curving line for the front of the bed and straight line for the back of the bed is also repeated through all the other borders, unifying all.

Unity is also set in the design by dominance, repetition, and interconnection. We have looked at the dominant colors, textures, and plants that create the focal points in this design. Repetition of both color and plant types (the dwarf conifers, ornamental grasses) is present, as is great interconnection: more often than not, plants are physically linked—there are no holes in this dense planting. The composition is further pulled together by the melders we discussed earlier and the layering of groundcovers, interplanting, and seeding that fill the spaces.

This border has so much rhythm, you can almost hear and feel its movement. Different plant heights and shapes along the length of the border undulate or alternate up and down, and gradations of rhythm occur as you move from the front of the border to the back, generally from lower to taller forms, from finer to coarser textures. There is movement in the grasses and the lazy swaying of the tropical leaves.

Diagram 19. Medium garden: Design II. Artist, Megan H. King; author's design, Heiberger garden.

DIAGRAM 19

Shrubs

1	(1)	*Rosa* Lyda Rose™	rose

Perennials

2	(6)	*Adiantum pedatum*	maidenhair fern
3	(5)	*Astilbe ×rosea* 'Peach Blossom'	astilbe
4	(5)	*Helleborus foetidus*	stinking hellebore
5	(3)	*Osmunda cinnamomea*	cinnamon fern
6	(7)	*Polygonatum odoratum* 'Variegatum'	variegated solomon's seal

Annuals

7	(3)	*Colocasia esculenta* 'Black Beauty'	elephant's ear
8	(2)	*Colocasia esculenta* 'Illustris'	elephant's ear
9	(3)	*Ipomoea batatas* 'Margarita'	sweet potato vine
10	(9)	*Solenostemon* 'Burgundy Columns'	coleus

Vines

11	(1)	*Clematis alpina* 'Constance'	alpine clematis
12	(1)	*Clematis macropetala* 'Markham's Pink'	clematis

Bulbs

13	(25)	*Narcissus* 'Petrel'	daffodil

This is a section from a medium-sized woodland mixed garden (be sure to check out Diagram 28, a larger shade border in Chapter 9). It was originally designed and installed in 1995. These photographs of the garden were taken in July 2000. One of the clients is a keen gardener and has maintained the border beautifully. She also has me return on a regular basis to consult on the garden and make any needed additions or changes, to keep it at its best. We have substituted, over the years, some newer plants where we lost some of the older ones.

Site: Located in Galena, Ohio, zone 5, adjacent to Hoover Reservoir, the garden is protected from strong winds off the lake by native deciduous trees. This is a 15 × 13 ft. section of a garden that is 55 ft. long and 10–29 ft. wide. The garden's proportions were set to balance the scale of the home and surrounding woodland. The soil was clay, low in organic matter, and neutral in pH. It was amended with 4 in. of organic matter. It is in the shade for most of the day, but this section in particular receives a few hours of late afternoon sun. An automated irrigation system helps maintain an evenly moist soil, so the plants thrive. Two inches of pine bark mini-chips, applied yearly as a mulch, also helps maintain moisture.

Objectives: The garden as a whole is fairly low maintenance. Some of the herbaceous woodland species and spring bulbs go dormant in the summer and require cutting back. Tropicals and different annuals are planted to fill these holes for summer and autumn interest. Every three years, starting in year three, we top-dress using 2 in. of a compost blend (1 part leaf humus, 1 part

Plate 113. Texture, form, and foliage color are the focus in this mid-sized shade garden. Author's design, Heiberger garden, Ohio.

Plate 114. Contrasting values, hues, and forms create arresting focal areas. Featuring *Caladium* 'Florida Cardinal', *Hakonechloa macra* 'Aureola'. Author's design, Heiberger garden, Ohio.

composted biosolids, 1 part topsoil). In years when no top-dressing occurs, plants are fertilized with an organic fertilizer, such as Espoma.

The garden's natural yet classy style employs both native and nonnative plants. As to function, this garden was planned solely for the enjoyment of the clients, their two cats, and their friends, who often come to visit the garden. It was designed to be viewed from the large picture window in the clients' home office.

Texture, form, and foliage color are the key focus in this shaded garden. The varying shades of green and, even more prominently, the contrasting leaf shapes create excitement and interest. Splashes of deep red foliage, which again add contrast but also weight and needed tension, are used throughout the border. The flowers of the Lyda Rose™ rose (1) and both clematis (11–12) are soft pinks, in keeping with the fairly broad flower color palette of mostly pinks, blues, whites, and yellows. The obelisk that the rose and clematis grow on creates a nice vertical element in the border, which repeats the verticals of both herbaceous and woody plants along the back of the border.

Flower color is at its peak in this garden in the spring; summer and autumn are also outstanding, in part because of various summer-blooming plants but mostly thanks to strong foliage.

Plant Selection: This border is predominantly herbaceous. In this portion of the garden, cinnamon fern (*Osmunda cinnamomea*) (5) was selected because it is such a reliable grower in the Midwest (most ferns are more fragile). Its 2-ft. height and "cinnamon stick" fertile frond add further to its charm. The variegated solomon's seal (*Polygonatum odoratum* 'Variegatum') (6) and stinking hellebore (*Helleborus foetidus*) (4) are probably my two favorite perennials for shade. The pink, white, and green new shoots of variegated solomon's seal are a sight in themselves; the awesome variegated leaves expand, and their beauty continues until the autumn, when a golden glow transforms them. The white flowers in the leaf axils are just a bonus! The plant is slow to establish, but after about the third year, it really starts to take hold and has formed a large colony in this border. The stinking hellebore is actually on the hardiness borderline here; it acts like a zone 6 plant and can be lost during a harsh winter in zone 5, but we haven't had any trouble in this garden. Plants have a tendency to reseed, and even if the parent plants are lost, these seedlings seem to make it. The deep green leaves have a fabulous toothed texture, and the plant sets green flower buds in the autumn that hold through the winter, opening in late winter or very early spring.

Burgundy Columns coleus (10) adds a splash of attitude to the grouping and was selected for its broad, deep red leaves. Another annual addition of Margarita sweet potato vine (9) brings a ray of yellow light into the grouping for relief from the heavier greens.

Bulbs such as netted iris (*Iris reticulata*) and *Narcissus* 'Petrel' (13) bloom in the spring in this section of the garden and throughout, along with Virginia bluebells (*Mertensia pulmonarioides (virginica)*), alpine columbine (*Aquilegia alpina*), and wood poppies (*Stylophorum diphyllum*).

Design Principles: There is a nice balance between the bolder forms of elephant's ear, *Colocasia esculenta* 'Black Beauty' and *C. esculenta* 'Illustris' (7–8), and the finer forms and textures of the solomon's seal and ferns, particularly maidenhair fern (*Adiantum pedatum*) (2). Different greens serve as a unifying element. Dominance is created by the stone birdbath. Depending on the lighting conditions during different times of the day, the colocasias can also be very dominant. Contrasts in leaf textures and color serve as secondary focal points. As with Diagram 18, of Hiddenhaven, mass collection, interconnection, and rhythm are present in the lush drifts of undulating plants.

Chapter 9

LARGE GARDENS

I feel blessed to have a large garden and to often have the opportunity to design large gardens for others. So much can be done with a lot of space! One can accomplish all the principles of design, attend to color, texture, and form issues, create season-long interest—and at the same time have an extraordinary collection of plants. Large areas may seem overwhelming at first, particularly for the new designer or owner, but with time I feel all the advantages of a large space win out. I suppose the terms small, medium, and large gardens are all relative, but I normally consider a large garden to be one that is more than 3,000 sq. ft.

In large garden, there is more room to play! You can afford to use more plants with a short season of interest than is usually the case with a small garden. Of course, the purposeful use of plants and various materials is still a requirement to be able to get away with a bit more frill. And although large gardens may require more time for maintenance, depending on their size and plant selection, you can sometimes get away with a few more less-than-perfect spots. This is, again, attributable to the scale; these areas are not as noticeable since viewers are distracted by all that is going on around them.

With more room for more plants, it is much easier to plan for season-long interest in larger gardens. It is particularly important, however, to remember the design principle of unity, to be sure the garden feels like a whole; repetition is a particular help in achieving this goal. In contrast to small gardens, where we may employ various techniques to create false perspective or an increased feeling of space, in large gardens we may want to accomplish just the opposite. Bold textures and warmer colors work effectively in large spaces to make areas appear smaller and more intimate. Larger masses of plants may be more appropriate, depending on the site, than smaller groups of plants. These may be needed to keep elements in proper scale and proportion. There is normally more space in large gardens for interesting hardscaping in walls or seating areas. Sections of open spaces of grass or meadow, for relief, can be added. Ponds, waterfalls, and other larger water features may be appropriate. Different sections of the gardens may be devoted to different color, plant, or design themes. Your imagination is limited only by budget and, most importantly, time for upkeep.

A word about commercial sites: do not get carried away with a great variety of plants (or plants requiring more maintenance) on large sites, as most landscape crews will not have the experience, time, or desire to care for choice or finicky specimens. This doesn't mean that some unusual plants can't be used. Exotic plant material is important to add interest and mystery to plantings. Care should be taken in the water requirements of plantings on commercial or public sites—always with a bias toward conservation. Large areas devoted to native drought-tolerant perennials and woody plants may be one solution. Public sites should be designed to offer a year-round oasis for peace and contemplation.

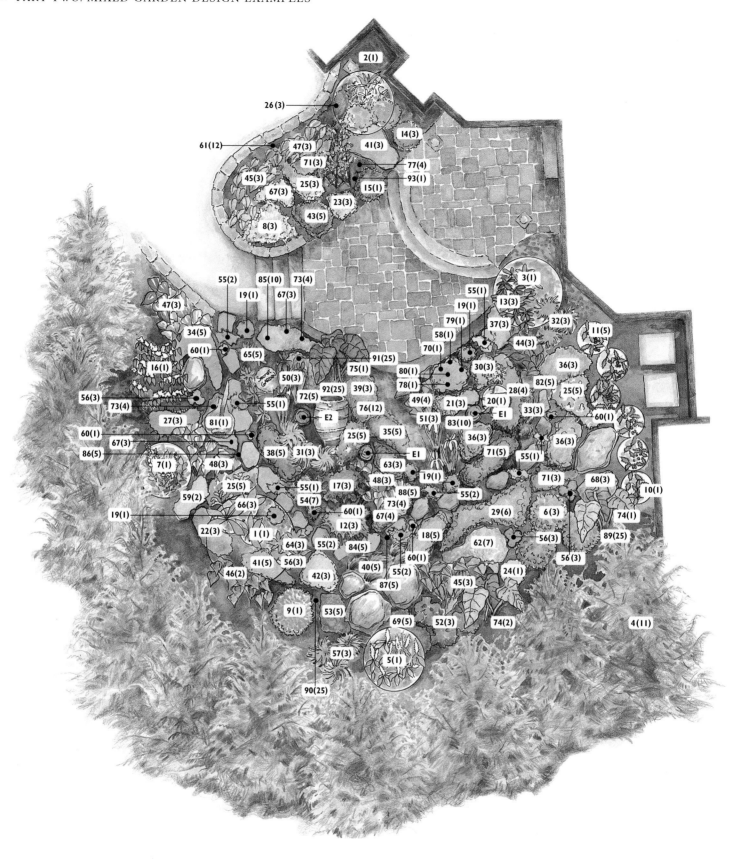

Diagram 20. Large garden: Design I. Artists, Megan H. King, Lisa Huddy, and the author; author's design, Marous garden.

⌞_____⌟ = 9 feet

N→

DIAGRAM 20

Trees

1	(1)	*Amelanchier ×grandiflora* 'Autumn Brilliance'	serviceberry
2	(1)	*Chionanthus virginicus*	white fringetree
3	(1)	*Magnolia virginiana*	sweetbay magnolia
4	(11)	*Tsuga canadensis*	Canadian hemlock

Existing trees

E1	(2)	*Pinus sylvestris*	Scots pine
E2	(1)	*Quercus palustris*	pin oak

Shrubs

5	(1)	*Aesculus parviflora*	bottlebrush buckeye
6	(3)	*Calycanthus floridus*	common sweetshrub
7	(1)	*Clethra alnifolia*	summersweet clethra
8	(3)	*Daphne ×burkwoodii* 'Carol Mackie'	Burkwood daphne
9	(1)	*Ilex glabra*	inkberry
10	(1)	*Ilex ×meserveae* 'Mesdob' (China boy)	Meserve holly
11	(5)	*Ilex ×meserveae* 'Mesog' (China girl)	Meserve holly
12	(3)	*Microbiota decussata*	Russian arborvitae
13	(3)	*Rhododendron* 'Mist Maiden'	rhododendron
14	(3)	*Rhododendron* 'Northern Starburst'	rhododendron
15	(1)	*Tsuga canadensis* 'Cole's Prostrate'	Canadian hemlock
16	(1)	*Viburnum plicatum* var. *tomentosum* 'Mariesii'	doublefile viburnum

Perennials

17	(3)	*Acanthus spinosus*	spiny bear's breeches
18	(5)	*Adiantum pedatum*	maidenhair fern
19	(5)	*Alchemilla mollis*	lady's mantle
20	(1)	*Amsonia elliptica*	amsonia
21	(3)	*Anemone ×hybrida* 'September Charm'	Japanese anemone
22	(3)	*Anemone ×hybrida* 'Queen Charlotte'	Japanese anemone
23	(3)	*Arisaema sikokianum*	jack-in-the-pulpit
24	(1)	*Aruncus dioicus*	goat's beard
25	(18)	*Astilbe ×arendsii* 'Snowdrift'	astilbe
26	(3)	*Astilbe chinensis* 'Purple Candle'	Chinese astilbe
27	(3)	*Astilbe chinensis* var. *taquetii* 'Superba'	Chinese astilbe
28	(4)	*Astilbe chinensis* 'Veronica Klose'	Chinese astilbe
29	(6)	*Astilbe ×rosea* 'Peach Blossom'	astilbe
30	(3)	*Athyrium niponicum* var. *pictum*	Japanese painted fern
31	(3)	*Calamagrostis ×acutiflora* 'Overdam'	feather reed grass
32	(3)	*Calamagrostis brachytricha*	Korean feather reed grass
33	(3)	*Carex morrowii* 'Variegata'	sedge
34	(5)	*Epimedium ×rubrum*	red barrenwort
35	(5)	*Geranium himalayense* 'Plenum'	lilac cranesbill
36	(9)	*Geranium ×oxonianum* 'Claridge Druce'	hardy geranium
37	(3)	*Geranium renardii*	hardy geranium
38	(5)	*Geranium wlassovianum*	hardy geranium
39	(3)	*Glaucidium palmatum*	Japanese woodlander
40	(5)	*Hakonechloa macra* 'Aureola'	golden-variegated Hakone grass
41	(8)	*Helleborus orientalis*	lenten rose
42	(3)	*Hemerocallis* 'Happy Returns'	daylily
43	(5)	*Heuchera micrantha* var. *diversifolia* 'Palace Purple'	coralbells
44	(3)	*Hosta* 'Fragrant Blue'	plantain-lily
45	(6)	*Hosta* 'Krossa Regal'	plantain-lily
46	(2)	*Hosta* 'Love Pat'	plantain-lily
47	(6)	*Hosta* 'Night Before Christmas'	plantain-lily
48	(6)	*Hosta* 'Patriot'	plantain-lily
49	(4)	*Hosta plantaginea* 'Aphrodite'	plantain-lily
50	(3)	*Iris sibirica* 'Caesar's Brother'	Siberian iris
51	(3)	*Iris sibirica* 'White Swirl'	Siberian iris
52	(3)	*Ligularia dentata* 'Dark Beauty'	bigleaf ligularia
53	(5)	*Lobelia* 'Royal Robe'	lobelia
54	(7)	*Luzula nivea*	snowy wood rush
55	(12)	*Mazus reptans*	mazus
56	(12)	*Mertensia pulmonarioides* (*virginica*)	Virginia bluebells
57	(3)	*Miscanthus sinensis* 'Morning Light'	miscanthus
58	(1)	*Origanum* 'Kent Beauty'	oregano
59	(2)	*Osmunda cinnamomea*	cinnamon fern
60	(5)	*Phlox stolonifera* 'Blue Ridge'	creeping phlox
61	(12)	*Phlox stolonifera* 'Bruce's White'	creeping phlox
62	(7)	*Polygonatum odoratum* 'Variegatum'	variegated solomon's seal
63	(3)	*Polystichum acrostichoides*	Christmas fern
64	(3)	*Pulmonaria* 'Majesté'	lungwort
65	(5)	*Pulmonaria* 'Viette's Deep Blue Sea'	lungwort
66	(3)	*Rodgersia pinnata*	rodgersia
67	(13)	*Stylophorum diphyllum*	wood poppy
68	(3)	*Thalictrum aquilegiifolium* 'Thundercloud'	meadow rue
69	(5)	*Thalictrum rochebruneanum*	lavender mist meadow rue
70	(1)	*Thymus ×citriodorus*	lemon thyme
71	(11)	*Tradescantia* (Andersoniana Group) 'Zwanenburg Blue'	spiderwort
72	(5)	*Trillium erectum*	trillium

Annuals

73	(12)	*Caladium* 'Florida Sweetheart'	caladium
74	(3)	*Colocasia esculenta*	elephant's ear
75	(1)	*Colocasia esculenta* 'Black Magic'	elephant's ear
76	(12)	*Fuchsia* 'Gartenmeister Bonstedt'	fuchsia
77	(4)	*Ipomoea tricolor* 'Heavenly Blue'	morning glory
78	(1)	*Ocimum* 'African Blue'	basil
79	(1)	*Plectranthus amboinicus*	Cuban oregano
80	(1)	*Salvia officinalis* 'Tricolor'	common sage

(*continued on next page*)

(*plant list cont.*)

Bulbs

81	(1)	*Amorphophallus konjac*	devil's tongue
82	(5)	*Camassia leichtlinii* 'Semiplena'	camass
83	(10)	*Erythronium* 'Pagoda'	trout lily
84	(5)	*Fritillaria persica*	fritillary
85	(10)	*Narcissus* 'Delnashaugh'	daffodil
86	(5)	*Narcissus* 'Fragrant Rose'	daffodil
87	(5)	*Narcissus* 'Mary Gay Lirette'	daffodil
88	(5)	*Narcissus* 'Mint Julep'	daffodil
89	(25)	*Narcissus* 'Stratosphere'	daffodil
90	(25)	*Triteleia laxa* 'Queen Fabiola'	triteleia
91	(25)	*Tulipa* 'Apricot Parrot'	tulip
92	(25)	*Tulipa* 'Black Parrot'	tulip

Vines

93	(1)	*Clematis* 'Hagley Hybrid'	clematis

Plate 115. The garden at planting, view from the terrace. Author's design, Marous garden, Ohio.

Site: This is a suburban garden but very distinct due to the spectacular 30- to 40-ft. Scots pines that were on the property when it was purchased. The garden is mostly shaded or at least partially shaded. This is a 3,365-sq.-ft. open border.

Consultation work began in the autumn, prior to construction of the home, in an effort to save the existing pines and oaks. Trying to avoid compaction in the garden area as much as possible involved a great deal of coordination with the builder and construction contractors. It was challenging at times to educate these individuals, who were from outside the typical landscape realm, about the special needs of herbaceous perennials and woody plants. Saving the trees involved setting standards and erecting boundary zones for the contractors. It also involved a bit of policing to see that the trees were indeed protected. It was always discouraging and infuriating to arrive on the site to see our snowfence protection plowed down, and an excavator sitting right up against the trunk of a gorgeous pine. Or for the tree barricades to become the trash bins!

Consultation, which continued during construction of the home, involved supervision of all other contractors, including an arborist and a landscape architect who was brought on site to lay out the grade, drainage, and hardscaping. All the garden space was to my design specifications. This was a treat, as a garden designer is often called onto the site only after bed spaces of inappropriate size and shape have been finalized. Design of the garden took place during the winter of that year; much of the house was completed by then, which made it easier to see the scale, color, and so on, for design purposes. Some construction on the hardscaping took place over the winter and was finished in the spring of the following year, before installation of the garden.

We installed the garden in the spring, by which time construction of the house was complete. The soil was prepared by adding 4 in. of organic matter (2 in. of Canadian sphagnum peat moss and 2 in. of a compost blend) and working it into the existing soil to a depth of at least 9 in. (12 in., in some locations, with a tiller). Hand-digging with forks and spades was necessary in some heavily compacted areas. Care was taken not to damage existing tree roots. An agricultural grade of fertilizer with an analysis of 8-32-16 was incorporated during tilling to be certain proper amounts of phosphorus were at root level (as it is immobile in the soil), for better root establishment. This analysis of fertilizer and percentage of soil amendments was based on soil tests run before installation. The soil was 5% organic matter content at the start, 16% after preparation.

Despite all our precautions, compaction by construction equipment caused a problem with drainage in the far north side of the garden (north of the stepping-stone path). Our normal bed preparation wasn't enough to combat the problem, and drainage tiles needed to be installed in this area late in the first season to correct the problem. Moisture-loving plants such as common sweetshrub (*Calycanthus floridus*) (6), inkberry (*Ilex glabra*) (9), summersweet clethra (*Clethra alnifolia*) (7), serviceberry (*Amelanchier* ×*grandiflora* 'Autumn Brilliance') (1), *Rodgersia pinnata* (66), bigleaf ligularia (*Ligularia dentata* 'Dark Beauty') (52), and *Lobelia* 'Royal Robe' (53) replaced plants that died due to the poor drainage (see list of moisture-loving plants in Appendix C). These plants have since prospered in the garden.

Water is supplied by automated irrigation systems, which are watched regularly for effectiveness. Separate timers are set for the

Plate 116. The garden five years later, view from the terrace. Author's design, Marous garden, Ohio.

Plate 117. Coming into the garden from the driveway. Author's design, Marous garden, Ohio.

Plate 118. View once in garden and approaching stepping-stone path. Author's design, Marous garden, Ohio.

Plate 119. Bold and fine textures contrast, as do varied leaf and overall plant forms, creating mystery and detail in the shade. Featuring *Polygonatum odoratum* 'Variegatum', *Adiantum pedatum, Hosta* 'Krossa Regal'. Author's design, Marous garden, Ohio.

Plate 120. Various greens and abundant textures and forms predominate in this vignette, accented by the variegated foliage of *Hosta* 'Patriot'. Also featuring *Acanthus spinosus, Luzula nivea.* Author's design, Marous garden, Ohio.

open border as compared to other garden areas and turf; this supplies less frequent but more thorough waterings for the perennials. The system is adjusted as needed based on annual weather conditions. Also known as the irritation system, it requires constant monitoring, as certain areas are always too dry, while other stay too wet.

Objectives: The secret garden, as this open border is known, was designed with varied objectives in mind. Its primary functions are to provide a secluded oasis for the owners to sit with their morning coffee, shielded from the busy outside world, and to provide a peaceful vista at any time, from indoors, to quiet the mind. The garden is also a retreat for friends; they meander down the stone path, discovering unusual colors, shapes, and textures, absorbing the lushness, perfumes, and sounds, all the while trying to guess rare-plant names.

As it is also admired from numerous windows in the home, this garden must have interest all year. It happily rises to the occasion with its ever-changing moods and pictures, not only from season to season but also from moment to moment, with mist, rain, frost, snow, and the play of sun and shadow providing endless vignettes. Soft evening lighting touches the romanticist in all. The garden is especially breathtaking in the spring and summer.

The style is natural elegance. Abundant masses of plants outlined by strong structural elements create a style in keeping with the artistic yet controlled nature of the interior décor. The bones of walls, terrace, stone path, and specimen boulders anchor the garden, harmonize with the house, and add to the wonderful

structure. The stone retaining wall at the entrance off the driveway and the screen of hemlocks creates this separate, enclosed world, hidden from outside view. Mixed containers carry excitement and life to the bluestone terrace. A pocket of herbs is located a short walk from the kitchen for seasoning the occasional omelet. The planted trees, shrubs, and herbaceous material offer a comforting understory to the impressive pines and oaks that were so carefully guarded through the entire construction phase.

This garden is one of several dynamic plantings on this site. Each has its own personality, design theme, and special maintenance requirements. Although this is a large garden, many combinations and vignettes could be utilized in gardens a fraction of its size. The stone-retaining-wall garden is an ideal smaller garden in itself.

Maintenance started in the secret garden the season before installation, as we tracked sun patterns through several days of the growing season, to see which areas in the diverse patterns created by the existing trees would actually be in the sun or shade. The design was then created using the right plant for the right lighting situation; for instance, some spots in this garden receive more sun and are planted with that in mind. Our aim was that at least 70% of the plants require lower maintenance. My company would be doing all the maintenance with some help from the homeowner; the objective was a mid-maintenance garden.

Many elements of installation (soil preparation, planting time and techniques, mulching, watering, fertilizing) interrelate to affect the long-term maintenance of the garden, so these were all addressed as needed. Most of the planting in this garden takes

Plate 121. Cooler colors prevail in the spring palette. Featuring *Tsuga canadensis* 'Cole's Prostrate', *Helleborus orientalis*, *Rhododendron* 'Northern Starburst'. Author's design, Marous garden, Ohio.

Plate 122. As the temperatures get warmer in the summer, so do the colors in the garden. Featuring *Colocasia esculenta*, *Ligularia dentata* 'Dark Beauty', *Lobelia* 'Royal Robe'. Author's design, Marous garden, Ohio.

place in the spring, before the heat and dry conditions of summer arrive; quart-sized plants are normally chosen, for their superior growth. With proper bed preparation, perennials double or triple in size the first season.

Mulching is done with a light organic pine soil conditioner similar to pine bark mini-chips. Two inches or less is added to moderate soil temperatures, retain moisture, and reduce weed competition. It is kept away from the crowns of the plants to avoid crown rot.

Maintenance is performed at the garden every two weeks. This involves any deadheading, cutting back, shearing, deadleafing, or staking that may be needed. Most shearing is done on the spring-blooming plants after they flower, for example the geraniums (35–38) are sheared to basal foliage as they decline to stimulate regrowth and rebloom. As the season continues, daylilies are deadheaded, the mazus (55) is kept trimmed to open the paths a bit. Wood poppy (*Stylophorum diphyllum*) (67) is cut to basal foliage as it declines in the summer heat. Most seedheads are left for the winter. *Tradescantia* (Andersoniana Group) 'Zwanenburg Blue' (71) is cut back by two-thirds with decline. Amsonia (20) is shaped by one-third after flowering to form structure in the garden. Approximately two-thirds of the lobelia (53) is dead-headed to avoid overcrowding but to allow some seeding to ensure the permanence of this hybrid in the garden. *Thalictrum rochebruneanum* (69) is one of the few perennials that are staked, as it does not respond well to cutting back before flowering in an effort to eliminate staking. We use tall, dead branches from trees in the woods on the property. Deadleafing is performed to keep plants looking good all summer. Many aesthetically pleasing perennials are left unpruned for winter. Cleanup continues in the spring, with the deadleafing of evergreens such as *Helleborus orientalis* (41), if needed, and cut back on perennials that were left for winter interest.

Topdressing with 2 in. of leaf humus and composted biosolids was done after four years to keep the organic matter high in the soil. No additional fertilizer is used on the perennials, as heavy-feeding perennials were not included in the design. Any fertilizing that is needed on the annuals is done with fish emulsion, every four weeks.

Plate 124. *Lobelia* 'Royal Robe'—red and dominant to the eyes of humans and hummingbirds. Also featuring *Miscanthus sinensis* 'Morning Light'. Author's design, Marous garden, Ohio.

Plate 123. Autumn brings beautiful and varied colors. Featuring *Carex morrowii* 'Variegata', *Geranium ×oxonianum* 'Claridge Druce', *Amsonia elliptica*. Author's design, Marous garden, Ohio.

Plate 125. *Chionanthus virginicus* is an ideal small tree to incorporate into mixed gardens. Also featuring *Hosta* 'Night Before Christmas', *H.* 'Krossa Regal', *Magnolia virginiana*, *Daphne ×burkwoodii* 'Carol Mackie'. Author's design, Marous garden, Ohio.

Plate 126. *Daphne ×burkwoodii* 'Carol Mackie' with *Heuchera micrantha* var. *diversifolia* 'Palace Purple'. Author's design, Marous garden, Ohio.

Plate 127. Ornamental lighting harmonizes with this combination of *Rhododendron* 'Mist Maiden', *Hosta* 'Fragrant Blue', and *Geranium renardii*. Escort Lighting; author's design, Marous garden, Ohio.

Hardly any pest or disease problems occur, as resistant plants were chosen, the soil is healthy, and the plants are stress-free. Diatomaceous earth is sometimes needed for slugs but very seldom. No chemicals are used for pests or disease or the herbaceous material. The only pest control that is normally needed is an application of dormant horticultural oil in the spring, to prevent mites and scale on the hemlocks. Woolly adelgid is more prominent in the Northeast but not a problem for us in the Midwest. Occasionally, black vine weevil is a slight problem, in which case a very low concentration of a low-toxicity pyrethrum is used; biological control with parasitic nematodes would be a very feasible alternative in this well-maintained, sheltered ecosystem. Persistent rabbits are captured and released as far away as possible.

Maintenance of herbaceous plant material requires only about one and a half hours of labor every other week through the season. Spring and autumn cleanups require approximately three hours of labor each. The arbor company that worked from the start of the project to help preserve the existing trees continues to maintain the trees as well as the woody landscape material. This requires less than 30 minutes in the spring and autumn, with occasional monitoring through the summer, along with the rest of the property. Acid-loving woody plants, such as the Canadian hemlocks (4), rhododendrons (13–14), hollies (9–11), and sweetbay magnolia (3), are treated with sulfur and ferous sulfate in the spring and autumn. The other flowering trees and shrubs are fertilized with a general-purpose fertilizer in the autumn when dormant. As you will note, the garden does not require a high maintenance schedule to keep it looking and performing great. Best of all, it is environmentally sound.

Flower color is abundant but foliage color, form, and texture are really key elements in this garden, as is the case in most shade gardens. Cool spring colors from numerous woodland species and bulbs, splashed with warm colors for focal interest, are followed by even warmer summer colors. In the summer, bolder shapes and textures and larger-sized herbaceous plants also come into play, tamed by varied soft and colorful foliage. Autumn is welcomed with rich golds and tans spotted with pinks from Japanese anemones (21–22), an echo of the earlier spring palette.

Plate 128. Unusual is the best way to describe *Arisaema sikokianum*. Marous garden, Ohio.

Plate 129. *Clematis* 'Hagley Hybrid' with *Arisaema sikokianum* and *Heuchera micrantha* var. *diversifolia* 'Palace Purple'. Escort Lighting; author's design, Marous garden, Ohio.

Plate 130. *Pulmonaria* 'Majesté' photographed in August. Note its spectacular clean foliage. Also featuring *Mazus reptans*. Author's design, Marous garden, Ohio.

Winter stands structurally strong, outlined with deep green Canadian hemlocks (4) and the evergreen leaves of both herbaceous and woody plants, and colored with red and green from the Meserve holly (11). The dark screen of hemlocks works effectively through all seasons to reduce the feeling of space, thus creating more intimacy in this garden. Lines of the seedheads from the ornamental grasses (31–32, 57), Siberian iris (50–51), and common sweetshrub (6) provide further relief from cabin fever during the cold months.

The color scheme is polychromatic. No limits were set on what colors would be used, yet there really isn't much in the yellow-orange or orange hue ranges, except for a couple of isolated pockets. One is provided by *Fuchsia* 'Gartenmeister Bonstedt' (76), near the large pot that serves as a strong focal point; another, by the bigleaf ligularia (*Ligularia dentata* 'Dark Beauty') (52). Greens, blues, pinks, and whites predominate and repeat through the garden, except in the summer, when the large mass of red from *Lobelia* 'Royal Robe' (53) becomes dominant in color, in strong vertical form, and in movement, thanks to the droves of hummingbirds surrounding it at this time.

Plant Selection: With 93 different plants in the garden, not including the plants in containers, there are many exciting and effective combinations. Underused plants prevail, although this garden contains predominantly hardy and reliable genera, species, and cultivars. As the garden matures, the vision of the design becomes more and more evident. The 7-ft. white fringetree (*Chionanthus virginicus*) (2) is spectacular, particularly when flow-

Plate 131. *Fritillaria persica*. Marous garden, Ohio.

ering, as it brings wonderful fragrance to the terrace. The 3 × 4 ft. group of *Daphne ×burkwoodii* 'Carol Mackie' (8) is stunning, and its vigor is extremely unusual for the zone 5 garden. Its fragrance is literally intoxicating.

The Meserve hollies (*Ilex ×meserveae* 'Mesog' (China girl)) (11) are 5 ft. tall and create a dynamic screen for the air conditioners. We have had a few losses with these plants in this particular section, which we've attributed to irrigation leaks; in other areas on the property, we've had great success with them. The inkberry (*Ilex glabra*) (9) is a 4-ft. specimen limbed up to reveal interesting lower branching. Reliable, small-growing *Rhododendron* 'Mist Maiden' (13) is also striking, with the white indumentum on the underside of its leaves and its dark pink buds, opening white. The

Plate 132. Dominance is set in the garden by many elements, including this large pot and the trunks of the existing trees. Featuring *Iris sibirica* 'Caesar's Brother'. Author's design, Marous garden, Ohio.

Plate 133. Design principles of order through mass collection and unity through interconnection are evident in this photograph. *Mazus reptans* is the groundcover that connects the whole. Author's design, Marous garden, Ohio.

Canadian hemlocks (4) have grown surprisingly well, as they were planted on a mound to keep the roots out of the heavy clay soil.

There are many exciting herbaceous plants as well as combinations in this design. Some of my favorites include *Arisaema sikokianum* (23) and *Geranium wlassovianum* (38), with its soft-textured foliage and repeat-blooming nature, paired with snowy wood rush (*Luzula nivea*) (54). Also of note is the unusual Japanese woodlander (*Glaucidium palmatum*) (39), with its palmately lobed leaves and poppylike mauve flowers, combined with *Trillium erectum* (72) and apricot and black tulips (91–92). The Japanese woodlander is temperamental in many ways; for one thing, it is only marginally hardy in zone 5 and really would prefer to be growing in a cooler, moister (perhaps Pacific Northwest) garden. But we like to try a few difficult species along with the tried-and-true that fill the majority of the gardens. When this spring combination dies down, it is replaced by the beautiful *Colocasia esculenta* 'Black Magic' (75) underplanted with various colorful annuals, depending on the year. *Clematis* 'Hagley Hybrid' (93) is charming growing on the obelisk with *Ipomoea tricolor* 'Heavenly Blue' (77).

To me, the best lungwort for outstanding silver foliage color that holds throughout the season without decline is *Pulmonaria* 'Majesté' (64). A striking, although marginally hardy bulb in zone 5 is *Fritillaria persica* (84), whose color and commanding vertical form add spice to the spring garden.

Design Principles: The comfortable balance between the weight of woody and herbaceous plants brings order to this design. Particularly obvious is the density that the hemlocks create as a frame to the many finer-massed groupings of herbaceous plants. The size of the terrace and the open relief it provides is an effective balance to the rest of the busy garden. The numerous drifts of perennials and annuals create mass collection, as do the shrub groupings.

Unity is provided by the connection between the stone retaining wall, the stepping-stone path, and the stone boulders. The curving lines of the terrace are also mimicked in the curve of the lines in the path and the hemlock screen.

Dominance is set in the design by the focal point of the pot, the vertical form of the obelisk in the raised bed, and by the contrasting bold forms from shrub groupings and plants such as elephant's ear (74–75), bigleaf ligularia (52), *Rodgersia pinnata* (66), and *Amorphophallus konjac* (81). Of special note is the dominance of the large existing pines and pin oak, which create a comforting overhead plane in this garden.

Repetition—of colors (blues, pinks, and, of course, greens) and of the many rounded forms from hostas and other plants—further unifies the design. Interconnection is evident throughout the lush, full planting, most strongly in the shrub groupings.

Rhythm is created through repetition of the hemlocks. Their full habit and 5-ft. spacing help slow movement in the garden they surround. The spacious stepping-stones coax visitors into meandering down the path. Plants that have been added among the stones, besides softening the path, also serve as small obstacles—they make people mindful of their movements, thus slowing the pace. One of my favorite forms of rhythm in the garden is the movement provided by the swaying of the 5-ft. meadow rue (*Thalictrum rochebruneanum*) (69) in the summer breeze.

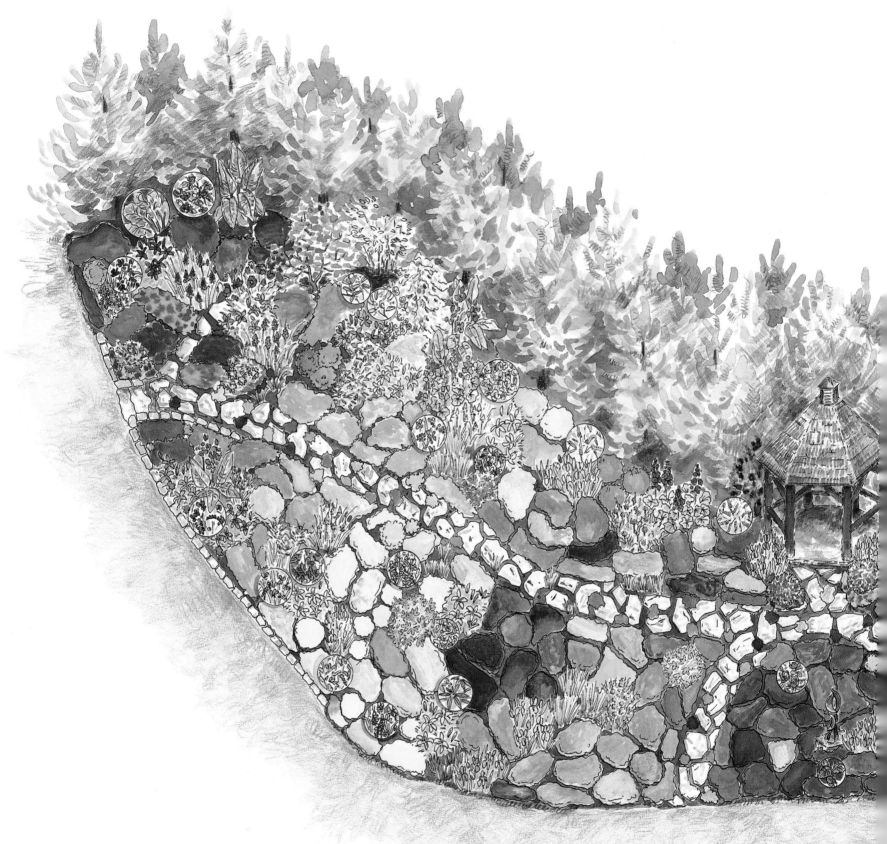

Diagram 21. Large garden: Design II, overall design. Artist, Megan H. King; author's design, Hendley garden.

DIAGRAM 21

Trees

1	(1)	*Acer griseum*	paperbark maple
2	(1)	*Acer palmatum* 'Sango-kaku'	Japanese maple
3	(1)	*Picea orientalis* 'Skylands'	oriental spruce
4	(1)	*Picea pungens* 'Iseli Foxtail'	Colorado spruce

Existing trees

E1		*Pinus strobus*	eastern white pine
E2		*Tsuga canadensis*	Canadian hemlock

Shrubs

5	(1)	*Abies procera* 'Glauca Prostrata'	noble fir
6	(1)	*Aralia elata* 'Aureovariegata'	aralia
7	(3)	*Berberis thunbergii* 'Monler' (Gold Nugget™)	Japanese barberry
8	(1)	*Berberis thunbergii* 'Monry' (Sunsation™)	Japanese barberry
9	(1)	*Berberis thunbergii* var. *atropurpurea* 'Bailtwo' (Burgundy Carousel™)	Japanese barberry
10	(1)	*Berberis thunbergii* var. *atropurpurea* 'Gentry Cultivar' (Royal Burgundy™)	Japanese barberry
11	(2)	*Berberis thunbergii* var. *atropurpurea* 'Royal Cloak'	Japanese barberry
12	(2)	*Buddleia davidii* 'Black Knight'	butterfly bush
13	(1)	*Buddleia davidii* 'Mongo' (Nanho blue)	butterfly bush
14	(1)	*Buddleia* 'Lochinch'	butterfly bush
15	(1)	*Callicarpa dichotoma* 'Issai'	purple beautyberry
16	(1)	*Caryopteris ×clandonensis* 'Longwood Blue'	bluebeard
17	(1)	*Caryopteris ×clandonensis* 'Worcester Gold'	bluebeard
18	(1)	*Chamaecyparis obtusa* 'Fernspray Gold'	Hinoki falsecypress
19	(1)	*Chamaecyparis pisifera* 'Golden Mop'	Japanese falsecypress
20	(1)	*Cotinus coggygria* 'Velvet Cloak'	smokebush
21	(1)	*Genista tinctoria* 'Royal Gold'	common woadwaxen
22	(1)	*Hypericum androsaemum* 'Albury Purple'	st. johnswort
23	(1)	*Ilex* 'Apollo'	winterberry holly
24	(2)	*Ilex verticillata* 'Afterglow'	winterberry holly
25	(3)	*Ilex verticillata* 'Christmas Cheer'	winterberry holly
26	(1)	*Ilex verticillata* 'Jim Dandy'	winterberry holly
27	(1)	*Ilex verticillata* 'Winter Red'	winterberry holly
28	(1)	*Picea abies* 'Mucronata'	Norway spruce
29	(1)	*Picea alcoquiana* 'Howell's Tigertail'	Alcock spruce
30	(3)	*Potentilla fruticosa* 'Sunset'	bush cinquefoil
31	(1)	*Rosa* 'Alchymist'	rose
32	(1)	*Rosa* 'Ausbuff' (English Garden®)	rose
33	(1)	*Rosa* 'Ausmas' (Graham Thomas®)	rose
34	(3)	*Rosa* 'Aussaucer' (Evelyn®)	rose
35	(1)	*Rosa* 'Ausvelvet' (The Prince®)	rose
36	(1)	*Rosa* 'Champlain'	rose
37	(1)	*Rosa* 'F. J. Grootendorst'	rose
38	(1)	*Rosa ×harisonii* 'Harison's Yellow'	rose
39	(1)	*Rosa* 'Nuits de Young'	rose
40	(1)	*Rosa* 'Scrivluv' (Baby Love®)	rose
41	(1)	*Sambucus racemosa* 'Sutherland Gold'	gold-leaved European red elder
42	(1)	*Vitex agnus-castus* var. *latifolia*	chastetree
43	(1)	*Yucca filamentosa* 'Color Guard'	yucca

Perennials

44	(3)	*Achillea* 'Anblo' (Anthea)	yarrow
45	(3)	*Achillea filipendulina* 'Altgold'	fernleaf yarrow
46	(3)	*Achillea* 'Heidi'	yarrow
47	(3)	*Achillea* 'Salmon Beauty'	yarrow
48	(6)	*Aconitum* 'Bressingham Spire'	monkshood
49	(6)	*Aconitum* 'Ivorine'	monkshood
50	(6)	*Aconitum lycoctonum* ssp. *neapolitanum*	monkshood
51	(3)	*Acorus gramineus* 'Ogon'	sweet flag
52	(3)	*Agastache* 'Blue Fortune'	anise hyssop
53	(6)	*Agastache rupestris*	rock anise hyssop
54	(6)	*Ajuga reptans* 'Purple Torch'	bugleweed
55	(3)	*Alcea rosea* 'Peaches and Dreams'	hollyhock
56	(3)	*Alcea rosea* 'The Watchman'	hollyhock
57	(5)	*Alcea rugosa*	Russian hollyhock
58	(11)	*Alchemilla mollis*	lady's mantle
59	(5)	*Alstroemeria* 'Sweet Laura'	Peruvian lily
60	(1)	*Amsonia hubrichtii*	Arkansas amsonia
61	(3)	*Anthriscus sylvestris* 'Ravenswing'	anthriscus
62	(3)	*Aquilegia alpina*	alpine columbine
63	(8)	*Aquilegia vulgaris* var. *stellata* 'Black Barlow'	columbine
64	(1)	*Arisaema sikokianum*	jack-in-the-pulpit
65	(6)	*Artemisia absinthium* 'Lambrook Silver'	artemisia
66	(3)	*Artemisia* 'Huntington'	artemisia
67	(6)	*Asclepias tuberosa*	butterfly weed
68	(3)	*Asclepias tuberosa* 'Hello Yellow'	butterfly weed
69	(3)	*Aster* 'Climax'	aster
70	(3)	*Aster laevis* 'Bluebird'	smooth aster
71	(3)	*Aster novae-angliae* 'Hella Lacy'	New England aster
72	(3)	*Aster novae-angliae* 'Hillside'	New England aster
73	(3)	*Aster novae-angliae* 'Purple Dome'	New England aster
74	(3)	*Aster novae-angliae* 'Wild Light Blue'	New England aster
75	(3)	*Aster oblongifolius* var. *angustatus* 'Raydon's Favorite'	Raydon's aster
76	(3)	*Aster tataricus* 'Jindai'	Tatarian aster
77	(1)	*Baptisia australis*	blue wild indigo
78	(1)	*Baptisia* 'Purple Smoke'	wild indigo
79	(1)	*Baptisia sphaerocarpa*	yellow wild indigo
80	(4)	*Belamcanda chinensis*	blackberry lily
81	(6)	*Belamcanda chinensis* 'Hello Yellow'	blackberry lily
82	(1)	*Buphthalmum speciosum*	scented oxeye

(*continued on next page*)

(plant list cont.)

83	(3)	*Calamagrostis* ×*acutiflora* 'Karl Foerster'	feather reed grass
84	(3)	*Campanula* 'Birch Hybrid'	bellflower
85	(3)	*Campanula* 'Constellation'	bellflower
86	(6)	*Campanula* 'Dwarf Tornado'	bellflower
87	(3)	*Campanula persicifolia* 'Chettle Charm'	peachleaf bellflower
88	(3)	*Campanula rapunculoides*	bellflower
89	(6)	*Campanula rotundifolia* 'Olympica'	Scotch bluebell
90	(3)	*Carex buchananii*	leatherleaf sedge
91	(7)	*Carex elata* 'Aurea (Bowles' golden)	tufted sedge
92	(5)	*Carex morrowii* 'Ice Dance'	sedge
93	(3)	*Centaurea montana*	mountain bluet
94	(1)	*Cephalaria gigantea*	Tatarian cephalaria
95	(3)	*Ceratostigma plumbaginoides*	plumbago
96	(3)	*Chrysanthemum* 'Pumpkin Harvest'	mum
97	(3)	*Chrysanthemum* 'Single Apricot'	mum
98	(3)	*Chrysanthemum* 'Single Peach'	mum
99	(3)	*Chrysanthemum* 'Viette's Apricot Glow'	mum
100	(3)	*Cimicifuga ramosa* 'Hillside Black Beauty'	bugbane
101	(3)	*Clematis integrifolia*	solitary clematis
102	(3)	*Coreopsis auriculata*	mouse ear coreopsis
103	(3)	*Coreopsis grandiflora* 'Walcoreop' (flying saucers)	tickseed
104	(1)	*Coreopsis tripteris*	tall coreopsis
105	(3)	*Coreopsis verticillata* 'Zagreb'	threadleaf coreopsis
106	(5)	*Crocosmia* ×*crocosmiiflora* 'Norwich Canary'	crocosmia
107	(7)	*Crocosmia* ×*crocosmiiflora* 'Solfatare'	crocosmia
108	(10)	*Crocosmia* ×*crocosmiiflora* 'Venus'	crocosmia
109	(14)	*Crocosmia* 'Emberglow'	crocosmia
110	(12)	*Crocosmia* 'Lucifer'	crocosmia
111	(6)	*Cryptotaenia japonica* f. *atropurpurea*	cryptotaenia
112	(5)	*Cynoglossum amabile* 'Firmament'	Chinese forget-me-not
113	(15)	*Delphinium* ×*bellamosum*	delphinium
114	(3)	*Delphinium* 'Centurion Sky Blue'	delphinium
115	(14)	*Delphinium exaltatum*	delphinium
116	(3)	*Deschampsia cespitosa* 'Goldgehänge'	tufted hair grass
117	(3)	*Dianthus* ×*allwoodii* 'Danielle Marie'	Allwood pink
118	(3)	*Dianthus barbatus* 'Sooty'	sweet william
119	(3)	*Dianthus deltoides* 'Leuchtfunk' (flashing light)	maiden pink
120	(18)	*Digitalis grandiflora*	yellow foxglove
121	(5)	*Digitalis lutea*	straw foxglove
122	(3)	*Digitalis purpurea* 'Apricot'	foxglove
123	(3)	*Echinops bannaticus* 'Taplow Blue'	globe thistle
124	(3)	*Echinops ritro* 'Blue Glow'	globe thistle
125	(3)	*Echinops ritro* 'Veitch's Blue'	globe thistle
126	(7)	*Epimedium davidii*	barrenwort
127	(5)	*Epimedium* ×*warleyense*	barrenwort
128	(6)	*Eryngium amethystinum*	sea holly
129	(3)	*Eryngium planum* 'Blaukappe'	sea holly
130	(3)	*Euphorbia amygdaloides* 'Purpurea'	purple wood spurge
131	(3)	*Euphorbia dulcis* 'Chameleon'	spurge
132	(6)	*Euphorbia griffithii* 'Fireglow'	Griffith's spurge
133	(3)	*Euphorbia polychroma*	cushion spurge
134	(3)	*Festuca glauca* 'Elijah Blue'	blue fescue
135	(3)	*Festuca glauca* 'Golden Toupee'	blue fescue
136	(6)	*Foeniculum vulgare* 'Purpureum'	copper fennel
137	(6)	*Galega* ×*hartlandii* 'Lady Wilson'	goat's rue
138	(8)	*Gentiana septemfida* var. *lagodechiana*	gentian
139	(3)	*Gentiana triflora* 'Royal Blue'	gentian
140	(6)	*Geranium* 'Ann Folkard'	hardy geranium
141	(6)	*Geranium* 'Brookside'	meadow cranesbill
142	(3)	*Geranium himalayense* 'Plenum'	lilac cranesbill
143	(3)	*Geranium* ×*magnificum*	showy geranium
144	(3)	*Geranium phaeum* 'Lily Lovell'	hardy geranium
145	(9)	*Geranium phaeum* 'Samobor'	hardy geranium
146	(6)	*Geranium* 'Phillippe Vapelle'	hardy geranium
147	(5)	*Geranium platypetalum*	broad-petaled geranium
148	(3)	*Geranium pratense* 'Mrs. Kendall Clark'	meadow cranesbill
149	(3)	*Geranium psilostemon*	Armenian geranium
150	(3)	*Geranium sanguineum* 'New Hampshire'	blood-red geranium
151	(5)	*Gladiolus* ×*gandavensis*	gladiolus
152	(7)	*Gladiolus* ×*gandavensis* 'Boone'	gladiolus
153	(3)	*Hakonechloa macra* 'Aureola'	golden-variegated Hakone grass
154	(3)	*Helenium* 'Kugelsonne'	common sneezeweed
155	(8)	*Helenium* 'Moerheim Beauty'	common sneezeweed
156	(3)	*Helianthemum* (double yellow)	sunrose
157	(6)	*Helianthemum* 'Fire Dragon'	sunrose
158	(2)	*Helianthus* 'Lemon Queen'	swamp sunflower
159	(1)	*Helianthus* 'Mellow Yellow'	swamp sunflower
160	(3)	*Helianthus salicifolius*	willow-leaved sunflower
161	(9)	*Helictotrichon sempervirens* 'Saphirsprudel' (sapphire fountain)	blue oat grass
162	(3)	*Heliopsis helianthoides* var. *scabra* 'Sommersonne' (summer sun)	heliopsis
163	(6)	*Helleborus* Royal Heritage™	lenten rose
164	(5)	*Helleborus orientalis* (single black)	lenten rose
165	(3)	*Hemerocallis* 'Alluring Peach'	daylily
166	(3)	*Hemerocallis* 'Carefree Peach'	daylily
167	(3)	*Hemerocallis* 'Peach Fairy'	daylily
168	(3)	*Hemerocallis* 'Red Razzamatazz'	daylily
169	(3)	*Hemerocallis* 'Scarlet Romance'	daylily
170	(3)	*Hemerocallis* 'Siloam Royal Prince'	daylily
171	(3)	*Hemerocallis* 'Staghorn Sumac'	daylily
172	(3)	*Hemerocallis* 'Sundried Tomatoes'	daylily
173	(3)	*Hemerocallis* 'Toy Trumpets'	daylily
174	(3)	*Hemerocallis* 'Welcome Mat'	daylily
175	(3)	*Hemerocallis* 'Yellow Lollipop'	daylily

(continued on next page)

(plant list cont.)

176	(8)	Heuchera 'Plum Pudding'	coralbells
177	(3)	Heuchera 'Velvet Night'	coralbells
178	(6)	×Heucherella 'Silver Streak'	foamy bells
179	(1)	Hibiscus moscheutos 'Lord Baltimore'	rose mallow
180	(1)	Hosta 'Big Daddy'	plantain-lily
181	(5)	Hosta 'Halcyon'	plantain-lily
182	(3)	Hosta 'Krossa Regal'	plantain-lily
183	(8)	Hosta 'Lemon Lime'	plantain-lily
184	(1)	Hosta 'Midas Touch'	plantain-lily
185	(5)	Hosta 'Paul's Glory'	plantain-lily
186	(3)	Hosta 'Sum and Substance'	plantain-lily
187	(1)	Hosta 'Sun Power'	plantain-lily
188	(3)	Hyssopus officinalis	hyssop
189	(7)	Impatiens omeiana	perennial impatiens
190	(5)	Imperata cylindrica var. koenigii 'Red Baron'	Japanese blood grass
191	(3)	Iris foetidissima	stinking iris
192	(13)	Iris pallida 'Variegata'	sweet iris
193	(3)	Iris sibirica 'Butter and Sugar'	Siberian iris
194	(3)	Iris sibirica 'Caesar's Brother'	Siberian iris
195	(5)	Iris sibirica 'Dianne's Daughter'	Siberian iris
196	(3)	Iris sibirica 'Orville Fay'	Siberian iris
197	(6)	Iris sibirica 'Pirate Prince'	Siberian iris
198	(3)	Iris sibirica 'Skywings'	Siberian iris
199	(3)	Iris sibirica 'Vi Luihn'	Siberian iris
200	(3)	Iris 'Sugar Blues'	bearded iris
201	(3)	Knautia macedonica	knautia
202	(6)	Kniphofia 'Alcazar'	red-hot poker
203	(6)	Kniphofia citrina	red-hot poker
204	(3)	Kniphofia 'Little Maid'	red-hot poker
205	(3)	Kniphofia 'Primrose Beauty'	red-hot poker
206	(3)	Kniphofia 'Royal Standard'	red-hot poker
207	(6)	Kniphofia 'Shining Sceptre'	red-hot poker
208	(3)	Lavandula ×intermedia 'Grosso'	lavender
209	(3)	Liatris spicata 'Kobold'	spike gayfeather
210	(1)	Ligularia wilsoniana	ligularia
211	(5)	Lilium 'Connecticut King'	lily
212	(3)	Lilium 'Conquistador'	lily
213	(9)	Lilium 'Eden's Dandy'	lily
214	(14)	Lilium 'Grand Cru'	lily
215	(7)	Lilium henryi	Henry's lily
216	(12)	Lilium 'Montenegro'	lily
217	(6)	Lilium 'Pretender'	lily
218	(6)	Lilium 'Royal Justice'	lily
219	(6)	Lilium 'Royal Perfume'	lily
220	(6)	Lilium 'Scarlet Emperor'	lily
221	(12)	Lilium 'Shirley'	lily
222	(6)	Lilium 'Sunset'	lily
223	(3)	Limonium platyphyllum 'Violetta'	sea lavender
224	(5)	Linum perenne 'Blau Saphir' (blue sapphire)	perennial flax
225	(8)	Lobelia 'Purple Towers'	lobelia
226	(13)	Lobelia 'Queen Victoria'	lobelia
227	(3)	Lobelia 'Ruby Slippers'	lobelia
228	(5)	Lobelia siphilitica	lobelia
229	(5)	Lychnis ×arkwrightii 'Vesuvius'	Arkwright's campion
230	(3)	Lychnis cognata	campion
231	(2)	Lysimachia nummularia 'Aurea'	golden creeping jenny
232	(3)	Miscanthus 'Purpurascens'	miscanthus
233	(1)	Monarda 'Jacob Cline'	beebalm
234	(1)	Monarda 'Violet Queen'	beebalm
235	(3)	Nepeta ×faassenii	catmint
236	(3)	Nepeta grandiflora 'Bramdean'	catmint
237	(3)	Nepeta racemosa 'Walker's Low'	catmint
238	(6)	Nepeta sibirica 'Souvenir d'André Chaudron'	catmint
239	(3)	Nepeta 'Six Hills Giant'	catmint
240	(5)	Oenothera fruticosa ssp. glauca 'Sonnenwende'	sundrops
241	(3)	Origanum laevigatum 'Herrenhausen'	oregano
242	(3)	Origanum vulgare 'Aureum'	oregano
243	(3)	Packera aurea (Senecio aureus)	golden ragwort
244	(1)	Paeonia 'America'	peony
245	(1)	Paeonia 'Coral Sunset'	peony
246	(1)	Paeonia 'Etched Salmon'	peony
247	(1)	Paeonia 'Prairie Moon'	peony
248	(2)	Panicum virgatum 'Dallas Blues'	switch grass
249	(3)	Panicum virgatum 'Heavy Metal'	switch grass
250	(3)	Papaver orientale 'Derwisch'	oriental poppy
251	(3)	Papaver orientale 'Patty's Plum'	oriental poppy
252	(5)	Papaver orientale 'Prince of Orange'	oriental poppy
253	(6)	Papaver orientale 'Turkenlouis'	oriental poppy
254	(3)	Patrinia scabiosifolia	patrinia
255	(3)	Pennisetum alopecuroides 'Hameln'	fountain grass
256	(3)	Perovskia atriplicifolia	Russian sage
257	(3)	Phlomis russeliana	Jerusalem sage
258	(5)	Phlox divaricata 'Dirigo Ice'	woodland phlox
259	(10)	Phlox divaricata ssp. laphamii	woodland phlox
260	(3)	Phlox paniculata 'Katherine'	border phlox
261	(3)	Phlox paniculata 'Laura'	border phlox
262	(3)	Phlox paniculata 'Orange Perfection'	border phlox
263	(3)	Phlox paniculata 'Tenor'	border phlox
264	(3)	Phlox paniculata 'The King'	border phlox
265	(1)	Phytolacca polyandra	pokeweed
266	(3)	Plantago major 'Rubrifolia'	plantain
267	(3)	Platycodon grandiflorus 'Double Blue'	balloon flower
268	(3)	Platycodon grandiflorus 'Komachi'	balloon flower
269	(6)	Polemonium caeruleum 'Blanjou' (brise d'Anjou)	jacob's ladder
270	(3)	Rheum palmatum var. tanguticum	ornamental rhubarb
271	(3)	Rudbeckia maxima	giant coneflower

(continued on next page)

(plant list cont.)

272	(6)	*Rumex sanguineus*	bloody dock
273	(6)	*Ruta graveolens* 'Blue Beauty'	common rue
274	(3)	*Salvia argentea*	silver sage
275	(1)	*Salvia azurea* var. *pitcheri*	azure sage
276	(3)	*Salvia nemorosa* 'Ostfriesland' (East Friesland)	perennial salvia
277	(3)	*Salvia nemorosa* 'Pusztaflamme' (plumosa)	perennial salvia
278	(3)	*Salvia* ×*sylvestris* 'Blauhügel' (blue hill)	perennial salvia
279	(3)	*Salvia* ×*sylvestris* 'Blaukönigin' (blue queen)	perennial salvia
280	(3)	*Salvia* ×*sylvestris* 'Mainacht' (May night)	perennial salvia
281	(3)	*Salvia* ×*sylvestris* 'Viola Klose'	perennial salvia
282	(3)	*Salvia verticillata* 'Purple Rain'	perennial salvia
283	(3)	*Sanguisorba tenuifolia* 'Purpurea'	purple burnet
284	(5)	*Saruma henryi*	saruma
285	(5)	*Scabiosa* Butterfly Blue®	pincushion flower
286	(3)	*Scabiosa columbaria* var. *ochroleuca*	cream pincushion flower
287	(3)	*Schizachyrium scoparium* 'The Blues'	little bluestem
288	(3)	*Sedum acre* 'Aureum'	sedum
289	(3)	*Sedum* 'Pork and Beans'	sedum
290	(3)	*Sedum telephium* ssp. *maximum* 'Atropurpureum'	sedum
291	(7)	*Silene regia*	wild pink
292	(5)	*Sisyrinchium bermudianum*	blue-eyed grass
293	(7)	*Sisyrinchium* 'Quaint and Queer'	blue-eyed grass
294	(3)	*Solidago* 'Golden Spangles'	goldenrod
295	(3)	*Solidago rugosa* 'Fireworks'	goldenrod
296	(3)	×*Solidaster luteus* 'Lemore'	golden aster
297	(3)	*Sorghastrum nutans* 'Sioux Blue'	Indian grass
298	(3)	*Stachys byzantina*	lamb's ear
299	(6)	*Stachys byzantina* 'Countess Helen von Stein'	lamb's ear
300	(6)	*Stachys byzantina* 'Primrose Heron'	lamb's ear
301	(3)	*Stokesia laevis* 'Klaus Jelitto'	Stokes' aster
302	(9)	*Stokesia laevis* 'Mary Gregory'	Stokes' aster
303	(5)	*Stokesia laevis* 'Omega Skyrocket'	Stokes' aster
304	(8)	*Stokesia laevis* 'Purple Parasols'	Stokes' aster
305	(7)	*Stylophorum diphyllum*	wood poppy
306	(6)	*Symphytum* 'Goldsmith'	comfrey
307	(3)	*Tanacetum* 'Golden Feathers'	tansy
308	(3)	*Thalictrum rochebruneanum*	lavender mist meadow rue
309	(3)	*Thermopsis villosa*	southern lupine
310	(3)	*Thymus* ×*citriodorus* 'Lemon Green'	lemon thyme
311	(3)	*Thymus pseudolanuginosus*	woolly thyme
312	(6)	*Tiarella cordifolia* 'Ninja'	foamflower
313	(3)	*Tradescantia* (Andersoniana Group) 'Purple Profusion'	spiderwort
314	(6)	*Verbascum* 'Jackie'	mullein
315	(3)	*Veronica austriaca* ssp. *teucrium* 'Crater Lake Blue'	Hungarian speedwell
316	(3)	*Veronica gentianoides* 'Nana'	gentian speedwell
317	(3)	*Veronica peduncularis* 'Georgia Blue'	speedwell
318	(3)	*Veronica prostrata* 'Trehane'	harebell speedwell
319	(3)	*Veronica repens* 'Sunshine'	golden creeping speedwell
320	(3)	*Veronica spicata* 'Blue Charm'	spike speedwell
321	(3)	*Veronica* 'Waterperry Blue'	speedwell
322	(14)	*Viola* 'Molly Sanderson'	violet
323	(5)	*Viola* 'Purple Showers'	violet

Annuals

324	(5)	*Alstroemeria aurea* 'Orange King'	Peruvian lily
325	(11)	*Alstroemeria psittacina*	parrot lily
326	(3)	*Alternanthera dentata* 'Rubiginosa'	joseph's coat
327	(5)	*Angelonia* 'Blue Pacific'	angelonia
328	(5)	*Antirrhinum majus* 'Rocket Red'	snapdragon
329	(7)	*Arctotis* ×*hybrida* 'Dark Red'	African daisy
330	(3)	*Arctotis* ×*hybrida* 'Flame'	African daisy
331	(14)	*Atriplex hortensis* var. *rubra*	mountain spinach
332	(3)	*Beta vulgaris* 'Golden'	Swiss chard
333	(3)	*Beta vulgaris* 'Ruby Queen'	Swiss chard
334	(12)	*Bouvardia ternifolia*	scarlet trompetilla
335	(7)	*Caladium* 'Florida Cardinal'	caladium
336	(5)	*Calendula officinalis* 'Orange King'	pot marigold
337	(3)	*Canna* 'Black Knight'	canna
338	(1)	*Canna indica* 'Red Stripe' (purpurea)	canna
339	(3)	*Canna* 'Omega'	canna
340	(3)	*Canna* 'Orange Punch'	canna
341	(1)	*Canna* 'Panache'	canna
342	(1)	*Canna* 'Phasion'	canna
343	(3)	*Canna* 'Roi Humbert' (red King Humbert)	canna
344	(3)	*Celosia spicata* 'Flamingo Purple'	celosia
345	(3)	*Centaurea cineraria*	knapweed
346	(16)	*Cerinthe major* 'Purpurascens'	cerinthe
347	(1)	*Colocasia esculenta* 'Fontanesii'	elephant's ear
348	(15)	*Consolida ajacis* 'Blue Spire'	larkspur
349	(7)	*Cosmos atrosanguineus*	cosmos
350	(1)	*Cynara cardunculus*	cardoon
351	(3)	*Dahlia* 'Arabian Night'	dahlia
352	(2)	*Dahlia* 'Bishop of Llandaff'	dahlia
353	(2)	*Dahlia* 'Ellen Houston'	dahlia
354	(3)	*Dahlia* 'Orange Nugget'	dahlia
355	(3)	*Dahlia* 'Susette'	dahlia
356	(1)	*Eucomis comosa* 'Sparkling Burgundy'	pineapple lily
357	(3)	*Hedychium coccineum*	red ginger lily
358	(3)	*Helichrysum petiolare* 'Limelight'	licorice plant
359	(3)	*Hibiscus acetosella* 'Red Shield'	hibiscus
360	(3)	*Ipomoea batatas* 'Blackie'	sweet potato vine
361	(6)	*Ipomoea batatas* 'Margarita'	sweet potato vine
362	(3)	*Lablab purpureus*	purple hyacinth bean
363	(7)	*Lactuca* 'Merlot'	lettuce
364	(6)	*Leonotis menthifolia*	leonotis
365	(3)	*Lysimachia congestiflora* 'Variegata'	variegated lysimachia

(continued on next page)

(*plant list cont.*)

366	(7)	*Melampodium paludosum* 'Million Gold'	melampodium
367	(3)	*Nicotiana langsdorffii*	flowering tobacco
368	(5)	*Papaver rhoeas*	corn poppy
369	(6)	*Papaver somniferum* 'Burnt Orange'	opium poppy
370	(5)	*Papaver somniferum* 'Lauren's Grape'	opium poppy
371	(3)	*Pennisetum setaceum* 'Rubrum'	purple fountain grass
372	(8)	*Perilla frutescens* var. *crispa*	perilla
373	(2)	*Phormium* 'Bronze Baby'	New Zealand flax
374	(3)	*Plectranthus argentatus*	plectranthus
375	(5)	*Portulaca grandiflora* 'Sundial Peach'	moss rose
376	(3)	*Ricinus communis* 'Carmencita'	castor bean
377	(3)	*Salvia coccinea* 'Lady in Red'	salvia
378	(1)	*Salvia guaranitica*	salvia
379	(2)	*Salvia* 'Indigo Spires'	salvia
380	(1)	*Salvia leucantha*	salvia
381	(5)	*Salvia patens*	salvia
382	(1)	*Salvia* 'Purple Majesty'	salvia
383	(5)	*Scabiosa atropurpurea* 'Ace of Spades'	pincushion flower
384	(8)	*Solenostemon* 'Burgundy Giant'	coleus
385	(7)	*Solenostemon* 'Olive'	coleus
386	(5)	*Solenostemon* 'Saturn'	coleus
387	(5)	*Tropaeolum majus* 'Alaska Salmon Orange'	nasturtium
388	(8)	*Tropaeolum majus* 'Apricot Trifle'	nasturtium
389	(3)	*Verbena bonariensis*	tall verbena
390	(9)	*Verbena* 'Romance Apricot'	verbena
391	(5)	*Verbena* Temari® Red	verbena
392	(5)	*Zinnia haageana* 'Orange Star'	zinnia

Bulbs

393	(3)	*Agapanthus* 'Bressingham Blue'	lily of the Nile
394	(25)	*Allium caeruleum*	blue globe onion
395	(25)	*Allium carinatum* ssp. *pulchellum*	keeled garlic
396	(5)	*Allium cristophii*	downy onion

397	(25)	*Allium hollandicum* (*aflatunense*) 'Purple Sensation'	ornamental onion
398	(50)	*Allium moly* 'Jeannine'	lily leek
399	(100)	*Allium sphaerocephalon*	drumstick allium
400	(10)	*Camassia leichtlinii* ssp. *suksdorfii* 'Blauwe Donau' (blue Danube)	camass
401	(10)	*Dichelostemma ida-maia*	firecracker flower
402	(5)	*Eremurus* ×*isabellinus* 'Pinokkio'	foxtail lily
403	(5)	*Fritillaria persica*	fritillary
404	(28)	*Hymenocallis* 'Sulphur Queen'	Peruvian daffodil
405	(15)	*Scadoxus multiflorus*	blood lily
406	(18)	*Tigridia pavonia* 'Speciosa'	tiger flower
407	(50)	*Tulipa* 'Apricot Parrot'	tulip
408	(25)	*Tulipa* 'Big Smile'	tulip
409	(100)	*Tulipa* 'Black Parrot'	tulip
410	(50)	*Tulipa* 'Blue Heron'	tulip
411	(25)	*Tulipa* 'Blue Parrot'	tulip
412	(75)	*Tulipa* 'Blushing Lady'	tulip
413	(50)	*Tulipa* 'Burgundy Lace'	tulip
414	(25)	*Tulipa* 'Carmine Parrot'	tulip
415	(25)	*Tulipa* 'Couleur Cardinal'	tulip
416	(25)	*Tulipa* 'Fringed Elegance'	tulip
417	(25)	*Tulipa* 'Queen of Night'	tulip
418	(50)	*Tulipa* 'Temple of Beauty'	tulip
419	(25)	*Tulipa* 'Uncle Tom'	tulip

Vines

420	(1)	*Campsis* ×*tagliabuana* 'Madame Galen'	trumpet creeper
421	(1)	*Clematis* 'Royal Velours'	clematis
422	(1)	*Humulus lupulus* 'Bianca'	golden hops
423	(1)	*Lonicera sempervirens* 'Blanche Sandman'	honeysuckle
424	(1)	*Passiflora incarnata*	wild passion flower
425	(1)	*Vitis vinifera* 'Purpurea'	purple-leaved grape

This garden is by far the most creatively stimulating project I have worked on. In many ways it has also been one of the most challenging—obviously, not a typical garden for just anyone to try at home. Yet the lessons to be garnered from it are countless, regardless of your garden's size or your budget or time constraints. Don't let its size or detail intimidate. Rather, let it inspire. Take your time getting to know this garden—the effort will be well rewarded. Many of the selected plants are on the hardiness borderline, new for this area, or just generally experimental in nature. It is an educational garden, for all who were involved and for all that experience it. The client has established his entire garden (these mixed borders included) as a trust that will one day be open to the public.

These borders, a renovation of existing herbaceous borders, required 150-plus hours of design time alone and countless hours of consulting in preparation for the design, of ordering, and of installation—to say nothing of the labor involved to make this project happen and to continue to maintain it. Follow-up recommendations continue years after. But as a fellow gardener with a passion for plants and everything involved with them, can you think of many better ways in life to use one's time or efforts? I can't. We will look at this design as a whole, for the design process is the same for all gardens, large or small. Then let's break this Dalai Lama down into digestible pieces. We have broken the large border into five sections; a shade border is shown separately.

Plate 134. A diverse and beautiful mixed garden combining over 2,400 plants from 188 genera. View from the south end facing north. Author's design, Hendley garden, Ohio; photograph by Ian Adams.

Site: These borders are within three acres of spectacular woodland gardens in a small neighborhood in Zanesville, Ohio. Driving by, one would never guess that such gardens exist behind the trees that surround the property. Although officially a zone 5 garden, these borders appear to be in a more protected microclimate that successfully sustains many zone 6 plants.

To be in proper proportion with the surrounding gardens, these borders needed to be large in scale—they total approximately 6,000 sq. ft. The large border is in full sun and is approximately 170 ft. long and 22–34 ft. wide. The smaller border, in shade and partial shade, is just less than 100 ft. long and 4–8 ft. wide.

Renovation began a year before installation. Existing plant material was evaluated and recorded through the entire growing season, so that we could decide whether a given plant would be saved, given away, or simply destroyed. Although there were many desirable plants in the garden, many had been overrun with weeds; other, aggressive perennials had declined or simply did not fit the new design objectives. Plants to be saved were dug in the autumn and placed in holding beds; when winter arrived, they were covered with thermal blanket. Any plants remaining in the borders that were not taken by happy neighbors were sprayed several times with nonselective herbicides. The borders were also evaluated the following spring, prior to planting, to be certain all weeds had been destroyed.

Other aspects of the site, such as sun patterns and soil conditions, were also evaluated during this year. A soil test revealed a clay loam with an organic matter content of 4% and a pH of 7.0. The soil was very poorly drained in certain locations of the borders. Drainage tiles were installed. The soil was prepared in the autumn prior to installation of the plants by incorporating approximately 40 cubic yards of a compost blend and 170 bales (each 4 cubic feet) of Canadian sphagnum peat moss. Follow-up soil tests revealed we had created a loam soil with an organic matter content of 19.4%.

Since the garden was already prone to poor drainage, and given the problems that might be involved designing a system for such a variety of plants, it was decided, after much debate, that there would not be an automatic irrigation system. The head gardener would be responsible for watching the plants and setting up sprinklers as needed. The gardens actually perform better during dryer years than wet ones, so supplying a great deal of water to sustain them has never been the priority—just the opposite is true. The only regular supplemental irrigation is along the front of the white pine screen, as they take a great deal of moisture from the area.

Objectives: Because of the size and diversity of the gardens, maintenance is quite involved. The plants don't require spraying for pest or disease control, but my assistant and I work anywhere from five to eight hours, one day a week, in the garden during the summer months, pruning and staking the herbaceous perennials. Two part-time gardeners may help periodically, particularly at planting times. Because the soil is high in organic matter, very little supplemental fertilizing is needed, except for feeding the annuals with an organic fertilizer twice a month.

Another area that requires a good deal of time is simply managing the garden to keep the integrity of the design. This type of monitoring and record keeping is vital to all mixed gardens, no matter the size, but particularly for one of this great diversity and detail. As a designer, I am blessed to have a client who cares so much about the garden, who cares that it fulfill its intended vision. This is rare—the best designs are too often let go, only to be lost over the years.

In the spring, several times through the summer, and again in the autumn, we evaluate the entire garden, noting the overall performance or color of the plants, recording losses, and deciding what we'll need to order. Gardening is often experimental and ever evolving; in the case of this garden, we are always evaluating a plant, gauging it to see if, for some reason or another, it just hasn't prospered. Mind, it may prosper in the same border, 5 ft. away! We often scratch our heads in amazement at both what is not doing well, and what—unexpectedly—is flourishing.

Ordering for this garden, be it a substitution for one species or simply a replacement, is often a nightmare. We may lose one plant here, two plants there, certain plants may no longer be available, and so on. We persevere, though, always with the big picture in mind: this is a unique and educational garden, and if we'd wanted it to be easy, we could have massed rudbeckia and autumn joy sedum and called it a day!

When I first met with the client, a keen plantsman and gardener, the only style objective I was given was that the garden not look like a typical American garden. I had free creative rein. The feel of the garden is of a British mixed colorist border with a touch of southern North American attitude, thanks in large part to the presence of tropicals. Tropicals were included for many reasons, but one important one is that the client's roots are in the South, and the tropicals spark childhood memories for him.

This is a designed collector's garden that in the future will function as a public trust, but as a private garden it is already used for education: busloads of tours come through on a regular basis. The fieldstone path in the large border was designed to bring these and all visitors into the garden; it allows them to be surrounded by the garden, to participate in it, rather than just to admire it from afar. It and the stepping-stone path make maintenance easier. The hut and seating area was put into place as a quiet spot for repose; the back side of the hut houses a storage shed for tools.

This is a colorist garden. Color was used in a controlled yet uninhibited fashion. Monochromatic color sections blend harmoniously into their neighbors as the colors move through the color wheel. Color on the north end of the large border starts with red, moves into orange, then peach (because I love this tint of orange and wanted entire sections of it), proceeds into yellow, softens to blue, and shifts to purple around the seating area. From this point the colors continue through the border in reverse order. Each section is designed to evoke a different mood. The warmer colors were used at the ends of the border to attract the eye, welcoming the visitor to this garden from within the larger garden. The cooler blues and purples were used around the seating area to encourage relaxation, tranquility, and inner calm.

Various tints, tones, and shades of the selected hues are not accomplished solely with flower color but with the use of colorful foliage, bark or stem color, and fruit. Foliage is key in this garden; yellow, blue, red, purple, and, of course, green foliage is repeated throughout the border, acting as unifying elements. Sometimes a plant in a contrasting color, or one close on the color wheel to the contrasting color (a split complement), was included within the various color sections to heighten the main color by simultaneous contrast.

It was great fun designing the different color sections. I was able to create 18 different monochromatic schemes, including sun and

Diagram 22. Large garden: Design II, overall color model. Artist, Megan H. King; author's design, Hendley garden.

Plate 135. The garden was designed primarily for summer and autumn interest. Trees and shrubs in the surrounding woods heighten the autumn glory. Author's design, Hendley garden, Ohio.

shade areas. This was also very challenging because it was often hard to locate true reds, blues, and peaches. No pinks and whites were used intentionally, but often something described as red or peach or purple (*Ajuga reptans* 'Purple Torch', for example) in a catalog would come into flower in an unwanted pink. Some of this was attributable to simultaneous contrast. Whatever the reason, we had to make several substitutions because the color just wasn't right.

Texture and form play a key role in the monochromatic garden. As we look at the different sections of the garden, we will see the continued orchestration of these elements in more detail.

We aimed to make the peak seasons of interest in the borders summer and autumn, because most of the rest of the garden shines in the spring. But with the varied forms, textures, and foliar tones offered, there is something of interest all through the year.

Plant Selection: This garden features more than 180 genera and over 2,400 plants, predominantly herbaceous perennials. Plants—including a wide selection of shrubs and annuals and various vines, bulbs, and trees—were procured nationwide from approximately 60 different nurseries. Many growers rallied and assisted tremendously in helping to make this project happen.

Because of the magnitude of plants ordered and the potential difficulty of locating the right plant for the right spot, for planting, the client came up with the idea to break the design into different sections within the sun and shade borders. As the orders arrived, each plant was placed in the appropriate holding area. This was a great help in the placement of the design, which still took several days.

Plate 136. Placing plants in a garden this large requires close attention to detail. Keep an eye on your measurements—or you may reach the far end of the border either out of space or out of plants. Empty pots hold the place of plants that have not yet arrived. Author's design, Hendley garden, Ohio.

Plate 137. The same view one year later. Author's design, Hendley garden, Ohio; photograph by Ian Adams.

The use of uncommon plants or common plants used in uncommon ways was my goal with this design. For one reason or another, it was my first time using some of them. For example, I would never have chosen Japanese barberries in the past, put off as I was by the poor manner in which they are commonly seen in landscapes. But in this garden, because of their interesting companions, they are much more appealing and extremely functional, providing foliar color and form (see Plate 141). Dwarf conifers appear as focal features throughout, adding weight or a vertical form where needed; they provide permanence among a sea of predominantly ephemeral treasures. Ten different disease-resistant roses were selected. Some, such as *Rosa ×harisonii* 'Harison's Yellow' and *R*. 'Scrivluv' (Baby Love®), have prospered, quickly becoming favorites, while some of the others have been slow to take hold. A sampling of the herbaceous material used would include asters, crocosmias, geraniums, daylilies, red-hot pokers, lilies, salvias, cannas, dahlias, alliums, and tulips. Various annuals that do not appear on the plant list are used from year to year as filler, if needed.

As we go through each section, I will discuss some of the key plants, but remember: you can get more information about the individual plants in Appendixes B and C.

Design Principles: Order is established with the placement of the fieldstone path, the seating area, and sculpture; the line of white pines also contributes to a sense of order. The arrange-ment of the color sections in the garden proceeds symmetrically from either side of the hut, creating subtle overall balance. Within the garden, colors, forms, and textures are asymmetrically balanced, using the two-thirds to one-third ratio—most obviously in the more numerous groupings of herbaceous plants balancing the weight of the fewer woody plants. I would have liked to make the blue sections larger, to better balance the

Plate 138. The hut, a dominant feature in the overall border, provides anchoring stability; it also functions as a meditative seating area. At its back is a small tool shed. Featuring *Helianthus salicifolius* (160), *Sorghastrum nutans* 'Sioux Blue' (297). Hut construction, Joe J. Miller Jr.; author's design, Hendley garden, Ohio; photograph by Ian Adams.

Plate 139. Plants within the fieldstone path slow the pace and sharpen one's attention to detail. Featuring *Plantago major* 'Rubrifolia' (266). Path construction, David Kridler; author's design, Hendley garden, Ohio; photograph by Ian Adams.

strong visual impact that the magnetizing yellow and (slightly less so) orange and red sections have, but since blue occurs so infrequently in flower and even foliage color, I had to keep these two sections about the same size as the others. Mass collection is evident in the drifts of herbaceous material and the masses of each color.

The individual sections of the gardens are strongly unified by monochromatic color schemes. This simplification helps the visitor take in the complexity of the whole. By repeating these color sections, the same genera in different colors, certain foliage colors, and the same types of plants, such as dwarf conifers and ornamental grasses, we unify the design as a whole.

Dominance in the overall design is apparent in the hut, which is a pivotal focal point for the entire border. The woody plants and, even more so, the large tropicals (such as the cannas, with their strong vertical form) attract and hold the eye. The warmer-colored sections, in particular the yellow sections, draw the eye. Unification through interconnection is accomplished through the lush, heavily layered planting.

Undulating rhythm, from taller to shorter plant material, is strong in the border. The fieldstone path sets a rhythm through the heart of the garden. Because one needs to be a bit careful when walking on a path, and the plants growing within it, the pace slows and attention to the detail of the garden is encouraged along the way. Various plants contribute so much movement to the border that it seems literally to dance at times.

Section 1:

This is the northern end of the border. It includes red, orange, and peach areas, and a portion of the first yellow area. The mood is bright and optimistic. We want people to feel happy to be here. A stepping-stone path is included in one of the wide parts of this section for maintenance; it also serves as a good spot to stand while explaining the surrounding plants to garden tour visitors. Besides the vertical forms provided by many of the plants, the post was installed and planted with vines to break the predominant horizontal plane. The red sections are my favorite parts of the border, and many people feel the same way. Many of their combinations really work well. Most visitors enter through this section of the border, where the abundance of contrasting red and green draws the eye and the person into the garden. The peach section was literally yummy to design, and it effectively smooths the transition from orange to yellow.

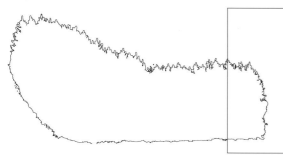

Diagram 23. Large garden: Design II, Section 1. Artist, Megan H. King; author's design, Hendley garden.

⌐————————⌐ = 6 feet

N→

Diagram 23

Trees

1	(1)	*Acer griseum*	paperbark maple

Existing trees

E1	*Pinus strobus*	eastern white pine

Shrubs

9	(1)	*Berberis thunbergii* var. *atropurpurea* 'Bailtwo' (Burgundy Carousel™)	Japanese barberry
19	(1)	*Chamaecyparis pisifera* 'Golden Mop'	Japanese falsecypress
20	(1)	*Cotinus coggygria* 'Velvet Cloak'	smokebush
22	(1)	*Hypericum androsaemum* 'Albury Purple'	st. johnswort
23	(1)	*Ilex* 'Apollo'	winterberry holly
25	(3)	*Ilex verticillata* 'Christmas Cheer'	winterberry holly
27	(1)	*Ilex verticillata* 'Winter Red'	winterberry holly
34	(3)	*Rosa* 'Aussaucer' (Evelyn®)	rose
36	(1)	*Rosa* 'Champlain'	rose
40	(1)	*Rosa* 'Scrivluv' (Baby Love®)	rose

Perennials

53	(3)	*Agastache rupestris*	rock anise hyssop
55	(3)	*Alcea rosea* 'Peaches and Dreams'	hollyhock
58	(3)	*Alchemilla mollis*	lady's mantle
67	(3)	*Asclepias tuberosa*	butterfly weed
80	(4)	*Belamcanda chinensis*	blackberry lily
83	(3)	*Calamagrostis* ×*acutiflora* 'Karl Foerster'	feather reed grass
96	(3)	*Chrysanthemum* 'Pumpkin Harvest'	mum
99	(3)	*Chrysanthemum* 'Viette's Apricot Glow'	mum
108	(5)	*Crocosmia* ×*crocosmiiflora* 'Venus'	crocosmia
109	(9)	*Crocosmia* 'Emberglow'	crocosmia
110	(7)	*Crocosmia* 'Lucifer'	crocosmia
119	(3)	*Dianthus deltoides* 'Leuchtfunk' (flashing light)	maiden pink
120	(4)	*Digitalis grandiflora*	yellow foxglove
131	(3)	*Euphorbia dulcis* 'Chameleon'	spurge
132	(3)	*Euphorbia griffithii* 'Fireglow'	Griffith's spurge
136	(3)	*Foeniculum vulgare* 'Purpureum'	copper fennel
155	(4)	*Helenium* 'Moerheim Beauty'	common sneezeweed
157	(3)	*Helianthemum* 'Fire Dragon'	sunrose
167	(3)	*Hemerocallis* 'Peach Fairy'	daylily
169	(3)	*Hemerocallis* 'Scarlet Romance'	daylily
174	(3)	*Hemerocallis* 'Welcome Mat'	daylily
190	(5)	*Imperata cylindrica* var. *koenigii* 'Red Baron'	Japanese blood grass
202	(3)	*Kniphofia* 'Alcazar'	red-hot poker
207	(3)	*Kniphofia* 'Shining Sceptre'	red-hot poker
212	(3)	*Lilium* 'Conquistador'	lily
213	(9)	*Lilium* 'Eden's Dandy'	lily
215	(7)	*Lilium henryi*	Henry's lily
216	(6)	*Lilium* 'Montenegro'	lily
220	(6)	*Lilium* 'Scarlet Emperor'	lily
232	(3)	*Miscanthus* 'Purpurascens'	miscanthus
233	(1)	*Monarda* 'Jacob Cline'	beebalm
244	(1)	*Paeonia* 'America'	peony
245	(1)	*Paeonia* 'Coral Sunset'	peony
253	(3)	*Papaver orientale* 'Turkenlouis'	oriental poppy
255	(3)	*Pennisetum alopecuroides* 'Hameln'	fountain grass
263	(3)	*Phlox paniculata* 'Tenor'	border phlox
272	(6)	*Rumex sanguineus*	bloody dock
286	(3)	*Scabiosa columbaria* var. *ochroleuca*	cream pincushion flower
288	(2)	*Sedum acre* 'Aureum'	sedum
289	(1)	*Sedum* 'Pork and Beans'	sedum
290	(3)	*Sedum telephium* ssp. *maximum* 'Atropurpureum'	sedum
295	(3)	*Solidago rugosa* 'Fireworks'	goldenrod
310	(1)	*Thymus* ×*citriodorus* 'Lemon Green'	lemon thyme
314	(3)	*Verbascum* 'Jackie'	mullein

Annuals

326	(3)	*Alternanthera dentata* 'Rubiginosa'	joseph's coat
328	(5)	*Antirrhinum majus* 'Rocket Red'	snapdragon
330	(3)	*Arctotis* ×*hybrida* 'Flame'	African daisy
333	(3)	*Beta vulgaris* 'Ruby Queen'	Swiss chard
334	(12)	*Bouvardia ternifolia*	scarlet trompetilla
336	(5)	*Calendula officinalis* 'Orange King'	pot marigold
341	(1)	*Canna* 'Panache'	canna
342	(1)	*Canna* 'Phasion'	canna
343	(3)	*Canna* 'Roi Humbert' (red King Humbert)	canna
352	(2)	*Dahlia* 'Bishop of Llandaff'	dahlia
353	(2)	*Dahlia* 'Ellen Houston'	dahlia
358	(3)	*Helichrysum petiolare* 'Limelight'	licorice plant
361	(4)	*Ipomoea batatas* 'Margarita'	sweet potato vine
368	(5)	*Papaver rhoeas*	corn poppy
369	(3)	*Papaver somniferum* 'Burnt Orange'	opium poppy
371	(3)	*Pennisetum setaceum* 'Rubrum'	purple fountain grass
373	(2)	*Phormium* 'Bronze Baby'	New Zealand flax
376	(3)	*Ricinus communis* 'Carmencita'	castor bean
386	(5)	*Solenostemon* 'Saturn'	coleus
390	(9)	*Verbena* 'Romance Apricot'	verbena
391	(5)	*Verbena* Temari® Red	verbena

Bulbs

401	(10)	*Dichelostemma ida-maia*	firecracker flower
405	(5)	*Scadoxus multiflorus*	blood lily
406	(8)	*Tigridia pavonia* 'Speciosa'	tiger flower
407	(25)	*Tulipa* 'Apricot Parrot'	tulip
412	(25)	*Tulipa* 'Blushing Lady'	tulip

(*continued on next page*)

(plant list cont.)

413	(25)	Tulipa 'Burgundy Lace'	tulip
414	(25)	*Tulipa* 'Carmine Parrot'	tulip
415	(25)	*Tulipa* 'Couleur Cardinal'	tulip

Vines

421	(1)	*Clematis* 'Royal Velours'	clematis
423	(1)	*Lonicera sempervirens* 'Blanche Sandman'	honeysuckle

Plate 141. At the north entrance to the border, reds greet the visitor. Common plants used in uncommon ways combine with more unusual plants. Featuring *Rumex sanguineus* (272), *Berberis thunbergii* var. *atropurpurea* 'Bailtwo' (Burgundy Carousel™) (9), *Papaver rhoeas* (368). Author's design, Hendley garden, Ohio.

Plate 140. A long shot of the garden from the north end facing south. Visible are reds, moving into yellow and blues. Featuring *Ricinus communis* 'Carmencita' (376). Author's design, Hendley garden, Ohio.

Plate 142. On the other side of the path, reds continue accented with yellow foliage. Red and yellow foliage act as a unifying element by repeating through the border in the different color sections. Author's design, Hendley garden, Ohio.

Plate 143. A close-up of a vignette in Plate 142. Featuring *Rumex sanguineus* (272), *Ipomoea batatas* 'Margarita' (361), *Phormium* 'Bronze Baby' (373), *Solenostemon* 'Saturn' (386), *Cotinus coggygria* 'Velvet Cloak' (20). Author's design, Hendley garden, Ohio.

Plate 144. Moving from the red into the orange section. The intense simultaneous contrast between the reds and greens is only accentuated by the wet foliage and overcast light. Featuring *Verbena* Temari® Red (391), *Belamcanda chinensis* (80), *Dahlia* 'Ellen Houston' (353). Author's design, Hendley garden, Ohio; photograph by Ian Adams.

Plate 146. Later in the season, in fruit, *Belamcanda chinensis* (80) shines. Author's design, Hendley garden, Ohio.

Plate 145. A view similar to the one shown in Plate 144 but from a bit further back and on a brighter, dry day. The reds, orange-reds, and oranges create an analogous transition between color sections. Plants as in Plate 144 with the addition of *Canna* 'Roi Humbert' (red King Humbert) (343), *Miscanthus* 'Purpurascens' (232). Author's design, Hendley garden, Ohio.

Plate 147. Color, texture, and form have equal roles in this autumn spectacle. Featuring *Dahlia* 'Ellen Houston' (353), *Miscanthus* 'Purpurascens' (232), *Ricinus communis* 'Carmencita' (376). Author's design, Hendley garden, Ohio.

Plate 148. Interplanted into the red-orange intersection for a dash of brilliance in the spring is the striking *Papaver orientale* 'Turkenlouis' (253). Also featuring *Helichrysum petiolare* 'Limelight' (358), *Alchemilla mollis* (58), *Dianthus deltoides* 'Leuchtfunk' (flashing light) (119). Author's design, Hendley garden, Ohio.

Plate 150. Natives and nonnatives fraternize throughout the garden. Featuring *Asclepias tuberosa* (67), *Bouvardia ternifolia* (334), *Helichrysum petiolare* 'Limelight' (358), *Verbena* Temari® Red (391). Author's design, Hendley garden, Ohio.

Plate 149. Coming into the oranges with *Helianthemum* 'Fire Dragon' (157), highlighted by *Helichrysum petiolare* 'Limelight' (358). Author's design, Hendley garden, Ohio.

Plate 152. Exotic is the first thing that comes to mind when people see the unbelievable red of tiger flower, *Tigridia pavonia* 'Speciosa' (406). With its fine narrow habit, this tender bulb is useful for interplanting. Author's design, Hendley garden, Ohio.

Plate 151. *Arctotis ×hybrida* 'Flame' (330) is an interesting, robust addition to the path in the orange section. Author's design, Hendley garden, Ohio.

Plate 153. *Rosa* 'Aussaucer' (Evelyn®) (34) is a highlight in the peach section. Author's design, Hendley garden, Ohio.

Plate 155. Foliage color, form, and texture rule throughout the garden. Featuring *Chamaecyparis pisifera* 'Golden Mop' (19), *Euphorbia amygdaloides* 'Purpurea' (130). Author's design, Hendley garden, Ohio.

Plate 154. Although *Verbascum* 'Jackie' (314) is short-lived and often needs replacing on an annual basis, its color, vertical form, and small stature make it a winner among peach-flowered plants. Author's design, Hendley garden, Ohio.

Plate 156. We start to move into yellow as we leave Section 1 and move into Section 2. This monochromatic color scheme in yellow features *Hakonechloa macra* 'Aureola' (153) and *Lysimachia nummularia* 'Aurea' (231). Author's design, Hendley garden, Ohio; photograph by Ian Adams.

Section 2:

In this section we continue with yellow and move into blue. The higher-valued yellows heighten the blues, which give the eyes a rest after experiencing the warmer colors. Spirit-soothing blues transition nicely into the calming violets of the next section. Limits are not as clearly defined through the blue sections; a more open airy feeling pervades this planting, compared to the warmer-colored sections.

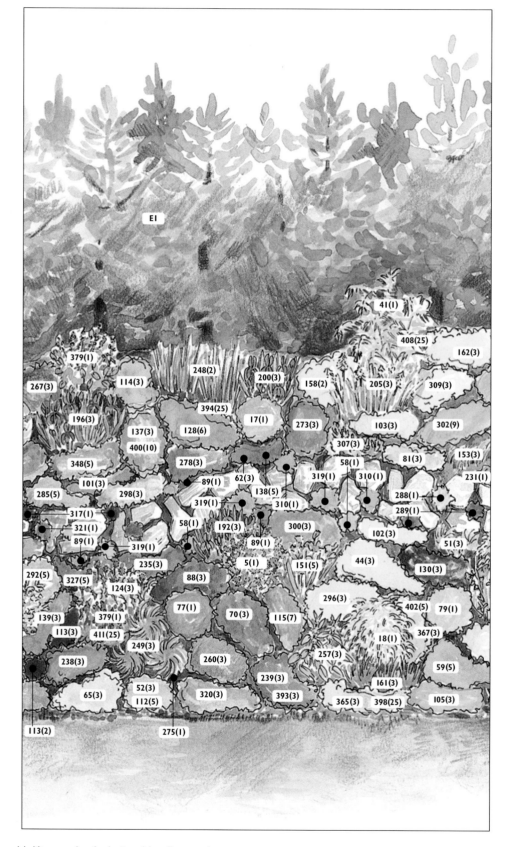

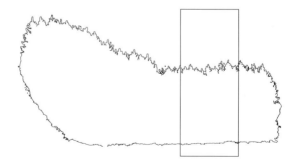

Diagram 24. Large garden: Design II, Section 2. Artist, Megan H. King; author's design, Hendley garden.

⊢——————————⊣ = 6 feet

N→

DIAGRAM 24

Existing trees

E1		Pinus strobus	eastern white pine

Shrubs

5	(1)	Abies procera 'Glauca Prostrata'	noble fir
17	(1)	Caryopteris ×clandonensis 'Worcester Gold'	bluebeard
18	(1)	Chamaecyparis obtusa 'Fernspray Gold'	Hinoki falsecypress
41	(1)	Sambucus racemosa 'Sutherland Gold'	gold-leaved European red elder

Perennials

44	(3)	Achillea 'Anblo' (Anthea)	yarrow
51	(3)	Acorus gramineus 'Ogon'	sweet flag
52	(3)	Agastache 'Blue Fortune'	anise hyssop
58	(2)	Alchemilla mollis	lady's mantle
59	(5)	Alstroemeria 'Sweet Laura'	Peruvian lily
62	(3)	Aquilegia alpina	alpine columbine
65	(3)	Artemisia absinthium 'Lambrook Silver'	artemisia
70	(3)	Aster laevis 'Bluebird'	smooth aster
77	(1)	Baptisia australis	blue wild indigo
79	(1)	Baptisia sphaerocarpa	yellow wild indigo
81	(3)	Belamcanda chinensis 'Hello Yellow'	blackberry lily
88	(3)	Campanula rapunculoides	bellflower
89	(3)	Campanula rotundifolia 'Olympica'	Scotch bluebell
101	(3)	Clematis integrifolia	solitary clematis
102	(3)	Coreopsis auriculata	mouse ear coreopsis
103	(3)	Coreopsis grandiflora 'Walcoreop (flying saucers)	tickseed
105	(3)	Coreopsis verticillata 'Zagreb'	threadleaf coreopsis
112	(5)	Cynoglossum amabile 'Firmament'	Chinese forget-me-not
113	(5)	Delphinium ×bellamosum	delphinium
114	(3)	Delphinium 'Centurion Sky Blue'	delphinium
115	(7)	Delphinium exaltatum	delphinium
124	(3)	Echinops ritro 'Blue Glow'	globe thistle
128	(6)	Eryngium amethystinum	sea holly
130	(3)	Euphorbia amygdaloides 'Purpurea'	purple wood spurge
137	(3)	Galega ×hartlandii 'Lady Wilson'	goat's rue
138	(5)	Gentiana septemfida var. lagodechiana	gentian
139	(3)	Gentiana triflora 'Royal Blue'	gentian
151	(5)	Gladiolus ×gandavensis	gladiolus
153	(3)	Hakonechloa macra 'Aureola'	golden-variegated Hakone grass
158	(2)	Helianthus 'Lemon Queen'	swamp sunflower
161	(3)	Helictotrichon sempervirens 'Saphirsprudel' (sapphire fountain)	blue oat grass
162	(3)	Heliopsis helianthoides var. scabra 'Sommersonne' (summer sun)	heliopsis
192	(3)	Iris pallida 'Variegata'	sweet iris

196	(3)	Iris sibirica 'Orville Fay'	Siberian iris
200	(3)	Iris 'Sugar Blues'	bearded iris
205	(3)	Kniphofia 'Primrose Beauty'	red-hot poker
231	(1)	Lysimachia nummularia 'Aurea'	golden creeping jenny
235	(3)	Nepeta ×faassenii	catmint
238	(3)	Nepeta sibirica 'Souvenir d'André Chaudron'	catmint
239	(3)	Nepeta 'Six Hills Giant'	catmint
248	(2)	Panicum virgatum 'Dallas Blues'	switch grass
249	(3)	Panicum virgatum 'Heavy Metal'	switch grass
257	(3)	Phlomis russeliana	Jerusalem sage
260	(3)	Phlox paniculata 'Katherine'	border phlox
267	(3)	Platycodon grandiflorus 'Double Blue'	balloon flower
273	(3)	Ruta graveolens 'Blue Beauty'	common rue
275	(1)	Salvia azurea var. pitcheri	azure sage
278	(3)	Salvia ×sylvestris 'Blauhügel' (blue hill)	perennial salvia
285	(5)	Scabiosa Butterfly Blue®	pincushion flower
288	(1)	Sedum acre 'Aureum'	sedum
289	(2)	Sedum 'Pork and Beans'	sedum
292	(5)	Sisyrinchium bermudianum	blue-eyed grass
296	(3)	×Solidaster luteus 'Lemore'	golden aster
298	(3)	Stachys byzantina	lamb's ear
300	(3)	Stachys byzantina 'Primrose Heron'	lamb's ear
302	(9)	Stokesia laevis 'Mary Gregory'	Stokes' aster
307	(3)	Tanacetum 'Golden Feathers'	tansy
309	(3)	Thermopsis villosa	southern lupine
310	(2)	Thymus ×citriodorus 'Lemon Green'	lemon thyme
317	(2)	Veronica peduncularis 'Georgia Blue'	speedwell
319	(3)	Veronica repens 'Sunshine'	golden creeping speedwell
320	(3)	Veronica spicata 'Blue Charm'	spike speedwell
321	(1)	Veronica 'Waterperry Blue'	speedwell

Annuals

327	(5)	Angelonia 'Blue Pacific'	angelonia
348	(5)	Consolida ajacis 'Blue Spire'	larkspur
365	(3)	Lysimachia congestiflora 'Variegata'	variegated lysimachia
367	(3)	Nicotiana langsdorffii	flowering tobacco
379	(2)	Salvia 'Indigo Spires'	salvia

Bulbs

393	(3)	Agapanthus 'Bressingham Blue'	lily of the Nile
394	(25)	Allium caeruleum	blue globe onion
398	(25)	Allium moly 'Jeannine'	lily leek
400	(10)	Camassia leichtlinii ssp. suksdorfii 'Blauwe Donau' (blue Danube)	camass
402	(5)	Eremurus ×isabellinus 'Pinokkio'	foxtail lily
408	(25)	Tulipa 'Big Smile'	tulip
411	(25)	Tulipa 'Blue Parrot'	tulip

Plate 157. Compare this combination of *Kniphofia* 'Primrose Beauty' (205) and *Sambucus racemosa* 'Sutherland Gold' (41) to the same kniphofia with *Picea orientalis* 'Skylands' in Plate 35. Notice how the change in texture and color saturation of the sambucus compared to the picea creates subtle changes in the mood of the combination. Both are very effective, just different. Author's design, Hendley garden, Ohio.

Plate 158. Tints and shades of yellow and yellow-green comprise this vignette. Featuring *Belamcanda chinensis* 'Hello Yellow' (81), *Tanacetum* 'Golden Feathers' (307), *Coreopsis grandiflora* 'Walcoreop' (flying saucers) (103), *Sambucus racemosa* 'Sutherland Gold' (41). Author's design, Hendley garden, Ohio.

Plate 159. A view facing north from the blue section into the yellow section. Blues, yellows, and greens (combinations of blues and yellows) create a sophisticated limited palette. Featuring *Salvia ×sylvestris* 'Blauhügel' (blue hill) (278), *Aquilegia alpina* (62), *Caryopteris ×clandonensis* 'Worcester Gold' (17). Author's design, Hendley garden, Ohio.

Plate 161. As the summer progresses, the yellow in *Caryopteris* ×*clandonensis* 'Worcester Gold' (17) will often fade, leaving us with its blue monochromatic combination with *Panicum virgatum* 'Dallas Blues' (248). Author's design, Hendley garden, Ohio.

Plate 160. Strong vertical forms of *Agastache* 'Blue Fortune' (52) contrast with the fine airy texture of *Panicum virgatum* 'Heavy Metal' (249). Author's design, Hendley garden, Ohio.

Plate 162. Vertical forms from the leaves and flowers of *Iris pallida* 'Variegata' (192) unify with the vertical flower stalks of *Baptisia australis* (77). The yellow in the iris leaves, however, is the light that draws the eye to the combination on this rainy May morning. Author's design, Hendley garden, Ohio.

Plate 164. Large-growing tender salvias are among my favorite plants: they provide a shrublike appearance by late summer and are covered with long spikes of incredible flowers. This one, *Salvia* 'Indigo Spires' (379), is an exceptional performer—but give it a wide berth. Also featuring *Panicum virgatum* 'Heavy Metal' (249). Author's design, Hendley garden, Ohio.

Plate 163. A completely different feel is accomplished with the same plants photographed in July, under brighter light, with a sprig of *Campanula rapunculoides* (88) vying for center stage. Author's design, Hendley garden, Ohio.

Plate 165. As we leave the blue section to cross the path into the purples, we are touched by *Picea alcoquiana* 'Howell's Tigertail' (29) keeping company with *Campanula* 'Birch Hybrid' (84) and *Nepeta racemosa* 'Walker's Low' (237). Author's design, Hendley garden, Ohio.

Section 3:

The hut and seating area is surrounded by purple.
It is a wonderfully centering spot, enclosed and secure.
The purples come alive with the sun. Silver and
yellow foliage is also used to enliven the purples.
Red and purple foliage is repeated in this section,
and black flowers add to the mystery.

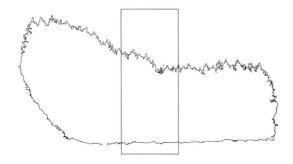

Diagram 25. Large garden: Design II, Section 3. Artist, Megan H. King; author's design, Hendley garden.

⊢————————⊣ = 6 feet

N➝

Diagram 25

Existing trees

E1		*Pinus strobus*	eastern white pine

Shrubs

7	(3)	*Berberis thunbergii* 'Monler' (Gold Nugget™)	Japanese barberry
11	(2)	*Berberis thunbergii* var. *atropurpurea* 'Royal Cloak'	Japanese barberry
12	(2)	*Buddleia davidii* 'Black Knight'	butterfly bush
13	(1)	*Buddleia davidii* 'Mongo' (Nanho blue)	butterfly bush
15	(1)	*Callicarpa dichotoma* 'Issai'	purple beautyberry
29	(1)	*Picea alcoquiana* 'Howell's Tigertail'	Alcock spruce
35	(1)	*Rosa* 'Ausvelvet' (The Prince®)	rose
39	(1)	*Rosa* 'Nuits de Young'	rose

Perennials

58	(1)	*Alchemilla mollis*	lady's mantle
61	(3)	*Anthriscus sylvestris* 'Ravenswing'	anthriscus
63	(3)	*Aquilegia vulgaris* var. *stellata* 'Black Barlow'	columbine
66	(3)	*Artemisia* 'Huntington'	artemisia
71	(3)	*Aster novae-angliae* 'Hella Lacy'	New England aster
72	(3)	*Aster novae-angliae* 'Hillside'	New England aster
73	(3)	*Aster novae-angliae* 'Purple Dome'	New England aster
75	(3)	*Aster oblongifolius* var. *angustatus* 'Raydon's Favorite'	Raydon's aster
78	(1)	*Baptisia* 'Purple Smoke'	wild indigo
84	(3)	*Campanula* 'Birch Hybrid'	bellflower
86	(2)	*Campanula* 'Dwarf Tornado'	bellflower
140	(6)	*Geranium* 'Ann Folkard'	hardy geranium
141	(3)	*Geranium* 'Brookside'	meadow cranesbill
142	(3)	*Geranium himalayense* 'Plenum'	lilac cranesbill
145	(3)	*Geranium phaeum* 'Samobor'	hardy geranium
146	(3)	*Geranium* 'Phillippe Vapelle'	hardy geranium
149	(3)	*Geranium psilostemon*	Armenian geranium
170	(3)	*Hemerocallis* 'Siloam Royal Prince'	daylily
176	(3)	*Heuchera* 'Plum Pudding'	coralbells
177	(3)	*Heuchera* 'Velvet Night'	coralbells
194	(3)	*Iris sibirica* 'Caesar's Brother'	Siberian iris
197	(6)	*Iris sibirica* 'Pirate Prince'	Siberian iris
208	(3)	*Lavandula* ×*intermedia* 'Grosso'	lavender
209	(3)	*Liatris spicata* 'Kobold'	spike gayfeather
223	(3)	*Limonium platyphyllum* 'Violetta'	sea lavender
225	(3)	*Lobelia* 'Purple Towers'	lobelia
227	(3)	*Lobelia* 'Ruby Slippers'	lobelia
234	(1)	*Monarda* 'Violet Queen'	beebalm
236	(3)	*Nepeta grandiflora* 'Bramdean'	catmint
237	(3)	*Nepeta racemosa* 'Walker's Low'	catmint
241	(3)	*Origanum laevigatum* 'Herrenhausen'	oregano
251	(3)	*Papaver orientale* 'Patty's Plum'	oriental poppy
256	(3)	*Perovskia atriplicifolia*	Russian sage
264	(3)	*Phlox paniculata* 'The King'	border phlox
265	(1)	*Phytolacca polyandra*	pokeweed
266	(3)	*Plantago major* 'Rubrifolia'	plantain
274	(3)	*Salvia argentea*	silver sage
276	(3)	*Salvia nemorosa* 'Ostfriesland' (East Friesland)	perennial salvia
280	(3)	*Salvia* ×*sylvestris* 'Mainacht' (May night)	perennial salvia
282	(3)	*Salvia verticillata* 'Purple Rain'	perennial salvia
283	(3)	*Sanguisorba tenuifolia* 'Purpurea'	purple burnet
299	(3)	*Stachys byzantina* 'Countess Helen von Stein'	lamb's ear
304	(8)	*Stokesia laevis* 'Purple Parasols'	Stokes' aster
308	(3)	*Thalictrum rochebruneanum*	lavender mist meadow rue
311	(3)	*Thymus pseudolanuginosus*	woolly thyme
313	(3)	*Tradescantia* (Andersoniana Group) 'Purple Profusion'	spiderwort
317	(1)	*Veronica peduncularis* 'Georgia Blue'	speedwell
321	(2)	*Veronica* 'Waterperry Blue'	speedwell
322	(8)	*Viola* 'Molly Sanderson'	violet
323	(4)	*Viola* 'Purple Showers'	violet

Annuals

329	(5)	*Arctotis* ×*hybrida* 'Dark Red'	African daisy
331	(14)	*Atriplex hortensis* var. *rubra*	mountain spinach
344	(3)	*Celosia spicata* 'Flamingo Purple'	celosia
345	(3)	*Centaurea cineraria*	knapweed
349	(7)	*Cosmos atrosanguineus*	cosmos
362	(3)	*Lablab purpureus*	purple hyacinth bean
370	(5)	*Papaver somniferum* 'Lauren's Grape'	opium poppy
372	(3)	*Perilla frutescens* var. *crispa*	perilla
374	(3)	*Plectranthus argentatus*	plectranthus
380	(1)	*Salvia leucantha*	salvia
382	(1)	*Salvia* 'Purple Majesty'	salvia
384	(3)	*Solenostemon* 'Burgundy Giant'	coleus
389	(3)	*Verbena bonariensis*	tall verbena

Bulbs

396	(5)	*Allium cristophii*	downy onion
397	(25)	*Allium hollandicum* (*aflatunense*) 'Purple Sensation'	ornamental onion
399	(100)	*Allium sphaerocephalon*	drumstick allium
403	(5)	*Fritillaria persica*	fritillary
409	(100)	*Tulipa* 'Black Parrot'	tulip

Vines

422	(1)	*Humulus lupulus* 'Bianca'	golden hops
424	(1)	*Passiflora incarnata*	wild passion flower
425	(1)	*Vitis vinifera* 'Purpurea'	purple-leaved grape

Plate 166. After the red sections, the purple section was the most delightful to create. Each time I see it, I receive great inspiration. "Biorhythms," a sculpture with proportions based on the Golden Mean, adds to the mystique. View from the north toward the south. Sculptor, Renate Burgyan; author's design, Hendley garden, Ohio.

Plate 168. Purple-fruited *Callicarpa dichotoma* 'Issai' (15) stops visitors in their tracks—one hears nothing but words of praise and questions about its identity and care. Also featuring *Tradescantia* (Andersoniana Group) 'Purple Profusion' (313). Author's design, Hendley garden, Ohio.

Plate 167. "Biorhythms" with *Perovskia atriplicifolia* (256) and *Salvia leucantha* (380). Author's design, Hendley garden, Ohio.

Plate 169. The hut frames the views from the purple section into the rest of the border, providing a different perspective. Author's design, Hendley garden, Ohio.

Plate 170. "One man's weed . . ." *Plantago major* 'Rubrifolia' (266) snuggles up with *Stokesia laevis* 'Purple Parasols' (304). Author's design, Hendley garden, Ohio.

Plate 171. Silver foliage accents the purple and blue sections. Featuring *Aster novae-angliae* 'Hillside' (72), *Plectranthus argentatus* (374), *Aster oblongifolius* var. *angustatus* 'Raydon's Favorite' (75). Author's design, Hendley garden, Ohio; photograph by Ian Adams.

Plate 172. Spots of black in the purple section add even more depth and intrigue. Yellow foliage accents the entire border. Here the bright eye of *Viola* 'Molly Sanderson' (322) echoes the foliage of *Berberis thunbergii* 'Monler' (Gold Nugget™) (7). Author's design, Hendley garden, Ohio.

Plate 173. *Papaver orientale* 'Patty's Plum' (251) is all about purple. Author's design, Hendley garden, Ohio.

Section 4:

We continue with a touch of purple then back into blue and yellow in this section, as we head south of the hut. Silver foliage ties the blue sections to its purple neighbors. The heat starts to go up again as we move away from the purples and blues to finish in areas of warmer colors.

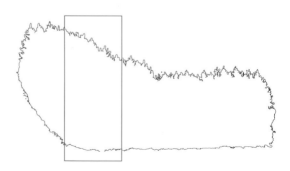

Diagram 26. Large garden: Design II, Section 4. Artist, Megan H. King; author's design, Hendley garden.

⊢——————⊣ = 8 feet

N→

Diagram 26

Trees

3	(1)	*Picea orientalis* 'Skylands'	oriental spruce
4	(1)	*Picea pungens* 'Iseli Foxtail'	Colorado spruce

Existing trees

E1		*Pinus strobus*	eastern white pine

Shrubs

14	(1)	*Buddleia* 'Lochinch'	butterfly bush
16	(1)	*Caryopteris* ×*clandonensis* 'Longwood Blue'	bluebeard
28	(1)	*Picea abies* 'Mucronata'	Norway spruce
31	(1)	*Rosa* 'Alchymist'	rose
33	(1)	*Rosa* 'Ausmas' (Graham Thomas®)	rose
38	(1)	*Rosa* ×*harisonii* 'Harison's Yellow'	rose
42	(1)	*Vitex agnus-castus* var. *latifolia*	chastetree

Perennials

45	(3)	*Achillea filipendulina* 'Altgold'	fernleaf yarrow
48	(3)	*Aconitum* 'Bressingham Spire'	monkshood
50	(3)	*Aconitum lycoctonum* ssp. *neapolitanum*	monkshood
53	(3)	*Agastache rupestris*	rock anise hyssop
56	(3)	*Alcea rosea* 'The Watchman'	hollyhock
57	(5)	*Alcea rugosa*	Russian hollyhock
58	(3)	*Alchemilla mollis*	lady's mantle
60	(1)	*Amsonia hubrichtii*	Arkansas amsonia
65	(3)	*Artemisia absinthium* 'Lambrook Silver'	artemisia
69	(3)	*Aster* 'Climax'	aster
74	(3)	*Aster novae-angliae* 'Wild Light Blue'	New England aster
76	(3)	*Aster tataricus* 'Jindai'	Tatarian aster
82	(1)	*Buphthalmum speciosum*	scented oxeye
85	(3)	*Campanula* 'Constellation'	bellflower
86	(4)	*Campanula* 'Dwarf Tornado'	bellflower
87	(3)	*Campanula persicifolia* 'Chettle Charm'	peachleaf bellflower
89	(3)	*Campanula rotundifolia* 'Olympica'	Scotch bluebell
93	(3)	*Centaurea montana*	mountain bluet
95	(3)	*Ceratostigma plumbaginoides*	plumbago
107	(7)	*Crocosmia* ×*crocosmiiflora* 'Solfatare'	crocosmia
113	(10)	*Delphinium* ×*bellamosum*	delphinium
115	(7)	*Delphinium exaltatum*	delphinium
116	(3)	*Deschampsia cespitosa* 'Goldgehänge'	tufted hair grass
121	(5)	*Digitalis lutea*	straw foxglove
123	(3)	*Echinops bannaticus* 'Taplow Blue'	globe thistle
125	(3)	*Echinops ritro* 'Veitch's Blue'	globe thistle
129	(3)	*Eryngium planum* 'Blaukappe'	sea holly
133	(3)	*Euphorbia polychroma*	cushion spurge
134	(3)	*Festuca glauca* 'Elijah Blue'	blue fescue

135	(3)	*Festuca glauca* 'Golden Toupee'	blue fescue
136	(3)	*Foeniculum vulgare* 'Purpureum'	copper fennel
137	(3)	*Galega* ×*hartlandii* 'Lady Wilson'	goat's rue
138	(3)	*Gentiana septemfida* var. *lagodechiana*	gentian
141	(3)	*Geranium* 'Brookside'	meadow cranesbill
143	(3)	*Geranium* ×*magnificum*	showy geranium
144	(3)	*Geranium phaeum* 'Lily Lovell'	hardy geranium
148	(3)	*Geranium pratense* 'Mrs. Kendall Clark'	meadow cranesbill
150	(3)	*Geranium sanguineum* 'New Hampshire'	blood-red geranium
159	(1)	*Helianthus* 'Mellow Yellow'	swamp sunflower
160	(3)	*Helianthus salicifolius*	willow-leaved sunflower
161	(6)	*Helictotrichon sempervirens* 'Saphirsprudel' (sapphire fountain)	blue oat grass
175	(3)	*Hemerocallis* 'Yellow Lollipop'	daylily
188	(3)	*Hyssopus officinalis*	hyssop
192	(5)	*Iris pallida* 'Variegata'	sweet iris
198	(3)	*Iris sibirica* 'Skywings'	Siberian iris
199	(3)	*Iris sibirica* 'Vi Luihn'	Siberian iris
201	(3)	*Knautia macedonica*	knautia
203	(6)	*Kniphofia citrina*	red-hot poker
211	(5)	*Lilium* 'Connecticut King'	lily
214	(7)	*Lilium* 'Grand Cru'	lily
218	(6)	*Lilium* 'Royal Justice'	lily
224	(5)	*Linum perenne* 'Blau Saphir (blue sapphire)	perennial flax
230	(3)	*Lychnis cognata*	campion
238	(3)	*Nepeta sibirica* 'Souvenir d'André Chaudron'	catmint
240	(5)	*Oenothera fruticosa* ssp. *glauca* 'Sonnenwende'	sundrops
242	(3)	*Origanum vulgare* 'Aureum'	oregano
246	(1)	*Paeonia* 'Etched Salmon'	peony
247	(1)	*Paeonia* 'Prairie Moon'	peony
254	(3)	*Patrinia scabiosifolia*	patrinia
261	(3)	*Phlox paniculata* 'Laura'	border phlox
268	(3)	*Platycodon grandiflorus* 'Komachi'	balloon flower
273	(3)	*Ruta graveolens* 'Blue Beauty'	common rue
277	(3)	*Salvia nemorosa* 'Pusztaflamme' (plumosa)	perennial salvia
279	(3)	*Salvia* ×*sylvestris* 'Blaukönigin' (blue queen)	perennial salvia
281	(3)	*Salvia* ×*sylvestris* 'Viola Klose'	perennial salvia
287	(3)	*Schizachyrium scoparium* 'The Blues'	little bluestem
297	(3)	*Sorghastrum nutans* 'Sioux Blue'	Indian grass
299	(3)	*Stachys byzantina* 'Countess Helen von Stein'	lamb's ear
300	(3)	*Stachys byzantina* 'Primrose Heron'	lamb's ear
301	(3)	*Stokesia laevis* 'Klaus Jelitto'	Stokes' aster
303	(5)	*Stokesia laevis* 'Omega Skyrocket'	Stokes' aster
315	(3)	*Veronica austriaca* ssp. *teucrium* 'Crater Lake Blue'	Hungarian speedwell
316	(3)	*Veronica gentianoides* 'Nana'	gentian speedwell
318	(3)	*Veronica prostrata* 'Trehane'	harebell speedwell

(*continued on next page*)

(plant list cont.)

| 323 | (1) | *Viola* 'Purple Showers' | violet |

Annuals

339	(3)	*Canna* 'Omega'	canna
346	(16)	*Cerinthe major* 'Purpurascens'	cerinthe
348	(5)	*Consolida ajacis* 'Blue Spire'	larkspur
350	(1)	*Cynara cardunculus*	cardoon
360	(3)	*Ipomoea batatas* 'Blackie'	sweet potato vine
366	(7)	*Melampodium paludosum* 'Million Gold'	melampodium
375	(2)	*Portulaca grandiflora* 'Sundial Peach'	moss rose
378	(1)	*Salvia guaranitica*	salvia
381	(5)	*Salvia patens*	salvia

Bulbs

395	(25)	*Allium carinatum* ssp. *pulchellum*	keeled garlic
410	(50)	*Tulipa* 'Blue Heron'	tulip
417	(25)	*Tulipa* 'Queen of Night'	tulip
418	(50)	*Tulipa* 'Temple of Beauty'	tulip

Vines

| 420 | (1) | *Campsis* ×*tagliabuana* 'Madame Galen' | trumpet creeper |

Plate 175. A different mood is created when we combine *Picea pungens* 'Iseli Foxtail' (4) with *Echinops ritro* 'Veitch's Blue' (125) and *Schizachyrium scoparium* 'The Blues' (287). Author's design, Hendley garden, Ohio.

Plate 174. As we move back into the blues, south of the hut, *Picea pungens* 'Iseli Foxtail' (4) provides a vertical corner focal point. Also featuring *Veronica austriaca* ssp. *teucrium* 'Crater Lake Blue' (315), *Stachys byzantina* 'Countess Helen von Stein' (299). Author's design, Hendley garden, Ohio.

Plate 177. Low-growing plants such as the ground-covering *Ceratostigma plumbaginoides* (95) and *Stachys byzantina* 'Primrose Heron' (300) effectively connect the blue section with the yellow section along the edge of the path. Author's design, Hendley garden, Ohio.

Plate 176. *Sorghastrum nutans* 'Sioux Blue' (297) makes a great background plant with the hedge of white pines. Author's design, Hendley garden, Ohio.

Plate 178. Another blue and yellow combination, this time accomplished with foliage color only. Featuring *Schizachyrium scoparium* 'The Blues' (287), *Origanum vulgare* 'Aureum' (242). Author's design, Hendley garden, Ohio.

Plate 179. A combination of blues, yes—but note the harmonizing autumnal shades of red and orange, present on the stems of the grass and the centers of the aster flowers. Featuring *Schizachyrium scoparium* 'The Blues' (287), *Aster* 'Climax' (69). Author's design, Hendley garden, Ohio.

Plate 180. A view looking south toward the yellows blending into oranges. The undulating forms of the plants create nice rhythm. The various greens, yellows, and yellow-greens unify the vignette. The diversity of plant material—trees, dwarf conifers, tropicals, vines, perennials, and annuals are all represented—creates excitement and stimulation. Author's design, Hendley garden, Ohio.

Plate 181. A vignette from Plate 180, showing an interesting combination of *Picea abies* 'Mucronata' (28), *Melampodium paludosum* 'Million Gold' (366), and *Euphorbia polychroma* (133). Author's design, Hendley garden, Ohio; photograph by Ian Adams.

Plate 183. The stately *Picea orientalis* 'Skylands' (3) looks great with just about everything. Here it is seen with *Coreopsis tripteris* (104) and a seedhead of *Rudbeckia maxima* (271) in a picturesque harmony of yellows, greens, and browns. Although this was designed as a monochromatic combination of yellows, we can see how other colors associated with plants—those present in their fruit or certain parts of their flowers, the green of their leaves and stems—bring more to the picture. Author's design, Hendley garden, Ohio.

Plate 182. Five different types of crocosmia add their tropical flair, gorgeous flowers, and fine texture to the border. Here *Crocosmia* ×*crocosmiiflora* 'Solfatare' (107) looks at home with *Canna* 'Omega' (339). Author's design, Hendley garden, Ohio.

Section 5:

Vibrant and bold is back as we leave the garden on the south end and pass through yellow, peach, orange, and red. Tender bulbs and tropicals steal the show in this section. The visitor is left with a strong impression of the garden upon exiting.

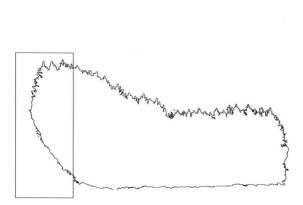

Diagram 27. Large garden: Design II, Section 5. Artist, Megan H. King; author's design, Hendley garden.

⊢——————⊣ = 7 feet

N→

DIAGRAM 27

Trees

2	(1)	*Acer palmatum* 'Sango-kaku'	Japanese maple

Existing trees

E1	*Pinus strobus*	eastern white pine

Shrubs

8	(1)	*Berberis thunbergii* 'Monry' (Sunsation™)	Japanese barberry
10	(1)	*Berberis thunbergii* var. *atropurpurea* 'Gentry Cultivar' (Royal Burgundy™)	Japanese barberry
21	(1)	*Genista tinctoria* 'Royal Gold'	common woadwaxen
24	(2)	*Ilex verticillata* 'Afterglow'	winterberry holly
26	(1)	*Ilex verticillata* 'Jim Dandy'	winterberry holly
30	(3)	*Potentilla fruticosa* 'Sunset'	bush cinquefoil
32	(1)	*Rosa* 'Ausbuff' (English Garden®)	rose
37	(1)	*Rosa* 'F. J. Grootendorst'	rose

Perennials

46	(3)	*Achillea* 'Heidi'	yarrow
47	(3)	*Achillea* 'Salmon Beauty'	yarrow
58	(2)	*Alchemilla mollis*	lady's mantle
67	(3)	*Asclepias tuberosa*	butterfly weed
68	(3)	*Asclepias tuberosa* 'Hello Yellow'	butterfly weed
81	(3)	*Belamcanda chinensis* 'Hello Yellow'	blackberry lily
90	(3)	*Carex buchananii*	leatherleaf sedge
94	(1)	*Cephalaria gigantea*	Tatarian cephalaria
97	(3)	*Chrysanthemum* 'Single Apricot'	mum
98	(3)	*Chrysanthemum* 'Single Peach'	mum
104	(1)	*Coreopsis tripteris*	tall coreopsis
106	(5)	*Crocosmia* ×*crocosmiiflora* 'Norwich Canary'	crocosmia
108	(5)	*Crocosmia* ×*crocosmiiflora* 'Venus'	crocosmia
109	(5)	*Crocosmia* 'Emberglow'	crocosmia
110	(5)	*Crocosmia* 'Lucifer'	crocosmia
117	(3)	*Dianthus* ×*allwoodii* 'Danielle Marie'	Allwood pink
118	(3)	*Dianthus barbatus* 'Sooty'	sweet william
122	(3)	*Digitalis purpurea* 'Apricot'	foxglove
132	(3)	*Euphorbia griffithii* 'Fireglow'	Griffith's spurge
152	(7)	*Gladiolus* ×*gandavensis* 'Boone'	gladiolus
154	(3)	*Helenium* 'Kugelsonne'	common sneezeweed
155	(4)	*Helenium* 'Moerheim Beauty'	common sneezeweed
156	(3)	*Helianthemum* (double yellow)	sunrose
157	(3)	*Helianthemum* 'Fire Dragon'	sunrose
165	(3)	*Hemerocallis* 'Alluring Peach'	daylily
166	(3)	*Hemerocallis* 'Carefree Peach'	daylily
168	(3)	*Hemerocallis* 'Red Razzamatazz'	daylily
171	(3)	*Hemerocallis* 'Staghorn Sumac'	daylily
172	(3)	*Hemerocallis* 'Sundried Tomatoes'	daylily
173	(3)	*Hemerocallis* 'Toy Trumpets'	daylily
179	(1)	*Hibiscus moscheutos* 'Lord Baltimore'	rose mallow
191	(3)	*Iris foetidissima*	stinking iris
193	(3)	*Iris sibirica* 'Butter and Sugar'	Siberian iris
202	(3)	*Kniphofia* 'Alcazar'	red-hot poker
204	(3)	*Kniphofia* 'Little Maid'	red-hot poker
206	(3)	*Kniphofia* 'Royal Standard'	red-hot poker
207	(3)	*Kniphofia* 'Shining Sceptre'	red-hot poker
214	(7)	*Lilium* 'Grand Cru'	lily
216	(6)	*Lilium* 'Montenegro'	lily
217	(6)	*Lilium* 'Pretender'	lily
219	(6)	*Lilium* 'Royal Perfume'	lily
221	(12)	*Lilium* 'Shirley'	lily
222	(6)	*Lilium* 'Sunset'	lily
226	(6)	*Lobelia* 'Queen Victoria'	lobelia
229	(5)	*Lychnis* ×*arkwrightii* 'Vesuvius'	Arkwright's campion
243	(3)	*Packera aurea* (*Senecio aureus*)	golden ragwort
250	(3)	*Papaver orientale* 'Derwisch'	oriental poppy
252	(5)	*Papaver orientale* 'Prince of Orange'	oriental poppy
253	(3)	*Papaver orientale* 'Turkenlouis'	oriental poppy
262	(3)	*Phlox paniculata* 'Orange Perfection'	border phlox
270	(3)	*Rheum palmatum* var. *tanguticum*	ornamental rhubarb
271	(3)	*Rudbeckia maxima*	giant coneflower
293	(7)	*Sisyrinchium* 'Quaint and Queer'	blue-eyed grass
294	(3)	*Solidago* 'Golden Spangles'	goldenrod
314	(3)	*Verbascum* 'Jackie'	mullein

Annuals

324	(5)	*Alstroemeria aurea* 'Orange King'	Peruvian lily
325	(11)	*Alstroemeria psittacina*	parrot lily
329	(2)	*Arctotis* ×*hybrida* 'Dark Red'	African daisy
332	(3)	*Beta vulgaris* 'Golden'	Swiss chard
335	(7)	*Caladium* 'Florida Cardinal'	caladium
338	(1)	*Canna indica* 'Red Stripe'	(purpurea) canna
340	(3)	*Canna* 'Orange Punch'	canna
351	(3)	*Dahlia* 'Arabian Night'	dahlia
354	(3)	*Dahlia* 'Orange Nugget'	dahlia
355	(3)	*Dahlia* 'Susette'	dahlia
356	(1)	*Eucomis comosa* 'Sparkling Burgundy'	pineapple lily
357	(3)	*Hedychium coccineum*	red ginger lily
359	(3)	*Hibiscus acetosella* 'Red Shield'	hibiscus
361	(2)	*Ipomoea batatas* 'Margarita'	sweet potato vine
363	(7)	*Lactuca* 'Merlot'	lettuce
364	(6)	*Leonotis menthifolia*	leonotis
369	(3)	*Papaver somniferum* 'Burnt Orange'	opium poppy
372	(5)	*Perilla frutescens* var. *crispa*	perilla
375	(3)	*Portulaca grandiflora* 'Sundial Peach'	moss rose

(continued on next page)

(plant list cont.)

377 (3)	*Salvia coccinea* 'Lady in Red'	salvia
383 (5)	*Scabiosa atropurpurea* 'Ace of Spades'	pincushion flower
387 (5)	*Tropaeolum majus* 'Alaska Salmon Orange'	nasturtium
388 (8)	*Tropaeolum majus* 'Apricot Trifle'	nasturtium
392 (5)	*Zinnia haageana* 'Orange Star'	zinnia

Bulbs

398 (25)	*Allium moly* 'Jeannine'	lily leek

404 (28)	*Hymenocallis* 'Sulphur Queen'	Peruvian daffodil
405 (10)	*Scadoxus multiflorus*	blood lily
406 (10)	*Tigridia pavonia* 'Speciosa'	tiger flower
407 (25)	*Tulipa* 'Apricot Parrot'	tulip
412 (50)	*Tulipa* 'Blushing Lady'	tulip
413 (25)	*Tulipa* 'Burgundy Lace'	tulip
416 (25)	*Tulipa* 'Fringed Elegance'	tulip
419 (25)	*Tulipa* 'Uncle Tom'	tulip

Plate 184. The light yellow, almost white flower of *Hymenocallis* 'Sulphur Queen' (404) and the light blue (containing a good deal of white) leaves of *Rudbeckia maxima* (271) are both high values, which creates unity. The sensual forms of the two add contrast. Author's design, Hendley garden, Ohio.

Plate 185. Outstanding foliage forms and textures are just as interesting in this combination as the warm flower colors. Featuring *Beta vulgaris* 'Golden' (332), *Tropaeolum majus* 'Alaska Salmon Orange' (387), *Crocosmia* ×*crocosmiiflora* 'Norwich Canary' (106), *Asclepias tuberosa* 'Hello Yellow' (68). Author's design, Hendley garden, Ohio.

Plate 186. Is this Ohio? Featuring *Hedychium coccineum* (357), *Hibiscus acetosella* 'Red Shield' (359). Author's design, Hendley garden, Ohio.

Plate 188. Seeing *Gladiolus* ×*gandavensis* 'Boone' (152) in flower makes one glad to be alive. Hendley garden, Ohio.

Plate 187. Looking back through peach toward the hut. Commoners such as *Hemerocallis* 'Alluring Peach' (165) rub shoulders with *Gladiolus* ×*gandav-ensis* 'Boone' (152) and other more unusual plants. Author's design, Hendley garden, Ohio.

Plate 189. An overall view of this section in autumn, with a prominence of peach offered by hardy mums. On the left is *Chrysanthemum* 'Single Peach' (98) and on the right, *C.* 'Single Apricot' (97). Author's design, Hendley garden, Ohio.

Plate 190. A close look at *Chrysanthemum* 'Single Peach' (98) through a veil of *Carex buchananii* (90). Peach (a tint of orange) and brown (which can be a shade of orange) actually have a lot in common (although not obviously so) and could be considered a monochromatic duo. Author's design, Hendley garden, Ohio.

Plate 191. *Carex buchananii* (90) again, this time seen at the base of *Kniphofia* 'Alcazar' (202). The kniphofia, with its orange volcanolike color pattern, effectively erupts from the carex. Author's design, Hendley garden, Ohio.

Plate 192. The deep orange bark and lighter orange new stems of *Acer palmatum* 'Sango-kaku' (2) make it an ideal woody plant for an orange or warm color scheme. It is complemented here by fiery *Helenium* 'Moerheim Beauty' (155). Author's design, Hendley garden, Ohio.

Plate 193. The heat continues to rise as we get into deeper oranges. *Canna* 'Orange Punch' (340) is a real knockout. Author's design, Hendley garden, Ohio.

Plate 194. *Dahlia* 'Orange Nugget' (354) defines orange. Hendley garden, Ohio.

Plate 196. The soft color and texture of *Pinus strobus* (E1) is just the backdrop needed to tone down, slightly, the vivacious enthusiasm of *Canna indica* 'Red Stripe' (338) and its partner *Hibiscus moscheutos* 'Lord Baltimore' (179), whose good weight anchors this south end of the border. Note that we are back to simultaneous contrast with red and green, as we were in Plates 141 and 144, at the north end of the border. Author's design, Hendley garden, Ohio.

Plate 195. Would you expect this garden of varied plant material to include lettuce? Of course. But not just any lettuce—one with red foliage, such as *Lactuca* 'Merlot' (363), to harmonize with *Dahlia* 'Arabian Night' (351) and other reds. Author's design, Hendley garden, Ohio.

Shade Border:

This border is separated from the large sun border by an 8-ft.-wide grass path. It is partially shaded; the northern section receives a few hours of late afternoon sun. For unification with the sun border, similar color themes, textures, and certain plant material are repeated in it. On the north end, the colors start in yellow, move to blue and then purple, and then reverse: back to blue, and then yellow, with a spot of orange, finishing in red. Foliage color and texture are key elements. Some of the larger hostas and perennials used along the rear of the border are slow to establish and continue to develop as the design's backbone. Various winterberries have been planted beyond the border, echoing the winterberries that appear in the sun border and better transitioning the garden into its native surroundings.

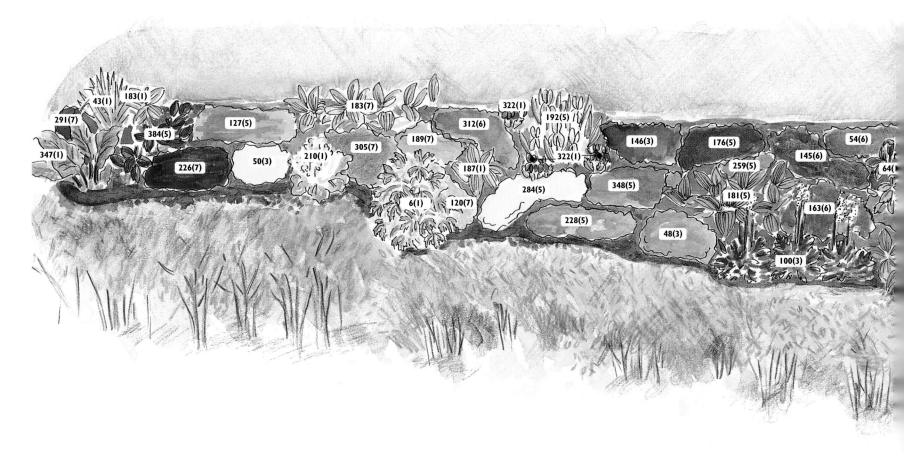

Diagram 28. Large garden: Design II, shade border. Artist, Megan H. King; author's design, Hendley garden.

⊢————————⊣ = 5½ feet

N⟶

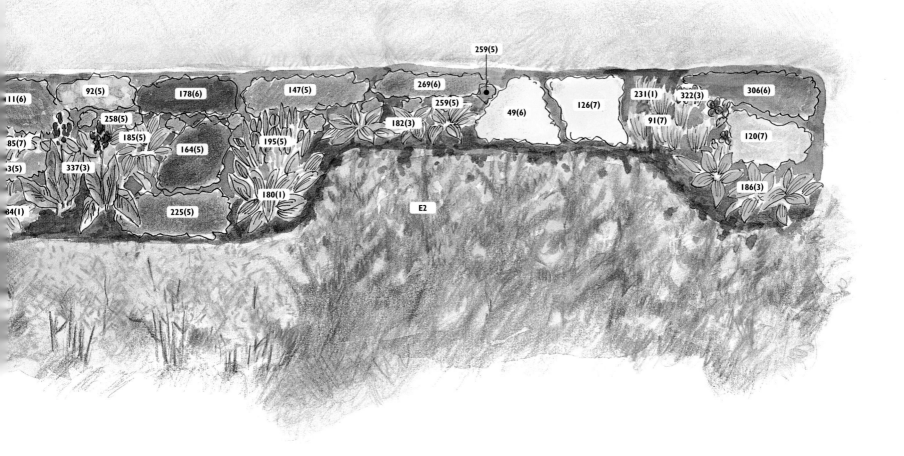

DIAGRAM 28

Existing trees

E2		*Tsuga canadensis*	Canadian hemlock

Shrubs

6	(1)	*Aralia elata* 'Aureovariegata'	aralia
43	(1)	*Yucca filamentosa* 'Color Guard'	yucca

Perennials

48	(3)	*Aconitum* 'Bressingham Spire'	monkshood
49	(6)	*Aconitum* 'Ivorine'	monkshood
50	(3)	*Aconitum lycoctonum* ssp. *neapolitanum*	monkshood
54	(6)	*Ajuga reptans* 'Purple Torch'	bugleweed
63	(5)	*Aquilegia vulgaris* var. *stellata* 'Black Barlow'	columbine
64	(1)	*Arisaema sikokianum*	jack-in-the-pulpit
91	(7)	*Carex elata* 'Aurea' (Bowles' golden)	tufted sedge
92	(5)	*Carex morrowii* 'Ice Dance'	sedge
100	(3)	*Cimicifuga ramosa* 'Hillside Black Beauty'	bugbane
111	(6)	*Cryptotaenia japonica* f. *atropurpurea*	cryptotaenia
120	(14)	*Digitalis grandiflora*	yellow foxglove
126	(7)	*Epimedium davidii*	barrenwort
127	(5)	*Epimedium ×warleyense*	barrenwort
145	(6)	*Geranium phaeum* 'Samobor'	hardy geranium
146	(3)	*Geranium* 'Phillippe Vapelle'	hardy geranium
147	(5)	*Geranium platypetalum*	broad-petaled geranium
163	(6)	*Helleborus* Royal Heritage™	lenten rose
164	(5)	*Helleborus orientalis* (single black)	lenten rose
176	(5)	*Heuchera* 'Plum Pudding'	coralbells
178	(6)	×*Heucherella* 'Silver Streak'	foamy bells
180	(1)	*Hosta* 'Big Daddy'	plantain-lily
181	(5)	*Hosta* 'Halcyon'	plantain-lily
182	(3)	*Hosta* 'Krossa Regal'	plantain-lily
183	(8)	*Hosta* 'Lemon Lime'	plantain-lily
184	(1)	*Hosta* 'Midas Touch'	plantain-lily
185	(5)	*Hosta* 'Paul's Glory'	plantain-lily
186	(3)	*Hosta* 'Sum and Substance'	plantain-lily
187	(1)	*Hosta* 'Sun Power'	plantain-lily
189	(7)	*Impatiens omeiana*	perennial impatiens
192	(5)	*Iris pallida* 'Variegata'	sweet iris
195	(5)	*Iris sibirica* 'Dianne's Daughter'	Siberian iris
210	(1)	*Ligularia wilsoniana*	ligularia
225	(5)	*Lobelia* 'Purple Towers'	lobelia
226	(7)	*Lobelia* 'Queen Victoria'	lobelia
228	(5)	*Lobelia siphilitica*	lobelia
231	(1)	*Lysimachia nummularia* 'Aurea'	golden creeping jenny
258	(5)	*Phlox divaricata* 'Dirigo Ice'	woodland phlox
259	(10)	*Phlox divaricata* ssp. *laphamii*	woodland phlox
269	(6)	*Polemonium caeruleum* 'Blanjou' (brise d'Anjou)	jacob's ladder
284	(5)	*Saruma henryi*	saruma
291	(7)	*Silene regia*	wild pink
305	(7)	*Stylophorum diphyllum*	wood poppy
306	(6)	*Symphytum* 'Goldsmith'	comfrey
312	(6)	*Tiarella cordifolia* 'Ninja'	foamflower
322	(6)	*Viola* 'Molly Sanderson'	violet

Annuals

337	(3)	*Canna* 'Black Knight'	canna
347	(1)	*Colocasia esculenta* 'Fontanesii'	elephant's ear
348	(5)	*Consolida ajacis* 'Blue Spire'	larkspur
384	(5)	*Solenostemon* 'Burgundy Giant'	coleus
385	(7)	*Solenostemon* 'Olive'	coleus

Plate 197. On the north end of the shade border, the new growth of *Tsuga canadensis* (E2) harmonizes with the yellows and yellow-greens of *Lysimachia nummularia* 'Aurea' (231) and *Carex elata* 'Aurea' (Bowles' golden) (91). Author's design, Hendley garden, Ohio.

Plate 198. This photograph and Plate 199 demonstrate some of the variables that affect color. In this photograph (taken in early August, when the plants were fresher and the light was brighter), yellows are more apparent; the color of the light is white with a tinge of yellow. Featuring *Hosta* 'Sun Power' (187), *Impatiens omeiana* (189). Author's design, Hendley garden, Ohio.

Plate 199. In this photograph, as compared with Plate 198, the light is lower, and we see an overall cast of blue shade light. The plants are also older: this was taken in October, by which time plant colors have faded a bit. No matter how you look at them, though, these plants are fabulous shade-dwellers. Featuring *Hosta* 'Sun Power' (187), *Impatiens omeiana* (189), *Saruma henryi* (284). Author's design, Hendley garden, Ohio.

Plate 200. Forms are the focus of this combination. The purple foliage of *Solenostemon* 'Burgundy Giant' (384), which appears even darker in the shade and moisture, creates a deep and mysterious background that contrasts with the lighter colors of the leaves of *Colocasia esculenta* 'Fontanesii' (347) and *Yucca filamentosa* 'Color Guard' (43), making their shapes and colors jump. Author's design, Hendley garden, Ohio; photograph by Ian Adams.

PART THREE

Encyclopedia of Plant Combinations

USING THE ENCYCLOPEDIA

This section features plant combinations that I hope, together with the combinations and designs featured in the first two parts of the book, will provide you with further artistic inspiration. Each combination discusses both design considerations and maintenance. Within the design considerations, we'll pull together much of the material we have already discussed, particularly color theory (Chapter 3) and design principles (Chapter 4). We will look at the relationships among these various elements, which are the heart of every outstanding combination. Refer back to these chapters and the color diagrams, to help recall the points discussed.

I think it is a fun and often challenging exercise to critique various combinations or designs—to try to really see what is happening within them. It is challenging because it involves the right and the left side of the brain. It is about trying to intellectualize a creative process. I hope such critical thinking will better train your eye, as it has mine, to be more present and aware. This awareness shouldn't be reserved for the garden alone—use it to enhance your appreciation of design in all facets of your life. Consider the shifts of hue and value, the textures, lines, and forms, and, most dramatically, the different effects of light, indoors and out, in the countryside and in interiors—paintings, photographs, textiles.

Take a moment to just look at each photograph and try to apply what we have discussed and what you already know about design. Then read to see how I have interpreted the combination. Sometimes we may have a similar analysis, other times something quite different. That is the beauty of design.

Because I feel so strongly about maintenance as a chief objective, I touch on the care that is needed to keep each combination performing as intended. Even if you can't grow a particular plant in your area, the design characteristics it provides can be incorporated using suitable plants with similar features that will grow for you.

I provide descriptive information for each plant featured in a combination, including its height and sometimes width, if pertinent. Mature heights and widths on plants will vary, depending on many factors, from seed or parent material to site issues, including climate, soil, and moisture levels. Some of the trees and shrubs have the potential to reach much larger proportions in their native habitat or if grown for eons in large public gardens. I have given sizes for expected growth under typical landscape conditions; we usually consider what the plant will look like about ten years from planting. Parenthetical height measurements indicate the height of the foliage and are provided only if it is significantly different from the height of the plant in flower.

If you like a particular plant within a combination, you can learn more about it and incorporate it into your designs or gardens in your own style, for your own purposes: the Design Chart and lists in Appendix B are in-depth references on what a featured plant offers—points such as its design color (cool or warm), texture, form, winter interest, and whether or not you can expect hummingbirds. For more information on what a featured plant needs, see the Culture Chart and lists in Appendix C.

I hope you will enjoy reading this section of the book as much as I enjoyed writing it. It often pushed me to dig deeper than the obvious. I trust it will do the same for you.

All combinations are from my garden except Combination 14 (author's design, Inniswood Metro Gardens, Ohio) and Combination 15 (Bobbie Schwartz garden, Ohio).

COMBINATION 1

1. Plant Phlox divaricata
   Common name woodland phlox
   Zone 4–9
   Type perennial
   Description fragrant white, light blue, or lavender flowers; small green leaves
   Height 10–15 in.
   Width 12 in.
   Light shade/pt shade
   Flowering month May–Jun

2. Plant Narcissus 'Sir Winston Churchill'
   Common name daffodil
   Zone 3–8
   Type hardy bulb
   Description fragrant double white blooms with orange flecks
   Height 15–17 in.
   Light sun/pt shade
   Flowering month Apr–May

Design Considerations: These two fragrant spring-flowering plants complement each other in charming fashion. The clean, simple form of the phlox flowers along with the crisp white color of the daffodil embody the freshness of spring. The double flowers of the daffodil add an almost rosebudlike appeal, further enhancing the romance of the duo. The full form of the daffodils adds weight to the composition and contrasts with the open form of the phlox. The pale blue-violet color of the phlox also contrasts nicely with the orange in the daffodil. The bright white from the daffodil in this partially shaded location draws the visitor to the combination, where, on close inspection, the fragrance and delicacy of the two small garden treasures is enjoyed.

Maintenance: Little care is involved in this combination. To create a naturalized appearance and cover open ground in the spring, allow the phlox to seed; to control its spread, deadhead it before seed-set. It is evergreen so does not require pruning for the winter. Simply deadhead the daffodil and allow the foliage to die down naturally under the foliage of other plants. If foliage is visible, cut it to base when decline occurs.

COMBINATION 2

1. Plant	Helleborus foetidus	
Common name	stinking hellebore	
Zone	(5)6–9	
Type	perennial	
Description	leathery dark green palmate leaves; large long-lasting green flowerheads	
Height	15–18 in.	
Width	18 in.	
Light	shade/pt shade	
Flowering month	Mar–Apr	
2. Plant	Fritillaria persica	
Common name	fritillary	
Zone	6–8	
Type	hardy bulb	
Description	nodding bell-shaped dark plum flowers	
Height	2–4 ft.	
Light	sun/pt shade	
Flowering month	Apr	

Design Considerations: This early spring combination is stunning and just the ticket to give hope for the rebirth of spring after a long winter. It is an intriguing study of texture and form. The vertical form of the fritillary emerging from the mounded form of the hellebore creates high contrast and therefore serves as an effective focal point. Such a strong vertical is unusual in the spring shade garden. The interesting, uniform leaf arrangement of the fritillary appears orderly and stiff in contrast to the loose, carefree appearance of the hellebore, yet the different leaf types are unified in their rather linear nature. Simultaneous contrast is at play: the hellebore foliage and flowers appear more yellow-green than if seen alone, while the fritillary appears more blue-green. Green is still the unifying hue, however. Also, the yellow-green of the hellebore flowers contrasts beautifully with the violet flowers of the fritillary, intensifying the colors of each. The hellebore flowers, which set in late autumn, and evergreen foliage are effective long before and after the fritillary has faded, making it a good companion for many shade-loving plants.

Maintenance: This species of hellebore is one of my two favorite perennials for shade. Although it can get killed to the ground during a hard winter in zone 5, it reseeds so profusely that permanence of the species in the garden is almost always assured. I leave the seedheads on the plants until they reach the intolerable stage, which is often mid-summer, to be certain of seed dispersal. Unwanted seedlings are easily yanked. Prune off winter damage in late spring. This species is tolerant of drought and heavy clay soils, which are the conditions of the plants in this picture. Oddly enough, the bulbs of the fritillary usually overwinter the first year they are planted, but they won't return in future springs. This has occurred for me in several garden settings, perhaps for different reasons. Bulbs may rot in irrigated summer gardens (not the case on this site); they are heavy feeders and prone to critter consumption. Whatever the reason for their demise, to me these beauties are worth the time it takes to replant them annually.

COMBINATION 3

1. Plant	Helleborus foetidus	
Common name	stinking hellebore	
Zone	(5)6–9	
Type	perennial	
Description	leathery dark green palmate leaves; large long-lasting green flowerheads	
Height	15–18 in.	
Width	18 in.	
Light	shade/pt shade	
Flowering month	Mar–Apr	
2. Plant	Osmunda regalis	
Common name	royal fern	
Zone	3–10	
Type	perennial	
Description	large green fronds; golden brown clusters of sporangia at tips of fertile fronds	
Height	24–30 in.	
Width	3 ft.	
Light	shade/pt shade	

Design Considerations: This is a wonderful example of form and texture, plus we get to see the same hellebore in a different light—literally—in this combination. Combination 2 was photographed on an overcast morning in the spring. This photograph was taken in the autumn with sidelighting and a touch of backlighting. This type of light increases contrast and emphasizes the three-dimensional nature of the plant, its texture, and the reflective qualities of glossy foliage. Notice the different values that are present in the hellebore and the royal fern leaves when lit from the side versus from the back. The backlit leaves, which are lighter or higher in value, appear to glow. The leaves with more direct light hitting them are darker and flat in appearance. The color of the hellebore leaves are also richer (darker and higher in saturation) in the autumn than in the spring, due to maturation. The tuftlike shoots of the hellebore are the clusters of flowers starting to form. The fabulous brown autumn foliage of the royal fern is a shade of orange (combination of reds and yellows) and contrasts beautifully with the darker green background of the hellebore, making the fern appear lighter in value; their association makes both colors appear more intense. Foliage form and texture are often much more appreciated in part-shade gardens such as this one, where magical light shows are few and far between. The fritillary in the previous combination is interplanted among the royal fern pictured here.

Maintenance: Maintenance for the hellebore is discussed in Combination 2. The royal fern works very well with the hellebore because it also tolerates partial shade and has proven to be fairly drought tolerant, once established in this dry-shade location. The fronds on this reliably hardy fern often fall off with heavy autumn winds, and stems are cut down at that time.

COMBINATION 4

1.	**Plant**	Aesculus parviflora
	Common name	bottlebrush buckeye
	Zone	4–8
	Type	shrub
	Description	palmate leaf; large pinkish white flower panicles; yellow fall color
	Height	8–12 ft.
	Width	8–15 ft.
	Light	shade/pt shade
	Flowering month	Jun–Jul
2.	**Plant**	Mertensia pulmonarioides (virginica)
	Common name	Virginia bluebells
	Zone	3–9
	Type	perennial
	Description	clusters of nodding blue flowers; bluish green leaves
	Height	18 in.
	Width	10 in.
	Light	partial shade
	Flowering month	Apr–May

Design Considerations: Virginia bluebells are a wonderful spring-flowering wildflower to interplant through a shady mixed border for early color. Here used as an underplanting for bottle-brush buckeye, it attracts attention to what might otherwise have gone unnoticed—the fabulous detail of the buckeye's newly emerging palmate leaves. The pastel-pink buds of Virgina bluebells harmonize with its pastel-blue open flowers and its blue-green foliage, creating total unification. These light colors contrasted with the dark soil really make the plant pop. The bluebells go dormant in peace beneath the buckeye as it comes into its own, with lush foliage and flowers that provide continued interest into the summer. The buckeye's bright yellow autumn color and winter stem formation make this vignette effective year-round. The buckeye can develop into a large multi-stemmed suckering shrub but is rather slow to do this. It creates good weight and an interesting layered form in the overall design. I like to use it as a specimen in mixed gardens.

Maintenance: Virginia bluebells are really no-brainers. After they die down in the summer, they are cut to the ground. In this combination the dying foliage is obscured by the maturing buckeye, and no pruning is necessary. The bottlebrush buckeye may require pruning after many years to control its suckering habit, depending on the size of the border. If you are fortunate enough to have a plant that is really putting on some nice growth, consider moving it to a location where it can develop its natural habit. It makes a spectacular lawn shrub after many years.

1. Plant	Valeriana officinalis
Common name	common valerian
Zone	4–9
Type	perennial
Description	fragrant pink-tinged white flowers; pinnately compound leaves
Height	24–60 in.
Width	12–18 in.
Light	sun/pt shade
Flowering month	May–Jun

2. Plant	Iris sanguinea 'Snow Queen'
Common name	iris
Zone	3–8
Type	perennial
Description	white flowers; straplike leaves; attractive seed pods
Height	30 in.
Width	24 in.
Light	sun/pt shade
Flowering month	May–Jun

3. Plant	Baptisia australis
Common name	blue wild indigo
Zone	3–9
Type	perennial
Description	indigo-blue flowers on spikes; blue-green leaves; black seed pods
Height	36 in.
Width	4 ft.
Light	sun/pt shade
Flowering month	Jun

4. Plant	Paeonia 'Monsieur Jules Elie'
Common name	peony
Zone	3–8
Type	perennial
Description	double dark pink flowers; coarse lobed dark green leaves
Height	36 in.
Width	36 in.
Light	full sun
Flowering month	May–Jun

COMBINATION 5

Design Considerations: The cooler colors of this classic, romantic early summer combination are relaxing and very appealing to most people. They definitely are a safe palette to work with and common colors for the time of year. A prominence of white from the valerian and the iris makes that part of the vignette dominate and come alive, particularly in the evening garden. The strong fragrance of the valerian, which intensifies late in the day, adds to its appeal as a draw for night owls. A variety of flower shapes adds greatly to the interest of this combination. The more vertical forms of the baptisia and iris flowers are separated by the more rounded form of the valerian flowers. The weight and mass of the peony flowers help to anchor this lighter mix of textures. A touch less white would make this combination a bit more balanced. Substituting a pale blue for the white iris, for example, would help get the colors in better proportion.

Maintenance: The valerian is the true maintenance magnet in this combination. It seeds excessively and can become a nuisance. Still, I find its fine texture, slender vertical habit, and fragrant flowers wonderful coming up among late-spring beauties, many of which are just awakening. It should be cut to the ground after flowering to prevent seeding and promote fresh, lush low growth. The baptisia can be sheared by one-third and shaped after flowering to create a shrublike mound that provides a structural element as a place for the eye to rest among a busy mixed garden display. The iris sets attractive seed pods, so allow at least one-third of the deadheads to remain for summer through winter interest. Its attractive golden autumn color also contributes to season-long interest. Although the heirloom peony adds to the classical charm of this vignette, its foliage gets tatty by midsummer. Avoid pruning plants back until after the first of September in zones 3, 4, and upper zone 5; leave until the end of September in the rest of zone 5 and wait until early October, if you can stand it, in zones 6, 7, and warmer. This allows the plant to continue to store energy for future bud formation. Plant it under other taller, later-blooming plants, which will help hide its unattractive appearance.

COMBINATION 6

1.	**Plant**	Humulus lupulus 'Bianca'
	Common name	golden hops
	Zone	3–8
	Type	perennial vine
	Description	yellow lobed and toothed leaves fade to yellow-green; red-tinted vining stems; yellow autumn foliage
	Height	10–15 ft.
	Light	sun/pt shade

2.	**Plant**	Rhodochiton atrosanguineus
	Common name	purple bell vine
	Type	annual vine
	Description	mauve and dark purple bell-shaped flowers; toothed and heart-shaped green leaves; outstanding purple spring growth
	Height	10 ft.
	Light	full sun
	Flowering month	Jun–Sep

Design Considerations: This simple yet stunning combination has all the ingredients of good design. It's a contrast—interesting bold foliage form and texture from the hops, with a finer yet just as interesting foliage form and texture from the purple bell vine. This spring shot is further enhanced by the contrast of the purple and yellow foliage colors. As the season progresses, the purple bell vine foliage will fade to green, yet its purple bell-shaped flowers will continue to contrast with the hops foliage, which fades to a yellow-green. Both plants are unified by their vining habit, and the way the purple bell vine climbs through and about the hops makes the two appear as one. These vines are growing on an obelisk in my garden; they add a nice vertical element that complements the mixed planting that surrounds them.

Maintenance: The hops are much more vigorous than the purple bell vine; care must be taken to keep them pruned off the purple bell vine, so that it can receive light. The gardener will also need to direct the vigorous, long, vining stems of the hops onto the support structure—and off the other plants growing around it. The purple bell vine will need a bit of assistance as well, to direct it through the hops. The purple bell vine may decline as the heat of the season increases. The hops will show some scorched leaves in heat and drought late in the season. These are easily pruned off, and healthy stems can be pulled over any open areas created by this clean-up pruning.

1. **Plant** — Ricinus communis
   Common name — castor bean
   Zone — (9)10–11
   Type — tropical
   Description — large maple-shaped leaves; rose-red seed pods, stalks, and veins
   Height — 6–8 ft.
   Width — 4 ft.
   Light — full sun
   Flowering month — Jul–Sep

2. **Plant** — Eupatorium purpureum ssp. maculatum 'Gateway'
   Common name — joe-pye weed
   Zone — 2–9
   Type — perennial
   Description — rose-pink flowerheads; whorled leaves
   Height — 5–6 ft.
   Width — 3–4 ft.
   Light — full sun
   Flowering month — Jul–Sep

3. **Plant** — Miscanthus sinensis var. condensatus 'Cosmopolitan'
   Common name — miscanthus
   Zone — (5)6–9
   Type — perennial
   Description — wide green and white variegated leaves; coppery red blooms fading to tan
   Height — 6–10 ft.
   Width — 4–5 ft.
   Light — full sun
   Flowering month — Sep–Oct

4. **Plant** — Heliopsis helianthoides var. scabra 'Sommersonne' (summer sun)
   Common name — heliopsis
   Zone — 3–9
   Type — perennial
   Description — golden yellow daisylike flowerheads; green leaves
   Height — 3–6 ft.
   Width — 4 ft.
   Light — sun/pt shade
   Flowering month — Jun–Aug

5. **Plant** — Echinacea purpurea
   Common name — purple coneflower
   Zone — 3–8
   Type — perennial
   Description — purplish pink daisylike flowers with orange conelike center; coarse leaves
   Height — 2–4 ft.
   Width — 2 ft.
   Light — full sun
   Flowering month — Jul–Sep

COMBINATION 7

Design Considerations: Wild is the overall mood of this vignette, thanks to the coneflower, heliopsis, and joe-pye weed, yet the boldness of the castor bean leaves contrasted with the refined texture and color of the miscanthus make it more eclectic than your typical meadow scene. It is long-flowering, lush, and exuberant, enlivening the viewer. The yellow flowers of the heliopsis are magnetizing—bringing the eye into the grouping, where it can then move on to the detail of the other plants—which is important, as this combination is predominantly viewed from a porch or windows that are a distance from the planting. The yellow of the heliopsis and the white on the miscanthus continue to shine into the evening, prolonging the pleasure of late-day porch-dwellers. Red or rose-pink is evident as a unifying color; it is present in the coneflowers, the joe-pye weed flowers and stems, and the stems of the castor bean. The repetition of the rounded flower forms of the joe-pye weed, heliopsis, and coneflower, and the dominance of the castor bean and miscanthus, are uniting elements. These two dominant features appear to frame the grouping, creating a sense of order through symmetrical balance. Good interconnection is established by the fullness of the planting; mass collection is evident in the drifts of plants. Wind provides good rhythm, particularly in the joe-pye weed and miscanthus.

Maintenance: Some time is involved in this grouping's upkeep. Particularly important is the deadheading of the heliopsis and coneflower, to prevent them from seeding and taking over the entire planting. Some deadheads are left for the goldfinches, which love to hang around this planting. Deadheading also prolongs bloom on the heliopsis. The castor bean needs staking. I usually allow it to go to seed; sometimes they take, and I don't have to replant the following year. The miscanthus and joe-pye weed are cut down in the spring; the joe-pye weed is good winter cover for the birds. This grouping is tolerant of short periods of drought once established.

1. Plant	Pinus flexilis 'Vanderwolf's Pyramid'
Common name	limber pine
Zone	4–7
Type	tree
Description	bluish gray-green needles; irregular open pyramidal form
Height	30 ft.
Width	30 ft.
Light	sun/pt shade

2. Plant	Sorghastrum nutans 'Sioux Blue'
Common name	Indian grass
Zone	5–8
Type	perennial
Description	upright to open form; blue foliage turning golden yellow in autumn; tan flower panicles
Height	4–6 ft.
Width	3–4 ft.
Light	full sun
Flowering month	Aug–Oct

3. Plant	Eschscholzia californica
Common name	California poppy
Type	annual
Description	bright orange flowers; ferny blue-green foliage
Height	10–12 in.
Width	8–10 in.
Light	full sun
Flowering month	Jun–Sep

4. Plant	Stokesia laevis 'Klaus Jelitto'
Common name	Stokes' aster
Zone	5–9
Type	perennial
Description	fringed daisylike sky-blue flowers; straplike green leaves
Height	12–15 in. (8 in.)
Width	15 in.
Light	full sun
Flowering month	Jul–Aug

5. Plant	Rudbeckia maxima
Common name	giant coneflower
Zone	4–9
Type	perennial
Description	yellow flowers; prominent brown cones; large blue-green leaves
Height	5–6 ft. (1½ ft.)
Width	2 ft.
Light	full sun
Flowering month	Aug–Sep

COMBINATION 8

Design Considerations: This vignette from an island bed in our driveway turnaround (see Plate 13) was photographed in August. The bed is not that large, approximately 20 ft. long by 9 ft. wide, yet it has fantastic multi-season interest, evident in this combination as well as in Combinations 9 and 10, which feature it in spring and autumn. As seen here, the overall colors in the summer are cool, unified by the predominance of the blue foliage of the plants. This is really a study in a monochromatic color scheme, where splashes of opposing colors—the orange of the California poppies, the yellow of the giant coneflower—add relief and drama. Simultaneous contrast brightens the intensity of both the blue and the orange. The California poppies, set above their blue-green foliage and hazed by the other blues, are a strong focal point. Because colors are limited, foliage textures and forms and the overall forms of the plants are more pronounced. The open, irregular form of the limber pine, the strongly vertical yet open form of the giant coneflower, the almost weeping appearance of the Indian grass, and the low, wide-spreading nature of the California poppy and Stokes' aster add great variety and contrast to the scene. The limber pine anchors the entire bed to the earth—it is a bastion of constancy among the ever-evolving herbaceous and deciduous plants that surround it. Compare the mood of this photograph to the next two photographs: all three shots were taken within a few feet of each other, from different angles, around this one limber pine

Maintenance: Not an overwhelming amount of care is needed to keep this vignette in shape. The California poppies and Stokes' asters are deadheaded regularly to keep them flowering longer. The inner foliage on the poppies is cleaned out periodically to improve the overall appearance. The giant coneflower is a carefree beauty. Allow it to set seed and enjoy it into the winter—the birds will. It isn't a heavy seeder. The tall stems may break in severe weather. The limber pine is fast growing at 18–24 in. a year; an 8-ft. plant, which is what we started with, can reach 30 ft. in about ten years. Since it can get tall and wide, it requires candling to keep it at the appropriate scale for this setting. The Indian grass is discussed in Combination 10.

COMBINATION 9

Design Considerations: The real beauty in our gardens lies in the details. This spring vignette from the border featured in Combination 8 is all about color. The red-orange buds of the limber pine would perhaps go unnoticed if not drawn into focus by the harmonizing red-orange of the oriental poppy. Both are intensified because they are surrounded by red's complement, green. The frontlighting on the beech makes its purple leaves appear almost black, a unifying link with the black basal blotches of the poppy and the black markings on top of its future seed capsule. All the colors appear richer (more saturated) and darker because they are wet from the morning dew. Notice how much more vibrant the color of the poppy is in the area where it is contrasted sharply by the dark background of the beech foliage, compared to where it is backed by the lighter, less contrastful, blue-gray background of the driveway.

Maintenance: The oriental poppy, bold both in its color and in its form, is also noticeably more stout and sturdy than most oriental poppies. The flowering stems hold up well into the summer, supporting the interesting seed capsules. Annuals fill the hole that is left when the poppy goes dormant. The limber pine was discussed in the previous combination. The weeping purple beech, a lovely specimen, was planted to hang over the edge of the raised stone island bed. It is grown as a large shrub in this garden, its height and spread easily controlled with pruning. Thinning of the plant is often desirable to emphasize the interesting weeping habit.

1. Plant	Pinus flexilis 'Vanderwolf's Pyramid'
Common name	limber pine
Zone	4–7
Type	tree
Description	bluish gray-green needles; irregular open pyramidal form
Height	30 ft.
Width	30 ft.
Light	sun/pt shade
2. Plant	Fagus sylvatica 'Purpurea Pendula'
Common name	weeping purple beech
Zone	4–7
Type	tree
Description	weeping purple-leaved form; small specimen
Height	10 ft.
Width	10 ft.
Light	sun/pt shade
3. Plant	Papaver orientale 'Feuerriese'
Common name	oriental poppy
Zone	3–7
Type	perennial
Description	single brick-red flowers; large coarse leaves
Height	30 in.
Width	24 in.
Light	full sun
Flowering month	May–Jun

COMBINATION 10

Design Considerations: Again we are looking at a combination from the garden featured in Combination 8, this time of an autumn highlight, demonstrating how a multi-seasonal effect can be accomplished in one rather small border by selecting from a diverse palette of plants and combining them with attention to detail. The unifying element of these warm colors is yellow. The yellow hue is obvious in the mum, but the brown of the Indian grass is really a version of orange, which is a yellow-red. This is more apparent in the leaves that are backlit. To me, looking at the mums through the grass softens their almost garish appearance. The fine texture of the grass contrasts with the bold texture of the mums, creating a focal feature. As if the mums couldn't do it on their own!

Maintenance: This is a very hardy mum. Cutting it back by half, before it flowers, would create a more compact habit, but I prefer to let it get tall behind the grass, which gives it a more natural appearance than a tight mound would. The Indian grass has a tendency to open up a bit and create a wide form; give it enough space to do this gracefully. Both plants are cut down in the early spring.

1. Plant	Chrysanthemum 'Autumn Moon'
Common name	mum
Zone	(5)6–9
Type	perennial
Description	large fully double pale yellow flowers
Height	24–30 in.
Width	24–30 in.
Light	full sun
Flowering month	Oct

2. Plant	Sorghastrum nutans 'Sioux Blue'
Common name	Indian grass
Zone	5–8
Type	perennial
Description	upright to open form; blue foliage turning golden yellow in autumn; tan flower panicles
Height	4–6 ft.
Width	3–4 ft.
Light	full sun
Flowering month	Aug–Oct

COMBINATION 11

1. Plant	Picea abies 'Pendula'
Common name	weeping Norway spruce
Zone	3–7
Type	tree
Description	dark green needles; weeping form
Height	12–15 ft.
Width	12–15 ft.
Light	full sun

2. Plant	Solenostemon 'Penny'
Common name	coleus
Type	annual
Description	parchment-yellow burgundy-infused leaves
Height	2–2½ ft.
Width	2 ft.
Light	full sun

3. Plant	Canna indica 'Red Stripe'
Common name	canna
Zone	7–10
Type	tropical
Description	large bananalike leaves striped green and red; orange-red flowers
Height	8–10 ft.
Width	2 ft.
Light	full sun
Flowering month	Jul–Sep

Design Considerations: This combination features summer-long interest using bold foliage colors and forms. The weeping Norway spruce's habit is interesting year-round, but it effectively pulls the eye from the tall canna down to the coleus in this summer vignette. The density and weight of its thick branching and deep green foliage grounds the transparency of the canna and coleus leaves, seen here with backlighting. The varied foliage and overall forms of these three plants add diversity and interest in a relatively limited color palette. We are looking at mostly greens, including yellow-greens, and various reds. Together these contrasting colors, along with the bold foliage and forms, create a focal area in this border. Yellow is present in both the coleus and the canna, creating unification. Because the spruce and the coleus are so interesting, they help take a touch of the spotlight away from the canna, which tends to overdominate a planting if given the chance.

Maintenance: This grouping is relatively low maintenance. Keeping the soil moist yet well draining (this planting is on a raised wall) will produce strong growth on the canna. The coleus is kept pinched to prevent flowering and maintain a neat growth habit. Although the spruce can eventually get large, it is relatively slow growing and can be kept pruned to a desirable height and width if needed. The cannas are dug, overwintered, and replanted annually. Various cultivars of coleus are chosen annually, depending on what is new and wild that year.

1. **Plant** — Euphorbia cotinifolia
   Common name — tropical smoketree
   Zone — 9–11
   Type — annual
   Description — rich red leaves reminiscent of a smokebush
   Height — 3–5 ft.
   Width — 3 ft.
   Light — full sun

2. **Plant** — Phlox paniculata 'Look Again'
   Common name — border phlox
   Zone — 4–8
   Type — perennial
   Description — large magenta flower clusters
   Height — 3½ ft.
   Width — 2 ft.
   Light — full sun
   Flowering month — Jul–Sep

3. **Plant** — Rudbeckia fulgida var. speciosa (newmannii)
   Common name — black-eyed susan
   Zone — 3–9
   Type — perennial
   Description — golden daisylike flowers with black centers; toothed leaves
   Height — 24 in. (12 in.)
   Width — 24 in.
   Light — full sun
   Flowering month — Jul–Sep

COMBINATION 12

Design Considerations: The backlighting on this combination increases the value and intensity of the colors, creating a glowing, striking ambience. The euphorbia is unbelievable under such conditions; an unusual plant and a real identification-stumper to even the savviest plants people, this woody annual is sometimes seen in containers, but it is a great addition to the mixed border, where it mimics a cotinus (smokebush). This is a harmonious warm combination, with analogous colors of red, yellow-orange, and magenta; red is the shared hue throughout. With careful association, the magenta phlox, being a shade of red-purple, can successfully be used in either warm or cool combinations. The fairly light (high-valued) and bright (saturated) phlox is a favorite of visitors to the garden. Black is a shade shared by some of leaves, stems, cones, and dead inner flowers through the vignette. The saturated red, verticality, and taller stature of the euphorbia make it the focal point. This black-eyed susan is preferred over the more common Goldsturm black-eyed susan because its flowers and leaves are smaller and the overall appearance of the plant is much more refined.

Maintenance: A well-drained soil is needed for this combination; short periods of dryness are tolerated. The euphorbia is not a heavy feeder, requiring fertilizing only once or twice the whole season; it can be overwintered indoors in a cool (65°F), very sunny window, with minimal water. Some leaf droppage is common when the plant is first brought inside, and it may maintain a slightly dormant look through the winter. This particular specimen was overwintered in a greenhouse and is trained as a tree form. The phlox is very low maintenance, being extremely free of disease even in tight quarters with minimal air circulation; it responds beautifully to pruning before flowering, to reduce its height or delay flowering time, if desired, and it doesn't seed heavily—truly a choice phlox. The black-eyed susan is a heavy seeder. Deadheading to control its spread may be desirable, but I often allow some seeding, so that this area of the garden is full and lush. Again, this coneflower, with its more refined nature, is not overbearing when it pops up between other plants; I simply dig out sections of the drift when it becomes too large.

COMBINATION 13

1. Plant   Amorpha canescens
   Common name   leadplant amorpha
   Zone   2–6
   Type   shrub
   Description   violet flower spikes with bright orange
                     anthers; pinnately compound gray-green
                     leaves
   Height   2–4 ft.
   Width   4–5 ft.
   Light   full sun
   Flowering month Jun–Jul

2. Plant   Eschscholzia californica 'Purple Gleam'
   Common name   California poppy
   Type   annual
   Description   pinkish purple flowers;
                     blue-green ferny foliage
   Height   10–12 in.
   Width   8–10 in.
   Light   full sun
   Flowering month Jun–Sep

3. Plant   Ocimum 'African Blue'
   Common name   basil
   Zone   9–10
   Type   annual
   Description   green foliage strongly tinted purple
   Height   24 in.
   Width   24 in.
   Light   full sun

Design Considerations: This unusual combination works for many reasons. The purple—in the basil foliage, in the amorpha flowers, and in the red-purple flowers of the California poppy—creates harmony. The blue-green foliage of the poppy emphasizes the blue element of these shared purples. The stray orange flower from the straight species of California poppy helps to emphasize the orange anthers of the amorpha. Although only a portion of the plants can be seen in this shot, both the amorpha and the basil form a shrublike mounded form. The delicate nature of the poppies interplanted among the two adds an airiness that softens the denser forms.

Maintenance: All members of this self-sufficient grouping are fairly tolerant of drought and relatively poor soil to boot. The basil should be kept pinched to prevent flowering and encourage a full shape. Periodic deadheading of the California poppy extends bloom. The amorpha can get large with maturity; prune plants back in late winter or early spring, if needed, to keep it in scale with its surroundings.

COMBINATION 14

1. Plant	Hosta 'Blue Cadet'	
Common name	plantain-lily	
Zone	3–8	
Type	perennial	
Description	lavender flowers; bluish green heart-shaped leaves fade to green by July	
Height	15 in.	
Width	24–36 in.	
Light	shade/pt shade	
Flowering month	Jun–Jul	
2. Plant	Arum italicum ssp. italicum 'Marmoratum'	
Common name	painted arum	
Zone	5–9	
Type	perennial	
Description	spear-shaped variegated deep green leaves; orange-red berries; jack-in-the-pulpit-type flowers	
Height	18 in.	
Width	18 in.	
Light	shade/pt shade	
Flowering month	May	
3. Plant	Ligularia dentata 'Desdemona'	
Common name	bigleaf ligularia	
Zone	4–8	
Type	perennial	
Description	yellow-orange daisylike flowerheads; large round leathery leaves with purple undersides; purple stems	
Height	3–4 ft. (3 ft.)	
Width	4 ft.	
Light	shade/pt shade	
Flowering month	Jul–Sep	

Design Considerations: The mood of this combination of blues and greens, with some hints of cooler purple, is cool and restful, an effect only enhanced in this shaded location by the blue light. Interesting foliage forms and textures are more apparent in the absence of strong colors. The verticality of the arum adds nice relief among the heart-shaped and rounded leaf forms of the hosta and the ligularia. The arum works well interplanted here because, as the foliage of its companions dies down in the autumn, the arum foliage returns, providing evergreen to semi-evergreen winter interest. When the arum fruit matures and turns orange-red, it contrasts with the blues and purples, adding a touch of warmth and creating a striking focal point, drawing greater attention to this combination. When the ligularia is in flower, its yellow-orange warms the vignette up even more, and its deadheads extend appeal into the cold months, while attracting goldfinches.

Maintenance: Although this selection of bigleaf ligularia appears to be more heat tolerant than the straight species, sufficient moisture is still key to keeping this combination in top shape. Line the planting hole of the ligularia with a plastic bag to help hold extra moisture around its roots. This vignette is as appealing to slugs as it is to the the shade gardener, so mulching with pine needles is in order. I don't bother to deadhead the ligularia, for the design reasons just mentioned. The arum needs a touch of deadleafing to clean-up declining summer foliage, but—obviously—deadheading this plant would be a major perennial pruning faux pas!

COMBINATION 15

1. **Plant**	Hydrangea quercifolia 'Snowflake'
Common name	oakleaf hydrangea
Zone	5–9
Type	shrub
Description	large white flower panicles; flowers appear double; red and purple fall color; cinnamon-colored exfoliating bark
Height	6–8 ft.
Width	6–8 ft.
Light	sun/pt shade
Flowering month	Jun–Jul

2. **Plant**	Cimicifuga ramosa 'Brunette'
Common name	bugbane
Zone	3 8
Type	perennial
Description	dark purple compound foliage; white bottlebrush flowers
Height	4–6 ft.
Width	2–4 ft.
Light	partial shade
Flowering month	Aug–Sep

Design Considerations: The first thing that strikes me as pleasing in this duo is the way the toothed leaf margins of the cimicifuga mimic the shape of the individual hydrangea flowers that brighten this partially shaded garden. This subtly similar pattern unifies the two plants, even as the difference between the light white (high value) and dark purplish green (lower value) creates strong contrast and a focal point. The white deepens and increases the saturation of the cimicifuga leaves by reflecting their color back upon them. The red-purple on the stems of the cimicifuga bleeds into the leaves; note how it and the green in the center of the hydrangea flowers complement each other. Because the texture of the hydrangea flowers is bold, the white has a more solid impact than it would have if delivered by open, airy flower panicles. Overall, the interesting textures of the hydrangea and cimicifuga leaves work well together. The cimicifuga starts to flower just as the hydrangea is finishing, further contributing white to this area, but not with near the impact of the larger, coarser-textured hydrangea blooms. In the autumn the hydrangea again takes center stage with its red and purple leaf colors, and it holds the spot in the winter, without the help of the cimicifuga, when its cinnamon-colored exfoliating stems continue to add a bold message.

Maintenance: Both plants prefer moist yet well-drained, fertile soil high in organic matter. Dry soil or too much sun will scorch the leaves of the cimicifuga. The hydrangea can be somewhat tender in cooler zones; young stems and buds may be injured with temperatures below –5°F. Prune the hydrangea after flowering if size control is needed.

COMBINATION 16

1. Plant		Scabiosa Butterfly Blue®
	Common name	pincushion flower
	Zone	3–7
	Type	perennial
	Description	light blue flowers; green leaves
	Height	12 in. (6 in.)
	Width	12 in.
	Light	full sun
	Flowering month	May–Oct
2. Plant		Salvia nemorosa 'Purple Glory'
	Common name	perennial salvia
	Zone	3–8
	Type	perennial
	Description	blue-violet flowers; oblong green leaves
	Height	24 in.
	Width	24 in.
	Light	full sun
	Flowering month	Jun–Aug
3. Plant		Antirrhinum majus 'Rocket Red'
	Common name	snapdragon
	Type	annual
	Description	dark red flowers
	Height	24 in.
	Width	12 in.
	Light	full sun
	Flowering month	Jun–Sep
4. Plant		Nepeta sibirica 'Souvenir d'André Chaudron'
	Common name	catmint
	Zone	3–8
	Type	perennial
	Description	lavender-blue flowers; gray-green leaves
	Height	24–36 in.
	Width	24–36 in.
	Light	full sun
	Flowering month	Jun–Jul

Design Considerations: This vignette is unified by repetition of vertical forms and the presence of shared hues of red and blue throughout, an analogous scheme that is very connected. I really like its yin and yang qualities: the spires of flowers create an active uplifting mood, as they seem to try to reach the heavens, while the mounded form of the scabiosa at the base is grounding, adding needed stability. The strong deep red of the snapdragons is enticing and dominant among the purples; its velvety flower texture only adds to its richness.

Maintenance: Deadhead all these plants to keep the display flowering for months. A sunny, well-drained, even rather dry location is ideal.

COMBINATION 17

1.	**Plant**	Angelica gigas
	Common name	angelica
	Zone	4–8
	Type	perennial
	Description	bold dissected foliage; 4- to 8-in.-wide burgundy flowerheads
	Height	3–6 ft.
	Width	2–3 ft.
	Light	sun/pt shade
	Flowering month	Jul–Aug
2.	**Plant**	Canna 'Striata' (Pretoria)
	Common name	canna
	Zone	7–10
	Type	tropical
	Description	green and yellow variegated leaves; orange flowers
	Height	5–9 ft.
	Width	2 ft.
	Light	full sun
	Flowering month	Jul–Sep

Design Considerations: This combination is all about line and form. Imagine this picture in black and white. Visualizing the different values of white, gray, and black will help you see its positive and negative spaces: the strong lines and forms would still be prominent. Note that the lines in the canna leaves repeat the lines of the angelica stems. The rounded outline of the angelica flowerheads are an inverted form of the rounded bases of the canna leaves. All these lines unite the two plants. Although color is secondary here, the yellow in the canna contrasts with the burgundy of the angelica, creating needed tension. Overall, the bold architectural nature of the plants exudes strength and dominance. When the canna is in bloom, its bodacious orange flowers can overwhelm the beauty we see here.

Maintenance: These plants are fairly low maintenance. The angelica is monocarpic, meaning it dies after setting seed, so the flowerheads should be cut off as soon as the flowers fade to prevent seed maturation; this can extend the life of the plant, which typically acts like a biennial or short-lived perennial. If allowed to seed in a very favorable location, angelica produces numerous offspring, but in my garden, unfortunately, seedlings occur only minimally. I allow each to develop (basal leaves year one, flowers year two) because I prize it so highly. Too many, though, could overpower even the largest garden.

COMBINATION 18

1. Plant	Gladiolus communis ssp. byzantinus
Common name	Byzantine gladiolus
Zone	(5)6–10
Type	perennial
Description	spikes of magenta flowers; irislike leaves
Height	24–36 in.
Width	4–6 in.
Light	sun/pt shade
Flowering month	Jun

2. Plant	Nigella damascena Miss Jekyll Series
Common name	love-in-a-mist
Type	annual
Description	white, blue, or pink flowers; feathery green foliage; decorative seed pods
Height	15 in.
Width	12 in.
Light	sun/pt shade
Flowering month	May–Jul

Design Considerations: The pastel colors and fine textures and lines of this combination give it a sweet, soft nature, which is quite a contrast to Combination 17. Also, compare the magenta (red-purple) of this gladiolus to the magenta of the phlox in Combination 12: this magenta has more white in it, making it a higher value than the phlox; it is also not as intense or saturated as the phlox. The white of the gladiolus flowers—evident both in the slightly open buds and the light green of its stems—is tied to the white of the nigella. The graceful habit of the gladiolus, combined with the ultrafine, intricately lacy texture of the nigella, contributes to the elegant effect of this duo. The gladiolus often dies back as summer progresses, and the nigella fills the space, continuing to flower and eventually setting outstanding seedheads that are perhaps even more ornamental than the flowers. This delicate combination needs to be sited at the front of a border or along a walkway, where it can be appreciated.

Maintenance: I allow the nigella to reseed in my gardens, where it acts almost perennial. In fact, I carried the seedheads to this location, where I wanted new plants. It was just by chance that the white-flowering plants developed here; however, the blues or even the pinks would have worked in this combination. The gladiolus is really only marginally hardy in my zone 5 garden (it is often listed as zone 7), but it makes it through most winters. It is worth replanting if losses should occur.

COMBINATION 19

1. Plant	Amsonia ciliata	
Common name	downy amsonia	
Zone	3–9	
Type	perennial	
Description	terminal clusters of star-shaped blue flowers; very fine foliage	
Height	24–36 in.	
Width	36 in.	
Light	sun/pt shade	
Flowering month	May–Jun	
2. Plant	Panicum virgatum 'Dallas Blues'	
Common name	switch grass	
Zone	5–9	
Type	perennial	
Description	wide blue leaves; large red-tinged airy panicles; strong vertical habit	
Height	6–8 ft.	
Width	3–4 ft.	
Light	full sun	
Flowering month	Aug–Oct	
3. Plant	Pinus parviflora 'Glauca'	
Common name	Japanese white pine	
Zone	4–7	
Type	tree	
Description	bluish gray-green needles	
Height	15–20 ft.	
Width	8–10 ft.	
Light	full sun	

Design Considerations: Textures and forms scream in this vignette. What an appreciation we feel for these elements, thanks here to the dazzle created by backlighting. When I view such scenes in the garden, I always feel overwhelmingly blessed to be surrounded by, to be a part of, such spectacular beauty. This combination explicitly illustrates the effective simplicity of a limited color palette. Low-profile greens, blue-greens, and tans allow contrasts of texture and form to shine. The angle of the light illuminates abundant details, such as the high (light) and low (dark) values throughout. The Japanese white pine is stabilizing among the wispy, fine textures of the panicum and amsonia; its form is cradling, adding a sense of security to the grouping.

Maintenance: Very little care is needed for this group of plants. The amsonia can be sheared and shaped for a better form after flowering by removing 4–6 in. off the top. The panicum, which has a tendency to open up a bit and therefore needs some room to perform naturally, is simply cut down in the spring. The Japanese white pine requires no care other than to be kept moist and free from the amsonia, the panicum, and other encroaching herbaceous plants, so that it receives sufficient light. It can be candled in the spring if size control is a factor.

1. Plant	Digitalis grandiflora
Common name	yellow foxglove
Zone	3–8
Type	perennial
Description	light yellow flower spikes; green leaves
Height	24–36 in.
Width	15–18 in.
Light	sun/pt shade
Flowering month	Jun–Jul

2. Plant	Nepeta 'Six Hills Giant'
Common name	catmint
Zone	3–8
Type	perennial
Description	lavender-blue flowers; gray-green leaves
Height	3 ft.
Width	3 ft.
Light	full sun
Flowering month	Jun–Jul

3. Plant	Rosa 'Nearly Wild'
Common name	rose
Zone	4–9
Type	shrub
Description	ever-blooming single pink flowers
Height	3 ft.
Width	3–4 ft.
Light	full sun
Flowering month	Jun–Sep

4. Plant	Geranium platypetalum
Common name	broad-petaled geranium
Zone	3–8
Type	perennial
Description	violet flowers on sticky stalks; rounded and lobed hairy leaves
Height	18–24 in.
Width	18–24 in.
Light	sun/pt shade
Flowering month	Jun

COMBINATION 20

Design Considerations: Victorian, classic, romantic, British—all thoughts that come to mind with this vignette. Grandma's garden may be another. However we choose to describe it, I think its restful style of predominantly soft and cooler colors still has broad appeal. An exception, the small spot of Leuchtfunk maiden pink, adds just the right amount of tension. Pastel color themes such as this one are more prevalent in the spring and early summer. Many people select this type of color scheme because it is relatively safe and fairly proper—it may be a favorite for those who still won't dare use orange! The rounded forms of the rose and geranium contrast with the vertical forms of the foxglove and nepeta. The scene is wonderfully interconnected, with layering and interplanting evident from top to bottom. Seedling plants of nigella and thyme, among others, seen at the bottom of the photograph, contribute to this interconnectedness.

Maintenance: With deadheading, this display will have a fairly long performance, with sporadic bloom into the autumn. The foxglove in particular will flower for a long time with deadheading; cut it back to the basal foliage after flowering is finished. I love this rose for its clean old-fashioned single flowers, long bloom period, good habit, and, most of all, its disease resistance. Japanese beetles love it too: they need to be picked off on a regular basis. Its habit is dense and round but can become open with age, particularly if it is part of a lush planting like this one. Prune in the early spring to improve a habit that may have gone astray, and in the summer, cut surrounding plants down a bit, so the rose gets sufficient sun. The geranium foliage holds up fairly well; shear it off to the base in stages to refurbish it, if needed. The nepeta can be sheared and shaped after flowering to prevent its falling over onto its neighbors.

COMBINATION 21

1. Plant   Papaver rhoeas
Common name   corn poppy
Type   annual
Description   brilliant red papery blooms
Height   12–18 in.
Width   3–5 in.
Light   full sun
Flowering month   May–Jul

2. Plant   Lychnis coronaria
Common name   rose campion
Zone   4–8
Type   perennial
Description   vivid magenta flowers; fuzzy gray stems and leaves
Height   24–36 in.
Width   18 in.
Light   full sun
Flowering month   Jun–Jul

3. Plant   Papaver rhoeas Angels' Choir
Common name   corn poppy
Type   annual
Description   a mix of double pink papery blooms and other pastel shades
Height   12–18 in.
Width   3–5 in.
Light   full sun
Flowering month   May–Jul

Design Considerations: This combination is fun, free-spirited, and wild—some of it was planned, some of it just seeded itself. Its intense colors are vibrant and cheerful; however, it may be a bit over-the-edge for some. Although the numerous flowerheads give it a busy quality, it is quite harmonious: all colors are various tints and shades of red or red-purple (magenta). Some of the Angels' Choir poppies have red central petals that effectively echo the red petals of the straight corn poppies. The gray stems of the lychnis combine more nicely with the cooler pinks and magentas they surround than with the warmer, taller reds. The contrastful greens and yellow-greens of the plants behind this grouping make all the colors even more intense. The dominance of this trio within the border is obvious—one such area is all that is needed. Its impressionistic nature is a painter's delight.

Maintenance: To keep this ethereal, short-lived combination full and abundant, reseed the poppies each spring and allow all deadheads to remain and drop seed. It is sacrilegious to deadhead poppies in my garden—several unfortunate student helpers have been reprimanded for even thinking about it! Be prepared, though, to live with straggly stems. The lychnis too must be allowed to seed, as it is short-lived and the permanence of the mother plants is never definite. This grouping is underplanted with plumbago, a wonderful groundcover that emerges late and fills in this spot to provide summer flowers and spectacular autumn color.

COMBINATION 22

1. **Plant**	Tradescantia (Andersoniana Group) 'Zwanenburg Blue'
Common name	spiderwort
Zone	3–9
Type	perennial
Description	blue-purple flowers; straplike leaves
Height	18–24 in.
Width	24 in.
Light	sun/pt shade
Flowering month	Jun–Aug

2. **Plant**	Rosa 'Seafoam'
Common name	rose
Zone	4–9
Type	shrub
Description	slightly fragrant recurrent white double flowers
Height	3 ft.
Width	4–5 ft.
Light	full sun
Flowering month	Jun–Aug

Design Considerations: The white of the rose lends this duo its clean, crisp appearance. The rose even imparts a touch of grandeur to the tradescantia, which is not typically associated with formality. The white of the rose is really a creamy white, which here is further enhanced by a haze of yellow-orange (blue-violet's complement). The white deepens the blue-violet of the tradescantia, increasing the contrast between the two. This rose is often listed as the first of the landscape roses, and it is still one of the best, with its abundant flowering and glossy, dark green foliage. A trailing rose, it is trained in this garden on heavy-gauge fishing line as an informal low hedge; it has many other outstanding associations with other plants along its length.

Maintenance: The rose is trouble-free (but do see the fertilizer recommendations in Chapter 7). I don't like the way white flowers die—so ungraceful! Deadhead to maintain attractive appearance and promote rebloom. Deadheading and then cutting back tatty foliage on the tradescantia will produce lush new growth and rebloom.

COMBINATION 23

1.	**Plant**	Pinus contorta 'Spaan's Dwarf'
	Common name	lodgepole pine
	Zone	5
	Type	tree
	Description	green needles; irregular open pyramidal form
	Height	12 ft.
	Width	8 ft.
	Light	sun/pt shade

2.	**Plant**	Hystrix patula
	Common name	bottle-brush grass
	Zone	4–8
	Type	perennial
	Description	green leaves; bottlebrush-shaped flowerheads
	Height	36 in.
	Width	15–18 in.
	Light	partial shade
	Flowering month	Jun–Aug

3.	**Plant**	Gillenia stipulata
	Common name	American ipecac
	Zone	4–8
	Type	perennial
	Description	white star-shaped flowers; trifoliate serrated leaves
	Height	24–36 in.
	Width	18 in.
	Light	sun/pt shade
	Flowering month	May–Jun

Design Considerations: Although this may not be the most striking of combinations, it is extremely useful and effective in a key trouble spot in the garden—dry shade. The vignette pictured here, situated under a maple tree, also features native plants that are not commonly seen growing in gardens, let alone growing together. For these reasons, I chose to share it. In this photograph, the combination is backlit by morning sun, which it receives for a short period. The open, irregular habit of the pine is interesting in itself, but the dark green plant would go unnoticed in this dark corner of the garden if it weren't associated with the white of the gillenia. The strong vertical form of the hystrix contrasts nicely with the loose and gracefully arching gillenia. The hystrix starts to flower in June, along with the gillenia; however, the hystrix flowers often shatter by late August. The gillenia exhibits nice golden tones in the autumn and attractive seedheads, which brings the focus back to this spot again later in the season. The pine creates permanence and winter interest.

Maintenance: Once established, all the plants in this grouping will tolerate dryness in partial shade. The hystrix is known to be somewhat short-lived, although I haven't experienced this. It will reseed. Allow this to occur to ensure permanence of the species. It is nice naturalized in dry shady areas and will require some pruning in late summer, after its flowerheads break down. The pine will be very slow-growing in dry conditions; size control is not an issue in such a location. The gillenia can be left for the winter and cut back in the spring.

COMBINATION 24

1.	**Plant**	Rodgersia aesculifolia
	Common name	fingerleaf rodgersia
	Zone	5–7
	Type	perennial
	Description	large clusters of white flowers; horsechestnut-like leaves
	Height	3–5 ft. (2–4 ft.)
	Width	4 ft.
	Light	partial shade
	Flowering month	May–Jun
2.	**Plant**	Sciadopitys verticillata
	Common name	Japanese umbrella-pine
	Zone	5–7
	Type	tree
	Description	long dark glossy green needles; conical form
	Height	15–20 ft.
	Width	10–15 ft.
	Light	sun/pt shade

Design Considerations: Monochromatic and magnificent! Textures and forms again star in this simple yet extremely effective combination, a perfect balance of harmony and contrast. Unification is accomplished in the various greens. Even in the details, we can note the yellow-green new growth of the Japanese umbrella-pine mimicked in the yellow-green of the declining rodgersia flowers. Contrast between the fine, delicately feminine texture and form of the pine and the strong, boldly masculine texture and form of the rodgersia is compelling.

Maintenance: Both players in this duo prefer rich, moist soil and protection from hot afternoon sun and strong winds. If the leaves on the rodgersia scorch, deadleaf to improve the plant's appearance. The Japanese umbrella-pine, although it would really prefer protection from winds, seems to tolerate them when young. Both plants are slow to extremely slow growing.

COMBINATION 25

1.	Plant	Hibiscus acetosella 'Red Shield'
	Common name	hibiscus
	Zone	10–11
	Type	tropical
	Description	dark red-purple palmately lobed and toothed leaves
	Height	5 ft.
	Width	3 ft.
	Light	full sun

2.	Plant	Aster laevis 'Bluebird'
	Common name	smooth aster
	Zone	4–8
	Type	perennial
	Description	lavender blue flowers with yellow eye
	Height	24–36 in.
	Width	18 in.
	Light	full sun
	Flowering month	Sep–Oct

Design Considerations: This autumn display is stunning and harmonious. The aster flowers (blue-purple) and the hibiscus leaves (red-purple) are united by the blues and purples they both contain. They contrast with each other, too: the darker or lower-valued shade of the hibiscus versus the lighter or higher-valued tint of the aster. The interesting cut-leaved form of the hibiscus leaf is a nice contrast to the common daisylike form of the aster. Together they enhance each other, as any good couple should. The hibiscus can be large and striking in a border; however, it is lost against a dark background or among similarly dark-shaded plants. Combining it with a lighter background or lighter plants, as is done here, makes it more visible and easier to enjoy.

Maintenance: Both plants are good, easy-to-grow performers. It may take a while for the hibiscus to reach mature size. Regular fertilizing is recommended to give it a boost. The aster doesn't appear to self-seed. Cut back in the spring. Its stems can be a bit lax; plan for this by siting the aster among plants that can act as support.

COMBINATION 26

1. Plant		Pinus contorta 'Chief Joseph'
	Common name	lodgepole pine
	Zone	5
	Type	tree
	Description	slow-growing small conifer; green needles turn bright yellow in autumn
	Height	15 ft.
	Width	6–7 ft.
	Light	sun/pt shade
2. Plant		Acorus gramineus 'Minimus Aureus'
	Common name	sweet flag
	Zone	6–8
	Type	perennial
	Description	chartreuse-yellow grasslike foliage
	Height	3–5 in.
	Width	3–5 in.
	Light	sun/pt shade

Design Considerations: Here two very different types of plants, a conifer and a grasslike perennial, are so alike they appear to be one. United by their yellow autumn foliage and fine-textured leaves, they create an eye-stopping combination. This photograph was actually taken in mid-November in Ohio, when a ray of such sunshine was as welcome as it was unexpected. The pine is small and young; it will eventually dwarf the acorus, but for now it works—and for once trying to speed up the growth of a plant is not the goal. A light snow will cover the acorus, but the top branches of the pine would still be evident, glowing more than ever in high contrast against the white.

Maintenance: This duo is actually situated on the west side of the house, where it gets some pretty strong afternoon sun. Such conditions are not recommended for an acorus, but plants don't always read books! It did, however, read that it was marginally hardy in my zone 5 garden and died during a winter with cold temperatures and very little snow cover. I think it is worth replanting. Moist but well-drained soil is preferred. The pine will be pruned to keep it shorter and more shrublike.

COMBINATION 27

1.	**Plant**	Rosa multiflora 'Grevillei'
		(seven sisters' rose)
	Common name	seven sisters' rose
	Zone	4–9
	Type	shrub
	Description	large clusters of small dark pink double
		flowers
	Height	10–12 ft.
	Width	4–5 ft.
	Light	full sun
	Flowering month	Jun–Jul
2.	**Plant**	Scabiosa columbaria var. ochroleuca
	Common name	cream pincushion flower
	Zone	3–7
	Type	perennial
	Description	cream yellow flowers on tall wiry stems
	Height	36 in. (3 in.)
	Width	24 in.
	Light	full sun
	Flowering month	Jun–Oct

Design Considerations: As the growing season comes to a close, we see the structural elements of our mixed gardens—trees, shrubs, conifers and other evergreens, hardscaping and art features, interesting seedheads and fruit, the outlines of perennials. And we focus on the details of what might still be happening—the little surprises that occur when you think everything is pretty much at rest never cease to amaze me. Here the foliage of a rose is candied by December's chill, among the remaining flowers and seedheads of the scabiosa. Although the rose has a short season, it remains in my garden, grown up a trellis on our home: it was a cutting I rooted from my grandmother's rose. The nomenclature for this rose is confused, but one of its common names (and the one I know it as) is seven sisters' rose—and my grandmother is one of seven sisters. No matter its color, texture, or form, or whether it combines properly with anything else, or that it gets mildew in the summer and all but defoliates—this rose will remain a part of my garden. I hope that even as we get more and more knowledgeable about plants and the art of design, we will always hold on to such sentimental associations and let them prevail over all else. Perhaps by showing such beauty, even once a year, this rose was placed as a reminder?

Maintenance: This rose is tolerant of poor soils and some shade, and can be damaged in severe winters. If hard pruned, it can be grown as a large shrub; if grown as a climber, remove dead wood in the spring and train new growth up the support structure. The scabiosa is wild and rangy and enjoys poor, dry soil. It can reseed heavily, but the fine texture of its long wiry stems keeps it from becoming a nuisance. Deadheading is somewhat overwhelming: the plant produces such masses of flowers, they seem to blur together after a while. I usually leave it alone and let it do its thing.

SCIENTIFIC AND COMMON NAMES

—A—

Abies lasiocarpa 'Arizonica Compacta'	corkbark fir
Abies procera 'Glauca Prostrata'	noble fir
Acanthus spinosus	spiny bear's breeches
Acer griseum	paperbark maple
Acer palmatum var. dissectum Dissectum Atropurpureum Group	cutleaf Japanese maple
Acer palmatum 'Sango-kaku'	Japanese maple
Achillea 'Anblo' (Anthea)	yarrow
Achillea 'Heidi'	yarrow
Achillea 'Salmon Beauty'	yarrow
Achillea filipendulina 'Altgold'	fernleaf yarrow
Aconitum 'Bressingham Spire'	monkshood
Aconitum 'Ivorine'	monkshood
Aconitum carmichaelii (Wilsonii Group) 'Spätlese'	monkshood
Aconitum episcopale	climbing monkshood
Aconitum lycoctonum ssp. neapolitanum	monkshood
Acorus gramineus 'Minimus Aureus'	sweet flag
Acorus gramineus 'Oborozuki'	sweet flag
Acorus gramineus 'Ogon'	sweet flag
Adiantum pedatum	maidenhair fern
Aesculus parviflora	bottlebrush buckeye
Agapanthus 'Bressingham Blue'	lily of the Nile
Agastache 'Blue Fortune'	anise hyssop
Agastache rupestris	rock anise hyssop
Agave havardiana	agave
Ageratum houstonianum 'Blue Horizon'	ageratum
Ajuga reptans 'Purple Torch'	bugleweed
Alcea rosea 'Peaches and Dreams'	hollyhock
Alcea rosea 'The Watchman'	hollyhock
Alcea rugosa	Russian hollyhock
Alchemilla mollis	lady's mantle
Allium caeruleum	blue globe onion
Allium carinatum ssp. pulchellum	keeled garlic
Allium cristophii	downy onion
Allium hollandicum (aflatunense) 'Purple Sensation'	ornamental onion
Allium moly 'Jeannine'	lily leek
Allium schubertii	ornamental onion
Allium sphaerocephalon	drumstick allium
Alstroemeria 'Sweet Laura'	Peruvian lily
Alstroemeria aurea 'Orange King'	Peruvian lily
Alstroemeria psittacina	parrot lily
Alternanthera dentata 'Rubiginosa'	joseph's coat
Amelanchier ×grandiflora 'Autumn Brilliance'	serviceberry
Amorpha canescens	leadplant amorpha
Amorphophallus konjac	devil's tongue
Ampelopsis glandulosa var. brevipedunculata 'Elegans'	porcelain berry
Amsonia ciliata	downy amsonia
Amsonia elliptica	amsonia
Amsonia hubrichtii	Arkansas amsonia
Amsonia tabernaemontana	willow amsonia
Anemone ×hybrida 'Queen Charlotte'	Japanese anemone

Anemone ×hybrida 'September Charm' . . . . Japanese anemone

Angelica gigas . . . . angelica

Angelonia 'Blue Pacific' . . . . angelonia

Angelonia angustifolia 'Purple Pinnacles' . . . . angelonia

Anthriscus sylvestris 'Ravenswing' . . . . anthriscus

Antirrhinum majus 'Rocket Red' . . . . snapdragon

Aquilegia alpina . . . . alpine columbine

Aquilegia vulgaris var. stellata 'Black Barlow' . . . . . columbine

Aralia elata 'Aureovariegata' . . . . aralia

Arctotis ×hybrida 'Dark Red' . . . . African daisy

Arctotis ×hybrida 'Flame' . . . . African daisy

Arisaema sikokianum . . . . jack-in-the-pulpit

Artemisia 'Huntington' . . . . artemisia

Artemisia 'Powis Castle' . . . . artemisia

Artemisia 'Silverado' . . . . artemisia

Artemisia absinthium 'Lambrook Silver' . . . . artemisia

Arum italicum ssp. italicum 'Marmoratum' . . . . . . painted arum

Aruncus dioicus . . . . goat's beard

Asclepias tuberosa . . . . butterfly weed

Asclepias tuberosa 'Hello Yellow' . . . . butterfly weed

Aster 'Climax' . . . . aster

Aster laevis 'Bluebird' . . . . smooth aster

Aster novae-angliae 'Hella Lacy' . . . . New England aster

Aster novae-angliae 'Hillside' . . . . New England aster

Aster novae-angliae 'Purple Dome' . . . . New England aster

Aster novae-angliae 'Wild Light Blue' . . . . New England aster

Aster oblongifolius var. angustatus
    'Raydon's Favorite' . . . . Raydon's aster

Aster tataricus 'Jindai' . . . . Tatarian aster

Astilbe ×arendsii 'Snowdrift' . . . . astilbe

Astilbe chinensis 'Purple Candle' . . . . Chinese astilbe

Astilbe chinensis var. taquetii 'Superba' . . . . Chinese astilbe

Astilbe chinensis 'Veronica Klose' . . . . Chinese astilbe

Astilbe ×rosea 'Peach Blossom' . . . . astilbe

Athyrium niponicum var. pictum . . . . Japanese painted fern

Atriplex hortensis var. rubra . . . . mountain spinach

—B—

Baptisia 'Purple Smoke' . . . . wild indigo

Baptisia australis . . . . blue wild indigo

Baptisia sphaerocarpa . . . . yellow wild indigo

Belamcanda chinensis . . . . blackberry lily

Belamcanda chinensis 'Hello Yellow' . . . . blackberry lily

Berberis thunbergii var. atropurpurea
    'Bailtwo' (Burgundy Carousel™) . . . . Japanese barberry

Berberis thunbergii var. atropurpurea
    'Gentry Cultivar' (Royal Burgundy™) . . . . Japanese barberry

Berberis thunbergii var. atropurpurea
    'Rose Glow' . . . . Japanese barberry

Berberis thunbergii var. atropurpurea
    'Royal Cloak' . . . . Japanese barberry

Berberis thunbergii 'Monler' (Gold Nugget™) . . . . Japanese barberry

Berberis thunbergii 'Monry' (Sunsation™) . . . . Japanese barberry

Beta vulgaris 'Bull's Blood' . . . . Swiss chard

Beta vulgaris 'Golden' . . . . Swiss chard

Beta vulgaris 'Ruby Queen' . . . . Swiss chard

Betula utilis var. jacquemontii . . . . whitebarked Himalayan
    birch

Bouvardia ternifolia . . . . scarlet trompetilla

Brachyscome 'Ultra' . . . . Swan River daisy

Brassica oleracea . . . . ornamental kale

Brunnera macrophylla . . . . Siberian bugloss

Buddleia 'Lochinch' . . . . butterfly bush

Buddleia davidii 'Black Knight' . . . . butterfly bush

Buddleia davidii 'Mongo' (Nanho blue) . . . . butterfly bush

Buphthalmum speciosum . . . . scented oxeye

Buxus 'Green Gem' . . . . boxwood

Buxus 'Green Velvet' . . . . boxwood

Buxus microphylla 'Winter Gem' . . . . boxwood

—C—

Caladium 'Florida Cardinal' . . . . caladium

Caladium 'Florida Sweetheart' . . . . caladium

Calamagrostis ×acutiflora 'Karl Foerster' . . . . feather reed grass

Calamagrostis ×acutiflora 'Overdam' . . . . feather reed grass

Calamagrostis brachytricha . . . . Korean feather reed
    grass

Calendula officinalis 'Orange King' . . . . pot marigold

Callicarpa dichotoma 'Issai' . . . . purple beautyberry

Calycanthus floridus . . . . common sweetshrub

Camassia leichtlinii 'Semiplena' . . . . camass

Camassia leichtlinii ssp. suksdorfii
    'Blauwe Donau' (blue Danube) . . . . camass

Campanula 'Birch Hybrid' . . . . bellflower

Campanula 'Constellation' . . . . bellflower

Campanula 'Dwarf Tornado' . . . . bellflower

Campanula 'Kent Belle' . . . . bellflower

Campanula persicifolia 'Chettle Charm' . . . . peachleaf bellflower

Campanula rapunculoides . . . . bellflower

Campanula rotundifolia 'Olympica' . . . . Scotch bluebell

Campsis ×tagliabuana 'Madame Galen' . . . . trumpet creeper

Canna 'Black Knight' . . . . canna

Canna 'Omega' . . . . canna

Canna 'Orange Punch' . . . . canna

Canna 'Panache' . . . . canna
Canna 'Phasion' . . . . canna
Canna 'Roi Humbert' (red King Humbert) . . . . . . canna
Canna 'Striata' (Pretoria) . . . . canna
Canna indica 'Red Stripe' (purpurea) . . . . canna
Carex buchananii . . . . leatherleaf sedge
Carex dolichostachya 'Kaga Nishiki'
    (gold fountains) . . . . sedge
Carex elata 'Aurea' (Bowles' golden) . . . . tufted sedge
Carex morrowii 'Ice Dance' . . . . sedge
Carex morrowii 'Variegata' . . . . sedge
Caryopteris ×clandonensis . . . . bluebeard
Caryopteris ×clandonensis 'Longwood Blue' . . . . bluebeard
Caryopteris ×clandonensis 'Worcester Gold' . . . . bluebeard
Catalpa bignonioides 'Aurea' . . . . southern catalpa
Celosia spicata 'Flamingo Purple' . . . . celosia
Centaurea cineraria . . . . knapweed
Centaurea montana . . . . mountain bluet
Cephalaria gigantea . . . . Tatarian cephalaria
Ceratostigma plumbaginoides . . . . plumbago
Cerinthe major 'Purpurascens' . . . . cerinthe
Chamaecyparis lawsoniana 'Sullivan' . . . . Lawson falsecypress
Chamaecyparis obtusa 'Fernspray Gold' . . . . Hinoki falsecypress
Chamaecyparis obtusa 'Mariesii' . . . . Hinoki falsecypress
Chamaecyparis pisifera 'Golden Mop' . . . . Japanese falsecypress
Chionanthus virginicus . . . . white fringetree
Chionodoxa forbesii (luciliae) Siehei Group . . . . . glory of the snow
Chrysanthemum 'Autumn Moon' . . . . mum
Chrysanthemum 'Pumpkin Harvest' . . . . mum
Chrysanthemum 'Single Apricot' . . . . mum
Chrysanthemum 'Single Peach' . . . . mum
Chrysanthemum 'Viette's Apricot Glow' . . . . mum
Cimicifuga ramosa 'Brunette' . . . . bugbane
Cimicifuga ramosa 'Hillside Black Beauty' . . . . . . bugbane
Clematis 'Elsa Späth' . . . . clematis
Clematis 'Hagley Hybrid' . . . . clematis
Clematis 'Lanuginosa Candida' . . . . clematis
Clematis 'Polish Spirit' . . . . clematis
Clematis 'Royal Velours' . . . . clematis
Clematis alpina 'Constance' . . . . alpine clematis
Clematis integrifolia . . . . solitary clematis
Clematis macropetala 'Markham's Pink' . . . . clematis
Clematis recta . . . . ground clematis
Clematis terniflora . . . . sweetautumn clematis
Clethra alnifolia . . . . summersweet clethra
Colchicum speciosum . . . . colchicum
Colocasia esculenta . . . . elephant's ear
Colocasia esculenta 'Black Beauty' . . . . elephant's ear
Colocasia esculenta 'Black Magic' . . . . elephant's ear

Colocasia esculenta 'Fontanesii' . . . . elephant's ear
Colocasia esculenta 'Illustris' . . . . elephant's ear
Consolida ajacis 'Blue Spire' . . . . larkspur
Coreopsis auriculata . . . . mouse ear coreopsis
Coreopsis grandiflora 'Walcoreop'
    (flying saucers) . . . . tickseed
Coreopsis tripteris . . . . tall coreopsis
Coreopsis verticillata 'Moonbeam' . . . . threadleaf coreopsis
Coreopsis verticillata 'Zagreb' . . . . threadleaf coreopsis
Cornus kousa . . . . Kousa dogwood
Cosmos atrosanguineus . . . . cosmos
Cotinus coggygria 'Velvet Cloak' . . . . smokebush
Crocosmia 'Blacro' (Jenny Bloom) . . . . crocosmia
Crocosmia 'Emberglow' . . . . crocosmia
Crocosmia 'Lucifer' . . . . crocosmia
Crocosmia ×crocosmiiflora 'Norwich Canary' . . . crocosmia
Crocosmia ×crocosmiiflora 'Solfatare' . . . . crocosmia
Crocosmia ×crocosmiiflora 'Venus' . . . . crocosmia
Crocus chrysanthus 'Blue Bird' . . . . crocus
Cryptotaenia japonica f. atropurpurea . . . . cryptotaenia
Cynara cardunculus . . . . cardoon
Cynoglossum amabile 'Firmament' . . . . Chinese forget-me-not
Cyperus alternifolius 'Stricta' . . . . umbrella plant

—D—

Dahlia 'Arabian Night' . . . . dahlia
Dahlia 'Bishop of Llandaff' . . . . dahlia
Dahlia 'Ellen Houston' . . . . dahlia
Dahlia 'Orange Nugget' . . . . dahlia
Dahlia 'Susette' . . . . dahlia
Daphne ×burkwoodii 'Carol Mackie' . . . . Burkwood daphne
Delphinium 'Centurion Sky Blue' . . . . delphinium
Delphinium ×bellamosum . . . . delphinium
Delphinium cashmerianum . . . . delphinium
Delphinium exaltatum . . . . delphinium
Deschampsia cespitosa 'Goldgehänge' . . . . tufted hair grass
Dianthus ×allwoodii 'Danielle Marie' . . . . Allwood pink
Dianthus barbatus 'Sooty' . . . . sweet william
Dianthus deltoides 'Leuchtfunk' (flashing light) . . . maiden pink
Dicentra 'Luxuriant' . . . . fringed bleeding heart
Dicentra spectabilis 'Gold Heart' . . . . showy bleeding heart
Dichelostemma ida-maia . . . . firecracker flower
Digitalis grandiflora . . . . yellow foxglove
Digitalis lutea . . . . straw foxglove
Digitalis purpurea 'Apricot' . . . . foxglove
Dracocephalum ruyschiana . . . . dracocephalum
Duranta erecta 'Golden Edge' . . . . pigeon berry

—E—

Echinacea purpurea. . . . . purple coneflower
Echinops bannaticus 'Taplow Blue' . . . . globe thistle
Echinops ritro 'Blue Glow' . . . . globe thistle
Echinops ritro 'Veitch's Blue'. . . . . globe thistle
Epimedium davidii. . . . . barrenwort
Epimedium ×rubrum. . . . . red barrenwort
Epimedium ×warleyense. . . . . barrenwort
Eranthis hyemalis . . . . winter aconite
Eremurus ×isabellinus 'Pinokkio' . . . . foxtail lily
Eryngium amethystinum . . . . sea holly
Eryngium planum 'Blaukappe' . . . . sea holly
Eryngium variifolium . . . . sea holly
Eryngium yuccifolium . . . . rattlesnake-master
Erythronium 'Pagoda' . . . . trout lily
Eschscholzia californica . . . . California poppy
Eschscholzia californica 'Purple Gleam' . . . . California poppy
Eucomis comosa 'Sparkling Burgundy' . . . . pineapple lily
Eupatorium purpureum ssp. maculatum
   'Gateway' . . . . joe-pye weed
Euphorbia 'Golden Towers' . . . . spurge
Euphorbia amygdaloides 'Purpurea' . . . . purple wood spurge
Euphorbia cotinifolia. . . . . tropical smoketree
Euphorbia cyparissias 'Fen's Ruby' . . . . cypress spurge
Euphorbia dulcis 'Chameleon'. . . . . spurge
Euphorbia griffithii 'Fireglow'. . . . . Griffith's spurge
Euphorbia ×martinii . . . . spurge
Euphorbia polychroma . . . . cushion spurge

—F—

Fagus sylvatica 'Purpurea Pendula'. . . . . weeping purple beech
Fagus sylvatica 'Tricolor' . . . . tricolor beech
Festuca glauca 'Elijah Blue' . . . . blue fescue
Festuca glauca 'Golden Toupee' . . . . blue fescue
Foeniculum vulgare 'Purpureum' . . . . copper fennel
Fothergilla gardenii . . . . dwarf fothergilla
Fritillaria persica . . . . fritillary
Fuchsia 'Gartenmeister Bonstedt'. . . . . fuchsia

—G—

Galega ×hartlandii 'Lady Wilson'. . . . . goat's rue
Galium odoratum . . . . sweet woodruff
Genista tinctoria 'Royal Gold'. . . . . common woadwaxen
Gentiana septemfida var. lagodechiana . . . . gentian

Gentiana triflora 'Royal Blue' . . . . gentian
Geranium 'Ann Folkard' . . . . hardy geranium
Geranium 'Brookside'. . . . . meadow cranesbill
Geranium 'Johnson's Blue' . . . . hardy geranium
Geranium 'Phillippe Vapelle' . . . . hardy geranium
Geranium 'Salome'. . . . . hardy geranium
Geranium himalayense 'Plenum'. . . . . lilac cranesbill
Geranium macrorrhizum 'Ingwersen's
   Variety' . . . . bigroot geranium
Geranium ×magnificum. . . . . showy geranium
Geranium ×oxonianum 'Claridge Druce'. . . . . hardy geranium
Geranium phaeum 'Lily Lovell' . . . . hardy geranium
Geranium phaeum 'Samobor' . . . . hardy geranium
Geranium platypetalum. . . . . broad-petaled
                        geranium
Geranium pratense 'Mrs. Kendall Clark' . . . . meadow cranesbill
Geranium pratense 'Victor Reiter Jr.' . . . . meadow cranesbill
Geranium psilostemon . . . . Armenian geranium
Geranium renardii. . . . . hardy geranium
Geranium sanguineum 'New Hampshire' . . . . blood-red geranium
Geranium wlassovianum . . . . hardy geranium
Gillenia stipulata . . . . American ipecac
Ginkgo biloba 'Autumn Gold' . . . . maidenhair tree
Gladiolus 'Atom'. gladiolus
Gladiolus 'Violetta' . . . . gladiolus
Gladiolus communis ssp. byzantinus . . . . Byzantine gladiolus
Gladiolus ×gandavensis . . . . gladiolus
Gladiolus ×gandavensis 'Boone' . . . . gladiolus
Glaucidium palmatum. . . . . Japanese woodlander
Gomphrena haageana 'Lavender Lady'. . . . . gomphrena

—H—

Hakonechloa macra 'Aureola'. . . . . golden-variegated
                        Hakone grass
Hedychium 'Daniel Weeks'. . . . . ginger lily
Hedychium coccineum . . . . red ginger lily
Helenium 'Kugelsonne'. . . . . common sneezeweed
Helenium 'Moerheim Beauty'. . . . . common sneezeweed
Helianthemum (double yellow). . . . . sunrose
Helianthemum 'Fire Dragon'. . . . . sunrose
Helianthus 'Lemon Queen'. . . . . swamp sunflower
Helianthus 'Mellow Yellow'. . . . . swamp sunflower
Helianthus salicifolius . . . . willow-leaved
                        sunflower
Helichrysum petiolare 'Limelight' . . . . licorice plant
Helictotrichon sempervirens 'Saphirsprudel'
   (sapphire fountain). . . . . blue oat grass

Heliopsis helianthoides var. scabra
    'Sommersonne' (summer sun) . . . . heliopsis
Helleborus Royal Heritage™ . . . . lenten rose
Helleborus foetidus. . . . . stinking hellebore
Helleborus orientalis. . . . . lenten rose
Helleborus orientalis (single black) . . . . lenten rose
Hemerocallis 'Alluring Peach' . . . . daylily
Hemerocallis 'Carefree Peach' . . . . daylily
Hemerocallis 'Happy Returns' . . . . daylily
Hemerocallis 'Peach Fairy' . . . . daylily
Hemerocallis 'Red Razzamatazz'. . . . . daylily
Hemerocallis 'Scarlet Romance' . . . . daylily
Hemerocallis 'Siloam Royal Prince' . . . . daylily
Hemerocallis 'Staghorn Sumac' . . . . daylily
Hemerocallis 'Sundried Tomatoes' . . . . daylily
Hemerocallis 'Toy Trumpets' . . . . daylily
Hemerocallis 'Welcome Mat' . . . . daylily
Hemerocallis 'Yellow Lollipop' . . . . daylily
Hesperis matronalis . . . . dame's rocket
Heuchera 'Chocolate Ruffles' . . . . coralbells
Heuchera 'Plum Pudding' . . . . coralbells
Heuchera 'Raspberry Regal' . . . . coralbells
Heuchera 'Velvet Night' . . . . coralbells
Heuchera micrantha var. diversifolia
    'Palace Purple' . . . . coralbells
×Heucherella 'Silver Streak' . . . . foamy bells
Hibiscus acetosella 'Red Shield' . . . . hibiscus
Hibiscus moscheutos 'Lord Baltimore' . . . . rose mallow
Hosta 'Big Daddy'. . . . . plantain-lily
Hosta 'Blue Cadet'. . . . . plantain-lily
Hosta 'Fragrant Blue' . . . . plantain-lily
Hosta 'Halcyon' . . . . plantain-lily
Hosta 'Krossa Regal' . . . . plantain-lily
Hosta 'Lemon Lime' . . . . plantain-lily
Hosta 'Love Pat' . . . . plantain-lily
Hosta 'Midas Touch' . . . . plantain-lily
Hosta 'Night Before Christmas' . . . . plantain-lily
Hosta 'Patriot' . . . . plantain-lily
Hosta 'Paul's Glory' . . . . plantain-lily
Hosta 'Sum and Substance'. . . . . plantain-lily
Hosta 'Sun Power' . . . . plantain-lily
Hosta plantaginea 'Aphrodite'. . . . . plantain-lily
Humulus lupulus 'Bianca'. . . . . golden hops
Hydrangea anomala ssp. petiolaris . . . . climbing hydrangea
Hydrangea quercifolia. oakleaf hydrangea
Hydrangea quercifolia 'Snowflake'. . . . . oakleaf hydrangea
Hymenocallis 'Sulphur Queen' . . . . Peruvian daffodil
Hypericum androsaemum 'Albury Purple'. . . . . . st. johnswort
Hyssopus officinalis. . . . . hyssop

Hystrix patula . . . . bottle-brush grass

—I—

Ilex 'Apollo' . . . . winterberry holly
Ilex glabra . . . . inkberry
Ilex ×meserveae 'Mesdob' (China boy). . . . . Meserve holly
Ilex ×meserveae 'Mesog' (China girl) . . . . Meserve holly
Ilex verticillata 'Afterglow'. . . . . winterberry holly
Ilex verticillata 'Christmas Cheer' . . . . winterberry holly
Ilex verticillata 'Jim Dandy' . . . . winterberry holly
Ilex verticillata 'Winter Red' . . . . winterberry holly
Impatiens omeiana . . . . perennial impatiens
Imperata cylindrica var. koenigii 'Red Baron'. . . . . Japanese blood grass
Ipomoea batatas 'Ace of Spades' . . . . sweet potato vine
Ipomoea batatas 'Blackie' . . . . sweet potato vine
Ipomoea batatas 'Margarita' . . . . sweet potato vine
Ipomoea lobata (Mina lobata). . . . . Spanish flag
Ipomoea tricolor 'Heavenly Blue' . . . . morning glory
Iris 'Blue Magic'. . . . . Dutch iris
Iris 'Flavescens' . . . . bearded iris
Iris 'Perfume Counter' . . . . bearded iris
Iris 'Sugar Blues' . . . . bearded iris
Iris foetidissima. . . . . stinking iris
Iris pallida 'Variegata' . . . . sweet iris
Iris pseudacorus 'Variegata'. . . . . yellow flag
Iris reticulata 'Harmony' . . . . netted iris
Iris sanguinea 'Snow Queen'. . . . . iris
Iris sibirica 'Butter and Sugar' . . . . Siberian iris
Iris sibirica 'Caesar's Brother' . . . . Siberian iris
Iris sibirica 'Dianne's Daughter'. . . . . Siberian iris
Iris sibirica 'Orville Fay'. . . . . Siberian iris
Iris sibirica 'Pirate Prince' . . . . Siberian iris
Iris sibirica 'Skywings' . . . . Siberian iris
Iris sibirica 'Vi Luihn' . . . . Siberian iris
Iris sibirica 'White Swirl' . . . . Siberian iris
Itea virginica . . . . Virginia sweetspire
Itea virginica 'Henry's Garnet'. . . . . Virginia sweetspire

—K—

Knautia macedonica . . . . knautia
Kniphofia 'Alcazar' . . . . red-hot poker
Kniphofia 'Little Maid'. red-hot poker
Kniphofia 'Primrose Beauty' . . . . red-hot poker
Kniphofia 'Prince Igor' . . . . red-hot poker
Kniphofia 'Royal Standard' . . . . red-hot poker

Kniphofia 'Shining Sceptre' . . . . red-hot poker
Kniphofia caulescens. . . . . red-hot poker
Kniphofia citrina . . . . red-hot poker
Kniphofia triangularis. . . . . red-hot poker

—L—

Lablab purpureus . . . . purple hyacinth bean
Lactuca 'Merlot' . . . . lettuce
Lamium maculatum 'White Nancy'. . . . . dead nettle
Lathyrus latifolius . . . . perennial sweet pea
Lathyrus odoratus. . . . . sweet pea
Lathyrus odoratus 'Henry Eckford'. . . . . sweet pea
Lathyrus odoratus 'King Size Navy Blue'. . . . . . . sweet pea
Lavandula angustifolia 'Munstead'. . . . . lavender
Lavandula ×intermedia 'Grosso' . . . . lavender
Leonotis menthifolia . . . . leonotis
Lespedeza cuneata . . . . bush clover
Liatris spicata 'Kobold' . . . . spike gayfeather
Ligularia 'The Rocket'. . . . . ligularia
Ligularia dentata 'Dark Beauty'. . . . . bigleaf ligularia
Ligularia dentata 'Desdemona' . . . . bigleaf ligularia
Ligularia wilsoniana. . . . . ligularia
Lilium 'Apricot Brandy'. lily
Lilium 'Casa Blanca' . . . . lily
Lilium 'Connecticut King' . . . . lily
Lilium 'Conquistador' . . . . lily
Lilium 'Eden's Dandy' . . . . lily
Lilium 'Grand Cru' . . . . lily
Lilium 'Montenegro' . . . . lily
Lilium 'Pretender'. . . . . lily
Lilium 'Royal Justice' . . . . lily
Lilium 'Royal Perfume' . . . . lily
Lilium 'Scarlet Emperor' . . . . lily
Lilium 'Shirley'. . . . . lily
Lilium 'Sunset'. . . . . lily
Lilium henryi. . . . . Henry's lily
Lilium lancifolium var. splendens . . . . lily
Lilium pumilum . . . . lily
Limonium platyphyllum 'Violetta' . . . . sea lavender
Linaria 'Natalie'. . . . . toadflax
Linaria purpurea . . . . purple toadflax
Linum perenne 'Blau Saphir' (blue sapphire) . . . . perennial flax
Lobelia 'Dark Crusader' . . . . lobelia
Lobelia 'Grape Knee High' . . . . lobelia
Lobelia 'Purple Towers' . . . . lobelia
Lobelia 'Queen Victoria' . . . . lobelia
Lobelia 'Royal Robe'. . . . . lobelia

Lobelia 'Ruby Slippers' . . . . lobelia
Lobelia siphilitica. . . . . lobelia
Lonicera periclymenum 'Graham Thomas' . . . . . . honeysuckle
Lonicera sempervirens 'Blanche Sandman' . . . . . . honeysuckle
Luzula nivea . . . . snowy wood rush
Lychnis ×arkwrightii 'Vesuvius' . . . . Arkwright's campion
Lychnis cognata. . . . . campion
Lychnis coronaria . . . . rose campion
Lysimachia congestiflora 'Variegata'. . . . . variegated lysimachia
Lysimachia nummularia 'Aurea'. . . . . golden creeping jenny

—M—

Magnolia virginiana . . . . sweetbay magnolia
Malus 'Lanzam' (Lancelot®). . . . . flowering crabapple
Mazus reptans. . . . . mazus
Melampodium paludosum 'Million Gold'. . . . . melampodium
Mertensia pulmonarioides (virginica). . . . . Virginia bluebells
Microbiota decussata . . . . Russian arborvitae
Miscanthus 'Purpurascens' . . . . miscanthus
Miscanthus sinensis var. condensatus
    'Cosmopolitan' . . . . miscanthus
Miscanthus sinensis 'Gracillimus'. . . . . miscanthus
Miscanthus sinensis 'Malepartus'. . . . . miscanthus
Miscanthus sinensis 'Morning Light'. . . . . miscanthus
Molinia caerulea ssp. arundinacea 'Skyracer' . . . . tall purple moor grass
Monarda 'Jacob Cline'. . . . . beebalm
Monarda 'Violet Queen' . . . . beebalm
Musa basjoo . . . . Japanese banana
Musa zebrina. . . . . bloodleaf banana

—N—

Narcissus 'Delnashaugh' . . . . daffodil
Narcissus 'Fragrant Rose' . . . . daffodil
Narcissus 'Mary Gay Lirette'. . . . . daffodil
Narcissus 'Mint Julep' . . . . daffodil
Narcissus 'Petrel' . . . . daffodil
Narcissus 'Sir Winston Churchill' . . . . daffodil
Narcissus 'Stratosphere' . . . . daffodil
Narcissus 'Tahiti'. . . . . daffodil
Nepeta 'Six Hills Giant'. . . . . catmint
Nepeta ×faassenii . . . . catmint
Nepeta grandiflora 'Bramdean'. . . . . catmint
Nepeta racemosa 'Walker's Low'. . . . . catmint
Nepeta sibirica 'Souvenir d'André Chaudron'. . . . catmint
Nicotiana langsdorffii . . . . flowering tobacco

Nierembergia scoparia 'Mont Blanc' . . . . nierembergia
Nigella damascena Miss Jekyll Series . . . . love-in-a-mist
Nymphaea 'Marliacea Chromatella' . . . . waterlily

—O—

Ocimum 'African Blue' . . . . basil
Ocimum basilicum 'Red Rubin' . . . . basil
Oenothera fremontii 'Lemon Silver' . . . . sundrops
Oenothera fruticosa ssp. glauca 'Sonnenwende' . . sundrops
Origanum 'Kent Beauty' . . . . oregano
Origanum laevigatum 'Herrenhausen' . . . . oregano
Origanum vulgare 'Aureum' . . . . oregano
Osmunda cinnamomea . . . . cinnamon fern
Osmunda regalis . . . . royal fern

—P—

Pachysandra procumbens . . . . Allegheny spurge
Packera aurea (Senecio aureus) . . . . golden ragwort
Paeonia 'America' . . . . peony
Paeonia 'Burma Ruby' . . . . peony
Paeonia 'Coral Sunset' . . . . peony
Paeonia 'Etched Salmon' . . . . peony
Paeonia 'Monsieur Jules Elie' . . . . peony
Paeonia 'Prairie Moon' . . . . peony
Paeonia obovata . . . . woodland peony
Panicum virgatum 'Dallas Blues' . . . . switch grass
Panicum virgatum 'Heavy Metal' . . . . switch grass
Panicum virgatum 'Rehbraun' . . . . switch grass
Papaver nudicaule 'Red Sails' . . . . Iceland poppy
Papaver orientale 'Curlilocks' . . . . oriental poppy
Papaver orientale 'Derwisch' . . . . oriental poppy
Papaver orientale 'Feuerriese' . . . . oriental poppy
Papaver orientale 'Harvest Moon' . . . . oriental poppy
Papaver orientale 'Lighthouse' . . . . oriental poppy
Papaver orientale 'Patty's Plum' . . . . oriental poppy
Papaver orientale 'Prince of Orange' . . . . oriental poppy
Papaver orientale 'Saffron' . . . . oriental poppy
Papaver orientale 'Turkenlouis' . . . . oriental poppy
Papaver rhoeas . . . . corn poppy
Papaver rhoeas Angels' Choir . . . . corn poppy
Papaver somniferum . . . . opium poppy
Papaver somniferum 'Black Peony' . . . . peony-flowered poppy
Papaver somniferum 'Burnt Orange' . . . . opium poppy
Papaver somniferum 'Lauren's Grape' . . . . opium poppy
Papaver somniferum 'Pepperbox' . . . . opium poppy

Passiflora incarnata . . . . wild passion flower
Patrinia scabiosifolia . . . . patrinia
Pennisetum alopecuroides 'Hameln' . . . . fountain grass
Pennisetum setaceum 'Rubrum' . . . . purple fountain grass
Penstemon digitalis 'Husker Red' . . . . foxglove penstemon
Penstemon ×mexicale 'Pike's Peak Purple' . . . . . . penstemon
Perilla frutescens var. crispa . . . . perilla
Perovskia atriplicifolia . . . . Russian sage
Perovskia atriplicifolia 'Longin' . . . . Russian sage
Persicaria microcephala 'Red Dragon' . . . . persicaria
Phlomis russeliana . . . . Jerusalem sage
Phlox divaricata . . . . woodland phlox
Phlox divaricata 'Dirigo Ice' . . . . woodland phlox
Phlox divaricata 'Eco Texas Purple' . . . . woodland phlox
Phlox divaricata ssp. laphamii . . . . woodland phlox
Phlox divaricata 'London Grove Blue' . . . . woodland phlox
Phlox divaricata 'Sweet Lilac' . . . . woodland phlox
Phlox paniculata 'David' . . . . border phlox
Phlox paniculata 'Fesselballon' . . . . border phlox
Phlox paniculata 'Katherine' . . . . border phlox
Phlox paniculata 'Laura' . . . . border phlox
Phlox paniculata 'Look Again' . . . . border phlox
Phlox paniculata 'Orange Perfection' . . . . border phlox
Phlox paniculata 'Pax' (peace) . . . . border phlox
Phlox paniculata 'Tenor' . . . . border phlox
Phlox paniculata 'The King' . . . . border phlox
Phlox paniculata 'Tracy's Treasure' . . . . border phlox
Phlox stolonifera 'Blue Ridge' . . . . creeping phlox
Phlox stolonifera 'Bruce's White' . . . . creeping phlox
Phormium 'Bronze Baby' . . . . New Zealand flax
Phormium 'Platt's Black' . . . . New Zealand flax
Phormium 'Yellow Wave' . . . . New Zealand flax
Phormium cookianum 'Chocolate' . . . . New Zealand flax
Phyllostachys nigra . . . . black bamboo
Phytolacca polyandra . . . . pokeweed
Picea abies 'Mucronata' . . . . Norway spruce
Picea abies 'Pendula' . . . . weeping Norway
                                                           spruce
Picea alcoquiana 'Howell's Tigertail' . . . . Alcock spruce
Picea orientalis 'Skylands' . . . . oriental spruce
Picea pungens 'Iseli Foxtail' . . . . Colorado spruce
Picea pungens 'Thomsen' . . . . Colorado spruce
Pinus cembra 'Silver Sheen' . . . . Swiss stone pine
Pinus contorta 'Chief Joseph' . . . . lodgepole pine
Pinus contorta 'Spaan's Dwarf' . . . . lodgepole pine
Pinus densiflora 'Oculus Draconis' . . . . dragon's eye pine
Pinus flexilis 'Vanderwolf's Pyramid' . . . . limber pine
Pinus parviflora 'Glauca' . . . . Japanese white pine
Pinus parviflora 'Yatsubusa' . . . . Japanese white pine

Pinus pumila 'Nana' . . . . dwarf Siberian pine
Pinus strobus . . . . eastern white pine
Pinus strobus 'Nana' . . . . dwarf eastern white pine
Pinus sylvestris . . . . Scots pine
Pinus sylvestris 'Albyn' . . . . Scots pine
Pinus sylvestris 'Fastigiata' . . . . fastigiate Scots pine
Pistia stratiotes . . . . water lettuce
Plantago major 'Rubrifolia' . . . . plantain
Platycodon grandiflorus 'Double Blue' . . . . balloon flower
Platycodon grandiflorus 'Komachi' . . . . balloon flower
Plectranthus amboinicus . . . . Cuban oregano
Plectranthus argentatus . . . . plectranthus
Polemonium caeruleum 'Blanjou'
   (brise d'Anjou) . . . . jacob's ladder
Polygonatum odoratum 'Variegatum' . . . . variegated solomon's seal
Polystichum acrostichoides . . . . Christmas fern
Portulaca grandiflora 'Sundial Peach' . . . . moss rose
Potentilla fruticosa 'Sunset' . . . . bush cinquefoil
Pseudotsuga menziesii 'Astro Blue' . . . . Douglas fir
Pulmonaria 'Majesté' . . . . lungwort
Pulmonaria 'Viette's Deep Blue Sea' . . . . lungwort
Puschkinia scilloides . . . . striped squill

—Q—

Quercus palustris . . . . pin oak
Quercus robur 'Pectinata' . . . . cutleaf English oak

—R—

Rheum palmatum var. tanguticum . . . . ornamental rhubarb
Rhodochiton atrosanguineus . . . . purple bell vine
Rhododendron 'Chionoides' . . . . Catawba rhododendron
Rhododendron 'Mist Maiden' . . . . rhododendron
Rhododendron 'Northern Starburst' . . . . rhododendron
Ricinus communis . . . . castor bean
Ricinus communis 'Carmencita' . . . . castor bean
Rodgersia aesculifolia . . . . fingerleaf rodgersia
Rodgersia pinnata . . . . rodgersia
Rosa 'Alchymist' . . . . rose
Rosa 'Ausbuff' (English Garden®) . . . . rose
Rosa 'Ausmas' (Graham Thomas®) . . . . rose
Rosa 'Aussaucer' (Evelyn®) . . . . rose
Rosa 'Ausvelvet' (The Prince®) . . . . rose

Rosa 'Champlain' . . . . rose
Rosa 'F. J. Grootendorst' . . . . rose
Rosa 'Hansa' . . . . rose
Rosa Lyda Rose™ . . . . rose
Rosa 'Meidomonac' (Bonica®) . . . . rose
Rosa 'Nearly Wild' . . . . rose
Rosa 'Nuits de Young' . . . . rose
Rosa 'Scrivluv' (Baby Love®) . . . . rose
Rosa 'Seafoam' . . . . rose
Rosa 'The Fairy' . . . . rose
Rosa ×harisonii 'Harison's Yellow' . . . . rose
Rosa multiflora 'Grevillei'
   (seven sisters' rose) . . . . seven sisters' rose
Rosa rugosa . . . . rose
Rudbeckia fulgida var. speciosa (newmannii) . . . . black-eyed susan
Rudbeckia hirta 'Irish Eyes' . . . . gloriosa daisy
Rudbeckia maxima . . . . giant coneflower
Rudbeckia triloba . . . . three-lobed cone flower
Rumex sanguineus . . . . bloody dock
Ruta graveolens 'Blue Beauty' . . . . common rue

—S—

Salvia 'Indigo Spires' . . . . salvia
Salvia 'Purple Majesty' . . . . salvia
Salvia argentea . . . . silver sage
Salvia azurea var. pitcheri . . . . azure sage
Salvia coccinea 'Lady in Red' . . . . salvia
Salvia guaranitica . . . . salvia
Salvia guaranitica 'Black and Blue' . . . . salvia
Salvia leucantha . . . . salvia
Salvia nemorosa 'Ostfriesland'
   (East Friesland) . . . . perennial salvia
Salvia nemorosa 'Purple Glory' . . . . perennial salvia
Salvia nemorosa 'Pusztaflamme' (plumosa) . . . . . perennial salvia
Salvia officinalis 'Tricolor' . . . . common sage
Salvia patens . . . . salvia
Salvia ×sylvestris 'Blauhügel' (blue hill) . . . . perennial salvia
Salvia ×sylvestris 'Blaukönigin' (blue queen) . . . . perennial salvia
Salvia ×sylvestris 'Mainacht' (May night) . . . . . . perennial salvia
Salvia ×sylvestris 'Viola Klose' . . . . perennial salvia
Salvia verticillata 'Purple Rain' . . . . perennial salvia
Sambucus racemosa 'Sutherland Gold' . . . . gold-leaved European red elder
Sanguisorba tenuifolia 'Purpurea' . . . . purple burnet
Saruma henryi . . . . saruma
Scabiosa Butterfly Blue® . . . . pincushion flower

Scabiosa 'Pink Mist'. pincushion flower
Scabiosa atropurpurea 'Ace of Spades'. . . . . pincushion flower
Scabiosa columbaria var. ochroleuca. . . . . cream pincushion
        flower
Scadoxus multiflorus. blood lily
Schizachyrium scoparium 'The Blues' . . . . little bluestem
Sciadopitys verticillata. . . . . Japanese umbrella-pine
Sedum 'Herbstfreude' (autumn joy) . . . . sedum
Sedum 'Pork and Beans' . . . . sedum
Sedum acre 'Aureum' . . . . sedum
Sedum telephium ssp. maximum
   'Atropurpureum' . . . . sedum
Silene regia . . . . wild pink
Sisyrinchium 'Quaint and Queer' . . . . blue-eyed grass
Sisyrinchium bermudianum. . . . . blue-eyed grass
Solenostemon 'Burgundy Columns' . . . . coleus
Solenostemon 'Burgundy Giant' . . . . coleus
Solenostemon 'Olive' . . . . coleus
Solenostemon 'Penny' . . . . coleus
Solenostemon 'Purple Emperor' . . . . coleus
Solenostemon 'Saturn' . . . . coleus
Solidago 'Golden Spangles' . . . . goldenrod
Solidago rugosa 'Fireworks' . . . . goldenrod
×Solidaster luteus 'Lemore' . . . . golden aster
Sorghastrum nutans 'Sioux Blue' . . . . Indian grass
Stachys byzantina . . . . lamb's ear
Stachys byzantina 'Countess Helen von Stein'. . . . lamb's ear
Stachys byzantina 'Primrose Heron' . . . . lamb's ear
Stachys macrantha . . . . big betony
Stokesia laevis 'Klaus Jelitto' . . . . Stokes' aster
Stokesia laevis 'Mary Gregory' . . . . Stokes' aster
Stokesia laevis 'Omega Skyrocket' . . . . Stokes' aster
Stokesia laevis 'Purple Parasols' . . . . Stokes' aster
Stylophorum diphyllum. . . . . wood poppy
Symphytum 'Goldsmith' . . . . comfrey
Syringa meyeri . . . . Meyer lilac

—T—

Tanacetum 'Golden Feathers' . . . . tansy
Thalictrum aquilegiifolium 'Thundercloud'. . . . . . meadow rue
Thalictrum rochebruneanum. . . . . lavender mist
        meadow rue
Thermopsis villosa . . . . southern lupine
Thuja occidentalis 'Techny' . . . . eastern arborvitae
Thunbergia battiscombei. . . . . thunbergia
Thymus ×citriodorus . . . . lemon thyme
Thymus ×citriodorus 'Lemon Green' . . . . lemon thyme

Thymus pseudolanuginosus. . . . . woolly thyme
Tiarella cordifolia 'Ninja' . . . . foamflower
Tigridia pavonia 'Speciosa' . . . . tiger flower
Tradescantia Andersoniana Group . . . . spiderwort
Tradescantia (Andersoniana Group)
   'Purple Profusion'. spiderwort
Tradescantia (Andersoniana Group)
   'Zwanenburg Blue'. . . . . spiderwort
Trillium erectum. . . . . trillium
Triteleia laxa 'Queen Fabiola' . . . . triteleia
Tropaeolum majus 'Apricot Trifle'. . . . . nasturtium
Tropaeolum majus 'Blush Double'. . . . . nasturtium
Tropaeolum majus 'Moonlight'. . . . . nasturtium
Tropaeolum majus 'Tip Top Mahogany' . . . . nasturtium
Tropaeolum majus Alaska Series. . . . . nasturtium
Tsuga canadensis. . . . . Canadian hemlock
Tsuga canadensis 'Cole's Prostrate'. . . . . Canadian hemlock
Tulipa 'Angelique' . . . . tulip
Tulipa 'Apricot Parrot' . . . . tulip
Tulipa 'Big Smile'. . . . . tulip
Tulipa 'Black Parrot'. . . . . tulip
Tulipa 'Blue Heron'. . . . . tulip
Tulipa 'Blue Parrot'. . . . . tulip
Tulipa 'Blushing Lady' . . . . tulip
Tulipa 'Burgundy Lace' . . . . tulip
Tulipa 'Carmine Parrot'. . . . . tulip
Tulipa 'Couleur Cardinal' . . . . tulip
Tulipa 'Fringed Elegance'. . . . . tulip
Tulipa 'Queen of Night' . . . . tulip
Tulipa 'Temple of Beauty' . . . . tulip
Tulipa 'Uncle Tom' . . . . tulip
Tulipa batalinii. . . . . tulip
Tulipa clusiana var. chrysantha. . . . . tulip

—V—

Valeriana officinalis . . . . common valerian
Verbascum 'Jackie' . . . . mullein
Verbascum bombyciferum . . . . Turkish mullein
Verbena 'Homestead Purple' . . . . verbena
Verbena 'Romance Apricot' . . . . verbena
Verbena Temari® Red. verbena
Verbena bonariensis . . . . tall verbena
Verbena hastata . . . . American blue vervain
Veronica 'Goodness Grows'. . . . . veronica
Veronica 'Waterperry Blue' . . . . speedwell
Veronica austriaca ssp. teucrium
   'Crater Lake Blue' . . . . Hungarian speedwell

Veronica austriaca ssp. teucrium
  'Royal Blue' . . . . Hungarian speedwell
Veronica gentianoides 'Nana' . . . . gentian speedwell
Veronica peduncularis 'Georgia Blue' . . . . speedwell
Veronica prostrata 'Trehane'. . . . . harebell speedwell
Veronica repens 'Sunshine' . . . . golden creeping
                                                     speedwell
Veronica spicata 'Blue Charm' . . . . spike speedwell
Veronica spicata 'Icicle'. spike speedwell
Veronicastrum virginicum 'Fascination' . . . . culver's root
Viburnum plicatum var. tomentosum
  'Mariesii'. . . . . doublefile viburnum
Viola 'Molly Sanderson' . . . . violet
Viola 'Purple Showers' . . . . violet

Viola labradorica. . . . . Labrador violet
Vitex agnus-castus var. latifolia . . . . chastetree
Vitis vinifera 'Purpurea'. purple-leaved grape

—Y—

Yucca filamentosa 'Color Guard' . . . . yucca
Yucca flaccida 'Golden Sword' . . . . yucca

—Z—

Zinnia haageana 'Orange Star' . . . . zinnia

PLANTS BY DESIGN CHARACTERISTICS

DESIGN CHART

Heights and widths listed are for expected growth under average landscape conditions.

	TYPE	ZONE	FORM	HEIGHT
Abies lasiocarpa 'Arizonica Compacta' Very beautiful and unusual plant with soft needles. Slow growing; great addition to small gardens. Plates 1–2.	tree	5–6	conical	10–15 ft.
Abies procera 'Glauca Prostrata' Provide this dwarf, slow-growing shrub with good drainage, or it can be lost.	shrub	5–6(7)	horizontal	2–2½ ft.
Acanthus spinosus Architectural plant. Use for a touch of drama from the foliage and outstanding long-lasting vertical flowers that can hold into autumn. Plates 95, 120.	perennial	5–10	vertical	24–48 in.
Acer griseum By far my favorite tree for its gorgeous bark, small habit, and outstanding autumn color, which develops even in partial shade. Plates 5, 102–103.	tree	5–7(8)	vertical	18–20 ft.
Acer palmatum var. dissectum Dissectum Atropurpureum Group Multiple uses for foliage color, form, and texture. Unusual cultivars make nice additions to containers. Plate 47.	tree	5–8	mound	6–8 ft.
Acer palmatum 'Sango-kaku' Beautiful small tree for orange-red young stems and bark. Can be subject to damage by strong winds and late frost. Best placed in protected location. Plate 192.	tree	5–8	vase	20–25 ft.
Achillea 'Anblo' (Anthea) Good selection. Performs without division longer than most yarrows. Does not require staking; not prone to melting out in hot climates.	perennial	3–8	mound	18–20 in.
Achillea 'Heidi' Often listed as having salmon flowers but actually more pink when in association with truer salmons.	perennial	3–8	mound	18–20 in.
Achillea 'Salmon Beauty' Hard-to-find color.	perennial	4–8	mound	24–36 in.
Achillea filipendulina 'Altgold' Sturdy form providing good height in a border.	perennial	3–8	mound	36 in.
Aconitum 'Bressingham Spire' Reminiscent of the English gardens that I worked in, so I use it in designs to evoke that mood.	perennial	4–8	vertical	24–36 in.
Aconitum 'Ivorine' Soft color, unexpected for the genus.	perennial	4–8	vertical	24 in.
Aconitum carmichaelii (Wilsonii Group) 'Spätlese' Sturdy robust grower. Very happy with performance.	perennial	4–8	vertical	36 in.

WIDTH	FLOWER COLOR	FLOWERING MONTH	FOLIAGE COLOR	FOLIAGE INTEREST	TEXTURE	DESIGN COLOR
6–10 ft.			blue	year-round	average	cool
4–6 ft.			blue	year-round	fine	cool
3 ft.	purple	Jun–Jul			bold	cool
10–15 ft.			red	autumn	bold	warm
6 ft.			purple	spring/summer	fine	warm or cool
18–22 ft.			yellow	autumn	fine	warm
18 in.	yellow	Jun–Aug	gray-green	spring/summer/ autumn	fine	warm
18 in.	pink	Jun–Aug			fine	warm
24 in.	peach	Jun–Aug			fine	warm
24 in.	yellow	Jun–Aug			fine	warm
18 in.	blue	Jun–Aug			average	cool
24 in.	yellow	Jun–Jul			average	warm
24 in.	blue	Jul–Sep			average	cool

	TYPE	ZONE	FORM	HEIGHT
Aconitum episcopale Just starting to experiment with this unusual vine. Appears slow to establish.	perennial	5–8	climbing	10–15 ft.
Aconitum lycoctonum ssp. neapolitanum	perennial	3–6	vertical	3–4 ft.
Acorus gramineus 'Minimus Aureus' Charming tiny yellow foliage. For edging or underplanting to create interconnection. Combination 26.	perennial	6–8	mound	3–5 in.
Acorus gramineus 'Oborozuki' Stunning foliage for yellow accent and fine texture. Plate 108.	perennial	(5)6–8	mound	12–15 in.
Acorus gramineus 'Ogon' Adaptable striking plant that I wish was in all my designs.	perennial	(5)6–8	mound	10–12 in.
Adiantum pedatum Reliable and invaluable as a textural element for the shade garden. Plate 119.	perennial	3–8	mound	16–18 in.
Aesculus parviflora I have always admired this suckering shrub and recall a 10 × 12 ft. lawn specimen at the garden where I worked in Belgium. It is slow to establish though, so I incorporate it without hesitation in mixed gardens and wait patiently for it to develop into even a small shrub. Combination 4.	shrub	4–8	mound	8–12 ft.
Agapanthus 'Bressingham Blue' Exotic touch of blue when coming up through other plants. Should be used more in total layering scheme of designs, 3–5 per sq. ft.	tender bulb	7–10	vertical	2–3 ft.
Agastache 'Blue Fortune' Reliable vertical design element. In flower all summer, and seedheads persist into autumn. Plates 5, 90, 160.	perennial	5–10	vertical	3–4 ft.
Agastache rupestris Interesting orange flowers and fragrant foliage for sunny dry spots.	perennial	5–8	vertical	3–4 ft.
Agave havardiana Great textural effect and form but need to grow-on indoors over winter to attain a good-sized plant. Plant into garden in a container and then lift for winter.	annual	7–10	mound	15–18 in.
Ageratum houstonianum 'Blue Horizon' A utilitarian plant but many more superior annuals are now available.	annual		mound	18 in.
Ajuga reptans 'Purple Torch' Really more pink than purple; disappointing in association with other truer violets. Should be called 'Pink Torch'.	perennial	4–9	horizontal	6–9 in.
Alcea rosea 'Peaches and Dreams' Yummy double peach flowers.	perennial	3–8	vertical	4–6 ft.

WIDTH	FLOWER COLOR	FLOWERING MONTH	FOLIAGE COLOR	FOLIAGE INTEREST	TEXTURE	DESIGN COLOR
2 ft.	blue	Aug–Oct			average	cool
2 ft.	yellow	Jul–Sep			average	warm
3–5 in.			yellow	spring/summer/autumn	fine	warm
12 in.			green/yellow	spring/summer/autumn	fine	warm
12 in.			green/yellow	spring/summer/autumn	fine	warm
18 in.					fine	warm or cool
8–15 ft.	white	Jun–Jul	yellow	autumn	bold	warm or cool
	blue	Jul–Sep			fine	cool
2–3 ft.	blue	Jul–Sep			average	cool
3 ft.	orange	Jun–Aug	gray-green	spring/summer/autumn	fine	warm
1½ ft.			gray-green	spring/summer/autumn	bold	warm or cool
12–18 in.	blue	Jul–Oct			average	cool
24 in.	pink	May		year-round	average	cool
3–4 ft.	peach	Jun–Aug			bold	warm

	TYPE	ZONE	FORM	HEIGHT
Alcea rosea 'The Watchman' Black flowers on bold vertical spikes—too cool for words. Inspirational to painters such as Georgia O'Keeffe as well as the artist within the garden designer. Short-lived but worth replanting.	perennial	3–8	vertical	4–6 ft.
Alcea rugosa Excellent vertical accent to add a classical touch to the mixed garden. Less prone to rust.	perennial	3–8	vertical	4–6 ft.
Alchemilla mollis My signature plant. Chartreuse color, mounded habit, and fabulous leaf form and texture make this an excellent blender in most color or texture schemes. Plates 94, 148.	perennial	4–7	mound	16–18 in.
Allium caeruleum Delicate blue addition, naturalizes, 10 per sq. ft.	hardy bulb	5–7	vertical	15–18 in.
Allium carinatum ssp. pulchellum Nice coming up through other plants due to delicate nature, 10 per sq. ft.	hardy bulb	5–8	vertical	24 in.
Allium cristophii Beautiful large flowers. Not overbearing, so it's easy to incorporate into combinations. One of my favorite bulbs, 5 per sq. ft. Plate 94.	hardy bulb	3–8	mound	15–20 in.
Allium hollandicum (aflatunense) 'Purple Sensation' A good height and flower size to incorporate into borders without being too overwhelming, 5 per sq. ft. Plate 98.	hardy bulb	3–8	vertical	24 in.
Allium moly 'Jeannine' Unexpected color for the genus. Great interplanted among blues and purples, 10 per sq. ft.	hardy bulb	3–8	mound	10–12 in.
Allium schubertii Crazy massive flowers that are truly a conversation piece in the garden. Seedheads last long into the autumn, although the stems loosen from the ground. I like to lift the seedheads and place them among other plants where a hole may have developed. Dominant in overall form but actually airy in texture. Treated as a short-lived bulb in my zone 5 garden. Often requires replanting, 3 per sq. ft. Plates 107, 110.	hardy bulb	(6)7–9	mound	18 in.
Allium sphaerocephalon I've used this bulb for years interplanted among various different types of plants and it has always been outstanding, 10 per sq. ft.	hardy bulb	4–8	vertical	2–2½ ft.
Alstroemeria 'Sweet Laura' Sweet indeed in flower fragrance, hardiness, and design effect. Plate 112.	perennial	5–10	vertical	24–36 in.
Alstroemeria aurea 'Orange King' Exotic touch to warm color schemes. Not an overly vigorous grower.	annual	(6)7–10	vertical	18–24 in.
Alstroemeria psittacina Fairly nice but not overwhelming. Good filler among other more prominent plants.	annual	(6)7–10	vertical	18–24 in.

WIDTH	FLOWER COLOR	FLOWERING MONTH	FOLIAGE COLOR	FOLIAGE INTEREST	TEXTURE	DESIGN COLOR
3–4 ft.	black	Jun–Aug			bold	warm or cool
3–4 ft.	yellow	Jun–Jul			bold	warm
24 in.	green	Jun–Aug			bold	warm or cool
	blue	May–Jun			fine	cool
	purple	Jul			fine	cool
	purple	Jun			fine	cool
	purple	May–Jun			average	cool
	yellow	Jun			fine	warm
	purple	Jun			fine	cool
	purple	Jul			fine	cool
18 in.	yellow	Jul–Sep			fine	warm
2 ft.	orange	Jun–Sep			fine	warm
2 ft.	red	Jun–Sep			fine	warm

	TYPE	ZONE	FORM	HEIGHT
Alternanthera dentata 'Rubiginosa' Makes an excellent groundcover or edger to pull purple down to the ground. Great for containers too.	annual	9–11	horizontal	10–12 in.
Amelanchier ×grandiflora 'Autumn Brilliance' Outstanding, adaptable, multi-season. Tolerant of wet locations.	tree	4–9	vase	20 ft.
Amorpha canescens Interesting rounded native shrub for its gray-green foliage and violet-blue flowers with complementary orange anthers. Adaptable to drought and poor soil. Pruning back hard in spring may be needed to maintain a good habit. Combination 13.	shrub	2–6	mound	2–4 ft.
Amorphophallus konjac To say this plant makes a statement is an understatement. Not for the timid designer. I like to use it as an annual in zone 5 gardens.	tender bulb	6–10	vertical	5–6 ft.
Ampelopsis glandulosa var. brevipedunculata 'Elegans' Great variegation and eye-catching blue berries. I like to use this as a low shrub and let its long twining stems cover the ground under perennials. Requires some policing to keep it where intended. Flowers on new wood so can be severely pruned in early spring to keep in control. Plate 45.	woody vine	5–8	climbing	15 ft.
Amsonia ciliata Extremely fine texture to foliage and nice mounded shrublike habit. Benefits from removing top 4–6 in. of stems after flowering to maintain good habit. Combination 19.	perennial	3–9	mound	24–36 in.
Amsonia elliptica Tough and reliable, excellent mounded form and glossy foliage. Should be used more. Plate 123.	perennial	3–9	mound	24–36 in.
Amsonia hubrichtii Fabulous fine texture, habit, and autumn color.	perennial	3–9	mound	24–36 in.
Amsonia tabernaemontana Good mounded form. To create a shrublike appearance, prune by one-third after flowering. Plate 28.	perennial	3–9	mound	24–36 in.
Anemone ×hybrida 'Queen Charlotte' Adds a rose-bud effect in a pale pastel during an unexpected time of year.	perennial	4–8	mound	24–48 in.
Anemone ×hybrida 'September Charm' Adds a pastel tint to the normal rich shades of autumn. Reliably hardy.	perennial	4–8	mound	24–48 in.
Angelica gigas Bold architectural plant for a focal point. Biennial; deadhead or allow to seed for permanence. Should be used more. Combination 17.	perennial	4–8	vertical	3–6 ft.

WIDTH	FLOWER COLOR	FLOWERING MONTH	FOLIAGE COLOR	FOLIAGE INTEREST	TEXTURE	DESIGN COLOR
24 in.			purple	spring/summer/autumn	average	warm or cool
8–10 ft.	white	Apr	red	autumn	average	warm or cool
4–5 ft.	purple	Jun–Jul	gray-green	spring/summer/autumn	fine	cool
1 ft.	red	Jul–Aug			bold	warm or cool
10 ft.		Jun–Aug	green/white	spring/summer/autumn	bold	cool
36 in.	blue	May–Jun	yellow	autumn	fine	cool
36 in.	blue	May–Jun	yellow	autumn	average	cool
36 in.	blue	May–Jun	yellow	autumn	fine	cool
36 in.	blue	May–Jun	yellow	autumn	fine	cool
2 ft.	pink	Sep			average	cool
2 ft.	pink	Sep			average	cool
2–3 ft.	purple	Jul–Aug			bold	warm or cool

	TYPE	ZONE	FORM	HEIGHT
Angelonia 'Blue Pacific' Reliable long-blooming annual, great as a short vertical element. Attracts attention of curious visitors, tolerates drought.	annual	9–10	vertical	18 in.
Angelonia angustifolia 'Purple Pinnacles' Exceptional deep purple flowers all summer long on nice vertical stems. Good filler in the purple garden, tolerates drought.	annual	9–10	vertical	18 in.
Anthriscus sylvestris 'Ravenswing' Provides excellent purple foliage. Use as cut flower or deadhead to keep from seeding. Has been listed as an invasive plant.	perennial	(5)6–8	mound	16–18 in.
Antirrhinum majus 'Rocket Red' Velvety dark red flowers make exceptional vertical accent. Combination 16.	annual		vertical	24 in.
Aquilegia alpina I wouldn't do without this plant in my gardens. Allow this charming mingler to self-seed through the mixed border. Blue spring flowers as well as scarlet autumn foliage. Plates 40, 103, 159.	perennial	3–9	mound	18–24 in.
Aquilegia vulgaris var. stellata 'Black Barlow' Cool black flowers to mix at the feet other perennials or shrubs.	perennial	3–9	mound	24 in.
Aralia elata 'Aureovariegata' Fabulous large shrub or small tree for variegated, tropical-looking foliage—definitely a dominant element in designs. Tolerant of many soil conditions, slow growing, may be prone to spider mites. Plates 15, 43.	shrub	(3)4–9	irregular	10–15 ft.
Arctotis ×hybrida 'Dark Red' I love arctotis for its flowers—which are like gazania, only better—and the gray-green leaves, which contrast nicely with most colors.	annual	9–11	mound	10–15 in.
Arctotis ×hybrida 'Flame' Gorgeous orange flowers for the dry, warm-color garden. Plate 151.	annual	9–11	mound	10–15 in.
Arisaema sikokianum Stunning spathe striped purple and brown, trifoliate leaves, and adaptable nature make this plant invaluable in the shady mixed garden. Plates 128–129.	perennial	5–9	vertical	15 in.
Artemisia 'Huntington' Keep it on the dry side and its silver foliage will shine in the sun and heighten colors around it. Disbud to maintain attractive form and foliage. Plate 44.	perennial	4–9	mound	24 in.
Artemisia 'Powis Castle' Forms a beautiful mound in a short period of time. Give it some space to develop in a design. Disbud to maintain attractive form and foliage.	perennial	5–8	mound	24–36 in.

WIDTH	FLOWER COLOR	FLOWERING MONTH	FOLIAGE COLOR	FOLIAGE INTEREST	TEXTURE	DESIGN COLOR
12 in.	blue	Jun–Sep			average	cool
12 in.	purple	Jun–Sep			average	cool
15–18 in.	white	May	purple	year-round	fine	warm or cool
12 in.	red	Jun–Sep			average	warm
12 in.	blue	May–Jun	red	autumn	average	cool
12 in.	black	May–Jun			average	warm or cool
8 ft.	white	Jul–Aug	green/yellow	spring/summer/ autumn	bold	warm
12 in.	red	Jun–Sep	gray-green	spring/summer/ autumn	average	warm
12 in.	orange	Jun–Sep	gray-green	spring/summer/ autumn	average	warm
6 in.	purple	May			average	warm or cool
24 in.	yellow	Aug–Sep	silver-gray	spring/summer/ autumn	fine	cool
36–48 in.	yellow	Aug–Sep	silver-gray	spring/summer/ autumn	fine	cool

	TYPE	ZONE	FORM	HEIGHT
Artemisia 'Silverado' Fantastic fine texture and low mounded habit on an underused plant. Disbud to maintain attractive form and foliage.	perennial	4–9	mound	18–20 in.
Artemisia absinthium 'Lambrook Silver' Useful due to noninvasive nature, silver autumn foliage, and mid-height habit. Disbud to maintain attractive form and foliage.	perennial	4–9	mound	24 in.
Arum italicum ssp. italicum 'Marmoratum' Multi-season effect from outstanding late-summer fruit and evergreen variegated autumn and winter foliage. Fruit adds warmth to the shade garden. Plan for a hole due to dormant foliage by early May. Combination 14.	perennial	5–9	mound	18 in.
Aruncus dioicus Bold habit useful where a large plant is needed for scale in a shady site.	perennial	3–7	mound	4–6 ft.
Asclepias tuberosa Native plant that offers hot orange flowers and "cool" seed pods. Exciting once established. Plate 150.	perennial	4–9	mound	24–36 in.
Asclepias tuberosa 'Hello Yellow' Yellow version of native for the hot garden. Plate 185.	perennial	4–9	mound	24–36 in.
Aster 'Climax' Charming light blue. Plate 179.	perennial	4–8	mound	36 in.
Aster laevis 'Bluebird' A unique aster for its violet-blue flowers borne in what look like large terminal panicles. Succulent green leaves. Only downside is lax habit. Combination 25.	perennial	4–8	mound	24–36 in.
Aster novae-angliae 'Hella Lacy' Nice large aster that should be pruned before flowering to prevent an ungainly appearance.	perennial	4–8	mound	24–36 in.
Aster novae-angliae 'Hillside' Adds a native feel to autumn border. Plate 171.	perennial	4–8	mound	36 in.
Aster novae-angliae 'Purple Dome' Deep purple flowers, heavy blooming, and compact habit make this a useful aster.	perennial	4–8	mound	18 in.
Aster novae-angliae 'Wild Light Blue' Nice addition for the blue garden in autumn. Prone to disease in high humidity.	perennial	4–8	mound	36 in.
Aster oblongifolius var. angustatus 'Raydon's Favorite' One of my favorite asters for habit and blue-lavender flower color. Plate 171.	perennial	4–8	mound	24–36 in.
Aster tataricus 'Jindai' Sometimes so late to flower in my zone 5 garden that just about everything else is finished, making its only companion fallen tree leaves. Still a great plant, can run if happy.	perennial	4–8	vertical	3–4 ft.

WIDTH	FLOWER COLOR	FLOWERING MONTH	FOLIAGE COLOR	FOLIAGE INTEREST	TEXTURE	DESIGN COLOR
15–18 in.	yellow	Jul–Sep	silver-gray	spring/summer/ autumn	fine	cool
24 in.	yellow	Aug–Sep	silver-gray	spring/summer/ autumn	fine	cool
18 in.	white	May	green/white	spring	bold	warm
6 ft.	white	Jun–Jul			bold	warm or cool
24 in.	orange	Jun–Aug			average	warm
24 in.	yellow	Jun–Aug			average	warm
3 ft.	blue	Sep			average	cool
18 in.	blue	Sep			average	cool
24 in.	purple	Sep			average	cool
2 ft.	purple	Sep			average	cool
24–36 in.	purple	Sep			average	cool
2 ft.	blue	Sep			average	cool
24 in.	blue	Sep			average	cool
3 ft.	blue	Oct–Nov			average	cool

	TYPE	ZONE	FORM	HEIGHT
Astilbe ×arendsii 'Snowdrift' Strong white that glows in the night garden.	perennial	3–8	vertical	18–24 in.
Astilbe chinensis 'Purple Candle' Tall spires of rose-purple flowers provide an often-needed tall vertical feature in the shade garden.	perennial	4–8	vertical	24–36 in.
Astilbe chinensis var. taquetii 'Superba' Tall spires add nice scale in the shade garden.	perennial	4–8	vertical	24 in.
Astilbe chinensis 'Veronica Klose' Nice vertical contribution for the lower layer of the border.	perennial	4–8	vertical	12–15 in.
Astilbe ×rosea 'Peach Blossom' More pink than peach yet still an outstanding color contribution.	perennial	4–9	vertical	24 in.
Athyrium niponicum var. pictum Adds light to the shade garden.	perennial	4–7	mound	18 in.
Atriplex hortensis var. rubra Nice purple-red foliage to use as filler. Great in combinations. Disbud, or seeding can be excessive.	annual	7–9	mound	3–4 ft.
Baptisia 'Purple Smoke' Smoky purple stems and dusty violet-blue flowers set this baptisia apart and make it great for the purple garden.	perennial	3–9	mound	36 in.
Baptisia australis Reliable and adaptable, a favorite for the blue garden. Plate 162; Combination 5.	perennial	3–9	mound	36 in.
Baptisia sphaerocarpa Excellent vertical yellow spikes in the early summer hot border.	perennial	5–9	mound	24 in.
Belamcanda chinensis Hot orange flowers and black fruit—still excellent for the mixed border. Plates 144, 146.	perennial	5–10	vertical	3–4 ft.
Belamcanda chinensis 'Hello Yellow' Useful in many design situations for its size, form, flower, and fruit color—yet often overlooked. Plate 158.	perennial	5–10	vertical	12–15 in.
Berberis thunbergii 'Monler' (Gold Nugget™) One of my favorite small-growing shrubs for mixed gardens: the awesome yellow foliage turns vibrant shades of orange and red in autumn. Plates 107–109, 172.	shrub	4–8	mound	15 in.
Berberis thunbergii 'Monry' (Sunsation™) The dazzling golden foliage color and graceful vase shape make this shrub a designer's delight.	shrub	4–8	vase	3–4 ft.
Berberis thunbergii var. atropurpurea 'Bailtwo' (Burgundy Carousel™) Colorful foliage useful for many different color schemes. Plate 141.	shrub	4–8	mound	3 ft.

WIDTH	FLOWER COLOR	FLOWERING MONTH	FOLIAGE COLOR	FOLIAGE INTEREST	TEXTURE	DESIGN COLOR
18 in.	white	Jun			average	warm or cool
24 in.	magenta	Jul–Aug			average	cool
24 in.	magenta	Jul–Aug			average	cool
12–15 in.	pink	Jul–Aug			average	cool
18 in.	peach	Jun			average	cool
12–18 in.			silver-gray	spring/summer/ autumn	fine	cool
1–1½ ft.			red	spring/summer/ autumn	average	warm or cool
4 ft.	purple	Jun			average	cool
4 ft.	blue	Jun			average	cool
24 in.	yellow	Jun			average	warm
2 ft.	orange	Jul–Aug			average	warm
15 in.	yellow	Jul–Aug			average	warm
24 in.			yellow	spring/summer/ autumn	fine	warm
4 ft.			yellow	spring/summer/ autumn	fine	warm
4–5 ft.			red	spring/summer/ autumn	fine	warm or cool

	TYPE	ZONE	FORM	HEIGHT
Berberis thunbergii var. atropurpurea 'Gentry Cultivar' (Royal Burgundy™) Compact habit and foliage color work great for front of mixed borders.	shrub	4–8	mound	1–2 ft.
Berberis thunbergii var. atropurpurea 'Rose Glow' Gorgeous mottled foliage makes it useful in a variety of situations. Interesting for bringing out the pink of pink-flowering plants in borders or even in containers. Plate 7.	shrub	4–8	mound	3 ft.
Berberis thunbergii var. atropurpurea 'Royal Cloak' Form and foliage color creates focal point in a border.	shrub	4–8	mound	4 ft.
Beta vulgaris 'Bull's Blood' Unusual plant, one of my favorite annuals. Outstanding deep red-purple foliage, compact habit, great as an edger or in containers. Plate 69.	annual		mound	10–12 in.
Beta vulgaris 'Golden' Bright yellow stalks are excellent in the yellow or warm-color-scheme garden. Plate 185.	annual		mound	12–15 in.
Beta vulgaris 'Ruby Queen' The red stems, midrib, and leaf veins of this autumn plant are intriguing under close inspection, as I noticed while painting them one day, but plants are also bold and glow—particularly with backlighting in the border.	annual		mound	12–15 in.
Betula utilis var. jacquemontii Stunning white bark. Reminds me of my days working in Belgium, where it was grown to perfection. Bark color may vary from milk-white (best form) to cream. Susceptible to Japanese beetle damage; often listed as resistant to borer. Plate 36.	tree	5–6	vertical	30 ft.
Bouvardia ternifolia Bright red-orange flowers on lax, sprawling stems are wonderful used as a groundcover or to clamber over other plants in a hot color scheme. Plate 150.	annual	9–11	mound	12–15 in.
Brachyscome 'Ultra' Purple-blue flowers on low groundcover.	annual	10–11	mound	10–12 in.
Brassica oleracea Some interesting forms for late foliage color when a hole appears in border. Most vivid colors are produced at temperatures below 50°F.	annual		mound	12–18 in.
Brunnera macrophylla Still a nice blue addition for the shade garden. Drought tolerant once established.	perennial	3–8	mound	12–18 in.
Buddleia 'Lochinch' Versatile shrub for blue or cool-color gardens.	shrub	5–9	vase	6–8 ft.
Buddleia davidii 'Black Knight' Outstanding deep purple flower color. Plants have proven hardier and more vigorous than other cultivars.	shrub	5–9	vase	8–10 ft.

WIDTH	FLOWER COLOR	FLOWERING MONTH	FOLIAGE COLOR	FOLIAGE INTEREST	TEXTURE	DESIGN COLOR
2 ft.			red	spring/summer/ autumn	fine	warm or cool
2–3 ft.			purple	spring/summer/ autumn	fine	cool
4 ft.			red	spring/summer/ autumn	fine	warm or cool
12 in.			red	spring/summer/ autumn	bold	warm or cool
18 in.			yellow	spring/summer/ autumn	bold	warm
18 in.			red	spring/summer/ autumn	bold	warm
18–20 ft.	tan	Apr			average	warm or cool
1–1½ ft.	red	Jun–Sep			average	warm
12 in.	purple	Jun–Sep			fine	cool
12–18 in.			purple	autumn	bold	cool
20 in.	blue	Apr–May			bold	cool
5–10 ft.	blue	Jun–Sep	gray-green	spring/summer/ autumn	bold	cool
5–10 ft.	purple	Jun–Sep			bold	cool

	TYPE	ZONE	FORM	HEIGHT
Buddleia davidii 'Mongo' (Nanho blue) More compact habit than other buddleias, with gray-green leaves and mauve-blue flowers—a great addition to blue or cool-color gardens. Deadhead before seeds mature to prevent excessive seeding; reportedly invasive when allowed to seed. Plate 78.	shrub	5–9	mound	6–8 ft.
Buphthalmum speciosum Big and bold and loved by the birds and butterflies. Adds often-needed weight to the garden.	perennial	4–7	mound	4–5 ft.
Buxus 'Green Gem' For hedging. Requires little pruning and performs well in colder climates.	shrub	5–9	mound	2 ft.
Buxus 'Green Velvet' For hedging. Requires little pruning and performs well in colder climates.	shrub	5–9	mound	3 ft.
Buxus microphylla 'Winter Gem' Good hedging plant for colder climates.	shrub	5–9	mound	2 ft.
Caladium 'Florida Cardinal' Cultivars in the Florida Series can tolerate sun with even moisture. They hate to be planted in cool soil. Plate 114.	tropical	10–11	mound	16 in.
Caladium 'Florida Sweetheart'	tropical	10–11	mound	16 in.
Calamagrostis ×acutiflora 'Karl Foerster' Still a favorite for use in narrow hard-to-design spots between walls and sidewalks—as well as just about anywhere else.	perennial	4–8	vertical	5–6 ft.
Calamagrostis ×acutiflora 'Overdam' Beautiful refined variegation and habit make for a classy plant.	perennial	5–8	vertical	4–5 ft.
Calamagrostis brachytricha Airy texture, mid height, and tolerant to partial shade—what more can we ask? Oh yes, drought tolerant once established.	perennial	4–8	vertical	4 ft.
Calendula officinalis 'Orange King' Sturdy orderly habit to flowers, which are upward-facing and close at night. Provides orange color in the lower layer of the border. Does not do well in high temperatures.	annual		mound	10–15 in.
Callicarpa dichotoma 'Issai' Graceful arching habit. Heavy lilac-violet fruit on young plants attracts a great deal of attention. Great for the purple garden. Coppicing may be beneficial to improve fruit production. Plate 168.	shrub	5–8	mound	3–4 ft.
Calycanthus floridus Fragrant flowers, persistent fruit, and adaptability to wet or poorly drained soils make this shrub useful as a mid-sized natural hedge or for use as a background shrub in the mixed border.	shrub	4–9	mound	6–9 ft.

WIDTH	FLOWER COLOR	FLOWERING MONTH	FOLIAGE COLOR	FOLIAGE INTEREST	TEXTURE	DESIGN COLOR
6–8 ft.	blue	Jun–Sep	gray-green	spring/summer/autumn	bold	cool
5 ft.	yellow	Jun–Aug			bold	warm
2 ft.					fine	warm or cool
3 ft.					fine	warm or cool
2 ft.					fine	warm or cool
12 in.			red	spring/summer/autumn	bold	warm
12 in.			red	spring/summer/autumn	bold	warm or cool
2 ft.	tan	Jun–Sep			fine	warm or cool
2 ft.	tan	Jun–Sep	green/white	spring/summer/autumn	fine	warm or cool
2–3 ft.	tan	Aug–Sep			fine	warm or cool
12–18 in.	orange	Jun–Sep			average	warm
4 ft.	pink	Jun–Aug			average	cool
6–12 ft.	red	May–Jun	yellow	autumn	bold	warm or cool

	TYPE	ZONE	FORM	HEIGHT
Camassia leichtlinii 'Semiplena' A different look to the flower spikes makes this interesting and a touch unusual, 5 per sq. ft.	hardy bulb	3–8	vertical	2½–3 ft.
Camassia leichtlinii ssp. suksdorfii 'Blauwe Donau' (blue Danube) Unusual bulb, great addition to the blue garden or as a spot of contrast in an orange theme, 5 per sq. ft.	hardy bulb	3–8	vertical	2–3 ft.
Campanula 'Birch Hybrid' Low, useful blue. Plate 165.	perennial	4–7	mound	4–8 in.
Campanula 'Constellation' Tiny, sweet blue for close observation along a path.	perennial	4–7	mound	4–6 in.
Campanula 'Dwarf Tornado' Fun, tiny campanula.	perennial	4–7	vertical	6 in.
Campanula 'Kent Belle' Fair performer but not on the top shelf in my experience.	perennial	5–9	vertical	24 in.
Campanula persicifolia 'Chettle Charm' Often listed as being blue but really more prominently white. Nice during a good year but often short-lived.	perennial	3–7	vertical	24–36 in.
Campanula rapunculoides Step aside for this running, flopping bellflower. Plate 163.	perennial	3–7	mound	24 in.
Campanula rotundifolia 'Olympica' This little self-seeding plant stole my heart years ago, and I still love it and get numerous questions about it from visitors to the gardens.	perennial	2–7	mound	6–12 in.
Campsis ×tagliabuana 'Madame Galen' Useful as a quick vining cover in spots where little else will grow. Has a reputation for being invasive.	woody vine	5–9	climbing	15–25 ft.
Canna 'Black Knight' Red flowers very attractive over dark foliage. Needs a light-colored background for plants to stand out.	tropical	(7)8–11	vertical	3–4 ft.
Canna 'Omega' Choice. Clean green leaves on tall plants topped with striking apricot flowers. Plate 182.	tropical	(7)8–11	vertical	8–10 ft.
Canna 'Orange Punch' Fantastic intense flowers for the orange garden—my favorite orange. Plate 193.	tropical	(7)8–11	vertical	36 in.
Canna 'Panache' Nice flower color.	tropical	(7)8–11	vertical	8–10 ft.
Canna 'Phasion' A stunning leaf variegation that is an excellent addition to hot color schemes. Flowers complement foliage nicely. Plate 43.	tropical	(7)8–11	vertical	5–7 ft.

WIDTH	FLOWER COLOR	FLOWERING MONTH	FOLIAGE COLOR	FOLIAGE INTEREST	TEXTURE	DESIGN COLOR
	white	May–Jun			average	warm or cool
	blue	May–Jun			average	cool
15 in.	blue	Jun–Jul			average	cool
6 in.	blue	Jun–Jul			average	cool
6 in.	blue	Jun–Jul			average	cool
18 in.	purple	Jul–Aug			average	cool
24 in.	blue	Jun–Jul			average	cool
48 in.	blue	Jun–Aug			average	cool
12 in.	blue	Jun–Sep			fine	cool
10–15 ft.	orange	Jul–Aug			bold	warm
2 ft.	red	Jul–Sep	purple	spring/summer/autumn	bold	warm
2 ft.	peach	Jul–Sep		spring/summer/autumn	bold	warm
2 ft.	orange	Jul–Sep		spring/summer/autumn	bold	warm
2 ft.	peach	Jul–Sep		spring/summer/autumn	bold	warm
2 ft.	orange	Jul–Sep	mixed	spring/summer/autumn	bold	warm

	TYPE	ZONE	FORM	HEIGHT
Canna 'Roi Humbert' (red King Humbert) Nice for bronze-red to deep green foliage and striking red-orange flowers. Plates 111, 145.	tropical	(7)8–11	vertical	5–7 ft.
Canna 'Striata' (Pretoria) Sometimes called 'Bengal Tiger'. I really prefer it when it isn't flowering: the foliage is a knockout—add the flowers, and it can get a bit over-the-edge hot. Plate 3; Combination 17.	tropical	(7)8–11	vertical	5–9 ft.
Canna indica 'Red Stripe' (purpurea) A great performer, probably my favorite canna due to its many uses and huge bold appearance. Leaves are stunning when backlit. In general, cannas can be planted 10–18 in. apart. Plates 8, 75, 196; Combination 11.	tropical	(7)8–11	vertical	8–10 ft.
Carex buchananii Some visitors to the garden aren't sure if this plant is dead or if it is supposed to look brown all year. Really an interesting character, bringing an unusual, fantastic color to combinations. Looks like fire when backlit. Provide good drainage in colder climates. Plates 190–191.	perennial	(5)6–9	vertical	24 in.
Carex dolichostachya 'Kaga Nishiki' (gold fountains) Nice low, variegated accent. Best with moisture.	perennial	5–9	mound	15–18 in.
Carex elata 'Aurea' (Bowles' golden) Memorable yellow glow, particularly when backlit. By far my favorite carex. Plate 197.	perennial	5–9	mound	15–18 in.
Carex morrowii 'Ice Dance' A robust variegated sedge, versatile in many situations.	perennial	5–9	mound	12–18 in.
Carex morrowii 'Variegata' Adaptable and useful variegated addition. Plate 123.	perennial	5–9	mound	12–18 in.
Caryopteris ×clandonensis Great summer-flowering shrub for the mixed garden. Plate 75.	shrub	(5)6–9	mound	3–4 ft.
Caryopteris ×clandonensis 'Longwood Blue' Gray-green foliage and blue flowers are excellent additions to cool color combinations. Prune back dead branch tips in spring; may need to prune to base of plant after severe winters. Well-draining soil essential.	shrub	(5)6–9	mound	3–4 ft.
Caryopteris ×clandonensis 'Worcester Gold' Yellow spring foliage is outstanding when combined with other blue-flowering spring plants. Not a vigorous grower and may require pruning of dead branch tips in the spring. Plates 40, 159, 161.	shrub	(5)6–9	mound	2–3 ft.
Catalpa bignonioides 'Aurea' Useful coppiced for dramatic foliage, form, and color, and to lend a shrublike appearance to the plant.	tree	5–9	mound	30 ft.
Celosia spicata 'Flamingo Purple' Striking (for a celosia), tall vertical purple element. Blends well yet is frequently asked about by visitors because it is not common. Vigorous.	annual		vertical	3–5 ft.

WIDTH	FLOWER COLOR	FLOWERING MONTH	FOLIAGE COLOR	FOLIAGE INTEREST	TEXTURE	DESIGN COLOR
2 ft.	red	Jul–Sep	red	spring/summer/ autumn	bold	warm
2 ft.	orange	Jul–Sep	green/yellow	spring/summer/ autumn	bold	warm
2 ft.	red	Jul–Sep	red	spring/summer/ autumn	bold	warm
15–18 in.			bronze	year-round	fine	warm
18 in.			green/yellow	spring/summer/ autumn	fine	warm
24 in.			yellow	spring/summer/ autumn	fine	warm
12 in.			green/white	year-round	fine	cool
12 in.			green/white	year-round	fine	cool
3–4 ft.	blue	Jul–Sep	gray-green	spring/summer/ autumn	fine	cool
3–4 ft.	blue	Jul–Sep	gray-green	spring/summer/ autumn	fine	cool
2–3 ft.	blue	Jul–Sep	yellow	spring/summer/ autumn	fine	warm or cool
30 ft.			yellow	spring/summer/ autumn	bold	warm
2 ft.	purple	Jul–Sep	purple	spring/summer/ autumn	average	cool

	TYPE	ZONE	FORM	HEIGHT
Centaurea cineraria Foliage is almost white, making this a bright highlight in the border. Intensifies cooler colors around it.	annual	7–9	mound	15–18 in.
Centaurea montana Still love this rather dated perennial, as the flowers lift my spirits. Good blue addition that will fill much space if not regularly deadheaded. Pulls out easily.	perennial	3–8	mound	18–24 in.
Cephalaria gigantea Airy, towering, soft yellow flowers anchored by bold basal foliage creates contrast. It's been around for years yet is still underutilized in designs.	perennial	3–8	vertical	5–7 ft.
Ceratostigma plumbaginoides Outstanding groundcover for late blue flowers and scarlet autumn color. Plates 100, 177.	perennial	5–9	mound	8–12 in.
Cerinthe major 'Purpurascens' By far my favorite annual for its blue succulent-like foliage, tinged purple at the tips, and the bell-shaped flowers that are purple, white, and yellow with a touch of rose to them. Combines beautifully with a variety of other cool colors: the numerous pictures through this book speak for themselves. Plates 34, 91, 98, 108.	annual	6(7)	mound	18 in.
Chamaecyparis lawsoniana 'Sullivan' Great for hedging. A hemlock substitute. Does not tolerate the heat of the South.	tree	5–7	conical	30–40 ft.
Chamaecyparis obtusa 'Fernspray Gold' Graceful habit. May be used as a small specimen tree or accent shrub. Creates interest in foliage color and texture. Needs moist well-draining soil and prefers a protected site. Plate 14.	shrub	5–8	conical	6–8 ft.
Chamaecyparis obtusa 'Mariesii' Dwarf, slow-growing specimen with a yellowish green overcast.	shrub	5–8	mound	2–3 ft.
Chamaecyparis pisifera 'Golden Mop' Excellent dwarf, yellow-foliaged specimen for a multitude of combinations. Plates 98, 155.	shrub	4–7	mound	2–3 ft.
Chionanthus virginicus Beautiful small three-season tree that I try to use whenever possible, particularly in partially shaded gardens. Pollution tolerant. Plate 125.	tree	4–9	vase	12–20 ft.
Chionodoxa forbesii (luciliae) Siehei Group Excellent blue, naturalizes. Foliage easily hidden in mixed gardens, 10–15 per sq. ft.	hardy bulb	3–8	mound	8 in.
Chrysanthemum 'Autumn Moon' Hardy and bold when in flower. Combination 10.	perennial	(5)6–9	mound	24–30 in.
Chrysanthemum 'Pumpkin Harvest' Dark peach—stunning.	perennial	5–9	mound	24 in.
Chrysanthemum 'Single Apricot' Another great flower color and performer. Plate 189.	perennial	5–9	mound	24 in.

WIDTH	FLOWER COLOR	FLOWERING MONTH	FOLIAGE COLOR	FOLIAGE INTEREST	TEXTURE	DESIGN COLOR
12 in.			silver-gray	spring/summer/ autumn	fine	cool
12 in.	blue	May–Jul			average	cool
3–6 ft.	yellow	Jun–Aug			bold	warm or cool
12–18 in.	blue	Aug–Sep	red	autumn	average	cool
15 in.	purple	May–Sep	blue	spring/summer/ autumn	average	cool
20–30 ft.					average	warm or cool
4–6 ft.			yellow	year-round	fine	warm
2–3 ft.					fine	warm
2–3 ft.			yellow	year-round	fine	warm
12–15 ft.	white	May–Jun	yellow	autumn	average	warm or cool
	blue	Apr			fine	cool
24–30 in.	yellow	Oct			average	warm
24 in.	peach	Sep			average	warm
24 in.	peach	Sep			average	warm

	TYPE	ZONE	FORM	HEIGHT
Chrysanthemum 'Single Peach' Good peach for late in season. Plates 189–190.	perennial	5–9	mound	24 in.
Chrysanthemum 'Viette's Apricot Glow' One of the hardiest and best apricots.	perennial	5–9	mound	24 in.
Cimicifuga ramosa 'Brunette' Great for foliage color and texture even if it never flowered. Combination 15.	perennial	3–8	vertical	4–6 ft.
Cimicifuga ramosa 'Hillside Black Beauty' Foliage to die for—should be in every shade garden. Plate 41.	perennial	3–8	vertical	4–6 ft.
Clematis 'Elsa Späth' Early large-flowering cultivar, good in association with climbing roses or in containers. Plate 37.	woody vine	4–8(9)	climbing	6–10 ft.
Clematis 'Hagley Hybrid' Jackman Group, vigorous and compact. Suitable for container culture. Plate 129.	woody vine	4–8(9)	climbing	6 ft.
Clematis 'Lanuginosa Candida' Strong grower, classic plant.	woody vine	5–8(9)	climbing	15 ft.
Clematis 'Polish Spirit' Viticella Group, reliable and vigorous. Nice purple. Plate 106.	woody vine	4–8(9)	climbing	10–15 ft.
Clematis 'Royal Velours' Viticella Group, reliable strong grower. Outstanding velvety flowers.	woody vine	4–8(9)	climbing	10–15 ft.
Clematis alpina 'Constance' Free-flowering, outstanding flower color and form.	woody vine	5–9	climbing	6–10 ft.
Clematis integrifolia Overlooked scrambling clematis that makes a good filler among other blue or cool colors.	perennial	4–9	mound	15–18 in.
Clematis macropetala 'Markham's Pink' Early, free-flowering, among the most reliably winter hardy.	woody vine	5–9	climbing	6–10 ft.
Clematis recta Can be trained on a small obelisk or over low arches to create a shrublike mound of starry white flowers. Plate 55.	perennial	3–7	mound	3–4 ft.
Clematis terniflora I still love this plant for late flowers and fragrance. Can be grown up obelisks or sturdy shrubs, creating a huge white cloud that attracts the eye. Plates 6, 73–74.	woody vine	5–8(9)	climbing	10–20 ft.
Clethra alnifolia Fragrant summer-flowering, stolonizing shrub. Can be used as a specimen in the mixed garden or as a naturalized mid-sized hedge. 'Hummingbird', an excellent compact selection, grows 2½–3½ ft. tall and wide. Plate 73.	shrub	4–9	vase	4–8 ft.
Colchicum speciosum Great for late-season color, really more pink than purple, 3–5 per sq. ft.	hardy bulb	4–9	mound	10 in.

WIDTH	FLOWER COLOR	FLOWERING MONTH	FOLIAGE COLOR	FOLIAGE INTEREST	TEXTURE	DESIGN COLOR
24 in.	peach	Sep			average	warm
24 in.	peach	Sep			average	warm
2–4 ft.	white	Aug–Sep	purple	spring/summer/ autumn	average	cool
2–4 ft.	white	Aug–Sep	purple	spring/summer/ autumn	average	warm or cool
3 ft.	purple	May–Jun			average	cool
3 ft.	pink	May–Jun			average	cool
6 ft.	white	Jun			average	warm or cool
6 ft.	purplc	Jun Jul			fine	cool
6 ft.	purple	Jun–Jul			average	cool
5 ft.	pink	Apr–Jun			average	cool
15–18 in.	blue	Jun			average	cool
5 ft.	pink	May–Jun			fine	cool
3 ft.	white	May–Jun			fine	warm or cool
15 ft.	white	Aug–Oct			fine	warm or cool
4–6 ft.	white	Jul–Aug	yellow	autumn	average	warm or cool
	pink	Sep			average	cool

	TYPE	ZONE	FORM	HEIGHT
Colocasia esculenta Striking bold foliage accents a variety of color schemes. Plate 122.	tropical	8–11	mound	4–6 ft.
Colocasia esculenta 'Black Beauty' A slightly smaller version of the selection 'Black Magic'.	tropical		mound	30–36 in.
Colocasia esculenta 'Black Magic' This is a striking bold dark plant, excellent in a variety of color combinations. Best contrasted with a light background or light-foliaged plants to increase its appearance.	tropical	8–11	mound	5–6 ft.
Colocasia esculenta 'Fontanesii' This is such a choice tropical plant, I think it should find a place in every large mixed garden. Purple in foliage and stems creates depth and mystery, and when in flower it will steal the show. Plates 97, 200.	tropical	8–11	vase	5–7 ft.
Colocasia esculenta 'Illustris' Interesting foliage but, in my experience, not as vigorous or as bold in the garden as some of the other colocasias.	tropical	7–10	mound	3–4 ft.
Consolida ajacis 'Blue Spire' Fantastic annual that, if allowed to reseed, acts perennial. Nice interplanted among perennials and shrubs, as these plants will hide declining larkspur foliage and resulting hole that develops in late summer. Plates 96, 110.	annual		vertical	3–4 ft.
Coreopsis auriculata Sturdy habit and long bloom period.	perennial	4–9	mound	15–18 in.
Coreopsis grandiflora 'Walcoreop' (flying saucers) Numerous flowers for a long time, yet plants are often short-lived. Prune in late summer to prevent plants from flowering to exhaustion. Plate 158.	perennial	4–9	mound	16–18 in.
Coreopsis tripteris Tall, light, and airy, with interesting foliage texture. Useful for height with minimal width and weight. May flop if not pruned before flowering. Plate 183.	perennial	4–8	vertical	4–8 ft.
Coreopsis verticillata 'Moonbeam' Lemon-yellow flowers, fine texture, and reliability make this a good utilitarian plant.	perennial	3–9	mound	18–20 in.
Coreopsis verticillata 'Zagreb' Stout in habit, fine in texture. Utilitarian plant.	perennial	3–9	mound	12 in.
Cornus kousa Good multi-season plant. I prefer to use as a small tree rather than shrub-form in mixed gardens. Requires pruning if used in smaller gardens, easier to grow than the native flowering dogwood.	tree	5–8	vase	20–30 ft.
Cosmos atrosanguineus Interesting and unusual flower color and scent to incorporate in purple or red color schemes or containers.	annual	7–10	mound	24 in.

WIDTH	FLOWER COLOR	FLOWERING MONTH	FOLIAGE COLOR	FOLIAGE INTEREST	TEXTURE	DESIGN COLOR
3 ft.					bold	warm or cool
30–36 in.			purple	spring/summer/autumn	bold	warm or cool
3–4 ft.			purple	spring/summer/autumn	bold	warm or cool
3–5 ft.	white	Aug–Sep	purple	spring/summer/autumn	bold	warm or cool
30 in.			purple	spring/summer/autumn	bold	warm or cool
1½ ft.	blue	Jun–Jul			fine	cool
12 in.	yellow	Jun–Jul			average	warm
15 in.	yellow	Jun–Aug			average	warm
2 ft.	yellow	Jul–Sep			fine	warm
18–20 in.	yellow	Jun–Oct			fine	warm
15–18 in.	yellow	Jun–Oct			fine	warm
20–30 ft.	white	May–Jun	red	autumn	average	warm or cool
18 in.	red	Jun–Sep			fine	warm or cool

	TYPE	ZONE	FORM	HEIGHT
Cotinus coggygria 'Velvet Cloak' Great designer shrub when stooled in spring for habit control and to intensify leaf color. Very adaptable, can be used in the red or purple garden. Plate 143.	shrub	(4)5–8	mound	10–15 ft.
Crocosmia 'Blacro' (Jenny Bloom) One of my favorite crocosmias for its reliable hardiness and flower color.	perennial	5–10	vertical	18 in.
Crocosmia 'Emberglow' Hot orange adds fire to garden. Marginal in most of Ohio.	perennial	6–9	vertical	24–36 in.
Crocosmia 'Lucifer' Reliable hardiness, eye-popping flowers, striking backlit foliage. Plates 25, 31, 97, 99.	perennial	5–9	vertical	24–36 in.
Crocosmia ×crocosmiiflora 'Norwich Canary' A nice yellow, unreliable hardiness. Plate 185.	perennial	6–9	vertical	12–15 in.
Crocosmia ×crocosmiiflora 'Solfatare' A cool crocosmia for a hot combination, interesting foliage color, fair hardiness. Plate 182.	perennial	6–9	vertical	20 in.
Crocosmia ×crocosmiiflora 'Venus' Good peachy yellow, unreliable hardiness but worth replanting if needed.	perennial	6–9	vertical	20 in.
Crocus chrysanthus 'Blue Bird' 10–15 per sq. ft.	hardy bulb	3–8	mound	3–6 in.
Cryptotaenia japonica f. atropurpurea I use this plant in shady spots strictly for its great purple foliage and interesting leaf dissection. Deadhead to avoid seeding into lawns and other adjacent areas.	perennial	5–7	mound	18 in.
Cynara cardunculus Gorgeous form and bold texture statement. Should be used more. Plate 84.	annual	7–9	vertical	3–5 ft.
Cynoglossum amabile 'Firmament' Excellent used as a groundcover or filler among other perennials or shrubs.	perennial	5–8	mound	12–15 in.
Cyperus alternifolius 'Stricta' A compact selection, offering interesting form and texture for the small water garden. Plate 71.	annual	9–11	vertical	18 in.
Dahlia 'Arabian Night' Spectacular deep shade of red, almost appearing black. Choice for drama, 1 per sq. ft. Plate 195.	tender bulb	(7)8–10	mound	24 in.
Dahlia 'Bishop of Llandaff' The king of dahlias as far as I'm concerned. Excellent in the red garden for flowers and foliage, 1 per sq. ft.	tender bulb	(7)8–10	mound	24 in.
Dahlia 'Ellen Houston' More orange-red than 'Bishop of Llandaff' dahlia. Useful as a blender from reds into oranges, 1 per sq. ft. Plates 144, 147.	tender bulb	(7)8–10	mound	18–24 in.

WIDTH	FLOWER COLOR	FLOWERING MONTH	FOLIAGE COLOR	FOLIAGE INTEREST	TEXTURE	DESIGN COLOR
10–15 ft.	purple	Jun–Sep	purple	spring/summer/ autumn	average	warm or cool
12 in.	yellow	Jul–Aug			fine	warm
12 in.	orange	Jul–Aug			fine	warm
12 in.	red	Jul–Aug			fine	warm
12 in.	yellow	Jul–Aug			fine	warm
12 in.	yellow	Jul–Aug			fine	warm
12 in.	yellow	Jul–Aug			fine	warm
	blue	Mar–Apr			average	cool
18 in.	white	Aug–Sep	purple	spring/summer/ autumn	average	cool
2–4 ft.	purple	Jul–Sep	silver-gray	spring/summer/ autumn	bold	cool
12 in.	blue	Aug–Sep			average	cool
18 in.					fine	warm or cool
	red	Jul–Oct			bold	warm
	red	Jul–Oct	red	spring/summer/ autumn	bold	warm
	orange	Jul–Oct	bronze	spring/summer/ autumn	bold	warm

	TYPE	ZONE	FORM	HEIGHT
Dahlia 'Orange Nugget' Wonderful, intense, large orange flowers for a hot touch, 1 per sq. ft. Plate 194.	tender bulb	(7)8–10	mound	12–18 in.
Dahlia 'Susette' Flowers so light they almost appear white, providing a soft appearance for an otherwise very bold genus, 1 per sq. ft.	tender bulb	(7)8–10	mound	16–20 in.
Daphne ×burkwoodii 'Carol Mackie' Gorgeous foliage and intoxicating flower fragrance, but this much-loved plant is temperamental and needs a well-drained, protected site. Often short-lived. Plates 125–126.	shrub	4–6(7)	mound	3–4 ft.
Delphinium 'Centurion Sky Blue' Beautiful but not vigorous, a high-maintenance prima donna of the border.	perennial	5–7	vertical	24–36 in.
Delphinium ×bellamosum Spectacular when it's happy. Long blooming yet short-lived. Worth replacing if needed.	perennial	3–7	vertical	30–36 in.
Delphinium cashmerianum Fairly pale flowers above finely cut leaves. Good for the blue garden.	perennial	5–7	vertical	24 in.
Delphinium exaltatum Interesting Ohio native that seems more adaptable than other delphiniums. Should be used more.	perennial	5–8	vertical	36 in.
Deschampsia cespitosa 'Goldgehänge'	perennial	4–9	mound	24–36 in.
Dianthus ×allwoodii 'Danielle Marie' Coral flowers. Somewhat short-lived, especially in wet soils.	perennial	5–8	mound	8–18 in.
Dianthus barbatus 'Sooty' Velvety dark red, almost maroon flowers are unusual and enticing—love it.	perennial	5–9	mound	12 in.
Dianthus deltoides 'Leuchtfunk' (flashing light) Bright red flower. Nice planted in paths or used as a groundcover. Plate 148.	perennial	4–9	mound	6–10 in.
Dicentra 'Luxuriant' Can be short-lived, needs well-drained soil.	perennial	3–9	mound	15–18 in.
Dicentra spectabilis 'Gold Heart' Fantastic yellow foliage accent for the spring garden. I could do without the pink flowers; to use plants in warm color combinations, I often disbud them before they open. Plate 41.	perennial	4–9	mound	24 in.
Dichelostemma ida-maia Unusual addition to hot color schemes, 10 per sq. ft.	hardy bulb	5–8	mound	20 in.
Digitalis grandiflora Such a reliable, beautiful, and useful plant in many settings and color schemes. Adds a romantic touch. Combination 20.	perennial	3–8	vertical	24–36 in.

WIDTH	FLOWER COLOR	FLOWERING MONTH	FOLIAGE COLOR	FOLIAGE INTEREST	TEXTURE	DESIGN COLOR
	orange	Jul–Oct			bold	warm
	yellow	Jul–Oct			bold	warm
3–4 ft.	pink	Apr–May	green/white	spring/summer/autumn	average	cool
18–24 in.	blue	Jun–Jul			average	cool
1½ ft.	blue	Jun–Jul			average	cool
12 in.	blue	Jun–Aug			average	cool
2 ft.	purple	Jul–Aug			average	cool
24 in.	yellow	Jun–Oct			fine	warm
12 in.	orange	Jun–Jul			fine	warm
15–18 in.	red	May–Jun			fine	warm
24 in.	red	May–Jun			fine	warm
18 in.	pink	Apr–Sep	blue	spring/summer autumn	fine	cool
18 in.	pink	May	yellow	spring/summer/autumn	average	warm or cool
	red	Jun–Aug			average	warm
15–18 in.	yellow	Jun–Jul			average	warm or cool

	TYPE	ZONE	FORM	HEIGHT
Digitalis lutea Narrow spikes in creamy yellow add a fine vertical accent. Reliable for years.	perennial	3–9	vertical	24 in.
Digitalis purpurea 'Apricot' Beautiful flower color. Biennial, will need replanting.	perennial	4–9	vertical	24–36 in.
Dracocephalum ruyschiana Tough, long-flowering plant whose persistent performance takes one by surprise.	perennial	4–8	mound	12–15 in.
Duranta erecta 'Golden Edge' Fabulous variegated foliage with a shrublike appearance. Great addition to the mixed border for its size and color. Plate 111.	tropical	8–10	mound	5–6 ft.
Echinacea purpurea Adaptable and long flowering but can become a thug and overtake any design if not deadheaded to prevent excess seeding. Combination 7.	perennial	3–8	mound	24–48 in.
Echinops bannaticus 'Taplow Blue' Coarse—creates dominance in a combination. Benefits from some softer plants for companions. Provide good drainage.	perennial	5–9	vertical	36 in.
Echinops ritro 'Blue Glow' Good bold blue.	perennial	3–9	vertical	3–3½ ft.
Echinops ritro 'Veitch's Blue' Stunning when happy: keep it dry. Plate 175.	perennial	3–9	vertical	3–3½ ft.
Epimedium davidii Useful and beautiful groundcover for a warm splash in dry shade.	perennial	5–9	mound	15 in.
Epimedium ×rubrum Workhorse groundcover. Great flowers, fall color, and dry-shade tolerance.	perennial	4–8	mound	8–12 in.
Epimedium ×warleyense Unusual orange flowers on this sturdy groundcover.	perennial	5–9	mound	20 in.
Eranthis hyemalis A welcome spot of color in late winter, very early spring. Reseeds when happy, especially in alkaline soil; scratch seed into soil to increase colony. Soak tubers before planting, 15 per sq. ft.	hardy bulb	5–8	mound	3–4 in.
Eremurus ×isabellinus 'Pinokkio' Great interplanted for vertical effect in early summer, 1 per sq. ft.	hardy bulb	5–8	vertical	4–5 ft.
Eryngium amethystinum Cool, deeply cut, spiny, steel-blue foliage and blue flowers. Very intolerant of wet clay soils.	perennial	3–8	vertical	24–36 in.
Eryngium planum 'Blaukappe'	perennial	3–8	vertical	24–36 in.

WIDTH	FLOWER COLOR	FLOWERING MONTH	FOLIAGE COLOR	FOLIAGE INTEREST	TEXTURE	DESIGN COLOR
12–18 in.	yellow	Jun–Jul			average	warm or cool
24 in.	peach	Jun			average	warm
12 in.	blue	Jun–Jul			average	cool
3 ft.			green/yellow	spring/summer/ autumn	bold	warm
2 ft.	pink	Jul–Sep			average	cool
2–3 ft.	blue	Jul–Sep	gray-green	spring/summer/ autumn	bold	cool
2–3 ft.	blue	Jul–Sep	gray-green	spring/summer/ autumn	bold	cool
2–3 ft.	blue	Jul–Sep	gray-green	spring/summer/ autumn	bold	cool
12 in.	yellow	Apr–May			fine	warm
12 in.	red	Apr–May	red	autumn	fine	warm
24 in.	orange	Apr–May	red	autumn	fine	warm
	yellow	Feb–Mar			fine	warm
	yellow	May–Jun			average	warm
24–36 in.	blue	Jul–Aug	blue	spring/summer/ autumn	bold	cool
24–36 in.	blue	Jul–Aug	blue	spring/summer/ autumn	bold	cool

	TYPE	ZONE	FORM	HEIGHT
Eryngium variifolium	perennial	5–9	vertical	18 in.
Eryngium yuccifolium Outstanding vertical effect from the tall, narrow, long-flowering stems. Great coarse texture also—one of my favorite plants for dry areas. Plate 4.	perennial	4–8	vertical	4 ft.
Erythronium 'Pagoda' Unusual early spring accent.	hardy bulb	3–8	mound	6–12 in.
Eschscholzia californica I love to seed this along the edges of paths and beds, and in between small shrubs, to provide intense flowers all season long. I can't get enough of them. Plate 13; Combination 8.	annual		mound	10–12 in.
Eschscholzia californica 'Purple Gleam' Nice seeded in among sturdier plants as filler. Combination 13.	annual		mound	10–12 in.
Eucomis comosa 'Sparkling Burgundy' Wonderful purple foliage, especially nice when emerging from surrounding yellow-foliaged plants. I haven't had any flowering on plants grown in the garden or containers in zone 5.	annual	(7)8–10	vertical	18 in.
Eupatorium purpureum ssp. maculatum 'Gateway' Provides great height and weight, serving as a dominant element in a large border. Plates 2, 32; Combination 7.	perennial	2–9	vertical	5–6 ft.
Euphorbia 'Golden Towers' Interesting stem and leaf color. Enjoy the plant early in the season—it gets a bit gangly by mid-summer.	perennial	5–8	mound	4 ft.
Euphorbia amygdaloides 'Purpurea' Outstanding foliage color, form, and textural effect. Plate 155.	perennial	5–9	mound	18 in.
Euphorbia cotinifolia To-die-for foliage color and shape. Outstanding in borders or containers as an accent. Forms a standardlike appearance with age. Should be used more. Plate 5; Combination 12.	tropical	9–11	mound	3–5 ft.
Euphorbia cyparissias 'Fen's Ruby' Vigorous spreader—can be invasive. Good container plant. Plate 41.	perennial	4–9	mound	12–16 in.
Euphorbia dulcis 'Chameleon' Fantastic foliage color that changes throughout the season.	perennial	4–9	mound	15–18 in.
Euphorbia griffithii 'Fireglow' Stunning for orange stem and flower effect in the hot-color spring garden. Plate 28.	perennial	5–8	mound	24–36 in.
Euphorbia ×martinii Interesting foliar color, form, and texture. Keep dry.	perennial	6–8	mound	18 in.
Euphorbia polychroma Plate 181.	perennial	4–8	mound	12–18 in.

WIDTH	FLOWER COLOR	FLOWERING MONTH	FOLIAGE COLOR	FOLIAGE INTEREST	TEXTURE	DESIGN COLOR
10 in.	blue	Jul–Aug	green/white	spring/summer/autumn	bold	cool
15–18 in.	green	Jul–Sep	gray-green	spring/summer/autumn	bold	warm or cool
6 in.	yellow	Apr–May			average	warm
8–10 in.	orange	Jun–Sep	blue	spring/summer/autumn	fine	warm
8–10 in.	purple	Jun–Sep	blue	spring/summer/autumn	fine	cool
18 in.	purple	Aug–Sep	purple	spring/summer/autumn	average	cool
3–4 ft.	pink	Jul–Sep			bold	cool
3 ft.	yellow	May–Jun			average	warm
18 in.	yellow	May–Jun	purple	autumn	average	warm
3 ft.			red	spring/summer/autumn	average	warm or cool
36 in.	yellow	Jun–Jul	red	spring	fine	warm
15–18 in.	yellow	May–Jun	purple	spring/summer/autumn	average	warm
24–36 in.	orange	May–Jun			average	warm
18 in.	yellow	Apr–May	blue	spring/summer/autumn	average	warm or cool
18 in.	yellow	Apr–May			fine	warm

	TYPE	ZONE	FORM	HEIGHT
Fagus sylvatica 'Purpurea Pendula' Purple foliage and weeping form make this an excellent specimen plant in designs. Many other plants play well off these features. Combination 9.	tree	4–7	weeping	10 ft.
Fagus sylvatica 'Tricolor' Good tree for perimeter of border due to outstanding foliage color in the spring—glows. Plate 1.	tree	4–7	vertical	30 ft.
Festuca glauca 'Elijah Blue' Still a favorite for blue foliage and compact habit.	perennial	4–8	mound	6–10 in.
Festuca glauca 'Golden Toupee' Interesting but has been a weak grower in my experience. Must have excellent drainage.	perennial	6–8	mound	8 in.
Foeniculum vulgare 'Purpureum' Love to use in designs for fine texture and depth provided by purple foliage.	perennial	4–9	vertical	3–4 ft.
Fothergilla gardenii Fantastic fragrant early spring flowers, wonderful autumn color. Excellent height and width for almost any garden.	shrub	5–8	mound	2–3 ft.
Fritillaria persica Outstanding—should be used more. Treated as a short-lived bulb in my zone 5 garden, often requires replanting, 5 per sq. ft. Plate 131; Combination 2.	hardy bulb	6–8	vertical	2–4 ft.
Fuchsia 'Gartenmeister Bonstedt'	annual	8–10	mound	24 in.
Galega ×hartlandii 'Lady Wilson' Unusual mounding plant with interesting foliage texture.	perennial	5–10	mound	3–5 ft.
Galium odoratum Invasive groundcover but tolerant of dry shade. Plate 36.	perennial	4–8	horizontal	6–8 in.
Genista tinctoria 'Royal Gold' Nice rounded form. Tolerant of poor, dry soil. May suffer some tip dieback in severe winters.	shrub	4–7	mound	2–3 ft.
Gentiana septemfida var. lagodechiana Deep blue flowers, useful sprawling at feet of other plants.	perennial	6–8	horizontal	6–8 in.
Gentiana triflora 'Royal Blue' Striking flowers. Lax habit; best placed between other plants for support.	perennial	5–8	vertical	15–18 in.
Geranium 'Ann Folkard' If I were a geranium, I'd want to be this dazzling schmoozer with its stunning chartreuse leaves and contrasting magenta black-eyed flowers.	perennial	5–8	mound	24 in.
Geranium 'Brookside' Nice flower color but habit is a bit too open for my liking.	perennial	4–8	mound	20 in.
Geranium 'Johnson's Blue' Good blue flowers but doggy habit. Many newer improved selections now available. Plate 29.	perennial	4–8	mound	18 in.

WIDTH	FLOWER COLOR	FLOWERING MONTH	FOLIAGE COLOR	FOLIAGE INTEREST	TEXTURE	DESIGN COLOR
10 ft.			purple	spring/summer/ autumn	average	warm or cool
20 ft.			purple	spring/summer/ autumn	average	cool
6–10 in.	tan	Jun	blue	year-round	fine	cool
8 in.			yellow	spring/summer/ autumn	fine	warm
1½–2 ft.	yellow	Jul–Aug	purple	spring/summer/ autumn	fine	warm
2–3 ft.	white	Apr–May	red	autumn	average	warm or cool
	purple	Apr			bold	cool
24 in.	red	Jun–Sep	red	spring/summer/ autumn	average	warm
3 ft.	blue	Jun–Sep			average	cool
	white	May			fine	warm or cool
2–3 ft.	yellow	Jun–Jul			fine	warm
12 in.	blue	Aug–Sep			average	cool
12 in.	blue	Aug–Sep			average	cool
24 in.	magenta	Jun–Sep	yellow	spring/summer/ autumn	average	warm or cool
24 in.	blue	Jun–Sep			average	cool
18 in.	blue	Jun–Jul			average	cool

	TYPE	ZONE	FORM	HEIGHT
Geranium 'Phillippe Vapelle' Flowers harmonize nicely with foliage. Good compact habit.	perennial	5–8	mound	12 in.
Geranium 'Salome' Interesting foliar and flower effect.	perennial	5–8	mound	8 in.
Geranium himalayense 'Plenum' Double flowers add weight to plant's appearance.	perennial	5–8	mound	10 in.
Geranium macrorrhizum 'Ingwersen's Variety' Excellent textural groundcover for dry, shady gardens.	perennial	3–8	mound	12–15 in.
Geranium ×magnificum Plate 38.	perennial	4–8	mound	18 in.
Geranium ×oxonianum 'Claridge Druce' Long-flowering plant that needs heavy pruning to keep a decent habit. Plate 123.	perennial	4–8	mound	18–24 in.
Geranium phaeum 'Lily Lovell' Have noticed it to be a bit temperamental about establishing.	perennial	5–8	mound	24 in.
Geranium phaeum 'Samobor' Very nice and, with its purple-blotched leaves, one of the best geraniums for foliage color effect.	perennial	5–8	mound	15–18 in.
Geranium platypetalum Good flower color, mounding habit, and minimal pruning requirements make this a useful plant in the border. Combination 20.	perennial	3–8	mound	18–24 in.
Geranium pratense 'Mrs. Kendall Clark'	perennial	4–8	mound	24 in.
Geranium pratense 'Victor Reiter Jr.' Charming for foliage color and texture.	perennial	5–8	mound	24 in.
Geranium psilostemon One of my favorite geraniums for its bold, striking flower color and larger than normal (for a geranium) size.	perennial	5–8	mound	24–36 in.
Geranium renardii Overall soft appearance due to soft foliage surface. Plate 127.	perennial	6–8	mound	12 in.
Geranium sanguineum 'New Hampshire' Reliable and utilitarian in a lower-maintenance border.	perennial	3–8	mound	12–15 in.
Geranium wlassovianum Outstanding in the shade garden for long bloom period and striking autumn foliage. Underutilized.	perennial	5–8	mound	24 in.
Gillenia stipulata I love this native for the shade for its interesting trifoliate leaves, airy nature, and flowers. Avoid afternoon sun. Combination 23.	perennial	4–8	vertical	24–36 in.
Ginkgo biloba 'Autumn Gold' Not normally a good addition to mixed gardens but remains dwarf and striking when grown in a container. Plate 70.	tree	5–9	vertical	50 ft.

WIDTH	FLOWER COLOR	FLOWERING MONTH	FOLIAGE COLOR	FOLIAGE INTEREST	TEXTURE	DESIGN COLOR
12 in.	purple	Jun–Jul	gray-green	spring/summer/autumn	average	cool
12 in.	blue	Jun–Sep	yellow	spring/summer/autumn	average	cool
24 in.	purple	Jun–Aug			average	cool
18 in.	pink	May–Jun			average	cool
24 in.	purple	Jun–Jul			average	cool
24 in.	pink	Jun–Sep			average	cool
18 in.	purple	May–Jun			average	cool
12 in.	purple	May–Jun	purple	spring/summer/autumn	average	cool
18–24 in.	purple	Jun			average	cool
24 in.	blue	May–Jun			average	cool
24 in.	blue	May–Jun	purple	spring	average	cool
3–4 ft.	magenta	Jun–Sep	red	autumn	average	warm or cool
12 in.	purple	Jun			average	cool
24 in.	magenta	May–Sep	red	autumn	average	warm or cool
24 in.	purple	Jul–Sep	red	autumn	average	cool
18 in.	white	May–Jun			fine	warm or cool
30 ft.			yellow	autumn	bold	warm

	TYPE	ZONE	FORM	HEIGHT
Gladiolus 'Atom' Charming small flowers with delicate silvery white edge—not for the color purist but one can definitely find a home for these, 5 per sq. ft.	tender bulb	7–9	vertical	24 in.
Gladiolus 'Violetta' Striking deep purple color with a velvet texture to the flowers. Great interplanted as a vertical form—I can't have enough of them, 5 per sq. ft. Plates 21, 97.	tender bulb	7–9	vertical	3 ft.
Gladiolus communis ssp. byzantinus Spreads freely from cormlets. Listed as zone 7 in some sources but has overwintered in my zone 5 garden for many years. Combination 18.	perennial	(5)6–10	vertical	24–36 in.
Gladiolus ×gandavensis Wonderful perennial form that can spread to a large clump; divide in spring if needed.	perennial	(5)6–9	vertical	24 in.
Gladiolus ×gandavensis 'Boone' Spectacular flowers that attract great attention. Plates 187–188.	perennial	(5)6–9	vertical	3–4 ft.
Glaucidium palmatum Spectacular plant but temperamental in my experience in Ohio gardens. Prefers cool, moist, high organic conditions.	perennial	6–9	mound	18 in.
Gomphrena haageana 'Lavender Lady' Great addition to the cutting garden for drying and craft purposes.	annual		mound	15–18 in.
Hakonechloa macra 'Aureola' Beautiful foliar color, texture, and habit when happy but not overly vigorous in most sites. Plates 114, 156.	perennial	5–9	mound	12–15 in.
Hedychium 'Daniel Weeks' Unbelievably fragrant flowers and foliage a bit more finely textured than some of the other tropicals make this a nice addition around entertaining areas, in beds or containers. Plate 20.	tropical	7–10	vertical	4–5 ft.
Hedychium coccineum Stunning in flower—will cause visitors to stop and drool. Plates 19, 186.	tropical	8–10	vertical	6–8 ft.
Helenium 'Kugelsonne' Great hot color for the autumn garden.	perennial	3–8	mound	3–5 ft.
Helenium 'Moerheim Beauty' Great addition to the autumn garden. Plate 192.	perennial	3–8	mound	3–5 ft.
Helianthemum (double yellow) Sweet, spring-flowering plant, requires well-draining soil.	perennial	5–7	mound	6–12 in.
Helianthemum 'Fire Dragon' Nice hot color for the spring garden. Requires well-draining soil. Plate 149.	perennial	5–7	mound	6–12 in.
Helianthus 'Lemon Queen' Stunning, large, long-flowering yellow that is a magnet for attention—much asked about.	perennial	3–9	mound	5–6 ft.

WIDTH	FLOWER COLOR	FLOWERING MONTH	FOLIAGE COLOR	FOLIAGE INTEREST	TEXTURE	DESIGN COLOR
	red	Jul–Aug			fine	warm
	purple	Jul–Aug			fine	cool
4–6 in.	magenta	Jun			fine	cool
18 in.	yellow	Jul			fine	warm
18 in.	peach	Jul			fine	warm
18 in.	purple	May			average	cool
24 in.	purple	Jun–Oct			average	cool
24 in.			green/yellow	spring/summer/autumn	fine	warm
2–3 ft.	yellow	Aug–Sep			bold	warm
3 ft.	orange	Jul–Sep			bold	warm
3 ft.	yellow	Jul–Oct			average	warm
3 ft.	red	Jul–Oct			average	warm
12–18 in.	yellow	May–Jun	gray-green	year-round	average	warm
12–18 in.	orange	May–Jun	gray-green	year-round	average	warm
2–3 ft.	yellow	Jun–Sep			average	warm

	TYPE	ZONE	FORM	HEIGHT
Helianthus 'Mellow Yellow'	perennial	3–9	mound	4–6 ft.
Helianthus salicifolius Fine texture, striking flowers, and size make this a must-have for autumn color. Plates 76, 138.	perennial	3–9	mound	5–6 ft.
Helichrysum petiolare 'Limelight' Foliage color and soft texture make an excellent accent. Use as groundcover, edger, or in containers. Foliage declines in late-summer heat and humidity. Plates 69, 148–150.	annual	10–11	horizontal	10–12 in.
Helictotrichon sempervirens 'Saphirsprudel' **(sapphire fountain)** Great blue-foliaged, mid-sized grass for accent or blending—very useful. Plates 95, 100.	perennial	4–8	mound	24 in.
Heliopsis helianthoides var. scabra **'Sommersonne' (summer sun)** Reliable long-flowering perennial that may be slow to establish. Color is magnetic. Plate 75; Combination 7.	perennial	3–9	mound	3–6 ft.
Helleborus Royal Heritage™ Royal Heritage™ hybrids are available in rose, green, white, and smoky purple; I usually select the smoky purple for my design work.	perennial	4–9	mound	16–18 in.
Helleborus foetidus Stunning for fantastic green flowerheads that set in autumn and open in early spring. Wonderful foliage texture. Combinations 2–3.	perennial	(5)6–9	mound	15–18 in.
Helleborus orientalis Flower colors of the straight species are pale green, rose, or white. Plate 121.	perennial	4–9	mound	16–18 in.
Helleborus orientalis (single black) A special selection chosen for its plum-black flowers.	perennial	4–9	mound	16–18 in.
Hemerocallis 'Alluring Peach' Pale peach color (good for use with other unsaturated colors) and deep purple foliage. One of my top five daylilies. Plates 4, 187.	perennial	3–9	mound	24–30 in.
Hemerocallis 'Carefree Peach'	perennial	3–9	mound	24 in.
Hemerocallis 'Happy Returns' Reliable and true yellow—another of my top five daylilies.	perennial	3–9	mound	18–20 in.
Hemerocallis 'Peach Fairy' Sweet, small peach flowers, smaller habit, and fine-textured foliage make this a very useful daylily.	perennial	3–9	mound	18–20 in.
Hemerocallis 'Red Razzamatazz' Hot and jazzy.	perennial	3–9	mound	24–30 in.
Hemerocallis 'Scarlet Romance'	perennial	3–9	mound	18–20 in.
Hemerocallis 'Siloam Royal Prince'	perennial	3–9	mound	18–20 in.

WIDTH	FLOWER COLOR	FLOWERING MONTH	FOLIAGE COLOR	FOLIAGE INTEREST	TEXTURE	DESIGN COLOR
2–3 ft.	yellow	Jun–Sep			average	warm
3 ft.	yellow	Sep			fine	warm
24–36 in.			yellow	spring/summer/autumn	average	warm
24 in.	tan	Jun	blue	year-round	fine	cool
3–4 ft.	yellow	Jun–Aug			average	warm
18 in.	purple	Mar–Apr			average	cool
18 in.	green	Mar–Apr			bold	warm or cool
15 in.	pink	Mar–Apr			average	cool
15 in.	black	Mar–Apr	purple	spring	average	warm or cool
24 in.	peach	Jul–Aug			fine	warm or cool
24 in.	peach	Jun–Jul			fine	warm
18 in.	yellow	Jul–Aug			fine	warm
20 in.	peach	Jun–Jul			fine	warm
24 in.	red	Jul–Aug			fine	warm
18 in.	red	Jul			fine	warm
18 in.	purple	Jul			fine	cool

	TYPE	ZONE	FORM	HEIGHT
Hemerocallis 'Staghorn Sumac' Nice heavy-substanced flower for the hot-color theme.	perennial	3–9	mound	24 in.
Hemerocallis 'Sundried Tomatoes' Nice red for the hot garden.	perennial	3–9	mound	30–36 in.
Hemerocallis 'Toy Trumpets' Delicate flowers on tall stems add great interest. Another of my top five daylilies.	perennial	3–9	mound	36 in.
Hemerocallis 'Welcome Mat' Large flowers with thick texture make this a winner. Another of my top five daylilies.	perennial	3–9	mound	24 in.
Hemerocallis 'Yellow Lollipop' Cute, small reblooming form.	perennial	3–9	mound	12 in.
Hesperis matronalis Beautiful for flowers, fragrance, and form in the spring garden. Avoid designing into natural areas where plants may become invasive. Plates 1, 39.	perennial	3–8	vertical	24–36 in.
Heuchera 'Chocolate Ruffles' Nice foliage color and texture.	perennial	4–9	mound	15–18 in.
Heuchera 'Plum Pudding' Beautiful foliage and habit. My second-favorite purple-leaved form. Plate 98.	perennial	4–9	mound	15–18 in.
Heuchera 'Raspberry Regal' Tall vertical red flowers are nice coming up through other plants.	perennial	3–8	mound	24 in.
Heuchera 'Velvet Night' Striking foliage color—my favorite purple-leaved heuchera. Plate 94.	perennial	4–9	mound	15–18 in.
Heuchera micrantha var. diversifolia 'Palace Purple' Superior purple-leaved forms are now available. Plates 126, 129.	perennial	4–9	mound	15–18 in.
×Heucherella 'Silver Streak' One of many fabulous foliage plants, this one is often reblooming.	perennial	4–7	mound	15 in.
Hibiscus acetosella 'Red Shield' Awesome foliage color and texture. Should be used in more designs. Plate 186; Combination 25.	tropical	10–11	mound	5 ft.
Hibiscus moscheutos 'Lord Baltimore' Big, bold, and beautiful is 'Lord Baltimore'—great for dominance. Plate 196.	perennial	4–9	mound	4–8 ft.
Hosta 'Big Daddy' Fabulous once mature.	perennial	3–8	mound	24 in.
Hosta 'Blue Cadet' Good small blue for edging or underplanting in the shade garden. Combination 14.	perennial	3–8	mound	15 in.

WIDTH	FLOWER COLOR	FLOWERING MONTH	FOLIAGE COLOR	FOLIAGE INTEREST	TEXTURE	DESIGN COLOR
24 in.	orange	Jul–Aug			fine	warm
24 in.	red	Jul–Aug			fine	warm
18 in.	yellow	Jul			fine	warm
24 in.	peach	Jul			fine	warm
12 in.	yellow	Jun–Aug			fine	warm
36 in.	purple	May–Jun			average	cool
12–18 in.	white	Jun–Jul	purple	year-round	average	warm or cool
12–18 in.	white	Jun–Jul	purple	year-round	average	warm or cool
12 in.	red	May			average	warm
12–18 in.	white	Jun–Jul	purple	year-round	average	warm or cool
12–18 in.	white	Jun–Jul	purple	year-round	average	warm or cool
12 in.	white	May–Jun	average	cool		
3 ft.			purple	spring/summer/autumn	bold	warm or cool
5 ft.	red	Jul–Oct			bold	warm
36 in.	white	Jun–Jul	blue	spring/summer/autumn	bold	cool
24–36 in.	purple	Jun–Jul	blue	spring/summer/autumn	bold	cool

	TYPE	ZONE	FORM	HEIGHT
Hosta 'Fragrant Blue' Nice blue foliage with an unusual added touch of fragrant flowers. Plate 127.	perennial	3–8	mound	20 in.
Hosta 'Halcyon' Good blue color, dense habit, and nice showy flowers. Great in the landscape.	perennial	3–8	mound	18 in.
Hosta 'Krossa Regal' Still one of my favorite for refined vase shape, foliage color, and flower height. Use at the back of the shade border. Plate 119.	perennial	3–8	vase	3–3½ ft.
Hosta 'Lemon Lime' Great yellow edger or groundcover that is rapid growing and dense, with a mass of purple flowers. May rebloom with deadheading.	perennial	3–8	mound	12 in.
Hosta 'Love Pat' Heavy-textured, bold, blue-gray foliage adds weight to fine-textured combinations.	perennial	3–8	mound	18 in.
Hosta 'Midas Touch' Bright gold color and intense corrugation gives this a special "touch" in shade designs.	perennial	3–8	mound	24 in.
Hosta 'Night Before Christmas' Best white-centered hosta to lighten shady spots. Nice tall flowers. Plate 125.	perennial	3–8	mound	24 in.
Hosta 'Patriot' Wide, clean, white margin is eye-catching. Plate 119.	perennial	3–8	mound	12–18 in.
Hosta 'Paul's Glory' Great gold center that may turn creamy white by late summer if it receives a few hours of direct sun each day.	perennial	3–8	mound	24 in.
Hosta 'Sum and Substance' Still my favorite big yellow to add scale and dominance to large shade gardens. Plate 6.	perennial	3–8	mound	30 in.
Hosta 'Sun Power' Bright gold creates excellent focal point. Plates 198–199.	perennial	3–8	mound	24 in.
Hosta plantaginea 'Aphrodite' Fragrant double flowers and apple-green leaves. Much desired in the garden.	perennial	3–8	mound	24 in.
Humulus lupulus 'Bianca' Outstanding chartreuse-yellow foliage from a vine. Fades to lime-green in summer. Plates 1–2; Combination 6.	perennial	3–8	climbing	10–15 ft.
Hydrangea anomala ssp. petiolaris Spectacular four-season clinging vine. Slow to establish but after a couple years takes hold and grows quickly. Best positioned with northern or eastern exposure.	woody vine	4–7(8)	climbing	30 ft.

WIDTH	FLOWER COLOR	FLOWERING MONTH	FOLIAGE COLOR	FOLIAGE INTEREST	TEXTURE	DESIGN COLOR
36–48 in.	purple	Aug	blue	spring/summer/autumn	bold	cool
24 in.	purple	Jul–Aug	blue	spring/summer/autumn	bold	cool
3 ft.	purple	Jul–Aug	blue	spring/summer/autumn	bold	cool
24 in.	purple	Jul	yellow	spring/summer/autumn	bold	warm
24–36 in.	white	Jul–Aug	blue	spring/summer/autumn	bold	cool
24 in.	white	Jun–Jul	yellow	spring/summer/autumn	bold	warm
2½ ft.	purple	Jul–Aug	green/white	spring/summer/autumn	bold	cool
24–30 in.	purple	Jul–Aug	green/white	spring/summer/autumn	bold	cool
36 in.	purple	Jul–Aug	green/yellow	spring/summer/autumn	bold	warm or cool
48–60 in.	purple	Jul–Aug	yellow	spring/summer/autumn	bold	warm or cool
24 in.	purple	Jul	yellow	spring/summer/autumn	bold	warm
24–36 in.	white	Aug			bold	warm or cool
			yellow	spring/summer/autumn	bold	warm
10–15 ft.	white	Jun–Jul			bold	warm or cool

	TYPE	ZONE	FORM	HEIGHT
Hydrangea quercifolia Bold habit and leaf color make this an outstanding addition to mixed gardens.	shrub	5–9	mound	4–6 ft.
Hydrangea quercifolia 'Snowflake' Outstanding shrub for the flowers that appear double as well as the bold textured leaves that turn beautiful shades of red and purple in the autumn. Good background shrub for the part-shade garden. Combination 15.	shrub	5–9	mound	6–8 ft.
Hymenocallis 'Sulphur Queen' Fantastic flowers with wonderful citrus fragrance add an unusual touch in the garden. Foliage is interesting long after the flowers fade. Choice, 3 per sq. ft. Plates 107, 110, 184.	tender bulb	(7)8–10	vertical	18–24 in.
Hypericum androsaemum 'Albury Purple' Unusual multi-season shrub for its outstanding foliage, fruit, and flowers. Great in warm combinations. Plates 110, 112.	shrub	(5)6–8	mound	1½–2 ft.
Hyssopus officinalis Good landscape herb.	perennial	4–9	mound	24 in.
Hystrix patula Great mid-sized grass for dry shade or moist, fertile sites. Combination 23.	perennial	4–8	vertical	36 in.
Ilex 'Apollo' Male form, pollinates 'Sparkleberry', 'Bonfire', 'Harvest Red'. Normally planted somewhere in the background, where it won't take space from more ornamental plants.	shrub	4–9	mound	6–9 ft.
Ilex glabra Cultivars such as 'Chamzin' (Nordic®) (3–4 ft. high and wide) are normally selected for compact growth. Creates a good evergreen mounded element or hedge in sun or shade, also a good "relief" plant among other more dominant plants.	shrub	(4)5–9(10)	mound	6–8 ft.
Ilex ×meserveae 'Mesdob' (China boy) Male form, pollinates 'Mesog'. Very hardy and vigorous grower.	shrub	5–7	mound	4–6 ft.
Ilex ×meserveae 'Mesog' (China girl) Hardy shrub for outstanding multi-season interest. Makes a good low screen.	shrub	5–7	mound	4–6 ft.
Ilex verticillata 'Afterglow' Great in warm combinations. Use 'Jim Dandy' as pollinator.	shrub	4–9	mound	3–6 ft.
Ilex verticillata 'Christmas Cheer' Excellent addition to warm border. Use 'Jim Dandy' as pollinator.	shrub	3–9	mound	6 ft.
Ilex verticillata 'Jim Dandy' Male form, pollinates 'Christmas Cheer' and 'Afterglow'.	shrub	4–9	mound	3–6 ft.
Ilex verticillata 'Winter Red' Can be used in masses, shrub borders, and wet areas. Use Ilex verticillata 'Southern Gentleman' to pollinate. Persistent red fruit.	shrub	3–9	mound	6–9 ft.

WIDTH	FLOWER COLOR	FLOWERING MONTH	FOLIAGE COLOR	FOLIAGE INTEREST	TEXTURE	DESIGN COLOR
4–6 ft.	white	Jun–Jul	red	autumn	bold	warm or cool
6–8 ft.	white	Jun–Jul	red	autumn	bold	warm or cool
	yellow	Jun			fine	warm
2 ft.	yellow	Jun–Jul	purple	spring	average	warm
18 in.	blue	Jul–Sep			average	cool
15–18 in.	tan	Jun–Aug			fine	warm or cool
6–9 ft.					average	warm or cool
6–8 ft.					fine	warm or cool
8 ft.					average	warm or cool
3–5 ft.					average	warm
3–6 ft.					average	warm
6 ft.					average	warm
3–6 ft.					average	warm or cool
6–9 ft.			bronze	autumn	average	warm

	TYPE	ZONE	FORM	HEIGHT
Impatiens omeiana Wonderful underused perennial impatiens for striking deep green leaves with cream stripe down center—a must for the shade garden. Plates 198–199.	perennial	6–9	mound	15 in.
Imperata cylindrica var. koenigii 'Red Baron' Excellent red for the hot garden, particularly alive with backlighting.	perennial	5–9	vertical	18 in.
Ipomoea batatas 'Ace of Spades' I prefer this heart-shaped leaf to the deeply lobed leaves of 'Blackie'. Plate 46.	annual	9–11	horizontal	15–18 in.
Ipomoea batatas 'Blackie' Excellent foliage color. Makes a useful wide-spreading groundcover. Leaves may develop holes from some sort of small beetle.	annual	9–11	horizontal	15–18 in.
Ipomoea batatas 'Margarita' Excellent foliage color. Makes a useful wide-spreading groundcover. Great in containers or trained up a small obelisk. Plates 65, 143.	annual	9–11	horizontal	15–18 in.
Ipomoea lobata (Mina lobata) This vine is so gorgeous—particularly nice in hot-color gardens. May reseed in a welcome way. Plate 66.	annual vine		climbing	8–15 ft.
Ipomoea tricolor 'Heavenly Blue' Beautiful in the garden enjoyed in the morning. Can reseed heavily. Interplants nicely with clematis or climbing roses. Plates 3, 18.	annual vine	10–11	climbing	10–12 ft.
Iris 'Blue Magic' Effective along the edge of borders, where it can be appreciated. Excellent for cutting, 5–10 per sq. ft.	hardy bulb	6–9	vertical	18–20 in.
Iris 'Flavescens' Striking yellow focal point in the spring garden. Plates 1, 39.	perennial	3–10	vertical	30 in.
Iris 'Perfume Counter' Very useful in the mixed border for its reblooming nature, which causes a surprise in autumn. Foliage seems to hold up fairly well.	perennial	3–10	vertical	24 in.
Iris 'Sugar Blues' A good blue, reblooms in autumn.	perennial	3–10	vertical	36 in.
Iris foetidissima Spectacular orange seeds but difficult to establish.	perennial	6–9	vertical	18 in.
Iris pallida 'Variegata' Wonderful variegated foliage—one of my favorite iris, even if it is short-lived and requires regular replanting. Plate 162.	perennial	4–9	vertical	24–30 in.
Iris pseudacorus 'Variegata' Useful in small water gardens. Plate 71.	perennial	5–8	vertical	36 in.

WIDTH	FLOWER COLOR	FLOWERING MONTH	FOLIAGE COLOR	FOLIAGE INTEREST	TEXTURE	DESIGN COLOR
15 in.	yellow	Sep			average	warm
12 in.			red	spring/summer/autumn	fine	warm
3–4 ft.			purple	spring/summer/autumn	bold	warm or cool
3–4 ft.			purple	spring/summer/autumn	bold	warm or cool
3–4 ft.			yellow	spring/summer/autumn	bold	warm
	red	Jul–Oct			fine	warm
	blue	Jun–Sep			average	cool
	blue	May			fine	cool
36 in.	yellow	May–Jun			fine	warm
24 in.	purple	Jun	gray-green	spring/summer/autumn	fine	cool
24 in.	blue	Jun			fine	cool
18 in.	blue	May–Jun			fine	warm or cool
24 in.	blue	May–Jun	green/yellow	spring/summer/autumn	fine	cool
18 in.	yellow	May–Jun	green/yellow	spring/summer/autumn	fine	warm

	TYPE	ZONE	FORM	HEIGHT
Iris reticulata 'Harmony'	hardy bulb	3–9	vertical	4–8 in.
I love netted iris for their very early (often in February) flowers and fragrance: they are a sign that spring is not far off. Their foliage hides easily among other plants; great planted under spring-flowering witchhazels, which are among the few other plants blooming at that time, 15 per sq. ft.				
Iris sanguinea 'Snow Queen'	perennial	3–8	vertical	30 in.
Good white followed by attractive seed pods and autumn color—year-round interest. Combination 5.				
Iris sibirica 'Butter and Sugar'	perennial	3–9	vertical	30 in.
Beautiful white and yellow combination.				
Iris sibirica 'Caesar's Brother'	perennial	3–9	vertical	30–36 in.
A classic, and my favorite for its foliage, height, deep purple flower color, velvety texture, and outstanding seed pods. Plate 132.				
Iris sibirica 'Dianne's Daughter'	perennial	3–9	vertical	30 in.
Iris sibirica 'Orville Fay'	perennial	3–9	vertical	36 in.
Reliable selection.				
Iris sibirica 'Pirate Prince'	perennial	3–9	vertical	30 in.
Beautiful deep purple flowers.				
Iris sibirica 'Skywings'	perennial	3–9	vertical	30 in.
Iris sibirica 'Vi Luihn'	perennial	3–9	vertical	30–36 in.
Iris sibirica 'White Swirl'	perennial	3–9	vertical	30 in.
Excellent and famous white.				
Itea virginica	shrub	5–9	mound	3–6 ft.
Larger-growing than 'Henry's Garnet' and slightly less attractive in flower and fall color but still wonderful. Good for massing.				
Itea virginica 'Henry's Garnet'	shrub	5–9	mound	3–5 ft.
Very attractive and versatile multi-season shrub. Love the autumn color in the gardens: leaves hold late into November, when many other plants are defoliated; glows when backlit. Larger flowers than the species.				
Knautia macedonica	perennial	5–8	mound	24–36 in.
Fine texture and different flower color and shape make for an interesting filler in borders.				
Kniphofia 'Alcazar'	perennial	5–9	vertical	36 in.
Accent form and color. Plate 191.				
Kniphofia 'Little Maid'	perennial	5–9	vertical	18 in.
Sweet, small soft-colored form.				
Kniphofia 'Primrose Beauty'	perennial	5–9	vertical	36 in.
Reliable yellow-flowering form—a favorite. Plates 35, 157.				

WIDTH	FLOWER COLOR	FLOWERING MONTH	FOLIAGE COLOR	FOLIAGE INTEREST	TEXTURE	DESIGN COLOR
	blue	Feb–Mar			fine	cool
24 in.	white	May–Jun			fine	warm or cool
24 in.	yellow	May–Jun			fine	warm
24 in.	purple	May–Jun			fine	cool
24 in.	blue	May–Jun			fine	cool
24 in.	blue	May–Jun			fine	cool
24 in.	purple	May–Jun			fine	cool
24 in.	blue	May–Jun			fine	cool
24 in.	blue	May–Jun			fine	cool
24 in.	white	May–Jun			fine	warm or cool
3–5 ft.	white	Jun	red	autumn	average	warm or cool
3–5 ft.	white	Jun	red	autumn	average	warm or cool
18 in.	purple	Jun–Sep			fine	warm or cool
24 in.	orange	Jul–Sep			fine	warm
12 in.	yellow	Jul–Sep			fine	warm
24 in.	yellow	Jul–Aug			fine	warm

	TYPE	ZONE	FORM	HEIGHT
Kniphofia 'Prince Igor' This large-growing orange kniphofia demands attention—a spectacular focal point. Plate 102.	perennial	6–9	vertical	6 ft.
Kniphofia 'Royal Standard' The standard in red-hot pokers, nice but not the best.	perennial	5–9	vertical	36 in.
Kniphofia 'Shining Sceptre' Interesting peach-yellow form.	perennial	5–9	vertical	30 in.
Kniphofia caulescens Interesting aloe-like foliage. Tender in zone 5 although has overwintered in a raised container in my garden. Seems to require a few years to mature before flowering. Plate 69.	perennial	(5)6–9	vertical	4 ft.
Kniphofia citrina	perennial	6–9	vertical	24 in.
Kniphofia triangularis Plate 23.	perennial	4–9	vertical	24–36 in.
Lablab purpureus Fantastic climbing purple vine to interplant with other vines or climbing roses. Some confusion in trade over nomenclature (often sold as Dolichos lablab 'Purpurea'); in any case, I prefer and always use the purple-leaved form.	annual vine		climbing	15 ft.
Lactuca 'Merlot' Could be used in the red or purple garden for unusual combinations with a common plant. Plate 195.	annual		mound	10–12 in.
Lamium maculatum 'White Nancy' Adds light to shady areas under other plants in the mixed garden.	perennial	3–8	horizontal	6–8 in.
Lathyrus latifolius Old-fashioned and reliable.	perennial	5–9	climbing	6–8 ft.
Lathyrus odoratus Classic and fragrant.	annual vine		climbing	6–8 ft.
Lathyrus odoratus 'Henry Eckford' Orange flowers, unusual for the genus—very nice. Plate 61.	annual vine		climbing	6 ft.
Lathyrus odoratus 'King Size Navy Blue' Excellent flower color and fragrance, try using as a climber or trailer in containers or raised beds.	annual vine		climbing	6 ft.
Lavandula angustifolia 'Munstead' Fairly reliable compact form.	perennial	5–8	mound	18 in.
Lavandula ×intermedia 'Grosso' A longtime favorite for its 18-in.-long flower spikes, which stand nicely above the foliage and are great for cutting.	perennial	(5)6–9	mound	24 in.
Leonotis menthifolia Beautiful orange flowers with interesting whorled arrangement. Nice height for an annual in the orange garden.	annual	10–11	vertical	3 ft.

WIDTH	FLOWER COLOR	FLOWERING MONTH	FOLIAGE COLOR	FOLIAGE INTEREST	TEXTURE	DESIGN COLOR
3 ft.	orange	Jul–Aug			fine	warm
24 in.	yellow	Jul–Aug			fine	warm
24 in.	yellow	Jul–Aug			fine	warm
2 ft.	yellow	Jul–Aug	blue	spring/summer/autumn	fine	warm
18 in.	yellow	Jun–Sep			fine	warm
18 in.	orange	Jul–Aug			fine	warm
	purple	Jul–Aug	purple	spring/summer/autumn	average	cool
12–15 in.			red	spring/summer/autumn	average	warm or cool
18 in.	white	Apr–Jun	silver-gray	spring/summer/autumn	average	cool
	pink	Jul–Sep	blue	spring/summer/autumn	average	cool
	purple	Jul–Oct			fine	cool
	orange	Jul–Oct			fine	warm
	blue	Jul–Oct			fine	cool
24 in.	purple	Jun–Jul	gray-green	spring/summer/autumn	fine	cool
24 in.	purple	Jul–Sep	gray-green	spring/summer/autumn	fine	cool
2–3 ft.	orange	Jun–Sep			average	warm

	TYPE	ZONE	FORM	HEIGHT
Lespedeza cuneata Nice texture. Reportedly invasive; it arrived as a volunteer in my gardens with another plant and has stayed, in well-behaved shrublike habit, producing only one other seedling in six years. Plate 5.	shrub	5–8	mound	3 ft.
Liatris spicata 'Kobold' Good vertical element.	perennial	3–9	vertical	24–30 in.
Ligularia 'The Rocket' Good vertical accent in shady moist locations. Plate 72.	perennial	4–8	vertical	4 ft.
Ligularia dentata 'Dark Beauty' A tropical feel from a perennial. Provides often-needed bold texture in the shade. Plate 122.	perennial	4–8	mound	3–4 ft.
Ligularia dentata 'Desdemona' Wonderful bold tropical feel. Combination 14.	perennial	4–8	mound	3–4 ft.
Ligularia wilsoniana	perennial	5–8	mound	4–6 ft.
Lilium 'Apricot Brandy' Good flower color. Plate 29.	perennial	4–9	vertical	3–3½ ft.
Lilium 'Casa Blanca'	perennial	4–8	vertical	24–36 in.
Lilium 'Connecticut King' Good yellow.	perennial	4–9	vertical	24–36 in.
Lilium 'Conquistador' Great for the hot garden.	perennial	4–9	vertical	3–4 ft.
Lilium 'Eden's Dandy' Flowers appear pink, particularly when in association with other truer peach hues.	perennial	4–9	vertical	24–36 in.
Lilium 'Grand Cru'	perennial	4–9	vertical	24–36 in.
Lilium 'Montenegro'	perennial	4–9	vertical	3–4 ft.
Lilium 'Pretender' Floriferous.	perennial	4–9	vertical	36 in.
Lilium 'Royal Justice' Good yellow.	perennial	4–9	vertical	24–36 in.
Lilium 'Royal Perfume'	perennial	4–9	vertical	36 in.
Lilium 'Scarlet Emperor' Good focal point.	perennial	4–9	vertical	30 in.
Lilium 'Shirley'	perennial	4–9	vertical	4½ ft.
Lilium 'Sunset' Pretty, with a slightly different flower color.	perennial	4–9	vertical	36 in.
Lilium henryi A classic lily. Sometimes listed as reaching 6 ft. in height, but it has always been a bit shorter in my experience. Plate 99.	perennial	3–9	vertical	3–4 ft.

WIDTH	FLOWER COLOR	FLOWERING MONTH	FOLIAGE COLOR	FOLIAGE INTEREST	TEXTURE	DESIGN COLOR
3 ft.	white	Aug			fine	warm or cool
18 in.	purple	Jul–Aug			average	cool
3 ft.	yellow	Jul–Sep			bold	warm
4 ft.	yellow	Jul–Sep	purple	spring/summer/autumn	bold	warm
4 ft.	yellow	Jul–Sep			bold	warm
4 ft.	yellow	Jul–Aug			bold	warm
	peach	Jun			average	warm
	white	Jul			average	warm or cool
	yellow	Jun			average	warm
	red	Jun			average	warm
	peach	Jun			average	warm
	yellow	Jun			average	warm
	red	Jun			average	warm
	orange	Jun			average	warm
	yellow	Jun			average	warm
	orange	Jun			average	warm
	red	Jun			average	warm
	peach	Jun–Jul			average	warm
	orange	Jun			average	warm
	orange	Jun–Jul			average	warm

	TYPE	ZONE	FORM	HEIGHT
Lilium lancifolium var. splendens I can't say enough about this spectacular "old" lily from around 1804. It's a knockout, and foliage holds until frost. Only problem is that it is a virus source—grow separate from other lilies. Plates 90, 95, 105.	perennial	3–9	vertical	4–5 ft.
Lilium pumilum	perennial	3–9	vertical	24 in.
Limonium platyphyllum 'Violetta' I love the contrast of the fine-textured, airy violet flowers with the bold, leathery basal foliage. Creates a cloudlike filler.	perennial	3–9	mound	18 in.
Linaria 'Natalie' A delicate beauty, with fine texture and light purple flowers that continue all summer.	perennial	5–9	vertical	24 in.
Linaria purpurea Love to use this plant as a filler among more prominent species.	perennial	5–9	vertical	36 in.
Linum perenne 'Blau Saphir' (blue sapphire) Delicate habit that moves in the slightest breeze. Short-lived—may require replanting.	perennial	5–8	mound	18–24 in.
Lobelia 'Dark Crusader' Vertical and red–makes for an outstanding focal point. Can be grown in sun with adequate moisture.	perennial	4–8	vertical	24–36 in.
Lobelia 'Grape Knee High' Nice smaller-growing purple form. Can be grown in sun with adequate moisture.	perennial	4–9	vertical	24 in.
Lobelia 'Purple Towers' Wonderful large-growing form; may require staking. Can be grown in sun with adequate moisture.	perennial	2–8	vertical	4–5 ft.
Lobelia 'Queen Victoria' A reliable favorite in zone 5. Performs well in sun with adequate moisture.	perennial	4–9	vertical	4–5 ft.
Lobelia 'Royal Robe' Can be grown in sun with adequate moisture and where summers are cool. Plates 122, 124.	perennial	2–9	vertical	36 in.
Lobelia 'Ruby Slippers' Dorothy would want this lobelia in her garden and so should you. Fabulous ruby-red flowers frequently asked about. Reliable in sun with adequate moisture.	perennial	3–9	vertical	36 in.
Lobelia siphilitica Still one of my favorites—a vertical blue in the part-shade garden.	perennial	5–9	vertical	24–48 in.
Lonicera periclymenum 'Graham Thomas' Gorgeous flowers and fragrance. Tip dieback can occur in severe winters. Plate 106.	woody vine	4–8	climbing	20 ft.
Lonicera sempervirens 'Blanche Sandman' Unique bright color.	woody vine	(3)4–9	climbing	20 ft.

WIDTH	FLOWER COLOR	FLOWERING MONTH	FOLIAGE COLOR	FOLIAGE INTEREST	TEXTURE	DESIGN COLOR
	orange	Aug			average	warm
	orange	Jun–Jul			average	warm
18 in.	purple	Jul–Aug			fine	cool
15 in.	purple	Jun–Sep			fine	cool
15–18 in.	purple	Jun–Oct			fine	cool
12 in.	blue	May–Aug			fine	cool
12–15 in.	red	Jul–Sep	red	spring/summer/autumn	average	cool
12 in.	purple	Jul–Aug			average	cool
2 ft.	purple	Jul–Sep			average	cool
2 ft.	red	Jul–Sep	red	spring/summer/autumn	average	warm
1½ ft.	red	Jul–Aug	red	spring/summer/autumn	average	warm
1½ ft.	purple	Jul–Sep			average	cool
18–24 in.	blue	Jul–Sep			average	cool
10–15 ft.	yellow	Jun–Jul			average	warm or cool
10–15 ft.	orange	Jun–Jul			average	warm

	TYPE	ZONE	FORM	HEIGHT
Luzula nivea An underused, adaptable grasslike plant that I find useful and very attractive in shade gardens. Needs moist but well-drained soil. Plate 120.	perennial	4–9	mound	15–18 in.
Lychnis ×arkwrightii 'Vesuvius' Wonderful strong orange for the hot garden but a weak plant that is often short-lived.	perennial	5–8	mound	18 in.
Lychnis cognata Pretty but not reliable for any length of time. Benefits from staking; stems can be lax.	perennial	5–9	mound	15 in.
Lychnis coronaria Bright focal point, loved by children for its high-energy color and soft velvety leaves. Combination 21.	perennial	4–8	vertical	24–36 in.
Lysimachia congestiflora 'Variegata' Thick-textured variegated leaves. Makes a wonderful groundcover for the summer.	annual	(6)7–9	horizontal	4 in.
Lysimachia nummularia 'Aurea' One of my favorite yellow-foliaged plants for use as a dense groundcover. Plates 112, 156, 197.	perennial	3–8	horizontal	1–2 in.
Magnolia virginiana Attractive small specimen tree. Great fragrant flowers for use near entrances or entertaining areas. Tolerates wide range of conditions, including wet sites. Plate 125.	tree	5–9	vase	10–20 ft.
Malus 'Lanzam' (Lancelot®) Outstanding narrow upright form makes this a good crabapple for smaller areas. Multi-season interest.	tree	4–7	vertical	10 ft.
Mazus reptans Have used this as a moss substitute in between stepping-stones. Requires pruning to keep in bounds when it is happy. Withstands light foot traffic. Plates 130, 133.	perennial	5–8	horizontal	1–2 in.
Melampodium paludosum 'Million Gold' Reliable, long-flowering yellow. May get a touch of mildew in crowded conditions. Plate 181.	annual		mound	8–10 in.
Mertensia pulmonarioides (virginica) Wonderful wildflower used as lower layer in the mixed garden. Dormant in summer. Combination 4.	perennial	3–9	mound	18 in.
Microbiota decussata Interesting evergreen for texture and habit in light shade. Moist, well-drained soil preferred.	shrub	3–8	horizontal	12–15 in.
Miscanthus 'Purpurascens' One of the best grasses for red-purple autumn color. Plates 5, 73, 145, 147.	perennial	4–9	vertical	3–5 ft.
Miscanthus sinensis 'Gracillimus'	perennial	5–9	vertical	6–7 ft.
Miscanthus sinensis 'Malepartus'	perennial	5–9	vertical	5–7 ft.

WIDTH	FLOWER COLOR	FLOWERING MONTH	FOLIAGE COLOR	FOLIAGE INTEREST	TEXTURE	DESIGN COLOR
12 in.	tan	Jun–Jul			fine	warm or cool
12 in.	orange	Jun–Jul			average	warm
15 in.	peach	Jun–Jul			average	warm
18 in.	magenta	Jun–Jul	silver-gray	spring/summer/autumn	average	warm or cool
12 in.	yellow	May–Jul	green/yellow	spring/summer/autumn	average	warm
24 in.			yellow	year-round	average	warm
10–20 ft.	white	May–Jun	yellow	autumn	average	warm or cool
8 ft.	white	Apr–May	yellow	autumn	average	warm
24 in.	purple	May–Jun			fine	cool
12 in.	yellow	Jun–Oct			average	warm
10 in.	blue	Apr–May			fine	cool
72–96 in.			bronze	autumn	fine	warm or cool
3 ft.	tan	Jul–Aug	red	autumn	fine	warm
4 ft.	tan	Sep			fine	warm or cool
4 ft.	tan	Sep	yellow	autumn	fine	warm or cool

	TYPE	ZONE	FORM	HEIGHT
Miscanthus sinensis 'Morning Light' Delicate variegation, narrow upright habit, and beautiful flowers make for an outstanding versatile grass. Plate 124.	perennial	5–9	vertical	4–5 ft.
Miscanthus sinensis var. condensatus 'Cosmopolitan' My favorite variegated miscanthus: not floppy, not too big, not too fussy—just right. Plate 2; Combination 7.	perennial	(5)6–9	vertical	6–10 ft.
Molinia caerulea ssp. arundinacea 'Skyracer' My favorite grass. Very tall yet narrow, and open flowers make an excellent see-through plant for a variety of locations. Foliage is very low, only about 18 in. in height. Added bonus of outstanding yellow autumn color. Plate 4.	perennial	4–9	vertical	7–8 ft.
Monarda 'Jacob Cline' Good red for dominance. Mildew resistant.	perennial	4–9	mound	3–4 ft.
Monarda 'Violet Queen' Lovely purple flowers. Mildew resistant.	perennial	4–9	mound	30–36 in.
Musa basjoo Supposedly cold hardy to –10°F. May overwinter in zones 5–8 but dies to the ground and regrows; it should be cut back in these areas, leaving about 1 ft. of the stem, which should be wrapped in burlap, and roots should be heavily mulched. If it dies completely back without protection, it will not likely return. Plate 6.	tropical	(5–6)7–11	vertical	6–14 ft.
Musa zebrina "Top banana" in my book for massive leaves streaked red and green and bold character. Has reached the 13-ft. ceiling in my conservatory, with leaves over 4 ft. long.	tropical	10–11	vertical	6–8 ft.
Narcissus 'Delnashaugh' Really a beauty, 5 per sq. ft.	hardy bulb	3–8	vertical	16–18 in.
Narcissus 'Fragrant Rose' Very charming, 5 per sq. ft.	hardy bulb	3–8	vertical	16–18 in.
Narcissus 'Mary Gay Lirette' 5 per sq. ft.	hardy bulb	3–8	vertical	14–16 in.
Narcissus 'Mint Julep' 5 per sq. ft.	hardy bulb	3–8	vertical	16–18 in.
Narcissus 'Petrel' Sweet, small addition to front of border, 5 per sq. ft.	hardy bulb	3–8	vertical	10 in.
Narcissus 'Sir Winston Churchill' Charming size and unbelievable fragrance—a real winner, 5 per sq. ft. Combination 1.	hardy bulb	3–8	vertical	15–17 in.
Narcissus 'Stratosphere' 10 per sq. ft.	hardy bulb	4–9	vertical	20 in.
Narcissus 'Tahiti' Reliable and attractive, 5 per sq. ft.	hardy bulb	3–8	vertical	18 in.
Nepeta 'Six Hills Giant' Reliable and useful for gray-green foliage, mid height, and lavender flowers. Combination 20.	perennial	3–8	mound	36 in.

WIDTH	FLOWER COLOR	FLOWERING MONTH	FOLIAGE COLOR	FOLIAGE INTEREST	TEXTURE	DESIGN COLOR
3 ft.	tan	Sep	green/white	spring/summer/autumn	fine	warm or cool
4–5 ft.	tan	Sep	green/white	spring/summer/autumn	fine	warm or cool
3 ft.	tan	Aug–Oct	yellow	autumn	fine	warm or cool
3 ft.	red	Jun–Aug			average	warm
24–36 in.	purple	Jun–Aug			average	cool
4–6 ft.					bold	warm or cool
3 ft.			red	spring/summer/autumn	bold	warm
	peach	Apr–May			fine	warm
	white	Apr–May			fine	cool
	peach	Apr–May			fine	warm
	yellow	Apr–May			fine	warm
	white	Apr–May			fine	warm or cool
	white	Apr–May			fine	warm
	yellow	Apr–May			fine	warm
	yellow	Apr–May			fine	warm
3 ft.	purple	Jun–Jul	gray-green	spring/summer/autumn	average	cool

	TYPE	ZONE	FORM	HEIGHT
Nepeta ×faassenii	perennial	3–8	mound	18–24 in.
Nepeta grandiflora 'Bramdean' Larger-than-typical tubular flowers borne on tall plants. Should be selected for more designs.	perennial	3–8	mound	3–3½ ft.
Nepeta racemosa 'Walker's Low' Great low groundcover or edger for gray-green foliage. Plate 165.	perennial	3–8	mound	15–18 in.
Nepeta sibirica 'Souvenir d'André Chaudron' Striking vertical form and flowers. Combination 16.	perennial	3–8	vertical	24–36 in.
Nicotiana langsdorffii Love the green flowers and narrow vertical habit. Useful as a neutral in many color schemes.	annual		vertical	4–5 ft.
Nierembergia scoparia 'Mont Blanc' Reliable long bloomer that adds light at ground level. Needs light shade in areas with hot, dry summers.	annual	7–10	mound	6 in.
Nigella damascena Miss Jekyll Series Versatile and beautiful annual—can't get enough of it. Allow to seed, and it will perform as a perennial. Interplant and use as filler. Combination 18.	annual		mound	15 in.
Nymphaea 'Marliacea Chromatella' Nice small form for small water gardens. Plate 71.	perennial	4–11	horizontal	3 in.
Ocimum 'African Blue' Classy-looking foliage color and habit. Disbud to maintain fullness. Plate 3; Combination 13.	annual	9–10	mound	24 in.
Ocimum basilicum 'Red Rubin' Old form, difficult to find.	annual	9–10	mound	12–15 in.
Oenothera fremontii 'Lemon Silver' Flowers during the day. Narrow silvery leaves and light yellow flowers shimmer in the sun. Not invasive.	perennial	5–9	horizontal	6–8 in.
Oenothera fruticosa ssp. glauca 'Sonnenwende'	perennial	3–8	mound	24 in.
Origanum 'Kent Beauty' Interesting pink flower bracts. Needs well-drained soil.	perennial	5–8	horizontal	6 in.
Origanum laevigatum 'Herrenhausen' Foliage often has a purple tint to it that, in combination with the long-blooming pinkish purple flowerheads and great purple-bronze autumn color, makes it a real winner.	perennial	5–9	mound	24 in.
Origanum vulgare 'Aureum' Good as yellow lower layer. Plate 178.	perennial	5–9	mound	12 in.
Osmunda cinnamomea Reliable and attractive fern for dominance in the shade garden.	perennial	3–8	vertical	36 in.

WIDTH	FLOWER COLOR	FLOWERING MONTH	FOLIAGE COLOR	FOLIAGE INTEREST	TEXTURE	DESIGN COLOR
24 in.	blue	Jun–Jul	gray-green	spring/summer/autumn	average	cool
2–3 ft.	purple	Jun–Jul	gray-green	spring/summer/autumn	average	cool
15–18 in.	purple	Jun–Jul	gray-green	spring/summer/autumn	average	cool
24–36 in.	blue	Jun–Jul	gray-green	spring/summer/autumn	average	cool
1½ ft.	green	Jun–Oct			bold	warm or cool
10–12 in.	white	Jun–Oct			fine	warm or cool
12 in.	white	May–Jul			fine	warm or cool
48–60 in.	yellow	Jun–Sep			average	warm
24 in.			purple	spring/summer/autumn	average	cool
12–15 in.			red	spring/summer/autumn	average	warm or cool
15 in.	yellow	Jun–Aug	silver-gray	spring/summer/autumn	fine	warm
15 in.	yellow	Jun–Aug	red	autumn	average	warm
10 in.	pink	Jun–Jul	gray-green	spring/summer/autumn	average	cool
18 in.	purple	Jun–Aug	purple	autumn	average	cool
12 in.			yellow	spring/summer/autumn	average	warm
3 ft.					fine	warm or cool

	TYPE	ZONE	FORM	HEIGHT
Osmunda regalis Reliable fern tolerant of drought once established. Attractive yellow autumn color. Combination 3.	perennial	3–10	vertical	24–30 in.
Pachysandra procumbens This native is an excellent replacement for Pachysandra terminalis as a groundcover for its more attractive form and leaf texture. Plate 47.	perennial	6–9	mound	12 in.
Packera aurea (Senecio aureus) Pretty but fast spreading.	perennial	4–8	mound	6 in.
Paeonia 'America' Excellent for a touch of hot color in the spring. Doesn't require staking, even in partial shade.	perennial	3–8	mound	30 in.
Paeonia 'Burma Ruby' Outstanding bold red flowers. Freestanding plants hold foliage late into season. Plate 56.	perennial	3–8	mound	24–30 in.
Paeonia 'Coral Sunset' Looks like a waterlily flower. Choice color.	perennial	3–8	mound	30 in.
Paeonia 'Etched Salmon' Beautiful flower form and color.	perennial	3–8	mound	36 in.
Paeonia 'Monsieur Jules Elie' Classic for the heirloom garden. Combination 5.	perennial	3–8	mound	36 in.
Paeonia 'Prairie Moon'	perennial	3–8	mound	30 in.
Paeonia obovata Rare woodland species grown more for its gorgeous and unusual fruit than its flowers. Underused. Plate 16.	perennial	4–8	mound	18–24 in.
Panicum virgatum 'Dallas Blues' Fantastic for wide blue leaves and large flower panicles. Plates 32, 161; Combination 19.	perennial	5–9	vertical	6–8 ft.
Panicum virgatum 'Heavy Metal' Stiff, vertical blue element—very useful. Plates 160, 164.	perennial	4–9	vertical	4–5 ft.
Panicum virgatum 'Rehbraun' Older selection but still a great performer. Needs space for wide spread. Plate 5.	perennial	5–9	vertical	3–4 ft.
Papaver nudicaule 'Red Sails' Good hot-red flowers on short-lived plants. Requires replanting every couple years for best effect.	perennial	2–8	mound	24 in.
Papaver orientale 'Curlilocks' Deep orange, serrated flowers create a nice focal point. Interplant at the base of plants that will hide the dying summer foliage.	perennial	3–7	mound	24–36 in.
Papaver orientale 'Derwisch'	perennial	3–7	mound	24–36 in.
Papaver orientale 'Feuerriese' Stout growth and wonderful red-orange flowers. Should be used more. Combination 9.	perennial	3–7	mound	30 in.

WIDTH	FLOWER COLOR	FLOWERING MONTH	FOLIAGE COLOR	FOLIAGE INTEREST	TEXTURE	DESIGN COLOR
3 ft.			yellow	autumn	fine	warm or cool
	white	Apr–May			bold	warm or cool
24 in.	yellow	Apr–May			average	warm
30 in.	red	May–Jun			bold	warm
24–30 in.	red	May–Jun			bold	warm
30 in.	peach	May–Jun			bold	warm
36 in.	peach	May–Jun			bold	warm
36 in.	pink	May–Jun			bold	cool
30 in.	yellow	May–Jun			bold	warm
18–24 in.	pink	May–Jun			average	cool
3–4 ft.	tan	Aug–Oct	blue	spring/summer	fine	cool
3 ft.	tan	Aug–Oct	blue	spring/summer	fine	cool
4 ft.	tan	Aug–Oct	yellow	autumn	fine	warm or cool
12 in.	red	Jun			average	warm
24 in.	orange	May–Jun			bold	warm
24 in.	peach	May–Jun			bold	warm
24 in.	red	May–Jun			bold	warm

	TYPE	ZONE	FORM	HEIGHT
Papaver orientale 'Harvest Moon' Nice golden orange.	perennial	3–7	mound	36 in.
Papaver orientale 'Lighthouse' Stunning large salmon flowers—my favorite salmon poppy.	perennial	3–7	mound	30 in.
Papaver orientale 'Patty's Plum' A to-die-for plant that you can't get enough of. Choice for the purple garden. Plate 173.	perennial	3–7	mound	24–36 in.
Papaver orientale 'Prince of Orange' Another good orange, provide well-draining soil.	perennial	3–7	mound	24–36 in.
Papaver orientale 'Saffron' A good orange, but I'm not crazy about white trim. Not for the color purist.	perennial	3–7	mound	24 in.
Papaver orientale 'Turkenlouis' An in-your-face red-orange that is not for the timid colorist—I love it. Plate 148.	perennial	3–7	mound	24–36 in.
Papaver rhoeas One of my top five favorite annuals. Bold, brilliant red color and dainty texture and habit. Interplant as filler anywhere and everywhere. Plates 91, 99, 141; Combination 21.	annual		mound	12–18 in.
Papaver rhoeas Angels' Choir Pretty mix with various tints and shades of reds and whites. Not for the color purist. Combination 21.	annual		mound	12–18 in.
Papaver somniferum Spectacular flower and foliage colors as well as seed pods. May be subject to the "poppy police." Plate 24.	annual		vertical	3–4 ft.
Papaver somniferum 'Black Peony' Not a strong grower in my experience but gorgeous when it does perform. I reseed annually in hopes of a bumper crop one year, or at least a slight display.	annual		vertical	2–3 ft.
Papaver somniferum 'Burnt Orange' Yummy, unusual color contrast with blue stems.	annual		vertical	3–4 ft.
Papaver somniferum 'Lauren's Grape' Fabulous color for the cool garden.	annual		vertical	3–4 ft.
Papaver somniferum 'Pepperbox' Another great poppy.	annual		vertical	3–4 ft.
Passiflora incarnata A tropical-looking tendril-climber that dies back to the ground in winter. Protect crowns with mulch. Late to emerge in the spring. May be invasive.	perennial	5–8	climbing	6 ft.
Patrinia scabiosifolia Love this plant when it's happy—but it seems temperamental. I keep trying in designs and have had occasional successes.	perennial	4–9	mound	3–6 ft.
Pennisetum alopecuroides 'Hameln' Good utilitarian plant but the many other superior grasses now available have pushed it to the back of the design palette.	perennial	5–9	mound	24–30 in.

WIDTH	FLOWER COLOR	FLOWERING MONTH	FOLIAGE COLOR	FOLIAGE INTEREST	TEXTURE	DESIGN COLOR
24 in.	orange	May–Jun			bold	warm
24 in.	pink	May–Jun			bold	cool
24 in.	purple	May–Jun			bold	cool
24 in.	orange	May–Jun			bold	warm
24 in.	orange	May–Jun			bold	warm
24 in.	orange	May–Jun			bold	warm
3–5 in.	red	May–Jul			fine	warm
3–5 in.	pink	May–Jul			average	cool
1 ft.	purple	Jun	blue	spring/summer	bold	cool
1 ft.	black	Jun	blue	spring/summer	bold	warm or cool
1 ft.	orange	Jun	blue	spring/summer	bold	warm
1 ft.	purple	Jun	blue	spring/summer	bold	cool
1 ft.	red	Jun	blue	spring/summer	bold	warm or cool
	purple	Jun–Sep			average	cool
2 ft.	yellow	Aug–Sep			fine	warm
24 in.	tan	Jul–Oct			fine	warm or cool

	TYPE	ZONE	FORM	HEIGHT
Pennisetum setaceum 'Rubrum' Could be used in the red or purple garden. Excellent as a specimen or massed. Plates 78, 84.	annual	9–10	vertical	3 ft.
Penstemon digitalis 'Husker Red' Used in designs for outstanding foliage color, which intensifies in the autumn. I often remove the so-so white flowers before they open.	perennial	2–8	vertical	24 in.
Penstemon ×mexicale 'Pike's Peak Purple' A gorgeous plant but short-lived for those of us without well-draining soil.	perennial	4–9	vertical	16–18 in.
Perilla frutescens var. crispa Fantastic foliage addition—still one of my favorites. Disbud to maintain habit. May seed excessively if allowed. Plate 44.	annual		mound	3 ft.
Perovskia atriplicifolia Good plant in blue or purple gardens, mainly for foliage effect. Needs well-drained soil. Plates 37, 167.	perennial	5–9	vertical	3–4 ft.
Perovskia atriplicifolia 'Longin' More upright and narrow than the species.	perennial	5–9	vertical	3–4 ft.
Persicaria microcephala 'Red Dragon' For use as foliage plant; cut off flowers. Not all it was claimed to be.	perennial	5–9	mound	24–36 in.
Phlomis russeliana I have had great success with this plant in dry shade, and I adore it for its form and flowers—a favorite.	perennial	4–9	vertical	36 in.
Phlox divaricata Great naturalizer if allowed to seed through a garden. Combination 1.	perennial	4–9	mound	10–15 in.
Phlox divaricata 'Dirigo Ice' Sweet fragrance. Interplant through shade gardens and allow to seed for a naturalized effect.	perennial	4–9	mound	10–15 in.
Phlox divaricata 'Eco Texas Purple' Wonderful deep purple flowers in the spring garden.	perennial	4–9	mound	10–15 in.
Phlox divaricata ssp. laphamii	perennial	4–9	mound	10–15 in.
Phlox divaricata 'London Grove Blue' Gorgeous blue and a reliable performer. Great to underplant through shade border or garden that receives morning sun.	perennial	4–9	mound	10–15 in.
Phlox divaricata 'Sweet Lilac' A bit disappointed with this one—mildew problems.	perennial	4–9	mound	10–15 in.
Phlox paniculata 'David' Still a good clean white in most garden settings.	perennial	4–8	vertical	3–4 ft.
Phlox paniculata 'Fesselballon' Fragrance is noticeable in border from a distance. Seems to never stop flowering. A great selection that should be used more often. Plate 4.	perennial	4–8	vertical	36 in.

WIDTH	FLOWER COLOR	FLOWERING MONTH	FOLIAGE COLOR	FOLIAGE INTEREST	TEXTURE	DESIGN COLOR
2 ft.	red	Jul–Oct	red	spring/summer/ autumn	fine	warm or cool
12 in.	white	Jun–Jul	red	year-round	average	warm or cool
12 in.	purple	Jul–Sep			fine	cool
1½ ft.			purple	spring/summer/ autumn	bold	warm or cool
3–4 ft.	purple	Jul–Sep	silver-gray	spring/summer/ autumn	fine	cool
2–3 ft.	purple	Jul–Sep	silver-gray	spring/summer/ autumn	fine	cool
24–48 in.	white	Jul–Oct	red	spring/summer/ autumn	average	warm or cool
24 in.	yellow	Jun			bold	warm
12 in.	blue	May–Jun			fine	cool
12 in.	blue	May–Jun			fine	cool
12 in.	purple	May–Jun			fine	cool
12 in.	blue	May–Jun			fine	cool
12 in.	blue	May–Jun			fine	cool
12 in.	purple	May–Jun			fine	cool
2 ft.	white	Jul–Sep			average	warm or cool
2 ft.	pink	Jul–Sep			average	cool

	TYPE	ZONE	FORM	HEIGHT
Phlox paniculata 'Katherine' One of the few wonderful and reliable blue selections. Normally mildew-free.	perennial	4–8	vertical	30–36 in.
Phlox paniculata 'Laura' Purple that looks pink at times, depending on its associated color and the light, but good disease resistance. Many people love it. Plate 73.	perennial	4–8	vertical	24–36 in.
Phlox paniculata 'Look Again' Eye-catching magenta that makes you "look again" and perfectly clean foliage all season—a real crowd pleaser. Plates 4–5; Combination 12.	perennial	4–8	vertical	3–4 ft.
Phlox paniculata 'Orange Perfection'	perennial	4–8	vertical	36 in.
Phlox paniculata 'Pax' (peace) Nice white with mildew-resistant foliage.	perennial	4–8	vertical	36 in.
Phlox paniculata 'Tenor' Not really a great red when used among other reds— still a hint of pink but good in other color schemes.	perennial	4–8	vertical	30–36 in.
Phlox paniculata 'The King' Good in the purple garden.	perennial	4–8	vertical	30–36 in.
Phlox paniculata 'Tracy's Treasure' Introduction found in my garden, likely a cross between the paniculata cultivars 'Speed Limit 45' and 'Pax'. Soft baby-pink flowers without magenta overtones, late flowering, and tall. Has been mildew- and disease-free in my garden, deep in the middle of hundreds of plants without good air circulation. Tough. Plate 26.	perennial	4–8	vertical	4–4½ ft.
Phlox stolonifera 'Blue Ridge' Good tucked into any empty hole as an interconnector or groundcover.	perennial	4–9	horizontal	6–12 in.
Phlox stolonifera 'Bruce's White' Brightens the base of any plant it creeps around.	perennial	4–9	horizontal	6–12 in.
Phormium 'Bronze Baby' Wonderful architectural feature in the red or purple garden. One of the best performers; tolerates drought once established. Love it. Plate 143.	tropical	8–10	vertical	24–30 in.
Phormium 'Platt's Black' Good deep foliage color as accent or focal point in garden or pots.	tropical	8–10	vertical	24–48 in.
Phormium 'Yellow Wave' Love the foliage color and form. Carefree. Plate 6.	tropical	8–10	vertical	36 in.
Phormium cookianum 'Chocolate' Great deep foliage color. Plates 107, 112.	tropical	8–10	vertical	24–48 in.

WIDTH	FLOWER COLOR	FLOWERING MONTH	FOLIAGE COLOR	FOLIAGE INTEREST	TEXTURE	DESIGN COLOR
24 in.	blue	Jul–Sep			average	cool
2 ft.	purple	Jul–Sep			average	cool
2 ft.	magenta	Jul–Sep			average	warm or cool
2 ft.	orange	Jul–Sep			average	warm
2 ft.	white	Jul–Sep			average	warm or cool
24 in.	red	Jul–Aug			average	warm or cool
24 in.	purple	Jul–Sep			average	cool
2 ft.	pink	Aug–Sep			average	cool
12–15 in.	blue	Apr–May			fine	cool
12–15 in.	white	Apr–May			fine	warm or cool
24–30 in.			bronze	spring/summer/ autumn	bold	warm or cool
24–48 in.			red	spring/summer/ autumn	bold	warm or cool
36 in.			yellow	spring/summer/ autumn	bold	warm
24–48 in.			bronze	spring/summer/ autumn	bold	warm or cool

	TYPE	ZONE	FORM	HEIGHT
Phyllostachys nigra Produces green stems that turn black in their second or third year. Invasive growth habit; use only in containers. Plate 54.	annual	7–10	vertical	10–15 ft.
Phytolacca polyandra Interesting "weed" to add to gardens to "ground" even the stuffiest visitor.	perennial	6–9	vertical	5–6 ft.
Picea abies 'Mucronata' Tight, slow-growing accent plant creates a bit of formality. Plate 181.	shrub	4	conical	6 ft.
Picea abies 'Pendula' Dominant form in designs. Pendulous branches bring the eye down to plantings below them. Train as a weeping form or else remains prostrate. Combination 11.	tree	3–7	weeping	12–15 ft.
Picea alcoquiana 'Howell's Tigertail' Beautiful, slow-growing conifer for the blue or cool-color garden. Adaptable to clay soils, resents drought. Plate 165.	shrub	5	mound	5–6 ft.
Picea orientalis 'Skylands' Excellent specimen for a warm border. Gold needles may fade in heat and burn in hot regions and winter wind. Plates 35, 183.	tree	4–7	conical	7 ft.
Picea pungens 'Iseli Foxtail' Lovely and interesting irregular habit, blue needle color, and a fairly adaptable nature make this a winning small conifer. Plates 38, 174–175.	tree	3–7(8)	conical	20 ft.
Picea pungens 'Thomsen' One of the best blues. Good symmetrical pyramidal habit, slow growth. Plates 25–27.	tree	3–7	conical	15–18 ft.
Pinus cembra 'Silver Sheen' Great for screening. Unusual.	tree	4–7	vertical	12–15 ft.
Pinus contorta 'Chief Joseph' Slow-growing specimen conifer. Yellow foliage intensifies in autumn and glows in winter. Combination 26.	shrub	5	irregular	15 ft.
Pinus contorta 'Spaan's Dwarf' Combination 23.	shrub	5	irregular	12 ft.
Pinus densiflora 'Oculus Draconis' I fall more in love with this plant every time I see its yellow and green needles backlit. Simply outstanding in the warm-color garden, great specimen. Plate 104.	shrub	3–7	irregular	8–10 ft.
Pinus flexilis 'Vanderwolf's Pyramid' Plate 13; Combinations 8–9.	tree	4–7	irregular	30 ft.
Pinus parviflora 'Glauca' Plate 6; Combination 19.	tree	4–7	irregular	15–20 ft.
Pinus parviflora 'Yatsubusa' Great specimen. Unusual, somewhat "twisted" habit. Plate 4.	shrub	4–7	irregular	6–8 ft.

WIDTH	FLOWER COLOR	FLOWERING MONTH	FOLIAGE COLOR	FOLIAGE INTEREST	TEXTURE	DESIGN COLOR
6–10 ft.					fine	warm or cool
2 ft.	purple	Aug	yellow	autumn	bold	cool
6 ft.					fine	warm or cool
12–15 ft.					fine	warm or cool
5–6 ft.			blue	year-round	fine	cool
7 ft.			yellow	year-round	fine	warm
15 ft.			blue	year-round	fine	cool
8–10 ft.			blue	year-round	fine	cool
10–15 ft.			blue	year-round	average	cool
6–7 ft.			yellow	autumn	fine	warm
8 ft.					fine	warm or cool
8–10 ft.			green/yellow	year-round	fine	warm
30 ft.			blue	year-round	fine	cool
8–10 ft.			blue	year-round	fine	cool
3 ft.			blue	year-round	fine	cool

	TYPE	ZONE	FORM	HEIGHT
Pinus pumila 'Nana' Beautiful semi-dwarf plant; sometimes sold incorrectly as Pinus cembra 'Nana'. Plate 45.	shrub	4–7	mound	6–9 ft.
Pinus strobus For use as a screen or backdrop in large gardens. Fast growing. Will not tolerate salt or pollution. Plates 14, 196.	tree	4–9	conical	60–80 ft.
Pinus strobus 'Nana' Nice, soft mounded form.	shrub	3–7	mound	2 ft.
Pinus sylvestris Not for small spaces.	tree	3–7	irregular	30–50 ft.
Pinus sylvestris 'Albyn' Low, spreading conifer. Nice in a cool or blue garden.	shrub	3–7	horizontal	1½ ft.
Pinus sylvestris 'Fastigiata' Excellent vertical form for corners of buildings, narrowest of any of the pines. Tends to break up in heavy ice and snow. Plate 10.	tree	3–7	vertical	20 ft.
Pistia stratiotes Invasive. Can quickly take over a small water garden but very attractive. Plate 71.	annual		mound	4 in.
Plantago major 'Rubrifolia' A refined "weed" with great foliage color and texture. Could be used in a red or purple garden. Deadhead before seed set to avoid it dominating the design. Plates 139, 170.	perennial	5–9	mound	12–18 in.
Platycodon grandiflorus 'Double Blue' Long bloomer for the blue or cool-color garden.	perennial	3–8	vertical	24 in.
Platycodon grandiflorus 'Komachi' To me this is the best platycodon because its flowers are large balloons that do not open at maturity. Plate 75.	perennial	3–8	vertical	24–36 in.
Plectranthus amboinicus Unusual herb.	annual	10–11	mound	8–12 in.
Plectranthus argentatus Wonderful silver-foliage addition to dry mixed gardens. Plate 171.	annual	10–11	horizontal	18 in.
Polemonium caeruleum 'Blanjou' (brise d'Anjou) I keep trying with this plant because of its cool variegated foliage, but it doesn't seem to like Midwest climates. Also prone to slug damage.	perennial	3–7	mound	18–24 in.
Polygonatum odoratum 'Variegatum' Ranks in the top five shade plants for its summer and autumn foliage color, habit, and tolerance to dry shade once established. Slow to take hold and then long-lived—a must-have in any shade garden. Plate 119.	perennial	3–9	vertical	24–36 in.
Polystichum acrostichoides Reliable and long-lived.	perennial	3–9	mound	18 in.

WIDTH	FLOWER COLOR	FLOWERING MONTH	FOLIAGE COLOR	FOLIAGE INTEREST	TEXTURE	DESIGN COLOR
6–9 ft.			gray-green	year-round	fine	warm or cool
15–20 ft.					fine	warm or cool
4 ft.					fine	warm or cool
20 ft.					average	warm or cool
5–6 ft.			blue	year-round	fine	cool
3 ft.			blue	year-round	fine	cool
					bold	warm or cool
8 in.	green	Sep	purple	spring/summer/autumn	bold	warm or cool
24 in.	blue	Jul–Sep	yellow	autumn	average	cool
24 in.	blue	Jul–Sep	yellow	autumn	average	cool
12 in.			gray-green	spring/summer/autumn	average	cool
36 in.	white	Jul–Sep	gray-green	spring/summer/autumn	bold	cool
18 in.	blue	Jun	green/white	spring/summer/autumn	fine	cool
24 in.	white	May–Jun	green/white	spring/summer	average	warm or cool
24 in.					fine	warm or cool

	TYPE	ZONE	FORM	HEIGHT
Portulaca grandiflora 'Sundial Peach' Nice addition to the peach garden or between stepping-stones that are set in sand or gravel.	annual		horizontal	8–10 in.
Potentilla fruticosa 'Sunset' Nice summer-flowering shrub addition to the warm garden.	shrub	2–6	mound	2 ft.
Pseudotsuga menziesii 'Astro Blue' Gorgeous, slow-growing specimen. May be difficult to locate in the trade. Plates 98, 107.	tree	4–6	conical	15–20 ft.
Pulmonaria 'Majesté' To me, this is "the" pulmonaria for fantastic silver-foliage effect that holds throughout the entire season. Plate 130.	perennial	3–8	mound	10 in.
Pulmonaria 'Viette's Deep Blue Sea' Intense blue flowers.	perennial	3–8	mound	9 in.
Puschkinia scilloides Carefree heirloom (1808) bulb, 15 per sq. ft.	hardy bulb	4–8	vertical	6 in.
Quercus palustris Not a tree to plant in a mixed garden due to its size, but often found existing in woodland gardens. Needs moist, acid, well-drained soil. Iron chlorosis can be a problem.	tree	4–8	vertical	60 ft.
Quercus robur 'Pectinata' Unusual small oak, outstanding for small gardens. Plate 6.	tree	5–8	vertical	15–20 ft.
Rheum palmatum var. tanguticum Gorgeous early in the season for bold texture and foliage color but declines as the night temperatures increase, leaving a disappointing hole in the garden. I have grown it in large containers in gardens and then moved it out of view as it declined.	perennial	5–9	mound	4–6 ft.
Rhodochiton atrosanguineus Excellent purple color to new foliage. Seems short-lived in summer heat. Combination 6.	annual vine		climbing	10 ft.
Rhododendron 'Chionoides' Easy to grow.	shrub	4–8	mound	4 ft.
Rhododendron 'Mist Maiden' One of my favorite rhododendrons for its apple-blossomy flowers and, especially, the silvery white undersides of the leaves. It has proven quite hardy in Ohio gardens. Plate 127.	shrub	4	mound	2–4 ft.
Rhododendron 'Northern Starburst' Reliably hardy. Plate 121.	shrub	4	mound	3 ft.
Ricinus communis Major textural statement. Great for size in large borders. Plate 75; Combination 7.	tropical	(9)10–11	vertical	6–8 ft.
Ricinus communis 'Carmencita' Superior cultivar for foliage color and interest. Plates 140, 147.	tropical	(9)10–11	vertical	6–8 ft.

WIDTH	FLOWER COLOR	FLOWERING MONTH	FOLIAGE COLOR	FOLIAGE INTEREST	TEXTURE	DESIGN COLOR
12 in.	peach	Jun–Sep			average	warm
2–3 ft.	orange	Jun–Sep			fine	warm
8 ft.			blue	year-round	fine	cool
18 in.	blue	Mar–Apr	silver-gray	spring/summer/autumn	average	cool
18 in.	blue	Mar–Apr	silver-gray	spring/summer/autumn	average	cool
	blue	Mar–Apr			fine	cool
25 ft.					average	warm or cool
15–20 ft.					fine	warm or cool
4–6 ft.	red	May–Jun	purple	spring/summer/autumn	bold	warm or cool
	purple	Jun–Sep	purple	spring	fine	cool
4 ft.	white	Apr–May			bold	warm or cool
2–4 ft.	white	Apr–May			average	cool
3 ft.	pink	Apr–May			average	cool
4 ft.					bold	warm or cool
4 ft.			red	spring/summer/autumn	bold	warm or cool

	TYPE	ZONE	FORM	HEIGHT
Rodgersia aesculifolia Good bold textural plant for moist, shady areas but resents standing water. Combination 24.	perennial	5–7	mound	3–5 ft.
Rodgersia pinnata Wonderful dominant feature in the shade garden. Reliable even in dryer conditions, although will get crispy around the margins of the leaves.	perennial	5–7	mound	3–4 ft.
Rosa 'Alchymist' Spectacular golden peach climber, worth growing even though it only flowers once.	shrub	4–9	climbing	12 ft.
Rosa 'Ausbuff' (English Garden®) Loved the pictures of this plant's double yellow-peach flowers and tales of its fragrance but have had trouble establishing it in mixed gardens, where it seems to get overshadowed. I will persist.	shrub	5–9	mound	3–4 ft.
Rosa 'Ausmas' (Graham Thomas®) Reliable, tall, good disease-resistant yellow for a spot of warmth in the border.	shrub	5–9	vertical	5 ft.
Rosa 'Aussaucer' (Evelyn®) Spectacular flower and extremely fragrant: used to make rose perfumes by English perfume company Crabtree & Evelyn. Not extremely vigorous. Plate 153.	shrub	5–10	mound	4 ft.
Rosa 'Ausvelvet' (The Prince®) Wonderful addition to the purple garden.	shrub	5–9	mound	3–4 ft.
Rosa 'Champlain' A good red for the red garden. Nice height. Have had some trouble with disease.	shrub	4–9	mound	3–4 ft.
Rosa 'F. J. Grootendorst' Appears somewhat pink-red when used among other truer reds. A good long-flowering and robust plant for hedging or specimen. Plate 78.	shrub	2–9	mound	5–6 ft.
Rosa 'Hansa' This to me is the epitome of a real rose for its fantastic fragrance and the shape of the flowers. Truly romantic. Habit can get leggy with age. Blackspot resistant.	shrub	2–7	mound	4–6 ft.
Rosa Lyda Rose™ Nice shrub that can be trained as small climber.	shrub	5–10	mound	4–5 ft.
Rosa 'Meidomonac' (Bonica®) A sturdy, long-flowering good pink. No spraying needed to keep it in fair condition. Good for hedging or as a specimen.	shrub	4–9	mound	3–5 ft.
Rosa 'Nearly Wild' Great multi-use rose in the cool-color vignette for its long bloom period, good height, habit, and clean foliage. Combination 20.	shrub	4–9	mound	3 ft.

WIDTH	FLOWER COLOR	FLOWERING MONTH	FOLIAGE COLOR	FOLIAGE INTEREST	TEXTURE	DESIGN COLOR
4 ft.	white	May–Jun			bold	warm or cool
2½ ft.	pink	Jul			bold	warm or cool
8 ft.	peach	May–Jun			average	warm
3 ft.	peach	Jun–Aug			average	warm
4 ft.	yellow	Jun–Aug			average	warm
3 ft.	peach	Jun–Aug			average	warm
2–3 ft.	purple	Jun–Aug			average	cool
3–4 ft.	red	Jun			average	warm
4–5 ft.	red	Jun–Sep			average	warm
4–6 ft.	pink	Jun–Sep			bold	cool
4 ft.	pink	Jun–Sep			average	cool
3–5 ft.	pink	Jun–Sep			average	cool
3–4 ft.	pink	Jun–Sep			average	cool

	TYPE	ZONE	FORM	HEIGHT
Rosa 'Nuits de Young' Classic rose (1845). Excellent for the purple garden but be prepared for the foliage to get horrid by mid-summer. Best not planted up-close-and-personal; if it is, allow herbaceous plants to fill in around it.	shrub	4–9	mound	4 ft.
Rosa 'Scrivluv' (Baby Love®) Charming single yellow. A well-behaved, disease-resistant selection.	shrub	5	mound	2–3 ft.
Rosa 'Seafoam' Ideal groundcover or may be grown as a climber. Stays in decent condition without spraying. Combination 22.	shrub	4–9	horizontal	3 ft.
Rosa 'The Fairy' Fairly disease resistant. A good low-maintenance landscape rose.	shrub	5–9	mound	2–3 ft.
Rosa ×harisonii 'Harison's Yellow' Beautiful yellow flowers cover entire shrub. Great in warm color combinations.	shrub	3–9	mound	4–6 ft.
Rosa multiflora 'Grevillei' (seven sisters' rose) Also known as 'Platyphylla'. Vigorous. Can be grown as a large shrub; better suited in the mixed border as a climber. Foliage gets tatty by late summer. Combination 27.	shrub	4–9	climbing	10–12 ft.
Rosa rugosa Sturdy, disease-free shrub but can be completely killed back by stem cankers that seem to develop on older, stressed plants. Plate 74.	shrub	2–9	mound	4–8 ft.
Rudbeckia fulgida var. speciosa (newmannii) Smaller, more refined flowers, foliage, and growth habit than the common black-eyed susan. More reliable and useful in mixed garden designs. Plate 5; Combination 12.	perennial	3–9	mound	24 in.
Rudbeckia hirta 'Irish Eyes' Bold and great for hot combinations. Biennial or short-lived perennial, often grown as an annual. Plate 23.	annual	3–7	mound	24–30 in.
Rudbeckia maxima Choice rudbeckia for its large blue-green leaves, tall narrow vertical habit, and long-lasting seedheads. Useful even in tight spots. Good see-through plant in front of border. Plates 13, 183–184; Combination 8.	perennial	4–9	vertical	5–6 ft.
Rudbeckia triloba Beautiful en masse, but I have not used it in any design work except my own gardens, where its wild, prolific self-seeding nature is tolerable. Too invasive for most gardens. Plate 3.	perennial	4–7	vertical	4–5 ft.
Rumex sanguineus Another ornamental "weed" for the red garden. Remove flowers to maintain healthy foliage. Plates 141, 143.	perennial	5–8	mound	18 in.
Ruta graveolens 'Blue Beauty' Blue foliage and fine texture make me lust for this plant in design work, but it doesn't tolerate less-than-ideal drainage. Good in pot culture, where moisture can be closely monitored.	perennial	4–9	mound	18 in.

WIDTH	FLOWER COLOR	FLOWERING MONTH	FOLIAGE COLOR	FOLIAGE INTEREST	TEXTURE	DESIGN COLOR
3 ft.	purple	Jun			average	cool
3 ft.	yellow	Jun–Sep			average	warm
4–5 ft.	white	Jun–Aug			average	warm or cool
2–3 ft.	pink	Jun–Sep			average	cool
2–3 ft.	yellow	Jun–Aug			fine	warm
4–5 ft.	pink	Jun–Jul			average	cool
3–8 ft.	pink	Jun–Oct			bold	cool
24 in.	yellow	Jul–Sep			average	warm
18 in.	yellow	Jul–Sep			bold	warm
2 ft.	yellow	Aug–Sep	blue	spring/summer/ autumn	bold	warm
3 ft.	yellow	Jul–Sep			average	warm
12 in.			red	spring/summer/ autumn	bold	warm
18 in.	yellow	Jul–Aug	blue	spring/summer/ autumn	fine	cool

	TYPE	ZONE	FORM	HEIGHT
Salvia 'Indigo Spires' Another wonderful large shrublike salvia with blue flowers on terminal spikes up to 15 in. long. Habit can open up by late summer, requiring support. Plants still fabulous, tolerant of several frosts without noticeable damage. Plate 164.	annual	7–10	mound	3–4 ft.
Salvia 'Purple Majesty' Striking 15-in.-long terminal spikes of purple flowers develop on shrublike plant in mid-late summer. Fantastic and should be used more. Tolerant of several frosts before damage is noticeable.	annual	8–10	mound	3–4 ft.
Salvia argentea Outstanding silver-gray foliage, bold and low. Plant is monocarpic but may produce offsets that live on. May take two or more years to flower. Plate 46.	perennial	5–8	mound	12–24 in.
Salvia azurea var. pitcheri Good interplanted among other structurally strong plants, to support its lax stems. Interesting for late blue flowers.	perennial	4–9	mound	5 ft.
Salvia coccinea 'Lady in Red' Brilliant red flowers.	annual		mound	16 in.
Salvia guaranitica Beautiful shrublike salvia.	annual	7–10	mound	4–6 ft.
Salvia guaranitica 'Black and Blue' Striking flower and bract combination on large shrublike plant. Fabulous.	annual	7–10	mound	4–6 ft.
Salvia leucantha Interesting narrow leaves and pubescent stems are attractive long before the flowers are evident. Another shrubby salvia winner. Plate 167.	annual		mound	4–5 ft.
Salvia nemorosa 'Ostfriesland' (East Friesland) Still a favorite for dark blue-violet vertical flowers and reliable performance.	perennial	3–8	mound	18 in.
Salvia nemorosa 'Purple Glory' Good purple form. Combination 16.	perennial	3–8	mound	24 in.
Salvia nemorosa 'Pusztaflamme' (plumosa) Interesting plumelike texture to flowers.	perennial	3–8	mound	18 in.
Salvia officinalis 'Tricolor' Varied foliage colors pair nicely with an assortment of other plants.	annual	7–8	mound	18–24 in.
Salvia patens Striking intense blue flower.	annual	8–9	mound	24 in.
Salvia ×sylvestris 'Blauhügel' (blue hill) The truest blue for the purist's blue garden. Long blooming. Plate 159.	perennial	3–8	mound	20 in.
Salvia ×sylvestris 'Blaukönigin' (blue queen) A blue-violet for the blue garden.	perennial	3–8	mound	24 in.

WIDTH	FLOWER COLOR	FLOWERING MONTH	FOLIAGE COLOR	FOLIAGE INTEREST	TEXTURE	DESIGN COLOR
3–4 ft.	blue	Jun–Oct			average	cool
3 ft.	purple	Jul–Oct			average	cool
18 in.			silver-gray	spring/summer/ autumn	bold	cool
3 ft.	blue	Aug–Oct			average	cool
12 in.	red	Jun–Oct			average	warm
3 ft.	blue	Jun–Oct			average	cool
3 ft.	blue	Jun–Oct			average	cool
3 ft.	purple	Aug–Oct			average	cool
24 in.	purple	Jun–Aug			average	cool
24 in.	purple	Jun–Aug			average	cool
24 in.	purple	Jun–Aug			average	cool
24 in.					average	cool
18 in.	blue	Jul–Oct			average	cool
24 in.	blue	Jun–Aug			average	cool
24 in.	blue	Jun–Aug			average	cool

	TYPE	ZONE	FORM	HEIGHT
Salvia ×sylvestris 'Mainacht' (May night) Old selection that is still effective for blue-purple vertical spikes.	perennial	3–8	mound	18 in.
Salvia ×sylvestris 'Viola Klose' Good dark blue.	perennial	3–8	mound	18 in.
Salvia verticillata 'Purple Rain' Mixed results with performance—can melt-out, flop, and be prone to mildew in poorly drained or rich soils. Excellent when happy in dry, infertile conditions. Plate 48.	perennial	5–8	mound	18 in.
Sambucus racemosa 'Sutherland Gold' Great accent shrub for foliage color and texture. Stooling will produce stronger-colored shoots and foliage. Resistant to sunburn. Plates 157–158.	shrub	4–6(7)	mound	8–10 ft.
Sanguisorba tenuifolia 'Purpurea' Strong vertical yet narrow growth habit, interesting toothed foliage, and dense purple-red catkinlike flowerheads. Often asked about. Useful in tight spots or coming up through other plants. Self-sows and makes its own great combinations. Good see-through plant.	perennial	4–8	vertical	5–6 ft.
Saruma henryi Underused, long-flowering shade plant—a favorite. Plate 199.	perennial	5–8	mound	15–18 in.
Scabiosa Butterfly Blue® Long bloomer with continual deadheading. For the blue garden. Must have well-drained soil. Combination 16.	perennial	3–7	mound	12 in.
Scabiosa 'Pink Mist' Long flowering with continual deadheading. Requires well-drained soil.	perennial	3–7	mound	12 in.
Scabiosa atropurpurea 'Ace of Spades' Interesting flowers, but plants are thin: quantities are required for any impact.	annual		vertical	2–3 ft.
Scabiosa columbaria var. ochroleuca Love to put this airy plant right up front in the border. Long flowering and sturdy with good drainage. Combination 27.	perennial	3–7	mound	36 in.
Scadoxus multiflorus Interesting large flowers on short stems for something different in the hot-color garden scheme, 3 per sq. ft.	tender bulb	7–10	mound	8–10 in.
Schizachyrium scoparium 'The Blues' Excellent blue foliage. Plates 175, 178–179.	perennial	3–9	vertical	24–36 in.
Sciadopitys verticillata Glossy foliage and outstanding texture and form make this a choice specimen in mixed gardens. Extremely slow growing. Combination 24.	tree	5–7	conical	15–20 ft.
Sedum 'Herbstfreude' (autumn joy) Still a useful addition to mixed borders.	perennial	3–10	mound	24 in.

WIDTH	FLOWER COLOR	FLOWERING MONTH	FOLIAGE COLOR	FOLIAGE INTEREST	TEXTURE	DESIGN COLOR
24 in.	purple	Jun–Aug			average	cool
24 in.	blue	Jun–Aug			average	cool
24 in.	purple	Jun–Aug	gray-green	spring/summer/autumn	average	cool
8–10 ft.			yellow	spring/summer/autumn	fine	warm
2–3 ft.	purple	Aug–Oct			fine	cool
24 in.	yellow	Apr–May			average	warm
12 in.	blue	May–Oct			fine	cool
12 in.	pink	May–Oct			fine	cool
1 ft.	red	Jun–Aug			fine	warm or cool
24 in.	yellow	Jun–Oct			fine	warm or cool
	red	Jul–Aug			fine	warm
15–18 in.	tan	Sep	blue	spring/summer/autumn	fine	cool
10–15 ft.					fine	warm or cool
18 in.	red	Aug–Sep			bold	warm or cool

	TYPE	ZONE	FORM	HEIGHT
Sedum 'Pork and Beans' Knobby appearance makes for a good filler between stepping-stones and in other dry nooks.	perennial	4–10	mound	2 in.
Sedum acre 'Aureum' Nice between stepping-stones and in other dry nooks to cover ground.	perennial	4–10	horizontal	3 in.
Sedum telephium ssp. maximum 'Atropurpureum' Nice height and foliage color but not always a reliable performer. Keep dry. Could be used in the red or purple garden.	perennial	4–9	mound	24 in.
Silene regia A bright warm touch in partially shaded sites. Pulls the eye.	perennial	5–8	vertical	36 in.
Sisyrinchium 'Quaint and Queer' Unique flower color. Should be used more in sites with good drainage.	perennial	5–8	mound	8–12 in.
Sisyrinchium bermudianum Excellent fine texture and sweet flowers. Useful along edges of paths laid in sand, so it can be seen, and to provide the drainage that is so essential.	perennial	5–8	mound	10–12 in.
Solenostemon 'Burgundy Columns' Another great burgundy.	annual	10	mound	24 in.
Solenostemon 'Burgundy Giant' Reliable. My favorite coleus for pure deep color. Plate 200.	annual	10	mound	3 ft.
Solenostemon 'Olive' Nice, almost a neutral color addition.	annual	10	mound	18–20 in.
Solenostemon 'Penny' Foliage appears red when backlit. Very interesting in different types of light. Combination 11.	annual	10	mound	2–2½ ft.
Solenostemon 'Purple Emperor' Excellent foliage plant.	annual	10	mound	2–3 ft.
Solenostemon 'Saturn' Sturdy, reliable performer. Plate 143.	annual	10	mound	2–3 ft.
Solidago 'Golden Spangles'	perennial	4–8	mound	24–36 in.
Solidago rugosa 'Fireworks' Fantastic arching sprays of flowers create a memorable form and lasting impression. Responds to pruning for use in smaller areas.	perennial	4–8	mound	4 ft.
×Solidaster luteus 'Lemore' Rather fine texture to the flowering panicle. I always think this plant seems a bit confused on how to act: like a goldenrod or an aster? Melts out in moist humid summers.	perennial	5–8	mound	24–30 in.

WIDTH	FLOWER COLOR	FLOWERING MONTH	FOLIAGE COLOR	FOLIAGE INTEREST	TEXTURE	DESIGN COLOR
10 in.					average	warm or cool
12 in.	yellow	Jun–Jul			average	warm
18 in.	red	Aug–Oct	purple	spring/summer/autumn	bold	warm or cool
24 in.	red	Jul–Sep			average	warm
8 in.	purple	May–Jun			fine	warm or cool
10 in.	purple	May–Jun			fine	cool
18 in.			purple	spring/summer/autumn	bold	warm or cool
3 ft.			purple	spring/summer/autumn	bold	warm or cool
15–18 in.					bold	warm or cool
2 ft.			yellow	spring/summer/autumn	bold	warm
2 ft.			purple	spring/summer/autumn	bold	warm or cool
2 ft.			red	spring/summer/autumn	bold	warm
18 in.	yellow	Aug–Oct			average	warm
2 ft.	yellow	Aug–Oct			average	warm
24–30 in.	yellow	Aug–Oct			fine	warm

	TYPE	ZONE	FORM	HEIGHT
Sorghastrum nutans 'Sioux Blue' Imposing tall blue form. Tends to open up as the season progresses—give it room to relax. Nice golden autumn color. Plates 13, 138, 176; Combinations 8, 10.	perennial	5–8	vertical	4–6 ft.
Stachys byzantina Disbud to maintain foliage appearance. New forms are more desirable.	perennial	4–8	mound	12–15 in.
Stachys byzantina 'Countess Helen von Stein' Striking, bold gray foliage mixes well in cool color schemes. Plate 174.	perennial	4–8	mound	12–15 in.
Stachys byzantina 'Primrose Heron' Nice yellow tinge to foliage for warm color schemes. Plate 177.	perennial	4–8	mound	12–15 in.
Stachys macrantha I don't see this plant used much, but it's beautiful for its vertical form, long-blooming flowers, and undemanding culture. Plate 34.	perennial	5–7	vertical	24 in.
Stokesia laevis 'Klaus Jelitto' In one of my open garden tours, this plant was voted the people's choice, out of thousands of other plants, for its large fringed blue flowers and sturdy growth. Plate 13; Combination 8.	perennial	5–9	mound	12–15 in.
Stokesia laevis 'Mary Gregory' I don't feel this really lives up to its press—not that impressive in my experience.	perennial	5–9	mound	18 in.
Stokesia laevis 'Omega Skyrocket' Useful for its taller flowers, which add a vertical form.	perennial	5–9	vertical	36 in.
Stokesia laevis 'Purple Parasols' Nice purple flowers. Plate 170.	perennial	5–9	mound	12–15 in.
Stylophorum diphyllum Another of my top five shade plants for its energizing yellow flowers, shimmering silver underside to the lobed leaves, interesting seed capsules, and ability to self-seed and naturalize.	perennial	4–9	mound	18–24 in.
Symphytum 'Goldsmith' Useful for variegated foliage in partial shade.	perennial	5–9	mound	12 in.
Syringa meyeri Can form a wide shrub or be pruned as a standard. Very floriferous.	shrub	3–7	mound	10 ft.
Tanacetum 'Golden Feathers' Grown for the outstanding yellow foliage color and fine texture. Disbud flowers to maintain attractive foliage. Plate 158.	perennial	4–8	mound	15 in.

WIDTH	FLOWER COLOR	FLOWERING MONTH	FOLIAGE COLOR	FOLIAGE INTEREST	TEXTURE	DESIGN COLOR
3–4 ft.	tan	Aug–Oct	blue	spring/summer	fine	cool
18 in.	purple	Jun–Jul	silver-gray	spring/summer/ autumn	bold	cool
18 in.	purple	Jun–Jul	silver-gray	spring/summer/ autumn	bold	cool
18 in.	purple	Jun–Jul	yellow	spring/summer/ autumn	bold	warm
12 in.	purple	Jun			average	cool
15 in.	blue	Jul–Aug			average	cool
15 in.	yellow	Jul–Aug			average	warm
15 in.	blue	Jul–Aug			average	cool
15 in.	purple	Jul–Aug			average	cool
18 in.	yellow	May–Jun			average	warm
12 in.	blue	Apr–May	green/yellow	spring/summer/ autumn	average	warm or cool
6–8 ft.	purple	May			average	cool
15 in.	white	Jun–Jul	yellow	spring/summer/ autumn	fine	warm

	TYPE	ZONE	FORM	HEIGHT
Thalictrum aquilegiifolium 'Thundercloud' Ornamental blue-green fine-textured foliage, purple flowers (larger than the species), and persistent three-winged fruit, along with the height, make this a useful addition to the part-shade garden. Underused.	perennial	5–8	vertical	36 in.
Thalictrum rochebruneanum Useful as a wonderful airy vertical element in the garden. Makes a good see-through plant. Often asked about.	perennial	4–7	vertical	5–6 ft.
Thermopsis villosa I use this as a lupine substitute. The flowers are a useful vertical element in the early summer garden. Fruit is persistent, but unfortunately the foliage has a tendency to decline by mid-late summer. Be patient—slow to establish.	perennial	3–8	mound	36 in.
Thuja occidentalis 'Techny' Great for hedging. One of the best for northern gardens.	tree	3–7	conical	10–15 ft.
Thunbergia battiscombei Unusual, fabulous, continuous purple-blue flowers. Robust and adaptable vine. Excellent grown on a short obelisk in the garden or in containers; can be brought inside for the winter as a houseplant on a very sunny, cool (60°F minimum) windowsill. Plate 17.	annual vine	10–11	climbing	3–4 ft.
Thymus ×citriodorus Nice tucked in flagstone paths laid in sand to provide essential drainage.	perennial	6–9	mound	9–12 in.
Thymus ×citriodorus 'Lemon Green' Interesting flecks of yellow on deep green foliage. Nice planted in flagstone paths.	perennial	5–8	mound	2 in.
Thymus pseudolanuginosus Useful planted in flagstone paths laid in sand or gravel to provide essential drainage.	perennial	5–8	horizontal	2 in.
Tiarella cordifolia 'Ninja' Reliable spreading groundcover or edger for shade with interesting purple markings on foliage.	perennial	3–8	mound	12 in.
Tigridia pavonia 'Speciosa' Unusual, to-die-for red flowers with yellow centers create quite a stir in the gardens. Flowers last one day, very choice, 5 per sq. ft. Plate 152.	tender bulb	8–10	vertical	18 in.
Tradescantia Andersoniana Group Seedlings will develop in garden. Extensive pruning required to maintain appearance.	perennial	3–9	mound	18–24 in.
Tradescantia (Andersoniana Group) 'Purple Profusion' Purple flowers, narrow foliage, and compact habit make this a useful long bloomer for the purple garden. Plate 168.	perennial	3–9	mound	16–18 in.
Tradescantia (Andersoniana Group) 'Zwanenburg Blue' Intense deep blue flowers are an appealing addition to the blue garden. Cutting foliage back promotes new growth and rebloom and keeps the plant aesthetically pleasing in designs. Combination 22.	perennial	3–9	mound	18–24 in.

WIDTH	FLOWER COLOR	FLOWERING MONTH	FOLIAGE COLOR	FOLIAGE INTEREST	TEXTURE	DESIGN COLOR
24 in.	purple	May–Jun	blue	spring/summer/ autumn	fine	cool
2–3 ft.	purple	May–Jun			fine	cool
3 ft.	yellow	May–Jun			average	warm
					average	warm or cool
	purple	Jul Sep			average	cool
12 in.	purple	May–Jun			fine	cool
12 in.	purple	May–Jun	green/yellow	spring/summer/ autumn	fine	warm
12 in.	purple	May–Jun	gray-green	spring/summer/ autumn	fine	cool
12 in.	white	May–Jun	purple	spring/summer/ autumn	average	warm or cool
	red	Aug–Sep			fine	warm
24 in.	blue	Jun–Aug			average	cool
24 in.	purple	Jun–Aug			average	cool
24 in.	blue	Jun–Aug			average	cool

	TYPE	ZONE	FORM	HEIGHT
Trillium erectum Excellent wildflower for the shade garden. Adds a touch of purple class. Dormant in summer.	perennial	4–9	mound	15 in.
Triteleia laxa 'Queen Fabiola' A different bulb, fun to incorporate, 10 per sq. ft.	hardy bulb	5–9	vertical	24 in.
Tropaeolum majus Alaska Series Flowers contrast nicely with variegated leaves. The only drawback: the mixed flowers are hard to use in more exact color schemes. Plate 185.	annual	9	mound	10 in.
Tropaeolum majus 'Apricot Trifle' Nice edger in peach color schemes.	annual	9	mound	10 in.
Tropaeolum majus 'Blush Double' Double apricot—a fantastic, unusual flower for a nasturtium. Should be used more but may be difficult to locate. Trailing habit great for containers. Plate 65.	annual	9	mound	10 in.
Tropaeolum majus 'Moonlight' Extremely long flowering, bright, and cheerful. Good performer in raised planters. Plate 69.	annual	9	mound	10 in.
Tropaeolum majus 'Tip Top Mahogany' Excellent contrast between flower and foliage attracts a lot of attention. Plant along edges or use as filler in containers or spilling over walls. Plates 92, 108.	annual	8–10	mound	10 in.
Tsuga canadensis Lovely used as a tall screen or specimen. Somewhat temperamental. Best sited in part or full shade with adequate moisture and protected from wind. Can be subject to spider mites and woolly adelgid. Plate 197.	tree	3–7	conical	40 ft.
Tsuga canadensis 'Cole's Prostrate' Gorgeous habit, multiple uses in designs. Plate 121.	shrub	4–7	horizontal	2 ft.
Tulipa 'Angelique' Perennializes in some climates, 5 per sq. ft.	hardy bulb	3–8	vertical	14–16 in.
Tulipa 'Apricot Parrot' Not crazy about the color combinations in this tulip, too busy, 5 per sq. ft.	hardy bulb	3–8	vertical	16–18 in.
Tulipa 'Big Smile' 5 per sq. ft.	hardy bulb	3–8	vertical	20 in.
Tulipa 'Black Parrot' Striking color and form. Makes an excellent subject for painting, 5 per sq. ft. Plate 98.	hardy bulb	3–8	vertical	18–20 in.
Tulipa 'Blue Heron' Interesting color and texture to flowers. Neat sturdy habit. Reliably returns, in my experience, particularly in dry gravelly areas, 5 per sq. ft.	hardy bulb	3–8	vertical	20 in.
Tulipa 'Blue Parrot' 5 per sq. ft.	hardy bulb	3–8	vertical	18–20 in.

WIDTH	FLOWER COLOR	FLOWERING MONTH	FOLIAGE COLOR	FOLIAGE INTEREST	TEXTURE	DESIGN COLOR
12 in.	purple	May			average	cool
	blue	Jun			fine	cool
15–18 in.	yellow	Jun–Oct	green/white	spring/summer/ autumn	average	warm
15–18 in.	peach	Jun–Oct			average	warm
15 in.	peach	Jun–Oct			average	warm
24 in.	yellow	Jun–Oct			average	warm
12–15 in.	red	Jun–Sep			average	warm
25 ft.					fine	warm or cool
3–5 ft.					fine	warm or cool
	pink	May			average	cool
	peach	May			average	warm
	yellow	May			average	warm
	black	Apr–May			bold	warm or cool
	blue	Apr–May			average	cool
	blue	May			bold	cool

	TYPE	ZONE	FORM	HEIGHT
Tulipa 'Blushing Lady' Very striking for the hot garden, 5 per sq. ft.	hardy bulb	3–7	vertical	2½–3 ft.
Tulipa 'Burgundy Lace' 5 per sq. ft.	hardy bulb	3–8	vertical	24 in.
Tulipa 'Carmine Parrot' Fantastic color. Long-lasting flowers open wide, creating a bold appearance, 5 per sq. ft. Plate 22.	hardy bulb	3–8	vertical	18–20 in.
Tulipa 'Couleur Cardinal' 5 per sq. ft.	hardy bulb	3–8	vertical	12–14 in.
Tulipa 'Fringed Elegance' 5 per sq. ft.	hardy bulb	3–8	vertical	20 in.
Tulipa 'Queen of Night' Great, almost black flowers. Fabulous with backlighting, 5 per sq. ft.	hardy bulb	3–7	vertical	24 in.
Tulipa 'Temple of Beauty' Tall and striking in hot combination, 5 per sq. ft.	hardy bulb	3–8	vertical	24 in.
Tulipa 'Uncle Tom' 5 per sq. ft.	hardy bulb	3–8	vertical	14–16 in.
Tulipa batalinii 5 per sq. ft.	hardy bulb	3–7	mound	8–10 in.
Tulipa clusiana var. chrysantha nice perennial form, 5 per sq. ft.	hardy bulb	3–7	mound	10 in.
Valeriana officinalis Fragrant flowers and strong narrow vertical habit make this plant appealing interplanted among other early summer plants. Cut down to basal foliage before seed set to prevent excessive seeding. Combination 5.	perennial	4–9	vertical	24–60 in.
Verbascum 'Jackie' Beautiful when happy but often short-lived in poorly drained soils. Worth replanting or treating as an annual for the peach garden. Plate 154.	perennial	3–8	vertical	18 in.
Verbascum bombyciferum Striking for vertical habit. Needs well-drained soil. Biennial or short-lived evergreen perennial. Plate 23.	perennial	4–8	vertical	6–8 ft.
Verbena 'Homestead Purple' Great to carry purple to ground level or used trailing over containers. May act perennial in mild winters in zone 5. Plate 65.	annual	6–10	horizontal	10 in.
Verbena 'Romance Apricot' Good low filler for the peach garden.	annual		horizontal	10 in.
Verbena Temari® Red Makes a nice groundcover for red gardens. Plates 144, 150.	annual		horizontal	10 in.

WIDTH	FLOWER COLOR	FLOWERING MONTH	FOLIAGE COLOR	FOLIAGE INTEREST	TEXTURE	DESIGN COLOR
	orange	May			average	warm
	red	Apr–May			average	warm
	red	May			bold	warm
	purple	May			average	cool
	yellow	May			average	warm
	black	May			average	warm or cool
	orange	May			average	warm
	red	May			average	warm
	yellow	Apr–May			fine	warm
	red	Apr–May			fine	warm
12–18 in.	white	May–Jun			fine	cool
12 in.	peach	Jul			average	warm
2 ft.	yellow	Jul–Aug	silver-gray	year-round	bold	warm
18–24 in.	purple	Jun–Sep			fine	cool
12 in.	peach	Jun–Oct			average	warm
12–18 in.	red	Jun–Oct			average	warm

	TYPE	ZONE	FORM	HEIGHT
Verbena bonariensis Often performs as a perennial; will at least reseed and come up through and around other plants. Delicate, tall airy habit. Great for interplanting.	annual	(6)7–11	vertical	3–4 ft.
Verbena hastata Interesting native for violet-blue flower color and vertical element of the flower spikes. Deadhead to prevent excess seeding. A bit floppy and overall coarse—may not be refined enough for a more formal garden setting. Subject to powdery mildew.	perennial	3–7	vertical	3–4 ft.
Veronica 'Goodness Grows' Requires frequent division to do its best. Nice when young.	perennial	3–8	vertical	15 in.
Veronica 'Waterperry Blue' Charming used as a lower layer, edger, or planted in stone paths in the blue border or cool color scheme.	perennial	3–8	mound	4–6 in.
Veronica austriaca ssp. teucrium 'Crater Lake Blue' Reliable, utilitarian plant. Cut back by one-half after flowering to maintain attractive mounding habit in design. Plates 38, 174.	perennial	3–8	mound	12–15 in.
Veronica austriaca ssp. teucrium 'Royal Blue' Reliable and useful for deep blue flowers. Shear by one-half after flowering to maintain mounded shape.	perennial	3–8	mound	18 in.
Veronica gentianoides 'Nana'	perennial	4–8	mound	12 in.
Veronica peduncularis 'Georgia Blue' I can't say enough about this underused veronica. It flowers like crazy early in the season, the habit is clean with just a touch of trimming, and the purple-tinged foliage intensifies in autumn.	perennial	5–8	mound	4–6 in.
Veronica prostrata 'Trehane' So-so. Yellow foliage is attractive, but plants get tatty after flowering, requiring severe pruning.	perennial	5–8	horizontal	6–12 in.
Veronica repens 'Sunshine' Beautiful yellow foliage to use as the lower layer interconnector at the feet of other plants, particularly purple-leaved ones. Great mulch hider.	perennial	(5)6–9	horizontal	1 in.
Veronica spicata 'Blue Charm' A good blue vertical element. May require staking; cutting back before flowering reduces the need to stake.	perennial	3–8	vertical	36 in.
Veronica spicata 'Icicle' A nice plant in its early years but starts to decline after about two years. Requires frequent division. Many new and better white plants now available.	perennial	3–8	vertical	24 in.
Veronicastrum virginicum 'Fascination' Interesting for its purple flowers, though they are a bit pale for my taste. Would be useful in a garden or vignette featuring other pale colors. Foliage is attractive once plants are deadheaded.	perennial	3–8	vertical	3–6 ft.

WIDTH	FLOWER COLOR	FLOWERING MONTH	FOLIAGE COLOR	FOLIAGE INTEREST	TEXTURE	DESIGN COLOR
1½ ft.	purple	Jul–Oct			fine	cool
2 ft.	purple	Jul–Sep			average	cool
15 in.	blue	Jun–Sep			average	cool
10 in.	blue	May–Jun	purple	year-round	average	cool
18 in.	blue	Jun			average	cool
24 in.	blue	Jun			average	cool
18 in.	blue	May–Jun			fine	cool
18 in.	blue	Apr–May			fine	cool
15 in.	blue	May–Jun	yellow	spring/summer/autumn	fine	cool
15 in.	white	May	yellow	spring/summer/autumn	fine	warm
24 in.	blue	Jun–Aug			average	cool
18 in.	white	Jun–Aug			average	warm or cool
3–4 ft.	purple	Aug–Sep			average	cool

	TYPE	ZONE	FORM	HEIGHT
Viburnum plicatum var. tomentosum 'Mariesii' Excellent three-season shrub. Outstanding layered habit.	shrub	5–7(8)	mound	8–10 ft.
Viola 'Molly Sanderson' Too cool for words are these black flowers with the yellow eye that can be effectively used in warm or cool color schemes. Particularly striking underplanted among yellow-foliaged low shrubs. Plate 172.	perennial	5–8	mound	6 in.
Viola 'Purple Showers' Great to use for underplanting or in a stone path.	perennial	5–8	mound	6 in.
Viola labradorica A great purple-foliaged violet used as the lower layer in a mixed garden. Can frost heave.	perennial	2–8	mound	3 in.
Vitex agnus-castus var. latifolia Interesting foliage form and texture as well as flower color. This hardier form is still killed to the base in severe winters in zone 5. Prune above visible growth in spring. Plate 76.	shrub	5–8	vase	6–8 ft.
Vitis vinifera 'Purpurea' Such a cool-colored vine but not vigorous or reliably hardy in zone 5 gardens. Nice interplanted with yellow-foliaged vines.	woody vine	(5)6–9	climbing	10–15 ft.
Yucca filamentosa 'Color Guard' Bold texture and interesting color addition to the border. Plate 200.	shrub	4–9	vertical	2–3 ft.
Yucca flaccida 'Golden Sword' Bright, bold addition to borders. Adds weight to a design. Plate 7.	shrub	5–9	vertical	2–3 ft.
Zinnia haageana 'Orange Star' Nice. Brings bright orange color to ground level.	annual		mound	10 in.

WIDTH	FLOWER COLOR	FLOWERING MONTH	FOLIAGE COLOR	FOLIAGE INTEREST	TEXTURE	DESIGN COLOR
9–12 ft.	white	May	purple	autumn	average	warm or cool
6 in.	black	Jun–Sep			fine	warm or cool
6 in.	purple	Jun–Sep			fine	cool
6 in.	purple	May–Jun	purple	year-round	fine	cool
6–8 ft.	blue	Jul–Sep			fine	cool
10–15 ft.			purple	spring/summer/autumn	bold	warm or cool
2 ft.	white	Jul–Aug	green/yellow	year-round	bold	warm
2 ft.	white	Jul–Aug	green/yellow	year-round	bold	warm
15 in.	orange	Jun–Sep			average	warm

PURPLE FLOWERS

List includes plants with magenta (violet-red) flowers.

Spring-blooming

Shrub
Syringa meyeri

Woody vine
Clematis 'Elsa Späth'

Perennial
Arisaema sikokianum
Baptisia 'Purple Smoke'
Glaucidium palmatum
Helleborus Royal Heritage™
Hesperis matronalis
Iris 'Perfume Counter'
Iris sibirica 'Caesar's Brother'
Iris sibirica 'Pirate Prince'
Mazus reptans
Papaver orientale 'Patty's Plum'
Phlox divaricata 'Eco Texas Purple'
Phlox divaricata 'Sweet Lilac'
Sisyrinchium 'Quaint and Queer'
Sisyrinchium bermudianum
Trillium erectum
Viola labradorica

Hardy bulb
Allium hollandicum (aflatunense)
    'Purple Sensation'
Fritillaria persica
Tulipa 'Couleur Cardinal'

Summer-blooming

Shrub
Amorpha canescens
Buddleia davidii 'Black Knight'
Cotinus coggygria 'Velvet Cloak'
Rosa 'Ausvelvet' (The Prince®)
Rosa 'Nuits de Young'

Woody vine
Clematis 'Polish Spirit'
Clematis 'Royal Velours'

Perennial
Acanthus spinosus
Angelica gigas
Astilbe chinensis 'Purple Candle'
Astilbe chinensis var. taquetii 'Superba'
Campanula 'Kent Belle'
Delphinium exaltatum
Geranium 'Ann Folkard'
Geranium 'Phillippe Vapelle'
Geranium himalayense 'Plenum'
Geranium ×magnificum
Geranium phaeum 'Lily Lovell'
Geranium phaeum 'Samobor'
Geranium platypetalum
Geranium psilostemon
Geranium renardii
Geranium sanguineum 'New Hampshire'
Geranium wlassovianum
Gladiolus communis ssp. byzantinus
Hemerocallis 'Siloam Royal Prince'
Hosta 'Blue Cadet'
Hosta 'Fragrant Blue'
Hosta 'Halcyon'
Hosta 'Krossa Regal'
Hosta 'Lemon Lime'
Hosta 'Night Before Christmas'
Hosta 'Patriot'
Hosta 'Paul's Glory'
Hosta 'Sum and Substance'
Hosta 'Sun Power'
Knautia macedonica
Lavandula angustifolia 'Munstead'
Lavandula ×intermedia 'Grosso'
Liatris spicata 'Kobold'
Limonium platyphyllum 'Violetta'
Linaria 'Natalie'
Linaria purpurea
Lobelia 'Grape Knee High'
Lobelia 'Purple Towers'
Lobelia 'Ruby Slippers'
Lychnis coronaria
Monarda 'Violet Queen'
Nepeta 'Six Hills Giant'
Nepeta grandiflora 'Bramdean'
Nepeta racemosa 'Walker's Low'
Origanum laevigatum 'Herrenhausen'
Passiflora incarnata
Penstemon ×mexicale 'Pike's Peak Purple'
Perovskia atriplicifolia
Perovskia atriplicifolia 'Longin'
Phlox paniculata 'Laura'
Phlox paniculata 'Look Again'
Phlox paniculata 'The King'
Phytolacca polyandra
Salvia nemorosa 'Ostfriesland' (East Friesland)
Salvia nemorosa 'Purple Glory'
Salvia nemorosa 'Pusztaflamme' (plumosa)
Salvia ×sylvestris 'Mainacht' (May night)
Salvia verticillata 'Purple Rain'
Sanguisorba tenuifolia 'Purpurea'
Stachys byzantina
Stachys byzantina 'Countess Helen von Stein'
Stachys byzantina 'Primrose Heron'
Stachys macrantha
Stokesia laevis 'Purple Parasols'
Thalictrum aquilegiifolium 'Thundercloud'
Thalictrum rochebruneanum
Thymus ×citriodorus
Thymus ×citriodorus 'Lemon Green'
Thymus pseudolanuginosus
Tradescantia (Andersoniana Group)
    'Purple Profusion'
Verbena hastata
Veronicastrum virginicum 'Fascination'
Viola 'Purple Showers'

Annual
Angelonia angustifolia 'Purple Pinnacles'
Brachyscome 'Ultra'
Celosia spicata 'Flamingo Purple'
Cerinthe major 'Purpurascens'
Cynara cardunculus
Eschscholzia californica 'Purple Gleam'
Eucomis comosa 'Sparkling Burgundy'
Gomphrena haageana 'Lavender Lady'
Papaver somniferum
Papaver somniferum 'Lauren's Grape'
Salvia 'Purple Majesty'
Salvia leucantha
Verbena 'Homestead Purple'
Verbena bonariensis

Annual vine
Lablab purpureus
Lathyrus odoratus
Rhodochiton atrosanguineus
Thunbergia battiscombei

Hardy bulb
Allium carinatum ssp. pulchellum
Allium cristophii
Allium schubertii
Allium sphaerocephalon

Tender bulb
Gladiolus 'Violetta'

Autumn-blooming

Perennial
Aster novae-angliae 'Hella Lacy'
Aster novae-angliae 'Hillside'
Aster novae-angliae 'Purple Dome'

PURPLE FRUIT

Shrub
Aralia elata 'Aureovariegata'
Callicarpa dichotoma 'Issai'

Woody vine
Vitis vinifera 'Purpurea'

Annual vine
Lablab 'Purpureus'

RED FLOWERS

Spring-blooming

Shrub
Calycanthus floridus

Perennial
Epimedium ×rubrum
Heuchera 'Raspberry Regal'
Paeonia 'America'
Paeonia 'Burma Ruby'
Papaver orientale 'Feuerriese'
Rheum palmatum var. tanguticum

Hardy bulb
Tulipa 'Burgundy Lace'
Tulipa 'Carmine Parrot'
Tulipa 'Uncle Tom'
Tulipa clusiana var. chrysantha

Tender bulb
Amorphophallus konjac

Summer-blooming

Shrub
Rosa 'Champlain'
Rosa 'F. J. Grootendorst'

Perennial
Crocosmia 'Lucifer'
Dianthus barbatus 'Sooty'
Dianthus deltoides 'Leuchtfunk' (flashing light)
Helenium 'Moerheim Beauty'
Hemerocallis 'Red Razzamatazz'
Hemerocallis 'Scarlet Romance'
Hemerocallis 'Sundried Tomatoes'
Hibiscus moscheutos 'Lord Baltimore'
Lilium 'Conquistador'
Lilium 'Montenegro'
Lilium 'Scarlet Emperor'
Lobelia 'Dark Crusader'
Lobelia 'Queen Victoria'
Lobelia 'Royal Robe'
Monarda 'Jacob Cline'
Papaver nudicaule 'Red Sails'
Phlox paniculata 'Tenor'
Sedum 'Herbstfreude' (autumn joy)

Sedum telephium ssp. maximum
  'Atropurpureum'
Silene regia

Annual
Alstroemeria psittacina
Antirrhinum majus 'Rocket Red'
Arctotis ×hybrida 'Dark Red'
Bouvardia ternifolia
Cosmos atrosanguineus
Fuchsia 'Gartenmeister Bonstedt'
Papaver rhoeas
Papaver somniferum 'Pepperbox'
Pennisetum setaceum 'Rubrum'
Salvia coccinea 'Lady in Red'
Scabiosa atropurpurea 'Ace of Spades'
Tropaeolum majus 'Tip Top Mahogany'
Verbena Temari® Red

Annual vine
Ipomoea lobata (Mina lobata)

Tropical
Canna 'Black Knight'
Canna 'Roi Humbert' (red King Humbert)
Canna indica 'Red Stripe'

Hardy bulb
Dichelostemma ida-maia

Tender bulb
Dahlia 'Arabian Night'
Dahlia 'Bishop of Llandaff'
Gladiolus 'Atom'
Scadoxus multiflorus
Tigridia pavonia 'Speciosa'

RED OR RED-ORANGE FRUIT

Tree
Cornus kousa
Magnolia virginiana

Shrub
Ilex ×meserveae 'Mesog' (China girl)
Ilex verticillata 'Christmas Cheer'
Ilex verticillata 'Winter Red'

Woody vine
Lonicera periclymenum 'Graham Thomas'
Lonicera sempervirens 'Blanche Sandman'

Tropical
Ricinus communis
Ricinus communis 'Carmencita'

PINK FLOWERS

Spring-blooming

Shrub
Daphne ×burkwoodii 'Carol Mackie'
Rhododendron 'Northern Starburst'

Woody vine
Clematis 'Hagley Hybrid'
Clematis alpina 'Constance'
Clematis macropetala 'Markham's Pink'

Perennial
Ajuga reptans 'Purple Torch'
Dicentra 'Luxuriant'
Dicentra spectabilis 'Gold Heart'
Helleborus orientalis
Paeonia 'Monsieur Jules Elie'
Paeonia obovata
Papaver orientale 'Lighthouse'

Hardy bulb
Tulipa 'Angelique'

Summer-blooming

Shrub
Callicarpa dichotoma 'Issai'
Rosa 'Hansa'
Rosa Lyda Rose™
Rosa 'Meidomonac'
Rosa 'Nearly Wild'
Rosa 'The Fairy'
Rosa multiflora 'Grevillei' (seven sisters' rose)
Rosa rugosa

Perennial
Achillea 'Heidi'
Astilbe chinensis 'Veronica Klose'
Echinacea purpurea
Eupatorium purpureum ssp. maculatum
  'Gateway'
Geranium macrorrhizum 'Ingwersen's Variety'
Geranium ×oxonianum 'Claridge Druce'
Lathyrus latifolius
Origanum 'Kent Beauty'
Phlox paniculata 'Fesselballon'
Phlox paniculata 'Tracy's Treasure'
Rodgersia pinnata
Scabiosa 'Pink Mist'

Annual
Papaver rhoeas Angels' Choir

Autumn-blooming

Perennial
Anemone ×hybrida 'Queen Charlotte'
Anemone ×hybrida 'September Charm'

Hardy bulb
Colchicum speciosum

RED, PURPLE, OR BRONZE FOLIAGE

Spring interest

Shrub
Hypericum androsaemum 'Albury Purple'

Perennial
Euphorbia cyparissias 'Fen's Ruby'
Euphorbia ×martinii
Geranium pratense 'Victor Reiter Jr.'
Helleborus orientalis (single black)

Annual vine
Rhodochiton atrosanguineus

Spring/summer interest

Tree
Acer palmatum var. dissectum Dissectum
  Atropurpureum Group

Autumn interest

Tree
Acer griseum
Amelanchier ×grandiflora 'Autumn Brilliance'
Cornus kousa

Shrub
Fothergilla gardenii
Hydrangea quercifolia
Hydrangea quercifolia 'Snowflake'
Ilex verticillata 'Winter Red'
Itea virginica
Itea virginica 'Henry's Garnet'
Microbiota decussata
Viburnum plicatum var. tomentosum 'Mariesii'

Perennial
Aquilegia alpina
Ceratostigma plumbaginoides
Epimedium ×rubrum
Epimedium ×warleyense
Euphorbia amygdaloides 'Purpurea'

Euphorbia ×martinii
Geranium psilostemon
Geranium sanguineum 'New Hampshire'
Geranium wlassovianum
Miscanthus 'Purpurascens'
Oenothera fruticosa ssp. glauca 'Sonnenwende'
Origanum laevigatum 'Herrenhausen'

Annual
Brassica oleracea

Spring/summer/autumn interest

Tree
Fagus sylvatica 'Purpurea Pendula'
Fagus sylvatica 'Tricolor'

Shrub
Berberis thunbergii var. atropurpurea
  'Bailtwo' (Burgundy Carousel™)
Berberis thunbergii var. atropurpurea
  'Gentry Cultivar' (Royal Burgundy™)
Berberis thunbergii var. atropurpurea
  'Rose Glow'
Berberis thunbergii var. atropurpurea
  'Royal Cloak'
Cotinus coggygria 'Velvet Cloak'

Woody vine
Vitis vinifera 'Purpurea'

Perennial
Cimicifuga ramosa 'Brunette'
Cimicifuga ramosa 'Hillside Black Beauty'
Cryptotaenia japonica f. atropurpurea
Euphorbia dulcis 'Chameleon'
Foeniculum vulgare 'Purpureum'
Geranium phaeum 'Samobor'
Imperata cylindrica var. koenigii 'Red Baron'
Ligularia dentata 'Dark Beauty'
Lobelia 'Dark Crusader'
Lobelia 'Queen Victoria'
Lobelia 'Royal Robe'
Persicaria microcephala 'Red Dragon'
Plantago major 'Rubrifolia'
Rheum palmatum var. tanguticum
Rumex sanguineus
Sedum telephium ssp. maximum
  'Atropurpureum'
Tiarella cordifolia 'Ninja'

Annual
Alternanthera dentata 'Rubiginosa'
Atriplex hortensis var. rubra
Beta vulgaris 'Bull's Blood'
Beta vulgaris 'Ruby Queen'
Celosia spicata 'Flamingo Purple'

Red, Purple, or Bronze Foliage,
spring/summer/autumn interest, cont.

Eucomis comosa 'Sparkling Burgundy'
Fuchsia 'Gartenmeister Bonstedt'
Ipomoea batatas 'Ace of Spades'
Ipomoea batatas 'Blackie'
Lactuca 'Merlot'
Ocimum 'African Blue'
Ocimum basilicum 'Red Rubin'
Pennisetum setaceum 'Rubrum'
Perilla frutescens var. crispa
Solenostemon 'Burgundy Columns'
Solenostemon 'Burgundy Giant'
Solenostemon 'Purple Emperor'
Solenostemon 'Saturn'

Annual vine
Lablab purpureus

Tropical
Caladium 'Florida Cardinal'
Caladium 'Florida Sweetheart'
Canna 'Black Knight'
Canna 'Roi Humbert' (red King Humbert)
Canna indica 'Red Stripe'
Colocasia esculenta 'Black Beauty'
Colocasia esculenta 'Black Magic'
Colocasia esculenta 'Fontanesii'
Colocasia esculenta 'Illustris'
Euphorbia cotinifolia
Hibiscus acetosella 'Red Shield'
Musa zebrina
Phormium 'Bronze Baby'
Phormium 'Platt's Black'
Phormium cookianum 'Chocolate'
Ricinus communis 'Carmencita'

Tender bulb
Dahlia 'Bishop of Llandaff'
Dahlia 'Ellen Houston'

Year-round interest

Perennial
Anthriscus sylvestris 'Ravenswing'
Carex buchananii
Heuchera 'Chocolate Ruffles'
Heuchera 'Plum Pudding'
Heuchera 'Velvet Night'
Heuchera micrantha var. diversifolia
    'Palace Purple'
Penstemon digitalis 'Husker Red'
Veronica 'Waterperry Blue'
Viola labradorica

ORANGE FLOWERS

Spring-blooming

Perennial
Epimedium ×warleyense
Helianthemum 'Fire Dragon'
Papaver orientale 'Curlilocks'
Papaver orientale 'Harvest Moon'
Papaver orientale 'Prince of Orange'
Papaver orientale 'Saffron'
Papaver orientale 'Turkenlouis'

Hardy bulb
Tulipa 'Blushing Lady'
Tulipa 'Temple of Beauty'

Summer-blooming

Shrub
Potentilla fruticosa 'Sunset'

Woody vine
Campsis ×tagliabuana 'Madame Galen'
Lonicera sempervirens 'Blanche Sandman'

Perennial
Agastache rupestris
Asclepias tuberosa
Belamcanda chinensis
Crocosmia 'Emberglow'
Dianthus ×allwoodii 'Danielle Marie'
Euphorbia griffithii 'Fireglow'
Hemerocallis 'Staghorn Sumac'
Kniphofia 'Alcazar'
Kniphofia 'Prince Igor'
Kniphofia triangularis
Lilium 'Pretender'
Lilium 'Royal Perfume'
Lilium 'Sunset'
Lilium henryi
Lilium lancifolium var. splendens
Lilium pumilum
Lychnis ×arkwrightii 'Vesuvius'
Phlox paniculata 'Orange Perfection'

Annual
Alstroemeria aurea 'Orange King'
Arctotis ×hybrida 'Flame'
Calendula officinalis 'Orange King'
Eschscholzia californica
Leonotis menthifolia
Papaver somniferum 'Burnt Orange'
Zinnia haageana 'Orange Star'

Annual vine
Lathyrus odoratus 'Henry Eckford'

Tropical
Canna 'Orange Punch'
Canna 'Phasion'
Canna 'Striata' (Pretoria)
Hedychium coccineum

Tender bulb
Dahlia 'Ellen Houston'
Dahlia 'Orange Nugget'

ORANGE OR ORANGE-RED FRUIT

Shrub
Ilex verticillata 'Afterglow'
Rosa 'Hansa'
Rosa 'Meidomonac' (Bonica®)
Rosa rugosa

PEACH FLOWERS

Spring-blooming

Perennial
Paeonia 'Coral Sunset'
Paeonia 'Etched Salmon'
Papaver orientale 'Derwisch'

Hardy bulb
Narcissus 'Delnashaugh'
Narcissus 'Mary Gay Lirette'
Tulipa 'Apricot Parrot'

Summer-blooming

Shrub
Rosa 'Alchymist'
Rosa 'Ausbuff' (English Garden®)
Rosa 'Aussaucer' (Evelyn®)

Perennial
Achillea 'Salmon Beauty'
Alcea rosea 'Peaches and Dreams'
Astilbe ×rosea 'Peach Blossom'
Digitalis purpurea 'Apricot'
Gladiolus ×gandavensis 'Boone'
Hemerocallis 'Alluring Peach'
Hemerocallis 'Carefree Peach'
Hemerocallis 'Peach Fairy'
Hemerocallis 'Welcome Mat'
Lilium 'Apricot Brandy'
Lilium 'Eden's Dandy'
Lilium 'Shirley'
Lychnis cognata

Verbascum 'Jackie'

Annual
Portulaca grandiflora 'Sundial Peach'
Tropaeolum majus 'Apricot Trifle'
Tropaeolum majus 'Blush Double'
Verbena 'Romance Apricot'

Tropical
Canna 'Omega'
Canna 'Panache'

Autumn-blooming

Perennial
Chrysanthemum 'Pumpkin Harvest'
Chrysanthemum 'Single Apricot'
Chrysanthemum 'Single Peach'
Chrysanthemum 'Viette's Apricot Glow'

YELLOW OR TAN FLOWERS

Spring-blooming

Tree
Betula utilis var. jacquemontii

Perennial
Baptisia sphaerocarpa
Epimedium davidii
Euphorbia ×martinii
Euphorbia polychroma
Helianthemum (double yellow)
Iris 'Flavescens'
Iris pseudacorus 'Variegata'
Iris sibirica 'Butter and Sugar'
Packera aurea (Senecio aureus)
Paeonia 'Prairie Moon'
Saruma henryi
Stylophorum diphyllum

Hardy bulb
Eranthis hyemalis
Erythronium 'Pagoda'
Narcissus 'Mint Julep'
Narcissus 'Stratosphere'
Narcissus 'Tahiti'
Tulipa 'Big Smile'
Tulipa 'Fringed Elegance'
Tulipa batalinii

Summer-blooming

Shrub

Genista tinctoria 'Royal Gold'
Hypericum androsaemum 'Albury Purple'
Rosa 'Ausmas' (Graham Thomas®)
Rosa 'Scrivluv' (Baby Love®)
Rosa ×harisonii 'Harison's Yellow'

Woody vine

Lonicera periclymenum 'Graham Thomas'

Perennial

Achillea 'Anblo' (Anthea)
Achillea filipendulina 'Altgold'
Aconitum 'Ivorine'
Aconitum lycoctonum ssp. neapolitanum
Alcea rugosa
Alstroemeria 'Sweet Laura'
Artemisia 'Huntington'
Artemisia 'Powis Castle'
Artemisia 'Silverado'
Artemisia absinthium 'Lambrook Silver'
Asclepias tuberosa 'Hello Yellow'
Belamcanda chinensis 'Hello Yellow'
Buphthalmum speciosum
Calamagrostis ×acutiflora 'Karl Foerster'
Calamagrostis ×acutiflora 'Overdam'
Calamagrostis brachytricha
Cephalaria gigantea
Coreopsis auriculata
Coreopsis grandiflora 'Walcoreop'
   (flying saucers)
Coreopsis tripteris
Coreopsis verticillata 'Moonbeam'
Coreopsis verticillata 'Zagreb'
Crocosmia 'Blacro' (Jenny Bloom)
Crocosmia ×crocosmiiflora 'Norwich Canary'
Crocosmia ×crocosmiiflora 'Solfatare'
Crocosmia ×crocosmiiflora 'Venus'
Deschampsia cespitosa 'Goldgehänge'
Digitalis grandiflora
Digitalis lutea
Euphorbia 'Golden Towers'
Euphorbia amygdaloides 'Purpurea'
Euphorbia cyparissias 'Fen's Ruby'
Euphorbia dulcis 'Chameleon'
Festuca glauca 'Elijah Blue'
Foeniculum vulgare 'Purpureum'
Gladiolus ×gandavensis
Helenium 'Kugelsonne'
Helianthus 'Lemon Queen'
Helianthus 'Mellow Yellow'
Helictotrichon sempervirens 'Saphirsprudel'
   (sapphire fountain)
Heliopsis helianthoides var. scabra
   'Sommersonne' (summer sun)
Hemerocallis 'Happy Returns'

Hemerocallis 'Toy Trumpets'
Hemerocallis 'Yellow Lollipop'
Hystrix patula
Kniphofia 'Little Maid'
Kniphofia 'Primrose Beauty'
Kniphofia 'Royal Standard'
Kniphofia 'Shining Sceptre'
Kniphofia caulescens
Kniphofia citrina
Ligularia 'The Rocket'
Ligularia dentata 'Dark Beauty'
Ligularia dentata 'Desdemona'
Ligularia wilsoniana
Lilium 'Connecticut King'
Lilium 'Grand Cru'
Lilium 'Royal Justice'
Luzula nivea
Miscanthus 'Purpurascens
Miscanthus sinensis var. condensatus
   'Cosmopolitan'
Miscanthus sinensis 'Gracillimus'
Miscanthus sinensis 'Malepartus'
Miscanthus sinensis 'Morning Light'
Molinia caerulea ssp. arundinacea 'Skyracer'
Nymphaea 'Marliacea Chromatella'
Oenothera fremontii 'Lemon Silver'
Oenothera fruticosa ssp. glauca 'Sonnenwende'
Panicum virgatum 'Dallas Blues'
Panicum virgatum 'Heavy Metal'
Panicum virgatum 'Rehbraun'
Patrinia scabiosifolia
Pennisetum alopecuroides 'Hameln'
Phlomis russeliana
Rudbeckia fulgida var. speciosa (newmannii)
Rudbeckia maxima
Rudbeckia triloba
Ruta graveolens 'Blue Beauty'
Scabiosa columbaria var. ochroleuca
Schizachyrium scoparium 'The Blues'
Sedum acre 'Aureum'
Sorghastrum nutans 'Sioux Blue'
Stokesia laevis 'Mary Gregory'
Thermopsis villosa
Verbascum bombyciferum

Annual

Lysimachia congestiflora 'Variegata'
Melampodium paludosum 'Million Gold'
Rudbeckia hirta 'Irish Eyes'
Tropaeolum majus Alaska Series
Tropaeolum majus 'Moonlight'

Tropical

Hedychium 'Daniel Weeks'

Hardy bulb

Allium moly 'Jeannine'
Eremurus ×isabellinus 'Pinokkio'

Tender bulb

Dahlia 'Susette'
Hymenocallis 'Sulphur Queen'

Autumn-blooming

Perennial

Calamagrostis ×acutiflora 'Karl Foerster'
Calamagrostis ×acutiflora 'Overdam'
Calamagrostis brachytricha
Chrysanthemum 'Autumn Moon'
Festuca glauca 'Elijah Blue'
Helianthus salicifolius
Helictotrichon sempervirens 'Saphirsprudel'
   (sapphire fountain)
Impatiens omeiana
Miscanthus 'Purpurascens
Miscanthus sinensis var. condensatus
   'Cosmopolitan'
Miscanthus sinensis 'Gracillimus'
Miscanthus sinensis 'Malepartus'
Miscanthus sinensis 'Morning Light'
Molinia caerulea ssp. arundinacea 'Skyracer'
Panicum virgatum 'Dallas Blues'
Panicum virgatum 'Heavy Metal'
Panicum virgatum 'Rehbraun'
Pennisetum alopecuroides 'Hameln'
Schizachyrium scoparium 'The Blues'
Solidago 'Golden Spangles'
Solidago rugosa 'Fireworks
×Solidaster luteus 'Lemore'
Sorghastrum nutans 'Sioux Blue'

YELLOW FRUIT

Tree

Malus 'Lanzam' (Lancelot®)

Perennial

Passiflora incarnata

YELLOW OR YELLOW-VARIEGATED FOLIAGE

Autumn interest

Tree

Acer palmatum 'Sango-kaku'
Chionanthus virginicus
Ginkgo biloba 'Autumn Gold'
Magnolia virginiana
Malus 'Lanzam' (Lancelot®)

Shrub

Aesculus parviflora
Calycanthus floridus
Clethra alnifolia
Pinus contorta 'Chief Joseph'

Perennial

Amsonia ciliata
Amsonia elliptica
Amsonia hubrichtii
Amsonia tabernaemontana
Molinia caerulea ssp. arundinacea 'Skyracer'
Osmunda regalis
Panicum virgatum 'Dallas Blues'
Panicum virgatum 'Heavy Metal'
Panicum virgatum 'Rehbraun'
Phytolacca polyandra
Platycodon grandiflorus 'Double Blue'
Platycodon grandiflorus 'Komachi'
Sorghastrum nutans 'Sioux Blue'

Spring/summer/autumn interest

Tree

Catalpa bignonioides 'Aurea'

Shrub

Aralia elata 'Aureovariegata'
Berberis thunbergii 'Monler' (Gold Nugget™)
Berberis thunbergii 'Monry' (Sunsation™)
Caryopteris ×clandonensis 'Worcester Gold'
Sambucus racemosa 'Sutherland Gold'

Perennial

Acorus gramineus 'Minimus Aureus'
Acorus gramineus 'Oborozuki'
Acorus gramineus 'Ogon'
Carex dolichostachya 'Kaga Nishiki'
   (gold fountains)
Carex elata 'Aurea' (Bowles' golden)
Dicentra spectabilis 'Gold Heart'
Festuca glauca 'Golden Toupee'
Geranium 'Ann Folkard'
Geranium 'Salome'
Hakonechloa macra 'Aureola'
Hosta 'Lemon Lime'
Hosta 'Midas Touch'
Hosta 'Paul's Glory'
Hosta 'Sum and Substance'
Hosta 'Sun Power'
Humulus lupulus 'Bianca'
Iris pallida 'Variegata'
Iris pseudacorus 'Variegata'
Origanum vulgare 'Aureum'
Stachys byzantina 'Primrose Heron'
Symphytum 'Goldsmith'
Tanacetum 'Golden Feathers'

Yellow or Yellow-Variegated Foliage,
spring/summer/autumn interest, cont.

Thymus ×citriodorus 'Lemon Green'
Veronica prostrata 'Trehane'
Veronica repens 'Sunshine'

Annual
Beta vulgaris 'Golden'
Helichrysum petiolare 'Limelight'
Ipomoea batatas 'Margarita'
Lysimachia congestiflora 'Variegata'
Solenostemon 'Penny'

Tropical
Canna 'Striata' (Pretoria)
Duranta erecta 'Golden Edge'
Phormium 'Yellow Wave'

Year-round interest

Tree
Picea orientalis 'Skylands'

Shrub
Chamaecyparis obtusa 'Fernspray Gold'
Chamaecyparis pisifera 'Golden Mop'
Pinus densiflora 'Oculus Draconis'
Yucca filamentosa 'Color Guard'
Yucca flaccida 'Golden Sword'

Perennial
Lysimachia nummularia 'Aurea'

BLUE FLOWERS

Spring-blooming

Perennial
Amsonia ciliata
Amsonia elliptica
Amsonia hubrichtii
Aquilegia alpina
Baptisia australis
Brunnera macrophylla
Iris 'Sugar Blues'
Iris foetidissima
Iris pallida 'Variegata'
Iris sibirica 'Dianne's Daughter'
Iris sibirica 'Orville Fay'
Iris sibirica 'Skywings'
Iris sibirica 'Vi Luihn'
Mertensia pulmonarioides (virginica)
Phlox divaricata
Phlox divaricata 'Dirigo Ice'
Phlox divaricata ssp. laphamii

Phlox divaricata 'London Grove Blue'
Phlox stolonifera 'Blue Ridge'
Pulmonaria 'Majesté'
Pulmonaria 'Viette's Deep Blue Sea'
Symphytum 'Goldsmith'
Veronica 'Waterperry Blue'
Veronica peduncularis 'Georgia Blue'
Veronica repens 'Sunshine'

Hardy bulb
Allium caeruleum
Camassia leichtlinii ssp. suksdorfii 'Blauwe
      Donau' (blue Danube)
Chionodoxa forbesii (luciliae) Siehei Group
Crocus chrysanthus 'Blue Bird'
Iris 'Blue Magic'
Iris reticulata 'Harmony'
Puschkinia scilloides
Tulipa 'Blue Heron'
Tulipa 'Blue Parrot'

Summer-blooming

Shrub
Buddleia 'Lochinch'
Buddleia davidii 'Mongo' (Nanho blue)
Caryopteris ×clandonensis
Caryopteris ×clandonensis 'Longwood Blue'
Caryopteris ×clandonensis 'Worcester Gold'
Vitex agnus-castus var. latifolia

Perennial
Aconitum 'Bressingham Spire'
Aconitum carmichaelii (Wilsonii Group)
      'Spätlese'
Aconitum episcopale
Agastache 'Blue Fortune'
Amsonia tabernaemontana
Campanula 'Birch Hybrid'
Campanula 'Constellation'
Campanula 'Dwarf Tornado'
Campanula persicifolia 'Chettle Charm'
Campanula rapunculoides
Campanula rotundifolia 'Olympica'
Centaurea montana
Ceratostigma plumbaginoides
Clematis integrifolia
Cynoglossum amabile 'Firmament'
Delphinium 'Centurion Sky Blue'
Delphinium ×bellamosum
Delphinium cashmerianum
Dracocephalum ruyschiana
Echinops bannaticus 'Taplow Blue'
Echinops ritro 'Blue Glow'
Echinops ritro 'Veitch's Blue'
Eryngium amethystinum
Eryngium planum 'Blaukappe'
Eryngium variifolium

Galega ×hartlandii 'Lady Wilson'
Gentiana septemfida var. lagodechiana
Gentiana triflora 'Royal Blue'
Geranium 'Brookside'
Geranium 'Johnson's Blue'
Geranium 'Salome'
Geranium pratense 'Mrs. Kendall Clark'
Geranium pratense 'Victor Reiter Jr.'
Hyssopus officinalis
Linum perenne 'Blau Saphir' (blue sapphire)
Lobelia siphilitica
Nepeta ×faassenii
Nepeta sibirica 'Souvenir d'André Chaudron'
Phlox paniculata 'Katherine'
Platycodon grandiflorus 'Double Blue'
Platycodon grandiflorus 'Komachi'
Polemonium caeruleum 'Blanjou' (brise d'Anjou)
Salvia ×sylvestris 'Blauhügel' (blue hill)
Salvia ×sylvestris 'Blaukönigin' (blue queen)
Salvia ×sylvestris 'Viola Klose'
Scabiosa Butterfly Blue®
Stokesia laevis 'Klaus Jelitto'
Stokesia laevis 'Omega Skyrocket'
Tradescantia Andersoniana Group
Tradescantia (Andersoniana Group)
      'Zwanenburg Blue'
Veronica 'Goodness Grows'
Veronica austriaca ssp. teucrium
      'Crater Lake Blue'
Veronica austriaca ssp. teucrium 'Royal Blue'
Veronica gentianoides 'Nana'
Veronica prostrata 'Trehane'
Veronica spicata 'Blue Charm'

Annual
Ageratum houstonianum 'Blue Horizon'
Angelonia 'Blue Pacific'
Consolida ajacis 'Blue Spire'
Plectranthus argentatus
Salvia 'Indigo Spires'
Salvia guaranitica
Salvia guaranitica 'Black and Blue'
Salvia patens

Annual vine
Ipomoea tricolor 'Heavenly Blue'
Lathyrus odoratus 'King Size Navy Blue'

Hardy bulb
Triteleia laxa 'Queen Fabiola'

Tender bulb
Agapanthus 'Bressingham Blue'

Autumn-blooming

Perennial
Aster 'Climax'

Aster laevis 'Bluebird'
Aster novae-angliae 'Wild Light Blue'
Aster oblongifolius var. angustatus
      'Raydon's Favorite'
Aster tataricus 'Jindai'
Salvia azurea var. pitcheri

BLUE FRUIT

Tree
Amelanchier ×grandiflora 'Autumn Brilliance'
Chionanthus virginicus

Woody vine
Ampelopsis glandulosa var. brevipedunculata
      'Elegans'

Perennial
Paeonia obovata

BLUE FOLIAGE

Spring/summer interest

Perennial
Panicum virgatum 'Dallas Blues'
Panicum virgatum 'Heavy Metal'
Sorghastrum nutans 'Sioux Blue'

Annual
Papaver somniferum
Papaver somniferum 'Black Peony'
Papaver somniferum 'Burnt Orange'
Papaver somniferum 'Lauren's Grape'
Papaver somniferum 'Pepperbox'

Spring/summer/
autumn interest

Perennial
Dicentra 'Luxuriant'
Eryngium amethystinum
Eryngium planum 'Blaukappe'
Euphorbia ×martinii
Hosta 'Big Daddy'
Hosta 'Blue Cadet'
Hosta 'Fragrant Blue'
Hosta 'Halcyon'
Hosta 'Krossa Regal'
Hosta 'Love Pat'
Kniphofia caulescens
Lathyrus latifolius
Rudbeckia maxima
Ruta graveolens 'Blue Beauty'

Schizachyrium scoparium 'The Blues'
Thalictrum aquilegiifolium 'Thundercloud'

Annual
Cerinthe major 'Purpurascens'
Eschscholzia californica
Eschscholzia californica 'Purple Gleam'

Year-round interest

Tree
Abies lasiocarpa 'Arizonica Compacta'
Picea pungens 'Iseli Foxtail'
Picea pungens 'Thomsen'
Pinus cembra 'Silver Sheen'
Pinus flexilis 'Vanderwolf's Pyramid'
Pinus parviflora 'Glauca'
Pinus sylvestris 'Fastigiata'
Pseudotsuga menziesii 'Astro Blue'

Shrub
Abies procera 'Glauca Prostrata'
Picea alcoquiana 'Howell's Tigertail'
Pinus parviflora 'Yatsubusa'
Pinus sylvestris 'Albyn'

Perennial
Festuca glauca 'Elijah Blue'
Helictotrichon sempervirens 'Saphirsprudel'
   (sapphire fountain)

GRAY OR SILVER FOLIAGE

Spring/summer/autumn interest

Shrub
Amorpha canescens
Buddleia 'Lochinch'
Buddleia davidii 'Mongo' (Nanho blue)
Caryopteris ×clandonensis
Caryopteris ×clandonensis 'Longwood Blue'

Perennial
Achillea 'Anblo' (Anthea)
Agastache rupestris
Artemisia 'Huntington'
Artemisia 'Powis Castle'
Artemisia 'Silverado'
Artemisia absinthium 'Lambrook Silver'
Athyrium niponicum var. pictum
Echinops bannaticus 'Taplow Blue'
Echinops ritro 'Blue Glow'
Echinops ritro 'Veitch's Blue'
Eryngium yuccifolium

Geranium 'Phillippe Vapelle'
Lamium maculatum 'White Nancy'
Lavandula angustifolia 'Munstead'
Lavandula ×intermedia 'Grosso'
Lychnis coronaria
Nepeta 'Six Hills Giant'
Nepeta ×faassenii
Nepeta grandiflora 'Bramdean'
Nepeta racemosa 'Walker's Low'
Nepeta sibirica 'Souvenir d'André Chaudron'
Oenothera fremontii 'Lemon Silver'
Origanum 'Kent Beauty'
Perovskia atriplicifolia
Perovskia atriplicifolia 'Longin'
Pulmonaria 'Majesté'
Salvia argentea
Salvia verticillata 'Purple Rain'
Stachys byzantina
Stachys byzantina 'Countess Helen von Stein'
Thymus pseudolanuginosus

Annual
Agave havardiana
Arctotis ×hybrida 'Dark Red'
Arctotis ×hybrida 'Flame'
Centaurea cineraria
Cynara cardunculus
Plectranthus amboinicus
Plectranthus argentatus

Year-round interest

Perennial
Helianthemum (double yellow)
Helianthemum 'Fire Dragon'
Verbascum bombyciferum

WHITE FLOWERS

Spring-blooming

Tree
Amelanchier ×grandiflora 'Autumn Brilliance'
Chionanthus virginicus
Cornus kousa
Magnolia virginiana
Malus 'Lanzam' (Lancelot®)

Shrub
Fothergilla gardenii
Rhododendron 'Chionoides'
Rhododendron 'Mist Maiden'
Viburnum plicatum var. tomentosum 'Mariesii'

Perennial
Anthriscus sylvestris 'Ravenswing'

Arum italicum ssp. italicum 'Marmoratum'
Galium odoratum
×Heucherella 'Silver Streak'
Iris sanguinea 'Snow Queen'
Iris sibirica 'White Swirl'
Lamium maculatum 'White Nancy'
Pachysandra procumbens
Phlox stolonifera 'Bruce's White'
Polygonatum odoratum 'Variegatum'
Rodgersia aesculifolia
Tiarella cordifolia 'Ninja'
Valeriana officinalis

Hardy bulb
Camassia leichtlinii 'Semiplena'
Narcissus 'Fragrant Rose'
Narcissus 'Petrel'
Narcissus 'Sir Winston Churchill'

Summer-blooming

Shrub
Aesculus parviflora
Aralia elata 'Aureovariegata'
Clethra alnifolia
Hydrangea quercifolia
Hydrangea quercifolia 'Snowflake'
Itea virginica
Itea virginica 'Henry's Garnet'
Lespedeza cuneata
Rosa 'Seafoam'
Yucca filamentosa 'Color Guard'
Yucca flaccida 'Golden Sword'

Woody vine
Clematis 'Lanuginosa Candida'
Hydrangea anomala ssp. petiolaris

Perennial
Aruncus dioicus
Astilbe ×arendsii 'Snowdrift'
Cimicifuga ramosa 'Brunette'
Cimicifuga ramosa 'Hillside Black Beauty'
Clematis recta
Cryptotaenia japonica f. atropurpurea
Gillenia stipulata
Heuchera 'Chocolate Ruffles'
Heuchera 'Plum Pudding'
Heuchera 'Velvet Night'
Heuchera micrantha var. diversifolia
   'Palace Purple'
Hosta 'Big Daddy'
Hosta 'Love Pat'
Hosta 'Midas Touch'
Hosta plantaginea 'Aphrodite'
Lilium 'Casa Blanca'
Penstemon digitalis 'Husker Red'
Persicaria microcephala 'Red Dragon'

Phlox paniculata 'David'
Phlox paniculata 'Pax' (peace)
Tanacetum 'Golden Feathers'
Veronica spicata 'Icicle'

Annual
Nierembergia scoparia 'Mont Blanc'
Nigella damascena Miss Jekyll Series

Tropical
Colocasia esculenta 'Fontanesii'

Autumn-blooming

Woody vine
Clematis terniflora

WHITE-VARIEGATED FOLIAGE

Spring interest

Perennial
Arum italicum ssp. italicum 'Marmoratum'

Spring/summer interest

Perennial
Polygonatum odoratum 'Variegatum'

Spring/summer/autumn interest

Shrub
Daphne ×burkwoodii 'Carol Mackie'

Woody vine
Ampelopsis glandulosa var. brevipedunculata
   'Elegans'

Perennial
Calamagrostis ×acutiflora 'Overdam'
Eryngium variifolium
Hosta 'Night Before Christmas'
Hosta 'Patriot'
Miscanthus sinensis var. condensatus
   'Cosmopolitan'
Miscanthus sinensis 'Morning Light'
Polemonium caeruleum 'Blanjou' (brise d'Anjou)

Annual
Tropaeolum majus Alaska Series

White-Variegated Foliage, cont.

Year-round interest

Perennial
Carex morrowii 'Ice Dance'
Carex morrowii 'Variegata'

GREEN FLOWERS

Spring-blooming

Perennial
Helleborus foetidus

Summer-blooming

Perennial
Alchemilla mollis
Eryngium yuccifolium

Annual
Nicotiana langsdorffii

Autumn-blooming

Perennial
Plantago major 'Rubrifolia'

BLACK FLOWERS

Spring-blooming

Perennial
Aquilegia vulgaris var. stellata 'Black Barlow'
Helleborus orientalis (single black)

Hardy bulb
Tulipa 'Black Parrot'
Tulipa 'Queen of Night'

Summer-blooming

Perennial
Alcea rosea 'The Watchman'
Viola 'Molly Sanderson'

Annual
Papaver somniferum 'Black Peony'

BLACK FRUIT

Shrub
Hypericum androsaemum 'Albury Purple'
Ilex glabra
Rosa 'Nuits de Young'
Rosa ×harisonii 'Harison's Yellow'
Viburnum plicatum var. tomentosum 'Mariesii'

Perennial
Baptisia 'Purple Smoke'
Baptisia australis
Belamcanda chinensis
Belamcanda chinensis 'Hello Yellow'
Phytolacca polyandra

COLOR SCHEMES

Warm

Tree
Acer griseum
Acer palmatum 'Sango-kaku'
Catalpa bignonioides 'Aurea'
Ginkgo biloba 'Autumn Gold'
Malus 'Lanzam' (Lancelot®)
Picea orientalis 'Skylands'

Shrub
Aralia elata 'Aureovariegata'
Berberis thunbergii 'Monler' (Gold Nugget™)
Berberis thunbergii 'Monry' (Sunsation™)
Chamaecyparis obtusa 'Fernspray Gold'
Chamaecyparis obtusa 'Mariesii'
Chamaecyparis pisifera 'Golden Mop'
Genista tinctoria 'Royal Gold'
Hypericum androsaemum 'Albury Purple'
Ilex ×meserveae 'Mesog' (China girl)
Ilex verticillata 'Afterglow'
Ilex verticillata 'Christmas Cheer'
Ilex verticillata 'Winter Red'
Pinus contorta 'Chief Joseph'
Pinus densiflora 'Oculus Draconis'
Potentilla fruticosa 'Sunset'
Rhododendron 'Chionoides'
Rosa 'Alchymist'
Rosa 'Ausbuff' (English Garden®)
Rosa 'Ausmas' (Graham Thomas®)
Rosa 'Aussaucer' (Evelyn®)
Rosa 'Champlain'
Rosa 'F. J. Grootendorst'
Rosa 'Scrivluv' (Baby Love®)
Rosa ×harisonii 'Harison's Yellow'
Sambucus racemosa 'Sutherland Gold'
Yucca filamentosa 'Color Guard'
Yucca flaccida 'Golden Sword'

Woody vine
Campsis ×tagliabuana 'Madame Galen'
Lonicera sempervirens 'Blanche Sandman'

Perennial
Achillea 'Anblo' (Anthea)
Achillea 'Heidi'
Achillea 'Salmon Beauty'
Achillea filipendulina 'Altgold'
Aconitum 'Ivorine'
Aconitum lycoctonum ssp. neapolitanum
Acorus gramineus 'Minimus Aureus'
Acorus gramineus 'Oborozuki'
Acorus gramineus 'Ogon'
Agastache rupestris
Alcea rosea 'Peaches and Dreams'
Alcea rugosa
Alstroemeria 'Sweet Laura'
Arum italicum ssp. italicum 'Marmoratum'
Asclepias tuberosa
Asclepias tuberosa 'Hello Yellow'
Baptisia sphaerocarpa
Belamcanda chinensis
Belamcanda chinensis 'Hello Yellow'
Buphthalmum speciosum
Carex buchananii
Carex dolichostachya 'Kaga Nishiki' (gold
    fountains)
Carex elata 'Aurea' (Bowles' golden)
Chrysanthemum 'Autumn Moon'
Chrysanthemum 'Pumpkin Harvest'
Chrysanthemum 'Single Apricot'
Chrysanthemum 'Single Peach'
Chrysanthemum 'Viette's Apricot Glow'
Coreopsis auriculata
Coreopsis grandiflora 'Walcoreop'
    (flying saucers)
Coreopsis tripteris
Coreopsis verticillata 'Moonbeam'
Coreopsis verticillata 'Zagreb'
Crocosmia 'Blacro' (Jenny Bloom)
Crocosmia 'Emberglow'
Crocosmia 'Lucifer'
Crocosmia ×crocosmiiflora 'Norwich Canary'
Crocosmia ×crocosmiiflora 'Solfatare'
Crocosmia ×crocosmiiflora 'Venus'
Deschampsia cespitosa 'Goldgehänge'
Dianthus ×allwoodii 'Danielle Marie'
Dianthus barbatus 'Sooty'
Dianthus deltoides 'Leuchtfunk' (flashing light)
Digitalis purpurea 'Apricot'
Epimedium davidii
Epimedium ×rubrum
Epimedium ×warleyense
Euphorbia 'Golden Towers'
Euphorbia amygdaloides 'Purpurea'
Euphorbia cyparissias 'Fen's Ruby'
Euphorbia dulcis 'Chameleon'

Euphorbia griffithii 'Fireglow'
Euphorbia polychroma
Festuca glauca 'Golden Toupee'
Foeniculum vulgare 'Purpureum'
Gladiolus ×gandavensis
Gladiolus ×gandavensis 'Boone'
Hakonechloa macra 'Aureola'
Helenium 'Kugelsonne'
Helenium 'Moerheim Beauty'
Helianthemum (double yellow)
Helianthemum 'Fire Dragon'
Helianthus 'Lemon Queen'
Helianthus 'Mellow Yellow'
Helianthus salicifolius
Heliopsis helianthoides var. scabra
    'Sommersonne' (summer sun)
Hemerocallis 'Carefree Peach'
Hemerocallis 'Happy Returns'
Hemerocallis 'Peach Fairy'
Hemerocallis 'Red Razzamatazz'
Hemerocallis 'Scarlet Romance'
Hemerocallis 'Staghorn Sumac'
Hemerocallis 'Sundried Tomatoes'
Hemerocallis 'Toy Trumpets'
Hemerocallis 'Welcome Mat'
Hemerocallis 'Yellow Lollipop'
Heuchera 'Raspberry Regal'
Hibiscus moscheutos 'Lord Baltimore'
Hosta 'Lemon Lime'
Hosta 'Midas Touch'
Hosta 'Sun Power'
Humulus lupulus 'Bianca'
Impatiens omeiana
Imperata cylindrica var. koenigii 'Red Baron'
Iris 'Flavescens'
Iris pseudacorus 'Variegata'
Iris sibirica 'Butter and Sugar'
Kniphofia 'Alcazar'
Kniphofia 'Little Maid'
Kniphofia 'Primrose Beauty'
Kniphofia 'Prince Igor'
Kniphofia 'Royal Standard'
Kniphofia 'Shining Sceptre'
Kniphofia caulescens
Kniphofia citrina
Kniphofia triangularis
Ligularia 'The Rocket'
Ligularia dentata 'Dark Beauty'
Ligularia dentata 'Desdemona'
Ligularia wilsoniana
Lilium 'Apricot Brandy'
Lilium 'Connecticut King'
Lilium 'Conquistador'
Lilium 'Eden's Dandy'
Lilium 'Grand Cru'
Lilium 'Montenegro'
Lilium 'Pretender'
Lilium 'Royal Justice'

Lilium 'Royal Perfume'
Lilium 'Scarlet Emperor'
Lilium 'Shirley'
Lilium 'Sunset'
Lilium henryi
Lilium lancifolium var. splendens
Lilium pumilum
Lobelia 'Queen Victoria'
Lobelia 'Royal Robe'
Lychnis ×arkwrightii 'Vesuvius'
Lychnis cognata
Lysimachia nummularia 'Aurea'
Miscanthus 'Purpurascens'
Monarda 'Jacob Cline'
Nymphaea 'Marliacea Chromatella'
Oenothera fremontii 'Lemon Silver'
Oenothera fruticosa ssp. glauca 'Sonnenwende'
Origanum vulgare 'Aureum'
Packera aurea (Senecio aureus)
Paeonia 'America'
Paeonia 'Burma Ruby'
Paeonia 'Coral Sunset'
Paeonia 'Etched Salmon'
Paeonia 'Prairie Moon'
Papaver nudicaule 'Red Sails'
Papaver orientale 'Curlilocks'
Papaver orientale 'Derwisch'
Papaver orientale 'Feuerriese'
Papaver orientale 'Harvest Moon'
Papaver orientale 'Prince of Orange'
Papaver orientale 'Saffron'
Papaver orientale 'Turkenlouis'
Patrinia scabiosifolia
Phlomis russeliana
Phlox paniculata 'Orange Perfection'
Rudbeckia fulgida var. speciosa (newmannii)
Rudbeckia maxima
Rudbeckia triloba
Rumex sanguineus
Saruma henryi
Sedum acre 'Aureum'
Silene regia
Solidago 'Golden Spangles'
Solidago rugosa 'Fireworks'
×Solidaster luteus 'Lemore'
Stachys byzantina 'Primrose Heron'
Stokesia laevis 'Mary Gregory'
Stylophorum diphyllum
Tanacetum 'Golden Feathers'
Thermopsis villosa
Thymus ×citriodorus 'Lemon Green'
Verbascum 'Jackie'
Verbascum bombyciferum
Veronica repens 'Sunshine'

Annual
Alstroemeria aurea 'Orange King'
Alstroemeria psittacina

Antirrhinum majus 'Rocket Red'
Arctotis ×hybrida 'Dark Red'
Arctotis ×hybrida 'Flame'
Beta vulgaris 'Golden'
Beta vulgaris 'Ruby Queen'
Bouvardia ternifolia
Calendula officinalis 'Orange King'
Eschscholzia californica
Fuchsia 'Gartenmeister Bonstedt'
Helichrysum petiolare 'Limelight'
Ipomoea batatas 'Margarita'
Leonotis menthifolia
Lysimachia congestiflora 'Variegata'
Melampodium paludosum 'Million Gold'
Papaver rhoeas
Papaver somniferum 'Burnt Orange'
Portulaca grandiflora 'Sundial Peach'
Rudbeckia hirta 'Irish Eyes'
Salvia coccinea 'Lady in Red'
Solenostemon 'Penny'
Solenostemon 'Saturn'
Tropaeolum majus Alaska Series
Tropaeolum majus 'Apricot Trifle'
Tropaeolum majus 'Blush Double'
Tropaeolum majus 'Moonlight'
Tropaeolum majus 'Tip Top Mahogany'
Verbena 'Romance Apricot'
Verbena Temari® Red
Zinnia haageana 'Orange Star'

Annual vine
Ipomoea lobata (Mina lobata)
Lathyrus odoratus 'Henry Eckford'

Tropical
Caladium 'Florida Cardinal'
Canna 'Black Knight'
Canna 'Omega'
Canna 'Orange Punch'
Canna 'Panache'
Canna 'Phasion'
Canna 'Roi Humbert' (red King Humbert)
Canna 'Striata' (Pretoria)
Canna indica 'Red Stripe' (purpurea)
Duranta erecta 'Golden Edge'
Hedychium 'Daniel Weeks'
Hedychium coccineum
Musa zebrina
Phormium 'Yellow Wave'

Hardy bulb
Allium moly 'Jeannine'
Dichelostemma ida-maia
Eranthis hyemalis
Eremurus ×isabellinus 'Pinokkio'
Erythronium 'Pagoda'
Narcissus 'Delnashaugh'
Narcissus 'Mary Gay Lirette'

Narcissus 'Mint Julep'
Narcissus 'Sir Winston Churchill'
Narcissus 'Stratosphere'
Narcissus 'Tahiti'
Tulipa 'Apricot Parrot'
Tulipa 'Big Smile'
Tulipa 'Blushing Lady'
Tulipa 'Burgundy Lace'
Tulipa 'Carmine Parrot'
Tulipa 'Fringed Elegance'
Tulipa 'Temple of Beauty'
Tulipa 'Uncle Tom'
Tulipa batalinii
Tulipa clusiana var. chrysantha

Tender bulb
Dahlia 'Arabian Night'
Dahlia 'Bishop of Llandaff'
Dahlia 'Ellen Houston'
Dahlia 'Orange Nugget'
Dahlia 'Susette'
Gladiolus 'Atom'
Hymenocallis 'Sulphur Queen'
Scadoxus multiflorus
Tigridia pavonia 'Speciosa'

Cool

Tree
Abies lasiocarpa 'Arizonica Compacta'
Fagus sylvatica 'Tricolor'
Picea pungens 'Iseli Foxtail'
Picea pungens 'Thomsen'
Pinus cembra 'Silver Sheen'
Pinus flexilis 'Vanderwolf's Pyramid'
Pinus parviflora 'Glauca'
Pinus sylvestris 'Fastigiata'
Pseudotsuga menziesii 'Astro Blue'

Shrub
Abies procera 'Glauca Prostrata'
Amorpha canescens
Berberis thunbergii var. atropurpurea
   'Rose Glow'
Buddleia 'Lochinch'
Buddleia davidii 'Black Knight'
Buddleia davidii 'Mongo' (Nanho blue)
Callicarpa dichotoma 'Issai'
Caryopteris ×clandonensis
Caryopteris ×clandonensis 'Longwood Blue'
Daphne ×burkwoodii 'Carol Mackie'
Picea alcoquiana 'Howell's Tigertail'
Pinus parviflora 'Yatsubusa'
Pinus sylvestris 'Albyn'
Rhododendron 'Mist Maiden'
Rhododendron 'Northern Starburst'
Rosa 'Ausvelvet' (The Prince®)
Rosa 'Hansa'

Rosa Lyda Rose™
Rosa 'Meidomonac' (Bonica®)
Rosa 'Nearly Wild'
Rosa 'Nuits de Young'
Rosa 'The Fairy'
Rosa multiflora 'Grevillei' (seven sisters' rose)
Rosa rugosa
Syringa meyeri
Vitex agnus-castus var. latifolia

Woody vine
Ampelopsis glandulosa var. brevipedunculata
   'Elegans'
Clematis 'Elsa Späth'
Clematis 'Hagley Hybrid'
Clematis 'Polish Spirit'
Clematis 'Royal Velours'
Clematis alpina 'Constance'
Clematis macropetala 'Markham's Pink'

Perennial
Acanthus spinosus
Aconitum 'Bressingham Spire'
Aconitum carmichaelii (Wilsonii Group)
   'Spätlese'
Aconitum episcopale
Agastache 'Blue Fortune'
Ajuga reptans 'Purple Torch'
Amsonia ciliata
Amsonia elliptica
Amsonia hubrichtii
Amsonia tabernaemontana
Anemone ×hybrida 'Queen Charlotte'
Anemone ×hybrida 'September Charm'
Aquilegia alpina
Artemisia 'Huntington'
Artemisia 'Powis Castle'
Artemisia 'Silverado'
Artemisia absinthium 'Lambrook Silver'
Aster 'Climax'
Aster laevis 'Bluebird'
Aster novae-angliae 'Hella Lacy'
Aster novae-angliae 'Hillside'
Aster novae-angliae 'Purple Dome'
Aster novae-angliae 'Wild Light Blue'
Aster oblongifolius var. angustatus
   'Raydon's Favorite'
Aster tataricus 'Jindai'
Astilbe chinensis 'Purple Candle'
Astilbe chinensis var. taquetii 'Superba'
Astilbe chinensis 'Veronica Klose'
Astilbe ×rosea 'Peach Blossom'
Athyrium niponicum var. pictum
Baptisia 'Purple Smoke'
Baptisia australis
Brunnera macrophylla
Campanula 'Birch Hybrid'
Campanula 'Constellation'

Color Schemes, cool, cont.
....

Campanula 'Dwarf Tornado'
Campanula 'Kent Belle'
Campanula persicifolia 'Chettle Charm'
Campanula rapunculoides
Campanula rotundifolia 'Olympica'
Carex morrowii 'Ice Dance'
Carex morrowii 'Variegata'
Centaurea montana
Ceratostigma plumbaginoides
Cimicifuga ramosa 'Brunette'
Clematis integrifolia
Cryptotaenia japonica f. atropurpurea
Cynoglossum amabile 'Firmament'
Delphinium 'Centurion Sky Blue'
Delphinium ×bellamosum
Delphinium cashmerianum
Delphinium exaltatum
Dicentra 'Luxuriant'
Dracocephalum ruyschiana
Echinacea purpurea
Echinops bannaticus 'Taplow Blue'
Echinops ritro 'Blue Glow'
Echinops ritro 'Veitch's Blue'
Eryngium amethystinum
Eryngium planum 'Blaukappe'
Eryngium variifolium
Eupatorium purpureum ssp. maculatum
    'Gateway'
Festuca glauca 'Elijah Blue'
Galega ×hartlandii 'Lady Wilson'
Gentiana septemfida var. lagodechiana
Gentiana triflora 'Royal Blue'
Geranium 'Brookside'
Geranium 'Johnson's Blue'
Geranium 'Phillippe Vapelle'
Geranium 'Salome'
Geranium himalayense 'Plenum'
Geranium macrorrhizum 'Ingwersen's Variety'
Geranium ×magnificum
Geranium ×oxonianum 'Claridge Druce'
Geranium phaeum 'Lily Lovell'
Geranium phaeum 'Samobor'
Geranium platypetalum
Geranium pratense 'Mrs. Kendall Clark'
Geranium pratense 'Victor Reiter Jr.'
Geranium renardii
Geranium wlassovianum
Gladiolus communis ssp. byzantinus
Glaucidium palmatum
Helictotrichon sempervirens 'Saphirsprudel'
    (sapphire fountain)
Helleborus Royal Heritage™
Helleborus orientalis
Hemerocallis 'Siloam Royal Prince'
Hesperis matronalis

×Heucherella 'Silver Streak'
Hosta 'Big Daddy'
Hosta 'Blue Cadet'
Hosta 'Fragrant Blue'
Hosta 'Halcyon'
Hosta 'Krossa Regal'
Hosta 'Love Pat'
Hosta 'Night Before Christmas'
Hosta 'Patriot'
Hyssopus officinalis
Iris 'Perfume Counter'
Iris 'Sugar Blues'
Iris pallida 'Variegata'
Iris sibirica 'Caesar's Brother'
Iris sibirica 'Dianne's Daughter'
Iris sibirica 'Orville Fay'
Iris sibirica 'Pirate Prince'
Iris sibirica 'Skywings'
Iris sibirica 'Vi Luihn'
Lamium maculatum 'White Nancy'
Lathyrus latifolius
Lavandula angustifolia 'Munstead'
Lavandula ×intermedia 'Grosso'
Liatris spicata 'Kobold'
Limonium platyphyllum 'Violetta
Linaria 'Natalie'
Linaria purpurea
Linum perenne 'Blau Saphir' (blue sapphire)
Lobelia 'Dark Crusader'
Lobelia 'Grape Knee High'
Lobelia 'Purple Towers'
Lobelia 'Ruby Slippers'
Lobelia siphilitica
Mazus reptans
Mertensia pulmonarioides (virginica)
Monarda 'Violet Queen'
Nepeta 'Six Hills Giant'
Nepeta ×faassenii
Nepeta grandiflora 'Bramdean'
Nepeta racemosa 'Walker's Low'
Nepeta sibirica 'Souvenir d'André Chaudron'
Origanum 'Kent Beauty'
Origanum laevigatum 'Herrenhausen'
Paeonia 'Monsieur Jules Elie'
Paeonia obovata
Panicum virgatum 'Dallas Blues'
Panicum virgatum 'Heavy Metal'
Papaver orientale 'Lighthouse'
Papaver orientale 'Patty's Plum'
Passiflora incarnata
Penstemon ×mexicale 'Pike's Peak Purple'
Perovskia atriplicifolia
Perovskia atriplicifolia 'Longin'
Phlox divaricata
Phlox divaricata 'Dirigo Ice'
Phlox divaricata 'Eco Texas Purple'
Phlox divaricata ssp. laphamii
Phlox divaricata 'London Grove Blue'

Phlox divaricata 'Sweet Lilac'
Phlox paniculata 'Fesselballon'
Phlox paniculata 'Katherine'
Phlox paniculata 'Laura'
Phlox paniculata 'The King'
Phlox paniculata 'Tracy's Treasure'
Phlox stolonifera 'Blue Ridge'
Phytolacca polyandra
Platycodon grandiflorus 'Double Blue'
Platycodon grandiflorus 'Komachi'
Polemonium caeruleum 'Blanjou' (brise d'Anjou)
Pulmonaria 'Majesté'
Pulmonaria 'Viette's Deep Blue Sea'
Ruta graveolens 'Blue Beauty'
Salvia argentea
Salvia azurea var. pitcheri
Salvia nemorosa 'Ostfriesland' (East Friesland)
Salvia nemorosa 'Purple Glory'
Salvia nemorosa 'Pusztaflamme' (plumosa)
Salvia ×sylvestris 'Blauhügel' (blue hill)
Salvia ×sylvestris 'Blaukönigin' (blue queen)
Salvia ×sylvestris 'Mainacht' (May night)
Salvia × sylvestris 'Viola Klose'
Salvia verticillata 'Purple Rain'
Sanguisorba tenuifolia 'Purpurea'
Scabiosa Butterfly Blue®
Scabiosa 'Pink Mist'
Schizachyrium scoparium 'The Blues'
Sisyrinchium bermudianum
Sorghastrum nutans 'Sioux Blue'
Stachys byzantina
Stachys byzantina 'Countess Helen von Stein'
Stachys macrantha
Stokesia laevis 'Klaus Jelitto'
Stokesia laevis 'Omega Skyrocket'
Stokesia laevis 'Purple Parasols'
Thalictrum aquilegiifolium 'Thundercloud'
Thalictrum rochebruneanum
Thymus ×citriodorus
Thymus pseudolanuginosus
Tradescantia Andersoniana Group
Tradescantia (Andersoniana Group)
    'Purple Profusion'
Tradescantia (Andersoniana Group)
    'Zwanenburg Blue'
Trillium erectum
Valeriana officinalis
Verbena hastata
Veronica 'Goodness Grows'
Veronica 'Waterperry Blue'
Veronica austriaca ssp. teucrium
    'Crater Lake Blue'
Veronica austriaca ssp. teucrium 'Royal Blue'
Veronica gentianoides 'Nana'
Veronica peduncularis 'Georgia Blue'
Veronica prostrata 'Trehane'
Veronica spicata 'Blue Charm'
Veronicastrum virginicum 'Fascination'

Viola 'Purple Showers'
Viola labradorica

Annual
Ageratum houstonianum 'Blue Horizon'
Angelonia 'Blue Pacific'
Angelonia angustifolia 'Purple Pinnacles'
Brachyscome 'Ultra'
Brassica oleracea
Celosia spicata 'Flamingo Purple'
Centaurea cineraria
Cerinthe major 'Purpurascens'
Consolida ajacis 'Blue Spire'
Cynara cardunculus
Eschscholzia californica 'Purple Gleam'
Eucomis comosa 'Sparkling Burgundy'
Gomphrena haageana 'Lavender Lady'
Ocimum 'African Blue'
Papaver rhoeas Angels' Choir
Papaver somniferum
Papaver somniferum 'Lauren's Grape'
Plectranthus amboinicus
Plectranthus argentatus
Salvia 'Indigo Spires'
Salvia 'Purple Majesty'
Salvia guaranitica
Salvia guaranitica 'Black and Blue'
Salvia leucantha
Salvia officinalis 'Tricolor'
Salvia patens
Verbena 'Homestead Purple
Verbena bonariensis

Annual vine
Ipomoea tricolor 'Heavenly Blue'
Lablab purpureus
Lathyrus odoratus
Lathyrus odoratus 'King Size Navy Blue'
Rhodochiton atrosanguineus
Thunbergia battiscombei

Hardy bulb
Allium caeruleum
Allium carinatum ssp. pulchellum
Allium cristophii
Allium hollandicum (aflatunense)
    'Purple Sensation'
Allium schubertii
Allium sphaerocephalon
Camassia leichtlinii ssp. suksdorfii 'Blauwe
    Donau' (blue Danube)
Chionodoxa forbesii (luciliae) Siehei Group
Colchicum speciosum
Crocus chrysanthus 'Blue Bird'
Fritillaria persica
Iris 'Blue Magic'
Iris reticulata 'Harmony'
Narcissus 'Fragrant Rose'

Puschkinia scilloides
Triteleia laxa 'Queen Fabiola'
Tulipa 'Angelique'
Tulipa 'Blue Heron'
Tulipa 'Blue Parrot'
Tulipa 'Couleur Cardinal'

Tender bulb
Agapanthus 'Bressingham Blue'
Gladiolus 'Violetta'

Warm or cool

Includes neutrals, such as whites, black, and greens, as well as very pale yellows, tans, magentas, maroons, and purple-red foliage, which can be used effectively in either warm or cool color schemes.

Tree
Acer palmatum var. dissectum Dissectum
    Atropurpureum Group
Amelanchier ×grandiflora 'Autumn Brilliance'
Betula utilis var. jacquemontii
Chamaecyparis lawsoniana 'Sullivan'
Chionanthus virginicus
Cornus kousa
Fagus sylvatica 'Purpurea Pendula'
Magnolia virginiana
Picea abies 'Pendula'
Pinus strobus
Pinus sylvestris
Quercus robur 'Pectinata'
Sciadopitys verticillata
Thuja occidentalis 'Techny'
Tsuga canadensis

Shrub
Aesculus parviflora
Berberis thunbergii var. atropurpurea 'Bailtwo'
    (Burgundy Carousel™)
Berberis thunbergii var. atropurpurea 'Gentry
    Cultivar' (Royal Burgundy™)
Berberis thunbergii var. atropurpurea
    'Royal Cloak'
Buxus 'Green Gem'
Buxus 'Green Velvet'
Buxus microphylla 'Winter Gem'
Calycanthus floridus
Caryopteris ×clandonensis 'Worcester Gold'
Clethra alnifolia
Cotinus coggygria 'Velvet Cloak'
Fothergilla gardenii
Hydrangea quercifolia
Hydrangea quercifolia 'Snowflake'
Ilex 'Apollo'
Ilex glabra
Ilex ×meserveae 'Mesdob' (China boy)

Ilex verticillata 'Jim Dandy'
Itea virginica
Itea virginica 'Henry's Garnet'
Lespedeza cuneata
Microbiota decussata
Picea abies 'Mucronata'
Pinus contorta 'Spaan's Dwarf'
Pinus pumila 'Nana'
Pinus strobus 'Nana'
Rhododendron 'Chionoides'
Rosa 'Seafoam'
Tsuga canadensis 'Cole's Prostrate'
Viburnum plicatum var. tomentosum 'Mariesii'

Woody vine
Clematis 'Lanuginosa Candida'
Clematis terniflora
Hydrangea anomala ssp. petiolaris
Lonicera periclymenum 'Graham Thomas'
Vitis vinifera 'Purpurea'

Perennial
Adiantum pedatum
Alcea rosea 'The Watchman'
Alchemilla mollis
Angelica gigas
Anthriscus sylvestris 'Ravenswing'
Aquilegia vulgaris var. stellata 'Black Barlow'
Arisaema sikokianum
Aruncus dioicus
Astilbe ×arendsii 'Snowdrift'
Calamagrostis ×acutiflora 'Karl Foerster'
Calamagrostis ×acutiflora 'Overdam'
Calamagrostis brachytricha
Cephalaria gigantea
Cimicifuga ramosa 'Hillside Black Beauty'
Clematis recta
Dicentra spectabilis 'Gold Heart'
Digitalis grandiflora
Digitalis lutea
Eryngium yuccifolium
Euphorbia ×martinii
Galium odoratum
Geranium 'Ann Folkard'
Geranium psilostemon
Geranium sanguineum 'New Hampshire'
Gillenia stipulata
Helleborus foetidus
Helleborus orientalis (single black)
Hemerocallis 'Alluring Peach'
Heuchera 'Chocolate Ruffles'
Heuchera 'Plum Pudding'
Heuchera 'Velvet Night'
Heuchera micrantha var. diversifolia
    'Palace Purple'
Hosta 'Paul's Glory'
Hosta 'Sum and Substance'
Hosta plantaginea 'Aphrodite'

Hystrix patula
Iris foetidissima
Iris sanguinea 'Snow Queen'
Iris sibirica 'White Swirl'
Knautia macedonica
Lilium 'Casa Blanca'
Luzula nivea
Lychnis coronaria
Miscanthus sinensis var. condensatus
    'Cosmopolitan'
Miscanthus sinensis 'Gracillimus'
Miscanthus sinensis 'Malepartus'
Miscanthus sinensis 'Morning Light'
Molinia caerulea ssp. arundinacea 'Skyracer'
Osmunda cinnamomea
Osmunda regalis
Pachysandra procumbens
Panicum virgatum 'Rehbraun'
Pennisetum alopecuroides 'Hameln'
Penstemon digitalis 'Husker Red'
Persicaria microcephala 'Red Dragon'
Phlox paniculata 'David'
Phlox paniculata 'Look Again'
Phlox paniculata 'Pax' (peace)
Phlox paniculata 'Tenor'
Phlox stolonifera 'Bruce's White'
Plantago major 'Rubrifolia'
Polygonatum odoratum 'Variegatum'
Polystichum acrostichoides
Rheum palmatum var. tanguticum
Rodgersia aesculifolia
Rodgersia pinnata
Scabiosa columbaria var. ochroleuca
Sedum 'Herbstfreude' (autumn joy)
Sedum 'Pork and Beans'
Sedum telephium ssp. maximum
    'Atropurpureum'
Sisyrinchium 'Quaint and Queer'
Symphytum 'Goldsmith'
Tiarella cordifolia 'Ninja'
Veronica spicata 'Icicle'
Viola 'Molly Sanderson'

Annual
Agave havardiana
Alternanthera dentata 'Rubiginosa'
Atriplex hortensis var. rubra
Beta vulgaris 'Bull's Blood'
Cosmos atrosanguineus
Cyperus alternifolius 'Stricta'
Ipomoea batatas 'Ace of Spades'
Ipomoea batatas 'Blackie'
Lactuca 'Merlot'
Nicotiana langsdorffii
Nierembergia scoparia 'Mont Blanc'
Nigella damascena Miss Jekyll Series
Ocimum basilicum 'Red Rubin'
Papaver somniferum 'Black Peony'

Papaver somniferum 'Pepperbox'
Pennisetum setaceum 'Rubrum'
Perilla frutescens var. crispa
Phyllostachys nigra
Pistia stratiotes
Scabiosa atropurpurea 'Ace of Spades'
Solenostemon 'Burgundy Columns'
Solenostemon 'Burgundy Giant'
Solenostemon 'Olive'
Solenostemon 'Purple Emperor'

Tropical
Caladium 'Florida Sweetheart'
Colocasia esculenta
Colocasia esculenta 'Black Beauty'
Colocasia esculenta 'Black Magic'
Colocasia esculenta 'Fontanesii'
Colocasia esculenta 'Illustris'
Euphorbia cotinifolia
Hibiscus acetosella 'Red Shield'
Musa basjoo
Phormium 'Bronze Baby'
Phormium 'Platt's Black'
Phormium cookianum 'Chocolate'
Ricinus communis
Ricinus communis 'Carmencita'

Hardy bulb
Camassia leichtlinii 'Semiplena'
Narcissus 'Petrel'
Tulipa 'Black Parrot'
Tulipa 'Queen of Night'

Tender bulb
Amorphophallus konjac

TEXTURE

Texture here refers to individual foliage texture. The overall texture of the plant may be different due to form, size, density, color, and so on.

Fine

Tree
Acer palmatum var. dissectum Dissectum
    Atropurpureum Group
Acer palmatum 'Sango-kaku'
Picea abies 'Pendula'
Picea orientalis 'Skylands'
Picea pungens 'Iseli Foxtail'
Picea pungens 'Thomsen'
Pinus flexilis 'Vanderwolf's Pyramid'
Pinus parviflora 'Glauca'
Pinus strobus
Pinus sylvestris 'Fastigiata'
Pseudotsuga menziesii 'Astro Blue'

Texture, fine, cont.

Quercus robur 'Pectinata'
Sciadopitys verticillata
Tsuga canadensis

Shrub

Abies procera 'Glauca Prostrata'
Amorpha canescens
Berberis thunbergii var. atropurpurea 'Bailtwo'
    (Burgundy Carousel™)
Berberis thunbergii var. atropurpurea 'Gentry
    Cultivar' (Royal Burgundy™)
Berberis thunbergii var. atropurpurea
    'Rose Glow'
Berberis thunbergii var. atropurpurea
    'Royal Cloak'
Berberis thunbergii 'Monler' (Gold Nugget™)
Berberis thunbergii 'Monry' (Sunsation™)
Buxus 'Green Gem'
Buxus 'Green Velvet'
Buxus microphylla 'Winter Gem'
Caryopteris ×clandonensis
Caryopteris ×clandonensis 'Longwood Blue'
Caryopteris ×clandonensis 'Worcester Gold'
Chamaecyparis obtusa 'Fernspray Gold'
Chamaecyparis obtusa 'Mariesii'
Chamaecyparis pisifera 'Golden Mop'
Genista tinctoria 'Royal Gold'
Ilex glabra
Lespedeza cuneata
Microbiota decussata
Picea abies 'Mucronata'
Picea alcoquiana 'Howell's Tigertail'
Pinus contorta 'Chief Joseph'
Pinus contorta 'Spaan's Dwarf'
Pinus densiflora 'Oculus Draconis'
Pinus parviflora 'Yatsubusa'
Pinus pumila 'Nana'
Pinus strobus 'Nana'
Pinus sylvestris 'Albyn'
Potentilla fruticosa 'Sunset'
Rosa ×harisonii 'Harison's Yellow'
Sambucus racemosa 'Sutherland Gold'
Tsuga canadensis 'Cole's Prostrate'
Vitex agnus-castus var. latifolia

Woody vine

Clematis 'Polish Spirit'
Clematis macropetala 'Markham's Pink'
Clematis terniflora

Perennial

Achillea 'Anblo' (Anthea)
Achillea 'Heidi'
Achillea 'Salmon Beauty'
Achillea filipendulina 'Altgold'

Acorus gramineus 'Minimus Aureus'
Acorus gramineus 'Oborozuki'
Acorus gramineus 'Ogon'
Adiantum pedatum
Agastache rupestris
Alstroemeria 'Sweet Laura'
Amsonia ciliata
Amsonia hubrichtii
Amsonia tabernaemontana
Anthriscus sylvestris 'Ravenswing'
Artemisia 'Huntington'
Artemisia 'Powis Castle'
Artemisia 'Silverado'
Artemisia absinthium 'Lambrook Silver'
Athyrium niponicum var. pictum
Calamagrostis ×acutiflora 'Karl Foerster'
Calamagrostis ×acutiflora 'Overdam'
Calamagrostis brachytricha
Campanula rotundifolia 'Olympica'
Carex buchananii
Carex dolichostachya 'Kaga Nishiki'
    (gold fountains)
Carex elata 'Aurea' (Bowles' golden)
Carex morrowii 'Ice Dance'
Carex morrowii 'Variegata'
Clematis recta
Coreopsis tripteris
Coreopsis verticillata 'Moonbeam'
Coreopsis verticillata 'Zagreb'
Crocosmia 'Blacro' (Jenny Bloom)
Crocosmia 'Emberglow'
Crocosmia 'Lucifer'
Crocosmia ×crocosmiiflora 'Norwich Canary'
Crocosmia ×crocosmiiflora 'Solfatare'
Crocosmia ×crocosmiiflora 'Venus'
Deschampsia cespitosa 'Goldgehänge'
Dianthus ×allwoodii 'Danielle Marie'
Dianthus barbatus 'Sooty'
Dianthus deltoides 'Leuchtfunk' (flashing light)
Dicentra 'Luxuriant'
Epimedium davidii
Epimedium ×rubrum
Epimedium ×warleyense
Euphorbia cyparissias 'Fen's Ruby'
Euphorbia polychroma
Festuca glauca 'Elijah Blue'
Festuca glauca 'Golden Toupee
Foeniculum vulgare 'Purpureum'
Galium odoratum
Gillenia stipulata
Gladiolus communis ssp. byzantinus
Gladiolus ×gandavensis
Gladiolus ×gandavensis 'Boone'
Hakonechloa macra 'Aureola'
Helianthus salicifolius
Helictotrichon sempervirens 'Saphirsprudel'
    (sapphire fountain)
Hemerocallis 'Alluring Peach'

Hemerocallis 'Carefree Peach'
Hemerocallis 'Happy Returns'
Hemerocallis 'Peach Fairy'
Hemerocallis 'Red Razzamatazz'
Hemerocallis 'Scarlet Romance'
Hemerocallis 'Siloam Royal Prince'
Hemerocallis 'Staghorn Sumac'
Hemerocallis 'Sundried Tomatoes'
Hemerocallis 'Toy Trumpets'
Hemerocallis 'Welcome Mat'
Hemerocallis 'Yellow Lollipop'
Hystrix patula
Imperata cylindrica var. koenigii 'Red Baron'
Iris 'Flavescens'
Iris 'Perfume Counter'
Iris 'Sugar Blues'
Iris foetidissima
Iris pallida 'Variegata'
Iris pseudacorus 'Variegata'
Iris sanguinea 'Snow Queen'
Iris sibirica 'Butter and Sugar'
Iris sibirica 'Caesar's Brother'
Iris sibirica 'Dianne's Daughter'
Iris sibirica 'Orville Fay'
Iris sibirica 'Pirate Prince'
Iris sibirica 'Skywings'
Iris sibirica 'Vi Luihn'
Iris sibirica 'White Swirl'
Knautia macedonica
Kniphofia 'Alcazar'
Kniphofia 'Little Maid'
Kniphofia 'Primrose Beauty'
Kniphofia 'Prince Igor'
Kniphofia 'Royal Standard'
Kniphofia 'Shining Sceptre'
Kniphofia caulescens
Kniphofia citrina
Kniphofia triangularis
Lavandula angustifolia 'Munstead'
Lavandula ×intermedia 'Grosso'
Limonium platyphyllum 'Violetta'
Linaria 'Natalie'
Linaria purpurea
Linum perenne 'Blau Saphir' (blue sapphire)
Luzula nivea
Mazus reptans
Mertensia pulmonarioides (virginica)
Miscanthus 'Purpurascens'
Miscanthus sinensis var. condensatus
    'Cosmopolitan'
Miscanthus sinensis 'Gracillimus'
Miscanthus sinensis 'Malepartus'
Miscanthus sinensis 'Morning Light'
Molinia caerulea ssp. arundinacea 'Skyracer'
Oenothera fremontii 'Lemon Silver'
Osmunda cinnamomea
Osmunda regalis
Panicum virgatum 'Dallas Blues'

Panicum virgatum 'Heavy Metal'
Panicum virgatum 'Rehbraun'
Patrinia scabiosifolia
Pennisetum alopecuroides 'Hameln'
Penstemon ×mexicale 'Pike's Peak Purple'
Perovskia atriplicifolia
Perovskia atriplicifolia 'Longin'
Phlox divaricata
Phlox divaricata 'Dirigo Ice'
Phlox divaricata 'Eco Texas Purple'
Phlox divaricata ssp. laphamii
Phlox divaricata 'London Grove Blue'
Phlox divaricata 'Sweet Lilac'
Phlox stolonifera 'Blue Ridge'
Phlox stolonifera 'Bruce's White'
Polemonium caeruleum 'Blanjou' (brise d'Anjou)
Polystichum acrostichoides
Ruta graveolens 'Blue Beauty'
Sanguisorba tenuifolia 'Purpurea'
Scabiosa Butterfly Blue®
Scabiosa 'Pink Mist'
Scabiosa columbaria var. ochroleuca
Schizachyrium scoparium 'The Blues'
Sisyrinchium 'Quaint and Queer'
Sisyrinchium bermudianum
×Solidaster luteus 'Lemore
Sorghastrum nutans 'Sioux Blue'
Tanacetum 'Golden Feathers'
Thalictrum aquilegiifolium 'Thundercloud'
Thalictrum rochebruneanum
Thymus ×citriodorus
Thymus ×citriodorus 'Lemon Green'
Thymus pseudolanuginosus
Valeriana officinalis
Veronica gentianoides 'Nana'
Veronica peduncularis 'Georgia Blue'
Veronica prostrata 'Trehane'
Veronica repens 'Sunshine'
Viola 'Molly Sanderson'
Viola 'Purple Showers'
Viola labradorica

Annual

Alstroemeria aurea 'Orange King'
Alstroemeria psittacina
Brachyscome 'Ultra'
Centaurea cineraria
Consolida ajacis 'Blue Spire'
Cosmos atrosanguineus
Cyperus alternifolius 'Stricta'
Eschscholzia californica
Eschscholzia californica 'Purple Gleam'
Nierembergia scoparia 'Mont Blanc'
Nigella damascena Miss Jekyll Series
Papaver rhoeas
Pennisetum setaceum 'Rubrum'
Phyllostachys nigra
Scabiosa atropurpurea 'Ace of Spades'

Verbena 'Homestead Purple'
Verbena bonariensis

Annual vine
Ipomoea lobata (Mina lobata)
Lathyrus odoratus
Lathyrus odoratus 'Henry Eckford'
Lathyrus odoratus 'King Size Navy Blue'
Rhodochiton atrosanguineus

Hardy bulb
Allium caeruleum
Allium carinatum ssp. pulchellum
Allium cristophii
Allium moly 'Jeannine'
Allium schubertii
Allium sphaerocephalon
Chionodoxa forbesii (luciliae) Siehei Group
Eranthis hyemalis
Iris 'Blue Magic'
Iris reticulata 'Harmony'
Narcissus 'Delnashaugh'
Narcissus 'Fragrant Rose'
Narcissus 'Mary Gay Lirette'
Narcissus 'Mint Julep'
Narcissus 'Petrel'
Narcissus 'Sir Winston Churchill'
Narcissus 'Stratosphere'
Narcissus 'Tahiti'
Puschkinia scilloides
Triteleia laxa 'Queen Fabiola'
Tulipa batalinii
Tulipa clusiana var. chrysantha

Tender bulb
Agapanthus 'Bressingham Blue'
Gladiolus 'Atom'
Gladiolus 'Violetta'
Hymenocallis 'Sulphur Queen'
Scadoxus multiflorus
Tigridia pavonia 'Speciosa'

Bold

Tree
Acer griseum
Catalpa bignonioides 'Aurea'
Ginkgo biloba 'Autumn Gold'

Shrub
Aesculus parviflora
Aralia elata 'Aureovariegata'
Buddleia 'Lochinch'
Buddleia davidii 'Black Knight'
Buddleia davidii 'Mongo' (Nanho blue)
Calycanthus floridus
Hydrangea quercifolia
Hydrangea quercifolia 'Snowflake'

Rhododendron 'Chionoides'
Rosa 'Hansa'
Rosa rugosa
Yucca filamentosa 'Color Guard'
Yucca flaccida 'Golden Sword'

Woody vine
Ampelopsis glandulosa var. brevipedunculata
 'Elegans'
Campsis ×tagliabuana 'Madame Galen'
Hydrangea anomala ssp. petiolaris
Vitis vinifera 'Purpurea'

Perennial
Acanthus spinosus
Alcea rosea 'Peaches and Dreams'
Alcea rosea 'The Watchman'
Alcea rugosa
Alchemilla mollis
Angelica gigas
Arum italicum ssp. italicum 'Marmoratum'
Aruncus dioicus
Brunnera macrophylla
Buphthalmum speciosum
Cephalaria gigantea
Echinops bannaticus 'Taplow Blue'
Echinops ritro 'Blue Glow'
Echinops ritro 'Veitch's Blue'
Eryngium amethystinum
Eryngium planum 'Blaukappe'
Eryngium variifolium
Eryngium yuccifolium
Eupatorium purpureum ssp. maculatum
 'Gateway'
Helleborus foetidus
Hibiscus moscheutos 'Lord Baltimore'
Hosta 'Big Daddy'
Hosta 'Blue Cadet'
Hosta 'Fragrant Blue'
Hosta 'Halcyon'
Hosta 'Krossa Regal'
Hosta 'Lemon Lime'
Hosta 'Love Pat'
Hosta 'Midas Touch'
Hosta 'Night Before Christmas'
Hosta 'Patriot'
Hosta 'Paul's Glory'
Hosta 'Sum and Substance'
Hosta 'Sun Power'
Hosta plantaginea 'Aphrodite'
Humulus lupulus 'Bianca'
Ligularia 'The Rocket'
Ligularia dentata 'Dark Beauty'
Ligularia dentata 'Desdemona'
Ligularia wilsoniana
Pachysandra procumbens
Paeonia 'America'
Paeonia 'Burma Ruby'

Paeonia 'Coral Sunset'
Paeonia 'Etched Salmon'
Paeonia 'Monsieur Jules Elie'
Paeonia 'Prairie Moon'
Papaver orientale 'Curlilocks'
Papaver orientale 'Derwisch'
Papaver orientale 'Feuerriese'
Papaver orientale 'Harvest Moon'
Papaver orientale 'Lighthouse'
Papaver orientale 'Patty's Plum'
Papaver orientale 'Prince of Orange'
Papaver orientale 'Saffron'
Papaver orientale 'Turkenlouis'
Phlomis russeliana
Phytolacca polyandra
Plantago major 'Rubrifolia'
Rheum palmatum var. tanguticum
Rodgersia aesculifolia
Rodgersia pinnata
Rudbeckia maxima
Rumex sanguineus
Salvia argentea
Sedum 'Herbstfreude' (autumn joy)
Sedum telephium ssp. maximum
 'Atropurpureum'
Stachys byzantina
Stachys byzantina 'Countess Helen von Stein'
Stachys byzantina 'Primrose Heron'
Verbascum bombyciferum

Annual
Agave havardiana
Beta vulgaris 'Bull's Blood'
Beta vulgaris 'Golden'
Beta vulgaris 'Ruby Queen'
Brassica oleracea
Cynara cardunculus
Ipomoea batatas 'Ace of Spades'
Ipomoea batatas 'Blackie'
Ipomoea batatas 'Margarita'
Nicotiana langsdorffii
Papaver somniferum
Papaver somniferum 'Black Peony'
Papaver somniferum 'Burnt Orange'
Papaver somniferum 'Lauren's Grape'
Papaver somniferum 'Pepperbox'
Perilla frutescens var. crispa
Pistia stratiotes
Plectranthus argentatus
Rudbeckia hirta 'Irish Eyes'
Solenostemon 'Burgundy Columns'
Solenostemon 'Burgundy Giant'
Solenostemon 'Olive'
Solenostemon 'Penny'
Solenostemon 'Purple Emperor'
Solenostemon 'Saturn'

Tropical
Caladium 'Florida Cardinal'
Caladium 'Florida Sweetheart'
Canna 'Black Knight'
Canna 'Omega'
Canna 'Orange Punch'
Canna 'Panache'
Canna 'Phasion'
Canna 'Roi Humbert' (red King Humbert)
Canna 'Striata' (Pretoria)
Canna indica 'Red Stripe' (purpurea)
Colocasia esculenta
Colocasia esculenta 'Black Beauty'
Colocasia esculenta 'Black Magic'
Colocasia esculenta 'Fontanesii'
Colocasia esculenta 'Illustris'
Duranta erecta 'Golden Edge'
Hedychium 'Daniel Weeks'
Hedychium coccineum
Hibiscus acetosella 'Red Shield'
Musa basjoo
Musa zebrina
Phormium 'Bronze Baby'
Phormium 'Platt's Black'
Phormium 'Yellow Wave'
Phormium cookianum 'Chocolate'
Ricinus communis
Ricinus communis 'Carmencita'

Hardy bulb
Fritillaria persica
Tulipa 'Black Parrot'
Tulipa 'Blue Parrot'
Tulipa 'Carmine Parrot'

Tender bulb
Amorphophallus konjac
Dahlia 'Arabian Night'
Dahlia 'Bishop of Llandaff'
Dahlia 'Ellen Houston'
Dahlia 'Orange Nugget'
Dahlia 'Susette'

FORM

Climbing

Shrub
Rosa 'Alchymist'
Rosa multiflora 'Grevillei' (seven sisters' rose)

Woody vine
Ampelopsis glandulosa var. brevipedunculata
 'Elegans'
Campsis ×tagliabuana 'Madame Galen'
Clematis 'Elsa Späth'

Form, climbing, cont.

Clematis 'Hagley Hybrid'
Clematis 'Lanuginosa Candida'
Clematis 'Polish Spirit'
Clematis 'Royal Velours'
Clematis alpina 'Constance'
Clematis macropetala 'Markham's Pink'
Clematis terniflora
Hydrangea anomala ssp. petiolaris
Lonicera periclymenum 'Graham Thomas'
Lonicera sempervirens 'Blanche Sandman'
Vitis vinifera 'Purpurea'

Perennial

Aconitum episcopale
Humulus lupulus 'Bianca'
Lathyrus latifolius
Passiflora incarnata

Annual vine

Ipomoea lobata (Mina lobata)
Ipomoea tricolor 'Heavenly Blue'
Lablab purpureus
Lathyrus odoratus
Lathyrus odoratus 'Henry Eckford'
Lathyrus odoratus 'King Size Navy Blue'
Rhodochiton atrosanguineus
Thunbergia battiscombei

Conical

Tree

Abies lasiocarpa 'Arizonica Compacta'
Chamaecyparis lawsoniana 'Sullivan'
Picea orientalis 'Skylands'
Picea pungens 'Iseli Foxtail'
Picea pungens 'Thomsen'
Pinus strobus
Pseudotsuga menziesii 'Astro Blue'
Sciadopitys verticillata
Thuja occidentalis 'Techny'
Tsuga canadensis

Shrub

Chamaecyparis obtusa 'Fernspray Gold'
Picea abies 'Mucronata'

Horizontal

Shrub

Abies procera 'Glauca Prostrata'
Microbiota decussata
Pinus sylvestris 'Albyn'
Rosa 'Seafoam'
Tsuga canadensis 'Cole's Prostrate'

Perennial

Ajuga reptans 'Purple Torch'
Galium odoratum
Gentiana septemfida var. lagodechiana
Lamium maculatum 'White Nancy'
Lysimachia nummularia 'Aurea'
Mazus reptans
Nymphaea 'Marliacea Chromatella'
Oenothera fremontii 'Lemon Silver'
Origanum 'Kent Beauty'
Phlox stolonifera 'Blue Ridge'
Phlox stolonifera 'Bruce's White'
Sedum acre 'Aureum'
Thymus pseudolanuginosus
Veronica prostrata 'Trehane'
Veronica repens 'Sunshine'

Annual

Alternanthera dentata 'Rubiginosa'
Helichrysum petiolare 'Limelight'
Ipomoea batatas 'Ace of Spades'
Ipomoea batatas 'Blackie'
Ipomoea batatas 'Margarita'
Lysimachia congestiflora 'Variegata'
Plectranthus argentatus
Portulaca grandiflora 'Sundial Peach'
Verbena 'Homestead Purple'
Verbena 'Romance Apricot'
Verbena Temari® Red

Irregular

Tree

Pinus flexilis 'Vanderwolf's Pyramid'
Pinus parviflora 'Glauca'
Pinus sylvestris

Shrub

Aralia elata 'Aureovariegata'
Pinus contorta 'Chief Joseph'
Pinus contorta 'Spaan's Dwarf'
Pinus densiflora 'Oculus Draconis'
Pinus parviflora 'Yatsubusa'

Vase

Tree

Acer palmatum 'Sango-kaku'
Amelanchier ×grandiflora 'Autumn Brilliance'
Chionanthus virginicus
Cornus kousa
Magnolia virginiana

Shrub

Berberis thunbergii 'Monry' (Sunsation™)
Buddleia 'Lochinch'
Buddleia davidii 'Black Knight'

Clethra alnifolia
Vitex agnus-castus var. latifolia

Perennial

Hosta 'Krossa Regal'

Tropical

Colocasia esculenta 'Fontanesii'

Vertical

Tree

Acer griseum
Betula utilis var. jacquemontii
Fagus sylvatica 'Tricolor'
Ginkgo biloba 'Autumn Gold'
Malus 'Lanzam' (Lancelot®)
Pinus cembra 'Silver Sheen'
Pinus sylvestris 'Fastigiata'
Quercus palustris
Quercus robur 'Pectinata'

Shrub

Rosa 'Ausmas' (Graham Thomas®)
Yucca filamentosa 'Color Guard'
Yucca flaccida 'Golden Sword'

Perennial

Acanthus spinosus
Aconitum 'Bressingham Spire'
Aconitum 'Ivorine'
Aconitum carmichaelii (Wilsonii Group)
  'Spätlese'
Aconitum lycoctonum ssp. neapolitanum
Agastache 'Blue Fortune'
Agastache rupestris
Alcea rosea 'Peaches and Dreams'
Alcea rosea 'The Watchman'
Alcea rugosa
Alstroemeria 'Sweet Laura'
Angelica gigas
Arisaema sikokianum
Aster tataricus 'Jindai'
Astilbe ×arendsii 'Snowdrift'
Astilbe chinensis 'Purple Candle'
Astilbe chinensis var. taquetii 'Superba'
Astilbe chinensis 'Veronica Klose'
Astilbe ×rosea 'Peach Blossom'
Belamcanda chinensis
Belamcanda chinensis 'Hello Yellow'
Calamagrostis ×acutiflora 'Karl Foerster'
Calamagrostis ×acutiflora 'Overdam'
Calamagrostis brachytricha
Campanula 'Dwarf Tornado'
Campanula 'Kent Belle'
Campanula persicifolia 'Chettle Charm'
Carex buchananii
Cephalaria gigantea

Cimicifuga ramosa 'Brunette'
Cimicifuga ramosa 'Hillside Black Beauty'
Coreopsis tripteris
Crocosmia 'Blacro' (Jenny Bloom)
Crocosmia 'Emberglow'
Crocosmia 'Lucifer'
Crocosmia ×crocosmiiflora 'Norwich Canary'
Crocosmia ×crocosmiiflora 'Solfatare'
Crocosmia ×crocosmiiflora 'Venus'
Delphinium 'Centurion Sky Blue'
Delphinium ×bellamosum
Delphinium cashmerianum
Delphinium exaltatum
Digitalis grandiflora
Digitalis lutea
Digitalis purpurea 'Apricot'
Echinops bannaticus 'Taplow Blue'
Echinops ritro 'Blue Glow'
Echinops ritro 'Veitch's Blue'
Eryngium amethystinum
Eryngium planum 'Blaukappe'
Eryngium variifolium
Eryngium yuccifolium
Eupatorium purpureum ssp. maculatum
  'Gateway'
Foeniculum vulgare 'Purpureum'
Gentiana triflora 'Royal Blue'
Gillenia stipulata
Gladiolus communis ssp. byzantinus
Gladiolus ×gandavensis
Gladiolus ×gandavensis 'Boone'
Hesperis matronalis
Hystrix patula
Imperata cylindrica var. koenigii 'Red Baron'
Iris 'Flavescens'
Iris 'Perfume Counter'
Iris 'Sugar Blues'
Iris foetidissima
Iris pallida 'Variegata'
Iris pseudacorus 'Variegata'
Iris sanguinea 'Snow Queen'
Iris sibirica 'Butter and Sugar'
Iris sibirica 'Caesar's Brother'
Iris sibirica 'Dianne's Daughter'
Iris sibirica 'Orville Fay'
Iris sibirica 'Pirate Prince'
Iris sibirica 'Skywings'
Iris sibirica 'Vi Luihn'
Iris sibirica 'White Swirl'
Kniphofia 'Alcazar'
Kniphofia 'Little Maid'
Kniphofia 'Primrose Beauty'
Kniphofia 'Prince Igor'
Kniphofia 'Royal Standard'
Kniphofia 'Shining Sceptre'
Kniphofia caulescens
Kniphofia citrina
Kniphofia triangularis

Liatris spicata 'Kobold'
Ligularia 'The Rocket'
Lilium 'Apricot Brandy'
Lilium 'Casa Blanca'
Lilium 'Connecticut King'
Lilium 'Conquistador'
Lilium 'Eden's Dandy'
Lilium 'Grand Cru'
Lilium 'Montenegro'
Lilium 'Pretender'
Lilium 'Royal Justice'
Lilium 'Royal Perfume'
Lilium 'Scarlet Emperor'
Lilium 'Shirley'
Lilium 'Sunset'
Lilium henryi
Lilium lancifolium var. splendens
Lilium pumilum
Linaria 'Natalie'
Linaria purpurea
Lobelia 'Dark Crusader'
Lobelia 'Grape Knee High'
Lobelia 'Purple Towers'
Lobelia 'Queen Victoria'
Lobelia 'Royal Robe'
Lobelia 'Ruby Slippers'
Lobelia siphilitica
Lychnis coronaria
Miscanthus 'Purpurascens'
Miscanthus sinensis var. condensatus
    'Cosmopolitan'
Miscanthus sinensis 'Gracillimus'
Miscanthus sinensis 'Malepartus'
Miscanthus sinensis 'Morning Light'
Molinia caerulea ssp. arundinacea 'Skyracer'
Nepeta sibirica 'Souvenir d'André Chaudron'
Osmunda cinnamomea
Osmunda regalis
Panicum virgatum 'Dallas Blues'
Panicum virgatum 'Heavy Metal'
Panicum virgatum 'Rehbraun'
Penstemon digitalis 'Husker Red'
Penstemon ×mexicale 'Pike's Peak Purple'
Perovskia atriplicifolia
Perovskia atriplicifolia 'Longin'
Phlomis russeliana
Phlox paniculata 'David'
Phlox paniculata 'Fesselballon'
Phlox paniculata 'Katherine'
Phlox paniculata 'Laura'
Phlox paniculata 'Look Again'
Phlox paniculata 'Orange Perfection'
Phlox paniculata 'Pax' (peace)
Phlox paniculata 'Tenor'
Phlox paniculata 'The King'
Phlox paniculata 'Tracy's Treasure'
Phytolacca polyandra
Platycodon grandiflorus 'Double Blue'

Platycodon grandiflorus 'Komachi'
Polygonatum odoratum 'Variegatum'
Rudbeckia maxima
Rudbeckia triloba
Sanguisorba tenuifolia 'Purpurea'
Schizachyrium scoparium 'The Blues'
Silene regia
Sorghastrum nutans 'Sioux Blue'
Stachys macrantha
Stokesia laevis 'Omega Skyrocket'
Thalictrum aquilegiifolium 'Thundercloud'
Thalictrum rochebruneanum
Valeriana officinalis
Verbascum 'Jackie'
Verbascum bombyciferum
Verbena hastata
Veronica 'Goodness Grows'
Veronica spicata 'Blue Charm'
Veronica spicata 'Icicle'
Veronicastrum virginicum 'Fascination'

Annual
Alstroemeria aurea 'Orange King'
Alstroemeria psittacina
Angelonia 'Blue Pacific'
Angelonia angustifolia 'Purple Pinnacles'
Antirrhinum majus 'Rocket Red'
Celosia spicata 'Flamingo Purple'
Consolida ajacis 'Blue Spire'
Cynara cardunculus
Cyperus alternifolius 'Stricta'
Eucomis comosa 'Sparkling Burgundy'
Leonotis menthifolia
Nicotiana langsdorffii
Papaver somniferum
Papaver somniferum 'Black Peony'
Papaver somniferum 'Burnt Orange'
Papaver somniferum 'Lauren's Grape'
Papaver somniferum 'Pepperbox'
Pennisetum setaceum 'Rubrum'
Phyllostachys nigra
Scabiosa atropurpurea 'Ace of Spades'
Verbena bonariensis

Tropical
Canna 'Black Knight'
Canna 'Omega'
Canna 'Orange Punch'
Canna 'Panache'
Canna 'Phasion'
Canna 'Roi Humbert' (red King Humbert)
Canna 'Striata' (Pretoria)
Canna indica 'Red Stripe' (purpurea)
Hedychium 'Daniel Weeks'
Hedychium coccineum
Musa basjoo
Musa zebrina
Phormium 'Bronze Baby'

Phormium 'Platt's Black'
Phormium 'Yellow Wave'
Phormium cookianum 'Chocolate'
Ricinus communis
Ricinus communis 'Carmencita'

Hardy bulb
Allium caeruleum
Allium carinatum ssp. pulchellum
Allium hollandicum (aflatunense) 'Purple
    Sensation'
Allium sphaerocephalon
Camassia leichtlinii 'Semiplena'
Camassia leichtlinii ssp. suksdorfii 'Blauwe
    Donau' (blue Danube)
Eremurus ×isabellinus 'Pinokkio'
Fritillaria persica
Iris 'Blue Magic'
Iris reticulata 'Harmony'
Narcissus 'Delnashaugh'
Narcissus 'Fragrant Rose'
Narcissus 'Mary Gay Lirette'
Narcissus 'Mint Julep'
Narcissus 'Petrel'
Narcissus 'Sir Winston Churchill'
Narcissus 'Stratosphere'
Narcissus 'Tahiti'
Puschkinia scilloides
Triteleia laxa 'Queen Fabiola'
Tulipa 'Angelique'
Tulipa 'Apricot Parrot'
Tulipa 'Big Smile'
Tulipa 'Black Parrot'
Tulipa 'Blue Heron'
Tulipa 'Blue Parrot'
Tulipa 'Blushing Lady'
Tulipa 'Burgundy Lace'
Tulipa 'Carmine Parrot'
Tulipa 'Couleur Cardinal'
Tulipa 'Fringed Elegance'
Tulipa 'Queen of Night'
Tulipa 'Temple of Beauty'
Tulipa 'Uncle Tom'

Tender bulb
Agapanthus 'Bressingham Blue'
Amorphophallus konjac
Gladiolus 'Atom'
Gladiolus 'Violetta'
Hymenocallis 'Sulphur Queen'
Tigridia pavonia 'Speciosa'

Weeping

Tree
Fagus sylvatica 'Purpurea Pendula'
Picea abies 'Pendula'

Mound

Tree
Acer palmatum var. dissectum Dissectum
    Atropurpureum Group
Catalpa bignonioides 'Aurea'

Shrub
Aesculus parviflora
Amorpha canescens
Berberis thunbergii var. atropurpurea 'Bailtwo'
    (Burgundy Carousel™)
Berberis thunbergii var. atropurpurea 'Gentry
    Cultivar' (Royal Burgundy™)
Berberis thunbergii var. atropurpurea
    'Rose Glow'
Berberis thunbergii var. atropurpurea
    'Royal Cloak'
Berberis thunbergii 'Monler' (Gold Nugget™)
Buddleia davidii 'Mongo' (Nanho blue)
Buxus 'Green Gem'
Buxus 'Green Velvet'
Buxus microphylla 'Winter Gem'
Callicarpa dichotoma 'Issai'
Calycanthus floridus
Caryopteris ×clandonensis
Caryopteris ×clandonensis 'Longwood Blue'
Caryopteris ×clandonensis 'Worcester Gold'
Chamaecyparis obtusa 'Mariesii'
Chamaecyparis pisifera 'Golden Mop'
Cotinus coggygria 'Velvet Cloak'
Daphne ×burkwoodii 'Carol Mackie'
Fothergilla gardenii
Genista tinctoria 'Royal Gold'
Hydrangea quercifolia
Hydrangea quercifolia 'Snowflake'
Hypericum androsaemum 'Albury Purple'
Ilex 'Apollo'
Ilex glabra
Ilex ×meserveae 'Mesdob' (China boy)
Ilex ×meserveae 'Mesog' (China girl)
Ilex verticillata 'Afterglow'
Ilex verticillata 'Christmas Cheer'
Ilex verticillata 'Jim Dandy'
Ilex verticillata 'Winter Red'
Itea virginica
Itea virginica 'Henry's Garnet'
Lespedeza cuneata
Picea alcoquiana 'Howell's Tigertail'
Pinus pumila 'Nana'
Pinus strobus 'Nana'
Potentilla fruticosa 'Sunset'
Rhododendron 'Chionoides'
Rhododendron 'Mist Maiden'
Rhododendron 'Northern Starburst'
Rosa 'Ausbuff' (English Garden®)
Rosa 'Aussaucer' (Evelyn®)
Rosa 'Ausvelvet' (The Prince®)

Form, mound, cont.

Rosa 'Champlain'
Rosa 'F. J. Grootendorst'
Rosa 'Hansa'
Rosa Lyda Rose™
Rosa 'Meidomonac' (Bonica®)
Rosa 'Nearly Wild'
Rosa 'Nuits de Young'
Rosa 'Scrivluv' (Baby Love®)
Rosa 'The Fairy'
Rosa ×harisonii 'Harison's Yellow'
Rosa rugosa
Sambucus racemosa 'Sutherland Gold'
Syringa meyeri
Viburnum plicatum var. tomentosum 'Mariesii'

Perennial

Achillea 'Anblo' (Anthea)
Achillea 'Heidi'
Achillea 'Salmon Beauty'
Achillea filipendulina 'Altgold'
Acorus gramineus 'Minimus Aureus'
Acorus gramineus 'Oborozuki'
Acorus gramineus 'Ogon'
Adiantum pedatum
Alchemilla mollis
Amsonia ciliata
Amsonia elliptica
Amsonia hubrichtii
Amsonia tabernaemontana
Anemone ×hybrida 'Queen Charlotte'
Anemone ×hybrida 'September Charm'
Anthriscus sylvestris 'Ravenswing'
Aquilegia alpina
Aquilegia vulgaris var. stellata 'Black Barlow'
Artemisia 'Huntington'
Artemisia 'Powis Castle'
Artemisia 'Silverado'
Artemisia absinthium 'Lambrook Silver'
Arum italicum ssp. italicum 'Marmoratum'
Aruncus dioicus
Asclepias tuberosa
Asclepias tuberosa 'Hello Yellow'
Aster 'Climax'
Aster laevis 'Bluebird'
Aster novae-angliae 'Hella Lacy'
Aster novae-angliae 'Hillside'
Aster novae-angliae 'Purple Dome'
Aster novae-angliae 'Wild Light Blue'
Aster oblongifolius var. angustatus
    'Raydon's Favorite'
Athyrium niponicum var. pictum
Baptisia 'Purple Smoke'
Baptisia australis
Baptisia sphaerocarpa
Brunnera macrophylla

Buphthalmum speciosum
Campanula 'Birch Hybrid'
Campanula 'Constellation'
Campanula rapunculoides
Campanula rotundifolia 'Olympica'
Carex dolichostachya 'Kaga Nishiki'
    (gold fountains)
Carex elata 'Aurea' (Bowles' golden)
Carex morrowii 'Ice Dance'
Carex morrowii 'Variegata'
Centaurea montana
Ceratostigma plumbaginoides
Chrysanthemum 'Autumn Moon'
Chrysanthemum 'Pumpkin Harvest'
Chrysanthemum 'Single Apricot'
Chrysanthemum 'Single Peach'
Chrysanthemum 'Viette's Apricot Glow'
Clematis integrifolia
Clematis recta
Coreopsis auriculata
Coreopsis grandiflora 'Walcoreop' (flying
    saucers)
Coreopsis verticillata 'Moonbeam'
Coreopsis verticillata 'Zagreb'
Cryptotaenia japonica f. atropurpurea
Cynoglossum amabile 'Firmament'
Deschampsia cespitosa 'Goldgehänge'
Dianthus ×allwoodii 'Danielle Marie'
Dianthus barbatus 'Sooty'
Dianthus deltoides 'Leuchtfunk' (flashing light)
Dicentra 'Luxuriant'
Dicentra spectabilis 'Gold Heart'
Dracocephalum ruyschiana
Echinacea purpurea
Epimedium davidii
Epimedium ×rubrum
Epimedium ×warleyense
Euphorbia 'Golden Towers'
Euphorbia amygdaloides 'Purpurea'
Euphorbia cyparissias 'Fen's Ruby'
Euphorbia dulcis 'Chameleon'
Euphorbia griffithii 'Fireglow'
Euphorbia ×martinii
Euphorbia polychroma
Festuca glauca 'Elijah Blue'
Festuca glauca 'Golden Toupee'
Galega ×hartlandii 'Lady Wilson'
Geranium 'Ann Folkard'
Geranium 'Brookside'
Geranium 'Johnson's Blue'
Geranium 'Phillippe Vapelle'
Geranium 'Salome'
Geranium himalayense 'Plenum'
Geranium macrorrhizum 'Ingwersen's Variety'
Geranium ×magnificum
Geranium ×oxonianum 'Claridge Druce'
Geranium phaeum 'Lily Lovell'
Geranium phaeum 'Samobor'

Geranium platypetalum
Geranium pratense 'Mrs. Kendall Clark'
Geranium pratense 'Victor Reiter Jr.'
Geranium psilostemon
Geranium renardii
Geranium sanguineum 'New Hampshire'
Geranium wlassovianum
Glaucidium palmatum
Hakonechloa macra 'Aureola'
Helenium 'Kugelsonne'
Helenium 'Moerheim Beauty'
Helianthemum (double yellow)
Helianthemum 'Fire Dragon'
Helianthus 'Lemon Queen'
Helianthus 'Mellow Yellow'
Helianthus salicifolius
Helictotrichon sempervirens 'Saphirsprudel'
    (sapphire fountain)
Heliopsis helianthoides var. scabra
    'Sommersonne' (summer sun)
Helleborus Royal Heritage™
Helleborus foetidus
Helleborus orientalis
Helleborus orientalis (single black)
Hemerocallis 'Alluring Peach'
Hemerocallis 'Carefree Peach'
Hemerocallis 'Happy Returns'
Hemerocallis 'Peach Fairy'
Hemerocallis 'Red Razzamatazz'
Hemerocallis 'Scarlet Romance'
Hemerocallis 'Siloam Royal Prince'
Hemerocallis 'Staghorn Sumac'
Hemerocallis 'Sundried Tomatoes'
Hemerocallis 'Toy Trumpets'
Hemerocallis 'Welcome Mat'
Hemerocallis 'Yellow Lollipop'
Heuchera 'Chocolate Ruffles'
Heuchera 'Plum Pudding'
Heuchera 'Raspberry Regal'
Heuchera 'Velvet Night'
Heuchera micrantha var. diversifolia
    'Palace Purple'
×Heucherella 'Silver Streak'
Hibiscus moscheutos 'Lord Baltimore'
Hosta 'Big Daddy'
Hosta 'Blue Cadet'
Hosta 'Fragrant Blue'
Hosta 'Halcyon'
Hosta 'Lemon Lime'
Hosta 'Love Pat'
Hosta 'Midas Touch'
Hosta 'Night Before Christmas'
Hosta 'Patriot'
Hosta 'Paul's Glory'
Hosta 'Sum and Substance'
Hosta 'Sun Power'
Hosta plantaginea 'Aphrodite'
Hyssopus officinalis

Impatiens omeiana
Knautia macedonica
Lavandula angustifolia 'Munstead'
Lavandula ×intermedia 'Grosso'
Ligularia dentata 'Dark Beauty'
Ligularia dentata 'Desdemona'
Ligularia wilsoniana
Limonium platyphyllum 'Violetta'
Linum perenne 'Blau Saphir' (blue sapphire)
Luzula nivea
Lychnis ×arkwrightii 'Vesuvius'
Lychnis cognata
Mertensia pulmonarioides (virginica)
Monarda 'Jacob Cline'
Monarda 'Violet Queen'
Nepeta 'Six Hills Giant'
Nepeta ×faassenii
Nepeta grandiflora 'Bramdean'
Nepeta racemosa 'Walker's Low'
Oenothera fruticosa ssp. glauca 'Sonnenwende'
Origanum laevigatum 'Herrenhausen'
Origanum vulgare 'Aureum'
Pachysandra procumbens
Packera aurea (Senecio aureus)
Paeonia 'America'
Paeonia 'Burma Ruby'
Paeonia 'Coral Sunset'
Paeonia 'Etched Salmon'
Paeonia 'Monsieur Jules Elie'
Paeonia 'Prairie Moon'
Paeonia obovata
Papaver nudicaule 'Red Sails'
Papaver orientale 'Curlilocks'
Papaver orientale 'Derwisch'
Papaver orientale 'Feuerriese'
Papaver orientale 'Harvest Moon'
Papaver orientale 'Lighthouse'
Papaver orientale 'Patty's Plum'
Papaver orientale 'Prince of Orange'
Papaver orientale 'Saffron'
Papaver orientale 'Turkenlouis'
Patrinia scabiosifolia
Pennisetum alopecuroides 'Hameln'
Persicaria microcephala 'Red Dragon'
Phlox divaricata
Phlox divaricata 'Dirigo Ice'
Phlox divaricata 'Eco Texas Purple'
Phlox divaricata ssp. laphamii
Phlox divaricata 'London Grove Blue'
Phlox divaricata 'Sweet Lilac'
Plantago major 'Rubrifolia'
Polemonium caeruleum 'Blanjou' (brise d'Anjou)
Polystichum acrostichoides
Pulmonaria 'Majesté'
Pulmonaria 'Viette's Deep Blue Sea'
Rheum palmatum var. tanguticum
Rodgersia aesculifolia
Rodgersia pinnata

Rudbeckia fulgida var. speciosa (newmannii)
Rumex sanguineus
Ruta graveolens 'Blue Beauty'
Salvia argentea
Salvia azurea var. pitcheri
Salvia nemorosa 'Ostfriesland' (East Friesland)
Salvia nemorosa 'Purple Glory'
Salvia nemorosa 'Pusztaflamme' (plumosa)
Salvia ×sylvestris 'Blauhügel' (blue hill)
Salvia ×sylvestris 'Blaukönigin' (blue queen)
Salvia ×sylvestris 'Mainacht' (May night)
Salvia ×sylvestris 'Viola Klose'
Salvia verticillata 'Purple Rain'
Saruma henryi
Scabiosa Butterfly Blue®
Scabiosa 'Pink Mist'
Scabiosa columbaria var. ochroleuca
Sedum 'Herbstfreude' (autumn joy)
Sedum 'Pork and Beans'
Sedum telephium ssp. maximum
    'Atropurpureum'
Sisyrinchium 'Quaint and Queer'
Sisyrinchium bermudianum
Solidago 'Golden Spangles'
Solidago rugosa 'Fireworks'
×Solidaster luteus 'Lemore'
Stachys byzantina
Stachys byzantina 'Countess Helen von Stein'
Stachys byzantina 'Primrose Heron'
Stokesia laevis 'Klaus Jelitto'
Stokesia laevis 'Mary Gregory'
Stokesia laevis 'Purple Parasols'
Stylophorum diphyllum
Symphytum 'Goldsmith'
Tanacetum 'Golden Feathers'
Thermopsis villosa
Thymus ×citriodorus
Thymus ×citriodorus 'Lemon Green'
Tiarella cordifolia 'Ninja'
Tradescantia Andersoniana Group
Tradescantia (Andersoniana Group)
    'Purple Profusion'
Tradescantia (Andersoniana Group)
    'Zwanenburg Blue'
Trillium erectum
Veronica 'Waterperry Blue'
Veronica austriaca ssp. teucrium
    'Crater Lake Blue'
Veronica austriaca ssp. teucrium 'Royal Blue'
Veronica gentianoides 'Nana'
Veronica peduncularis 'Georgia Blue'
Viola 'Molly Sanderson'
Viola 'Purple Showers'
Viola labradorica

Annual

Agave havardiana
Ageratum houstonianum 'Blue Horizon'

Arctotis ×hybrida 'Dark Red'
Arctotis ×hybrida 'Flame'
Atriplex hortensis var. rubra
Beta vulgaris 'Bull's Blood'
Beta vulgaris 'Golden'
Beta vulgaris 'Ruby Queen'
Bouvardia ternifolia
Brachyscome 'Ultra'
Brassica oleracea
Calendula officinalis 'Orange King'
Centaurea cineraria
Cerinthe major 'Purpurascens'
Cosmos atrosanguineus
Eschscholzia californica
Eschscholzia californica 'Purple Gleam'
Fuchsia 'Gartenmeister Bonstedt'
Gomphrena haageana 'Lavender Lady'
Lactuca 'Merlot'
Melampodium paludosum 'Million Gold'
Nierembergia scoparia 'Mont Blanc'
Nigella damascena Miss Jekyll Series
Ocimum 'African Blue'
Ocimum basilicum 'Red Rubin'
Papaver rhoeas
Papaver rhoeas Angels' Choir
Perilla frutescens var. crispa
Pistia stratiotes
Plectranthus amboinicus
Rudbeckia hirta 'Irish Eyes'
Salvia 'Indigo Spires'
Salvia 'Purple Majesty'
Salvia coccinea 'Lady in Red'
Salvia guaranitica
Salvia guaranitica 'Black and Blue'
Salvia leucantha
Salvia officinalis 'Tricolor'
Salvia patens
Solenostemon 'Burgundy Columns'
Solenostemon 'Burgundy Giant'
Solenostemon 'Olive'
Solenostemon 'Penny'
Solenostemon 'Purple Emperor'
Solenostemon 'Saturn'
Tropaeolum majus 'Apricot Trifle'
Tropaeolum majus 'Blush Double'
Tropaeolum majus 'Moonlight'
Tropaeolum majus 'Tip Top Mahogany'
Tropaeolum majus Alaska Series
Zinnia haageana 'Orange Star'

Tropical

Caladium 'Florida Cardinal'
Caladium 'Florida Sweetheart'
Colocasia esculenta
Colocasia esculenta 'Black Beauty'
Colocasia esculenta 'Black Magic'
Colocasia esculenta 'Illustris'
Duranta erecta 'Golden Edge

Euphorbia cotinifolia
Hibiscus acetosella 'Red Shield'

Hardy bulb

Allium cristophii
Allium moly 'Jeannine'
Allium schubertii
Chionodoxa forbesii (luciliae) Siehei Group
Colchicum speciosum
Crocus chrysanthus 'Blue Bird'
Dichelostemma ida-maia
Eranthis hyemalis
Erythronium 'Pagoda'
Tulipa batalinii
Tulipa clusiana var. chrysantha

Tender bulb

Dahlia 'Arabian Night'
Dahlia 'Bishop of Llandaff'
Dahlia 'Ellen Houston'
Dahlia 'Orange Nugget'
Dahlia 'Susette'
Scadoxus multiflorus

HEIGHTS

Tree

Small (under 30 ft.)

Abies lasiocarpa 'Arizonica Compacta'
Acer griseum
Acer palmatum var. dissectum Dissectum
    Atropurpureum Group
Acer palmatum 'Sango-kaku'
Amelanchier ×grandiflora 'Autumn Brilliance'
Chionanthus virginicus
Cornus kousa
Fagus sylvatica 'Purpurea Pendula'
Magnolia virginiana
Malus 'Lanzam' (Lancelot®)
Picea abies 'Pendula'
Picea orientalis 'Skylands'
Picea pungens 'Iseli Foxtail'
Picea pungens 'Thomsen'
Pinus cembra 'Silver Sheen'
Pinus parviflora 'Glauca'
Pinus sylvestris 'Fastigiata'
Pseudotsuga menziesii 'Astro Blue'
Quercus robur 'Pectinata'
Sciadopitys verticillata
Thuja occidentalis 'Techny'

Medium (30–40 ft.)

Betula utilis var. jacquemontii
Catalpa bignonioides 'Aurea'
Chamaecyparis lawsoniana 'Sullivan'

Fagus sylvatica 'Tricolor'
Ginkgo biloba 'Autumn Gold'
Pinus flexilis 'Vanderwolf's Pyramid'
Pinus sylvestris
Tsuga canadensis

Large (50 ft. or greater)

Pinus strobus
Quercus palustris

Shrub

Small (under 4 ft.)

Abies procera 'Glauca Prostrata'
Amorpha canescens
Berberis thunbergii var. atropurpurea 'Bailtwo'
    (Burgundy Carousel™)
Berberis thunbergii var. atropurpurea 'Gentry
    Cultivar' (Royal Burgundy™)
Berberis thunbergii var. atropurpurea
    'Rose Glow'
Berberis thunbergii 'Monler' (Gold Nugget™)
Berberis thunbergii 'Monry' (Sunsation™)
Buxus 'Green Gem'
Buxus 'Green Velvet'
Buxus microphylla 'Winter Gem'
Callicarpa dichotoma 'Issai'
Caryopteris ×clandonensis
Caryopteris ×clandonensis 'Longwood Blue'
Caryopteris ×clandonensis 'Worcester Gold'
Chamaecyparis obtusa 'Mariesii'
Chamaecyparis pisifera 'Golden Mop'
Daphne ×burkwoodii 'Carol Mackie'
Fothergilla gardenii
Genista tinctoria 'Royal Gold'
Hypericum androsaemum 'Albury Purple'
Ilex verticillata 'Afterglow'
Ilex verticillata 'Jim Dandy'
Itea virginica
Itea virginica 'Henry's Garnet'
Lespedeza cuneata
Microbiota decussata
Pinus strobus 'Nana'
Pinus sylvestris 'Albyn'
Potentilla fruticosa 'Sunset'
Rhododendron 'Mist Maiden'
Rhododendron 'Northern Starburst'
Rosa 'Ausbuff' (English Garden®)
Rosa 'Ausvelvet' (The Prince®)
Rosa 'Champlain'
Rosa 'Meidomonac' (Bonica®)
Rosa 'Nearly Wild'
Rosa 'Scrivluv' (Baby Love®)
Rosa 'Seafoam'
Rosa 'The Fairy'
Tsuga canadensis 'Cole's Prostrate'
Yucca filamentosa 'Color Guard'
Yucca flaccida 'Golden Sword'

Heights, shrub, cont.

Medium (4–8 ft.)
Berberis thunbergii var. atropurpurea
   'Royal Cloak'
Buddleia 'Lochinch'
Buddleia davidii 'Mongo' (Nanho blue)
Calycanthus floridus
Chamaecyparis obtusa 'Fernspray Gold'
Clethra alnifolia
Hydrangea quercifolia
Hydrangea quercifolia 'Snowflake'
Ilex 'Apollo'
Ilex glabra
Ilex ×meserveae 'Mesdob' (China boy)
Ilex ×meserveae 'Mesog' (China girl)
Ilex verticillata 'Christmas Cheer'
Ilex verticillata 'Winter Red'
Picea abies 'Mucronata'
Picea alcoquiana 'Howell's Tigertail'
Pinus parviflora 'Yatsubusa'
Pinus pumila 'Nana'
Rhododendron 'Chionoides'
Rosa 'Ausmas' (Graham Thomas®)
Rosa 'Aussaucer' (Evelyn®)
Rosa 'F. J. Grootendorst'
Rosa 'Hansa'
Rosa Lyda Rose™
Rosa 'Nuits de Young'
Rosa ×harisonii 'Harison's Yellow'
Rosa rugosa
Viburnum plicatum var. tomentosum 'Mariesii'

Large (over 8 ft.)
Aesculus parviflora
Aralia elata 'Aureovariegata'
Buddleia davidii 'Black Knight'
Cotinus coggygria 'Velvet Cloak'
Pinus contorta 'Chief Joseph'
Pinus contorta 'Spaan's Dwarf'
Pinus densiflora 'Oculus Draconis'
Rosa 'Alchymist'
Rosa multiflora 'Grevillei' (seven sisters' rose)
Sambucus racemosa 'Sutherland Gold'
Syringa meyeri
Vitex agnus-castus var. latifolia

Woody vine

Medium (6–10 ft.)
Clematis 'Elsa Späth'
Clematis 'Hagley Hybrid'
Clematis alpina 'Constance'
Clematis macropetala 'Markham's Pink'

Large (over 10 ft.)
Ampelopsis glandulosa var. brevipedunculata
   'Elegans'
Campsis ×tagliabuana 'Madame Galen'
Clematis 'Lanuginosa Candida'
Clematis 'Polish Spirit'
Clematis 'Royal Velours'
Clematis terniflora
Hydrangea anomala ssp. petiolaris
Lonicera periclymenum 'Graham Thomas'
Lonicera sempervirens 'Blanche Sandman'
Vitis vinifera 'Purpurea'

Perennial

Small (under 16 in.)
Acorus gramineus 'Minimus Aureus'
Acorus gramineus 'Oborozuki'
Acorus gramineus 'Ogon'
Ajuga reptans 'Purple Torch'
Arisaema sikokianum
Astilbe chinensis 'Veronica Klose'
Belamcanda chinensis 'Hello Yellow'
Brunnera macrophylla
Campanula 'Birch Hybrid'
Campanula 'Constellation'
Campanula 'Dwarf Tornado'
Campanula rotundifolia 'Olympica'
Carex dolichostachya 'Kaga Nishiki'
   (gold fountains)
Carex elata 'Aurea' (Bowles' golden)
Carex morrowii 'Ice Dance'
Carex morrowii 'Variegata'
Ceratostigma plumbaginoides
Clematis integrifolia
Coreopsis auriculata
Coreopsis verticillata 'Zagreb'
Crocosmia ×crocosmiiflora 'Norwich Canary'
Cynoglossum amabile 'Firmament'
Dianthus ×allwoodii 'Danielle Marie'
Dianthus barbatus 'Sooty'
Dianthus deltoides 'Leuchtfunk' (flashing light)
Dicentra 'Luxuriant'
Dracocephalum ruyschiana
Epimedium davidii
Epimedium ×rubrum
Euphorbia cyparissias 'Fen's Ruby'
Euphorbia dulcis 'Chameleon'
Euphorbia polychroma
Festuca glauca 'Elijah Blue'
Festuca glauca 'Golden Toupee'
Galium odoratum
Gentiana septemfida var. lagodechiana
Gentiana triflora 'Royal Blue'
Geranium 'Phillippe Vapelle'
Geranium 'Salome'
Geranium himalayense 'Plenum'
Geranium macrorrhizum 'Ingwersen's Variety'

Geranium phaeum 'Samobor'
Geranium renardii
Geranium sanguineum 'New Hampshire'
Hakonechloa macra 'Aureola'
Helianthemum (double yellow)
Helianthemum 'Fire Dragon'
Helleborus foetidus
Hemerocallis 'Yellow Lollipop'
Heuchera 'Chocolate Ruffles'
Heuchera 'Plum Pudding'
Heuchera 'Velvet Night'
Heuchera micrantha var. diversifolia
   'Palace Purple'
×Heucherella 'Silver Streak'
Hosta 'Blue Cadet'
Hosta 'Lemon Lime'
Hosta 'Patriot'
Impatiens omeiana
Lamium maculatum 'White Nancy'
Luzula nivea
Lychnis cognata
Lysimachia nummularia 'Aurea'
Mazus reptans
Nepeta racemosa 'Walker's Low'
Nymphaea 'Marliacea Chromatella'
Oenothera fremontii 'Lemon Silver'
Origanum 'Kent Beauty'
Origanum vulgare 'Aureum'
Pachysandra procumbens
Packera aurea (Senecio aureus)
Phlox divaricata
Phlox divaricata 'Dirigo Ice'
Phlox divaricata 'Eco Texas Purple'
Phlox divaricata ssp. laphamii
Phlox divaricata 'London Grove Blue'
Phlox divaricata 'Sweet Lilac'
Phlox stolonifera 'Blue Ridge'
Phlox stolonifera 'Bruce's White'
Plantago major 'Rubrifolia'
Pulmonaria 'Majesté'
Pulmonaria 'Viette's Deep Blue Sea'
Salvia argentea
Saruma henryi
Scabiosa Butterfly Blue®
Scabiosa 'Pink Mist'
Sedum 'Pork and Beans'
Sedum acre 'Aureum'
Sisyrinchium 'Quaint and Queer'
Sisyrinchium bermudianum
Stachys byzantina
Stachys byzantina 'Countess Helen von Stein'
Stachys byzantina 'Primrose Heron'
Stokesia laevis 'Klaus Jelitto'
Stokesia laevis 'Purple Parasols'
Symphytum 'Goldsmith'
Tanacetum 'Golden Feathers'
Thymus ×citriodorus
Thymus ×citriodorus 'Lemon Green'

Thymus pseudolanuginosus
Tiarella cordifolia 'Ninja'
Trillium erectum
Veronica 'Goodness Grows'
Veronica 'Waterperry Blue'
Veronica austriaca ssp. teucrium
   'Crater Lake Blue'
Veronica gentianoides 'Nana'
Veronica peduncularis 'Georgia Blue'
Veronica prostrata 'Trehane'
Veronica repens 'Sunshine'
Viola 'Molly Sanderson'
Viola 'Purple Showers'
Viola labradorica

Medium (16–36 in.)
Acanthus spinosus
Achillea 'Anblo' (Anthea)
Achillea 'Heidi'
Achillea 'Salmon Beauty'
Achillea filipendulina 'Altgold'
Aconitum 'Bressingham Spire'
Aconitum 'Ivorine'
Aconitum carmichaelii (Wilsonii Group)
   'Spätlese'
Adiantum pedatum
Alchemilla mollis
Alstroemeria 'Sweet Laura'
Amsonia ciliata
Amsonia elliptica
Amsonia hubrichtii
Amsonia tabernaemontana
Anemone ×hybrida 'Queen Charlotte'
Anemone ×hybrida 'September Charm'
Anthriscus sylvestris 'Ravenswing'
Aquilegia alpina
Aquilegia vulgaris var. stellata 'Black Barlow'
Artemisia 'Huntington'
Artemisia 'Powis Castle'
Artemisia 'Silverado'
Artemisia absinthium 'Lambrook Silver'
Arum italicum ssp. italicum 'Marmoratum'
Asclepias tuberosa
Asclepias tuberosa 'Hello Yellow'
Aster 'Climax'
Aster laevis 'Bluebird'
Aster novae-angliae 'Hella Lacy'
Aster novae-angliae 'Hillside'
Aster novae-angliae 'Purple Dome'
Aster novae-angliae 'Wild Light Blue'
Aster oblongifolius var. angustatus
   'Raydon's Favorite'
Astilbe ×arendsii 'Snowdrift'
Astilbe chinensis 'Purple Candle'
Astilbe chinensis var. taquetii 'Superba'
Astilbe ×rosea 'Peach Blossom'
Athyrium niponicum var. pictum
Baptisia 'Purple Smoke'

Baptisia australis
Baptisia sphaerocarpa
Campanula 'Kent Belle'
Campanula persicifolia 'Chettle Charm'
Campanula rapunculoides
Carex buchananii
Centaurea montana
Chrysanthemum 'Autumn Moon'
Chrysanthemum 'Pumpkin Harvest'
Chrysanthemum 'Single Apricot'
Chrysanthemum 'Single Peach'
Chrysanthemum 'Viette's Apricot Glow'
Coreopsis grandiflora 'Walcoreop'
    (flying saucers)
Coreopsis verticillata 'Moonbeam'
Crocosmia 'Blacro' (Jenny Bloom)
Crocosmia 'Emberglow'
Crocosmia 'Lucifer'
Crocosmia ×crocosmiiflora 'Solfatare'
Crocosmia ×crocosmiiflora 'Venus'
Cryptotaenia japonica f. atropurpurea
Delphinium 'Centurion Sky Blue'
Delphinium ×bellamosum
Delphinium cashmerianum
Delphinium exaltatum
Deschampsia cespitosa 'Goldgehänge'
Dicentra spectabilis 'Gold Heart'
Digitalis grandiflora
Digitalis lutea
Digitalis purpurea 'Apricot'
Echinacea purpurea
Echinops bannaticus 'Taplow Blue'
Epimedium ×warleyense
Eryngium amethystinum
Eryngium planum 'Blaukappe'
Eryngium variifolium
Euphorbia amygdaloides 'Purpurea'
Euphorbia griffithii 'Fireglow'
Euphorbia ×martinii
Geranium 'Ann Folkard'
Geranium 'Brookside'
Geranium 'Johnson's Blue'
Geranium ×magnificum
Geranium ×oxonianum 'Claridge Druce'
Geranium phaeum 'Lily Lovell'
Geranium platypetalum
Geranium pratense 'Mrs. Kendall Clark'
Geranium pratense 'Victor Reiter Jr.'
Geranium psilostemon
Geranium wlassovianum
Gillenia stipulata
Gladiolus communis ssp. byzantinus
Gladiolus ×gandavensis
Glaucidium palmatum
Helictotrichon sempervirens 'Saphirsprudel'
    (sapphire fountain)
Helleborus Royal Heritage™
Helleborus orientalis

Helleborus orientalis (single black)
Hemerocallis 'Alluring Peach'
Hemerocallis 'Carefree Peach'
Hemerocallis 'Happy Returns'
Hemerocallis 'Peach Fairy'
Hemerocallis 'Red Razzamatazz'
Hemerocallis 'Scarlet Romance'
Hemerocallis 'Siloam Royal Prince'
Hemerocallis 'Staghorn Sumac'
Hemerocallis 'Sundried Tomatoes'
Hemerocallis 'Toy Trumpets'
Hemerocallis 'Welcome Mat'
Hesperis matronalis
Heuchera 'Raspberry Regal'
Hosta 'Big Daddy'
Hosta 'Fragrant Blue'
Hosta 'Halcyon'
Hosta 'Love Pat'
Hosta 'Midas Touch'
Hosta 'Night Before Christmas'
Hosta 'Paul's Glory'
Hosta 'Sum and Substance'
Hosta 'Sun Power'
Hosta plantaginea 'Aphrodite'
Hyssopus officinalis
Hystrix patula
Imperata cylindrica var. koenigii 'Red Baron'
Iris 'Flavescens'
Iris 'Perfume Counter'
Iris 'Sugar Blues'
Iris foetidissima
Iris pallida 'Variegata'
Iris pseudacorus 'Variegata'
Iris sanguinea 'Snow Queen'
Iris sibirica 'Butter and Sugar'
Iris sibirica 'Caesar's Brother'
Iris sibirica 'Dianne's Daughter'
Iris sibirica 'Orville Fay'
Iris sibirica 'Pirate Prince'
Iris sibirica 'Skywings'
Iris sibirica 'Vi Luihn'
Iris sibirica 'White Swirl'
Knautia macedonica
Kniphofia 'Alcazar'
Kniphofia 'Little Maid'
Kniphofia 'Primrose Beauty'
Kniphofia 'Royal Standard'
Kniphofia 'Shining Sceptre'
Kniphofia citrina
Kniphofia triangularis
Lavandula angustifolia 'Munstead'
Lavandula ×intermedia 'Grosso'
Liatris spicata 'Kobold'
Lilium 'Casa Blanca'
Lilium 'Connecticut King'
Lilium 'Eden's Dandy'
Lilium 'Grand Cru'
Lilium 'Pretender'

Lilium 'Royal Justice'
Lilium 'Royal Perfume'
Lilium 'Scarlet Emperor'
Lilium 'Sunset'
Lilium pumilum
Limonium platyphyllum 'Violetta'
Linaria 'Natalie'
Linaria purpurea
Linum perenne 'Blau Saphir' (blue sapphire)
Lobelia 'Dark Crusader'
Lobelia 'Grape Knee High'
Lobelia 'Royal Robe'
Lobelia 'Ruby Slippers'
Lobelia siphilitica
Lychnis ×arkwrightii 'Vesuvius'
Lychnis coronaria
Mertensia pulmonarioides (virginica)
Monarda 'Violet Queen'
Nepeta 'Six Hills Giant'
Nepeta ×faassenii
Nepeta sibirica 'Souvenir d'André Chaudron'
Oenothera fruticosa ssp. glauca 'Sonnenwende'
Origanum laevigatum 'Herrenhausen'
Osmunda cinnamomea
Osmunda regalis
Paeonia 'America'
Paeonia 'Burma Ruby'
Paeonia 'Coral Sunset'
Paeonia 'Etched Salmon'
Paeonia 'Monsieur Jules Elie'
Paeonia 'Prairie Moon'
Paeonia obovata
Papaver nudicaule 'Red Sails'
Papaver orientale 'Curlilocks'
Papaver orientale 'Derwisch'
Papaver orientale 'Feuerriese'
Papaver orientale 'Harvest Moon'
Papaver orientale 'Lighthouse'
Papaver orientale 'Patty's Plum'
Papaver orientale 'Prince of Orange'
Papaver orientale 'Saffron'
Papaver orientale 'Turkenlouis'
Pennisetum alopecuroides 'Hameln'
Penstemon digitalis 'Husker Red'
Penstemon ×mexicale 'Pike's Peak Purple'
Persicaria microcephala 'Red Dragon'
Phlomis russeliana
Phlox paniculata 'Fesselballon'
Phlox paniculata 'Katherine'
Phlox paniculata 'Laura'
Phlox paniculata 'Orange Perfection'
Phlox paniculata 'Pax' (peace)
Phlox paniculata 'Tenor'
Phlox paniculata 'The King'
Platycodon grandiflorus 'Double Blue'
Platycodon grandiflorus 'Komachi'
Polemonium caeruleum 'Blanjou' (brise d'Anjou)
Polygonatum odoratum 'Variegatum'

Polystichum acrostichoides
Rudbeckia fulgida var. speciosa (newmannii)
Rumex sanguineus
Ruta graveolens 'Blue Beauty'
Salvia nemorosa 'Ostfriesland' (East Friesland)
Salvia nemorosa 'Purple Glory'
Salvia nemorosa 'Pusztaflamme' (plumosa)
Salvia ×sylvestris 'Blauhügel' (blue hill)
Salvia ×sylvestris 'Blaukönigin' (blue queen)
Salvia ×sylvestris 'Mainacht' (May night)
Salvia ×sylvestris 'Viola Klose'
Salvia verticillata 'Purple Rain'
Scabiosa columbaria var. ochroleuca
Schizachyrium scoparium 'The Blues'
Sedum 'Herbstfreude' (autumn joy)
Sedum telephium ssp. maximum
    'Atropurpureum'
Silene regia
Solidago 'Golden Spangles'
×Solidaster luteus 'Lemore'
Stachys macrantha
Stokesia laevis 'Mary Gregory'
Stokesia laevis 'Omega Skyrocket'
Stylophorum diphyllum
Thalictrum aquilegiifolium 'Thundercloud'
Thermopsis villosa
Tradescantia Andersoniana Group
Tradescantia (Andersoniana Group)
    'Purple Profusion'
Tradescantia (Andersoniana Group)
    'Zwanenburg Blue'
Valeriana officinalis
Verbascum 'Jackie'
Veronica austriaca ssp. teucrium 'Royal Blue'
Veronica spicata 'Blue Charm'
Veronica spicata 'Icicle'

Large (over 3 ft.)
Aconitum episcopale
Aconitum lycoctonum ssp. neapolitanum
Agastache 'Blue Fortune'
Agastache rupestris
Alcea rosea 'Peaches and Dreams'
Alcea rosea 'The Watchman'
Alcea rugosa
Angelica gigas
Aruncus dioicus
Aster tataricus 'Jindai'
Belamcanda chinensis
Buphthalmum speciosum
Calamagrostis ×acutiflora 'Karl Foerster'
Calamagrostis ×acutiflora 'Overdam'
Calamagrostis brachytricha
Cephalaria gigantea
Cimicifuga ramosa 'Brunette'
Cimicifuga ramosa 'Hillside Black Beauty'
Clematis recta
Coreopsis tripteris

Heights, perennial, cont.

Echinops ritro 'Blue Glow'
Echinops ritro 'Veitch's Blue'
Eryngium yuccifolium
Eupatorium purpureum ssp. maculatum
  'Gateway'
Euphorbia 'Golden Towers'
Foeniculum vulgare 'Purpureum'
Galega ×hartlandii 'Lady Wilson'
Gladiolus ×gandavensis 'Boone'
Helenium 'Kugelsonne'
Helenium 'Moerheim Beauty'
Helianthus 'Lemon Queen'
Helianthus 'Mellow Yellow'
Helianthus salicifolius
Heliopsis helianthoides var. scabra
  'Sommersonne' (summer sun)
Hibiscus moscheutos 'Lord Baltimore'
Hosta 'Krossa Regal'
Humulus lupulus 'Bianca'
Kniphofia 'Prince Igor'
Kniphofia caulescens
Lathyrus latifolius
Ligularia 'The Rocket'
Ligularia dentata 'Dark Beauty'
Ligularia dentata 'Desdemona'
Ligularia wilsoniana
Lilium 'Apricot Brandy'
Lilium 'Conquistador'
Lilium 'Montenegro'
Lilium 'Shirley'
Lilium henryi
Lilium lancifolium var. splendens
Lobelia 'Purple Towers'
Lobelia 'Queen Victoria'
Miscanthus 'Purpurascens'
Miscanthus sinensis var. condensatus
  'Cosmopolitan'
Miscanthus sinensis 'Gracillimus'
Miscanthus sinensis 'Malepartus'
Miscanthus sinensis 'Morning Light'
Molinia caerulea ssp. arundinacea 'Skyracer'
Monarda 'Jacob Cline'
Nepeta grandiflora 'Bramdean'
Panicum virgatum 'Dallas Blues'
Panicum virgatum 'Heavy Metal'
Panicum virgatum 'Rehbraun'
Passiflora incarnata
Patrinia scabiosifolia
Perovskia atriplicifolia
Perovskia atriplicifolia 'Longin'
Phlox paniculata 'David'
Phlox paniculata 'Look Again'
Phlox paniculata 'Tracy's Treasure'
Phytolacca polyandra
Rheum palmatum var. tanguticum

Rodgersia aesculifolia
Rodgersia pinnata
Rudbeckia maxima
Rudbeckia triloba
Salvia azurea var. pitcheri
Sanguisorba tenuifolia 'Purpurea'
Solidago rugosa 'Fireworks'
Sorghastrum nutans 'Sioux Blue'
Thalictrum rochebruneanum
Verbascum bombyciferum
Verbena hastata
Veronicastrum virginicum 'Fascination'

Annual

Small (under 12 in.)
Alternanthera dentata 'Rubiginosa'
Arctotis ×hybrida 'Dark Red'
Arctotis ×hybrida 'Flame'
Beta vulgaris 'Bull's Blood'
Brachyscome 'Ultra'
Calendula officinalis 'Orange King'
Eschscholzia californica
Eschscholzia californica 'Purple Gleam'
Helichrysum petiolare 'Limelight'
Lactuca 'Merlot'
Lysimachia congestiflora 'Variegata'
Melampodium paludosum 'Million Gold'
Nierembergia scoparia 'Mont Blanc'
Pistia stratiotes
Plectranthus amboinicus
Portulaca grandiflora 'Sundial Peach'
Tropaeolum majus 'Apricot Trifle'
Tropaeolum majus 'Blush Double'
Tropaeolum majus 'Moonlight'
Tropaeolum majus 'Tip Top Mahogany'
Tropaeolum majus Alaska Series
Verbena 'Homestead Purple'
Verbena 'Romance Apricot'
Verbena Temari® Red
Zinnia haageana 'Orange Star'

Medium (12–24 in.)
Agave havardiana
Ageratum houstonianum 'Blue Horizon'
Alstroemeria aurea 'Orange King'
Alstroemeria psittacina
Angelonia 'Blue Pacific'
Angelonia angustifolia 'Purple Pinnacles'
Antirrhinum majus 'Rocket Red'
Beta vulgaris 'Golden'
Beta vulgaris 'Ruby Queen'
Bouvardia ternifolia
Brassica oleracea
Centaurea cineraria
Cerinthe major 'Purpurascens'
Cosmos atrosanguineus
Cyperus alternifolius 'Stricta'

Eucomis comosa 'Sparkling Burgundy'
Fuchsia 'Gartenmeister Bonstedt'
Gomphrena haageana 'Lavender Lady'
Ipomoea batatas 'Ace of Spades'
Ipomoea batatas 'Blackie'
Ipomoea batatas 'Margarita'
Nigella damascena Miss Jekyll Series
Ocimum 'African Blue'
Ocimum basilicum 'Red Rubin'
Papaver rhoeas
Papaver rhoeas Angels' Choir
Plectranthus argentatus
Rudbeckia hirta 'Irish Eyes'
Salvia coccinea 'Lady in Red'
Salvia officinalis 'Tricolor'
Salvia patens
Solenostemon 'Burgundy Columns'
Solenostemon 'Olive'

Large (over 2 ft.)
Atriplex hortensis var. rubra
Celosia spicata 'Flamingo Purple'
Consolida ajacis 'Blue Spire'
Cynara cardunculus
Leonotis menthifolia
Nicotiana langsdorffii
Papaver somniferum
Papaver somniferum 'Black Peony'
Papaver somniferum 'Burnt Orange'
Papaver somniferum 'Lauren's Grape'
Papaver somniferum 'Pepperbox'
Pennisetum setaceum 'Rubrum'
Perilla frutescens var. crispa
Phyllostachys nigra
Salvia 'Indigo Spires'
Salvia 'Purple Majesty'
Salvia guaranitica
Salvia guaranitica 'Black and Blue'
Salvia leucantha
Scabiosa atropurpurea 'Ace of Spades'
Solenostemon 'Burgundy Giant'
Solenostemon 'Penny'
Solenostemon 'Purple Emperor'
Solenostemon 'Saturn'
Verbena bonariensis

Annual vine

Small (3–4 ft.)
Thunbergia battiscombei

Medium (5–8 ft.)
Lathyrus odoratus
Lathyrus odoratus 'Henry Eckford'
Lathyrus odoratus 'King Size Navy Blue'

Large (over 8 ft.)
Ipomoea lobata (Mina lobata)

Ipomoea tricolor 'Heavenly Blue'
Lablab purpureus
Rhodochiton atrosanguineus

Tropical

Medium (16–36 in.)
Caladium 'Florida Cardinal'
Caladium 'Florida Sweetheart'
Canna 'Orange Punch'
Colocasia esculenta 'Black Beauty'
Phormium 'Bronze Baby'
Phormium 'Platt's Black'
Phormium 'Yellow Wave'
Phormium cookianum 'Chocolate'

Large (over 3 ft.)
Canna 'Black Knight'
Canna 'Omega'
Canna 'Panache'
Canna 'Phasion'
Canna 'Roi Humbert' (red King Humbert)
Canna 'Striata' (Pretoria)
Canna indica 'Red Stripe' (purpurea)
Colocasia esculenta
Colocasia esculenta 'Black Magic'
Colocasia esculenta 'Fontanesii'
Colocasia esculenta 'Illustris'
Duranta erecta 'Golden Edge'
Euphorbia cotinifolia
Hedychium 'Daniel Weeks'
Hedychium coccineum
Hibiscus acetosella 'Red Shield'
Musa basjoo
Musa zebrina
Ricinus communis
Ricinus communis 'Carmencita'

Hardy bulb

Small (under 12 in.)
Allium moly 'Jeannine'
Chionodoxa forbesii (luciliae) Siehei Group
Colchicum speciosum
Crocus chrysanthus 'Blue Bird'
Eranthis hyemalis
Erythronium 'Pagoda'
Iris reticulata 'Harmony'
Narcissus 'Petrel'
Puschkinia scilloides
Tulipa batalinii
Tulipa clusiana var. chrysantha

Medium (12–24 in.)
Allium caeruleum
Allium carinatum ssp. pulchellum
Allium cristophii

Allium hollandicum (aflatunense)
  'Purple Sensation'
Allium schubertii
Dichelostemma ida-maia
Iris 'Blue Magic'
Narcissus 'Delnashaugh'
Narcissus 'Fragrant Rose'
Narcissus 'Mary Gay Lirette'
Narcissus 'Mint Julep'
Narcissus 'Sir Winston Churchill'
Narcissus 'Stratosphere'
Narcissus 'Tahiti'
Triteleia laxa 'Queen Fabiola'
Tulipa 'Angelique'
Tulipa 'Apricot Parrot'
Tulipa 'Big Smile'
Tulipa 'Black Parrot'
Tulipa 'Blue Heron'
Tulipa 'Blue Parrot'
Tulipa 'Burgundy Lace'
Tulipa 'Carmine Parrot'
Tulipa 'Couleur Cardinal'
Tulipa 'Fringed Elegance'
Tulipa 'Queen of Night'
Tulipa 'Temple of Beauty'

Large (over 2 ft.)
Allium sphaerocephalon
Camassia leichtlinii 'Semiplena'
Camassia leichtlinii ssp. suksdorfii 'Blauwe
  Donau' (blue Danube)
Eremurus ×isabellinus 'Pinokkio'
Fritillaria persica
Tulipa 'Blushing Lady'
Tulipa 'Uncle Tom'

Tender bulb

Small (under 12 in.)
Scadoxus multiflorus

Medium (12–24 in.)
Dahlia 'Arabian Night'
Dahlia 'Bishop of Llandaff'
Dahlia 'Ellen Houston'
Dahlia 'Orange Nugget'
Dahlia 'Susette'
Gladiolus 'Atom'
Hymenocallis 'Sulphur Queen'
Tigridia pavonia 'Speciosa'

Large (over 2 ft.)
Agapanthus 'Bressingham Blue'
Amorphophallus konjac
Gladiolus 'Violetta'

WINTER INTEREST

Tree
Abies lasiocarpa 'Arizonica Compacta'
Acer griseum
Acer palmatum 'Sango-kaku'
Amelanchier ×grandiflora 'Autumn Brilliance'
Betula utilis var. jacquemontii
Chamaecyparis lawsoniana 'Sullivan'
Malus 'Lanzam' (Lancelot®)
Picea abies 'Pendula'
Picea orientalis 'Skylands'
Picea pungens 'Iseli Foxtail'
Picea pungens 'Thomsen'
Pinus cembra 'Silver Sheen'
Pinus flexilis 'Vanderwolf's Pyramid'
Pinus parviflora 'Glauca'
Pinus strobus
Pinus sylvestris
Pinus sylvestris 'Fastigiata'
Pseudotsuga menziesii 'Astro Blue'
Sciadopitys verticillata
Thuja occidentalis 'Techny'
Tsuga canadensis

Shrub
Abies procera 'Glauca Prostrata'
Buxus 'Green Gem'
Buxus 'Green Velvet'
Buxus microphylla 'Winter Gem'
Chamaecyparis obtusa 'Fernspray Gold'
Chamaecyparis obtusa 'Mariesii'
Chamaecyparis pisifera 'Golden Mop'
Hydrangea quercifolia
Hydrangea quercifolia 'Snowflake'
Ilex glabra
Ilex ×meserveae 'Mesdob (China boy)
Ilex ×meserveae 'Mesog (China girl)
Ilex verticillata 'Afterglow'
Ilex verticillata 'Christmas Cheer
Ilex verticillata 'Winter Red
Microbiota decussata
Picea abies 'Mucronata'
Picea alcoquiana 'Howell's Tigertail'
Pinus contorta 'Chief Joseph'
Pinus contorta 'Spaan's Dwarf'
Pinus densiflora 'Oculus Draconis'
Pinus parviflora 'Yatsubusa'
Pinus pumila 'Nana'
Pinus strobus 'Nana'
Pinus sylvestris 'Albyn'
Rhododendron 'Chionoides'
Rhododendron 'Mist Maiden'
Rhododendron 'Northern Starburst'
Tsuga canadensis 'Cole's Prostrate'
Yucca filamentosa 'Color Guard'
Yucca flaccida 'Golden Sword'

Woody vine
Hydrangea anomala ssp. petiolaris

Perennial
Ajuga reptans 'Purple Torch'
Amsonia ciliata
Amsonia elliptica
Amsonia hubrichtii
Arum italicum ssp. italicum 'Marmoratum'
Calamagrostis ×acutiflora 'Karl Foerster'
Calamagrostis ×acutiflora 'Overdam'
Carex buchananii
Carex morrowii 'Ice Dance'
Carex morrowii 'Variegata'
Deschampsia cespitosa 'Goldgehänge'
Epimedium davidii
Epimedium ×rubrum
Epimedium ×warleyense
Gillenia stipulata
Helianthemum (double yellow)
Helianthemum 'Fire Dragon'
Helictotrichon sempervirens 'Saphirsprudel'
  (sapphire fountain)
Helleborus foetidus
Helleborus orientalis
Heuchera 'Chocolate Ruffles'
Heuchera 'Plum Pudding'
Heuchera 'Velvet Night'
Heuchera micrantha var. diversifolia 'Palace
  Purple'
Iris sanguinea 'Snow Queen'
Iris sibirica 'Caesar's Brother'
Kniphofia caulescens
Lamium maculatum 'White Nancy'
Luzula nivea
Lysimachia nummularia 'Aurea'
Miscanthus 'Purpurascens'
Miscanthus sinensis 'Gracillimus'
Miscanthus sinensis 'Malepartus'
Miscanthus sinensis 'Morning Light'
Miscanthus sinensis var. condensatus
  'Cosmopolitan'
Molinia caerulea ssp. arundinacea 'Skyracer'
Panicum virgatum 'Dallas Blues'
Panicum virgatum 'Heavy Metal'
Panicum virgatum 'Rehbraun'
Perovskia atriplicifolia
Perovskia atriplicifolia 'Longin'
Phlox divaricata
Phlox stolonifera 'Blue Ridge'
Phlox stolonifera 'Bruce's White'
Polystichum acrostichoides
Schizachyrium scoparium 'The Blues'
Sedum 'Herbstfreude' (autumn joy)
Sorghastrum nutans 'Sioux Blue'
Veronica 'Waterperry Blue'

FRUIT, SEEDHEADS

Tree
Abies lasiocarpa 'Arizonica Compacta'
Acer griseum
Acer palmatum 'Sango-kaku'
Amelanchier ×grandiflora 'Autumn Brilliance'
Chamaecyparis lawsoniana 'Sullivan'
Chionanthus virginicus
Cornus kousa
Magnolia virginiana
Malus 'Lanzam' (Lancelot®)
Picea abies 'Pendula'
Picea orientalis 'Skylands'
Picea pungens 'Iseli Foxtail'
Picea pungens 'Thomsen'
Pinus cembra 'Silver Sheen'
Pinus flexilis 'Vanderwolf's Pyramid'
Pinus parviflora 'Glauca'
Pinus strobus
Pinus sylvestris
Pinus sylvestris 'Fastigiata'
Pseudotsuga menziesii 'Astro Blue'
Quercus robur 'Pectinata'
Sciadopitys verticillata
Thuja occidentalis 'Techny'
Tsuga canadensis

Shrub
Abies procera 'Glauca Prostrata'
Aesculus parviflora
Aralia elata 'Aureovariegata'
Callicarpa dichotoma 'Issai'
Calycanthus floridus
Clethra alnifolia
Hypericum androsaemum 'Albury Purple'
Ilex glabra
Ilex ×meserveae 'Mesog' (China girl)
Ilex verticillata 'Afterglow'
Ilex verticillata 'Christmas Cheer'
Ilex verticillata 'Winter Red'
Picea abies 'Mucronata'
Picea alcoquiana 'Howell's Tigertail'
Pinus contorta 'Chief Joseph'
Pinus contorta 'Spaan's Dwarf'
Pinus densiflora 'Oculus Draconis'
Pinus parviflora 'Yatsubusa'
Pinus pumila 'Nana'
Pinus strobus 'Nana'
Pinus sylvestris 'Albyn'
Rosa 'Hansa'
Rosa 'Meidomonac' (Bonica®)
Rosa 'Nuits de Young'
Rosa ×harisonii 'Harison's Yellow'
Rosa rugosa
Tsuga canadensis 'Cole's Prostrate'
Viburnum plicatum var. tomentosum 'Mariesii'

Fruit, Seedheads, cont.
....

Woody vine

Ampelopsis glandulosa var. brevipedunculata
   'Elegans'
Clematis 'Elsa Späth'
Clematis 'Hagley Hybrid'
Clematis 'Lanuginosa Candida'
Clematis alpina 'Constance'
Clematis macropetala 'Markham's Pink'
Lonicera periclymenum 'Graham Thomas'
Lonicera sempervirens 'Blanche Sandman'
Vitis vinifera 'Purpurea'

Perennial

Acanthus spinosus
Aquilegia alpina
Aquilegia vulgaris var. stellata 'Black Barlow'
Arum italicum ssp. italicum 'Marmoratum'
Asclepias tuberosa
Asclepias tuberosa 'Hello Yellow'
Astilbe ×arendsii 'Snowdrift'
Astilbe chinensis 'Purple Candle'
Astilbe chinensis var. taquetii 'Superba'
Astilbe chinensis 'Veronica Klose'
Astilbe ×rosea 'Peach Blossom'
Baptisia 'Purple Smoke'
Baptisia australis
Baptisia sphaerocarpa
Belamcanda chinensis
Belamcanda chinensis 'Hello Yellow
Buphthalmum speciosum
Calamagrostis ×acutiflora 'Karl Foerster'
Calamagrostis ×acutiflora 'Overdam'
Calamagrostis brachytricha
Ceratostigma plumbaginoides
Coreopsis verticillata 'Moonbeam'
Coreopsis verticillata 'Zagreb'
Crocosmia 'Emberglow'
Crocosmia 'Lucifer'
Crocosmia ×crocosmiiflora 'Norwich Canary'
Crocosmia ×crocosmiiflora 'Solfatare'
Crocosmia ×crocosmiiflora 'Venus'
Deschampsia cespitosa 'Goldgehänge'
Echinacea purpurea
Echinops bannaticus 'Taplow Blue'
Echinops ritro 'Blue Glow'
Echinops ritro 'Veitch's Blue'
Eryngium amethystinum
Eryngium planum 'Blaukappe'
Eryngium variifolium
Eryngium yuccifolium
Festuca glauca 'Elijah Blue'
Gillenia stipulata
Helictotrichon sempervirens 'Saphirsprudel'
   (sapphire fountain)
Hystrix patula

Iris foetidissima
Iris sanguinea 'Snow Queen'
Iris sibirica 'Caesar's Brother'
Lathyrus latifolius
Ligularia 'The Rocket'
Ligularia dentata 'Dark Beauty'
Ligularia dentata 'Desdemona'
Ligularia wilsoniana
Luzula nivea
Miscanthus 'Purpurascens'
Miscanthus sinensis var. condensatus
   'Cosmopolitan'
Miscanthus sinensis 'Gracillimus'
Miscanthus sinensis 'Malepartus'
Miscanthus sinensis 'Morning Light'
Molinia caerulea ssp. arundinacea 'Skyracer'
Paeonia obovata
Panicum virgatum 'Dallas Blues'
Panicum virgatum 'Heavy Metal'
Panicum virgatum 'Rehbraun'
Papaver nudicaule 'Red Sails'
Papaver orientale 'Curlilocks'
Papaver orientale 'Derwisch'
Papaver orientale 'Feuerriese'
Papaver orientale 'Harvest Moon'
Papaver orientale 'Lighthouse'
Papaver orientale 'Patty's Plum'
Papaver orientale 'Prince of Orange'
Papaver orientale 'Saffron'
Papaver orientale 'Turkenlouis'
Passiflora incarnata
Pennisetum alopecuroides 'Hameln'
Phlomis russeliana
Phytolacca polyandra
Rheum palmatum var. tanguticum
Rudbeckia fulgida var. speciosa (newmannii)
Rudbeckia maxima
Rudbeckia triloba
Schizachyrium scoparium 'The Blues'
Sedum 'Herbstfreude' (autumn joy)
Sorghastrum nutans 'Sioux Blue'
Stylophorum diphyllum
Thalictrum aquilegiifolium 'Thundercloud'
Thalictrum rochebruneanum
Thermopsis villosa

Annual

Gomphrena haageana 'Lavender Lady'
Nigella damascena Miss Jekyll Series
Papaver rhoeas
Papaver rhoeas Angels' Choir
Papaver somniferum
Papaver somniferum 'Black Peony'
Papaver somniferum 'Burnt Orange'
Papaver somniferum 'Lauren's Grape'
Papaver somniferum 'Pepperbox'
Pennisetum setaceum 'Rubrum'

Annual vine

Lablab purpureus
Lathyrus odoratus 'Henry Eckford'
Lathyrus odoratus 'King Size Navy Blue'

Tropical

Ricinus communis
Ricinus communis 'Carmencita'

Hardy bulb

Allium cristophii
Allium hollandicum (aflatunense) 'Purple
   Sensation'
Allium schubertii

EVERGREEN FOLIAGE
_____

Tree

Abies lasiocarpa 'Arizonica Compacta'
Chamaecyparis lawsoniana 'Sullivan'
Picea abies 'Pendula'
Picea orientalis 'Skylands'
Picea pungens 'Iseli Foxtail'
Picea pungens 'Thomsen'
Pinus cembra 'Silver Sheen'
Pinus flexilis 'Vanderwolf's Pyramid'
Pinus parviflora 'Glauca'
Pinus strobus
Pinus sylvestris
Pinus sylvestris 'Fastigiata'
Pseudotsuga menziesii 'Astro Blue'
Sciadopitys verticillata
Thuja occidentalis 'Techny'
Tsuga canadensis

Shrub

Abies procera 'Glauca Prostrata'
Buxus 'Green Gem'
Buxus 'Green Velvet'
Buxus microphylla 'Winter Gem'
Chamaecyparis obtusa 'Fernspray Gold'
Chamaecyparis obtusa 'Mariesii'
Chamaecyparis pisifera 'Golden Mop'
Ilex glabra
Ilex ×meserveae 'Mesdob' (China boy)
Ilex ×meserveae 'Mesog' (China girl)
Microbiota decussata
Picea abies 'Mucronata'
Picea alcoquiana 'Howell's Tigertail'
Pinus contorta 'Chief Joseph'
Pinus contorta 'Spaan's Dwarf'
Pinus densiflora 'Oculus Draconis'
Pinus parviflora 'Yatsubusa'
Pinus pumila 'Nana'
Pinus strobus 'Nana'
Pinus sylvestris 'Albyn'
Rhododendron 'Chionoides'

Rhododendron 'Mist Maiden'
Rhododendron 'Northern Starburst'
Tsuga canadensis 'Cole's Prostrate'
Yucca filamentosa 'Color Guard'
Yucca flaccida 'Golden Sword'

Perennial

*Many perennials not listed also hold evergreen
foliage.*

Ajuga reptans 'Purple Torch'
Anthriscus sylvestris 'Ravenswing'
Arum italicum ssp. italicum 'Marmoratum'
Carex morrowii 'Ice Dance'
Carex morrowii 'Variegata'
Deschampsia cespitosa 'Goldgehänge'
Epimedium davidii
Epimedium ×rubrum
Epimedium ×warleyense
Festuca glauca 'Elijah Blue'
Helianthemum (double yellow)
Helianthemum 'Fire Dragon'
Helictotrichon sempervirens 'Saphirsprudel'
   (sapphire fountain)
Helleborus foetidus
Helleborus orientalis
Kniphofia caulescens
Lamium maculatum 'White Nancy'
Luzula nivea
Lysimachia nummularia 'Aurea'
Phlox divaricata
Phlox divaricata 'Dirigo Ice'
Phlox divaricata 'Eco Texas Purple'
Phlox divaricata ssp. laphamii
Phlox divaricata 'London Grove Blue'
Phlox divaricata 'Sweet Lilac'
Polystichum acrostichoides
Veronica 'Waterperry Blue'
Veronica peduncularis 'Georgia Blue'

CUT FLOWERS
_____

Spring

Shrub

Daphne ×burkwoodii 'Carol Mackie'
Syringa meyeri

Perennial

Amsonia ciliata
Amsonia elliptica
Amsonia hubrichtii
Anthriscus sylvestris 'Ravenswing'
Aquilegia alpina
Aquilegia vulgaris var. stellata 'Black Barlow'
Baptisia 'Purple Smoke'

Baptisia australis
Baptisia sphaerocarpa
Helleborus Royal Heritage™
Helleborus orientalis
Helleborus orientalis (single black)
Hesperis matronalis
Heuchera 'Raspberry Regal'
Iris 'Flavescens'
Iris 'Perfume Counter'
Iris 'Sugar Blues'
Iris pallida 'Variegata'
Iris sanguinea 'Snow Queen'
Iris sibirica 'Butter and Sugar'
Iris sibirica 'Caesar's Brother'
Iris sibirica 'Dianne's Daughter'
Iris sibirica 'Orville Fay'
Iris sibirica 'Pirate Prince'
Iris sibirica 'Skywings'
Iris sibirica 'Vi Luihn'
Iris sibirica 'White Swirl'
Paeonia 'America'
Paeonia 'Burma Ruby'
Paeonia 'Coral Sunset'
Paeonia 'Etched Salmon'
Paeonia 'Monsieur Jules Elie'
Paeonia 'Prairie Moon'
Papaver orientale 'Curlilocks'
Papaver orientale 'Derwisch'
Papaver orientale 'Feuerriese'
Papaver orientale 'Harvest Moon'
Papaver orientale 'Lighthouse'
Papaver orientale 'Patty's Plum'
Papaver orientale 'Prince of Orange'
Papaver orientale 'Saffron'
Papaver orientale 'Turkenlouis'
Valeriana officinalis

Hardy bulb
Allium caeruleum
Allium hollandicum (aflatunense) 'Purple
    Sensation'
Camassia leichtlinii 'Semiplena'
Camassia leichtlinii ssp. suksdorfii 'Blauwe
    Donau' (blue Danube)
Chionodoxa forbesii (luciliae) Siehei Group
Iris 'Blue Magic'
Iris reticulata 'Harmony'
Narcissus 'Delnashaugh'
Narcissus 'Fragrant Rose'
Narcissus 'Mary Gay Lirette'
Narcissus 'Mint Julep'
Narcissus 'Petrel'
Narcissus 'Sir Winston Churchill'
Narcissus 'Stratosphere'
Narcissus 'Tahiti'
Tulipa 'Angelique'
Tulipa 'Apricot Parrot'
Tulipa 'Big Smile'

Tulipa 'Black Parrot'
Tulipa 'Blue Heron'
Tulipa 'Blue Parrot'
Tulipa 'Blushing Lady'
Tulipa 'Burgundy Lace'
Tulipa 'Carmine Parrot'
Tulipa 'Couleur Cardinal'
Tulipa 'Fringed Elegance'
Tulipa 'Queen of Night'
Tulipa 'Temple of Beauty'
Tulipa 'Uncle Tom'
Tulipa batalinii
Tulipa clusiana var. chrysantha

Summer

Shrub
Buddleia 'Lochinch'
Buddleia davidii 'Black Knight'
Buddleia davidii 'Mongo' (Nanho blue)
Clethra alnifolia
Hydrangea quercifolia
Hydrangea quercifolia 'Snowflake'
Rosa 'Alchymist'
Rosa 'Ausbuff' (English Garden®)
Rosa 'Ausmas' (Graham Thomas®)
Rosa 'Aussaucer' (Evelyn®)
Rosa 'Ausvelvet' (The Prince®)
Rosa 'Champlain'
Rosa 'F. J. Grootendorst'
Rosa 'Nuits de Young'
Rosa 'Scrivluv' (Baby Love®)
Rosa 'Seafoam'
Rosa ×harisonii 'Harison's Yellow'
Rosa multiflora 'Grevillei' (seven sisters' rose)
Rosa rugosa
Vitex agnus-castus var. latifolia

Perennial
Acanthus spinosus
Achillea 'Anblo' (Anthea)
Achillea 'Heidi'
Achillea 'Salmon Beauty'
Achillea filipendulina 'Altgold'
Aconitum 'Bressingham Spire'
Aconitum 'Ivorine'
Aconitum carmichaelii (Wilsonii Group)
    'Spätlese'
Aconitum lycoctonum ssp. neapolitanum
Agastache 'Blue Fortune'
Agastache rupestris
Alcea rosea 'Peaches and Dreams'
Alcea rosea 'The Watchman'
Alcea rugosa
Alchemilla mollis
Alstroemeria 'Sweet Laura'
Aruncus dioicus
Asclepias tuberosa

Asclepias tuberosa 'Hello Yellow'
Astilbe ×arendsii 'Snowdrift'
Astilbe chinensis 'Purple Candle'
Astilbe chinensis var. taquetii 'Superba'
Astilbe chinensis 'Veronica Klose'
Astilbe ×rosea 'Peach Blossom'
Belamcanda chinensis
Belamcanda chinensis 'Hello Yellow'
Calamagrostis ×acutiflora 'Karl Foerster'
Calamagrostis ×acutiflora 'Overdam'
Calamagrostis brachytricha
Campanula 'Kent Belle'
Campanula persicifolia 'Chettle Charm'
Campanula rapunculoides
Centaurea montana
Cephalaria gigantea
Clematis integrifolia
Coreopsis auriculata
Coreopsis grandiflora 'Walcoreop'
    (flying saucers)
Coreopsis tripteris
Crocosmia 'Blacro' (Jenny Bloom)
Crocosmia 'Emberglow'
Crocosmia 'Lucifer'
Crocosmia ×crocosmiiflora 'Norwich Canary'
Crocosmia ×crocosmiiflora 'Solfatare'
Crocosmia ×crocosmiiflora 'Venus'
Delphinium 'Centurion Sky Blue'
Delphinium ×bellamosum
Delphinium cashmerianum
Delphinium exaltatum
Dianthus barbatus 'Sooty'
Digitalis grandiflora
Digitalis lutea
Digitalis purpurea 'Apricot'
Dracocephalum ruyschiana
Echinacea purpurea
Echinops bannaticus 'Taplow Blue'
Echinops ritro 'Blue Glow'
Echinops ritro 'Veitch's Blue'
Eryngium amethystinum
Eryngium planum 'Blaukappe'
Eryngium variifolium
Foeniculum vulgare 'Purpureum'
Geranium phaeum 'Lily Lovell'
Gladiolus communis ssp. byzantinus
Gladiolus ×gandavensis
Gladiolus ×gandavensis 'Boone'
Helenium 'Kugelsonne'
Helenium 'Moerheim Beauty'
Helianthus 'Lemon Queen'
Helianthus 'Mellow Yellow'
Helictotrichon sempervirens 'Saphirsprudel'
    (sapphire fountain)
Heliopsis helianthoides var. scabra
    'Sommersonne' (summer sun)
Hyssopus officinalis
Hystrix patula

Knautia macedonica
Kniphofia triangularis
Lathyrus latifolius
Lavandula angustifolia 'Munstead'
Lavandula ×intermedia 'Grosso'
Liatris spicata 'Kobold'
Ligularia 'The Rocket'
Lilium 'Apricot Brandy'
Lilium 'Casa Blanca'
Lilium 'Connecticut King'
Lilium 'Conquistador'
Lilium 'Eden's Dandy'
Lilium 'Grand Cru'
Lilium 'Montenegro'
Lilium 'Pretender'
Lilium 'Royal Justice'
Lilium 'Royal Perfume'
Lilium 'Scarlet Emperor'
Lilium 'Shirley'
Lilium 'Sunset'
Lilium henryi
Lilium lancifolium var. splendens
Lilium pumilum
Limonium platyphyllum 'Violetta'
Linaria 'Natalie'
Linaria purpurea
Lobelia 'Dark Crusader'
Lobelia 'Grape Knee High'
Lobelia 'Purple Towers'
Lobelia 'Queen Victoria'
Lobelia 'Royal Robe'
Lobelia 'Ruby Slippers'
Lobelia siphilitica
Lychnis ×arkwrightii 'Vesuvius'
Miscanthus 'Purpurascens'
Miscanthus sinensis var. condensatus
    'Cosmopolitan'
Miscanthus sinensis 'Gracillimus'
Miscanthus sinensis 'Malepartus'
Miscanthus sinensis 'Morning Light'
Molinia caerulea ssp. arundinacea 'Skyracer'
Origanum laevigatum 'Herrenhausen'
Panicum virgatum 'Dallas Blues'
Panicum virgatum 'Heavy Metal'
Panicum virgatum 'Rehbraun'
Papaver nudicaule 'Red Sails'
Patrinia scabiosifolia
Pennisetum alopecuroides 'Hameln'
Pennisetum setaceum 'Rubrum'
Penstemon digitalis 'Husker Red'
Penstemon ×mexicale 'Pike's Peak Purple'
Phlox paniculata 'David'
Phlox paniculata 'Fesselballon'
Phlox paniculata 'Katherine'
Phlox paniculata 'Laura'
Phlox paniculata 'Look Again'
Phlox paniculata 'Orange Perfection'
Phlox paniculata 'Pax' (peace)

Cut Flowers, summer, cont.

Phlox paniculata 'Tenor'
Phlox paniculata 'The King'
Phlox paniculata 'Tracy's Treasure'
Platycodon grandiflorus 'Double Blue'
Platycodon grandiflorus 'Komachi'
Rudbeckia fulgida var. speciosa (newmannii)
Rudbeckia triloba
Salvia nemorosa 'Ostfriesland' (East Friesland)
Salvia nemorosa 'Purple Glory'
Salvia nemorosa 'Pusztaflamme' (plumosa)
Salvia ×sylvestris 'Blauhügel' (blue hill)
Salvia ×sylvestris 'Blaukönigin' (blue queen)
Salvia ×sylvestris 'Mainacht' (May night)
Salvia ×sylvestris 'Viola Klose'
Salvia verticillata 'Purple Rain'
Sanguisorba tenuifolia 'Purpurea'
Schizachyrium scoparium 'The Blues'
Silene regia
Sorghastrum nutans 'Sioux Blue'
Stachys macrantha
Veronica 'Goodness Grows'
Veronica spicata 'Blue Charm'
Veronica spicata 'Icicle'

Annual

Ageratum houstonianum 'Blue Horizon'
Alstroemeria aurea 'Orange King'
Alstroemeria psittacina
Angelonia 'Blue Pacific'
Angelonia angustifolia 'Purple Pinnacles'
Antirrhinum majus 'Rocket Red'
Arctotis ×hybrida 'Dark Red'
Arctotis ×hybrida 'Flame'
Calendula officinalis 'Orange King'
Celosia spicata 'Flamingo Purple'
Consolida ajacis 'Blue Spire'
Cosmos atrosanguineus
Cynara cardunculus
Eschscholzia californica
Eschscholzia californica 'Purple Gleam'
Gomphrena haageana 'Lavender Lady'
Nigella damascena Miss Jekyll Series
Papaver rhoeas
Papaver rhoeas Angels' Choir
Papaver somniferum
Papaver somniferum 'Black Peony'
Papaver somniferum 'Burnt Orange'
Papaver somniferum 'Lauren's Grape'
Papaver somniferum 'Pepperbox'
Rudbeckia hirta 'Irish Eyes'
Salvia 'Indigo Spires'
Salvia 'Purple Majesty'
Salvia coccinea 'Lady in Red'
Salvia guaranitica

Salvia guaranitica 'Black and Blue'
Salvia leucantha
Scabiosa atropurpurea 'Ace of Spades'
Tropaeolum majus 'Apricot Trifle'
Tropaeolum majus 'Blush Double'
Tropaeolum majus 'Moonlight'
Tropaeolum majus 'Tip Top Mahogany'
Tropaeolum majus Alaska Series
Verbena 'Romance Apricot'
Verbena Temari® Red
Zinnia haageana 'Orange Star'

Annual vine

Lathyrus odoratus
Lathyrus odoratus 'Henry Eckford'
Lathyrus odoratus 'King Size Navy Blue'

Hardy bulb

Allium carinatum ssp. pulchellum
Allium cristophii
Allium moly 'Jeannine'
Allium schubertii
Allium sphaerocephalon
Dichelostemma ida-maia
Eremurus ×isabellinus 'Pinokkio'
Triteleia laxa 'Queen Fabiola'

Tender bulb

Agapanthus 'Bressingham Blue'
Dahlia 'Arabian Night'
Dahlia 'Bishop of Llandaff'
Dahlia 'Ellen Houston'
Dahlia 'Orange Nugget'
Dahlia 'Susette'
Gladiolus 'Atom'
Gladiolus 'Violetta'
Hymenocallis 'Sulphur Queen'

Autumn

Perennial

Aster 'Climax'
Aster laevis 'Bluebird'
Aster novae-angliae 'Hella Lacy'
Aster novae-angliae 'Hillside'
Aster novae-angliae 'Purple Dome'
Aster novae-angliae 'Wild Light Blue'
Aster oblongifolius var. angustatus
    'Raydon's Favorite'
Aster tataricus 'Jindai'
Calamagrostis ×acutiflora 'Karl Foerster'
Calamagrostis ×acutiflora 'Overdam'
Calamagrostis brachytricha
Chrysanthemum 'Autumn Moon'
Chrysanthemum 'Pumpkin Harvest'
Chrysanthemum 'Single Apricot'

Chrysanthemum 'Single Peach'
Chrysanthemum 'Viette's Apricot Glow'
Helianthus salicifolius
Helictotrichon sempervirens 'Saphirsprudel'
    (sapphire fountain)
Miscanthus sinensis var. condensatus
    'Cosmopolitan'
Miscanthus sinensis 'Gracillimus'
Miscanthus sinensis 'Malepartus'
Molinia caerulea ssp. arundinacea 'Skyracer'
Panicum virgatum 'Dallas Blues'
Panicum virgatum 'Heavy Metal'
Panicum virgatum 'Rehbraun'
Pennisetum alopecuroides 'Hameln'
Penstemon digitalis 'Husker Red'
Penstemon ×mexicale 'Pike's Peak Purple'
Schizachyrium scoparium 'The Blues'
Solidago 'Golden Spangles'
Solidago rugosa 'Fireworks'
×Solidaster luteus 'Lemore'
Sorghastrum nutans 'Sioux Blue'

FRAGRANCE

List includes plants with fragrant flowers or foliage.

Tree

Chionanthus virginicus
Magnolia virginiana

Shrub

Buddleia 'Lochinch'
Buddleia davidii 'Black Knight'
Buddleia davidii 'Mongo' (Nanho blue)
Calycanthus floridus
Clethra alnifolia
Daphne ×burkwoodii 'Carol Mackie'
Fothergilla gardenii
Hydrangea quercifolia
Itea virginica
Itea virginica 'Henry's Garnet'
Rosa 'Alchymist'
Rosa 'Ausbuff' (English Garden®)
Rosa 'Ausmas' (Graham Thomas®)
Rosa 'Aussaucer' (Evelyn®)
Rosa 'Ausvelvet' (The Prince®)
Rosa 'Hansa'
Rosa 'Nuits de Young'
Rosa 'Scrivluv' (Baby Love®)
Rosa 'Seafoam'
Rosa rugosa
Syringa meyeri
Vitex agnus-castus var. latifolia

Woody vine

Clematis terniflora
Hydrangea anomala ssp. petiolaris
Lonicera periclymenum 'Graham Thomas'

Perennial

Agastache 'Blue Fortune'
Agastache rupestris
Alstroemeria 'Sweet Laura'
Cimicifuga ramosa 'Brunette'
Clematis recta
Dianthus ×allwoodii 'Danielle Marie'
Dianthus barbatus 'Sooty'
Foeniculum vulgare 'Purpureum'
Galium odoratum
Geranium macrorrhizum 'Ingwersen's Variety'
Helleborus orientalis
Hemerocallis 'Happy Returns'
Hesperis matronalis
Hosta 'Fragrant Blue'
Hosta plantaginea 'Aphrodite'
Hyssopus officinalis
Iris 'Perfume Counter'
Iris 'Sugar Blues'
Lavandula angustifolia 'Munstead'
Lavandula ×intermedia 'Grosso'
Lilium 'Casa Blanca'
Monarda 'Jacob Cline'
Monarda 'Violet Queen'
Origanum 'Kent Beauty'
Origanum laevigatum 'Herrenhausen'
Origanum vulgare 'Aureum'
Pachysandra procumbens
Paeonia 'Etched Salmon'
Phlox paniculata 'Fesselballon'
Ruta graveolens 'Blue Beauty'
Thymus ×citriodorus
Thymus ×citriodorus 'Lemon Green'
Thymus pseudolanuginosus
Valeriana officinalis

Annual

Calendula officinalis 'Orange King'
Cosmos atrosanguineus
Ocimum 'African Blue'
Ocimum basilicum 'Red Rubin'
Plectranthus amboinicus
Salvia officinalis 'Tricolor'

Annual vine

Lathyrus odoratus
Lathyrus odoratus 'Henry Eckford'
Lathyrus odoratus 'King Size Navy Blue'

Tropical

Hedychium 'Daniel Weeks'
Hedychium coccineum

Hardy bulb
Iris reticulata 'Harmony'
Narcissus 'Fragrant Rose'
Narcissus 'Sir Winston Churchill'
Narcissus 'Stratosphere'
Tulipa 'Angelique'
Tulipa 'Apricot Parrot'
Tulipa 'Couleur Cardinal'

Tender bulb
Hymenocallis 'Sulphur Queen'

SONGBIRDS

Tree
Amelanchier ×grandiflora 'Autumn Brilliance'
Chionanthus virginicus
Cornus kousa

Shrub
Aralia elata 'Aureovariegata'
Callicarpa dichotoma 'Issai'
Ilex ×meserveae 'Mesog' (China girl)
Ilex verticillata 'Afterglow'
Ilex verticillata 'Christmas Cheer'
Ilex verticillata 'Winter Red'
Viburnum plicatum var. tomentosum 'Mariesii'

Woody vine
Lonicera periclymenum 'Graham Thomas'
Lonicera sempervirens 'Blanche Sandman'

Perennial
Asclepias tuberosa
Asclepias tuberosa 'Hello Yellow'
Buphthalmum speciosum
Echinacea purpurea
Echinops bannaticus 'Taplow Blue'
Echinops ritro 'Blue Glow'
Echinops ritro 'Veitch's Blue'
Eupatorium purpureum ssp. maculatum 'Gateway'
Helianthus salicifolius
Heliopsis helianthoides var. scabra 'Sommersonne' (summer sun)
Hosta 'Big Daddy'
Hosta 'Blue Cadet'
Hosta 'Fragrant Blue'
Hosta 'Halcyon'
Hosta 'Krossa Regal'
Hosta 'Lemon Lime'
Hosta 'Love Pat'
Hosta 'Midas Touch'
Hosta 'Night Before Christmas'
Hosta 'Patriot'
Hosta 'Paul's Glory'
Hosta 'Sum and Substance'

Hosta 'Sun Power'
Hosta plantaginea 'Aphrodite'
Liatris spicata 'Kobold'
Ligularia 'The Rocket'
Ligularia dentata 'Dark Beauty'
Ligularia dentata 'Desdemona'
Ligularia wilsoniana
Monarda 'Jacob Cline'
Monarda 'Violet Queen'
Rudbeckia fulgida var. speciosa (newmannii)
Rudbeckia maxima
Rudbeckia triloba
Schizachyrium scoparium 'The Blues'

HUMMINGBIRDS

Shrub
Aralia elata 'Aureovariegata'
Buddleia 'Lochinch'
Buddleia davidii 'Black Knight'
Buddleia davidii 'Mongo' (Nanho blue)

Woody vine
Campsis ×tagliabuana 'Madame Galen'
Lonicera periclymenum 'Graham Thomas'
Lonicera sempervirens 'Blanche Sandman'

Perennial
Agastache 'Blue Fortune'
Agastache rupestris
Ajuga reptans 'Purple Torch'
Alcea rosea 'Peaches and Dreams'
Alcea rosea 'The Watchman'
Alcea rugosa
Aquilegia alpina
Aquilegia vulgaris var. stellata 'Black Barlow'
Asclepias tuberosa
Asclepias tuberosa 'Hello Yellow'
Delphinium 'Centurion Sky Blue'
Delphinium ×bellamosum
Delphinium cashmerianum
Delphinium exaltatum
Digitalis grandiflora
Digitalis lutea
Digitalis purpurea 'Apricot'
Gentiana septemfida var. lagodechiana
Gentiana triflora 'Royal Blue'
Hemerocallis 'Alluring Peach'
Hemerocallis 'Carefree Peach'
Hemerocallis 'Happy Returns'
Hemerocallis 'Peach Fairy'
Hemerocallis 'Red Razzamatazz'
Hemerocallis 'Scarlet Romance'
Hemerocallis 'Siloam Royal Prince'
Hemerocallis 'Staghorn Sumac'
Hemerocallis 'Sundried Tomatoes'
Hemerocallis 'Toy Trumpets'

Hemerocallis 'Welcome Mat'
Hemerocallis 'Yellow Lollipop'
Hibiscus moscheutos 'Lord Baltimore'
Hosta 'Big Daddy'
Hosta 'Blue Cadet'
Hosta 'Fragrant Blue'
Hosta 'Halcyon'
Hosta 'Krossa Regal'
Hosta 'Lemon Lime'
Hosta 'Love Pat'
Hosta 'Midas Touch'
Hosta 'Night Before Christmas'
Hosta 'Patriot'
Hosta 'Paul's Glory'
Hosta 'Sum and Substance'
Hosta 'Sun Power'
Hosta plantaginea 'Aphrodite'
Hyssopus officinalis
Kniphofia 'Alcazar'
Kniphofia 'Little Maid'
Kniphofia 'Primrose Beauty'
Kniphofia 'Prince Igor'
Kniphofia 'Royal Standard'
Kniphofia 'Shining Sceptre'
Kniphofia caulescens
Kniphofia citrina
Kniphofia triangularis
Lilium 'Apricot Brandy'
Lilium 'Casa Blanca'
Lilium 'Connecticut King'
Lilium 'Conquistador'
Lilium 'Eden's Dandy'
Lilium 'Grand Cru'
Lilium 'Montenegro'
Lilium 'Pretender'
Lilium 'Royal Justice'
Lilium 'Royal Perfume'
Lilium 'Scarlet Emperor'
Lilium 'Shirley'
Lilium 'Sunset'
Lilium henryi
Lilium lancifolium var. splendens
Lilium pumilum
Lobelia 'Dark Crusader'
Lobelia 'Grape Knee High'
Lobelia 'Purple Towers'
Lobelia 'Queen Victoria'
Lobelia 'Royal Robe'
Lobelia 'Ruby Slippers'
Monarda 'Jacob Cline'
Monarda 'Violet Queen'
Penstemon digitalis 'Husker Red'
Penstemon ×mexicale 'Pike's Peak Purple'
Salvia azurea var. pitcheri
Salvia nemorosa 'Ostfriesland' (East Friesland)
Salvia nemorosa 'Pusztaflamme' (plumosa)
Salvia ×sylvestris 'Blauhügel' (blue hill)
Salvia ×sylvestris 'Blaukönigin' (blue queen)

Salvia ×sylvestris 'Mainacht' (May night)
Salvia ×sylvestris 'Viola Klose'
Salvia verticillata 'Purple Rain'
Silene regia

Annual
Bouvardia ternifolia
Salvia 'Purple Majesty'
Salvia coccinea 'Lady in Red'
Salvia guaranitica
Salvia guaranitica 'Black and Blue'

Tropical
Canna 'Black Knight'
Canna 'Orange Punch'
Canna 'Phasion'
Canna 'Roi Humbert' (red King Humbert)
Canna 'Striata' (Pretoria)
Canna indica 'Red Stripe' (purpurea)
Hedychium 'Daniel Weeks'

Tender bulb
Agapanthus 'Bressingham Blue'

BUTTERFLIES

Shrub
Aesculus parviflora
Buddleia 'Lochinch'
Buddleia davidii 'Black Knight'
Buddleia davidii 'Mongo' (Nanho blue)
Caryopteris ×clandonensis
Caryopteris ×clandonensis 'Longwood Blue'
Caryopteris ×clandonensis 'Worcester Gold'
Clethra alnifolia
Fothergilla gardenii
Itea virginica
Itea virginica 'Henry's Garnet'
Rhododendron 'Mist Maiden'
Rhododendron 'Northern Starburst'
Rosa 'Hansa'
Rosa rugosa
Syringa meyeri
Vitex agnus-castus var. latifolia

Woody vine
Campsis ×tagliabuana 'Madame Galen'
Clematis terniflora
Lonicera periclymenum 'Graham Thomas'
Lonicera sempervirens 'Blanche Sandman'

Perennial
Achillea 'Anblo' (Anthea)
Achillea 'Heidi'
Achillea 'Salmon Beauty'
Achillea filipendulina 'Altgold'
Agastache 'Blue Fortune'

Butterflies, cont.

Agastache rupestris
Alcea rosea 'Peaches and Dreams'
Alcea rosea 'The Watchman'
Alstroemeria 'Sweet Laura'
Angelica gigas
Asclepias tuberosa
Asclepias tuberosa 'Hello Yellow'
Aster 'Climax'
Aster laevis 'Bluebird'
Aster novae-angliae 'Hella Lacy'
Aster novae-angliae 'Hillside'
Aster novae-angliae 'Purple Dome'
Aster novae-angliae 'Wild Light Blue'
Aster oblongifolius var. angustatus
    'Raydon's Favorite'
Aster tataricus 'Jindai'
Buphthalmum speciosum
Ceratostigma plumbaginoides
Chrysanthemum 'Pumpkin Harvest'
Chrysanthemum 'Single Apricot'
Chrysanthemum 'Single Peach'
Chrysanthemum 'Viette's Apricot Glow'
Clematis recta
Coreopsis auriculata
Coreopsis grandiflora 'Walcoreop'
    (flying saucers)
Coreopsis tripteris
Coreopsis verticillata 'Zagreb'
Dianthus ×allwoodii 'Danielle Marie'
Dianthus barbatus 'Sooty'
Dianthus deltoides 'Leuchtfunk' (flashing light)
Echinacea purpurea
Echinops bannaticus 'Taplow Blue'
Echinops ritro 'Blue Glow'
Echinops ritro 'Veitch's Blue'
Eupatorium purpureum ssp. maculatum
    'Gateway'
Foeniculum vulgare 'Purpureum'
Helenium 'Kugelsonne'
Helenium 'Moerheim Beauty'

Helianthus 'Lemon Queen'
Helianthus 'Mellow Yellow'
Helianthus salicifolius
Hemerocallis 'Alluring Peach'
Hemerocallis 'Carefree Peach'
Hemerocallis 'Happy Returns'
Hemerocallis 'Peach Fairy'
Hemerocallis 'Red Razzamatazz'
Hemerocallis 'Scarlet Romance'
Hemerocallis 'Siloam Royal Prince'
Hemerocallis 'Staghorn Sumac'
Hemerocallis 'Sundried Tomatoes'
Hemerocallis 'Toy Trumpets'
Hemerocallis 'Welcome Mat'
Hemerocallis 'Yellow Lollipop'
Hesperis matronalis
Hyssopus officinalis
Lavandula angustifolia 'Munstead'
Lavandula ×intermedia 'Grosso'
Liatris spicata 'Kobold'
Lilium 'Apricot Brandy'
Lilium 'Casa Blanca'
Lilium 'Connecticut King'
Lilium 'Conquistador'
Lilium 'Eden's Dandy'
Lilium 'Grand Cru'
Lilium 'Montenegro'
Lilium 'Pretender'
Lilium 'Royal Justice'
Lilium 'Royal Perfume'
Lilium 'Scarlet Emperor'
Lilium 'Shirley'
Lilium 'Sunset'
Lilium henryi
Lilium lancifolium var. splendens
Lilium pumilum
Monarda 'Jacob Cline'
Monarda 'Violet Queen'
Nepeta 'Six Hills Giant'
Nepeta ×faassenii
Nepeta grandiflora 'Bramdean'
Nepeta racemosa 'Walker's Low'
Nepeta sibirica 'Souvenir d'André Chaudron'
Origanum laevigatum 'Herrenhausen'

Packera aurea (Senecio aureus)
Penstemon digitalis 'Husker Red'
Penstemon ×mexicale 'Pike's Peak Purple'
Phlox divaricata 'Dirigo Ice'
Phlox divaricata 'Eco Texas Purple'
Phlox divaricata ssp. laphamii
Phlox divaricata 'London Grove Blue'
Phlox divaricata 'Sweet Lilac'
Phlox paniculata 'David'
Phlox paniculata 'Fesselballon'
Phlox paniculata 'Katherine'
Phlox paniculata 'Laura'
Phlox paniculata 'Look Again'
Phlox paniculata 'Orange Perfection'
Phlox paniculata 'Pax' (peace)
Phlox paniculata 'Tenor'
Phlox paniculata 'The King'
Phlox paniculata 'Tracy's Treasure'
Phlox stolonifera 'Blue Ridge'
Phlox stolonifera 'Bruce's White'
Rudbeckia fulgida var. speciosa (newmannii)
Rudbeckia maxima
Ruta graveolens 'Blue Beauty'
Salvia azurea var. pitcheri
Salvia nemorosa 'Ostfriesland' (East Friesland)
Salvia nemorosa 'Purple Glory'
Salvia nemorosa 'Pusztaflamme' (plumosa)
Salvia ×sylvestris 'Blauhügel' (blue hill)
Salvia ×sylvestris 'Blaukönigin' (blue queen)
Salvia ×sylvestris 'Mainacht' (May night)
Salvia ×sylvestris 'Viola Klose'
Salvia verticillata 'Purple Rain'
Scabiosa Butterfly Blue®
Scabiosa 'Pink Mist'
Scabiosa columbaria var. ochroleuca
Sedum 'Herbstfreude' (autumn joy)
Sedum telephium ssp. maximum
    'Atropurpureum'
Silene regia
Solidago 'Golden Spangles'
Solidago rugosa 'Fireworks'
×Solidaster luteus 'Lemore'
Stachys macrantha

Verbascum bombyciferum
Verbena hastata
Veronica 'Goodness Grows'
Veronica 'Waterperry Blue'
Veronica austriaca ssp. teucrium
    'Crater Lake Blue'
Veronica austriaca ssp. teucrium 'Royal Blue'
Veronica gentianoides 'Nana'
Veronica peduncularis 'Georgia Blue'
Veronica prostrata 'Trehane'
Veronica spicata 'Blue Charm'
Veronica spicata 'Icicle'

Annual
Ageratum houstonianum 'Blue Horizon'
Arctotis ×hybrida 'Dark Red'
Arctotis ×hybrida 'Flame'
Bouvardia ternifolia
Brachyscome 'Ultra'
Calendula officinalis 'Orange King'
Eschscholzia californica
Eschscholzia californica 'Purple Gleam'
Gomphrena haageana 'Lavender Lady'
Melampodium paludosum 'Million Gold'
Ocimum basilicum 'Red Rubin'
Plectranthus amboinicus
Rudbeckia hirta 'Irish Eyes'
Salvia 'Indigo Spires'
Salvia 'Purple Majesty'
Salvia coccinea 'Lady in Red'
Verbena 'Homestead Purple'
Verbena 'Romance Apricot'
Verbena Temari® Red
Verbena bonariensis
Zinnia haageana 'Orange Star'

Annual vine
Lathyrus odoratus
Lathyrus odoratus 'Henry Eckford'
Lathyrus odoratus 'King Size Navy Blue'

Hardy bulb
Eremurus ×isabellinus 'Pinokkio'

PLANTS BY MAINTENANCE CHARACTERISTICS

CULTURE CHART

Note: if all other requirements have been met and it is still difficult to grow the plant, it may relate to soil pH.

	TYPE	ZONE	SOIL MOISTURE	LIGHT	SOIL pH
Abies lasiocarpa 'Arizonica Compacta' Small conifer; conical form; blue-gray needles. Plates 1–2.	tree	5–6	average	sun/pt shade	acid
Abies procera 'Glauca Prostrata' Very blue foliage; numerous cones.	shrub	5–6(7)	average	sun/pt shade	acid
Acanthus spinosus Spikes of mauve flowers; shiny thistlelike leaves. Plates 95, 120.	perennial	5–10	average	sun/pt shade	average
Acer griseum Cinnamon-colored exfoliating bark; red and bronze fall color; trifoliate leaves. Plates 5, 102–103.	tree	5–7(8)	average	sun/pt shade	average
Acer palmatum var. dissectum Dissectum Atropurpureum Group Deeply cut ferny foliage emerges red-purple in spring, fades to purple-green in summer, turns bright orange in autumn; mounded pendulous form. Plate 47.	tree	5–8	average	sun/pt shade	average
Acer palmatum 'Sango-kaku' Lobed and serrated green leaves turn golden yellow in autumn; young stems coral-red in autumn and winter. Plate 192.	tree	5–8	average	sun/pt shade	average
Achillea 'Anblo' (Anthea) Light yellow flowerheads; gray-green foliage.	perennial	3–8	dry	full sun	average
Achillea 'Heidi' Pink-salmon flowerheads; fernlike foliage.	perennial	3–8	dry	full sun	average
Achillea 'Salmon Beauty' Salmon flowerheads; fernlike green foliage.	perennial	4–8	dry	full sun	average
Achillea filipendulina 'Altgold' Golden yellow flowerheads; fernlike green foliage.	perennial	3–8	dry	full sun	average
Aconitum 'Bressingham Spire' Blue-violet spikes of hooded flowers; deep green palmately divided foliage.	perennial	4–8	average	sun/pt shade	average
Aconitum 'Ivorine' Creamy yellow hooded flowers; green palmately divided foliage.	perennial	4–8	average	sun/pt shade	average
Aconitum carmichaelii (Wilsonii Group) 'Spätlese' Deep blue hooded flowers; green palmately divided foliage.	perennial	4–8	average	sun/pt shade	average

	TYPE	ZONE	SOIL MOISTURE	LIGHT	SOIL pH
Aconitum episcopale Blue-lavender hooded flowers; green palmately divided foliage; vinelike habit.	perennial	5–8	average	sun/pt shade	average
Aconitum lycoctonum ssp. neapolitanum Yellow hooded flowers; green palmately divided foliage.	perennial	3–6	average	sun/pt shade	average
Acorus gramineus 'Minimus Aureus' Chartreuse-yellow grasslike foliage. Combination 26.	perennial	6–8	wet	sun/pt shade	average
Acorus gramineus 'Oborozuki' Green and yellow variegated grasslike foliage. Plate 108.	perennial	(5)6–8	wet	sun/pt shade	average
Acorus gramineus 'Ogon' Light green and yellow variegated grasslike foliage.	perennial	(5)6–8	wet	sun/pt shade	average
Adiantum pedatum Lacy green fronds; dark reddish brown stalks. Plate 119.	perennial	3–8	average	shade/pt shade	average
Aesculus parviflora Palmate leaf; large pinkish white flower panicles; yellow fall color. Combination 4.	shrub	4–8	average	shade/pt shade	acid
Agapanthus 'Bressingham Blue' Umbels of blue tubular flowers; linear green leaves.	tender bulb	7–10	average	full sun	average
Agastache 'Blue Fortune' Long bottlebrush spikes of blue flowers. Plates 5, 90, 160.	perennial	5–10	dry	full sun	average
Agastache rupestris Pinkish orange tubular flowers; gray-green foliage.	perennial	5–8	dry	full sun	average
Agave havardiana Rosette-forming dark gray-green lance-shaped leaves with reddish brown marginal and terminal spines.	annual	7–10	dry	full sun	average
Ageratum houstonianum 'Blue Horizon' Blue rounded brushlike flower clusters.	annual		average	full sun	average
Ajuga reptans 'Purple Torch' Pink-lavender flower spikes; glossy green foliage.	perennial	4–9	average	shade/pt shade	average
Alcea rosea 'Peaches and Dreams' Double peach flowers; large rounded and scalloped leaves.	perennial	3–8	average	full sun	average
Alcea rosea 'The Watchman' Single black-maroon flowers; large rounded and scalloped leaves.	perennial	3–8	average	full sun	average
Alcea rugosa Single yellow flowers; large rounded and scalloped leaves.	perennial	3–8	average	full sun	average
Alchemilla mollis Frothy chartreuse flowerheads; round, scalloped, soft, smoky yellow-green leaves. Plates 94, 148.	perennial	4–7	average	sun/pt shade	average

	TYPE	ZONE	SOIL MOISTURE	LIGHT	SOIL pH
Allium caeruleum 2-in. umbels of deep blue flowers.	hardy bulb	5–7	average	full sun	average
Allium carinatum ssp. pulchellum Loose umbels of pendulous violet-red flowers on purple stems.	hardy bulb	5–8	average	full sun	average
Allium cristophii Softball-sized spidery pinkish lavender flowerheads. Plate 94.	hardy bulb	3–8	average	full sun	average
Allium hollandicum (aflatunense) 'Purple Sensation' Baseball-sized violet flowerheads. Plate 98.	hardy bulb	3–8	average	full sun	average
Allium moly 'Jeannine' 2- to 3-in. loose umbels of star-shaped bright yellow flowers.	hardy bulb	3–8	average	full sun	average
Allium schubertii Huge (10–12 in. across) violet-rose spidery flowerheads. Plates 107, 110.	hardy bulb	(6)7–9	average	full sun	average
Allium sphaerocephalon 1- to 2-in. oval reddish purple flowerheads.	hardy bulb	4–8	average	full sun	average
Alstroemeria 'Sweet Laura' Fragrant bright yellow flowers with red-orange highlights. Plate 112.	perennial	5–10	average	full sun	average
Alstroemeria aurea 'Orange King' Bright yellowy orange flowers with purple streaks.	annual	(6)7–10	average	full sun	average
Alstroemeria psittacina Dark red flowers with green tips.	annual	(6)7–10	average	full sun	average
Alternanthera dentata 'Rubiginosa' Dark burgundy-purple foliage; sprawling habit.	annual	9–11	average	full sun	average
Amelanchier ×grandiflora 'Autumn Brilliance' White flowers; edible dark blue berries; red fall color; handsome gray bark.	tree	4–9	wet	sun/pt shade	average
Amorpha canescens Violet flower spikes with bright orange anthers; pinnately compound gray-green leaves. Combination 13.	shrub	2–6	dry	full sun	average
Amorphophallus konjac Maroon-speckled stalk; dark red spathe; 3-ft.-tall dark red spadix; bulblike plant.	tender bulb	6–10	average	shade/pt shade	average
Ampelopsis glandulosa var. brevipedunculata 'Elegans' Green lobed leaves mottled white and pink; inconspicuous flowers; bright blue berries. Plate 45.	woody vine	5–8	average	sun/pt shade	average
Amsonia ciliata Terminal clusters of star-shaped blue flowers; very fine threadlike foliage. Combination 19.	perennial	3–9	dry	sun/pt shade	average

	TYPE	ZONE	SOIL MOISTURE	LIGHT	SOIL pH
Amsonia elliptica Terminal clusters of star-shaped blue flowers; glossy elliptic leaves. Plate 123.	perennial	3–9	dry	sun/pt shade	average
Amsonia hubrichtii Terminal clusters of star-shaped blue flowers; very fine foliage.	perennial	3–9	dry	sun/pt shade	average
Amsonia tabernaemontana Light blue star-shaped flowers; glossy slender leaves; nice yellow autumn color. Plate 28.	perennial	3–9	dry	sun/pt shade	average
Anemone ×hybrida 'Queen Charlotte' Semi-double pink flowers; trifoliate leaves.	perennial	4–8	average	sun/pt shade	average
Anemone ×hybrida 'September Charm' Single pink flowers; trifoliate leaves.	perennial	4–8	average	sun/pt shade	average
Angelica gigas Bold dissected foliage; 4- to 8-in.-wide dark purple-burgundy flowerheads. Combination 17.	perennial	4–8	average	sun/pt shade	average
Angelonia 'Blue Pacific' Narrow lance-shaped dark green leaves; blue flowers sometimes with white markings.	annual	9–10	dry	full sun	average
Angelonia angustifolia 'Purple Pinnacles' Narrow lance-shaped dark green leaves; deep purple flowers.	annual	9–10	dry	full sun	average
Anthriscus sylvestris 'Ravenswing' Dark purple fernlike foliage; white flowers.	perennial	(5)6–8	average	sun/pt shade	average
Antirrhinum majus 'Rocket Red' Dark red flowers. Combination 16.	annual		average	full sun	average
Aquilegia alpina Nodding solid blue flowers; gray-green compound foliage turns scarlet in autumn. Plates 40, 103, 159.	perennial	3–9	average	sun/pt shade	average
Aquilegia vulgaris var. stellata 'Black Barlow' Dark black-purple double flowers.	perennial	3–9	average	sun/pt shade	average
Aralia elata 'Aureovariegata' Yellow-edged green leaves turn shades of violet in autumn; lacy white flowers; dark purple fruit. Plates 15, 43.	shrub	(3)4–9	dry	sun/pt shade	average
Arctotis ×hybrida 'Dark Red' Brick-red daisylike flowers; gray-green foliage.	annual	9–11	dry	full sun	average
Arctotis ×hybrida 'Flame' Orange daisylike flowers; gray-green foliage. Plate 151.	annual	9–11	dry	full sun	average
Arisaema sikokianum Trifoliate leaves; white clublike spadix; spathe striped purple and brown. Plates 128–129.	perennial	5–9	average	shade/pt shade	average

	TYPE	ZONE	SOIL MOISTURE	LIGHT	SOIL pH
Artemisia 'Huntington' Silvery gray deeply divided foliage; yellow flowers. Plate 44.	perennial	4–9	dry	full sun	alkaline
Artemisia 'Powis Castle' Finely cut silver foliage; insignificant flowerheads.	perennial	5–8	dry	full sun	alkaline
Artemisia 'Silverado' Fine-textured silver foliage.	perennial	4–9	dry	full sun	alkaline
Artemisia absinthium 'Lambrook Silver' Silvery gray deeply divided foliage; yellow flowers.	perennial	4–9	dry	full sun	alkaline
Arum italicum ssp. italicum 'Marmoratum' Spear-shaped variegated deep green leaves; orange-red berries; jack-in-the-pulpit-type flowers. Combination 14.	perennial	5–9	average	shade/pt shade	average
Aruncus dioicus Plumelike creamy white flowers; pinnately compound astilbelike foliage.	perennial	3–7	wet	shade/pt shade	average
Asclepias tuberosa Orange flowers; narrow foliage. Plate 150.	perennial	4–9	dry	full sun	acid
Asclepias tuberosa 'Hello Yellow' Yellow flowers; narrow foliage. Plate 185.	perennial	4–9	dry	full sun	acid
Aster 'Climax' Large light blue flowers. Plate 179.	perennial	4–8	average	full sun	average
Aster laevis 'Bluebird' Blue-lavender flowers with yellow eye. Combination 25.	perennial	4–8	average	full sun	average
Aster novae-angliae 'Hella Lacy' Violet-blue flowers with yellow eye.	perennial	4–8	average	full sun	average
Aster novae-angliae 'Hillside' Dark purple flowers with yellow eye. Plate 171.	perennial	4–8	average	full sun	average
Aster novae-angliae 'Purple Dome' Purple flowers with yellow eye.	perennial	4–8	average	full sun	average
Aster novae-angliae 'Wild Light Blue' Light blue flowers.	perennial	4–8	average	full sun	average
Aster oblongifolius var. angustatus 'Raydon's Favorite' Blue-lavender flowers. Plate 171.	perennial	4–8	dry	full sun	average
Aster tataricus 'Jindai' Blue-lavender flowerheads; large basal leaves.	perennial	4–8	dry	sun/pt shade	average
Astilbe ×arendsii 'Snowdrift' Clear white flowers; serrated compound leaves.	perennial	3–8	average	shade/pt shade	acid
Astilbe chinensis 'Purple Candle' Rose-purple flowers; serrated compound leaves.	perennial	4–8	average	shade/pt shade	acid

	TYPE	ZONE	SOIL MOISTURE	LIGHT	SOIL pH
Astilbe chinensis 'Veronica Klose' Dark pink flowers; serrated compound leaves.	perennial	4–8	average	shade/pt shade	acid
Astilbe chinensis var. taquetii 'Superba' Reddish purple flowers; serrated compound leaves.	perennial	4–8	average	shade/pt shade	acid
Astilbe ×rosea 'Peach Blossom' Light peach-pink flowers; serrated compound leaves.	perennial	4–9	average	shade/pt shade	acid
Athyrium niponicum var. pictum Maroon stems; silvery green leaves.	perennial	4–7	average	shade/pt shade	average
Atriplex hortensis var. rubra Dark purple-red foliage.	annual	7–9	average	full sun	average
Baptisia 'Purple Smoke' Dark smoky green stems; dusty lavender-blue flowers on spikes; black seed pods.	perennial	3–9	dry	sun/pt shade	acid
Baptisia australis Indigo-blue flowers on spikes; blue-green leaves, typical of pea family; black seed pods. Plate 162; Combination 5.	perennial	3–9	dry	sun/pt shade	acid
Baptisia sphaerocarpa Yellow flowers on spikes; blue-green leaves; tan seed pods.	perennial	5–9	dry	sun/pt shade	acid
Belamcanda chinensis Orange star-shaped flowers; irislike leaves; black fruit. Plates 144, 146.	perennial	5–10	average	full sun	average
Belamcanda chinensis 'Hello Yellow' Yellow star-shaped flowers; irislike leaves; black fruit. Plate 158.	perennial	5–10	average	full sun	average
Berberis thunbergii 'Monler' (Gold Nugget™) Golden yellow foliage with hints of green, orange, and red; colors intensify in autumn. Plates 107–109, 172.	shrub	4–8	dry	sun/pt shade	average
Berberis thunbergii 'Monry' (Sunsation™) Green new foliage matures to gold.	shrub	4–8	dry	sun/pt shade	average
Berberis thunbergii var. atropurpurea 'Bailtwo' (Burgundy Carousel™) Burgundy-purple foliage. Plate 141.	shrub	4–8	dry	full sun	average
Berberis thunbergii var. atropurpurea 'Gentry Cultivar' (Royal Burgundy™) Rich burgundy foliage turns black-red in autumn.	shrub	4–8	dry	full sun	average
Berberis thunbergii var. atropurpurea 'Rose Glow' Rose-pink and reddish purple mottled foliage. Plate 7.	shrub	4–8	dry	full sun	average
Berberis thunbergii var. atropurpurea 'Royal Cloak' Large dark red-purple leaves.	shrub	4–8	dry	full sun	average

	TYPE	ZONE	SOIL MOISTURE	LIGHT	SOIL pH
Beta vulgaris 'Bull's Blood' Dark maroon-purple leaves with ruffled edges. Plate 69.	annual		average	full sun	average
Beta vulgaris 'Golden' Bright yellow stalks, midrib, and leaf veins; green leaves. Plate 185.	annual		average	full sun	average
Beta vulgaris 'Ruby Queen' Red stalks, midrib, and leaf veins; green leaves.	annual		average	full sun	average
Betula utilis var. jacquemontii Pyramidal-oval form; brown catkins; milky-white exfoliating bark. Plate 36.	tree	5–6	wet	full sun	acid
Bouvardia ternifolia Terminal clusters of scarlet-red tubular flowers; sprawling habit. Plate 150.	annual	9–11	average	full sun	average
Brachyscome 'Ultra' Lavender daisylike flowers; finely divided foliage.	annual	10–11	average	full sun	average
Brassica oleracea Loose rosettes of large ruffled rose and smoky purple leaves.	annual		average	full sun	average
Brunnera macrophylla Small true-blue flowers; coarse heart-shaped leaves.	perennial	3–8	dry	shade/pt shade	average
Buddleia 'Lochinch' Sweetly fragrant blue-lavender flowers; gray-green leaves.	shrub	5–9	dry	full sun	average
Buddleia davidii 'Black Knight' Dark purple flowers.	shrub	5–9	dry	full sun	average
Buddleia davidii 'Mongo' (Nanho blue) Blue-mauve flowers; small gray-green leaves. Plate 78.	shrub	5–9	dry	full sun	average
Buphthalmum speciosum Yellow daisylike flowerheads; large coarse heart-shaped leaves.	perennial	4–7	average	sun/pt shade	average
Buxus 'Green Gem' Very slow growing; small deep green leaves; evergreen.	shrub	5–9	average	sun/pt shade	average
Buxus 'Green Velvet' Very slow growing; small deep green leaves; evergreen.	shrub	5–9	average	sun/pt shade	average
Buxus microphylla 'Winter Gem' Small deep green leaves; evergreen.	shrub	5–9	average	shade/pt shade	average
Caladium 'Florida Cardinal' Red leaves edged in green. Plate 114.	tropical	10–11	average	shade/pt shade	average
Caladium 'Florida Sweetheart' Translucent rose-red leaves with darker veins, edged in green.	tropical	10–11	average	shade/pt shade	average

	TYPE	ZONE	SOIL MOISTURE	LIGHT	SOIL pH
Calamagrostis brachytricha Green foliage; inflorescences open purplish red then fade to silvery tan.	perennial	4–8	dry	shade/pt shade	average
Calamagrostis ×acutiflora 'Karl Foerster' Green foliage; loose inflorescences open with a tint of purple turning to buff.	perennial	4–8	dry	full sun	average
Calamagrostis ×acutiflora 'Overdam' Cream and green variegated foliage; purplish inflorescences turning to buff.	perennial	5–8	dry	sun/pt shade	average
Calendula officinalis 'Orange King' Orange daisylike flowerheads; thick oblong leaves.	annual		average	full sun	average
Callicarpa dichotoma 'Issai' Arching branches; outstanding lilac-violet fruit. Plate 168.	shrub	5–8	average	sun/pt shade	average
Calycanthus floridus Dark green leaves; fruity-scented maroon-red spring flowers; persistent capsulelike fruit.	shrub	4–9	wet	sun/pt shade	average
Camassia leichtlinii 'Semiplena' Tall spikes of large white semi-double flowers; straplike basal leaves.	hardy bulb	3–8	average	sun/pt shade	average
Camassia leichtlinii ssp. suksdorfii 'Blauwe Donau' (blue Danube) Tall spikes of blue flowers; straplike basal leaves.	hardy bulb	3–8	average	sun/pt shade	average
Campanula 'Birch Hybrid' Blue-mauve flowers; spreading habit. Plate 165.	perennial	4–7	average	sun/pt shade	average
Campanula 'Constellation' Star-shaped deep blue flowers; dense mound of small toothed leaves.	perennial	4–7	average	sun/pt shade	average
Campanula 'Dwarf Tornado' Clusters of deep blue star-shaped flowers.	perennial	4–7	average	sun/pt shade	average
Campanula 'Kent Belle' Large violet bell-shaped flowers; relaxed habit.	perennial	5–9	average	sun/pt shade	average
Campanula persicifolia 'Chettle Charm' White flowers rimmed in pale blue-lavender.	perennial	3–7	average	sun/pt shade	average
Campanula rapunculoides Spikes of blue-violet flowers. Plate 163.	perennial	3–7	average	sun/pt shade	average
Campanula rotundifolia 'Olympica' Tiny blue bell-shaped flowers; round leaves often disappear by the time flowering occurs.	perennial	2–7	average	sun/pt shade	average
Campsis ×tagliabuana 'Madame Galen' Vigorous vine; pinnate foliage; orange-red trumpet flowers.	woody vine	5–9	dry	sun/pt shade	average
Canna 'Black Knight' Blackish purple-green lance-shaped leaves; scarlet flowers.	tropical	(7)8–11	wet	full sun	average

	TYPE	ZONE	SOIL MOISTURE	LIGHT	SOIL pH
Canna 'Omega' Green lance-shaped leaves; apricot flowers. Plate 182.	tropical	(7)8–11	wet	full sun	average
Canna 'Orange Punch' Green leaves; tangerine-orange self-cleaning flowers with a yellow throat. Plate 193.	tropical	(7)8–11	wet	full sun	average
Canna 'Panache' Green lance-shaped leaves; yellow buds open to pinky peach flowers.	tropical	(7)8–11	wet	full sun	average
Canna 'Phasion' Leaves striped deep green, orange, purple, red, and yellow; orange flowers. Plate 43.	tropical	(7)8–11	wet	full sun	average
Canna 'Roi Humbert' (red King Humbert) Bronze-red leaves; red-orange flowers. Plates 111, 145.	tropical	(7)8–11	wet	full sun	average
Canna 'Striata' (Pretoria) Green and yellow variegated leaves; orange flowers. Plate 3; Combination 17.	tropical	(7)8–11	wet	full sun	average
Canna indica 'Red Stripe' (purpurea) Large bananalike leaves striped green and red; red-orange flowers. Plates 8, 75, 196; Combination 11.	tropical	(7)8–11	wet	full sun	average
Carex buchananii Narrow copper-bronze foliage. Plates 190–191.	perennial	(5)6–9	average	sun/pt shade	average
Carex dolichostachya 'Kaga Nishiki' (gold fountains) Narrow green and yellow variegated leaves.	perennial	5–9	wet	sun/pt shade	average
Carex elata 'Aurea' (Bowles' golden) Yellow leaves with faint green variegation. Plate 197.	perennial	5–9	wet	sun/pt shade	average
Carex morrowii 'Ice Dance' Green and cream variegated leaves.	perennial	5–9	wet	sun/pt shade	average
Carex morrowii 'Variegata' Green leaves with white margins. Plate 123.	perennial	5–9	wet	sun/pt shade	average
Caryopteris ×clandonensis Blue late-summer flowers; narrow gray-green foliage. Plate 75.	shrub	(5)6–9	dry	sun/pt shade	average
Caryopteris ×clandonensis 'Longwood Blue' Bright blue late-summer flowers; narrow gray-green foliage.	shrub	(5)6–9	dry	sun/pt shade	average
Caryopteris ×clandonensis 'Worcester Gold' Yellow foliage often turning chartreuse-green in summer; bright blue late-summer flowers. Plates 40, 159, 161.	shrub	(5)6–9	dry	sun/pt shade	average
Catalpa bignonioides 'Aurea' Large heart-shaped chartreuse-yellow foliage.	tree	5–9	dry	full sun	average
Celosia spicata 'Flamingo Purple' Purple foliage; spikes of fluffy purple flowers.	annual		average	full sun	average

	TYPE	ZONE	SOIL MOISTURE	LIGHT	SOIL pH
Centaurea cineraria Felted silvery gray divided leaves.	annual	7–9	average	full sun	average
Centaurea montana Fringed blue flowers; green leaves.	perennial	3–8	dry	sun/pt shade	average
Cephalaria gigantea Yellow pincushion flowers on tall wiry stems; compound leaves.	perennial	3–8	average	full sun	average
Ceratostigma plumbaginoides Small blue flowers; small green leaves turn red in autumn. Plates 100, 177.	perennial	5–9	dry	sun/pt shade	average
Cerinthe major 'Purpurascens' Grayish blue-green leaves; small purple-pink bell- shaped flowers. Plates 34, 91, 98, 108.	annual	6(7)	average	full sun	average
Chamaecyparis lawsoniana 'Sullivan' Graceful, deep green foliage.	tree	5–7	average	sun/pt shade	average
Chamaecyparis obtusa 'Fernspray Gold' Yellow-green flattened fernlike foliage. Plate 14.	shrub	5–8	average	sun/pt shade	average
Chamaecyparis obtusa 'Mariesii' Yellowish green to yellowish white needles; branches thin and slightly nodding.	shrub	5–8	average	sun/pt shade	average
Chamaecyparis pisifera 'Golden Mop' Yellow stringy branchlets; dwarf evergreen. Plates 98, 155.	shrub	4–7	average	sun/pt shade	average
Chionanthus virginicus Medium green leaves; fragrant white flowers; dark blue fruit. Plate 125.	tree	4–9	wet	sun/pt shade	average
Chionodoxa forbesii (luciliae) Siehei Group Bright gentian-blue flowers.	hardy bulb	3–8	average	sun/pt shade	average
Chrysanthemum 'Autumn Moon' Large fully double pale yellow flowers. Combination 10.	perennial	(5)6–9	average	full sun	average
Chrysanthemum 'Pumpkin Harvest' Single daisylike dark peach flowers.	perennial	5–9	average	full sun	average
Chrysanthemum 'Single Apricot' Single daisylike apricot flowers. Plate 189.	perennial	5–9	average	full sun	average
Chrysanthemum 'Single Peach' Single daisylike peach flowers. Plates 189–190.	perennial	5–9	average	full sun	average
Chrysanthemum 'Viette's Apricot Glow' Single daisylike apricot flowers.	perennial	5–9	average	full sun	average
Cimicifuga ramosa 'Brunette' Dark purple compound foliage; white bottlebrush flowers. Combination 15.	perennial	3–8	wet	shade/pt shade	acid

	TYPE	ZONE	SOIL MOISTURE	LIGHT	SOIL pH
Cimicifuga ramosa 'Hillside Black Beauty' Dark purple compound foliage; white bottlebrush flowers. Plate 41.	perennial	3–8	wet	shade/pt shade	acid
Clematis 'Elsa Späth' Mauve-blue flowers; silvery seedheads. Plate 37.	woody vine	4–8(9)	average	sun/pt shade	alkaline
Clematis 'Hagley Hybrid' Large pink flowers with brown anthers; silvery seedheads; repeat bloom. Plate 129.	woody vine	4–8(9)	average	sun/pt shade	alkaline
Clematis 'Lanuginosa Candida' Large white flowers; silvery seedheads.	woody vine	5–8(9)	average	sun/pt shade	alkaline
Clematis 'Polish Spirit' Purple flowers; sporadic rebloom throughout the summer; seedheads are of little garden value. Plate 106.	woody vine	4–8(9)	average	sun/pt shade	alkaline
Clematis 'Royal Velours' Dark velvety purple-red flowers; seedheads are of little garden value.	woody vine	4–8(9)	average	sun/pt shade	alkaline
Clematis alpina 'Constance' Semi-double purplish pink bell-shaped flowers; sporadic rebloom throughout the summer; silvery seedheads.	woody vine	5–9	average	sun/pt shade	alkaline
Clematis integrifolia blue-violet bell-shaped flowers; sprawling habit.	perennial	4–9	average	sun/pt shade	alkaline
Clematis macropetala 'Markham's Pink' Pink semi-double open bell-shaped flowers; sporadic rebloom; silvery seedheads.	woody vine	5–9	average	sun/pt shade	alkaline
Clematis recta Fragrant fringed white flowers; compound blue-green leaves. Plate 55.	perennial	3–7	average	sun/pt shade	alkaline
Clematis terniflora Very vigorous vine covered in small fragrant white flowers. Plates 6, 73–74.	woody vine	5–8(9)	average	sun/pt shade	alkaline
Clethra alnifolia Fragrant white flowers; green leaves turn golden yellow-brown in autumn. Plate 73.	shrub	4–9	wet	sun/pt shade	acid
Colchicum speciosum Pink-lavender cup-shaped flowers on naked stems in autumn; hostalike leaves appear in spring.	hardy bulb	4–9	average	sun/pt shade	average
Colocasia esculenta Huge velvety green heart-shaped leaves. Plate 122.	tropical	8–11	wet	sun/pt shade	average
Colocasia esculenta 'Black Beauty' Large heart-shaped purple-black leaves; purple-black stems.	tropical		wet	sun/pt shade	average
Colocasia esculenta 'Black Magic' Large heart-shaped purple-black leaves and stems.	tropical	8–11	wet	sun/pt shade	average

	TYPE	ZONE	SOIL MOISTURE	LIGHT	SOIL pH
Colocasia esculenta 'Fontanesii' Huge heart-shaped purple-tinted green leaves with purple-black stalks, veins, and margins; creamy yellow-white spathe. Plates 97, 200.	tropical	8–11	wet	sun/pt shade	average
Colocasia esculenta 'Illustris' Large heart-shaped purple-black leaves with green veins.	tropical	7–10	wet	sun/pt shade	average
Consolida ajacis 'Blue Spire' Finely dissected fernlike foliage; spikes of blue flowers. Plates 96, 110.	annual		average	full sun	average
Coreopsis auriculata Bright yellow flowers.	perennial	4–9	dry	full sun	average
Coreopsis grandiflora 'Walcoreop' **(flying saucers)** Golden yellow flowerheads; narrow green leaves on bushy plants. Plate 158.	perennial	4–9	dry	full sun	average
Coreopsis tripteris Pale yellow flowers with brown-purple centers. Plate 183.	perennial	4–8	dry	full sun	average
Coreopsis verticillata 'Moonbeam' Soft yellow flowerheads; feathery green leaves.	perennial	3–9	dry	full sun	average
Coreopsis verticillata 'Zagreb' Golden yellow flowerheads; feathery green leaves.	perennial	3–9	dry	full sun	average
Cornus kousa Vase-shaped in youth; rounded form with horizontal branching at maturity; purple-red autumn color; creamy white flowers; red fruit.	tree	5–8	average	sun/pt shade	acid
Cosmos atrosanguineus Chocolate-scented maroon flowers.	annual	7–10	average	full sun	average
Cotinus coggygria 'Velvet Cloak' Dark purple foliage turning red-purple in autumn. Plate 143.	shrub	(4)5–8	dry	full sun	average
Crocosmia 'Blacro' (Jenny Bloom) Orange buds open to golden yellow flowers; sword-shaped foliage.	perennial	5–10	average	full sun	average
Crocosmia 'Emberglow' Sword-shaped foliage; orange flowers.	perennial	6–9	average	full sun	average
Crocosmia 'Lucifer' Sword-shaped foliage; red-orange bloom. Plates 25, 31, 97, 99.	perennial	5–9	average	full sun	average
Crocosmia ×crocosmiiflora 'Norwich Canary' Sword-shaped foliage; yellow flowers. Plate 185.	perennial	6–9	average	full sun	average
Crocosmia ×crocosmiiflora 'Solfatare' Bronze-green sword-shaped foliage; yellow-apricot flowers. Plate 182.	perennial	6–9	average	full sun	average

	TYPE	ZONE	SOIL MOISTURE	LIGHT	SOIL pH
Crocosmia ×crocosmiiflora 'Venus' Sword-shaped foliage; peachy yellow flowers.	perennial	6–9	average	full sun	average
Crocus chrysanthus 'Blue Bird' Blue-violet flowers with creamy white interiors.	hardy bulb	3–8	average	sun/pt shade	average
Cryptotaenia japonica f. atropurpurea Purple-black leaves; white flowers.	perennial	5–7	average	shade/pt shade	average
Cynara cardunculus Large spiny silvery gray leaves; purple flowerheads. Plate 84.	annual	7–9	dry	full sun	average
Cynoglossum amabile 'Firmament' Gray-green hairy leaves; tiny blue flowers.	perennial	5–8	average	sun/pt shade	average
Cyperus alternifolius 'Stricta' Leafless stems topped with long narrow leaves that radiate outward. Plate 71.	annual	9–11	wet	full sun	average
Dahlia 'Arabian Night' Dark velvety red double flowers. Plate 195.	tender bulb	(7)8–10	average	full sun	average
Dahlia 'Bishop of Llandaff' Dark red foliage; red flowers.	tender bulb	(7)8–10	average	full sun	average
Dahlia 'Ellen Houston' Dark greenish black foliage; orange-red flowers. Plates 144, 147.	tender bulb	(7)8–10	average	full sun	average
Dahlia 'Orange Nugget' Bright orange flowers. Plate 194.	tender bulb	(7)8–10	average	full sun	average
Dahlia 'Susette' Soft yellow flowers.	tender bulb	(7)8–10	average	full sun	average
Daphne ×burkwoodii 'Carol Mackie' Dark green leaves edged with cream; highly perfumed pink flowers. Plates 125–126.	shrub	4–6(7)	average	sun/pt shade	alkaline
Delphinium 'Centurion Sky Blue' Pale blue flower spikes.	perennial	5–7	average	sun/pt shade	alkaline
Delphinium ×bellamosum Dark blue flowers on spikes; palmately divided leaves.	perennial	3–7	average	sun/pt shade	alkaline
Delphinium cashmerianum Blue-purple flower spikes; lobed and finely cut leaves.	perennial	5–7	average	sun/pt shade	alkaline
Delphinium exaltatum Purple flower spikes.	perennial	5–8	average	sun/pt shade	average
Deschampsia cespitosa 'Goldgehänge' Long-lasting, pendulous golden yellow inflorescences.	perennial	4–9	average	sun/pt shade	average
Dianthus ×allwoodii 'Danielle Marie' Double coral flowers.	perennial	5–8	dry	full sun	alkaline
Dianthus barbatus 'Sooty' Velvety dark red flowers; green foliage tinged dark red.	perennial	5–9	dry	full sun	alkaline

	TYPE	ZONE	SOIL MOISTURE	LIGHT	SOIL pH
Dianthus deltoides 'Leuchtfunk' (flashing light) Carmine-red flowers; green foliage. Plate 148.	perennial	4–9	dry	full sun	alkaline
Dicentra 'Luxuriant' Cherry-red heart-shaped flowers; gray-green feathery leaves.	perennial	3–9	average	shade/pt shade	average
Dicentra spectabilis 'Gold Heart' Yellow foliage; pink heart-shaped pendent flowers. Plate 41.	perennial	4–9	average	shade/pt shade	average
Dichelostemma ida-maia Tubular pendent red flowers with greenish yellow tips.	hardy bulb	5–8	average	full sun	average
Digitalis grandiflora Light yellow flower spikes; green leaves. Combination 20.	perennial	3–8	average	sun/pt shade	average
Digitalis lutea Creamy yellow flowers; glossy dark green leaves.	perennial	3–9	average	sun/pt shade	average
Digitalis purpurea 'Apricot' Creamy apricot flowers.	perennial	4–9	dry	sun/pt shade	average
Dracocephalum ruyschiana Blue flower spikes; lance-shaped leaves.	perennial	4–8	dry	sun/pt shade	average
Duranta erecta 'Golden Edge' Golden yellow and green variegated foliage. Plate 111.	tropical	8–10	average	full sun	average
Echinacea purpurea Purplish pink daisylike flowers with orange conelike center; coarse leaves. Combination 7.	perennial	3–8	dry	full sun	average
Echinops bannaticus 'Taplow Blue' Round blue flowerheads; rough spiny leaves.	perennial	5–9	dry	full sun	average
Echinops ritro 'Blue Glow' Round blue flowerheads; rough spiny leaves.	perennial	3–9	dry	full sun	average
Echinops ritro 'Veitch's Blue' Round blue flowerheads; rough spiny leaves. Plate 175.	perennial	3–9	dry	full sun	average
Epimedium davidii Delicate yellow flowers; spiny evergreen leaflets.	perennial	5–9	dry	shade/pt shade	average
Epimedium ×rubrum Red flowers; heart-shaped leaves.	perennial	4–8	dry	shade/pt shade	average
Epimedium ×warleyense Orange and yellow flowers; reddish green leaves.	perennial	5–9	dry	shade/pt shade	average
Eranthis hyemalis Yellow flowers; frilly green collar of leaves.	hardy bulb	5–8	average	shade/pt shade	alkaline
Eremurus ×isabellinus 'Pinokkio' Tall spikes of golden yellow flowers with orange anthers.	hardy bulb	5–8	average	full sun	average

	TYPE	ZONE	SOIL MOISTURE	LIGHT	SOIL pH
Eryngium amethystinum Deeply cut spiny steel-blue foliage; small blue flowers.	perennial	3–8	dry	full sun	average
Eryngium planum 'Blaukappe' Deeply cut spiny steel-blue foliage and flowers.	perennial	3–8	dry	full sun	average
Eryngium variifolium Spiny green leaves with white veins; blue-gray flowers with sharply pointed bracts.	perennial	5–9	dry	full sun	average
Eryngium yuccifolium Rosette of spiny, sword-shaped bluish gray-green leaves; small green oval flowerheads on tall stems. Plate 4.	perennial	4–8	dry	full sun	average
Erythronium 'Pagoda' Maroon-mottled green foliage; yellow flowers; plant goes dormant after flowering.	hardy bulb	3–8	wet	shade/pt shade	average
Eschscholzia californica Bright orange flowers; blue-green ferny foliage. Plate 13; Combination 8.	annual		dry	full sun	average
Eschscholzia californica 'Purple Gleam' Pinkish purple flowers; blue-green ferny foliage. Combination 13.	annual		dry	full sun	average
Eucomis comosa 'Sparkling Burgundy' Purple foliage; tufted purple flower spikes resemble a pineapple.	annual	(7)8–10	average	full sun	average
Eupatorium purpureum ssp. maculatum 'Gateway' Rose-pink flowerheads; whorled leaves. Plates 2, 32; Combination 7.	perennial	2–9	wet	full sun	average
Euphorbia 'Golden Towers' Coral-red stems; blue-green leaves with narrow red margins; yellow flowers.	perennial	5–8	dry	full sun	average
Euphorbia amygdaloides 'Purpurea' Foliage tinged red and purple; dark red stems; greenish yellow flowers. Plate 155.	perennial	5–9	dry	sun/pt shade	average
Euphorbia cotinifolia Rich red leaves reminiscent of a smokebush. Plate 5; Combination 12.	tropical	9–11	dry	full sun	average
Euphorbia cyparissias 'Fen's Ruby' Narrow feathery leaves emerge red then fade to blue-green; yellow flowers. Plate 41.	perennial	4–9	dry	full sun	average
Euphorbia dulcis 'Chameleon' Reddish purple and green leaves; yellow flowers; foliage colors intensify in autumn.	perennial	4–9	dry	full sun	average
Euphorbia griffithii 'Fireglow' Bright orange flower bracts; orange stems. Plate 28.	perennial	5–8	dry	full sun	average

	TYPE	ZONE	SOIL MOISTURE	LIGHT	SOIL pH
Euphorbia ×martinii Blue-green leaves tinged red-purple in spring and turn burgundy in fall and winter; chartreuse flowers.	perennial	6–8	dry	full sun	average
Euphorbia polychroma Yellow flowers in clustered inflorescences; green leaves. Plate 181.	perennial	4–8	dry	full sun	average
Fagus sylvatica 'Purpurea Pendula' Weeping purple-leaved form; small specimen. Combination 9.	tree	4–7	average	sun/pt shade	acid
Fagus sylvatica 'Tricolor' Purple leaves with rose and cream margins emerging bright rose-pink in spring; foliage may scorch in hot sun. Plate 1.	tree	4–7	average	sun/pt shade	acid
Festuca glauca 'Elijah Blue' Silver-blue foliage.	perennial	4–8	dry	sun/pt shade	average
Festuca glauca 'Golden Toupee' Chartreuse-yellow foliage.	perennial	6–8	dry	full sun	average
Foeniculum vulgare 'Purpureum' Feathery purple foliage; yellow-green umbel flowers.	perennial	4–9	dry	full sun	average
Fothergilla gardenii Fragrant white bottlebrush flowers; orange, yellow, and red fall color.	shrub	5–8	average	sun/pt shade	acid
Fritillaria persica Nodding bell-shaped dark plum flowers. Plate 131; Combination 2.	hardy bulb	6–8	average	sun/pt shade	average
Fuchsia 'Gartenmeister Bonstedt' Dark bronze-red leaves with purple undersides; dark red flowers.	annual	8–10	average	sun/pt shade	average
Galega ×hartlandii 'Lady Wilson' Spikes of blue-violet flowers tinged white; pinnate soft green leaves.	perennial	5–10	average	sun/pt shade	average
Galium odoratum Small white flowers; green whorled leaves; quickly spreading groundcover. Plate 36.	perennial	4–8	dry	shade/pt shade	average
Genista tinctoria 'Royal Gold' Long panicles of golden yellow flowers.	shrub	4–7	dry	full sun	average
Gentiana septemfida var. lagodechiana Prostrate stems; deep blue bell-shaped flowers.	perennial	6–8	average	sun/pt shade	average
Gentiana triflora 'Royal Blue' Bell-shaped blue-purple flowers.	perennial	5–8	average	sun/pt shade	average
Geranium 'Ann Folkard' Chartreuse-green leaves; black-eyed magenta flowers; trailing habit.	perennial	5–8	average	sun/pt shade	average
Geranium 'Brookside' Finely divided leaves; small blue flowers.	perennial	4–8	average	sun/pt shade	average

	TYPE	ZONE	SOIL MOISTURE	LIGHT	SOIL pH
Geranium 'Johnson's Blue' Blue flowers; palmately lobed leaves. Plate 29.	perennial	4–8	average	sun/pt shade	average
Geranium 'Phillippe Vapelle' Soft bluish gray-green leaves; bluish purple flowers with dark veins.	perennial	5–8	average	sun/pt shade	average
Geranium 'Salome' Large blue-lavender flowers marked with maroon; chartreuse-yellow foliage.	perennial	5–8	average	sun/pt shade	average
Geranium himalayense 'Plenum' Small round divided leaves; double purple flowers.	perennial	5–8	average	sun/pt shade	average
Geranium macrorrhizum 'Ingwersen's Variety' Pink flowers; fragrant palmately lobed green leaves; groundcover.	perennial	3–8	dry	shade/pt shade	average
Geranium ×magnificum Rounded divided leaves; large dark-veined violet flowers. Plate 38.	perennial	4–8	average	sun/pt shade	average
Geranium ×oxonianum 'Claridge Druce' Glossy gray-green foliage; pink trumpet-shaped flowers. Plate 123.	perennial	4–8	average	sun/pt shade	average
Geranium phaeum 'Lily Lovell' Long-stemmed purplish plum flowers; light green foliage.	perennial	5–8	average	sun/pt shade	average
Geranium phaeum 'Samobor' Dark purple blotches on leaves; dark purple-plum flowers.	perennial	5–8	average	sun/pt shade	average
Geranium platypetalum Violet flowers on sticky stalks; rounded and lobed hairy leaves. Combination 20.	perennial	3–8	average	sun/pt shade	average
Geranium pratense 'Mrs. Kendall Clark' Pearl-gray flowers tinged with blue-lavender and veined with rose.	perennial	4–8	average	sun/pt shade	average
Geranium pratense 'Victor Reiter Jr.' Deeply divided purplish green foliage; dark blue flowers.	perennial	5–8	average	sun/pt shade	average
Geranium psilostemon Deeply cut and toothed leaves; black-eyed magenta flowers.	perennial	5–8	average	sun/pt shade	average
Geranium renardii Wrinkled velvety rounded and divided leaves; pearly white flowers with purple veins. Plate 127.	perennial	6–8	average	sun/pt shade	average
Geranium sanguineum 'New Hampshire' Magenta flowers; cranelike seedheads; small lobed leaves.	perennial	3–8	dry	sun/pt shade	average
Geranium wlassovianum Purple-pink with violet veins; red leaves in autumn.	perennial	5–8	average	shade/pt shade	average

	TYPE	ZONE	SOIL MOISTURE	LIGHT	SOIL pH
Gillenia stipulata White star-shaped flowers; trifoliate serrated leaves. Combination 23.	perennial	4–8	average	sun/pt shade	average
Ginkgo biloba 'Autumn Gold' Broadly conical form; gray furrowed bark; green fan-shaped leaves turn golden yellow in autumn. Plate 70.	tree	5–9	dry	full sun	average
Gladiolus 'Atom' Red flowers with silvery white edging; irislike leaves.	tender bulb	7–9	average	full sun	average
Gladiolus 'Violetta' Tall deep purple velvety flowers; irislike leaves. Plates 21, 97.	tender bulb	7–9	average	full sun	average
Gladiolus communis ssp. byzantinus Spikes of magenta flowers; irislike leaves. Combination 18.	perennial	(5)6–10	average	sun/pt shade	average
Gladiolus ×gandavensis Soft yellow flowers; irislike leaves.	perennial	(5)6–9	average	full sun	average
Gladiolus ×gandavensis 'Boone' Spikes of soft yellowy peach flowers; irislike leaves. Plates 187–188.	perennial	(5)6–9	average	full sun	average
Glaucidium palmatum Palmately lobed and toothed leaves; pinkish purple poppylike flowers.	perennial	6–9	average	shade/pt shade	average
Gomphrena haageana 'Lavender Lady' Spherical cloverlike lavender-pink flowerheads.	annual		average	full sun	average
Hakonechloa macra 'Aureola' Foliage striped bright yellow and green tinged with pink in autumn. Plates 114, 156.	perennial	5–9	average	shade/pt shade	average
Hedychium 'Daniel Weeks' Long lance-shaped leaves; fragrant yellow flowers with gold throat. Plate 20.	tropical	7–10	average	sun/pt shade	average
Hedychium coccineum Long lance-shaped leaves; fragrant pale orange flowers with prominent red stamens. Plates 19, 186.	tropical	8–10	average	sun/pt shade	average
Helenium 'Kugelsonne' Yellow daisylike flowerheads; narrow green leaves.	perennial	3–8	dry	full sun	average
Helenium 'Moerheim Beauty' Copper-red daisylike flowerheads; narrow green leaves. Plate 192.	perennial	3–8	dry	full sun	average
Helianthemum (double yellow) Crepe-papery yellow flowers; narrow gray-green leaves.	perennial	5–7	dry	full sun	alkaline
Helianthemum 'Fire Dragon' Crepe-papery orange-red flowers; narrow gray-green leaves. Plate 149.	perennial	5–7	dry	full sun	alkaline

	TYPE	ZONE	SOIL MOISTURE	LIGHT	SOIL pH
Helianthus 'Lemon Queen' Lemon-yellow daisylike flowerheads.	perennial	3–9	dry	full sun	average
Helianthus 'Mellow Yellow' Yellow daisylike flowerheads.	perennial	3–9	dry	full sun	average
Helianthus salicifolius Golden yellow daisylike flowerheads; narrow leaves. Plates 76, 138.	perennial	3–9	dry	full sun	average
Helichrysum petiolare 'Limelight' Silvery lime-green woolly leaves. Plates 69, 148–150.	annual	10–11	average	full sun	average
Helictotrichon sempervirens 'Saphirsprudel' **(sapphire fountain)** Silver-blue foliage; tan flower. Plates 95, 100.	perennial	4–8	dry	full sun	average
Heliopsis helianthoides var. scabra **'Sommersonne' (summer sun)** Golden yellow daisylike flowerheads; green leaves. Plate 75; Combination 7.	perennial	3–9	dry	full sun	average
Helleborus Royal Heritage™ Nodding flowers in rose, green, white, and smoky purple; deep green palmate leaves.	perennial	4–9	average	shade/pt shade	alkaline
Helleborus foetidus Leathery dark green palmate leaves; large long- lasting green flowerheads. Combinations 2–3.	perennial	(5)6–9	average	shade/pt shade	alkaline
Helleborus orientalis Rose-pink flowers; deep green palmate leaves. Plate 121.	perennial	4–9	average	shade/pt shade	alkaline
Helleborus orientalis (single black) Plum-black nodding flowers; rich purple new growth; palmate leaves.	perennial	4–9	average	shade/pt shade	alkaline
Hemerocallis 'Alluring Peach' Large peach flowers; green straplike leaves. Plates 4, 187.	perennial	3–9	average	sun/pt shade	average
Hemerocallis 'Carefree Peach' Large peach flowers; green straplike leaves; reblooming.	perennial	3–9	average	sun/pt shade	average
Hemerocallis 'Happy Returns' Lemon-yellow flowers; green straplike leaves; reblooming.	perennial	3–9	average	full sun	average
Hemerocallis 'Peach Fairy' Small melon-pink flowers; green straplike leaves.	perennial	3–9	average	sun/pt shade	average
Hemerocallis 'Red Razzamatazz' Bright red flowers; green straplike leaves.	perennial	3–9	average	full sun	average
Hemerocallis 'Scarlet Romance' Red flowers; green straplike leaves.	perennial	3–9	average	full sun	average
Hemerocallis 'Siloam Royal Prince' Ruffled purple-red flowers; green straplike leaves.	perennial	3–9	average	full sun	average

	TYPE	ZONE	SOIL MOISTURE	LIGHT	SOIL pH
Hemerocallis 'Staghorn Sumac' Large ruffled burnt-orange flowers; green straplike leaves.	perennial	3–9	average	full sun	average
Hemerocallis 'Sundried Tomatoes' Large tomato-red blooms with yellow and light green throat; green straplike leaves.	perennial	3–9	average	full sun	average
Hemerocallis 'Toy Trumpets' Small yellow self-cleaning flowers on 3-ft. stems; green straplike leaves.	perennial	3–9	average	full sun	average
Hemerocallis 'Welcome Mat' Large peach-pink flowers with yellow throat; green straplike leaves.	perennial	3–9	average	sun/pt shade	average
Hemerocallis 'Yellow Lollipop' Bright yellow flowers; green straplike leaves; reblooming.	perennial	3–9	average	full sun	average
Hesperis matronalis Fragrant purple or white flowers; narrow serrated leaves. Plates 1, 39.	perennial	3–8	average	sun/pt shade	alkaline
Heuchera 'Chocolate Ruffles' Chocolate-purple ruffled leaves; tiny white flowers on spikes.	perennial	4–9	average	sun/pt shade	average
Heuchera 'Plum Pudding' Plum-purple scalloped leaves; tiny white flowers on spikes. Plate 98.	perennial	4–9	average	sun/pt shade	average
Heuchera 'Raspberry Regal' Raspberry-red flower spikes; scalloped green leaves.	perennial	3–8	average	sun/pt shade	average
Heuchera 'Velvet Night' Dark plum-purple scalloped leaves; tiny white flowers on spikes. Plate 94.	perennial	4–9	average	sun/pt shade	average
Heuchera micrantha var. diversifolia 'Palace Purple' Greenish purple to reddish purple ivy-shaped leaves; tiny white flowers on spikes. Plates 126, 129.	perennial	4–9	average	sun/pt shade	average
×Heucherella 'Silver Streak' White flowers tinged lavender; greenish purple leaves overlaid with silver.	perennial	4–7	average	sun/pt shade	average
Hibiscus acetosella 'Red Shield' Dark red-purple palmately lobed and toothed leaves. Plate 186; Combination 25.	tropical	10–11	average	full sun	average
Hibiscus moscheutos 'Lord Baltimore' Deeply lobed triangular leaves; huge brilliant red ruffled flowers. Plate 196.	perennial	4–9	wet	full sun	average
Hosta 'Big Daddy' White flowers; large puckered and cupped blue-green leaves.	perennial	3–8	average	shade/pt shade	average

	TYPE	ZONE	SOIL MOISTURE	LIGHT	SOIL pH
Hosta 'Blue Cadet' Lavender flowers; bluish green heart-shaped leaves that turn more green in late summer. Combination 14.	perennial	3–8	average	shade/pt shade	average
Hosta 'Fragrant Blue' Fragrant pale lavender flowers; blue leaves. Plate 127.	perennial	3–8	average	shade/pt shade	average
Hosta 'Halcyon' Pale bluish lavender flowers; gray-blue leaves.	perennial	3–8	average	shade/pt shade	average
Hosta 'Krossa Regal' Pale lavender flowers; greenish blue leaves. Plate 119.	perennial	3–8	average	shade/pt shade	average
Hosta 'Lemon Lime' Purple flowers; narrow yellow-green leaves.	perennial	3–8	average	shade/pt shade	average.
Hosta 'Love Pat' White flowers; thick puckered blue-gray leaves.	perennial	3–8	average	shade/pt shade	average
Hosta 'Midas Touch' White flowers; large puckered yellow leaves.	perennial	3–8	average	shade/pt shade	average
Hosta 'Night Before Christmas' Pale lavender flowers; creamy white leaves with wide dark green margins. Plate 125.	perennial	3–8	average	shade/pt shade	average
Hosta 'Patriot' Lavender flowers; green leaves with creamy white margins. Plate 119.	perennial	3–8	average	shade/pt shade	average
Hosta 'Paul's Glory' Pale lavender-gray flowers; yellow leaves with green margins.	perennial	3–8	average	shade/pt shade	average
Hosta 'Sum and Substance' Pale lavender flowers; large chartreuse to gold leaves. Plate 6.	perennial	3–8	average	shade/pt shade	average
Hosta 'Sun Power' Pale lavender flowers; wavy yellow leaves. Plates 198–199.	perennial	3–8	average	shade/pt shade	average
Hosta plantaginea 'Aphrodite' Fragrant double white flowers; shiny green leaves.	perennial	3–8	average	shade/pt shade	average
Humulus lupulus 'Bianca' Chartreuse-yellow lobed and toothed leaves; vining red-tinted stems; yellow autumn foliage. Plates 1–2; Combination 6.	perennial	3–8	average	sun/pt shade	average
Hydrangea anomala ssp. petiolaris Cinnamon-colored exfoliating bark; glossy green leaves may turn yellow in autumn; white flowers in summer.	woody vine	4–7(8)	average	sun/pt shade	average
Hydrangea quercifolia Large creamy white flower panicles; large green oakleaf-shaped leaves turn red and purple in autumn; cinnamon-colored exfoliating bark.	shrub	5–9	average	sun/pt shade	average

	TYPE	ZONE	SOIL MOISTURE	LIGHT	SOIL pH
Hydrangea quercifolia 'Snowflake' Large white flower panicles; flowers appear double; large green oakleaf-shaped leaves turn red and purple in autumn; cinnamon-colored exfoliating bark. Combination 15.	shrub	5–9	average	sun/pt shade	average
Hymenocallis 'Sulphur Queen' Fragrant soft yellow flowers; attractive straplike foliage. Plates 107, 110, 184.	tender bulb	(7)8–10	average	full sun	average
Hypericum androsaemum 'Albury Purple' Foliage tinged purple and red; yellow flowers; black berries. Plates 110, 112.	shrub	(5)6–8	dry	sun/pt shade	average
Hyssopus officinalis Blue-violet flower spikes; leaves and flowers have camphorlike odor.	perennial	4–9	average	full sun	average
Hystrix patula Green leaves; bottlebrush-shaped flowerheads. Combination 23.	perennial	4–8	dry	sun/pt shade	average
Ilex 'Apollo' Green glossy leaves; abundant pollen.	shrub	4–9	wet	sun/pt shade	acid
Ilex glabra Small dark evergreen leaves; black persistent fruit.	shrub	(4)5–9(10)	wet	sun/pt shade	acid
Ilex ×meserveae 'Mesdob' (China boy) Glossy evergreen leaves.	shrub	5–7	average	shade/pt shade	acid
Ilex ×meserveae 'Mesog' (China girl) Glossy evergreen leaves; red fruit.	shrub	5–7	average	shade/pt shade	acid
Ilex verticillata 'Afterglow' Compact habit; small glossy leaves; large orange-red fruit.	shrub	4–9	wet	sun/pt shade	acid
Ilex verticillata 'Christmas Cheer' Compact habit; abundant red fruit.	shrub	3–9	wet	sun/pt shade	acid
Ilex verticillata 'Jim Dandy' Compact habit; dark green foliage.	shrub	4–9	wet	sun/pt shade	acid
Ilex verticillata 'Winter Red' Abundant large red fruit persisting into winter; glossy green foliage turns bronze in autumn.	shrub	3–9	wet	sun/pt shade	acid
Impatiens omeiana Palmately divided dark green leaves w7ith cream stripe center; small yellow flowers. Plates 198–199.	perennial	6–9	average	shade/pt shade	average
Imperata cylindrica var. koenigii 'Red Baron' Bright red leaves.	perennial	5–9	average	sun/pt shade	average
Ipomoea batatas 'Ace of Spades' Heart-shaped near-black foliage; trailing habit. Plate 46.	annual	9–11	average	full sun	average
Ipomoea batatas 'Blackie' Lobed near-black foliage; trailing habit.	annual	9–11	average	full sun	average

	TYPE	ZONE	SOIL MOISTURE	LIGHT	SOIL pH
Ipomoea batatas 'Margarita' Lobed chartreuse foliage; trailing habit. Plates 65, 143.	annual	9–11	average	full sun	average
Ipomoea lobata (Mina lobata) Climber with lobed green leaves; panicles of red, orange, and yellow tubular flowers. Plate 66.	annual vine		average	full sun	average
Ipomoea tricolor 'Heavenly Blue' Sky-blue flowers with white throat; heart-shaped leaves. Plates 3, 18.	annual vine	10–11	average	full sun	average
Iris 'Blue Magic' Bright blue-violet and yellow flowers.	hardy bulb	6–9	average	full sun	average
Iris 'Flavescens' Bearded yellow flowers with dark speckling at the heart of petals. Plates 1, 39.	perennial	3–10	average	full sun	average
Iris 'Perfume Counter' Large fragrant bearded purple flowers; swordlike flat gray-green leaves; reblooms in autumn.	perennial	3–10	average	full sun	average
Iris 'Sugar Blues' Fragrant bearded blue-lavender flowers; swordlike gray-green leaves; reblooms in autumn.	perennial	3–10	average	full sun	average
Iris foetidissima Light blue-lavender flowers; capsules containing bright orange seeds in autumn.	perennial	6–9	average	sun/pt shade	average
Iris pallida 'Variegata' Soft blue-lavender flowers; light creamy yellow and green variegated leaves. Plate 162.	perennial	4–9	average	sun/pt shade	average
Iris pseudacorus 'Variegata' Green and yellow variegated foliage; yellow flower. Plate 71.	perennial	5–8	wet	full sun	average
Iris reticulata 'Harmony' Fragrant blue and yellow flowers.	hardy bulb	3–9	average	sun/pt shade	average
Iris sanguinea 'Snow Queen' White flowers; straplike leaves. Combination 5.	perennial	3–8	average	sun/pt shade	average
Iris sibirica 'Butter and Sugar' Yellow and white flowers; straplike leaves.	perennial	3–9	average	sun/pt shade	average
Iris sibirica 'Caesar's Brother' Violet flowers; straplike leaves; black-brown seed pods. Plate 132.	perennial	3–9	average	sun/pt shade	average
Iris sibirica 'Dianne's Daughter' Blue flowers; straplike leaves.	perennial	3–9	average	sun/pt shade	average
Iris sibirica 'Orville Fay' Blue flower with darker veins; straplike leaves.	perennial	3–9	average	sun/pt shade	average
Iris sibirica 'Pirate Prince' Deep purple-blue flowers; straplike leaves.	perennial	3–9	average	sun/pt shade	average

	TYPE	ZONE	SOIL MOISTURE	LIGHT	SOIL pH
Iris sibirica 'Skywings' Light blue flowers; straplike leaves.	perennial	3–9	average	sun/pt shade	average
Iris sibirica 'Vi Luihn' Cobalt-blue flowers; straplike leaves.	perennial	3–9	average	sun/pt shade	average
Iris sibirica 'White Swirl' White flowers; straplike leaves.	perennial	3–9	average	sun/pt shade	average
Itea virginica Fragrant white flowers; green foliage turns red in autumn.	shrub	5–9	wet	sun/pt shade	acid
Itea virginica 'Henry's Garnet' Large fragrant white flowers; green foliage turns reddish purple in autumn.	shrub	5–9	wet	sun/pt shade	acid
Knautia macedonica Purple-red pincushion flowers held on wiry stems.	perennial	5–8	dry	full sun	average
Kniphofia 'Alcazar' Light orange flower spikes deepen to orange-red at the tips; grasslike foliage. Plate 191.	perennial	5–9	average	full sun	average
Kniphofia 'Little Maid' Pale creamy yellow flower spikes; grasslike foliage.	perennial	5–9	average	full sun	average
Kniphofia 'Primrose Beauty' Deep yellow flower spikes; grasslike foliage. Plates 35, 157.	perennial	5–9	average	full sun	average
Kniphofia 'Prince Igor' Orange-red flower spikes; grasslike foliage. Plate 102.	perennial	6–9	average	full sun	average
Kniphofia 'Royal Standard' Scarlet buds opening to bright yellow flower spikes; grasslike foliage.	perennial	5–9	average	full sun	average
Kniphofia 'Shining Sceptre' Peachy yellow flower spikes; grasslike foliage.	perennial	5–9	average	full sun	average
Kniphofia caulescens Buds are coral-pink to flame-red and open to pale greenish yellow to cream; foliage is blue-green and resembles an aloe. Plate 69.	perennial	(5)6–9	average	full sun	average
Kniphofia citrina Lemon-yellow flower spikes; grasslike foliage.	perennial	6–9	average	full sun	average
Kniphofia triangularis Reddish orange flower spikes; grasslike foliage. Plate 23.	perennial	4–9	average	full sun	average
Lablab purpureus Trifoliate purple-tinged green leaves; dark purple stems and seed pods; purple flowers.	annual vine		average	full sun	average
Lactuca 'Merlot' Glossy purple-red ruffled leaves. Plate 195.	annual		average	full sun	average

	TYPE	ZONE	SOIL MOISTURE	LIGHT	SOIL pH
Lamium maculatum 'White Nancy' White flowers; silver leaves with green margins; groundcover.	perennial	3–8	dry	shade/pt shade	average
Lathyrus latifolius Purplish pink flowers; vining blue-green foliage.	perennial	5–9	average	full sun	average
Lathyrus odoratus Climber with fragrant purple and wine-red flowers.	annual vine		average	full sun	average
Lathyrus odoratus 'Henry Eckford' Climber with fragrant orange flowers; green seed pods, typical of pea family. Plate 61.	annual vine		average	full sun	average
Lathyrus odoratus 'King Size Navy Blue' Climber with large fragrant dark purplish blue flowers; green seed pods, typical of pea family.	annual vine		average	full sun	average
Lavandula angustifolia 'Munstead' Lavender-blue flower spikes; narrow fragrant gray-green leaves.	perennial	5–8	dry	full sun	alkaline
Lavandula ×intermedia 'Grosso' Large dark violet flower spikes; narrow fragrant gray-green leaves.	perennial	(5)6–9	dry	full sun	alkaline
Leonotis menthifolia Whorls of orange tubular flowers at intervals along stem.	annual	10–11	average	full sun	average
Lespedeza cuneata Trifoliate leaves; arching branches; white flowers. Plate 5.	shrub	5–8	dry	full sun	average
Liatris spicata 'Kobold' Spikes of purple flowers; linear leaves.	perennial	3–9	dry	full sun	average
Ligularia 'The Rocket' Large toothed leaves; tall black stems form spikes of yellow flowers. Plate 72.	perennial	4–8	wet	shade/pt shade	average
Ligularia dentata 'Dark Beauty' Yellow-orange daisylike flowerheads; large rounded purplish green leaves. Plate 122.	perennial	4–8	wet	shade/pt shade	average
Ligularia dentata 'Desdemona' Yellow-orange daisylike flowerheads; large rounded leathery leaves with purple undersides; purple stems. Combination 14.	perennial	4–8	wet	shade/pt shade	average
Ligularia wilsoniana Yellow-orange daisylike flowerheads; large dark green serrated leaves.	perennial	5–8	wet	shade/pt shade	average
Lilium 'Apricot Brandy' Apricot flowers; foliage dies down in summer. Plate 29.	perennial	4–9	average	sun/pt shade	average
Lilium 'Casa Blanca' Fragrant white flowers.	perennial	4–8	average	full sun	average

	TYPE	ZONE	SOIL MOISTURE	LIGHT	SOIL pH
Lilium 'Connecticut King' Bright yellow flowers; foliage dies down in summer.	perennial	4–9	average	sun/pt shade	average
Lilium 'Conquistador' Red-orange flowers; foliage dies down in summer.	perennial	4–9	average	sun/pt shade	average
Lilium 'Eden's Dandy' Peach-pink flowers; foliage dies down in summer.	perennial	4–9	average	sun/pt shade	average
Lilium 'Grand Cru' Buff-yellow flowers with red-brown hearts; foliage dies down in summer.	perennial	4–9	average	sun/pt shade	average
Lilium 'Montenegro' Deep red flowers; foliage dies down in summer.	perennial	4–9	average	sun/pt shade	average
Lilium 'Pretender' Orange flowers; foliage dies down in summer.	perennial	4–9	average	sun/pt shade	average
Lilium 'Royal Justice' Yellow flowers; foliage dies down in summer.	perennial	4–9	average	sun/pt shade	average
Lilium 'Royal Perfume' Orange flowers; foliage dies down in summer.	perennial	4–9	average	sun/pt shade	average
Lilium 'Scarlet Emperor' Red flowers; foliage dies down in summer.	perennial	4–9	average	sun/pt shade	average
Lilium 'Shirley' Pinkish peach flowers; foliage dies down in summer.	perennial	4–9	average	sun/pt shade	average
Lilium 'Sunset' Salmon-orange flowers; foliage dies down in summer.	perennial	4–9	average	sun/pt shade	average
Lilium henryi Brown-speckled tangerine-orange flowers with recurved petals. Plate 99.	perennial	3–9	average	full sun	average
Lilium lancifolium var. splendens Large brown-speckled orange flowers with recurved petals. Plates 90, 95, 105.	perennial	3–9	average	full sun	average
Lilium pumilum Small reddish orange flowers with recurved petals.	perennial	3–9	average	full sun	average
Limonium platyphyllum 'Violetta' Clouds of tiny violet-blue flowers above narrow leathery basal leaves.	perennial	3–9	dry	full sun	average
Linaria 'Natalie' Lavender snapdragonlike flowers; narrow blue-green leaves.	perennial	5–9	dry	sun/pt shade	average
Linaria purpurea Purple snapdragonlike flowers; narrow blue-green leaves.	perennial	5–9	dry	sun/pt shade	average
Linum perenne 'Blau Saphir' (blue sapphire) Sky-blue flowers; small narrow leaves.	perennial	5–8	dry	full sun	average

	TYPE	ZONE	SOIL MOISTURE	LIGHT	SOIL pH
Lobelia 'Dark Crusader' Red flower spikes; narrow dark maroon foliage.	perennial	4–8	wet	sun/pt shade	average
Lobelia 'Grape Knee High' Purple flower spikes; narrow foliage.	perennial	4–9	wet	sun/pt shade	average
Lobelia 'Purple Towers' Purple flower spikes; narrow foliage.	perennial	2–8	wet	sun/pt shade	average
Lobelia 'Queen Victoria' Red flower spikes; narrow dark maroon foliage.	perennial	4–9	wet	sun/pt shade	average
Lobelia 'Royal Robe' Red flower spikes; narrow red foliage. Plates 122, 124.	perennial	2–9	wet	sun/pt shade	average
Lobelia 'Ruby Slippers' Violet-red flower spikes; narrow foliage.	perennial	3–9	wet	sun/pt shade	average
Lobelia siphilitica True-blue flower spikes; narrow foliage.	perennial	5–9	wet	sun/pt shade	average
Lonicera periclymenum 'Graham Thomas' Extremely fragrant light yellow flowers; red fruit; rebloom throughout the summer. Plate 106.	woody vine	4–8	dry	sun/pt shade	average
Lonicera sempervirens 'Blanche Sandman' Bright reddish orange flowers; rebloom throughout the summer.	woody vine	(3)4–9	dry	sun/pt shade	average
Luzula nivea Light tan-white flowers; tufted evergreen grasslike foliage. Plate 120.	perennial	4–9	average	shade/pt shade	average
Lychnis ×arkwrightii 'Vesuvius' Orange flowers; dark bronze foliage.	perennial	5–8	average	full sun	average
Lychnis cognata Melon flowers with frilled edges.	perennial	5–9	average	sun/pt shade	average
Lychnis coronaria Vivid magenta flowers; fuzzy gray stems and leaves. Combination 21.	perennial	4–8	dry	full sun	average
Lysimachia congestiflora 'Variegata' Mat-forming yellow and green variegated leaves; golden yellow flowers.	annual	(6)7–9	wet	full sun	average
Lysimachia nummularia 'Aurea' Inconspicuous yellow flowers; mat-forming yellow foliage. Plates 112, 156, 197.	perennial	3–8	average	sun/pt shade	average
Magnolia virginiana Large white fragrant flowers; dark red seed capsule; leaves have silver undersides. Plate 125.	tree	5–9	wet	sun/pt shade	acid
Malus 'Lanzam' (Lancelot®) Red buds open to white flowers; green leaves turn yellow in autumn; gold fruit persistent into new year.	tree	4–7	average	full sun	average

	TYPE	ZONE	SOIL MOISTURE	LIGHT	SOIL pH
Mazus reptans Tiny purple flowers; mat-forming light green foliage. Plates 130, 133.	perennial	5–8	average	sun/pt shade	average
Melampodium paludosum 'Million Gold' Golden yellow daisylike flowers. Plate 181.	annual		average	full sun	average
Mertensia pulmonarioides (virginica) Clusters of nodding blue flowers; bluish green leaves. Combination 4.	perennial	3–9	average	sun/pt shade	average
Microbiota decussata Branchlets formed from medium green flattened sprays; turns bronze in autumn and winter.	shrub	3–8	average	shade/pt shade	average
Miscanthus 'Purpurascens' Gray-green leaves turn red-purple in autumn; silvery tan flowers. Plates 5, 73, 145, 147.	perennial	4–9	average	full sun	average
Miscanthus sinensis 'Gracillimus' Narrow green leaves; blooms emerge coppery red then fade to tan; golden yellow autumn color.	perennial	5–9	average	full sun	average
Miscanthus sinensis 'Malepartus' Wider green leaves; silvery tan flowers fade to golden tan; golden yellow autumn color infused with reds and oranges.	perennial	5–9	average	full sun	average
Miscanthus sinensis 'Morning Light' Green leaves with white margins; reddish tan flowers. Plate 124.	perennial	5–9	average	full sun	average
Miscanthus sinensis var. condensatus 'Cosmopolitan' Wide green and white variegated leaves; blooms emerge coppery red then fade to tan. Plate 2; Combination 7.	perennial	(5)6–9	average	full sun	average
Molinia caerulea ssp. arundinacea 'Skyracer' Green foliage turns yellow in autumn; golden tan inflorescences on tall wiry stems. Plate 4.	perennial	4–9	average	full sun	average
Monarda 'Jacob Cline' Red flowers.	perennial	4–9	dry	full sun	average
Monarda 'Violet Queen' Violet flowers.	perennial	4–9	dry	full sun	average
Musa basjoo Huge oblong bright green leaves. Plate 6.	tropical	(5–6)7–11	average	full sun	average
Musa zebrina Huge leaves streaked dark red and green with red undersides.	tropical	10–11	average	sun/pt shade	average
Narcissus 'Delnashaugh' White petals with apricot-pink centers; roselike blooms.	hardy bulb	3–8	average	sun/pt shade	average
Narcissus 'Fragrant Rose' White and pink rose-scented flowers with large cups.	hardy bulb	3–8	average	sun/pt shade	average

	TYPE	ZONE	SOIL MOISTURE	LIGHT	SOIL pH
Narcissus 'Mary Gay Lirette' Cup is split and ruffled, opens yellow then fades to salmon; white petals.	hardy bulb	3–8	average	sun/pt shade	average
Narcissus 'Mint Julep' Small cupped pale yellow flowers with green eyes.	hardy bulb	3–8	average	sun/pt shade	average
Narcissus 'Petrel' Nodding white flowers, several to a stem.	hardy bulb	3–8	average	sun/pt shade	average
Narcissus 'Sir Winston Churchill' Fragrant double white blooms with orange flecks. Combination 1.	hardy bulb	3–8	average	sun/pt shade	average
Narcissus 'Stratosphere' Golden yellow fragrant flowers, several to a stem.	hardy bulb	4–9	average	sun/pt shade	average
Narcissus 'Tahiti' Double yellow flowers with orange centers.	hardy bulb	3–8	average	sun/pt shade	average
Nepeta 'Six Hills Giant' Lavender-blue flowers; gray-green leaves. Combination 20.	perennial	3–8	dry	full sun	average
Nepeta ×faassenii Small blue-lavender flowers; gray-green leaves.	perennial	3–8	dry	full sun	average
Nepeta grandiflora 'Bramdean' Lavender-blue flowers; gray-green leaves.	perennial	3–8	dry	full sun	average
Nepeta racemosa 'Walker's Low' Lavender-blue flowers; gray-green leaves. Plate 165.	perennial	3–8	dry	full sun	average
Nepeta sibirica 'Souvenir d'André Chaudron' Blue-violet flowers; gray-green leaves. Combination 16.	perennial	3–8	dry	full sun	average
Nicotiana langsdorffii Small nodding apple-green bell-shaped flowers; large green leaves.	annual		dry	full sun	average
Nierembergia scoparia 'Mont Blanc' Yellow-centered white flowers; narrow leaves.	annual	7–10	average	full sun	average
Nigella damascena Miss Jekyll Series White, blue, or pink flowers; feathery green foliage; decorative seed pod. Combination 18.	annual		average	full sun	average
Nymphaea 'Marliacea Chromatella' Soft yellow flowers; sometimes purple-speckled leaves. Plate 71.	perennial	4–11	wet	full sun	average
Ocimum 'African Blue' Green foliage strongly tinted purple. Plate 3; Combination 13.	annual	9–10	average	full sun	average
Ocimum basilicum 'Red Rubin' Red-purple foliage.	annual	9–10	average	full sun	average
Oenothera fremontii 'Lemon Silver' Large lemon-yellow flowers; elongated silver foliage.	perennial	5–9	dry	full sun	average

	TYPE	ZONE	SOIL MOISTURE	LIGHT	SOIL pH
Oenothera fruticosa ssp. glauca 'Sonnenwende' Lemon-yellow flowers; red buds; narrow green leaves turn red in autumn.	perennial	3–8	dry	full sun	average
Origanum 'Kent Beauty' unique rose-pink flower bracts; rounded gray-green leaves.	perennial	5–8	dry	full sun	average
Origanum laevigatum 'Herrenhausen' Pinkish purple flowers; green foliage turns purple-bronze in autumn.	perennial	5–9	dry	full sun	average
Origanum vulgare 'Aureum' Yellow foliage. Plate 178.	perennial	5–9	dry	full sun	average
Osmunda cinnamomea Cinnamon-colored fertile fronds; green pinnately compound leaves.	perennial	3–8	average	shade/pt shade	average
Osmunda regalis Large green fronds; golden brown clusters of sporangia at tips of fertile fronds. Combination 3.	perennial	3–10	average	shade/pt shade	acid
Pachysandra procumbens Whorls of coarsely toothed leaves; small white fragrant flowers; slow-growing groundcover. Plate 47.	perennial	6–9	average	shade/pt shade	average
Packera aurea (Senecio aureus) Golden yellow flowers; shiny green foliage.	perennial	4–8	wet	sun/pt shade	average
Paeonia 'America' Large single red flowers; golden stamen centers; coarse lobed dark green leaves.	perennial	3–8	average	full sun	alkaline
Paeonia 'Burma Ruby' Single scarlet-red flowers; golden stamen centers; coarse lobed dark green leaves. Plate 56.	perennial	3–8	average	full sun	alkaline
Paeonia 'Coral Sunset' Semi-double coral flowers; golden stamen centers; coarse lobed dark green leaves.	perennial	3–8	average	full sun	alkaline
Paeonia 'Etched Salmon' Double salmon-coral flowers; coarse lobed dark green leaves.	perennial	3–8	average	full sun	alkaline
Paeonia 'Monsieur Jules Elie' Double dark pink flowers; coarse lobed dark green leaves. Combination 5.	perennial	3–8	average	full sun	alkaline
Paeonia 'Prairie Moon' Semi-double pale cream-yellow flowers; golden stamen centers; coarse lobed dark green leaves.	perennial	3–8	average	full sun	alkaline
Paeonia obovata Single rosy pink flowers; seed capsule opens to a bright red interior holding metallic dark blue seeds. Plate 16.	perennial	4–8	average	shade/pt shade	average

	TYPE	ZONE	SOIL MOISTURE	LIGHT	SOIL pH
Panicum virgatum 'Dallas Blues' Wide blue leaves; large red-tinged airy panicles; strong vertical habit. Plates 32, 161; Combination 19.	perennial	5–9	dry	full sun	average
Panicum virgatum 'Heavy Metal' Metallic blue leaves turn yellow in autumn; airy panicles tinted pink; stiff upright clump. Plates 160, 164.	perennial	4–9	dry	full sun	average
Panicum virgatum 'Rehbraun' Narrow green foliage turns reddish yellow in autumn; feathery tan panicles. Plate 5.	perennial	5–9	dry	full sun	average
Papaver nudicaule 'Red Sails' Red-orange flowers with yellow stamens.	perennial	2–8	average	full sun	average
Papaver orientale 'Curlilocks' Single orange-red flowers with serrated petals; black blotch at base; large coarse leaves.	perennial	3–7	average	full sun	average
Papaver orientale 'Derwisch' Single salmon-red flowers; small black blotch at base; large coarse leaves.	perennial	3–7	average	full sun	average
Papaver orientale 'Feuerriese' Single brick-red flowers; large coarse leaves. Combination 9.	perennial	3–7	average	full sun	average
Papaver orientale 'Harvest Moon' Ruffled semi-double golden orange flowers; large coarse leaves.	perennial	3–7	average	full sun	average
Papaver orientale 'Lighthouse' Single salmon-pink flowers with red blotch at base; large coarse leaves.	perennial	3–7	average	full sun	average
Papaver orientale 'Patty's Plum' Single plum-purple flowers; black blotch at base; large coarse leaves. Plate 173.	perennial	3–7	average	full sun	average
Papaver orientale 'Prince of Orange' Single bright orange flowers; large coarse leaves.	perennial	3–7	average	full sun	average
Papaver orientale 'Saffron' Single light orange flower fading to near white at edges; large coarse leaves.	perennial	3–7	average	full sun	average
Papaver orientale 'Turkenlouis' Single orange-scarlet fringed flowers; black blotch at base; large coarse leaves. Plate 148.	perennial	3–7	average	full sun	average
Papaver rhoeas Brilliant red papery blooms. Plates 91, 99, 141; Combination 21.	annual		average	full sun	average
Papaver rhoeas Angels' Choir A mix of double pink papery blooms and other pastel shades. Combination 21.	annual		full sun	average	

	TYPE	ZONE	SOIL MOISTURE	LIGHT	SOIL pH
Papaver somniferum Mauve-purple or red flowers; toothed blue-green leaves; ornamental seed pods. Plate 24.	annual		average	full sun	average
Papaver somniferum 'Black Peony' Peonylike deep purple-maroon, almost black flowers.	annual		average	full sun	average
Papaver somniferum 'Burnt Orange' Dark orange-red deeply fringed petals.	annual		average	full sun	average
Papaver somniferum 'Lauren's Grape' Mauve-purple flowers.	annual		average	full sun	average
Papaver somniferum 'Pepperbox' Bright red and dark purple papery blooms; toothed blue-green leaves; ornamental seed pods.	annual		average	full sun	average
Passiflora incarnata Deeply lobed and finely toothed leaves; pale purple flowers; yellow fruit; reblooms throughout the summer.	perennial	5–8	average	sun/pt shade	average
Patrinia scabiosifolia Clusters of tiny yellow flowers on tall stems; pinnately divided leaves.	perennial	4–9	average	full sun	average
Pennisetum alopecuroides 'Hameln' Narrow green leaves; tan flowers.	perennial	5–9	dry	full sun	average
Pennisetum setaceum 'Rubrum' Rich burgundy leaves; foxtail-like flowers. Plates 78, 84.	annual	9–10	dry	full sun	average
Penstemon digitalis 'Husker Red' Tubular white flowers; long narrow red-purple leaves.	perennial	2–8	dry	full sun	average
Penstemon ×mexicale 'Pike's Peak Purple' Spikes of tubular bell-shaped purple flowers.	perennial	4–9	dry	full sun	average
Perilla frutescens var. crispa Dark purple ruffled foliage. Plate 44.	annual		average	full sun	average
Perovskia atriplicifolia Spikes of lavender-blue flowers; fine gray leaves. Plates 37, 167.	perennial	5–9	dry	full sun	average
Perovskia atriplicifolia 'Longin' Spikes of lavender-blue flowers; fine gray leaves.	perennial	5–9	dry	full sun	average
Persicaria microcephala 'Red Dragon' Small white flowers; red-purple, silver, and green leaves.	perennial	5–9	average	full sun	average
Phlomis russeliana Hooded pale yellow flowers on tall stems; large softly hairy basal leaves.	perennial	4–9	average	sun/pt shade	average
Phlox divaricata Light blue, white, or lavender flowers; small green leaves. Combination 1.	perennial	4–9	average	shade/pt shade	acid

	TYPE	ZONE	SOIL MOISTURE	LIGHT	SOIL pH
Phlox divaricata 'Dirigo Ice' Pale blue flowers; small green leaves.	perennial	4–9	average	shade/pt shade	acid
Phlox divaricata 'Eco Texas Purple' Purple flowers; small green leaves.	perennial	4–9	average	shade/pt shade	acid
Phlox divaricata ssp. laphamii Blue-lavender flowers; small green leaves.	perennial	4–9	average	shade/pt shade	acid
Phlox divaricata 'London Grove Blue' Small blue flowers; small green leaves.	perennial	4–9	average	shade/pt shade	acid
Phlox divaricata 'Sweet Lilac' Lilac flowers; small green leaves.	perennial	4–9	average	shade/pt shade	acid
Phlox paniculata 'David' Large white flower clusters.	perennial	4–8	average	full sun	acid
Phlox paniculata 'Fesselballon' Large pink dark-eyed flower clusters. Plate 4.	perennial	4–8	average	full sun	acid
Phlox paniculata 'Katherine' Large blue-lavender white-eyed flower clusters.	perennial	4–8	average	full sun	acid
Phlox paniculata 'Laura' Large purple white-eyed flower clusters. Plate 73.	perennial	4–8	average	full sun	acid
Phlox paniculata 'Look Again' Large magenta flower clusters. Plates 4–5; Combination 12.	perennial	4–8	average	full sun	acid
Phlox paniculata 'Orange Perfection' Large salmon-orange flower clusters.	perennial	4–8	average	full sun	acid
Phlox paniculata 'Pax' (peace) Large white flower clusters.	perennial	4–8	average	full sun	acid
Phlox paniculata 'Tenor' Large rosy red flower clusters.	perennial	4–8	average	full sun	acid
Phlox paniculata 'The King' Large lavender-purple flower clusters.	perennial	4–8	average	full sun	acid
Phlox paniculata 'Tracy's Treasure' Large baby-pink flower clusters. Plate 26.	perennial	4–8	average	full sun	acid
Phlox stolonifera 'Blue Ridge' Blue flowers; small oval leaves.	perennial	4–9	average	shade/pt shade	acid
Phlox stolonifera 'Bruce's White' White flowers; small oval leaves.	perennial	4–9	average	shade/pt shade	acid
Phormium 'Bronze Baby' Bronze straplike leaves. Plate 143.	tropical	8–10	dry	full sun	average
Phormium 'Platt's Black' Dark burgundy-black straplike leaves.	tropical	8–10	dry	full sun	average
Phormium 'Yellow Wave' Yellow and green variegated straplike leaves. Plate 6.	tropical	8–10	dry	full sun	average

	TYPE	ZONE	SOIL MOISTURE	LIGHT	SOIL pH
Phormium cookianum 'Chocolate' Bronze-chocolate straplike leaves. Plates 107, 112.	tropical	8–10	dry	full sun	average
Phyllostachys nigra Lance-shaped dark green leaves; hollow jointed black stems. Plate 54.	annual	7–10	average	sun/pt shade	average
Phytolacca polyandra Pinkish purple flowers; red stalks and stems; green leaves; black inedible berries.	perennial	6–9	average	sun/pt shade	average
Picea abies 'Mucronata' Deep green glossy needles; strong pyramidal growth. Plate 181.	shrub	4	average	full sun	average
Picea abies 'Pendula' Dark green needles; weeping form; if left untrained will grow 5 ft. tall, 20 ft. wide. Combination 11.	tree	3–7	average	full sun	acid
Picea alcoquiana 'Howell's Tigertail' Blue-green short needles; wide, layered somewhat flat-topped appearance to habit. Plate 165.	shrub	5	average	full sun	acid
Picea orientalis 'Skylands' Horizontal branching; golden yellow needles. Plates 35, 183.	tree	4–7	average	sun/pt shade	acid
Picea pungens 'Iseli Foxtail' Stiff 1-in. blue-gray needles. Plates 38, 174–175.	tree	3–7(8)	average	full sun	acid
Picea pungens 'Thomsen' Symmetrical, pyramidal habit; intense silver-blue needles. Plates 25–27.	tree	3–7	average	full sun	acid
Pinus cembra 'Silver Sheen' Silvery blue-green needles.	tree	4–7	average	full sun	acid
Pinus contorta 'Chief Joseph' Slow-growing small conifer; green needles turn bright yellow in autumn. Combination 26.	shrub	5	dry	sun/pt shade	acid
Pinus contorta 'Spaan's Dwarf' Green needles; irregular open pyramidal form. Combination 23.	shrub	5	dry	sun/pt shade	acid
Pinus densiflora 'Oculus Draconis' Yellow-banded green needles; reddish brown flaky bark. Plate 104.	shrub	3–7	average	full sun	acid
Pinus flexilis 'Vanderwolf's Pyramid' Bluish green needles; irregular broad pyramidal form. Plate 13; Combinations 8–9.	tree	4–7	average	sun/pt shade	acid
Pinus parviflora 'Glauca' Silvery blue-green needles; irregular form. Plate 6; Combination 19.	tree	4–7	average	full sun	acid
Pinus parviflora 'Yatsubusa' Short, slightly bluish green needles; ascending branches; irregular form. Plate 4.	shrub	4–7	average	full sun	acid

	TYPE	ZONE	SOIL MOISTURE	LIGHT	SOIL pH
Pinus pumila 'Nana' Globose habit; gray-green needles. Plate 45.	shrub	4–7	average	full sun	acid
Pinus strobus Long gray-green needles; conical in youth becoming irregular with age. Plates 14, 196.	tree	4–9	average	full sun	acid
Pinus strobus 'Nana' Long gray-green needles; mounded form.	shrub	3–7	average	full sun	acid
Pinus sylvestris Conical in youth becoming domed or flat-topped with age; flaky red-brown bark; bluish green needles.	tree	3–7	average	full sun	acid
Pinus sylvestris 'Albyn' Prostrate bluish gray-green foliage; bottlebrush-shaped branches.	shrub	3–7	average	full sun	acid
Pinus sylvestris 'Fastigiata' Columnar; very narrow habit; blue-green needles. Plate 10.	tree	3–7	average	full sun	acid
Pistia stratiotes Floating rosettes of bluish green fluted and ribbed leaves. Plate 71.	annual		wet	full sun	average
Plantago major 'Rubrifolia' Basal rosette of spoon-shaped leaves tinted maroon. Plates 139, 170.	perennial	5–9	average	full sun	average
Platycodon grandiflorus 'Double Blue' "Inflated" blue flowers that pop open with maturity; oval green leaves.	perennial	3–8	average	full sun	average
Platycodon grandiflorus 'Komachi' "Inflated" blue flowers that do not open with maturity; oval green leaves. Plate 75.	perennial	3–8	average	full sun	average
Plectranthus amboinicus Small rounded and pubescent fragrant gray-green leaves.	annual	10–11	average	full sun	average
Plectranthus argentatus Bluish white flowers; woolly silvery gray foliage. Plate 171.	annual	10–11	dry	full sun	average
Polemonium caeruleum 'Blanjou' **(brise d'Anjou)** Small blue-violet flowers on spikes; pinnately compound green and white variegated leaves.	perennial	3–7	average	sun/pt shade	average
Polygonatum odoratum 'Variegatum' White bell-shaped flowers; broad leaves variegated green and creamy white turn outstanding yellow in autumn. Plate 119.	perennial	3–9	dry	shade/pt shade	average
Polystichum acrostichoides Dark green fronds.	perennial	3–9	wet	shade/pt shade	average
Portulaca grandiflora 'Sundial Peach' Peach flowers; green succulent leaves.	annual		average	full sun	average

	TYPE	ZONE	SOIL MOISTURE	LIGHT	SOIL pH
Potentilla fruticosa 'Sunset' Green pinnate leaves; pale yellowy orange flowers.	shrub	2–6	dry	full sun	average
Pseudotsuga menziesii 'Astro Blue' Bluish green needles; open broadly conical form. Plates 98, 107.	tree	4–6	average	full sun	average
Pulmonaria 'Majesté' Wide silver leaves; pink and blue flowers. Plate 130.	perennial	3–8	average	shade/pt shade	average
Pulmonaria 'Viette's Deep Blue Sea' Silver-spotted leaves; royal-blue flowers.	perennial	3–8	average	shade/pt shade	average
Puschkinia scilloides Small straplike leaves; clusters of star-shaped blue-striped, bluish white flowers.	hardy bulb	4–8	average	sun/pt shade	average
Quercus palustris Deeply lobed glossy green leaves; russet to bronze autumn color.	tree	4–8	wet	full sun	acid
Quercus robur 'Pectinata' Leaves deeply cut into narrow feathery lobes. Plate 6.	tree	5–8	dry	full sun	average
Rheum palmatum var. tanguticum Large toothed green leaves tinted purple; massive rose-red flower panicles.	perennial	5–9	wet	sun/pt shade	average
Rhodochiton atrosanguineus Mauve and dark purple bell-shaped flowers; toothed heart-shaped leaves emerge purple then fade to green. Combination 6.	annual vine		average	full sun	average
Rhododendron 'Chionoides' White flowers with yellow centers; broad dense form; narrow leaves.	shrub	4–8	average	shade/pt shade	acid
Rhododendron 'Mist Maiden' Underside of leaves covered with silvery white in dumentum; dark pink buds open to white flowers. Plate 127.	shrub	4	average	shade/pt shade	acid
Rhododendron 'Northern Starburst' Large purplish pink blossoms. Plate 121.	shrub	4	average	shade/pt shade	acid
Ricinus communis Large maple-shaped leaves; rose-red seed pods, stalks, and veins. Plate 75; Combination 7.	tropical	(9)10–11	average	full sun	average
Ricinus communis 'Carmencita' Large maple-shaped purple-red leaves; rose-red seed pods. Plates 140, 147.	tropical	(9)10–11	average	full sun	average
Rodgersia aesculifolia Large clusters of white flowers; horsechestnut- like leaves. Combination 24.	perennial	5–7	wet	shade/pt shade	average
Rodgersia pinnata Large clusters of rose-pink flowers; pinnately compound leaves.	perennial	5–7	wet	shade/pt shade	average

	TYPE	ZONE	SOIL MOISTURE	LIGHT	SOIL pH
Rosa 'Alchymist' Climbing shrub rose; once blooming; very fragrant; double golden peach flowers.	shrub	4–9	average	full sun	average
Rosa 'Ausbuff' (English Garden®) Modern shrub; repeat blooming; rosette-shaped double yellow-peach flowers; tea-rose fragrance.	shrub	5–9	average	full sun	average
Rosa 'Ausmas' (Graham Thomas®) Modern shrub rose; repeat blooming; yellow cupped double flowers; tea-rose fragrance; disease resistant foliage; may be trained as a 12-ft. climber.	shrub	5–9	average	full sun	average
Rosa 'Aussaucer' (Evelyn®) Large many-petaled apricot-yellow rosettes; repeat blooming; fragrant; may be trained as a 6-ft. climber. Plate 153.	shrub	5–10	average	full sun	average
Rosa 'Ausvelvet' (The Prince®) Rich royal-purple cup-shaped rosettes; old-rose fragrance.	shrub	5–9	average	full sun	average
Rosa 'Champlain' Shrub rose; repeat blooming; cherry-red double flowers.	shrub	4–9	average	full sun	average
Rosa 'F. J. Grootendorst' Rugosa rose; small red carnationlike blossoms produced in clusters of 20 per stem. Plate 78.	shrub	2–9	average	full sun	average
Rosa 'Hansa' Fragrant semi-double dark pink-purple; glossy green foliage; large orange-red hips.	shrub	2–7	average	full sun	average
Rosa Lyda Rose™ Single white flowers edged in pink-lavender.	shrub	5–10	average	full sun	average
Rosa 'Meidomonac' (Bonica®) Ever-blooming fully double pink flowers; bright orange-red hips.	shrub	4–9	average	full sun	average
Rosa 'Nearly Wild' Ever-blooming single pink flowers. Combination 20.	shrub	4–9	average	full sun	average
Rosa 'Nuits de Young' Moss rose; fragrant and once blooming; dark velvety purple-maroon blossoms.	shrub	4–9	average	full sun	average
Rosa 'Scrivluv' (Baby Love®) Sweetly fragrant; single buttercup-yellow blossoms.	shrub	5	average	full sun	average
Rosa 'Seafoam' Slightly fragrant and recurrent; small white double flowers. Combination 22.	shrub	4–9	average	full sun	average
Rosa 'The Fairy' Clusters of small light pink flowers.	shrub	5–9	average	full sun	average
Rosa multiflora 'Grevillei' (seven sisters' rose) Large clusters of small dark pink double flowers. Combination 27.	shrub	4–9	average	full sun	average

	TYPE	ZONE	SOIL MOISTURE	LIGHT	SOIL pH
Rosa rugosa Leathery dark green leaves; very thorny stems; single fragrant dark pink flowers; large orange-red hips. Plate 74.	shrub	2–9	dry	full sun	average
Rosa ×harisonii 'Harison's Yellow' Semi-double bright yellow flowers; blackish red hips.	shrub	3–9	average	full sun	average
Rudbeckia fulgida var. speciosa Small golden daisylike flowers with black centers; toothed leaves. Plate 5; Combination 12.	perennial	3–9	dry	full sun	average
Rudbeckia hirta 'Irish Eyes' Yellow daisylike flowers with green centers. Plate 23.	annual	3–7	dry	full sun	average
Rudbeckia maxima Yellow flowers; prominent brown cones; large blue-green leaves. Plates 13, 183–184; Combination 8.	perennial	4–9	dry	full sun	average
Rudbeckia triloba Small golden daisylike flowers with brown-black centers on tall branched stems. Plate 3.	perennial	4–7	dry	full sun	average
Rumex sanguineus Large red-tinted green leaves with dark red veins. Plates 141, 143.	perennial	5–8	average	full sun	average
Ruta graveolens 'Blue Beauty' Blue-green aromatic foliage; small yellow flowers.	perennial	4–9	dry	full sun	average
Salvia 'Indigo Spires' Long blue-purple flower spikes. Plate 164.	annual	7–10	dry	full sun	average
Salvia 'Purple Majesty' Deep purple flowers borne on long spikes.	annual	8–10	dry	full sun	average
Salvia argentea Large basal rosettes of silver woolly leaves. Plate 46.	perennial	5–8	dry	full sun	average
Salvia azurea var. pitcheri Large sky-blue flowers.	perennial	4–9	dry	full sun	average
Salvia coccinea 'Lady in Red' Cherry-red flower spikes.	annual		dry	full sun	average
Salvia guaranitica Royal-blue flowers.	annual	7–10	dry	full sun	average
Salvia guaranitica 'Black and Blue' Blue flowers in smoky black bracts.	annual	7–10	dry	full sun	average
Salvia leucantha Downy white stems; fuzzy purple flower spikes; narrow lance-shaped leaves. Plate 167.	annual		dry	full sun	average
Salvia nemorosa 'Ostfriesland' (East Friesland) Dark violet-blue flowers; oblong green leaves.	perennial	3–8	dry	full sun	average
Salvia nemorosa 'Purple Glory' Violet flowers; oblong green leaves. Combination 16.	perennial	3–8	dry	full sun	average

	TYPE	ZONE	SOIL MOISTURE	LIGHT	SOIL pH
Salvia nemorosa 'Pusztaflamme' (plumosa) Light purple flowers; oblong green leaves.	perennial	3–8	dry	full sun	average
Salvia officinalis 'Tricolor' Gray-green aromatic leaves with cream and pink-purple variegation.	annual	7–8	dry	full sun	average
Salvia patens Deep blue flowers.	annual	8–9	dry	sun/pt shade	average
Salvia ×sylvestris 'Blauhügel' (blue hill) Blue flowers; oblong green leaves. Plate 159.	perennial	3–8	dry	full sun	average
Salvia ×sylvestris 'Blaukönigin' (blue queen) Blue-violet flowers; oblong green leaves.	perennial	3–8	dry	full sun	average
Salvia ×sylvestris 'Mainacht' (May night) Purple-blue flowers; oblong green leaves.	perennial	3–8	dry	full sun	average
Salvia ×sylvestris 'Viola Klose' Dark blue flowers; oblong green leaves.	perennial	3–8	dry	full sun	average
Salvia verticillata 'Purple Rain' Long racemes of purple flowers; gray-green pubescent foliage. Plate 48.	perennial	5–8	dry	full sun	average
Sambucus racemosa 'Sutherland Gold' Golden yellow finely divided foliage. Plates 157–158.	shrub	4–6(7)	average	sun/pt shade	average
Sanguisorba tenuifolia 'Purpurea' Short terminal dark reddish purple catkinlike flowers; toothed compound foliage.	perennial	4–8	average	sun/pt shade	average
Saruma henryi Fuzzy heart-shaped leaves; soft yellow flowers. Plate 199.	perennial	5–8	average	shade/pt shade	average
Scabiosa Butterfly Blue® Light blue pincushion flowers; green leaves. Combination 16.	perennial	3–7	average	full sun	average
Scabiosa 'Pink Mist' Pink pincushion flowers; green leaves.	perennial	3–7	average	full sun	average
Scabiosa atropurpurea 'Ace of Spades' Velvety blood-red pincushion flowers.	annual		average	full sun	average
Scabiosa columbaria var. ochroleuca Small cream-yellow pincushion flowers on tall wiry stems. Combination 27.	perennial	3–7	average	full sun	average
Scadoxus multiflorus Softball-sized red-orange flowerheads; broad green leaves emerge after flowering.	tender bulb	7–10	average	full sun	average
Schizachyrium scoparium 'The Blues' Blue foliage turning copper-red in autumn; flowers inconspicuous; seedheads silvery tan. Plates 175, 178–179.	perennial	3–9	dry	full sun	average

	TYPE	ZONE	SOIL MOISTURE	LIGHT	SOIL pH
Sciadopitys verticillata Long dark glossy green needles; conical form. Combination 24.	tree	5–7	average	sun/pt shade	acid
Sedum 'Herbstfreude' (autumn joy) Rose-red (changing to rust) flowers in flat heads; fleshy green leaves.	perennial	3–10	dry	full sun	average
Sedum 'Pork and Beans' Small bean-shaped succulent green foliage; groundcover.	perennial	4–10	dry	sun/pt shade	average
Sedum acre 'Aureum' Light green foliage with yellow new growth; bright yellow flowers.	perennial	4–10	dry	sun/pt shade	average
Sedum telephium ssp. maximum 'Atropurpureum' Dark red-purple stems and leaves; rose-red flowers.	perennial	4–9	dry	full sun	average
Silene regia Bright red star-shaped flowers.	perennial	5–8	average	shade/pt shade	average
Sisyrinchium 'Quaint and Queer' Small chocolate purple-maroon, yellow-throated flowers; narrow irislike foliage.	perennial	5–8	average	sun/pt shade	average
Sisyrinchium bermudianum Purple-blue, yellow-throated flowers; narrow irislike foliage.	perennial	5–8	average	sun/pt shade	average
Solenostemon 'Burgundy Columns' Dark red-purple foliage; light green stems.	annual	10	average	sun/pt shade	average
Solenostemon 'Burgundy Giant' Dark burgundy-purple leaves. Plate 200.	annual	10	average	sun/pt shade	average
Solenostemon 'Olive' Yellow-green foliage.	annual	10	average	sun/pt shade	average
Solenostemon 'Penny' Parchment-yellow burgundy-infused leaves. Combination 11.	annual	10	average	sun/pt shade	average
Solenostemon 'Purple Emperor' Dark purple-maroon ruffled leaves.	annual	10	average	sun/pt shade	average
Solenostemon 'Saturn' Lime-green wavy leaves edged in maroon-red. Plate 143.	annual	10	average	sun/pt shade	average
Solidago 'Golden Spangles' Yellow-flecked green foliage; golden yellow flowers.	perennial	4–8	dry	full sun	average
Solidago rugosa 'Fireworks' Arching sprays of golden yellow flowers.	perennial	4–8	dry	full sun	average
×Solidaster luteus 'Lemore' Corymbs of small pale lemon-yellow daisylike flowers.	perennial	5–8	average	full sun	average

	TYPE	ZONE	SOIL MOISTURE	LIGHT	SOIL pH
Sorghastrum nutans 'Sioux Blue' Upright to open form; blue foliage turns golden yellow in autumn; tan flower panicles. Plates 13, 138, 176; Combinations 8, 10.	perennial	5–8	dry	full sun	average
Stachys byzantina Woolly, soft gray leaves; unattractive pinkish purple flowers on silvery spike.	perennial	4–8	dry	full sun	average
Stachys byzantina 'Countess Helen von Stein' Large woolly, soft gray leaves. Plate 174.	perennial	4–8	dry	full sun	average
Stachys byzantina 'Primrose Heron' Woolly, soft yellow-gray-green leaves. Plate 177.	perennial	4–8	dry	full sun	average
Stachys macrantha Spikes of pinkish purple flowers; rosettes of scalloped and wrinkled leaves. Plate 34.	perennial	5–7	dry	sun/pt shade	average
Stokesia laevis 'Klaus Jelitto' Sky-blue, fringed daisylike flowers; straplike green leaves. Plate 13; Combination 8.	perennial	5–9	dry	full sun	average
Stokesia laevis 'Mary Gregory' Soft yellow, fringed daisylike flowers; straplike green leaves.	perennial	5–9	dry	full sun	average
Stokesia laevis 'Omega Skyrocket' Pale blue, fringed daisylike flowers; straplike green leaves.	perennial	5–9	dry	full sun	average
Stokesia laevis 'Purple Parasols' Purple, fringed daisylike flowers; straplike green leaves. Plate 170.	perennial	5–9	dry	full sun	average
Stylophorum diphyllum Bright yellow flowers; lobed green leaves with silver undersides.	perennial	4–9	average	shade/pt shade	average
Symphytum 'Goldsmith' Small pink, white, and blue flowers; yellow and green variegated leaves.	perennial	5–9	average	sun/pt shade	average
Syringa meyeri Dense mounded form; purple flowers.	shrub	3–7	average	full sun	average
Tanacetum 'Golden Feathers' Yellow fernlike foliage; small white daisylike flowers. Plate 158.	perennial	4–8	average	sun/pt shade	average
Thalictrum aquilegiifolium 'Thundercloud' Fluffy deep purple flowerheads; blue-green columbinelike leaves.	perennial	5–8	wet	shade/pt shade	average
Thalictrum rochebruneanum Fluffy lavender flowerheads; columbinelike leaves; purple-tinged stems.	perennial	4–7	wet	sun/pt shade	average
Thermopsis villosa Yellow lupinelike flowers; palmately compound leaves; dark brown seed pods.	perennial	3–8	dry	full sun	average

	TYPE	ZONE	SOIL MOISTURE	LIGHT	SOIL pH
Thuja occidentalis 'Techny' Broad-based pyramidal form; flats sprays of dark green foliage.	tree	3–7	average	full sun	average
Thunbergia battiscombei Vine with large yellow-throated, trumpet-shaped purple-blue flowers. Plate 17.	annual vine	10–11	average	full sun	average
Thymus ×citriodorus Pinkish lavender flowers; small green lemon-scented leaves.	perennial	6–9	dry	full sun	average
Thymus ×citriodorus 'Lemon Green' Mat-forming yellow-flecked green foliage.	perennial	5–8	dry	full sun	average
Thymus pseudolanuginosus Lavender flowers; gray-green mats of foliage.	perennial	5–8	dry	full sun	average
Tiarella cordifolia 'Ninja' White, peach-flushed flower spikes; dark purple markings on leaves.	perennial	3–8	average	shade/pt shade	average
Tigridia pavonia 'Speciosa' Bright red with red-spotted yellow centers; swordlike leaves. Plate 152.	tender bulb	8–10	average	full sun	average
Tradescantia Andersoniana Group Blue or purple flowers; straplike leaves.	perennial	3–9	wet	sun/pt shade	average
Tradescantia (Andersoniana Group) 'Purple Profusion' Purple flowers; straplike leaves. Plate 168.	perennial	3–9	wet	sun/pt shade	average
Tradescantia (Andersoniana Group) 'Zwanenburg Blue' Deep blue-purple flowers; straplike leaves. Combination 22.	perennial	3–9	wet	sun/pt shade	average
Trillium erectum Deep purple-red flowers; three large whorled leaves.	perennial	4–9	average	shade/pt shade	average
Triteleia laxa 'Queen Fabiola' Blue up-facing bells in loose clusters.	hardy bulb	5–9	average	sun/pt shade	average
Tropaeolum majus Alaska Series Orange-red, salmon, or yellow flowers; cream-speckled green leaves. Plate 185.	annual	9	average	full sun	average
Tropaeolum majus 'Apricot Trifle' Peach flowers.	annual	9	average	full sun	average
Tropaeolum majus 'Blush Double' Double peach pom-pom flowers; trailing habit. Plate 65.	annual	9	average	full sun	average
Tropaeolum majus 'Moonlight' Large soft yellow flowers; trailing habit. Plate 69.	annual	9	average	full sun	average
Tropaeolum majus 'Tip Top Mahogany' Dark red flowers; chartreuse-green foliage. Plates 92, 108.	annual	8–10	average	full sun	average

	TYPE	ZONE	SOIL MOISTURE	LIGHT	SOIL pH
Tsuga canadensis Elegant and fine-textured soft green needles. Plate 197.	tree	3–7	average	shade/pt shade	acid
Tsuga canadensis 'Cole's Prostrate' Low-spreading evergreen. Plate 121.	shrub	4–7	average	shade/pt shade	acid
Tulipa 'Angelique' Fragrant pale blush-pink with darker pink and creamy yellow, variable color.	hardy bulb	3–8	average	full sun	average
Tulipa 'Apricot Parrot' Scalloped and fringed yellowy apricot petals with a hint of rose.	hardy bulb	3–8	average	full sun	average
Tulipa 'Big Smile' Long-lasting amber-yellow flowers.	hardy bulb	3–8	average	full sun	average
Tulipa 'Black Parrot' Scalloped and fringed burgundy, almost black petals. Plate 98.	hardy bulb	3–8	average	full sun	average
Tulipa 'Blue Heron' Blue-lilac petals with a frosty fringe.	hardy bulb	3–8	average	full sun	average
Tulipa 'Blue Parrot' Scalloped and fringed blue-violet petals.	hardy bulb	3–8	average	full sun	average
Tulipa 'Blushing Lady' Lily-shaped light orange and pale yellow flowers with a blush-rose flame.	hardy bulb	3–7	average	full sun	average
Tulipa 'Burgundy Lace' Long-lasting burgundy-red flowers.	hardy bulb	3–8	average	full sun	average
Tulipa 'Carmine Parrot' Scalloped and fringed cherry-red petals. Plate 22.	hardy bulb	3–8	average	full sun	average
Tulipa 'Couleur Cardinal' Fragrant reddish plum flowers.	hardy bulb	3–8	average	full sun	average
Tulipa 'Fringed Elegance' Bright yellow with an occasional red fleck.	hardy bulb	3–8	average	full sun	average
Tulipa 'Queen of Night' Velvety maroon-black flowers.	hardy bulb	3–7	average	full sun	average
Tulipa 'Temple of Beauty' Lily-shaped salmon-rose flowers flushed with orange.	hardy bulb	3–8	average	full sun	average
Tulipa 'Uncle Tom' Peonylike dark maroon flowers.	hardy bulb	3–8	average	full sun	average
Tulipa batalinii Pale yellow flowers; gray-green leaves with wavy red margins.	hardy bulb	3–7	average	full sun	average
Tulipa clusiana var. chrysantha Interior of petals yellow, exterior of petals red.	hardy bulb	3–7	average	full sun	average

	TYPE	ZONE	SOIL MOISTURE	LIGHT	SOIL pH
Valeriana officinalis Fragrant pink-tinged white flowers; pinnately compound leaves. Combination 5.	perennial	4–9	average	full sun	average
Verbascum 'Jackie' Peach flowers along spiky stems. Plate 154.	perennial	3–8	dry	full sun	alkaline
Verbascum bombyciferum Basal rosette of large, silvery woolly leaves; tall spikes of golden yellow flowers. Plate 23.	perennial	4–8	dry	full sun	alkaline
Verbena 'Homestead Purple' Low-spreading form; purple flowerheads. Plate 65.	annual	6–10	average	full sun	average
Verbena 'Romance Apricot' Peach flowerheads.	annual		average	full sun	average
Verbena Temari® Red Bright red flowerheads. Plates 144, 150.	annual		average	full sun	average
Verbena bonariensis Lilac-purple flowerheads on tall wiry stems.	annual	(6)7–11	dry	full sun	average
Verbena hastata Numerous small violet-blue flower spikes. Subject to powdery mildew.	perennial	3–7	wet	full sun	average
Veronica 'Goodness Grows' Blue flower spikes.	perennial	3–8	average	full sun	average
Veronica 'Waterperry Blue' Light blue flowers; evergreen to semi-evergreen purple-tinged foliage.	perennial	3–8	average	full sun	average
Veronica austriaca ssp. teucrium 'Crater Lake Blue' Blue flower spikes; narrow toothed leaves. Plates 38, 174.	perennial	3–8	average	full sun	average
Veronica austriaca ssp. teucrium 'Royal Blue' Deep blue flower spikes; narrow toothed leaves.	perennial	3–8	average	full sun	average
Veronica gentianoides 'Nana' Pale blue flower spikes.	perennial	4–8	average	full sun	average
Veronica peduncularis 'Georgia Blue' Deep blue flowers with white eyes; small purple-tinged leaves.	perennial	5–8	average	full sun	average
Veronica prostrata 'Trehane' Deep blue flowers; yellow-green foliage.	perennial	5–8	average	full sun	average
Veronica repens 'Sunshine' Occasional tiny white flower spikes; low-growing mat of yellow foliage.	perennial	(5)6–9	average	full sun	average
Veronica spicata 'Blue Charm' Pale blue-lavender flower spikes.	perennial	3–8	average	full sun	average
Veronica spicata 'Icicle' White flower spikes.	perennial	3–8	average	full sun	average

	TYPE	ZONE	SOIL MOISTURE	LIGHT	SOIL pH
Veronicastrum virginicum 'Fascination' Lavender flower spikes; narrow green whorled leaves.	perennial	3–8	dry	sun/pt shade	average
Viburnum plicatum var. tomentosum 'Mariesii' Serrated dark green leaves turn reddish purple in autumn; white flowers; black fruit.	shrub	5–7(8)	dry	sun/pt shade	average
Viola 'Molly Sanderson' Black flowers with a yellow eye. Plate 172.	perennial	5–8	average	sun/pt shade	average
Viola 'Purple Showers' Purple flowers.	perennial	5–8	average	sun/pt shade	average
Viola labradorica Groundcover; purple-tinged dark green leaves; small pale purple flowers.	perennial	2–8	average	sun/pt shade	average
Vitex agnus-castus var. latifolia Palmate leaves; long blue panicles. Plate 76.	shrub	5–8	average	full sun	average
Vitis vinifera 'Purpurea' Lobed and toothed leaves, plum-purple color that intensifies in autumn.	woody vine	(5)6–9	average	sun/pt shade	average
Yucca filamentosa 'Color Guard' Sword-shaped green leaves with creamy yellow central variegation tinged rose in winter; large panicles of white bell-shaped flowers. Plate 200.	shrub	4–9	dry	full sun	average
Yucca flaccida 'Golden Sword' Sword-shaped leaves with green margins and yellow centers; large panicles of white bell-shaped flowers. Plate 7.	shrub	5–9	dry	full sun	average
Zinnia haageana 'Orange Star' Small bright orange daisylike flowers.	annual		average	full sun	average

LIGHT REQUIREMENTS

Full sun

Tree

Betula utilis var. jacquemontii
Catalpa bignonioides 'Aurea'
Ginkgo biloba 'Autumn Gold'
Malus 'Lanzam' (Lancelot®)
Picea abies 'Pendula'
Picea pungens 'Iseli Foxtail'
Picea pungens 'Thomsen'
Pinus cembra 'Silver Sheen'
Pinus parviflora 'Glauca'
Pinus strobus
Pinus sylvestris
Pinus sylvestris 'Fastigiata'
Pseudotsuga menziesii 'Astro Blue'
Quercus palustris
Quercus robur 'Pectinata'
Thuja occidentalis 'Techny'

Shrub

Amorpha canescens
Berberis thunbergii var. atropurpurea
    'Bailtwo' (Burgundy Carousel™)
Berberis thunbergii var. atropurpurea
    'Gentry Cultivar' (Royal Burgundy™)
Berberis thunbergii var. atropurpurea
    'Rose Glow'
Berberis thunbergii var. atropurpurea
    'Royal Cloak'
Buddleia 'Lochinch'
Buddleia davidii 'Black Knight'
Buddleia davidii 'Mongo' (Nanho blue)
Cotinus coggygria 'Velvet Cloak'
Genista tinctoria 'Royal Gold'
Lespedeza cuneata
Picea abies 'Mucronata'
Picea alcoquiana 'Howell's Tigertail'
Pinus densiflora 'Oculus Draconis'
Pinus parviflora 'Yatsubusa'
Pinus pumila 'Nana'
Pinus strobus 'Nana'
Pinus sylvestris 'Albyn'
Potentilla fruticosa 'Sunset'
Rosa 'Alchymist'
Rosa 'Ausbuff' (English Garden®)
Rosa 'Ausmas' (Graham Thomas®)
Rosa 'Aussaucer' (Evelyn®)
Rosa 'Ausvelvet' (The Prince®)
Rosa 'Champlain'
Rosa 'F. J. Grootendorst'
Rosa 'Hansa'
Rosa Lyda Rose™
Rosa 'Meidomonac' (Bonica®)
Rosa 'Nearly Wild'

Rosa 'Nuits de Young'
Rosa 'Scrivluv' (Baby Love®)
Rosa 'Seafoam'
Rosa 'The Fairy'
Rosa ×harisonii 'Harison's Yellow'
Rosa multiflora 'Grevillei' (seven sisters' rose)
Rosa rugosa
Syringa meyeri
Vitex agnus-castus var. latifolia
Yucca filamentosa 'Color Guard'
Yucca flaccida 'Golden Sword'

Perennial

Achillea 'Anblo' (Anthea)
Achillea 'Heidi'
Achillea 'Salmon Beauty'
Achillea filipendulina 'Altgold'
Agastache 'Blue Fortune'
Agastache rupestris
Alcea rosea 'Peaches and Dreams'
Alcea rosea 'The Watchman'
Alcea rugosa
Alstroemeria 'Sweet Laura'
Artemisia 'Huntington'
Artemisia 'Powis Castle'
Artemisia 'Silverado'
Artemisia absinthium 'Lambrook Silver'
Asclepias tuberosa
Asclepias tuberosa 'Hello Yellow'
Aster 'Climax'
Aster laevis 'Bluebird'
Aster novae-angliae 'Hella Lacy'
Aster novae-angliae 'Hillside'
Aster novae-angliae 'Purple Dome'
Aster novae-angliae 'Wild Light Blue'
Aster oblongifolius var. angustatus
    'Raydon's Favorite'
Belamcanda chinensis
Belamcanda chinensis 'Hello Yellow'
Calamagrostis ×acutiflora 'Karl Foerster'
Cephalaria gigantea
Chrysanthemum 'Autumn Moon'
Chrysanthemum 'Pumpkin Harvest'
Chrysanthemum 'Single Apricot'
Chrysanthemum 'Single Peach'
Chrysanthemum 'Viette's Apricot Glow'
Coreopsis auriculata
Coreopsis grandiflora 'Walcoreop'
    (flying saucers)
Coreopsis tripteris
Coreopsis verticillata 'Moonbeam'
Coreopsis verticillata 'Zagreb'
Crocosmia 'Blacro' (Jenny Bloom)
Crocosmia 'Emberglow'
Crocosmia 'Lucifer'
Crocosmia ×crocosmiiflora 'Norwich Canary'
Crocosmia ×crocosmiiflora 'Solfatare'
Crocosmia ×crocosmiiflora 'Venus'

Dianthus ×allwoodii 'Danielle Marie'
Dianthus barbatus 'Sooty'
Dianthus deltoides 'Leuchtfunk' (flashing light)
Echinacea purpurea
Echinops bannaticus 'Taplow Blue'
Echinops ritro 'Blue Glow'
Echinops ritro 'Veitch's Blue'
Eryngium amethystinum
Eryngium planum 'Blaukappe'
Eryngium variifolium
Eryngium yuccifolium
Eupatorium purpureum ssp. maculatum
    'Gateway'
Euphorbia 'Golden Towers'
Euphorbia cyparissias 'Fen's Ruby'
Euphorbia dulcis 'Chameleon'
Euphorbia griffithii 'Fireglow'
Euphorbia ×martinii
Euphorbia polychroma
Festuca glauca 'Golden Toupee'
Foeniculum vulgare 'Purpureum'
Gladiolus ×gandavensis
Gladiolus ×gandavensis 'Boone'
Helenium 'Kugelsonne'
Helenium 'Moerheim Beauty'
Helianthemum (double yellow)
Helianthemum 'Fire Dragon'
Helianthus 'Lemon Queen'
Helianthus 'Mellow Yellow'
Helianthus salicifolius
Helictotrichon sempervirens 'Saphirsprudel'
    (sapphire fountain)
Heliopsis helianthoides var. scabra
    'Sommersonne' (summer sun)
Hemerocallis 'Happy Returns'
Hemerocallis 'Red Razzamatazz'
Hemerocallis 'Scarlet Romance'
Hemerocallis 'Siloam Royal Prince'
Hemerocallis 'Staghorn Sumac'
Hemerocallis 'Sundried Tomatoes'
Hemerocallis 'Toy Trumpets'
Hemerocallis 'Yellow Lollipop'
Hibiscus moscheutos 'Lord Baltimore'
Hyssopus officinalis
Iris 'Flavescens'
Iris 'Perfume Counter'
Iris 'Sugar Blues'
Iris pseudacorus 'Variegata'
Knautia macedonica
Kniphofia 'Alcazar'
Kniphofia 'Little Maid'
Kniphofia 'Primrose Beauty'
Kniphofia 'Prince Igor'
Kniphofia 'Royal Standard'
Kniphofia 'Shining Sceptre'
Kniphofia caulescens
Kniphofia citrina
Kniphofia triangularis

Lathyrus latifolius
Lavandula angustifolia 'Munstead'
Lavandula ×intermedia 'Grosso'
Liatris spicata 'Kobold'
Lilium 'Casa Blanca'
Lilium henryi
Lilium lancifolium var. splendens
Lilium pumilum
Limonium platyphyllum 'Violetta'
Linum perenne 'Blau Saphir' (blue sapphire)
Lychnis ×arkwrightii 'Vesuvius'
Lychnis coronaria
Miscanthus 'Purpurascens'
Miscanthus sinensis var. condensatus
    'Cosmopolitan'
Miscanthus sinensis 'Gracillimus'
Miscanthus sinensis 'Malepartus'
Miscanthus sinensis 'Morning Light'
Molinia caerulea ssp. arundinacea 'Skyracer'
Monarda 'Jacob Cline'
Monarda 'Violet Queen'
Nepeta 'Six Hills Giant'
Nepeta ×faassenii
Nepeta grandiflora 'Bramdean'
Nepeta racemosa 'Walker's Low'
Nepeta sibirica 'Souvenir d'André Chaudron'
Nymphaea 'Marliacea Chromatella'
Oenothera fremontii 'Lemon Silver'
Oenothera fruticosa ssp. glauca 'Sonnenwende'
Origanum 'Kent Beauty'
Origanum laevigatum 'Herrenhausen'
Origanum vulgare 'Aureum'
Paeonia 'America'
Paeonia 'Burma Ruby'
Paeonia 'Coral Sunset'
Paeonia 'Etched Salmon'
Paeonia 'Monsieur Jules Elie'
Paeonia 'Prairie Moon'
Panicum virgatum 'Dallas Blues'
Panicum virgatum 'Heavy Metal'
Panicum virgatum 'Rehbraun'
Papaver nudicaule 'Red Sails'
Papaver orientale 'Curlilocks'
Papaver orientale 'Derwisch'
Papaver orientale 'Feuerriese'
Papaver orientale 'Harvest Moon'
Papaver orientale 'Lighthouse'
Papaver orientale 'Patty's Plum'
Papaver orientale 'Prince of Orange'
Papaver orientale 'Saffron'
Papaver orientale 'Turkenlouis'
Patrinia scabiosifolia
Pennisetum alopecuroides 'Hameln'
Penstemon digitalis 'Husker Red'
Penstemon ×mexicale 'Pike's Peak Purple'
Perovskia atriplicifolia
Perovskia atriplicifolia 'Longin'
Persicaria microcephala 'Red Dragon'

Light Requirements, full sun, cont.

Phlox paniculata 'David'
Phlox paniculata 'Fesselballon'
Phlox paniculata 'Katherine'
Phlox paniculata 'Laura'
Phlox paniculata 'Look Again'
Phlox paniculata 'Orange Perfection'
Phlox paniculata 'Pax' (peace)
Phlox paniculata 'Tenor'
Phlox paniculata 'The King'
Phlox paniculata 'Tracy's Treasure'
Plantago major 'Rubrifolia'
Platycodon grandiflorus 'Double Blue'
Platycodon grandiflorus 'Komachi'
Rudbeckia fulgida var. speciosa (newmannii)
Rudbeckia maxima
Rudbeckia triloba
Rumex sanguineus
Ruta graveolens 'Blue Beauty'
Salvia argentea
Salvia azurea var. pitcheri
Salvia nemorosa 'Ostfriesland' (East Friesland)
Salvia nemorosa 'Purple Glory'
Salvia nemorosa 'Pusztaflamme' (plumosa)
Salvia ×sylvestris 'Blauhügel' (blue hill)
Salvia ×sylvestris 'Blaukönigin' (blue queen)
Salvia ×sylvestris 'Mainacht' (May night)
Salvia ×sylvestris 'Viola Klose'
Salvia verticillata 'Purple Rain'
Scabiosa Butterfly Blue®
Scabiosa 'Pink Mist'
Scabiosa columbaria var. ochroleuca
Schizachyrium scoparium 'The Blues'
Sedum 'Herbstfreude' (autumn joy)
Sedum telephium ssp. maximum
    'Atropurpureum'
Solidago 'Golden Spangles'
Solidago rugosa 'Fireworks'
×Solidaster luteus 'Lemore'
Sorghastrum nutans 'Sioux Blue'
Stachys byzantina
Stachys byzantina 'Countess Helen von Stein'
Stachys byzantina 'Primrose Heron'
Stokesia laevis 'Klaus Jelitto'
Stokesia laevis 'Mary Gregory'
Stokesia laevis 'Omega Skyrocket'
Stokesia laevis 'Purple Parasols'
Thermopsis villosa
Thymus ×citriodorus
Thymus ×citriodorus 'Lemon Green'
Thymus pseudolanuginosus
Valeriana officinalis
Verbascum 'Jackie'
Verbascum bombyciferum
Verbena hastata
Veronica 'Goodness Grows'

Veronica 'Waterperry Blue'
Veronica austriaca ssp. teucrium
    'Crater Lake Blue'
Veronica austriaca ssp. teucrium 'Royal Blue'
Veronica gentianoides 'Nana'
Veronica peduncularis 'Georgia Blue'
Veronica prostrata 'Trehane'
Veronica repens 'Sunshine'
Veronica spicata 'Blue Charm'
Veronica spicata 'Icicle'

Annual

Agave havardiana
Ageratum houstonianum 'Blue Horizon'
Alstroemeria aurea 'Orange King'
Alstroemeria psittacina
Alternanthera dentata 'Rubiginosa'
Angelonia 'Blue Pacific'
Angelonia angustifolia 'Purple Pinnacles'
Antirrhinum majus 'Rocket Red'
Arctotis ×hybrida 'Dark Red'
Arctotis ×hybrida 'Flame'
Atriplex hortensis var. rubra
Beta vulgaris 'Bull's Blood'
Beta vulgaris 'Golden'
Beta vulgaris 'Ruby Queen'
Bouvardia ternifolia
Brachyscome 'Ultra'
Brassica oleracea
Calendula officinalis 'Orange King'
Celosia spicata 'Flamingo Purple'
Centaurea cineraria
Cerinthe major 'Purpurascens'
Consolida ajacis 'Blue Spire'
Cosmos atrosanguineus
Cynara cardunculus
Cyperus alternifolius 'Stricta'
Eschscholzia californica
Eschscholzia californica 'Purple Gleam'
Eucomis comosa 'Sparkling Burgundy'
Gomphrena haageana 'Lavender Lady'
Helichrysum petiolare 'Limelight'
Ipomoea batatas 'Ace of Spades'
Ipomoea batatas 'Blackie'
Ipomoea batatas 'Margarita'
Lactuca 'Merlot'
Leonotis menthifolia
Lysimachia congestiflora 'Variegata'
Melampodium paludosum 'Million Gold'
Nicotiana langsdorffii
Nierembergia scoparia 'Mont Blanc'
Nigella damascena Miss Jekyll Series
Ocimum 'African Blue'
Ocimum basilicum 'Red Rubin'
Papaver rhoeas
Papaver rhoeas Angels' Choir
Papaver somniferum
Papaver somniferum 'Black Peony'

Papaver somniferum 'Burnt Orange'
Papaver somniferum 'Lauren's Grape'
Papaver somniferum 'Pepperbox'
Pennisetum setaceum 'Rubrum'
Perilla frutescens var. crispa
Pistia stratiotes
Plectranthus amboinicus
Plectranthus argentatus
Portulaca grandiflora 'Sundial Peach'
Rudbeckia hirta 'Irish Eyes'
Salvia 'Indigo Spires'
Salvia 'Purple Majesty'
Salvia coccinea 'Lady in Red'
Salvia guaranitica
Salvia guaranitica 'Black and Blue'
Salvia leucantha
Salvia officinalis 'Tricolor'
Scabiosa atropurpurea 'Ace of Spades'
Tropaeolum majus 'Apricot Trifle'
Tropaeolum majus 'Blush Double'
Tropaeolum majus 'Moonlight'
Tropaeolum majus 'Tip Top Mahogany'
Tropaeolum majus Alaska Series
Verbena 'Homestead Purple'
Verbena 'Romance Apricot'
Verbena Temari® Red
Verbena bonariensis
Zinnia haageana 'Orange Star'

Annual vine

Ipomoea lobata (Mina lobata)
Ipomoea tricolor 'Heavenly Blue'
Lablab purpureus
Lathyrus odoratus
Lathyrus odoratus 'Henry Eckford'
Lathyrus odoratus 'King Size Navy Blue'
Rhodochiton atrosanguineus
Thunbergia battiscombei

Tropical

Canna 'Black Knight'
Canna 'Omega'
Canna 'Orange Punch'
Canna 'Panache'
Canna 'Phasion'
Canna 'Roi Humbert' (red King Humbert)
Canna 'Striata' (Pretoria)
Canna indica 'Red Stripe' (purpurea)
Duranta erecta 'Golden Edge'
Euphorbia cotinifolia
Hibiscus acetosella 'Red Shield'
Musa basjoo
Phormium 'Bronze Baby'
Phormium 'Platt's Black'
Phormium 'Yellow Wave'
Phormium cookianum 'Chocolate'
Ricinus communis
Ricinus communis 'Carmencita'

Hardy bulb

Allium caeruleum
Allium carinatum ssp. pulchellum
Allium cristophii
Allium hollandicum (aflatunense)
    'Purple Sensation'
Allium moly 'Jeannine'
Allium schubertii
Allium sphaerocephalon
Dichelostemma ida-maia
Eremurus ×isabellinus 'Pinokkio'
Iris 'Blue Magic'
Tulipa 'Angelique'
Tulipa 'Apricot Parrot'
Tulipa 'Big Smile'
Tulipa 'Black Parrot'
Tulipa 'Blue Heron'
Tulipa 'Blue Parrot'
Tulipa 'Blushing Lady'
Tulipa 'Burgundy Lace'
Tulipa 'Carmine Parrot'
Tulipa 'Couleur Cardinal'
Tulipa 'Fringed Elegance'
Tulipa 'Queen of Night'
Tulipa 'Temple of Beauty'
Tulipa 'Uncle Tom'
Tulipa batalinii
Tulipa clusiana var. chrysantha

Tender bulb

Agapanthus 'Bressingham Blue'
Dahlia 'Arabian Night'
Dahlia 'Bishop of Llandaff'
Dahlia 'Ellen Houston'
Dahlia 'Orange Nugget'
Dahlia 'Susette'
Gladiolus 'Atom'
Gladiolus 'Violetta'
Hymenocallis 'Sulphur Queen'
Scadoxus multiflorus
Tigridia pavonia 'Speciosa'

Sun/pt shade

These plants prefer sun but can tolerate some shade; those marked with an asterisk are especially tolerant of shade.

Tree

Abies lasiocarpa 'Arizonica Compacta'
Acer griseum
Acer palmatum var. dissectum Dissectum
    Atropurpureum Group*
Acer palmatum 'Sango-kaku'
Amelanchier ×grandiflora 'Autumn Brilliance'*
Chamaecyparis lawsoniana 'Sullivan'
Chionanthus virginicus*
Cornus kousa*

Fagus sylvatica 'Purpurea Pendula'
Fagus sylvatica 'Tricolor'
Magnolia virginiana*
Picea orientalis 'Skylands'
Pinus flexilis 'Vanderwolf's Pyramid'
Sciadopitys verticillata*

Shrub

Abies procera 'Glauca Prostrata'
Aralia elata 'Aureovariegata'
Berberis thunbergii 'Monler' (Gold Nugget™)
Berberis thunbergii 'Monry' (Sunsation™)
Buxus 'Green Gem'*
Buxus 'Green Velvet'*
Callicarpa dichotoma 'Issai'
Calycanthus floridus*
Caryopteris ×clandonensis
Caryopteris ×clandonensis 'Longwood Blue'
Caryopteris ×clandonensis 'Worcester Gold'
Chamaecyparis obtusa 'Fernspray Gold'
Chamaecyparis obtusa 'Mariesii'
Chamaecyparis pisifera 'Golden Mop'
Clethra alnifolia*
Daphne ×burkwoodii 'Carol Mackie'*
Fothergilla gardenii*
Hydrangea quercifolia*
Hydrangea quercifolia 'Snowflake'*
Hypericum androsaemum 'Albury Purple'
Ilex 'Apollo'*
Ilex glabra*
Ilex verticillata 'Afterglow'*
Ilex verticillata 'Christmas Cheer'*
Ilex verticillata 'Jim Dandy'*
Ilex verticillata 'Winter Red'*
Itea virginica 'Henry's Garnet'*
Itea virginica*
Pinus contorta 'Chief Joseph'
Pinus contorta 'Spaan's Dwarf'*
Sambucus racemosa 'Sutherland Gold'
Viburnum plicatum var. tomentosum 'Mariesii'*

Woody vine

Ampelopsis glandulosa var. brevipedunculata 'Elegans'
Campsis ×tagliabuana 'Madame Galen'
Clematis 'Elsa Späth'
Clematis 'Hagley Hybrid'
Clematis 'Lanuginosa Candida'
Clematis 'Polish Spirit'
Clematis 'Royal Velours'
Clematis alpina 'Constance'
Clematis macropetala 'Markham's Pink'
Clematis terniflora
Hydrangea anomala ssp. petiolaris*
Lonicera periclymenum 'Graham Thomas'
Lonicera sempervirens 'Blanche Sandman'
Vitis vinifera 'Purpurea'

Perennial

Acanthus spinosus*
Aconitum 'Bressingham Spire'*
Aconitum 'Ivorine'*
Aconitum carmichaelii (Wilsonii Group) 'Spätlese'
Aconitum episcopale
Aconitum lycoctonum ssp. neapolitanum
Acorus gramineus 'Minimus Aureus'*
Acorus gramineus 'Oborozuki'
Acorus gramineus 'Ogon'*
Alchemilla mollis
Amsonia ciliata
Amsonia elliptica
Amsonia hubrichtii
Amsonia tabernaemontana
Anemone ×hybrida 'Queen Charlotte'*
Anemone ×hybrida 'September Charm'*
Angelica gigas
Anthriscus sylvestris 'Ravenswing'
Aquilegia alpina*
Aquilegia vulgaris var. stellata 'Black Barlow'*
Aster tataricus 'Jindai'
Baptisia 'Purple Smoke'
Baptisia australis
Baptisia sphaerocarpa
Buphthalmum speciosum
Calamagrostis ×acutiflora 'Overdam'
Campanula 'Birch Hybrid'
Campanula 'Constellation'
Campanula 'Dwarf Tornado'
Campanula 'Kent Belle'
Campanula persicifolia 'Chettle Charm'
Campanula rapunculoides
Campanula rotundifolia 'Olympica'
Carex buchananii
Carex dolichostachya 'Kaga Nishiki' (gold fountain)*
Carex elata 'Aurea' (Bowles' golden)*
Carex morrowii 'Ice Dance'*
Carex morrowii 'Variegata'*
Centaurea montana
Ceratostigma plumbaginoides
Clematis integrifolia
Clematis recta
Cynoglossum amabile 'Firmament'
Delphinium 'Centurion Sky Blue'
Delphinium ×bellamosum
Delphinium cashmerianum
Delphinium exaltatum*
Deschampsia cespitosa 'Goldgehänge'
Digitalis grandiflora*
Digitalis lutea*
Digitalis purpurea 'Apricot'
Dracocephalum ruyschiana
Euphorbia amygdaloides 'Purpurea'
Festuca glauca 'Elijah Blue'
Galega ×hartlandii 'Lady Wilson'

Gentiana septemfida var. lagodechiana*
Gentiana triflora 'Royal Blue'
Geranium 'Ann Folkard'
Geranium 'Brookside'
Geranium 'Johnson's Blue'
Geranium 'Phillippe Vapelle'
Geranium 'Salome'
Geranium himalayense 'Plenum'
Geranium ×magnificum
Geranium ×oxonianum 'Claridge Druce'
Geranium phaeum 'Lily Lovell'
Geranium phaeum 'Samobor'*
Geranium platypetalum
Geranium pratense 'Mrs. Kendall Clark'
Geranium pratense 'Victor Reiter Jr.'
Geranium psilostemon
Geranium renardii
Geranium sanguineum 'New Hampshire'
Gillenia stipulata
Gladiolus communis ssp. byzantinus
Hemerocallis 'Alluring Peach'
Hemerocallis 'Carefree Peach'
Hemerocallis 'Peach Fairy'
Hemerocallis 'Welcome Mat'
Hesperis matronalis
Heuchera 'Chocolate Ruffles'*
Heuchera 'Plum Pudding'*
Heuchera 'Raspberry Regal'*
Heuchera 'Velvet Night'*
Heuchera micrantha var. diversifolia 'Palace Purple'*
×Heucherella 'Silver Streak'*
Humulus lupulus 'Bianca'
Hystrix patula*
Imperata cylindrica var. koenigii 'Red Baron'
Iris foetidissima
Iris pallida 'Variegata'*
Iris sanguinea 'Snow Queen'
Iris sibirica 'Butter and Sugar'
Iris sibirica 'Caesar's Brother'
Iris sibirica 'Dianne's Daughter'
Iris sibirica 'Orville Fay'
Iris sibirica 'Pirate Prince'
Iris sibirica 'Skywings'
Iris sibirica 'Vi Luihn'
Iris sibirica 'White Swirl'
Lilium 'Apricot Brandy'
Lilium 'Connecticut King'
Lilium 'Conquistador'
Lilium 'Eden's Dandy'
Lilium 'Grand Cru'
Lilium 'Montenegro'
Lilium 'Pretender'
Lilium 'Royal Justice'
Lilium 'Royal Perfume'
Lilium 'Scarlet Emperor'
Lilium 'Shirley'
Lilium 'Sunset'

Linaria 'Natalie'
Linaria purpurea
Lobelia 'Dark Crusader'*
Lobelia 'Grape Knee High'*
Lobelia 'Purple Towers'*
Lobelia 'Queen Victoria'*
Lobelia 'Royal Robe'*
Lobelia 'Ruby Slippers'*
Lobelia siphilitica*
Lychnis cognata
Lysimachia nummularia 'Aurea'
Mazus reptans*
Mertensia pulmonarioides (virginica)*
Packera aurea (Senecio aureus)
Passiflora incarnata
Phlomis russeliana*
Phytolacca polyandra
Polemonium caeruleum 'Blanjou' (brise d'Anjou)*
Rheum palmatum var. tanguticum
Sanguisorba tenuifolia 'Purpurea'
Sedum 'Pork and Beans'
Sedum acre 'Aureum'
Sisyrinchium 'Quaint and Queer'
Sisyrinchium bermudianum
Stachys macrantha
Symphytum 'Goldsmith'
Tanacetum 'Golden Feathers'
Thalictrum rochebruneanum
Tradescantia Andersoniana Group*
Tradescantia (Andersoniana Group) 'Purple Profusion'*
Tradescantia (Andersoniana Group) 'Zwanenburg Blue'*
Veronicastrum virginicum 'Fascination'
Viola 'Molly Sanderson'*
Viola 'Purple Showers'
Viola labradorica*

Annual

Fuchsia 'Gartenmeister Bonstedt'
Phyllostachys nigra
Salvia patens
Solenostemon 'Burgundy Columns'
Solenostemon 'Burgundy Giant'
Solenostemon 'Olive'
Solenostemon 'Penny'
Solenostemon 'Purple Emperor'
Solenostemon 'Saturn'

Tropical

Colocasia esculenta
Colocasia esculenta 'Black Beauty'
Colocasia esculenta 'Black Magic'
Colocasia esculenta 'Fontanesii'
Colocasia esculenta 'Illustris'*
Hedychium 'Daniel Weeks'
Hedychium coccineum
Musa zebrina

Light Requirements, sun/pt shade, cont.

Hardy bulb

Camassia leichtlinii 'Semiplena'
Camassia leichtlinii ssp. suksdorfii 'Blauwe Donau' (blue Danube)
Chionodoxa forbesii (luciliae) Siehei Group*
Colchicum speciosum*
Crocus chrysanthus 'Blue Bird'*
Fritillaria persica*
Iris reticulata 'Harmony'*
Narcissus 'Delnashaugh'*
Narcissus 'Fragrant Rose'*
Narcissus 'Mary Gay Lirette'*
Narcissus 'Mint Julep'*
Narcissus 'Petrel'*
Narcissus 'Sir Winston Churchill'*
Narcissus 'Stratosphere'*
Narcissus 'Tahiti'*
Puschkinia scilloides*
Triteleia laxa 'Queen Fabiola'*

Shade/pt shade

These plants prefer shade but will take some light sun, such as morning sun.

Tree

Tsuga canadensis

Shrub

Aesculus parviflora
Buxus microphylla 'Winter Gem'
Ilex ×meserveae 'Mesdob' (China boy)
Ilex ×meserveae 'Mesog' (China girl)
Microbiota decussata
Rhododendron 'Chionoides'
Rhododendron 'Mist Maiden'
Rhododendron 'Northern Starburst'
Tsuga canadensis 'Cole's Prostrate'

Perennial

Adiantum pedatum
Ajuga reptans 'Purple Torch'
Arisaema sikokianum
Arum italicum ssp. italicum 'Marmoratum'
Aruncus dioicus
Astilbe ×arendsii 'Snowdrift'
Astilbe chinensis 'Purple Candle'
Astilbe chinensis var. taquetii 'Superba'
Astilbe chinensis 'Veronica Klose'
Astilbe ×rosea 'Peach Blossom'
Athyrium niponicum var. pictum
Brunnera macrophylla
Calamagrostis brachytricha
Cimicifuga ramosa 'Brunette'
Cimicifuga ramosa 'Hillside Black Beauty'

Cryptotaenia japonica f. atropurpurea
Dicentra 'Luxuriant'
Dicentra spectabilis 'Gold Heart'
Epimedium davidii
Epimedium ×rubrum
Epimedium ×warleyense
Galium odoratum
Geranium macrorrhizum 'Ingwersen's Variety'
Geranium wlassovianum
Glaucidium palmatum
Hakonechloa macra 'Aureola'
Helleborus Royal Heritage™
Helleborus foetidus
Helleborus orientalis
Helleborus orientalis (single black)
Hosta 'Big Daddy'
Hosta 'Blue Cadet'
Hosta 'Fragrant Blue'
Hosta 'Halcyon'
Hosta 'Krossa Regal'
Hosta 'Lemon Lime'
Hosta 'Love Pat'
Hosta 'Midas Touch'
Hosta 'Night Before Christmas'
Hosta 'Patriot'
Hosta 'Paul's Glory'
Hosta 'Sum and Substance'
Hosta 'Sun Power'
Hosta plantaginea 'Aphrodite'
Impatiens omeiana
Lamium maculatum 'White Nancy'
Ligularia 'The Rocket'
Ligularia dentata 'Dark Beauty'
Ligularia dentata 'Desdemona'
Ligularia wilsoniana
Luzula nivea
Osmunda cinnamomea
Osmunda regalis
Pachysandra procumbens
Paeonia obovata
Phlox divaricata
Phlox divaricata 'Dirigo Ice'
Phlox divaricata 'Eco Texas Purple'
Phlox divaricata ssp. laphamii
Phlox divaricata 'London Grove Blue'
Phlox divaricata 'Sweet Lilac'
Phlox stolonifera 'Blue Ridge'
Phlox stolonifera 'Bruce's White'
Polygonatum odoratum 'Variegatum'
Polystichum acrostichoides
Pulmonaria 'Majesté'
Pulmonaria 'Viette's Deep Blue Sea'
Rodgersia aesculifolia
Rodgersia pinnata
Saruma henryi
Silene regia
Stylophorum diphyllum
Thalictrum aquilegiifolium 'Thundercloud'

Tiarella cordifolia 'Ninja'
Trillium erectum

Tropical

Caladium 'Florida Cardinal'
Caladium 'Florida Sweetheart'

Hardy bulb

Eranthis hyemalis
Erythronium 'Pagoda'

Tender bulb

Amorphophallus konjac

DRY SHADE

These plants will tolerate dry conditions once established; those marked with an asterisk can tolerate both shade and sun.

Shade/pt shade

Perennial

Brunnera macrophylla
Calamagrostis brachytricha
Epimedium davidii
Epimedium ×rubrum
Epimedium ×warleyense
Galium odoratum
Geranium macrorrhizum 'Ingwersen's Variety'
Lamium maculatum 'White Nancy'
Polygonatum odoratum 'Variegatum'

Sun/pt shade

Shrub

Aralia elata 'Aureovariegata'
Berberis thunbergii 'Monler' (Gold Nugget™)
Berberis thunbergii 'Monry' (Sunsation™)
Caryopteris ×clandonensis
Caryopteris ×clandonensis 'Longwood Blue'
Caryopteris ×clandonensis 'Worcester Gold'
Hypericum androsaemum 'Albury Purple'
Pinus contorta 'Chief Joseph'
Pinus contorta 'Spaan's Dwarf'*

Woody vine

Campsis ×tagliabuana 'Madame Galen'
Lonicera periclymenum 'Graham Thomas'
Lonicera sempervirens 'Blanche Sandman'

Perennial

Amsonia ciliata
Amsonia elliptica

Amsonia hubrichtii
Amsonia tabernaemontana
Aster tataricus 'Jindai'
Baptisia 'Purple Smoke'
Baptisia australis
Baptisia sphaerocarpa
Calamagrostis ×acutiflora 'Overdam'
Centaurea montana
Ceratostigma plumbaginoides
Dracocephalum ruyschiana
Euphorbia amygdaloides 'Purpurea'
Festuca glauca 'Elijah Blue'
Geranium sanguineum 'New Hampshire'
Hystrix patula*
Linaria 'Natalie'
Linaria purpurea
Sedum 'Pork and Beans'
Sedum acre 'Aureum'
Stachys macrantha
Veronicastrum virginicum 'Fascination'

Annual

Salvia patens

DRY SOIL

Tree

Catalpa bignonioides 'Aurea'
Ginkgo biloba 'Autumn Gold'
Quercus robur 'Pectinata'

Shrub

Amorpha canescens
Aralia elata 'Aureovariegata'
Berberis thunbergii var. atropurpurea 'Bailtwo' (Burgundy Carousel™)
Berberis thunbergii var. atropurpurea 'Gentry Cultivar' (Royal Burgundy™)
Berberis thunbergii var. atropurpurea 'Rose Glow'
Berberis thunbergii var. atropurpurea 'Royal Cloak'
Berberis thunbergii 'Monler' (Gold Nugget™)
Berberis thunbergii 'Monry' (Sunsation™)
Buddleia 'Lochinch'
Buddleia davidii 'Black Knight'
Buddleia davidii 'Mongo' (Nanho blue)
Caryopteris ×clandonensis
Caryopteris ×clandonensis 'Longwood Blue'
Caryopteris ×clandonensis 'Worcester Gold'
Cotinus coggygria 'Velvet Cloak'
Genista tinctoria 'Royal Gold'
Hypericum androsaemum 'Albury Purple'
Lespedeza cuneata
Pinus contorta 'Chief Joseph'
Pinus contorta 'Spaan's Dwarf'

Potentilla fruticosa 'Sunset'
Rosa rugosa
Viburnum plicatum var. tomentosum 'Mariesii'
Yucca filamentosa 'Color Guard'
Yucca flaccida 'Golden Sword'

Woody vine

Campsis ×tagliabuana 'Madame Galen'
Lonicera periclymenum 'Graham Thomas'
Lonicera sempervirens 'Blanche Sandman'

Perennial

Achillea 'Anblo' (Anthea)
Achillea 'Heidi'
Achillea 'Salmon Beauty'
Achillea filipendulina 'Altgold'
Agastache 'Blue Fortune'
Agastache rupestris
Amsonia ciliata
Amsonia elliptica
Amsonia hubrichtii
Amsonia tabernaemontana
Artemisia 'Huntington'
Artemisia 'Powis Castle'
Artemisia 'Silverado'
Artemisia absinthium 'Lambrook Silver'
Asclepias tuberosa
Asclepias tuberosa 'Hello Yellow'
Aster oblongifolius var. angustatus
    'Raydon's Favorite'
Aster tataricus 'Jindai'
Baptisia 'Purple Smoke'
Baptisia australis
Baptisia sphaerocarpa
Brunnera macrophylla
Calamagrostis ×acutiflora 'Karl Foerster'
Calamagrostis ×acutiflora 'Overdam'
Calamagrostis brachytricha
Centaurea montana
Ceratostigma plumbaginoides
Coreopsis auriculata
Coreopsis grandiflora 'Walcoreop'
    (flying saucers)
Coreopsis tripteris
Coreopsis verticillata 'Moonbeam'
Coreopsis verticillata 'Zagreb'
Dianthus ×allwoodii 'Danielle Marie'
Dianthus barbatus 'Sooty'
Dianthus deltoides 'Leuchtfunk' (flashing light)
Digitalis purpurea 'Apricot'
Dracocephalum ruyschiana
Echinacea purpurea
Echinops bannaticus 'Taplow Blue'
Echinops ritro 'Blue Glow'
Echinops ritro 'Veitch's Blue'
Epimedium davidii
Epimedium ×rubrum
Epimedium ×warleyense

Eryngium amethystinum
Eryngium planum 'Blaukappe'
Eryngium variifolium
Eryngium yuccifolium
Euphorbia 'Golden Towers'
Euphorbia amygdaloides 'Purpurea'
Euphorbia cyparissias 'Fen's Ruby'
Euphorbia dulcis 'Chameleon'
Euphorbia griffithii 'Fireglow'
Euphorbia ×martinii
Euphorbia polychroma
Festuca glauca 'Elijah Blue'
Festuca glauca 'Golden Toupee'
Foeniculum vulgare 'Purpureum'
Galium odoratum
Geranium macrorrhizum 'Ingwersen's Variety'
Geranium sanguineum 'New Hampshire'
Helenium 'Kugelsonne'
Helenium 'Moerheim Beauty'
Helianthemum (double yellow)
Helianthemum 'Fire Dragon'
Helianthus 'Lemon Queen'
Helianthus 'Mellow Yellow'
Helianthus salicifolius
Helictotrichon sempervirens 'Saphirsprudel'
    (sapphire fountain)
Heliopsis helianthoides var. scabra
    'Sommersonne' (summer sun)
Hystrix patula
Knautia macedonica
Lamium maculatum 'White Nancy'
Lavandula angustifolia 'Munstead'
Lavandula ×intermedia 'Grosso'
Liatris spicata 'Kobold'
Limonium platyphyllum 'Violetta'
Linaria 'Natalie'
Linaria purpurea
Linum perenne 'Blau Saphir' (blue sapphire)
Lychnis coronaria
Monarda 'Jacob Cline'
Monarda 'Violet Queen'
Nepeta 'Six Hills Giant'
Nepeta ×faassenii
Nepeta grandiflora 'Bramdean'
Nepeta racemosa 'Walker's Low'
Nepeta sibirica 'Souvenir d'André Chaudron'
Oenothera fremontii 'Lemon Silver'
Oenothera fruticosa ssp. glauca 'Sonnenwende'
Origanum 'Kent Beauty'
Origanum laevigatum 'Herrenhausen'
Origanum vulgare 'Aureum'
Panicum virgatum 'Dallas Blues'
Panicum virgatum 'Heavy Metal'
Panicum virgatum 'Rehbraun'
Pennisetum alopecuroides 'Hameln'
Penstemon digitalis 'Husker Red'
Penstemon ×mexicale 'Pike's Peak Purple'
Perovskia atriplicifolia

Perovskia atriplicifolia 'Longin'
Polygonatum odoratum 'Variegatum'
Rudbeckia fulgida var. speciosa (newmannii)
Rudbeckia maxima
Rudbeckia triloba
Ruta graveolens 'Blue Beauty'
Salvia argentea
Salvia azurea var. pitcheri
Salvia nemorosa 'Ostfriesland' (East Friesland)
Salvia nemorosa 'Purple Glory'
Salvia nemorosa 'Pusztaflamme' (plumosa)
Salvia ×sylvestris 'Blauhügel' (blue hill)
Salvia ×sylvestris 'Blaukönigin' (blue queen)
Salvia ×sylvestris 'Mainacht' (May night)
Salvia ×sylvestris 'Viola Klose'
Salvia verticillata 'Purple Rain'
Schizachyrium scoparium 'The Blues'
Sedum 'Herbstfreude' (autumn joy)
Sedum 'Pork and Beans'
Sedum acre 'Aureum'
Sedum telephium ssp. maximum
    'Atropurpureum'
Solidago 'Golden Spangles'
Solidago rugosa 'Fireworks'
Sorghastrum nutans 'Sioux Blue'
Stachys byzantina
Stachys byzantina 'Countess Helen von Stein'
Stachys byzantina 'Primrose Heron'
Stachys macrantha
Stokesia laevis 'Klaus Jelitto'
Stokesia laevis 'Mary Gregory'
Stokesia laevis 'Omega Skyrocket'
Stokesia laevis 'Purple Parasols'
Thermopsis villosa
Thymus ×citriodorus
Thymus ×citriodorus 'Lemon Green'
Thymus pseudolanuginosus
Verbascum 'Jackie'
Verbascum bombyciferum
Veronicastrum virginicum 'Fascination'

Annual

Agave havardiana
Angelonia 'Blue Pacific'
Angelonia angustifolia 'Purple Pinnacles'
Arctotis ×hybrida 'Dark Red'
Arctotis ×hybrida 'Flame'
Cynara cardunculus
Eschscholzia californica
Eschscholzia californica 'Purple Gleam'
Nicotiana langsdorffii
Pennisetum setaceum 'Rubrum'
Plectranthus argentatus
Rudbeckia hirta 'Irish Eyes'
Salvia 'Indigo Spires'
Salvia 'Purple Majesty'
Salvia coccinea 'Lady in Red'
Salvia guaranitica

Salvia guaranitica 'Black and Blue'
Salvia leucantha
Salvia officinalis 'Tricolor'
Salvia patens
Verbena bonariensis

Tropical

Euphorbia cotinifolia
Phormium 'Bronze Baby'
Phormium 'Platt's Black'
Phormium 'Yellow Wave'
Phormium cookianum 'Chocolate'

WET SOIL

Tree

Amelanchier ×grandiflora 'Autumn Brilliance'
Betula utilis var. jacquemontii
Chionanthus virginicus
Magnolia virginiana

Shrub

Calycanthus floridus
Clethra alnifolia
Ilex 'Apollo'
Ilex glabra
Ilex verticillata 'Afterglow'
Ilex verticillata 'Christmas Cheer'
Ilex verticillata 'Jim Dandy'
Ilex verticillata 'Winter Red'
Itea virginica
Itea virginica 'Henry's Garnet'

Perennial

Acorus gramineus 'Minimus Aureus'
Acorus gramineus 'Oborozuki'
Acorus gramineus 'Ogon'
Aruncus dioicus
Carex dolichostachya 'Kaga Nishiki'
    (gold fountains)
Carex elata 'Aurea' (Bowles' golden)
Carex morrowii 'Ice Dance'
Carex morrowii 'Variegata'
Cimicifuga ramosa 'Brunette'
Cimicifuga ramosa 'Hillside Black Beauty'
Eupatorium purpureum ssp. maculatum
    'Gateway'
Hibiscus moscheutos 'Lord Baltimore'
Iris pseudoacorus 'Variegata'
Ligularia 'The Rocket'
Ligularia dentata 'Dark Beauty'
Ligularia dentata 'Desdemona'
Ligularia wilsoniana
Lobelia 'Dark Crusader'
Lobelia 'Grape Knee High'
Lobelia 'Purple Towers'
Lobelia 'Queen Victoria'

Wet Soil, cont.

Lobelia 'Royal Robe'
Lobelia 'Ruby Slippers'
Lobelia siphilitica
Nymphaea 'Marliacea Chromatella'
Packera aurea (Senecio aureus)
Polystichum acrostichoides
Rheum palmatum var. tanguticum
Rodgersia aesculifolia
Rodgersia pinnata
Thalictrum aquilegiifolium 'Thundercloud'
Thalictrum rochebruneanum
Tradescantia Andersoniana Group
Tradescantia (Andersoniana Group)
    'Purple Profusion'
Tradescantia (Andersoniana Group)
    'Zwanenburg Blue'
Verbena hastata

Annual

Cyperus alternifolius 'Stricta'
Lysimachia congestiflora 'Variegata'
Pistia stratiotes

Tropical

Canna 'Black Knight'
Canna 'Omega'
Canna 'Orange Punch'
Canna 'Panache'
Canna 'Phasion'
Canna 'Roi Humbert' (red King Humbert)
Canna 'Striata' (Pretoria)
Canna indica 'Red Stripe' (purpurea)
Colocasia esculenta
Colocasia esculenta 'Black Beauty'
Colocasia esculenta 'Black Magic'
Colocasia esculenta 'Fontanesii'
Colocasia esculenta 'Illustris'

Hardy bulb

Erythronium 'Pagoda'

LOWER MAINTENANCE

Tree

Abies lasiocarpa 'Arizonica Compacta'
Acer griseum
Acer palmatum var. dissectum Dissectum
    Atropurpureum Group
Acer palmatum 'Sango-kaku'
Amelanchier ×grandiflora 'Autumn Brilliance'
Chamaecyparis lawsoniana 'Sullivan'
Chionanthus virginicus
Cornus kousa
Fagus sylvatica 'Purpurea Pendula'

Fagus sylvatica 'Tricolor'
Ginkgo biloba 'Autumn Gold'
Magnolia virginiana
Malus 'Lanzam' (Lancelot®)
Picea orientalis 'Skylands'
Picea pungens 'Iseli Foxtail'
Picea pungens 'Thomsen'
Pinus cembra 'Silver Sheen'
Pinus flexilis 'Vanderwolf's Pyramid'
Pinus parviflora 'Glauca'
Pinus strobus
Pinus sylvestris
Pinus sylvestris 'Fastigiata'
Pseudotsuga menziesii 'Astro Blue'
Quercus robur 'Pectinata'
Sciadopitys verticillata
Thuja occidentalis 'Techny'

Shrub

Abies procera 'Glauca Prostrata'
Aesculus parviflora
Amorpha canescens
Berberis thunbergii var. atropurpurea
    'Bailtwo' (Burgundy Carousel™)
Berberis thunbergii var. atropurpurea
    'Gentry Cultivar' (Royal Burgundy™)
Berberis thunbergii var. atropurpurea
    'Rose Glow'
Berberis thunbergii var. atropurpurea
    'Royal Cloak'
Berberis thunbergii 'Monler' (Gold Nugget™)
Berberis thunbergii 'Monry' (Sunsation™)
Buddleia 'Lochinch'
Buddleia davidii 'Black Knight'
Buddleia davidii 'Mongo' (Nanho blue)
Buxus 'Green Gem'
Buxus 'Green Velvet'
Buxus microphylla 'Winter Gem'
Callicarpa dichotoma 'Issai'
Calycanthus floridus
Chamaecyparis obtusa 'Fernspray Gold'
Chamaecyparis obtusa 'Mariesii'
Chamaecyparis pisifera 'Golden Mop'
Clethra alnifolia
Cotinus coggygria 'Velvet Cloak'
Fothergilla gardenii
Genista tinctoria 'Royal Gold'
Hydrangea quercifolia
Hydrangea quercifolia 'Snowflake'
Ilex 'Apollo'
Ilex glabra
Ilex ×meserveae 'Mesdob' (China boy)
Ilex ×meserveae 'Mesog' (China girl)
Ilex verticillata 'Afterglow'
Ilex verticillata 'Christmas Cheer'
Ilex verticillata 'Jim Dandy'
Ilex verticillata 'Winter Red'
Itea virginica

Itea virginica 'Henry's Garnet'
Microbiota decussata
Picea abies 'Mucronata'
Picea alcoquiana 'Howell's Tigertail'
Pinus contorta 'Chief Joseph'
Pinus contorta 'Spaan's Dwarf'
Pinus densiflora 'Oculus Draconis'
Pinus parviflora 'Yatsubusa'
Pinus pumila 'Nana'
Pinus strobus 'Nana'
Pinus sylvestris 'Albyn'
Rhododendron 'Mist Maiden'
Rhododendron 'Northern Starburst'
Rosa 'Hansa'
Rosa Lyda Rose™
Rosa 'Meidomonac' (Bonica®)
Rosa 'Nearly Wild'
Rosa 'Scrivluv' (Baby Love®)
Rosa 'Seafoam'
Rosa 'The Fairy'
Rosa rugosa
Sambucus racemosa 'Sutherland Gold'
Syringa meyeri
Tsuga canadensis 'Cole's Prostrate'
Viburnum plicatum var. tomentosum 'Mariesii'
Vitex agnus-castus var. latifolia
Yucca filamentosa 'Color Guard'
Yucca flaccida 'Golden Sword'

Woody vine

Clematis 'Polish Spirit'
Clematis alpina 'Constance'
Clematis macropetala 'Markham's Pink'
Hydrangea anomala ssp. petiolaris
Lonicera periclymenum 'Graham Thomas'
Lonicera sempervirens 'Blanche Sandman'

Perennial

Acanthus spinosus
Achillea filipendulina 'Altgold'
Aconitum carmichaelii (Wilsonii Group)
    'Spätlese'
Acorus gramineus 'Ogon'
Adiantum pedatum
Agastache 'Blue Fortune'
Agastache rupestris
Amsonia ciliata
Amsonia elliptica
Amsonia hubrichtii
Amsonia tabernaemontana
Anemone ×hybrida 'Queen Charlotte'
Anemone ×hybrida 'September Charm'
Aquilegia alpina
Arisaema sikokianum
Arum italicum ssp. italicum 'Marmoratum'
Aruncus dioicus
Asclepias tuberosa
Asclepias tuberosa 'Hello Yellow'

Aster tataricus 'Jindai'
Astilbe ×arendsii 'Snowdrift'
Astilbe chinensis 'Purple Candle'
Astilbe chinensis 'Veronica Klose'
Astilbe chinensis var. taquetii 'Superba'
Astilbe ×rosea 'Peach Blossom'
Baptisia 'Purple Smoke'
Baptisia australis
Baptisia sphaerocarpa
Brunnera macrophylla
Buphthalmum speciosum
Calamagrostis ×acutiflora 'Karl Foerster'
Calamagrostis ×acutiflora 'Overdam'
Calamagrostis brachytricha
Carex buchananii
Carex dolichostachya 'Kaga Nishiki'
    (gold fountains)
Carex elata 'Aurea' (Bowles' golden)
Carex morrowii 'Ice Dance'
Carex morrowii 'Variegata'
Cephalaria gigantea
Ceratostigma plumbaginoides
Chrysanthemum 'Autumn Moon'
Chrysanthemum 'Pumpkin Harvest'
Chrysanthemum 'Single Apricot'
Chrysanthemum 'Single Peach'
Chrysanthemum 'Viette's Apricot Glow'
Cimicifuga ramosa 'Brunette'
Cimicifuga ramosa 'Hillside Black Beauty'
Clematis integrifolia
Coreopsis tripteris
Coreopsis verticillata 'Moonbeam'
Coreopsis verticillata 'Zagreb'
Cynoglossum amabile 'Firmament'
Delphinium exaltatum
Deschampsia cespitosa 'Goldgehänge'
Digitalis grandiflora
Digitalis lutea
Dracocephalum ruyschiana
Echinops bannaticus 'Taplow Blue'
Echinops ritro 'Blue Glow'
Echinops ritro 'Veitch's Blue'
Epimedium davidii
Epimedium ×rubrum
Epimedium ×warleyense
Eupatorium purpureum ssp. maculatum
    'Gateway'
Euphorbia griffithii 'Fireglow'
Geranium 'Ann Folkard'
Geranium 'Phillippe Vapelle'
Geranium 'Salome'
Geranium himalayense 'Plenum'
Geranium macrorrhizum 'Ingwersen's Variety'
Geranium ×magnificum
Geranium ×oxonianum 'Claridge Druce'
Geranium phaeum 'Samobor'
Geranium platypetalum
Geranium pratense 'Mrs. Kendall Clark'

Geranium pratense 'Victor Reiter Jr.'
Geranium psilostemon
Geranium renardii
Geranium sanguineum 'New Hampshire'
Geranium wlassovianum
Gillenia stipulata
Gladiolus ×gandavensis
Gladiolus ×gandavensis 'Boone'
Helianthus 'Lemon Queen'
Helianthus 'Mellow Yellow'
Helianthus salicifolius
Helictotrichon sempervirens 'Saphirsprudel'
    (sapphire fountain)
Heliopsis helianthoides var. scabra
    'Sommersonne' (summer sun)
Helleborus Royal Heritage™
Helleborus orientalis
Helleborus orientalis (single black)
Hemerocallis 'Alluring Peach'
Hemerocallis 'Carefree Peach'
Hemerocallis 'Happy Returns'
Hemerocallis 'Peach Fairy'
Hemerocallis 'Red Razzamatazz'
Hemerocallis 'Scarlet Romance'
Hemerocallis 'Siloam Royal Prince'
Hemerocallis 'Staghorn Sumac'
Hemerocallis 'Sundried Tomatoes'
Hemerocallis 'Toy Trumpets'
Hemerocallis 'Welcome Mat'
Hemerocallis 'Yellow Lollipop'
×Heucherella 'Silver Streak'
Hibiscus moscheutos 'Lord Baltimore'
Hosta 'Big Daddy'
Hosta 'Blue Cadet'
Hosta 'Fragrant Blue'
Hosta 'Halcyon'
Hosta 'Krossa Regal'
Hosta 'Lemon Lime'
Hosta 'Love Pat'
Hosta 'Midas Touch'
Hosta 'Night Before Christmas'
Hosta 'Patriot'
Hosta 'Paul's Glory'
Hosta 'Sum and Substance'
Hosta 'Sun Power'
Hosta plantaginea 'Aphrodite'
Humulus lupulus 'Bianca'
Hyssopus officinalis
Hystrix patula
Impatiens omeiana
Iris 'Sugar Blues'
Iris pseudacorus 'Variegata'
Iris sanguinea 'Snow Queen'
Iris sibirica 'Butter and Sugar'
Iris sibirica 'Caesar's Brother'
Iris sibirica 'Dianne's Daughter'
Iris sibirica 'Orville Fay'
Iris sibirica 'Pirate Prince'

Iris sibirica 'Skywings'
Iris sibirica 'Vi Luihn'
Iris sibirica 'White Swirl'
Lathyrus latifolius
Liatris spicata 'Kobold'
Ligularia 'The Rocket'
Ligularia dentata 'Dark Beauty'
Ligularia dentata 'Desdemona'
Ligularia wilsoniana
Lilium henryi
Lilium lancifolium var. splendens
Lilium pumilum
Limonium platyphyllum 'Violetta'
Linaria 'Natalie'
Linaria purpurea
Luzula nivea
Lysimachia nummularia 'Aurea'
Mazus reptans
Miscanthus 'Purpurascens'
Miscanthus sinensis var. condensatus
    'Cosmopolitan'
Miscanthus sinensis 'Gracillimus'
Miscanthus sinensis 'Malepartus'
Miscanthus sinensis 'Morning Light'
Molinia caerulea ssp. arundinacea 'Skyracer'
Nepeta 'Six Hills Giant'
Origanum 'Kent Beauty'
Origanum laevigatum 'Herrenhausen'
Origanum vulgare 'Aureum'
Osmunda cinnamomea
Paeonia obovata
Panicum virgatum 'Dallas Blues'
Panicum virgatum 'Heavy Metal'
Panicum virgatum 'Rehbraun'
Pennisetum alopecuroides 'Hameln'
Penstemon digitalis 'Husker Red'
Perovskia atriplicifolia
Perovskia atriplicifolia 'Longin'
Persicaria microcephala 'Red Dragon'
Phlomis russeliana
Phlox divaricata
Phlox divaricata 'Dirigo Ice'
Phlox divaricata 'Eco Texas Purple'
Phlox divaricata ssp. laphamii
Phlox divaricata 'London Grove Blue'
Phlox divaricata 'Sweet Lilac'
Phlox paniculata 'David'
Phlox paniculata 'Fesselballon'
Phlox paniculata 'Katherine'
Phlox paniculata 'Laura'
Phlox paniculata 'Look Again'
Phlox paniculata 'Orange Perfection'
Phlox paniculata 'Pax' (peace)
Phlox paniculata 'Tenor'
Phlox paniculata 'The King'
Phlox paniculata 'Tracy's Treasure'
Phlox stolonifera 'Blue Ridge'
Phlox stolonifera 'Bruce's White'

Plantago major 'Rubrifolia'
Platycodon grandiflorus 'Double Blue'
Platycodon grandiflorus 'Komachi'
Polygonatum odoratum 'Variegatum'
Polystichum acrostichoides
Pulmonaria 'Majesté'
Pulmonaria 'Viette's Deep Blue Sea'
Rodgersia aesculifolia
Rodgersia pinnata
Rudbeckia maxima
Rumex sanguineus
Salvia azurea var. pitcheri
Salvia nemorosa 'Ostfriesland'
    (East Friesland)
Salvia nemorosa 'Purple Glory'
Salvia nemorosa 'Pusztaflamme' (plumosa)
Salvia ×sylvestris 'Blauhügel' (blue hill)
Salvia ×sylvestris 'Blaukönigin' (blue queen)
Salvia ×sylvestris 'Mainacht' (May night)
Salvia ×sylvestris 'Viola Klose'
Salvia verticillata 'Purple Rain'
Sanguisorba tenuifolia 'Purpurea'
Saruma henryi
Schizachyrium scoparium 'The Blues'
Sedum 'Herbstfreude' (autumn joy)
Silene regia
Solidago 'Golden Spangles'
Solidago rugosa 'Fireworks'
×Solidaster luteus 'Lemore'
Sorghastrum nutans 'Sioux Blue'
Stachys byzantina 'Countess Helen von Stein'
Stachys byzantina 'Primrose Heron'
Stachys macrantha
Stokesia laevis 'Klaus Jelitto'
Stokesia laevis 'Mary Gregory'
Stokesia laevis 'Omega Skyrocket'
Stokesia laevis 'Purple Parasols'
Stylophorum diphyllum
Thalictrum aquilegiifolium 'Thundercloud'
Thalictrum rochebruneanum
Thermopsis villosa
Tiarella cordifolia 'Ninja'
Veronica 'Waterperry Blue'
Veronica austriaca ssp. teucrium
    'Crater Lake Blue'
Veronica austriaca ssp. teucrium 'Royal Blue'
Veronica gentianoides 'Nana'
Veronica peduncularis 'Georgia Blue'
Veronica prostrata 'Trehane'
Veronica repens 'Sunshine'
Veronica spicata 'Blue Charm'
Veronica spicata 'Icicle'
Veronicastrum virginicum 'Fascination'
Viola 'Molly Sanderson'
Viola 'Purple Showers'
Viola labradorica

Annual

Ageratum houstonianum 'Blue Horizon'
Alternanthera dentata 'Rubiginosa'
Angelonia 'Blue Pacific'
Angelonia angustifolia 'Purple Pinnacles'
Antirrhinum majus 'Rocket Red'
Arctotis ×hybrida 'Dark Red'
Arctotis ×hybrida 'Flame'
Atriplex hortensis var. rubra
Beta vulgaris 'Bull's Blood'
Beta vulgaris 'Golden'
Beta vulgaris 'Ruby Queen'
Bouvardia ternifolia
Brachyscome 'Ultra'
Brassica oleracea
Calendula officinalis 'Orange King'
Celosia spicata 'Flamingo Purple'
Centaurea cineraria
Cerinthe major 'Purpurascens'
Consolida ajacis 'Blue Spire'
Cosmos atrosanguineus
Cynara cardunculus
Eschscholzia californica
Eschscholzia californica 'Purple Gleam'
Fuchsia 'Gartenmeister Bonstedt'
Gomphrena haageana 'Lavender Lady'
Ipomoea batatas 'Ace of Spades'
Ipomoea batatas 'Blackie'
Ipomoea batatas 'Margarita'
Lactuca 'Merlot'
Leonotis menthifolia
Lysimachia congestiflora 'Variegata'
Melampodium paludosum 'Million Gold'
Nicotiana langsdorffii
Nierembergia scoparia 'Mont Blanc'
Ocimum 'African Blue'
Ocimum basilicum 'Red Rubin'
Papaver rhoeas
Papaver rhoeas Angels' Choir
Papaver somniferum
Papaver somniferum 'Burnt Orange'
Papaver somniferum 'Lauren's Grape'
Papaver somniferum 'Pepperbox'
Pennisetum setaceum 'Rubrum'
Perilla frutescens var. crispa
Plectranthus amboinicus
Plectranthus argentatus
Portulaca grandiflora 'Sundial Peach'
Salvia 'Indigo Spires'
Salvia 'Purple Majesty'
Salvia coccinea 'Lady in Red'
Salvia guaranitica
Salvia guaranitica 'Black and Blue'
Salvia leucantha
Salvia officinalis 'Tricolor'
Salvia patens
Scabiosa atropurpurea 'Ace of Spades'
Solenostemon 'Burgundy Columns'

Lower Maintenance, cont.
....

Solenostemon 'Burgundy Giant'
Solenostemon 'Olive'
Solenostemon 'Penny'
Solenostemon 'Purple Emperor'
Solenostemon 'Saturn'
Tropaeolum majus 'Apricot Trifle'
Tropaeolum majus 'Blush Double'
Tropaeolum majus 'Moonlight'
Tropaeolum majus 'Tip Top Mahogany'

Tropaeolum majus Alaska Series
Verbena 'Homestead Purple'
Verbena 'Romance Apricot'
Verbena Temari® Red
Verbena bonariensis
Zinnia haageana 'Orange Star'

Annual vine
Ipomoea lobata (Mina lobata)
Ipomoea tricolor 'Heavenly Blue'
Lablab purpureus
Thunbergia battiscombei

Hardy bulb
Allium caeruleum
Allium carinatum ssp. pulchellum
Allium cristophii
Allium hollandicum (aflatunense)
    'Purple Sensation'
Allium moly 'Jeannine'
Allium sphaerocephalon
Chionodoxa forbesii (luciliae) Siehei Group
Colchicum speciosum
Crocus chrysanthus 'Blue Bird'
Dichelostemma ida-maia
Eranthis hyemalis

Iris 'Blue Magic'
Iris reticulata 'Harmony'
Narcissus 'Delnashaugh'
Narcissus 'Fragrant Rose'
Narcissus 'Mary Gay Lirette'
Narcissus 'Mint Julep'
Narcissus 'Petrel'
Narcissus 'Sir Winston Churchill'
Narcissus 'Stratosphere'
Narcissus 'Tahiti'
Puschkinia scilloides
Tulipa 'Angelique'

USDA PLANT HARDINESS ZONE MAP

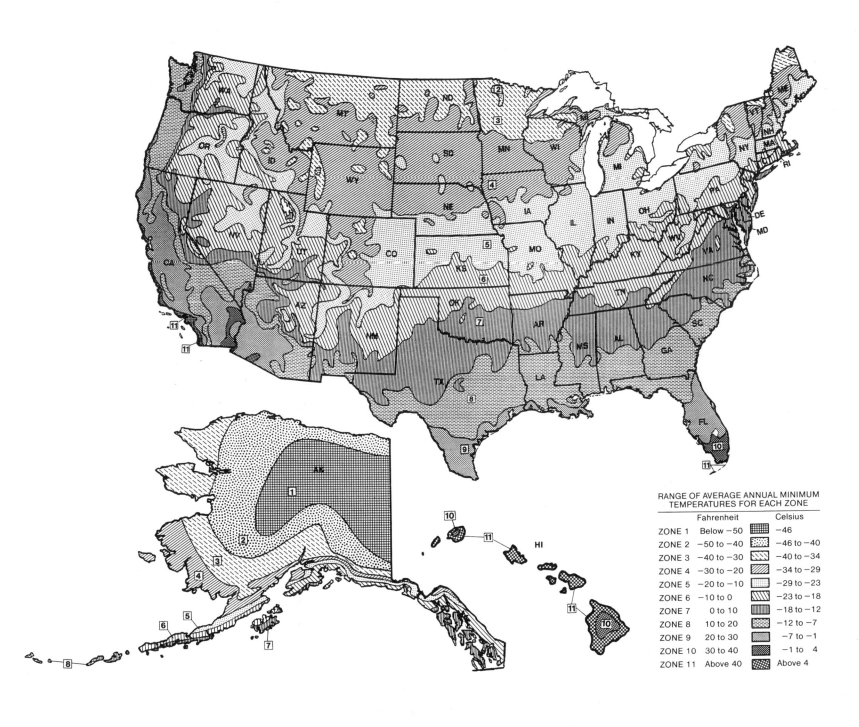

RANGE OF AVERAGE ANNUAL MINIMUM
TEMPERATURES FOR EACH ZONE

	Fahrenheit	Celsius
ZONE 1	Below −50	−46
ZONE 2	−50 to −40	−46 to −40
ZONE 3	−40 to −30	−40 to −34
ZONE 4	−30 to −20	−34 to −29
ZONE 5	−20 to −10	−29 to −23
ZONE 6	−10 to 0	−23 to −18
ZONE 7	0 to 10	−18 to −12
ZONE 8	10 to 20	−12 to −7
ZONE 9	20 to 30	−7 to −1
ZONE 10	30 to 40	−1 to 4
ZONE 11	Above 40	Above 4

METRIC CONVERSION CHART

INCHES	CENTIMETERS		FEET	METERS
⅛	0.3		¼	0.08
⅙	0.4		⅓	0.1
⅕	0.5		½	0.15
¼	0.6		1	0.3
⅓	0.8		1½	0.5
⅜	0.9		2	0.6
⅖	1.0		2½	0.8
½	1.25		3	0.9
⅗	1.5		4	1.2
⅝	1.6		5	1.5
⅔	1.7		6	1.8
¾	1.9		7	2.1
⅞	2.2		8	2.4
1	2.5		9	2.7
1¼	3.1		10	3.0
1⅓	3.3		12	3.6
1½	3.75		15	4.5
1¾	4.4		18	5.4
2	5.0		20	6.0
3	7.5		25	7.5
4	10		30	9.0
5	12.5		35	10.5
6	15		40	12
7	17.5		45	13.5
8	20		50	15
9	22.5		60	18
10	25		70	21
12	30		75	22.5
15	37.5		80	24
18	45		90	27
20	50		100	30
24	60		125	37.5
30	75		150	45
32	80		175	52.5
36	90		200	60

$$°C = \tfrac{5}{9} \times (°F - 32)$$

$$°F = (\tfrac{9}{5} \times °C) + 32$$

GLOSSARY

ALTERNATION: the repeating of design elements that are different from each other; achieves the design principles of unity and rhythm.

ANALOGOUS COLORS: colors that are adjacent on the color wheel.

ANALOGOUS SCHEME: a color scheme that predominantly uses two or three colors that are adjacent to each other on the color wheel.

ANNUAL: a plant that completes its life cycle in one growing season and then dies.

BALANCE: the feeling that different elements of a design are in equilibrium.

BASAL FOLIAGE: the leaves that grow from the base or crown of a plant.

BIENNIAL: a plant that completes its life cycle in two growing seasons and then dies.

BORDER: a garden that is bordered by a wall, fence, or hedge.

BULBS: fleshy leaf bases consisting of scales attached to a basal plate; tulips are one example.

CANDLING: a pruning technique for Pinus species in which the candle (the soft new growth that develops on the tips of the branches in spring) is pinched or pruned off by one-half to two-thirds, before the needles are fully elongated.

CLOCHE: a bell-shaped glass structure used for cold weather protection or for starting early crops in open ground.

COMPLEMENTARY (OR CONTRASTING) COLORS: colors that are opposite each other on the color wheel.

COMPLEMENTARY SCHEME: a scheme that focuses on two colors opposite each other on the color wheel.

COMPOUND: refers to leaves with blades that are fully divided into leaflets.

CONIFER: mostly evergreen trees or shrubs, usually with needle-like linear leaves and seeds borne naked on the scales of cones.

COOLER COLORS: blue-green, blue, blue-violet.

COPPICING. See stooling

CORM: the swollen base of a stem; corms are replaced by new corms every year; gladioli are one example.

CUTTING BACK: pruning off foliage and possibly flower buds or deadheads to renew a plant's appearance, to encourage a new flush of growth and flowering, or to control the plant's height or flowering time.

DAPPLED SHADE. See full shade

DEADHEADING: removing spent flowers or flowerheads for aesthetics, to prolong bloom or promote rebloom, or to prevent seeding.

DEADLEAFING: removing dead leaves to improve the appearance of a plant or in an effort to prevent or reduce pests and diseases.

DISBUDDING: removing side buds to encourage larger terminal buds, or removing terminal buds to produce smaller but more numerous side buds.

DOMINANCE: accomplished when one element or group of elements is more dominant than other elements; can be thought of as creating an accent or focal point.

FENG SHUI: the ancient Chinese art of design and placement that balances the chi, or energies, within your surroundings.

FIBONACCI SERIES: a series of numbers based on the Golden Mean.

FORM: refers to the overall size and shape of an object.

FULL SHADE: less than two hours of direct sun with some filtered sun during part of the day.

FULL SUN: at least six hours of strong sun each day.

GOLDEN MEAN: the ratio 1:1.618 and a rule of proportion common throughout nature that can be applied to garden design.

GRADATION: a gradual change in one or more elements in a repeating sequence.

HARDINESS ZONES: determined by the average annual frost-free days and minimum winter temperatures.

HARMONIOUS SCHEME: a color scheme created when colors are related by a shared hue.

HEADING BACK: a pruning technique for conifers in which the tips of stems are pruned back to a side or lateral bud or branch for size control.

HEAT ZONES: determined by the average number of days per year above 86∞F.

HOT COLORS. See warmer colors

HUE: a dimension of color; pure color, containing no white, black, or gray.

INDUMENTUM: a covering of hairs.

INFLORESCENCE: many flowers grouped to form one flowerhead; types of inflorescence include umbels, spikes, racemes, and panicles.

INTENSITY: a dimension of color; refers to the relative colorfulness or grayness of a color, also known as saturation, purity, or chroma.

INTERCONNECTION: when various elements of the design physically link together.

INTERPLANTING: planting in between plant material to achieve a layered look and extend the season of interest.

ISLAND BED: a freestanding area in a lawn, paved area, or garden.

LAYERING: utilizing all space in the garden from the ground to the mid and top levels; achieved by using a mix of herbaceous and woody plant material of differing heights.

LINE: related to eye movement or overall flow; inferred by bed layout and the way different beds work or flow together; also related to the lines created by different plant forms or forms of garden elements.

MASS COLLECTION: grouping like plants together in masses or drifts.

MIXED BORDER: a garden planted with combinations of herbaceous and woody plant material that may or may not be bordered by a wall, fence, or hedge.

MIXED GARDEN: a garden that is planted with combinations of herbaceous and woody plant material.

MONOCARPIC: a type of plant that flowers and fruits only once and then dies; monocarpic perennials may grow for several years before flowering.

MONOCHROMATIC SCHEME: a color scheme that incorporates shades, tints, and tones of a single pure hue.

NEUTRAL COLORS: green, violet, black, white, gray, brown.

OBELISK: a tall, four-sided, pyramidal structure usually made of iron or wood and used to support the growth of vines; may also be a similarly shaped garden ornament made of stone.

OPEN BORDERS: a garden that is a combination of a border and an island bed.

ORDER: a design principle; the underlying visual structure or organization of a design.

PALMATE: lobed or divided as in the shape of a fan, with all divisions originating from the same point; used to describe the arrangement of a plant's leaves.

PARTIAL SHADE: areas that receive morning or early afternoon sun but that are protected by the shade of trees during burning late sun from the west; often refers to the location on east side of a house.

PARTIAL SUN: three to five hours of direct sun per day with protection from the hottest part of the day.

PINNATE: fully divided into leaflets that arise on both sides of a single axis; used to describe the arrangement of a plant's leaves.

POLYCHROMATIC SCHEME: a scheme that includes many different colors.

PRIMARY HUES: red, yellow, blue.

PRINCIPLES OF DESIGN: order, unity, rhythm.

PROPORTION: the relationship of the elements' sizes to each other, or the ratio of one dimension to another.

PUBESCENT: covered with short, soft hairs.

REPETITION: the repeating of certain design elements throughout a garden to achieve the design principles of unity and rhythm.

RHIZOME: swollen, horizontal underground stem; cannas are one example.

RHYTHM: a design principle; related to time and movement in the garden; can be established through repetition, alternation, and gradation.

SCALE: the relative size of an element or area.

SECONDARY HUES: orange, green, violet (purple).

SHADE: a darker or lower-valued version of a color; contains black; implies weight or solidity.

SHEARING: pruning or cutting back with hedge shears.

SIMULTANEOUS CONTRAST: responsible for heightened contrast in hue, value, and intensity; when two colors are placed side by side, each color is tinged or hazed with the neighboring color's complement.

SPADIX: a type of inflorescence; a spike of tiny flowers, often surrounded by a spathe.

SPATHE: a flower structure; a modified, hoodlike bract surrounding a spike of tiny flowers (spadix).

STOLONIZING: refers to plant material with horizontal stems that produce roots and new shoots at the tips.

STOOLING: heavily pruning a shrub at the beginning of the season; also referred to as coppicing.

SUCCESSIVE CONTRAST: similar to simultaneous contrast but involves the element of time; a phenomenon in which, having stared at a color for 15 to 30 seconds, we have the tendency to see a ghost or afterimage of that color's complement when we look at another color, particularly white.

SUCKERING: describes plant material with adventitious shoots arising from below soil level, usually from the roots rather than the crown or stem of the plant.

SYMMETRY: elements in a design placed in an equal fashion around an axis; establishes balance.

TERTIARY (OR INTERMEDIATE) HUES: a mix of a primary hue and a secondary hue; red-orange is one example.

TEXTURE: refers to the surface quality of an object that can either be felt or seen.

TINT: a lighter or higher-valued version of a color; contains white; implies lightness or fragility and often refers to pastels.

TONE: relative brightness or grayness of a color; contains gray.

TRIADIC HARMONY: a scheme created by selecting three colors that are equal distances from each other on the color wheel.

TROPICAL: refers to plant material that gives a tropical feel to the garden; plants that provide bold texture.

TUBER: a swollen, irregularly shaped stem or root used for food storage; dahlias are one example.

UMBEL: a type of inflorescence in which stalked flowers radiate from a single point at the top of a stem.

UNDERPLANTING: planting at the base of trees, shrubs, or other plant material to create layers in the garden.

UNITY: a design principle; brings a design together, creating an aesthetically pleasing and functional whole composition; harmony, oneness.

UNITY OF THREE: when three elements of the same kind are grouped together to create a sense of oneness.

VALUE: a dimension of color; the degree of a color's luminosity, or the amount of light reflected back from it.

VIGNETTE: a part or small section of a garden.

WARMER COLORS: yellow, yellow-green, yellow-orange, orange, red-orange, red, and red-violet (magenta).

BIBLIOGRAPHY

Albers, Josef. 1963. *Interaction of Color*. New Haven, CT: Yale University Press.

American Conifer Society. http://www.conifersociety.org/conifer-info.html

American Horticultural Society. 1997. *Plant Heat-Zone Map*. Alexandria, VA: American Horticultural Society.

American National Standards Institute. 1996. *American Standard for Nursery Stock*. Washington, D.C.: American Association of Nurserymen.

Armitage, Allan. 1989. *Herbaceous Perennial Plants*. Athens, GA: Varsity Press.

Austin, Sandra. 1998. *Color in Garden Design*. Newtown, CT: Taunton Press.

Booth, Norman, and James Hiss. 1991. *Residential Landscape Architecture*. Englewood Cliffs, NJ: Prentice Hall Career and Technology.

Brickell, Christopher, and Elvin McDonald, eds. 1993. *The American Horticultural Society Encyclopedia of Gardening*. New York: Dorling Kindersley.

Brickell, Christopher, and Judith Zuk, eds. 1996. *The American Horticultural Society A—Z Encyclopedia of Garden Plants*. New York: Dorling Kindersley.

Brookes, John. 1991. *The Book of Garden Design*. New York: Macmillan Publishing.

Burrell, Colston. 1999. *Perennial Combinations*. Emmaus, PA: Rodale Press.

———. 2000. *Perennials for Today's Gardens*. Des Moines, IA: Meredith Publishing.

Chatto, Beth. 1989. *The Green Tapestry*. London: Harper Collins Publishing.

Darke, Rick. 1999. *The Color Encyclopedia of Ornamental Grasses*. Portland, OR: Timber Press.

Davies, Dilys. 1992. *Alliums*. Portland, OR: Timber Press.

Dirr, Michael. 1997. *Dirr's Hardy Trees and Shrubs*. Portland, OR: Timber Press.

———. 1998. *Manual of Woody Landscape Plants*. Champaign, IL: Stipes Publishing.

———. 2002. *Dirr's Trees and Shrubs for Warm Climates*. Portland, OR: Timber Press.

DiSabato-Aust, Tracy. 1998. *The Well-Tended Perennial Garden*. Portland, OR: Timber Press.

———. 2001. Planting with a limited color palette. *Fine Gardening* (April): 43—47.

Doczi, Gyorgy. 1984. *The Power of Limits: Proportional Harmonies in Nature, Art and Architecture*. Boston, MA: Shambhala Press.

Evison, Raymond. 1998. *Clematis*. Portland, OR: Timber Press.

Ferguson, Nicola. 1998. *Take Two Plants*. Lincolnwood, IL: Contemporary Books.

Frederick, William H., Jr. 1992. *The Exuberant Garden*. Boston, MA: Little, Brown.

Gelderen, D. M. van, and J. R. P. van Hoey Smith. 1996. *Conifers: The Illustrated Encyclopedia*. 2 vols. Portland, OR: Timber Press.

Goethe, Johann Wolfgang von. 1840. *Theory of Colours*. Reprint, Cambridge, MA: MIT Press, 1970.

Greenlee, John. 1992. *The Encyclopedia of Ornamental Grasses*. Emmaus, PA: Rodale Press.

Grey-Wilson, Christopher. 2000. *Poppies*. Portland, OR: Timber Press.

Hartman, John, Thomas Pirone, and Mary Ann Sall. 2000. *Pirone's Tree Maintenance*. New York: Oxford University Press.

Hawke, Richard. 1999. Clematis: the queen of vines. In *Flowering Vines*. Karan Davis Cutler, ed. Brooklyn, NY: Brooklyn Botanic Garden.

Hill, Lewis. 1997. *Pruning Made Easy*. Pownal, VT: Storey Publishing.

Hobhouse, Penelope. 1985. *Color in Your Garden*. Boston, MA: Little, Brown.

———.1989. *Borders*. New York: Harper and Row Publishers.

Hudak, Joseph. 2000. *Design for Gardens*. Portland, OR: Timber Press.

Jekyll, Gertrude. *Wood and Garden*. 1899. Reprint, Woodbridge, England: Antique Collectors' Club, 1981.

———. *Colour Schemes for the Flower Garden*. 1908. Reprint, Woodbridge, England: Antique Collectors' Club, 1982.

Keim, Gary R. 2001. Hardy shrubs for containers. In *The Potted Garden*. Scott D. Appell, ed. Brooklyn, NY: Brooklyn Botanic Garden.

Kingsbury, Noel. 1997. *Design and Plant a Mixed Border*. London: Ward Lock.

Knapp, Martin. 2001. Color scheme diagrams. www.makart.com/

Krussman, Gerd. 1985. *Manual of Cultivated Conifers*. Portland, OR: Timber Press.

Lord, Tony, ed. 2001. *RHS Plant Finder*. London: Dorling Kindersley.

Lovejoy, Ann. 1993. *American Mixed Border*. New York: Macmillan Publishing.

———. 2001. *Organic Garden Design School*. Emmaus, PA: Rodale Press.

Macunovich, Janet. 1992. *Easy Garden Design*. Pownal, VT: Storey Books.

McClure, Susan. 1999. *Midwest Landscape Design*. Dallas, TX: Taylor Publishing.

McKeon, Judith. 1997. *Gardening with Roses*. New York: Michael Friedman Publishing.

M'Mahon, Bernard. 1806. *The American Gardeners Calendar*. Philadelphia: B. Graves.

Moody, Mary, and Peter Harkness, eds. 1992. *The Illustrated Encyclopedia of Roses*. Portland, OR: Timber Press.

O'Byrne, Marietta. 2001. Well-placed shrubs make borders better. In *Creating Beds and Borders*. Newtown, CT: Taunton Press.

Oudolf, Piet, and Noel Kingsbury. 1999. *Designing with Plants*. Portland, OR: Timber Press.

Patterson, J. C., J. J. Murray, and J. R. Short. 1980. The impact of urban soils on vegetation. *M.E.T.R.I.A. Proceedings* 3:33—56.

Pope, Nori, and Sandra Pope. 1998. *Color by Design*. San Francisco, CA: SOMA Books.

Rawlings, Roma. 1998. *Healing Gardens*. Minocqua, WI: Willow Creek Press.

Rice, Graham. 1999. *Discovering Annuals*. Portland, OR: Timber Press.

Robinson, William, ed. 1879. *Gardening, Illustrated for Town and Country* 1(37):587.

Roth, Susan, and Dennis Schrader. 2000. *Hot Plants for Cool Climates*. New York: Houghton Mifflin.

The Royal Horticultural Society. 2001. *RHS Color Chart*. London: The Royal Horticultural Society.

Schwartz, Bobbie. 2001. *The Design Puzzle: Putting the Pieces Together*. Shaker Heights, OH: Bobbie Schwartz.

Smith, Linda. 1998. *Garden Ornament*. New York: Workman Publishing.

Springer, Lauren, and Rob Proctor. 2000. *Passionate Gardening*. Golden, CO: Fulcrum Publishing.

Still, Steven. 1994. *Manual of Herbaceous Ornamental Plants*. Champaign, IL: Stipes Publishing.

Strong, Roy. 1992. *Small Period Gardens*. New York: Rizzoli International Publications.

Sunset Books and Sunset Magazine Editors. 1972. *Sunset Pruning Handbook*. Menlo Park, CA: Lane Publishing.

Thomas, R. William, Susan F. Martin, and Kim Tripp, eds. 1997. *Growing Conifers*. Brooklyn, NY: Brooklyn Botanic Garden.

Turner Luke, Joy. 1996. *The Munsell Color System: A Language for Color*. New York: Fairchild Publications.

Verey, Rosemary. 1990. *The Art of Planting*. Boston, MA: Little, Brown.

Wilder, Louise Beebe. 1918. *Color in My Garden: An American Gardener's Palette*. Reprint, New York: Atlantic Monthly Press, 1990.

Williams, Robin. 1990. *The Garden Planner*. New York: Barron's Educational Series.

Wydra, Nancilee. 1997. *Feng Shui in the Garden*. Lincolnwood, IL: Contemporary Books.

Zilis, Mark. 2000. *The Hosta Handbook*. Rochelle, IL: Q & Z Nursery.

SOURCES

GENERAL

Acorn Farms
7679 Worthington Rd.
Galena, OH 43021
1.800.340.9348
wholesale
trees, shrubs, perennials

André Viette Farm and Nursery
P.O. Box 1109
Fisherville, VA 22939
1.800.575.5538
www.viette.com
mail order and retail
choice perennials, legendary family
nursery

Asiatica
P.O. Box 270
Lewisberry, PA 17339
717.938.8677
www.asiatica-pa.com
mail order
exclusive plants mostly from Asia, mostly
for shade garden

Baker's Acres Greenhouse
3388 Castle Rd.
Alexandria, OH 43001
1.800.934.6525
retail
great selection and service, predominantly
perennials and annuals

Beds and Borders, Inc.
P.O. Box 616
Laurel Lane
Laurel, NY 11948
631.298.1836
www.bedsandborders.com
retail
unusual annuals and tropicals, container
gardening specialists

Blanchette Gardens
223 Rutland St.
Carlisle, MA 01741
978.369.2962
www.blanchettegardens.com
mail order and retail
superb assortment of unusual perennials

Brotzman's Nursery
6899 Chapel Rd.
Madison, OH 44057
440.428.3361
wholesale
unusual trees and shrubs, premier
plantsman

Carroll Gardens
444 East Main St.
Westminster, MD 21157
1.800.638.6334
mail order and retail
broad selection

Dave Dannaher, Dannaher Landscaping,
    Inc.
12200 Vans Valley Rd.
Galena, OH 43021
740.965.3789
retail and wholesale
unusual conifers, dwarf conifers, trees

Essentially English Gardens
6599 US Route 35 East
Jamestown, OH 45335
937.675.7055
www.eegardens.com
craig@eegardens.com
retail
rare and unusual trees, shrubs, perennials

Fairweather Gardens
P.O. Box 330
Greenwich, NJ 08323
856.451.6261
www.fairweathergardens.com
mail order
unusual trees, shrubs, herbaceous plants,
and tropicals

Glasshouse Works
P.O. Box 97
Church St.
Stewart, OH 45778
740.662.2142
mail order and retail
rare and unusual plants, tropicals

Herman Losely & Son
3410 Shepard Rd.
Perry, OH 44081
440.259.2725
www.losely.com
wholesale
choice trees and shrubs, large sizes

Heronswood Nursery
7530 NE 288th St.
Kingston, WA 98346
360.297.4172
www.heronswood.com
mail order
unusual and rare plants, catalog is a great
reference

Homewood Farm
19520 Nunda Rd.
Howard, OH 43028
740.599.6638
retail
great selection of unusual plants

Joy Creek Nursery
20300 NW Watson Rd.
Scappoose, OR 97056
503.543.7474
www.joycreek.com
mail order and retail
nice quality plants, predominantly perennials, some vines and shrubs

Klehm's Song Sparrow Perennial Farm
13101 East Rye Rd.
Avalon, WI 53505
1.800.553.3715
www.songsparrow.com
mail order and retail
wide selection of perennials, trees, and
shrubs, specializing in peonies and
daylilies

Klyn Nurseries, Inc.
3322 South Ridge Rd.
P.O. Box 343
Perry, OH 44081
1.800.860.8104
wholesale
excellent selection of trees, shrubs, and
perennials, including bamboo and bog
plants

Kurt Bluemel, Inc.
2740 Greene Ln.
Baldwin, MD 21013
1.800.498.1560
www.bluemel.com
wholesale mail order
great grasses, perennials

Lake County Nursery
Route 84
P.O. Box 122
Perry, OH 44081
1.800.522.5253
www.lakecountynursery.com
wholesale
trees and shrubs, with many lower-maintenance plant introductions exclusive to
the nursery

Millcreek Gardens
15088 Smart-Cole Rd.
Ostrander, OH 43061
1.800.948.1234
wholesale
high quality perennials and herbs

Mountain Laurel Nursery
906 Round Bottom Rd.
Milford, OH 45150
513.831.5800
retail and wholesale
wide selection of perennials,
knowledgeable staff

Niche Gardens
111 Dawson Rd.
Chapel Hill, NC 27516
919.967.0078
www.nichegardens.com
mail order and retail
nursery-propagated wildflowers, native
perennials, grasses, unusual trees, and
shrubs

North Creek Nursery
388 North Creek Rd.
Landenberg, PA 19350
1.877.326.7584
wholesale
starter plant plugs, specializing in eastern
North American native perennials and
grasses

Plant Delights Nursery
9241 Sauls Rd.
Raleigh, NC 27603
919.772.4794
www.plantdelights.com
mail order
excellent unusual perennials, tropicals

The Planter's Palette
28 W. 571 Roosevelt Rd.
Winfield, IL 60190
630.293.1040
retail and wholesale
specializing in flowering perennials

Prairie Nursery
P.O. Box 306
Westfield, WI 53964
1.800.476.9453
www.prairienursery.com
mail order and retail
great nursery-propagated prairie plants,
seeds, and advice

Roslyn Nursery
211 Burrs Ln.
Dix Hills, NY 11746
631.643.9347
www.roslynnursery.com
mail order and retail
extensive selection of unusual trees and
shrubs, herbaceous plants

Seely's Landscape Nursery
3265 Walcutt Rd.
Hilliard, OH 43026
614.876.1838
retail and wholesale
unusual trees and shrubs

Seneca Hill Perennials
3712 County Route 57
Oswego, NY 13126
315.342.5915
www.senecahill.com
mail order
eclectic, emphasizing species cyclamen,
aroids, species peonies, and hardy South
African plants

Singing Springs Nursery
8802 Wilkerson Rd.
Cedar Grove, NC 27231
919.732.9403
mail order
wonderful unusual tropicals, personal
service

Sunny Border
3637 State Route 167
Jefferson, OH 44047
1.800.577.1760
www.sunnyborderohio.com
wholesale
outstanding new varieties

Sunshine Farms and Gardens
HC 67, Box 539B
Renick, WV 24966
304.497.2208
www.sunfarm.com
retail and wholesale
unusual herbaceous, excellent Internet
photos and information

Tranquil Lake Nursery
45 River St.
Rehoboth, MA 02769
508.252.4002
www.tranquil-lake.com
mail order and retail
New England–grown daylilies and iris

Wade and Gatton
1288 Gatton Rocks Rd.
Bellville, OH 44813
419.883.3191
retail
choice perennials and woody plants,
leading hosta specialist

Walters Gardens
96th Ave. and Business I-196
P.O. Box 137
Zeeland, MI 49464
1.888.925.8377
www.waltersgardens.com
wholesale
perennials

Woodside Gardens
1191 Egg & I Rd.
Chimacum, WA 98325
1.800.453.1152
www.woodsidegardens.com
mail order and retail
wide selection of unusual plants, great
service

ROSES

Heirloom Old Garden Roses
24062 Riverside Dr. NE
St. Paul, Oregon 97137
503.538.1576
mail order
large selection of roses

Roses Unlimited
Rt. 1, Box 587
Laurens, SC 29360
864.682.7673
mail order
large selection of own-root roses

The Rose Ranch
P.O. Box 10087
Salinas, CA 93912
408.758.6965
mail order
old, rare, and selected modern roses

MAIL-ORDER BULBS

Brent and Becky's Bulbs
7463 Heath Trail
Gloucester, VA 23061
1.877.661.2852
www.brentandbeckybulbs.com
great bulbs and informative, friendly
service

McClure & Zimmerman
108 West Winnebago St.
P.O. Box 368
Friesland, WI 53935
1.800.883.6998
www.mzbulb.com

Old House Gardens
536 Third St.
Ann Arbor, MI 48103
734.995.1486
www.oldhousegardens.com
heirloom bulbs and informative, friendly
service

MAIL-ORDER SEEDS

Seeds of Change
P.O. Box 15700
Santa Fe, NM 87506
1.888.762.7333
www.seedsofchange.com
specializing in organic seeds

Seeds of Distinction
P.O. Box 86, Station A
Toronto, Ont. M9C 4V2
Canada
416.255.3060
www.seedsofdistinction.com
interesting and unusual selection

Select Seeds
180 Stickney Hill Rd.
Union, CT 06076
860.684.9310
www.selectseeds.com
specializing in antique flowers

Thompson & Morgan
P.O. Box 1308
Jackson, NJ 08527
1.800.274.7333
www.thompson-morgan.com
extensive selection, new varieties

Wildseed Farms
425 Wildflower Hills
P.O. Box 3000
Fredericksburg, TX 78624
1.800.990.8090
www.wildseedfarms.com
specializing in regional wildflower mixtures

ART

Ian Adams Photography
2200 Bailey Rd.
Cuyahoga Falls, OH 44221
330.920.7401
www.ianadamsphotography.com

Mark Bokenkamp, Bokenkamp's Forge
3404 County Rd. 959
Loudonville, OH 44842
419.994.3405
specializing in forged iron trellises

Renate Burgyan
72 Overbrook Dr.
Columbus, OH 43214
614.832.6444
specializing in bronze sculpture

Escort Lighting
51 North Elm St.
Wernersville, PA 19565
1.800.856.7948
fine garden lighting fixtures

Connie Huston, tile mosaic artist
Galena Glass Art/S.E.M.K. Studio
owned and operated by glass artist Susie
Kossmann
46 West Columbus St.
P.O. Box 203
Galena, OH 43021
specializing in stained glass and glass
mosaic stepping-stones

Phil Kimball, Riverbend Studio
1812 Stratford Rd.
Delaware, OH 43015
1.800.584.2657
www.riverbendart.com
specializing in eclectic sculpture

Megan H. King
20913 Cotton Slash Rd.
Marysville, OH 43040
937.642.3780
specializing in design rendering,
illustration

David Kridler
Twp. Rd. 215
Fresno, OH 43824
740.623.8706
stonemason

Daniel Mathewson, The Copper Frog
7614 Harmony Church Rd.
Efland, NC 27243
919.304.3222
specializing in personalized copper frog
sculpture, recycled steel sculpture, and
fountains

Joe J. Miller, Jr.
8076 Kidron Rd.
Apple Creek, OH 44606
330.857.2021
timber framer, furniture

Stacey Renee Peters
5237 Norwich St.
Hilliard, OH 43026
614.771.8649
specializing in watercolors, instruction

Walt Rickli, The Garden Studio
R.R. 2
Milton, Ont. L9T 2X6
Canada
905.319.6369
www.waltrickli.com
specializing in stone sculpture

Terra Cotta
4055 The Strand West
Columbus, OH 43219
614.476.1218
retail
home and garden ornaments, pots,
furniture

SUPPLIES

A. M. Leonard
241 Fox Dr.
P.O. Box 816
Piqua, OH 45356
1.800.543.8955
www.amleo.com
mail order
landscape and nursery supply

Espoma
6 Espoma Rd.
Millville, NJ 08332
1.800.634.0603
www.espoma.com
organic fertilizers available at garden
centers

Kurtz Brothers, Inc.
2850 Rohr Rd.
Groveport, OH 43215
614.491.0868
retail and wholesale
topsoil, garden loam, compost, and
mulch

MacKenzie Nursery Supply, Inc.
P.O. Box 322
3891 Shepard Rd.
Perry, OH 44081
1.800.777.5030
or
P.O. Box 5368
704 Buffalo Shoals Rd.
Statesville, NC 28687
1.800.223.2784
www.mackenzie-nsy-supply.com
mail order
landscape and nursery supply

Smith & Hawken
P.O. Box 431
Milwaukee, WI 53201
1.800.776.3336
www.smithandhawken.com
mail order and retail
garden tools, ornaments, pots, furniture

Urban Gardener
940 North High St.
Columbus, OH 43201
614.299.4769
retail
garden ornaments, pots, supplies, plants

INDEX

Japanese maple. See *Acer palmatum*
Japanese painted fern. See *Athyrium niponicum* var. *pictum*
Japanese umbrella-pine. See *Sciadopitys verticillata*
Japanese white pine. See *Pinus parviflora*
Japanese woodlander. See *Glaucidium palmatum*
Jerusalem sage. See *Phlomis russeliana*
joe-pye weed. See *Eupatorium purpureum*
joseph's coat. See *Alternanthera dentata*
juniper. See *Juniperus*
Juniperus, 86

keeled garlic. See *Allium carinatum* ssp. *pulchellum*
knapweed. See *Centaurea cineraria*
Knautia macedonica, 140, 169
Kniphofia
   'Alcazar', 140, 149, 175, 179
   'Little Maid', 140, 175
   'Primrose Beauty', 49, 140, 157, 158
   'Prince Igor', 106, 112
   'Royal Standard', 140, 175
   'Shining Sceptre', 140, 149, 175
   caulescens, 81
   citrina, 140, 169
   triangularis, 40
Korean feather reed grass. See *Calamagrostis brachytricha*
Kousa dogwood. See *Cornus kousa*

Lablab purpureus, 141, 163
Labrador violet. See *Viola labradorica*
Lactuca 'Merlot', 141, 175, 181
lady's mantle. See *Alchemilla mollis*
lamb's ear. See *Stachys byzantina*
Lamium maculatum 'White Nancy', 103
larkspur. See *Consolida*
Lathyrus
   latifolius, 67, 72
   odoratus 'Henry Eckford', 77, 106, 118
   odoratus 'King Size Navy Blue', 106, 118
Lavandula
   angustifolia 'Munstead', 66, 70
   ×*intermedia* 'Grosso', 140, 163
lavender. See *Lavandula*

lavender mist meadow rue. See *Thalictrum rochebruneanum*
Lawson falsecypress. See *Chamaecyparis lawsoniana*
leadplant amorpha. See *Amorpha canescens*
leatherleaf sedge. See *Carex buchananii*
lemon thyme. See *Thymus* ×*citriodorus*
lenten rose. See *Helleborus*
Leonotis menthifolia, 141, 175
Lespedeza cuneata, 19
lettuce. See *Lactuca*
Liatris spicata 'Kobold', 97, 140, 163
licorice plant. See *Helichrysum petiolare*
Ligularia
   'The Rocket', 47, 82
   dentata 'Dark Beauty', 125, 126, 129, 133, 135
   dentata 'Desdemona', 217
   wilsoniana, 140, 184
lilac. See *Syringa*
lilac cranesbill. See *Geranium himalayense*
Lilium
   'Apricot Brandy', 44
   'Casa Blanca', 67, 72
   'Connecticut King', 140, 169
   'Conquistador', 140, 149
   'Eden's Dandy', 140, 149
   'Grand Cru', 140, 169, 175
   'Montenegro', 140, 149, 175
   'Pretender', 140, 175
   'Royal Justice', 140, 169
   'Royal Perfume', 140, 175
   'Scarlet Emperor', 140, 149
   'Shirley', 140, 175
   'Sunset', 140, 175
   henryi, 106, 112, 140, 149
   lancifolium var. *splendens*, 106, 109, 111, 115
   pumilum, 106
lily. See *Lilium*
lily leek. See *Allium moly*
lily of the Nile. See *Agapanthus*
limber pine. See *Pinus flexilis*
Limonium platyphyllum 'Violetta', 67, 72, 140, 163
Linaria,
   'Natalie', 106, 115
   purpurea, 106, 115

Linum
   perenne, 47
   perenne 'Blau Saphir' (blue sapphire), 140, 169
little bluestem. See *Schizachyrium scoparium*
Lobelia
   'Dark Crusader', 106
   'Grape Knee High', 106
   'Purple Towers', 106, 140, 163, 184
   'Queen Victoria', 140, 175, 184
   'Royal Robe', 125, 126, 129, 130, 133
   'Ruby Slippers', 140, 163
   siphilitica, 140, 184
lodgepole pine. See *Pinus contorta*
Lonicera, 88
   periclymenum 'Graham Thomas', 106, 115, 117
   sempervirens 'Blanche Sandman', 142, 150
love-in-a-mist. See *Nigella damascena*
lungwort. See *Pulmonaria*
Luzula nivea, 125, 128, 135
Lychnis
   ×*arkwrightii* 'Vesuvius', 140, 175
   cognata, 140, 169
   coronaria, 76, 106, 231
Lysimachia
   congestiflora 'Variegata', 141, 157
   nummularia 'Aurea', 106, 118, 119, 140, 155, 157, 184, 185

Magnolia
   stellata, 20
   virginiana, 85, 125, 130, 131
maidenhair fern. See *Adiantum pedatum*
maidenhair tree. See *Ginkgo biloba*
maiden pink. See *Dianthus deltoides*
Malus 'Lanzam' (Lancelot®), 66, 70
Mazus reptans, 125, 129, 133, 134
meadow cranesbill. See *Geranium pratense*
meadow rue. See *Thalictrum*
Melampodium paludosum 'Million Gold', 142, 169, 172
Mertensia
   pulmonarioides, 122, 125, 197
   virginica. See *Mertensia pulmonarioides*
Meserve holly. See *Ilex* ×*meserveae*